T0302096

AFTER THE ACCORD

In this book, Kenneth Garbade, a former analyst at a primary dealer firm and researcher at the Federal Reserve Bank of New York, traces the evolution of open market operations, Treasury debt management, and the structure of the US government securities markets following the 1951 Treasury-Federal Reserve Accord. The volume examines how these institutions evolved, responding both to external forces and to one another. Utilizing a vast scope of primary materials, the work provides insight into how officials fashioned the facilities and procedures needed to advance their policy objectives in light of their novel freedoms and responsibilities. Students and scholars of macroeconomics, financial regulation, and the history of central banking will find this volume a welcome addition to Garbade's earlier studies of Treasury debt operations during World War I, the 1920s, and the Great Depression and since 1983.

Kenneth D. Garbade is a former economist and senior vice president at the Federal Reserve Bank of New York. He has been a Professor of Economics and Finance in the Graduate School of Business Administration at New York University, and a Managing Director at Bankers Trust Company working in the primary dealer department for US Treasury securities. He is the author of *Fixed Income Analytics* (1996), *Birth of a Market: The US Treasury Securities Market from the Great War to the Great Depression* (2012), and *Treasury Debt Management under the Rubric of Regular and Predictable Issuance: 1983-2012* (2015).

STUDIES IN MACROECONOMIC HISTORY

The titles in this series investigate themes of interest to economists and economic historians in the rapidly developing field of macroeconomic history. The four areas covered include the application of monetary and finance theory, international economics, and quantitative methods to historical problems; the historical application of growth and development theory and theories of business fluctuations; the history of domestic and international monetary, financial, and other macroeconomic institutions; and the history of international monetary and financial systems. The series amalgamates the former Cambridge University Press series Studies in Monetary and Financial History and Studies in Quantitative Economic History.

Other Books in the Series:

Claudio Borio, Stijn Claessens, Piet Clement, Robert N. McCauley, and Hyun Song Shin, Editors, *Promoting Global Monetary and Financial Stability: The Bank for International Settlements after Bretton Woods, 1973–2020* (2020)

Patrick Honohan, *Currency, Credit and Crisis: Central Banking in Ireland and Europe* (2019)

William A. Allen, *The Bank of England and the Government Debt: Operations in the Gilt-Edged Market, 1928–1972* (2019)

Eric Monnet, *Controlling Credit: Central Banking and the Planned Economy in Postwar France, 1948–1973* (2018)

Laurence M. Ball, *The Fed and Lehman Brothers: Setting the Record Straight on a Financial Disaster* (2018)

Rodney Edvinsson, Tor Jacobson, and Daniel Waldenström, Editors, *Sveriges Riksbank and the History of Central Banking* (2018)

Peter L. Rousseau and Paul Wachtel, Editors, *Financial Systems and Economic Growth: Credit, Crises, and the Regulation from the 19th Century to the Present* (2017)

Ernst Baltensperger and Peter Kugler, *Swiss Monetary History since the Early 19th Century* (2017)

Øyvind Eitrheim, Jan Tore Klovland, and Lars Fredrik Øksendal, *A Monetary History of Norway, 1816–2016* (2016)

Jan Fredrik Qvigstad, *On Central Banking* (2016)

Michael D. Bordo, Øyvind Eitrheim, Marc Flandreau, and Jan F. Qvigstad, Editors, *Central Banks at a Crossroads: What Can We Learn from History?* (2016)

Michael D. Bordo and Mark A. Wynne, Editors, *The Federal Reserve's Role in the Global Economy: A Historical Perspective* (2016)

Owen F. Humpage, Editor, *Current Federal Reserve Policy Under the Lens of Economic History: Essays to Commemorate the Federal Reserve System's Centennial* (2015)

Michael D. Bordo and William Roberds, Editors, *The Origins, History, and Future of the Federal Reserve: A Return to Jekyll Island* (2013)

Michael D. Bordo and Ronald MacDonald, Editors, *Credibility and the International Monetary Regime: A Historical Perspective* (2012)

Robert L. Hetzel, *The Great Recession: Market Failure or Policy Failure?* (2012)

Tobias Straumann, *Fixed Ideas of Money: Small States and Exchange Rate Regimes in Twentieth-Century Europe* (2010)

Forrest Capie, *The Bank of England: 1950s to 1979* (2010)

Aldo Musacchio, *Experiments in Financial Democracy: Corporate Governance and Financial Development in Brazil, 1882–1950* (2009)

Claudio Borio, Gianni Toniolo, and Piet Clement, Editors, *The Past and Future of Central Bank Cooperation* (2008)

Robert L. Hetzel, *The Monetary Policy of the Federal Reserve: A History* (2008)

Caroline Fohlin *Finance Capitalism and Germany's Rise to Industrial Power* (2007)

John H. Wood, *A History of Central Banking in Great Britain and the United States* (2005)

Gianni Toniolo (with the assistance of Piet Clement), *Central Bank Cooperation at the Bank for International Settlements, 1930–1973* (2005)

Richard Burdekin and Pierre Siklos, Editors, *Deflation: Current and Historical Perspectives* (2004)

Pierre Siklos, *The Changing Face of Central Banking: Evolutionary Trends since World War II* (2002)

Michael D. Bordo and Roberto Cortés-Conde, Editors, *Transferring Wealth and Power from the Old to the New World: Monetary and Fiscal Institutions in the 17th through the 19th Centuries* (2001)

Howard Bodenhorn, *A History of Banking in Antebellum America: Financial Markets and Economic Development in an Era of Nation-Building* (2000)

Mark Harrison, Editor, *The Economics of World War II: Six Great Powers in International Comparison* (2000)

Angela Redish, *Bimetallism: An Economic and Historical Analysis* (2000)

Elmus Wicker, *Banking Panics of the Gilded Age* (2000)

Michael D. Bordo, *The Gold Standard and Related Regimes: Collected Essays* (1999)

Michele Fratianni and Franco Spinelli, *A Monetary History of Italy* (1997)

Mark Toma, *Competition and Monopoly in the Federal Reserve System, 1914–1951* (1997)

Barry Eichengreen Editor, *Europe's Postwar Recovery* (1996)

Lawrence H. Officer, *Between the Dollar-Sterling Gold Points: Exchange Rates, Parity and Market Behavior* (1996)

Elmus Wicker, *The Banking Panics of the Great Depression* (1996)

Norio Tamaki, *Japanese Banking: A History, 1859–1959* (1995)

Barry Eichengreen, *Elusive Stability: Essays in the History of International Finance, 1919–1939* (1993)

Michael D. Bordo and Forrest Capie, Editors, *Monetary Regimes in Transition* (1993)

Larry Neal, *The Rise of Financial Capitalism: International Capital Markets in the Age of Reason* (1993)

S. N. Broadberry and N. F. R. Crafts, Editors, *Britain in the International Economy, 1870–1939* (1992)

Aurel Schubert, *The Credit-Anstalt Crisis of 1931* (1992)

Trevor J. O. Dick and John E. Floyd, *Canada and the Gold Standard: Balance of Payments Adjustment under Fixed Exchange Rates, 1871–1913* (1992)

Kenneth Mouré, *Managing the Franc Poincaré: Economic Understanding and Political Constraint in French Monetary Policy, 1928–1936* (1991)

David C. Wheelock, *The Strategy and Consistency of Federal Reserve Monetary Policy, 1924–1933* (1991)

After the Accord

A History of Federal Reserve Open Market Operations, the US Government Securities Market, and Treasury Debt Management from 1951 to 1979

KENNETH D. GARBADE

CAMBRIDGE
UNIVERSITY PRESS

University Printing House, Cambridge CB2 8BS, United Kingdom

One Liberty Plaza, 20th Floor, New York, NY 10006, USA

477 Williamstown Road, Port Melbourne, VIC 3207, Australia

314–321, 3rd Floor, Plot 3, Splendor Forum, Jasola District Centre,
New Delhi – 110025, India

79 Anson Road, #06–04/06, Singapore 079906

Cambridge University Press is part of the University of Cambridge.

It furthers the University's mission by disseminating knowledge in the pursuit of education, learning, and research at the highest international levels of excellence.

www.cambridge.org
Information on this title: www.cambridge.org/9781108839891
DOI: 10.1017/9781108885386

First published 2021

A catalogue record for this publication is available from the British Library.

Library of Congress Cataloging-in-Publication Data
Names: Garbade, Kenneth D., author.
Title: After the accord : a history of Federal Reserve open market operations, the US government securities market, and Treasury debt management from 1951 to 1979 / Kenneth D. Garbade, Federal Reserve Bank of New York.
Description: Cambridge, United Kingdom ; New York, NY : Cambridge University Press, 2021. | Includes bibliographical references and index.
Identifiers: LCCN 2020022765 (print) | LCCN 2020022766 (ebook) | ISBN 9781108839891 (hardback) | ISBN 9781108813808 (paperback) | ISBN 9781108885386 (epub)
Subjects: LCSH: United States. Federal Reserve Board. | United States. Department of the Treasury. | Open market operations–United States–History–20th century. | Monetary policy–United States–History–20th century. | Finance–Government policy–United States–History–20th century. | Government securities–United States–History–20th century.
Classification: LCC HG2562.O5 .G37 2020 (print) | LCC HG2562.O5 (ebook) | DDC 332.1/140973–dc23
LC record available at https://lccn.loc.gov/2020022765
LC ebook record available at https://lccn.loc.gov/2020022766

ISBN 978-1-108-83989-1 Hardback

This book is dedicated to the librarians and archivists of the Federal Reserve System, conservators of our institutional memory and guides through the labyrinths of that memory.

Contents

Charts

Tables

Boxes

Foreword

The Merriam-Webster Dictionary defines the word "institution" as "a significant practice, relationship, or organization in a society or culture."

Institutions – such as contract law, central banks, and a wide variety of markets – constitute the structural framework of an economy. They make today look pretty much like yesterday and allow us to expect tomorrow to look pretty much like today; they facilitate planning and investment for the future.

Nevertheless, economic conditions change, new products appear, and new ideas come to mind, all of which provide a reason for institutions to evolve – sometimes gradually, in a succession of small steps; at other times discontinuously, in a single leap. The Federal Reserve Act of 1913 is an example of discontinuous evolution – a statutory prescription for an entirely new framework for US monetary policy.

This book examines an episode of more gradual institutional change: the development of open market operations, the market for US Treasury securities, and Treasury debt management practices during the quarter century following the termination of the pegged interest rate regime put in place during World War II. This book describes how the Fed and the Treasury fashioned the instruments, facilities, and procedures needed to advance their respective policy objectives in the context of a free market for Treasury debt. It describes how open market operations evolved from little more than buying whatever securities were offered at yields above the prescribed wartime ceiling rates to the dynamic management of bank reserves and money market conditions. It also describes how Treasury debt management evolved from selling coupon-bearing securities in fixed-price subscription offerings to regular and predictable auction offerings. Finally, it describes how the Fed came to take a leading role in mapping out the evolution of Treasury market infrastructures, including book-entry securities, securities lending, and secondary market governance.

Acknowledgments

This book would not have been written but for the many interactions I have enjoyed over the past four and a half decades with staff of the Federal Reserve System and the US Treasury, and with participants in the market for US Treasury securities.

At the Federal Reserve Bank of New York, I have benefited from working with Tobias Adrian, Paul Agueci, Chris Burke, Richard Crump, Bob Elsasser, Michael Fleming, Steve Friedman, Joshua Frost, Oliver Giannotte, Warren Hrung, Sandra Krieger, David Lucca, Jim Mahoney, Antoine Martin, John McGowan, John Partlan, Debby Perelmuter, Paul Santoro, Pari Sastry, Charles Steindel, and Nate Wuerffel. Jim Close was similarly helpful at the Federal Reserve Board. I owe a particular debt of gratitude to the past and present librarians of the New York Bank, including Pat Buckley, Maryalice Cassidy, Megan Cohen, Amy Farber, Kara Masciangelo, Kathleen McKiernan, Hayley Mink, Deidre O'Brien, and Mary Tao, and to the Bank's archivist, Joseph Komljenovich.

At the US Treasury, Chuck Andreatta, Steve Barardi, Francis Cavanaugh, Kurt Eidemiller, Lee Grandy, Jennifer Imler, Colin Kim, Paul Malvey, Dave Monroe, Fred Pietrangeli, Karthik Ramanathan, Amar Reganti, and Mark Stalnecker patiently answered my many questions.

Mead Briggs, Dave Buckmaster, Al Clark, Lou Crandall, Jeff Ingber, Arlen Klinger, Allan Rogers, Doug and Rita Skoknick, and Tom Wipf shared their thoughts on how the market really works.

I have been especially fortunate, over the past decades, to have been able to work with particularly thoughtful people, including Ken Abbott, Ken Baron, Clinton Lively, and Marcy Recktenwald at Bankers Trust Company; Frank Keane, Lorie Logan, Tony Rodrigues, and Jennifer Wolgemuth at the New York Reserve Bank; Jeff Huther, Mary Miller, Matt Rutherford, and Lori Santamorena at the Treasury; and my longtime colleague and coauthor, William Silber.

I have a special obligation to the present and past directors of the Research and Statistics Function at the New York Bank: Christine Cumming, Joe Tracy, Jamie McAndrews, Simon Potter, and Beverly Hirtle, for tolerating, and encouraging, a project that must have seemed endless.

Last, but hardly least, Bernice, Larissa, Edward, and Rachel have been extraordinarily tolerant of a husband and father who regularly disappeared into his files in the basement.

I am grateful to the MIT Press for permission to use narrative material from the last chapter of *Birth of a Market: The U.S. Treasury Securities Market from the Great War to the Great Depression*, in Chapters 2, 5, and 28.

Try as I might, I have been unable to slough off any responsibility for the errors and omissions that follow – they are mine alone.

The views expressed in this book are those of the author and do not necessarily reflect the position of the Federal Reserve Bank of New York or the Federal Reserve System.

Treasury Officials

Secretary of the Treasury

Henry Morgenthau	Jan. 1934–Jul. 1945
Fred Vinson	Jul. 1945–Jun. 1946
John Snyder	Jun. 1946–Jan. 1953
George Humphrey	Jan. 1953–Jul. 1957
Robert Anderson	Jul. 1957–Jan. 1961
Douglas Dillon	Jan. 1961–Apr. 1965
Henry Fowler	Apr. 1965–Dec. 1968
Joseph Barr	Dec. 1968–Jan. 1969
David Kennedy	Jan. 1969–Feb. 1971
John Connally	Feb. 1971–Jun. 1972
George Schultz	Jun. 1972–May 1974
William Simon	May 1974–Jan. 1977
W. Michael Blumenthal	Jan. 1977–Aug. 1979
G. William Miller	Aug. 1979–Jan. 1981

Under Secretary for Monetary Affairs[1]

W. Randolph Burgess	Aug. 1954–Sep. 1957
Julian Baird	Sep. 1957–Jan. 1961
Robert Roosa	Jan. 1961–Dec. 1964
Frederick Deming	Feb. 1965–Jan. 1969

[1] Established by the Act of July 22, 1954.

Paul Volcker	Jan. 1969–Jul. 1974
Jack Bennett	Jul. 1974–Jun. 1975
Edwin Yeo	Aug. 1975–Jan. 1977
Anthony Solomon	May 1977–Feb. 1980

Federal Reserve Officials

Chairman of the Board of Governors

Marriner Eccles	Nov. 1934–Jan. 1948
Thomas McCabe	Apr. 1948–Mar. 1951
William McChesney Martin	Apr. 1951–Jan. 1970
Arthur Burns	Feb. 1970–Jan. 1978
G. William Miller	May 1978–Aug. 1979
Paul Volcker	Aug. 1979–Aug. 1987

President of the Federal Reserve Bank of New York

George Harrison	Nov. 1928–Dec. 1940
Allan Sproul	Jan. 1941–Jun. 1956
Alfred Hayes	Aug. 1956–Aug. 1975
Paul Volcker	Aug. 1975–Aug. 1979

Manager of the System Open Market Account

W. Randolph Burgess	Mar. 1936–Sep. 1938
Allan Sproul	Sep. 1938–Dec. 1939
Robert Rouse	Dec. 1939–May 1962
Robert Stone	May 1962–Mar. 1965
Alan Holmes	Mar. 1965–Sep. 1979
Peter Sternlight	Sep. 1979–Sep. 1992

The Many Varieties of Dealer

A dealer is a partnership, bank, or corporation that, on a regular basis, bids on securities that market participants want to sell and makes offerings of securities that market participants want to buy.

Dealers are among the principal actors in this book. They come in many varieties: A "government securities dealer" is a dealer that provides bids and offers in US Treasury and federal agency securities. It can be a commercial bank – that is, a "bank dealer" or a partnership or corporation other than a bank, a "non-bank dealer." A nonbank dealer may do a general securities business, or it may specialize in government securities.

Government securities dealers that provide bids and offers to the Federal Reserve Bank of New York when that bank is conducting open market operations are generally referred to as "primary dealers," but have had other names from time to time. (From the late 1930s to mid-1944, they were described as "recognized dealers"[1]; between mid-1944 and the spring of 1953, they were described as "qualified dealers.") A primary dealer could be a bank dealer or a nonbank dealer. The most significant difference between the two was that, between August 1949 and June 1975, the Open Market Desk did not lend to bank primary dealers on repurchase agreements, because those dealers had access to the Fed's discount window.

A "reporting dealer" is a government securities dealer who reports its transactions, positions, and financing arrangements to the Federal Reserve Bank of New York pursuant to a reporting regime put in place in 1960. All primary dealers are reporting dealers, but there have been instances where

[1] Over the same interval, the Open Market Desk sometimes entered into transactions with nonbank dealers who were not "recognized" dealers but whom the Desk considered "responsible."

a reporting dealer was not also a primary dealer – generally when it was seeking to become a primary dealer but had not yet qualified.

A broker is a market participant who, for a commission, puts buyers and sellers together. Unlike a dealer, a broker does not purchase or sell securities for its own account. "Interdealer brokers" are the most important type of broker in the government securities market. Over the specific time period addressed in this book, interdealer brokers limited their business to brokering transactions between reporting dealers. They did not serve other government securities dealers and did not serve nondealers like pension funds and corporate cash managers.

A clearing bank is a commercial bank that maintains the inventory, paper or digital, of a dealer, receives (and makes payment for) securities purchased by the dealer, and delivers (and accepts payment for) securities sold by the dealer. A clearing bank may also be a bank dealer, but the two businesses are separate and distinct.

1

Introduction

The market for US Treasury securities has been the keystone of American finance for more than a century. It is where, in war and peace, the federal government finances deficits and refinances maturing debt; it has been the principle arena of Federal Reserve policy operations.

The fiscal demands of World War I propelled the Treasury market from a late-nineteenth-century backwater to a twentieth-century behemoth, in the process providing the foundation for the reorientation of the Federal Reserve System from a passive lender of last resort to an active manager of bank reserves and money market conditions. Robert Roosa, an economist at the New York Reserve Bank from 1946 to 1961 and Under Secretary of the Treasury for Monetary Affairs from 1961 to 1965, emphasized the "shift-over from a purely defensive to what might be called a dynamic conception of Federal Reserve responsibility."[1]

World War II brought comparably far-reaching changes. Government consumption of goods and services increased from 10 percent of real GNP in 1939 to 21 percent in 1944. Federal indebtedness grew from $41 billion at the end of 1939 to $276 billion at the end of 1945. The ratio of federal debt to nominal GNP rose from 0.45 to 1.30.

Monetary policy during the war was limited to enforcing ceilings on Treasury yields, which were justified as necessary to facilitate war loan drives and limit interest expenses. The Fed held thirteen-week bill yields at ⅜ percent, a one-year certificate of indebtedness[2] yields at ⅞ percent,

[1] Roosa (1956, pp. 8–9). Roosa states that the shift was "evident all through the [nineteen] twenties . . ."

[2] A certificate of indebtedness was a coupon-bearing security payable in not more than one year.

and long-term bond yields at or below 2½ percent by purchasing Treasury debt for its own account whenever private demand flagged.

Following the cessation of hostilities, soldiers and sailors returned to civilian life (by 1950, the armed forces accounted for 2.6 percent of the labor force, down from 17.3 percent in 1944) and government expenditures receded (government consumption of goods and services fell back to 9 percent of real GNP in 1950). Some progress was made with respect to the national debt, but much remained to be done. By the end of 1950, the Treasury had paid down federal indebtedness to $254 billion and the debt-to-GNP ratio had receded to 0.89. Seeking to refocus monetary policy on managing bank reserves, the Fed, acting with Treasury acquiescence, removed the ceiling on bill yields and raised the ceiling on certificate yields. However, the ceiling on long-term bond yields remained unchanged in the face of strenuous Treasury resistance to further change.

Following several months of intense interagency conflict, Treasury and Federal Reserve officials reached an accommodation in March 1951. The Treasury-Federal Reserve Accord removed the remaining interest rate ceilings but committed the System to ensuring the success of Treasury offerings priced at market levels.

This book traces the subsequent evolution of open market operations, Treasury debt management, and the secondary market for US Treasury securities, focusing on how officials fashioned the instruments, facilities, and procedures needed to advance their policy objectives in light of their newfound freedoms and responsibilities.

OPEN MARKET OPERATIONS AFTER THE ACCORD

For its part, the Fed demonstrated a strong and persistent interest in bolstering and accessing liquidity. A more liquid Treasury market would support less costly and (when required) larger open market operations.

Bills Preferably

In 1953, the Federal Open Market Committee (FOMC) adopted a set of operating principles that it believed would foster a more liquid market. Seeking to promote competition among dealers and other market participants, the Fed announced that it would neither target interest rates nor directly support Treasury offerings. The related doctrine of "bills preferably" emphasized purchases and sales of Treasury bills, deemphasized operations in short-term coupon-bearing debt and rejected operations in longer-term debt.

Repurchase Agreements

The Fed supplemented outright operations in bills with repurchase agreements, in which it bought Treasury securities from a dealer and simultaneously agreed to sell the same securities back to the same dealer at a higher price on a later date. System repos were used during World War I and in the 1920s, fell into disuse in the 1930s, and were revived in 1947.

After the Accord, repos proved useful in short-term "defensive operations" that were aimed at neutralizing transient fluctuations in autonomous reserve factors such as public demand for currency, float, and Treasury balances at Federal Reserve Banks.[3] The bill market was not large enough or liquid enough to absorb the largest operations that the System had occasion to undertake, and officials were leery of confusing market participants with in-and-out purchases and sales unrelated to longer-run policy objectives. Repos were well suited for short-term operations because reserves injected with repos automatically ran off when the repos matured.

At the outset, officials used repurchase agreements sparingly. The FOMC limited repo collateral to short-term Treasury securities held in dealer inventories, conventionally (but not always) fixed the repo rate at the discount rate, and excluded bank dealers from repo operations (because banks had access to the discount window).

When interest rates rose and became more volatile in the mid-1960s and dealers became reluctant to carry more than minimal inventories, the Committee expanded the scope and scale of its repo operations. The Committee

- terminated the maturity limit on repo collateral and introduced back-to-back contracts, with nonbank dealers intermediating between their customers and the Fed, in June 1966;

[3] Roosa (1956, pp. 13–14) originated the term "defensive operations," as well as its complement, "dynamic operations." He defined the former as "keeping a given volume of reserves in being and helping with the economical distribution of that given total." He defined "dynamic operations" as a matter of varying "the quantity of reserves (after allowance for seasonal variations) by such amounts, and through such methods, as to make the banking system, and the money market as well, an active force in the economy – promoting growth, resisting depression, and limiting inflation."

- introduced matched sale-purchase agreements (a form of reverse repurchase agreement used to drain reserves from the banking system) in July 1966; and
- accepted federal agency securities as repo collateral beginning in December 1966.

In the first half of the 1970s, the FOMC introduced repo auctions and accepted bank dealers as repo counterparties. The successive adjustments forged repurchase agreements into a powerful tool for managing short-run fluctuations in bank reserves.

Open Market Operations in Coupon-Bearing Debt

Open market operations in bills and repos sufficed for managing reserves but not for the additional task of keeping the price of gold at $35 per ounce.

The US commitment to $35 gold was the foundation of the international financial system set in place in Bretton Woods, New Hampshire, in the summer of 1944. The central understanding of Bretton Woods was that countries other than the United States would fix the *dollar* value of their currencies, while the US maintained the *gold* value of the dollar. The system worked as long as payments between the United States and the rest of the world approximately balanced but faltered when the US balance of payments began to deteriorate in the late 1950s. Some countries, believing the deterioration a temporary phenomenon, parked their accumulating dollar balances in Treasury bills. Others took up the Treasury's standing offer to sell gold at $35 per ounce.

Operation Twist, initiated in February 1961, aimed at maintaining or raising the level of short-term interest rates (to keep foreign central banks invested in bills rather than demanding gold) while providing ample reserves to the banking system (to hasten recovery from an ongoing recession). In its weakest form, Operation Twist contemplated System purchases of intermediate- and long-term Treasury debt when reserves had to be added to the banking system and sales of short-term securities when reserves had to be drained. A more robust version included purchases of intermediate- and long-term debt against *concurrent* sales of short-term debt when there was no reason to either add or remove reserves. System support for such operations led to the formal abandonment of bills preferably in December 1961.

The abandonment of bills preferably had important consequences for the management of the Open Market Account and for Federal Reserve oversight of the Treasury market. Throughout the bills preferably period, from 1954 to 1960, Federal Reserve holdings of coupon-bearing debt – a legacy of World War II – hardly varied. The single significant exception was the acquisition of $1 billion of certificates in connection with the rescue of a failing Treasury offering in 1958. Purchases of coupon-bearing securities on a regular basis beginning in 1961 was a novel activity and officials began to pay more attention to aspects of the government securities market beyond the bill and repo markets. In particular, they became involved with market infrastructure issues – many of which were identified and discussed during the 1966–69 production of the Joint Treasury–Federal Reserve Study of the Government Securities Market – including dealer oversight, dealer finance, settlement fails, securities lending, settlement systems, and book-entry securities.

TREASURY DEBT MANAGEMENT AFTER THE ACCORD

The Treasury's main concern, in the wake of the Accord, was refinancing maturing debt and raising new money, reliably and at least cost over time. It was not unconcerned with liquidity – a more liquid market would make government securities more attractive – but concentrated on how to structure and sell its marketable debt.

As they had since 1938, Treasury officials auctioned thirteen-week bills on a regular and predictable basis[4] and relied on large, sporadic fixed-price subscription offerings of coupon-bearing debt to raise new money and to refinance maturing certificates, notes, and bonds. Each offering required identifying a maturity sector of current interest to market participants. The only strategic objective of any note aimed at extending the average maturity of marketable debt by issuing long-term securities whenever possible.

Because the Treasury relied on fixed-price offerings to sell coupon-bearing debt, the Federal Reserve was obliged to keep the market on an "even keel" during marketing periods that stretched from a few days before the announcement of a new issue to as much as a week after settlement. Some interpreted the obligation as a matter of abstaining from unexpected policy initiatives; others interpreted it more broadly as a matter of keeping interest rates steady.

[4] "Regular" meaning offered at a fixed frequency, such as weekly in the case of thirteen-week bills, and "predictable" in terms of amount, because new issues were generally the same size as maturing issues – a little larger if the Treasury needed new money, a little smaller if it was running a surplus.

Even with the Fed's even keeling, it was not unknown for an offering to falter and for Treasury officials to request assistance. Following the near failure of an offering of one-year certificates in the summer of 1958, officials expanded their reliance on regular and predictable issuance by introducing weekly twenty-six-week bill auctions and quarterly one-year bill auctions and by regularizing refundings of coupon-bearing debt to the middle of every calendar quarter. They continued to seek to extend average maturity but adopted the more flexible framework of advance refundings: fixed-price offers to issue longer-term debt in exchange for shorter-term debt that was not close to maturity. Advance refundings allowed the Treasury to offer long-term securities to market participants most likely to be interested in the securities – that is, to holders of intermediate-term debt.

The pace of innovation in Treasury debt management accelerated in the 1970s as indebtedness continued to grow. Officials began auctioning coupon-bearing debt after a second refunding debacle in May 1970. Regular and predictable offerings of two-year notes were introduced in 1972. Following a sharp increase in the deficit in 1975, officials introduced regular and predictable offerings of four- and five-year notes. By the end of the decade the Treasury had identified an issuance program and a method of sale – regular and predictable auction offerings – that meshed with the post-Accord free market in Treasury debt.

PART I

THE SYSTEM AND THE MARKET IN THE 1940S

The three chapters in this part survey the relationship between the Federal Reserve System and the government securities market during the 1940s. Chapter 2 describes the market, focusing on the Fed's decision to put a ceiling on Treasury yields during World War II and the gradual lifting of the ceiling in the front end of the yield curve following the cessation of hostilities. Chapter 3 describes the fulcrum of monetary policy, the requirement that member commercial banks maintain reserves with Federal Reserve Banks and the ability of the System to vary the supply of reserves with open market operations.[1] Chapter 4 examines the channel through which the System executed open market operations: transactions with a limited number of what would later become known as "primary" dealers in Treasury securities.

[1] In 1958, Ralph Young, then the director of the Division of Research and Statistics at the Board of Governors, remarked that "the required reserve balances of all member banks serve as the fulcrum of monetary management by the Federal Reserve System." Young (1958, p. 14).

2

The Government Securities Market

At the beginning of 1941, the public debt of the United States amounted to $44.4 billion, including $35.6 billion of marketable debt:

- $1.3 billion of bills,
- $6.2 billion of notes, and
- $28.2 billion of marketable bonds;

and $8.8 billion of nonmarketable debt:

- $3.2 billion of savings bonds,
- $5.4 billion of special issues to government investment accounts (such as the social security trust fund), and
- $200 million of other nonmarketable securities.[1]

Chart 2.1 shows the subsequent growth in marketable debt during the 1940s – growth driven entirely by US participation in World War II.

Table 2.1 shows that 23 percent of the $224 billion increase in Treasury debt from the beginning of 1941 to mid-1946 was financed with short-term bills and certificates. Sixty-one percent was financed with conventional bonds and savings bonds. The remaining 16 percent was spread over conventional notes, tax and savings notes (nonmarketable securities sold to investors anticipating future tax liabilities), and special trust fund issues.

Treasury Secretary Henry Morgenthau had hoped to finance the war with savings bonds sold individually and through payroll savings plans. He wanted to attract the rising incomes of wage earners in hopes of containing inflationary pressures, and he wanted to do so without the intense – and sometimes coercive – bond drives of World War I.[2] However, by mid-

[1] Board of Governors of the Federal Reserve System (1976, table 13.2).

[2] Morse (1971) and Samuel (1997).

Table 2.1 *Interest-bearing Treasury debt.*

	Beginning of 1941 ($ billions)	Mid-1946 ($ billions)	Increase ($ billions)	Percent of total increase
Marketable debt				
Bills	1.3	17.0	15.7	7.0
Certificates	0.0	34.8	34.8	15.6
Notes	6.2	18.3	12.1	5.4
Bonds	28.2	119.5	91.3	40.8
Nonmarketable debt				
Savings bonds	3.2	49.0	45.8	20.5
Tax and savings notes	0.0	6.7	6.7	3.0
Special issues	5.4	22.3	16.9	7.6
Other	0.2	0.4	0.2	0.1
Total	44.4	268.1	223.7	100.0

Board of Governors of the Federal Reserve System (1976, table 13.2).

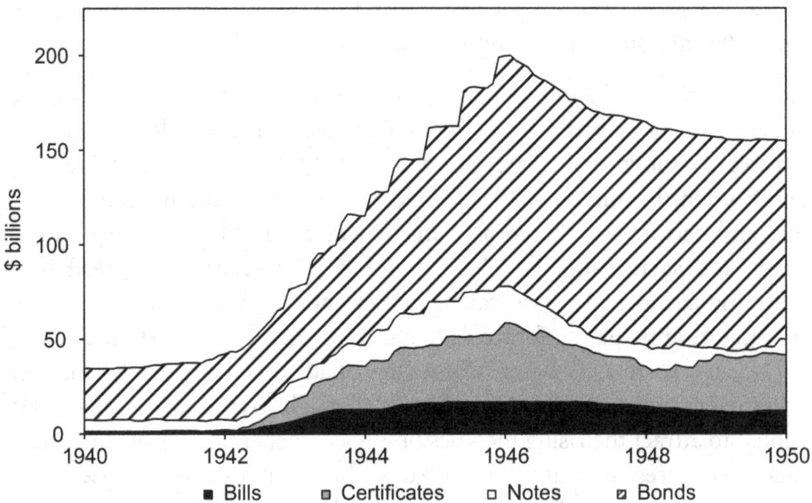

Chart 2.1 Marketable Treasury debt. End of month.
Board of Governors of the Federal Reserve System (1976, table 13.2).

1942, it was clear that the savings bonds were not attracting enough money and that the Treasury would have to reintroduce bond drives and sell marketable debt as well as savings bonds.[3]

The Treasury ultimately launched seven War Loan drives and one postwar Victory Loan drive (Table 2.2). Unlike the Liberty Loan drives of World War I, each of which offered only a single security, the loan drives of World War II offered a variety of securities, reflecting a marketing strategy of "something for everyone."[4] The contribution of the drives is evident in the stepwise increases in marketable debt between late 1942 and late 1945 (Chart 2.1).

At the end of 1949, the public debt stood at $255 billion – a more than fivefold increase from the beginning of 1941 – including $155 billion of marketable debt:

- $12.3 billion of bills,
- $29.6 billion of certificates,
- $8.2 billion of notes, and
- $104.9 billion of marketable bonds;

and $100 billion of nonmarketable debt:

- $56.7 billion of savings bonds,
- $33.9 billion of special issues, and
- $9.3 billion of other nonmarketable securities.[5]

Bills and certificates were owned in roughly equal shares by commercial banks, other private investors, and Federal Reserve Banks. Notes and bonds with not more than five years to maturity were owned primarily by banks. Long-term bonds with more than ten years to maturity were held by insurance companies and other private investors, with smaller amounts held by government trust funds, Federal Reserve Banks, and mutual savings banks.[6]

WARTIME INTEREST RATE CEILINGS[7]

The key debt management decision of World War II was the 1942 agreement between Treasury and Federal Reserve officials that interest rates on

[3] Gaines (1962, p. 51).

[4] See "Report to Congress by Secretary Morgenthau," July 21, 1945, reprinted in 1945 Treasury Annual Report, p. 397, stating (p. 410) that "the second major objective of the Treasury in its war borrowing – second only to the objective of avoiding inflation – has been to adapt the securities, which it has offered to the public to the requirements of the various classes of investors."

[5] Board of Governors of the Federal Reserve System (1976, table 13.2).

[6] Board of Governors of the Federal Reserve System (1976, table 13.5).

[7] The narrative in this section and the following section first appeared in Garbade (2012, pp. 339–46).

Table 2.2 *World War II war loan drives.*

Term and type	Maturity	Coupon rate (percent)	Sales ($ billions)
First War Loan, November 30 to December 23, 1942			
1-year certificate	Dec. 1, 1943	⅞	3.80
5½-year bond	Jun. 15, 1948	1¾	3.06
26-year bond	Dec. 15, 1968	2½	2.83
Second War Loan, April 12 to May 1, 1943			
1-year certificate	Apr. 1, 1944	⅞	5.25
9½-year bond	Sep. 15, 1952	2	4.94
26¼-year bond	Jun. 15, 1969	2½	3.76
Third War Loan, September 9 to October 2, 1943			
1-year certificate	Sep. 1, 1944	⅞	4.12
10-year bond	Sep. 15, 1953	2	5.26
26¼-year bond	Dec. 15, 1969	2½	3.78
Fourth War Loan, January 18 to February 15, 1944			
1-year certificate	Feb. 1, 1945	⅞	5.05
15½-year bond	Sep. 15, 1959	2¼	3.73
26-year bond	Mar. 15, 1970	2½	2.21
Fifth War Loan, June 12 to July 8, 1944			
1-year certificate	Jun. 1, 1945	⅞	3.56
2¾-year note	Mar. 15, 1947	1¼	1.29
10-year bond	Jun. 15, 1954	2	4.21
25¾-year bond	Mar. 15, 1970	2½	2.50
Sixth War Loan, November 20 to December 16, 1944			
1-year certificate	Dec. 1, 1945	⅞	4.40
2¾-year note	Sep. 15, 1947	1¼	1.55
10-year bond	Dec. 15, 1954	2	7.92
26¼-year bond	Mar. 15, 1971	2½	3.45
Seventh War Loan, May 14 to June 30, 1945			
1-year certificate	Jun. 1, 1946	⅞	4.46
5½-year bond	Dec. 15, 1950	1½	2.37
17-year bond	Jun. 15, 1962	2¼	4.51
27-year bond	Jun. 15, 1972	2½	7.97
Victory Loan, October 29 to December 8, 1945			
1-year certificate	Dec. 1, 1946	⅞	3.77
17-year bond	Dec. 15, 1962	2¼	3.47
27-year bond	Dec. 15, 1972	2½	11.69

Treasury annual reports.

long-term Treasury debt maturing in twenty to twenty-five years would be capped at 2½ percent for the duration of the war.[8] The cap was intended to solve a problem that had plagued Treasury Secretary William McAdoo

[8] Murphy (1950), Walker (1954), and Wicker (1969).

during World War I: Investors were reluctant to buy long-term fixed-rate bonds when the duration of the war was uncertain and there was a risk that an unexpectedly lengthy war would result in higher yields in the future.[9] Conversely, as Emanuel Goldenweiser, director of the Division of Research and Statistics at the Board of Governors, noted in a mid-1941 memo to the Federal Open Market Committee, "when the public is assured that the rate will not rise, prospective investors will realize that there is nothing to be gained by waiting, and a flow [of funds] into Government securities . . . may be confidently expected."[10] A 2½ percent ceiling was deemed appropriate because that was the rate at which the Treasury had been able to sell long-term bonds in October and December 1941[11] and because senior Federal Reserve officials believed that higher rates would not prevent inflation, would increase the cost of government borrowing and would burden existing bondholders with capital losses.[12]

In addition to capping the rate on long-term bonds, the Fed agreed in the spring of 1942 to cap the thirteen-week bill rate at ⅜ percent[13] – a rate

9 Garbade (2012, p. 72).

10 Minutes of the Federal Open Market Committee, June 10, 1941, p. 8. Thomas and Young (1947, p. 91) state that a policy of stable rates was adopted to "encourage prompt buying of securities by investors, who might otherwise have awaited higher rates." Thomas (1951, p. 622) states that the policy was adopted "with the recognition that with almost unlimited borrowing always in prospect, interest rates would tend to rise and that such a prospect would tend to hold back purchases of securities."

11 Murphy (1950, pp. 93–94), Treasury Circular no. 670, October 9, 1941, reprinted 1942 Treasury Annual Report, p. 212, and Treasury Circular no. 672, December 4, 1941, reprinted 1942 Treasury Annual Report, p. 216.

12 Minutes of the Federal Open Market Committee, September 27, 1941, p. 7, summarizing Goldenweiser's view that higher rates "would not be a feasible policy for the reason that it would increase the cost of Government borrowing without being effective in preventing price rises, and it could not be carried out with the approval of other agencies of Government. It would also raise serious problems about the decline in the capital value of outstanding securities." See also Thomas and Young (1947, p. 91), stating that maintenance of interest rates at the level prevailing prior to US entry into the war served to "keep down the interest cost on the Government's war debt" and Meltzer (2003, p. 580), noting Secretary Morgenthau's "passionate attachment to low interest rates."

13 Federal Reserve Bank of New York Circular no. 2430, May 8, 1942, stating that "As an added means of assuring the liquidity of investments in Treasury bills, aside from the short maturity and ready marketability of the securities, the Board of Governors of the Federal Reserve System announced on April 30 that the Federal Open Market Committee had directed the Federal Reserve banks to purchase for the System Open Market Account all Treasury bills that may be offered to them, on a discount basis at the rate of ⅜ per cent per annum. This arrangement gives assurance to purchasers of Treasury bills that, in case they have a need for cash before the maturity of the bills, they can obtain it by selling Treasury bills to the Federal Reserve Bank, if necessary." See also "Treasury to Issue New

only marginally above the contemporaneous market rate. When wartime expenditures began to stimulate rapid growth in economic activity, Federal Reserve officials tried to get their Treasury counterparts to agree to an increase in the bill rate. The latter refused and the ⅜ percent ceiling rate held for the duration.[14] Maximum yields at maturities between three months and twenty years were interpolated to give a smooth curve: yields on one-year certificates were capped at ⅞ percent, and yields on seven- to nine-year bonds were capped at 2 percent.[15]

There were two important consequences of the Fed's commitment to capping interest rates at prewar levels and to stabilizing the yield curve with a slope that reflected prewar expectations of rising rates.[16] First, the *levels* were too low for the hothouse economy required to fight a world war. The Federal Reserve ended up monetizing a significant quantity of war debt, with adverse consequences for postwar inflation.

Second, the *shape* of the curve was inconsistent with the decision to stabilize rates. As market participants became aware of the inconsistency, they increasingly evidenced a preference for higher-yielding – but hardly riskier – long-term debt.[17] Virtually all of the $15.7 billion increase in Treasury bills from the beginning of 1941 to mid-1946 ended up on Federal Reserve Bank balance sheets (Table 2.3); $6.8 billion of the $34.8 billion increase in certificates ended up in the same place. In contrast, only a modest portion of the wartime increase in notes ended up with the Fed and the Fed actually reduced its bond holdings during the war.

The disproportionate increase in Federal Reserve holdings of short-term Treasury debt reflects (1) the decision of the Treasury to issue across the curve during the war and (2) the preference of public investors for intermediate-term notes and longer-term bonds. In keeping to its

Type of Bond," *New York Times*, May 1, 1942, p. 29; "Treasury Plans New 'Tap' Issue: An Innovation," *Wall Street Journal*, May 1, 1942, p. 6; and Murphy (1950, pp. 98–99).

14 Wicker (1969, p. 453) argues that Federal Reserve officials did not interpret their 1942 support of a ⅜ percent bill rate as an indefinite commitment: "The evidence on this point is overwhelming – the record of continuous requests made to the Treasury during the war period to approve an increase in the bill rate." Wicker (1969, p. 457) states that Treasury officials "repeatedly rejected requests by the FOMC to increase bill rates."

15 Walker (1954, p. 27).

16 Lutz (1940, p. 59) states that "In recent years we have had a situation where future short rates . . . were expected to rise, which accounts for the fact that we have a series of yields which ascends with the length of the maturities. . . . Direct evidence [of such expectations] is to be found in the financial journals, which are full of warnings that present interest rates are unusually low."

17 Walker (1954, pp. 31–33), Wicker (1969, pp. 455–56), and Meltzer (2003, pp. 580 and 596).

Table 2.3 *Selected assets and liabilities of Federal Reserve Banks.*

	Beginning of 1941 ($ billions)	Mid-1946 ($ billions)	Increase ($ billions)
Assets			
Gold and gold certificates[a]	19.8	18.1	−1.7
Loans and advances	0.0	0.2	0.2
Treasury securities			
Bills	0.0	14.5	14.5
Certificates	0.0	6.8	6.8
Notes	0.9	1.7	0.8
Bonds	1.3	0.8	−0.5
Liabilities			
Federal Reserve notes	5.9	24.2	18.3
Member bank reserve balances	14.0	16.1	2.1

[a] Includes redemption fund for Federal Reserve notes.
Federal Reserve Bulletin, February 1941, p. 131; and August 1946, p. 883.

commitment to stabilize interest rates, the Fed had to purchase all of the bills that the public did not want to hold at the ⅜ percent ceiling rate – which, as it turned out, was most of the bills that the Treasury issued for new money. The resulting debt monetization fueled a doubling of high-powered money (the sum of Federal Reserve notes and member bank reserve balances in Table 2.3) and laid the foundation for the postwar inflation. The consumer price index rose 34 percent between 1945 and 1948.[18]

FROM THE END OF THE WAR TO THE END OF 1949

World War II ended with the surrender of Germany in May 1945 and Japan three months later. The key debt management issue in the postwar period was how the Federal Reserve would exit from the wartime interest rate stabilization program.[19] System officials wanted to avoid precipitous

[18] US Department of Commerce (1975, p. 210).

[19] Sproul (1964, p. 228) states that "In the reconversion period, at the end of the war in 1945, the problem facing the Federal Reserve System was how to proceed, and at what speed, to recapture [the initiative on creation of reserves], and to restore the ability of the Federal Reserve Banks to place a price upon reserve credit and a check on its availability which could be varied to meet changes in economic circumstances."

action that might destabilize the swollen Treasury market[20] but they also wanted to restrain inflation. Some – including, most prominently, Allan Sproul, president of the Federal Reserve Bank of New York from January 1941 to June 1956 – were willing to accept higher interest rates in the process.[21] Treasury officials resisted, concerned that higher rates would add to Federal expenditures. Sproul later observed that "the hesitations and refusals of the Treasury meant that the defrosting of the wartime 'pattern of rates' took place distressingly slowly."[22]

The defrosting started with thirteen-week bills, frozen at ⅜ percent since the spring of 1942. Sproul notes that "from the closing months of 1945, all through 1946, the [Federal Reserve] was pressing for an end of [the] artificially low buying rate."[23] At a meeting of the Executive Committee of the Federal Open Market Committee in January 1947, Sproul proposed that the committee should "discuss with the Treasury and recommend to the full Committee that the Committee authorize the abandonment of the posted buying rate."[24] As a "sweetener" to Treasury, he suggested that the Federal Open Market Committee (FOMC) and the Reserve Banks should seek restoration of a franchise tax on excess Bank earnings that had been eliminated in 1933. Restoration of the tax would offset the cost to the Treasury of higher bill rates.

Federal Reserve and Treasury officials discussed Sproul's proposals as well as the prospect of an increase in the ⅞ percent ceiling rate on certificates at a meeting on February 26, but the Treasury pronounced itself unready to reach a decision.[25] Another meeting followed on Friday, April 18. The Treasury again deferred a decision but said it would "express its views the following week."[26] More discussions, but no decision,

[20] Thomas and Young (1947) note (p. 100) the Fed's "responsibilities for maintaining an orderly and stable market for Government debt" and (p. 101) the System's "new responsibility, inherited from war finance, of maintaining a stable market for the public debt." Gaines (1962, p. 63) states that "the principal officials of [the Fed and the Treasury] were in substantial agreement on basic policies through most of the first four postwar years, differing principally on the levels of interest rates that should be maintained not on the root question of whether *any* level of rates should be maintained." Emphasis in the original.

[21] Meltzer (2003, pp. 634–35, 637).

[22] Sproul (1964, p. 228).

[23] Sproul (1964, p. 228).

[24] Minutes of the Executive Committee of the Federal Open Market Committee, January 10, 1947, pp. 11–12.

[25] Minutes of the Executive Committee of the Federal Open Market Committee, February 27, 1947, p. 2.

[26] Minutes of the Executive Committee of the Federal Open Market Committee, May 2, 1947, pp. 3–4.

followed in May, and Federal Reserve officials came to the conclusion that the Treasury was unlikely to take any action before the end of June.[27]

In late June, Marriner Eccles, the Chairman of the Board of Governors of the Federal Reserve System from November 1934 to January 1948, put it bluntly to Treasury officials that,

> the elimination of the posted rate on Treasury bills was long overdue, that the rate was a wartime measure that had long since ceased to serve the purpose for which it was established, [and] that the elimination of the rate was a matter for decision by the Federal Open Market Committee and did not require the assumption of any responsibility by the Treasury.[28]

The FOMC announced the termination of the posted rate program on July 2.[29]

Under the new policy, the bill rate was left to "find its level in the market in proper relation to the yields on certificates of indebtedness."[30] Bill rates rose to 0.75 percent in August (Chart 2.2), forcing a reconsideration of certificate yields.[31] Officials raised the ceiling rate on one-year certificates to 1 percent in September and 1⅛ percent in November (Table 2.4).

Higher yields on bills and certificates – as well as the prospect of rising yields (and, therefore, falling prices) on longer-term securities – incentivized investors to move in on the yield curve, selling bonds and buying shorter-term securities. The System accommodated the reallocation, reducing its bill portfolio to $4.8 billion and expanding its holdings of bonds to $7.2 billion by the end of 1949 (Chart 2.3).[32] At the same time, the Treasury refrained from issuing bonds and did all of its refinancing with bills, certificates, and notes.

27 Minutes of the Executive Committee of the Federal Open Market Committee, June 5, 1947, pp. 3–4; and the Federal Open Market Committee, June 5, 1947, pp. 4–6 and 12. In the meantime, the Board of Governors acted to transfer to the Treasury most of the excess earnings of the Reserve Banks by charging the Banks interest on Federal Reserve notes and remitting the proceeds to the Treasury. "Transfer to Treasury of Excess Earnings of Federal Reserve Banks," *Federal Reserve Bulletin*, May 1947, p. 518; and minutes of the Board of Governors of the Federal Reserve System, April 11, 1947, pp. 12–14, and April 23, 1947, pp. 1–6.

28 Minutes of the Executive Committee of the Federal Open Market Committee, June 30, 1947, pp. 6–8.

29 "Unpegs Interest on Treasury Bills," *New York Times*, July 3, 1947, p. 25; "Federal Reserve Announces the End of 'Pegged' ⅜% Interest Rate on Government Short Term Bills," *Wall Street Journal*, July 3, 1947, p. 8; and Federal Reserve Bank of New York Circular no. 3230, July 3, 1947. See also Meltzer (2003, pp. 642–43), Thomas (1951, p. 626), and Sproul (1964, p. 228).

30 Federal Reserve Bank of New York Circular no. 3230, July 3, 1947.

31 Meltzer (2003, p. 643).

32 Board of Governors of the Federal Reserve System (1976, table 9.5A).

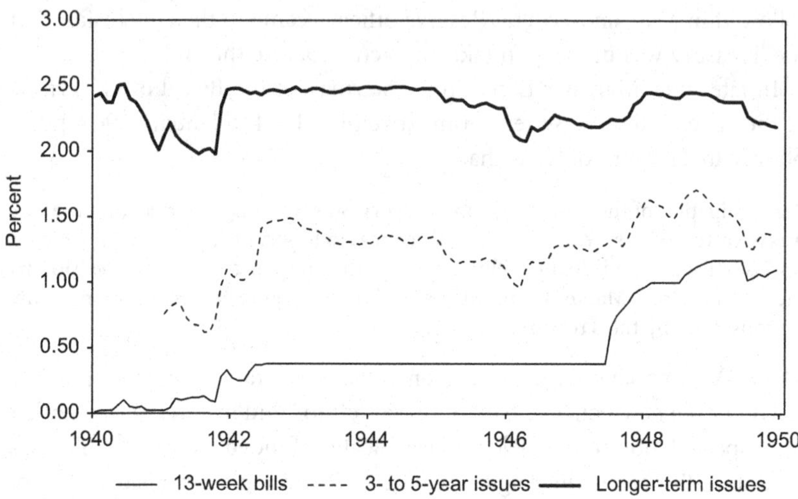

Chart 2.2 Treasury yields. Monthly averages.
Board of Governors of the Federal Reserve System (1976, tables 12.7A and 12.12A).

Treasury and Federal Reserve officials raised the rate on one-year certificates to 1¼ percent in September 1948,[33] but that was as high as it got before the end of the 1940s. System officials continued to seek further relaxation of the interest rate ceilings, but the onset of a recession in November 1948 undercut the urgency of their requests: by the fall of 1949, the Treasury was back to selling one-year certificates with a 1⅛ percent coupon.

THE PRIMARY MARKET

Treasury officials relied on three mechanisms to raise new money and refinance maturing debt during the 1940s – auctions, fixed-price cash subscription offerings, and fixed-price exchange offerings. Bills were sold only by auction; certificates, notes, and bonds were sold only in fixed-price offerings.

Bill Auctions

Treasury officials had been auctioning bills since 1929 and thirteen-week bills on a regular and predictable weekly basis since 1938.[34] By the end of the 1940s, they were auctioning $800 million to $1 billion of thirteen-week

[33] Sproul (1964, p. 229). [34] Garbade (2012, pp. 298–302).

Table 2.4 *Treasury offerings of coupon-bearing debt.*

Issue date	Term (months)	Coupon rate (percent)	Amount issued ($ billions)
1947			
Jan. 2	12	7/8	3.13
Feb. 1	12	7/8	3.95
Mar. 1	12	7/8	2.14
Apr. 1	12	7/8	1.32
Jun. 2	12	7/8	1.78
Jul. 1	12	7/8	2.74
Aug. 1	11	7/8	1.13
Sep. 2	10	7/8	2.21
Sep. 15	12½	1	4.09
Oct. 1	12	1	1.35
Nov. 1	11	1	1.47
Dec. 1	13	1⅛	3.54
1948			
Jan. 2	12	1⅛	2.59
Feb. 2	12	1⅛	2.19
Mar. 1	12	1⅛	3.55
Apr. 1	12	1⅛	1.06
Jun. 1	12	1⅛	4.30
Jul. 1	12	1⅛	5.78
Sep. 15	18½	1⅜	3.60
Oct. 1	12	1¼	6.54
Dec. 15	12	1¼	0.52
1949			
Jan. 3	12	1¼	5.70
Feb. 1	12	1¼	1.99
Mar. 1	12	1¼	2.92
Apr. 1	12	1¼	0.96
Jun. 1	12	1¼	5.02
Jul. 1	12	1¼	5.60
Sep. 15	12	1⅛	1.20
Oct. 1	12	1⅛	6.24
Dec. 15	51	1⅜	4.68

Treasury annual reports and offering circulars.

bills every week, applying most or all of the proceeds to the redemption of maturing bills. New offerings were announced on Friday, auctions closed at 2:00 p.m. (New York time) the following Monday, and awards were announced later the same day. The new bills were issued and paid for three days later, to mature on Thursday thirteen weeks hence.

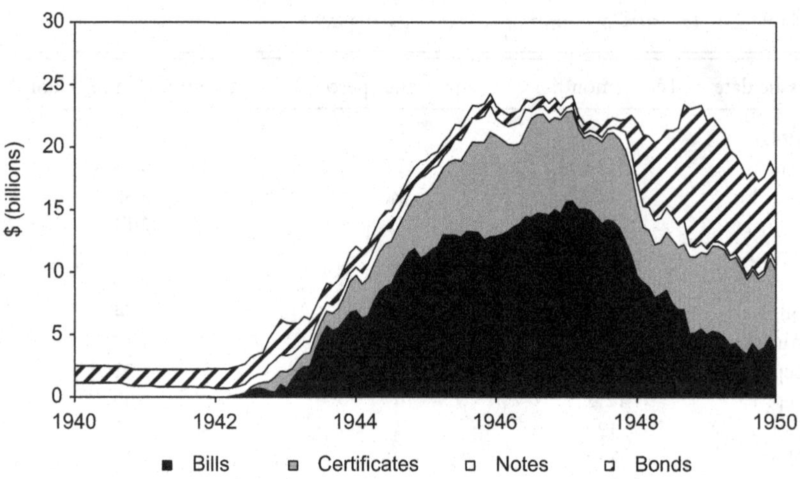

Chart 2.3 Treasury securities in the System Open Market Account. End of month. Board of Governors of the Federal Reserve System (1976, table 9.5A).

Bill auctions were conducted as discriminating, or multiple-price, auctions in which each successful bidder paid its bid price. Bidders who bid above the lowest accepted price (commonly called the "stop-out" price) were filled in full; those who bid at the stop-out price were subject to pro rata rationing. Auction participation was open to anyone, although participants other than a bank or recognized dealer[35] had to make a 2 percent down payment or provide a bank guaranty of payment.

Cash Subscription Offerings

Certificates, notes, and bonds were sold on a fixed-price cash subscription basis during the war. Treasury officials fixed the coupon rate on a new issue, priced the offering at par, and solicited subscriptions. Subscription books were open to individuals for more than a month and to other subscribers for about a week. Treasury's cash needs were essentially unlimited and all subscriptions were filled in full. The Victory Loan offerings in the fall of 1945 were the last cash offerings of coupon-bearing securities in the 1940s.

[35] As discussed in Chapter 4, the Federal Reserve Bank of New York formalized the concept of a "recognized dealer" in 1939.

Exchange Offerings

The Treasury began paying down debt soon after the end of the Victory Loan drive. Since it had no need to raise new cash, it switched to making exchange offerings to refinance maturing debt. Officials set the coupon rate on a new issue and offered it in exchange, on a par-for-par basis, for one or more maturing issues. Holders of exchange-eligible maturing debt could tender that debt, receiving in return the new securities (tenders were always filled in full), or they could sit tight and receive repayment of principal at maturity.

Exchange-eligible issues were commonly referred to as "rights" because holders had the right to exchange the issues for whatever new security the Treasury was offering. Short-dated rights usually traded above par because new issues typically had coupon rates in excess of current market yields.[36] (Rights couldn't trade much below par because they could always be redeemed at par at maturity.)

An Example. On December 5, 1949, the Treasury offered a new 1⅜ percent 4¼-year note in exchange for any of four issues due to be redeemed on December 15, including,

- $519 million of a 1¼ percent certificate maturing December 15;
- $2,098 million of a 2 percent bond due December 15, 1951, and called for early redemption on December 15, 1949;
- $491 million of a 3⅛ percent bond due December 15, 1952, and called for early redemption on December 15, 1949; and
- $1,786 million of a 2½ percent bond due December 15, 1953 and called for early redemption on December 15, 1949.[37]

Treasury received tenders for $4.7 billion of the 4¼-year notes prior to the close of the subscription books on December 8. On December 15, it issued notes to everyone who had accepted the exchange offer and made cash redemption payments (commonly called "attrition") of $219 million to those who had not.[38]

Federal Reserve Participation in the Primary Market

Section 14(b) of the Federal Reserve Act of December 23, 1913, authorized Federal Reserve Banks to "buy and sell, at home and abroad, bonds and

[36] Market participants sometimes found an exchange offering so attractive that the rights to the offering had a negative yield to maturity. See Garbade (2012, p. 312) and Cecchetti (1988).

[37] Federal Reserve Bank of New York Circular no. 3517, December 5, 1949.

[38] 1950 Treasury Annual Report, p. 18.

notes of the United States." The Act did not make any distinction between purchases in the primary market, directly from the Treasury, and secondary market purchases.

Section 206 of the Banking Act of 1935 amended Section 14(b) by adding the words "but only in the open market." The qualification appeared to exclude Reserve Banks from participating in primary market offerings, and in 1936 they purchased securities only from dealers, a limitation that proved to be both expensive and burdensome.[39]

The objective of Section 206 is obscure but, as discussed in the appendix to this chapter, one interpretation is that Congress wanted to deter the executive branch from forcing the Fed to extend credit to the government on terms and in amounts that did not reflect the realities of the market. System officials consequently concluded, in early 1937, that the Fed could participate in exchange offerings because those offerings did not provide the Treasury with new money and did not treat the Fed differently from other market participants.[40]

In 1947, the Treasury began to accept maturing bills in payment for new bills.[41] Reasoning analogous to the 1937 decision led the FOMC to allow the System Open Market Account to participate in auctions of thirteen-week bills up to the amount of maturing bills held in the account. Officials on the open market trading desk at the New York Fed – hereafter, "the Desk" – had to bid like other auction market participants and a SOMA tender was subject to pro rata rationing if the auction stopped at the tender's bid price, just like tenders from other auction participants. More

[39] Minutes of the Federal Open Market Committee, January 26, 1937, p. 11, noting "the present practice of selling maturing securities in the market and replacing them with other securities purchased in the market" and stating that, in the course of replacing maturing securities, the Banks paid in excess of $25 thousand in commissions to dealers during 1936.

[40] Minutes of the Federal Open Market Committee, January 26, 1937, pp. 11–12, noting that Federal Reserve participation in Treasury exchange offerings was limited "to the *replacement* of maturing securities with securities of *an issue being offered to the public.*" Emphasis added. The FOMC authorized the Federal Reserve Bank of New York to exchange "directly with the Treasury Department maturing securities held in the [System Open Market Account] for securities being offered to the public under terms which permit the tender of the maturing securities in exchange." Minutes of the Federal Open Market Committee, January 26, 1937, p. 12.

[41] "New Treasury Rule," *New York Times*, April 25, 1947, p. 31. See also the difference between the notice of public offering of the July 24, 1947, bills (Federal Reserve Bank of New York Circular no. 3204, April 18, 1947) and the notice of public offering of the July 31, 1947, bills (Federal Reserve Bank of New York Circular no. 3206, April 25, 1947).

generally, the Fed did not receive any preferential treatment in bill auctions.

An FOMC press release announcing the policy change emphasized that the new authority would not provide the Treasury with any new money and that the Open Market Account would be treated the same as other market participants:

> The Federal Reserve Banks will receive the *same percentage allotment of bills as will other bidders at the same price.* Acquisitions of bills by the Federal Reserve Banks, in this manner, will represent the *replacement of bills originally purchased in the market* and, like other exchanges of maturing securities for new securities, would not be subject to the limitation contained in [section 14(b)] of the Federal Reserve Act. *No new credit will be made available to the Treasury* by the Federal Reserve Banks as a result of this change in procedure.[42]

The Committee explained that the change was intended to simplify the process of reinvesting maturing bills held in the Open Market Account:

> These related actions were taken to relieve a situation which has become less and less appropriate, as weekly maturities of bills held by the Federal Reserve Banks have increased, until recently they have ordinarily been more than $1,100 million of a total weekly maturity of $1,300 million. In the past the market has taken all of each week's offerings of Treasury bills and has promptly sold to the Federal Reserve Banks that portion of the offering which it did not wish to hold. Thus the Federal Reserve Banks indirectly replaced part or all of their Treasury bill maturities. Such a procedure means that the market places tenders for new issues of bills in amounts bearing no relation to market requirements, the excess being taken for the purpose of immediate sale to the Federal Reserve Banks. In these circumstances, a more direct method of replacing maturing bills held by the Federal Reserve Banks has been deemed desirable.

At the end of the 1940s, the Federal Reserve was a full participant in exchange offerings of coupon-bearing debt and participated in auctions of thirteen-week bills up to the amount of its maturing bills. It could not invest new money through bill auctions, and it could not participate in cash offerings of coupon-bearing debt.

THE SECONDARY MARKET

The over-the-counter market for outstanding Treasury debt first took shape in the 1920s in the wake of the dramatic expansion in Treasury debt, primarily certificates and bonds, during World War I.

[42] Federal Reserve Bank of New York Circular no. 3207, April 25, 1947. Emphasis added.

Treasury bonds traded actively on the New York Stock Exchange during the war, but certificates did not trade in a free market until the spring of 1920.[43] In 1921, the Treasury began to issue notes to facilitate its debt management operations.[44] Certificates and notes were not eligible for listing on the Exchange and an active over-the-counter market quickly developed. Early dealers included C. F. Childs, Discount Corp., Charles E. Quincey & Co., Salomon Brothers & Hutzler, and Bankers Trust Co.[45] Bond trading migrated to the over-the-counter market before the middle of the decade, both because dealers were willing to use their capital to facilitate large, albeit sporadic, customer trades, and because customers swapping long-term bonds for shorter-term debt (and vice versa) found it more efficient to execute both legs of the swap at the same time with a single counterparty.[46]

The postwar market in Treasury debt was national in scope but centered in New York. Large dealers had their main offices in that city, keeping in close contact with branch offices in other cities and with regional dealers by telegraph and telephone. The development of an integrated national market was facilitated by the introduction, in 1921, of wire transfers of certificates and notes between Federal Reserve Banks and branches.[47] (The significance of such transfers is explained in chapter 25 below.)

The government securities market underwent a second significant expansion during the Great Depression. Marketable Treasury debt increased from $15.4 billion at the end of 1929 to $35.6 billion at the end of 1940.[48] The Depression-linked decline in private economic activity and increase in marketable Treasury debt provided strong incentives for financial institutions to expand their activities in Treasury securities.[49] Almost a dozen firms, all located in New York and including C. J.

[43] Garbade (2012, pp. 185–92). [44] Garbade (2012, pp. 161–66 and 185–92).

[45] Beckhart, Smith, and Brown (1932, p. 335). [46] Garbade (2012, pp. 196–98).

[47] Smith (1956, p. 86). Bills became wireable in December 1930, shortly after they were introduced; bonds became wireable in March 1948. Smith (1956, pp. 88 and 91). See also "Telegraphic Transfer of U.S. Bonds Slated to Broaden the Market for Such Securities," *New York Times*, February 5, 1948, p. 35, "Treasury Approves Title Transfer on U.S. Bonds by Telegraph March 1," *Wall Street Journal*, February 5, 1948, p. 8, and 1948 Federal Reserve Bank of New York Annual Report, p. 50.

[48] Statement of the Public Debt of the United States, December 31, 1929, and December 31, 1940.

[49] Federal Reserve Bank of New York (1940, pp. 10–11). See also Sobel (1986, p. 45), stating that, in the early 1930s, "Salomon Brothers expanded its operations in government paper while cutting back in the corporate sector."

Devine & Co. and New York Hanseatic Corp., joined the half-dozen firms already active in the market.[50]

The growth of the market in the 1930s also led to the appearance of several significant regional dealers. A 1940 Federal Reserve Bank of New York study stated that "the First National Bank of Chicago operates as a dealer and is the most important Government security dealer having the principal office outside New York." The study further noted that "the Continental Illinois National Bank and Trust Company of Chicago is considered a dealer ... in Treasury bills."[51]

The core of the market nevertheless remained in New York. The 1940 New York Bank study observed that,

> All of the facilities existing outside New York for trading in Government securities are operated "on the basis" of the New York market, both with respect to price quotations and the relative breadth of the market existing for various issues of Government securities. Except for a small amount of orders which are "matched off" by banks and investment firms in local markets (on the basis of New York quotations), all of the trading is ultimately with or through the Government security dealers in New York. For example, the First National Bank of Chicago ... keeps in close touch with the New York market by telegraph and has a staff member permanently located in New York who checks quotations and condition of markets for individual issues, and executes transactions for the bank with the dealers in New York. Most of the other banks located outside New York transact their Government securities business ... through the branches and representatives of the New York dealers ... or directly by wire with New York.[52]

THE POSTWAR SECONDARY MARKET

At the end of the 1940s there were about twenty active dealers in the over-the-counter market for Treasury debt.[53] New York continued to be the center of activity.[54]

[50] Childs (1947, pp. 383–84). Other new entrants included R.W. Pressprich & Co., Harvey Fisk & Sons, Harriman Ripley & Co., and J.B. Roll & Co.

[51] Federal Reserve Bank of New York (1940, p. 14).

[52] Federal Reserve Bank of New York (1940, pp. 14–15).

[53] Federal Open Market Committee (1952, p. 261).

[54] A 1952 study stated that "all of the larger Government securities dealers have their principal offices in New York City and Chicago but they operate on a national scale, serving the principal cities through the medium of branch offices, representatives, banks and a variety of firms doing a general securities business with which they maintain contact by telephone or teletype facilities." Federal Reserve Bank of New York (1952, p. 10-1).

Despite the relatively large number of dealers and the lack of a central trading floor, the market was well integrated and trading was essentially continuous. A 1952 study by the Federal Reserve Bank of New York remarked that "through maintaining from minute to minute during each trading day a set of posted quotations . . . the dealers attempt to provide investors in the Government securities market with the closest practicable approximation to a 'full and continuous market.'"[55]

The 1952 study also emphasized the tight integration of the interdealer market:

> Making and maintaining a market not only requires a broad and continuous contact with major investors but also depends on constant checking and cross checking among the individual dealers themselves as to their competitor's markets. This provides the dealer with a composite view of the market as a whole and, to the extent that quoted prices may be a clue, guides him in the location of fresh sources of supply and demand.[56]

The study observed that "in a well-organized dealer market, anything more than a nominal disparity between dealers' markets cannot last for long" and concluded that "the concerted action of the dealers engaging in searching inquiry and continual refinement of their quotations" gave the market "the necessary degree of cohesion and makes it a collective reflection of the many judgments that are brought to bear in the valuation process."[57]

Bid-ask spreads for Treasury securities ranged from about 1 basis point for thirteen-week bills to 1/32nd of 1 percent of par value (or $312.50 per million dollars of par value) for long-term bonds. Transactions for as much as $1 million of long-term bonds and up to $5 million or more for shorter-term securities could usually be executed "on-the-wire" with a dealer.[58]

THE ROLE OF DEALERS IN PRIMARY MARKET OFFERINGS

Dealers played an important role in both cash auctions of Treasury bills and fixed-price exchange offerings of coupon-bearing securities.

Following the uncapping of bill yields in 1947, many smaller, and not a few midsized, participants in the bill market were reluctant to bid for bills in primary market auctions; they were fearful that they might suffer the

[55] Federal Reserve Bank of New York (1952, p. 2–5).
[56] Federal Reserve Bank of New York (1952, p. 10-3).
[57] Federal Reserve Bank of New York (1952, pp. 10-3 to 10-4).
[58] Federal Open Market Committee (1952, p. 261).

"winner's curse" of paying more than other successful bidders. They preferred, instead, to buy in the secondary market following the close of bidding from whatever dealer was quoting the lowest price. Dealers were left as the principle participants in bill auctions, bidding not for investment but to resell to retail investors, usually on a when-issued basis for settlement on the Thursday following an auction.

Dealers also played an important role in exchange offerings of Treasury debt. Holders of maturing debt frequently had no interest in rolling over their investments, preferring instead to cash out their positions. Investors interested in acquiring a new offering, on the other hand, frequently did not own any of the maturing debt. Dealers facilitated both parties in either of two ways. The simplest was for a dealer to purchase maturing debt, that is, "rights," from a current holder (thereby cashing the seller out of its investment) and then sell the rights to a prospective new investor, who could tender the rights in exchange for the new issue. Alternatively, a dealer could purchase maturing debt from a current holder and sell the new issue on a "when-issued" basis, for settlement on the exchange date fixed by the Treasury, obtaining the security it had sold by exercising the exchange rights on the security it had purchased. Both processes were cumbersome and required the completion of two separate transactions, but both served to limit attrition and allowed the Treasury to refinance the bulk of its maturing debt.

APPENDIX. THE OBJECTIVE OF THE PROHIBITION ON DIRECT PURCHASES OF TREASURY SECURITIES BY FEDERAL RESERVE BANKS

The Banking Act of 1935 amended Section 14(b) of the Federal Reserve Act by limiting System purchases of Treasury securities to purchases "in the open market."

The 1935 Act was introduced into the 74th Congress as H.R. 7617. Following passage by the House of Representatives, H.R. 7617 moved to the Senate, where it was referred to the Senate Banking Committee. The committee reported out an amended version of the bill that included the amendment to Section 14(b).

The report of the Senate Banking Committee does not explain the reason for prohibiting direct purchases from the Treasury. The sole reference to the prohibition in committee hearings came during the testimony of Winthrop Aldrich, chairman of the Chase National Bank in New York. Aldrich decried the prospective power of the revamped FOMC, prospectively dominated by presidential appointees, to compel the Reserve Banks to purchase securities directly from the Treasury. He recommended that "the direct purchase of Government obligations from the Treasury . . . be specifically declared not to be open-market operations within the meaning of the act."[59]

Treasury officials were not happy with the amended version of H.R. 7617. In a letter to the chairman of the Senate Banking Committee, Under Secretary of the Treasury T. J. Coolidge questioned whether "in times of emergency it might not be important to permit a direct loan. This might have been the case in the bank holiday in 1933 had there been a sizeable note issue coming due when the banks were closed; it might be the case in time of war."[60] A House-Senate conference committee chose to retain the proviso in spite of Coolidge's objections[61] and the prohibition passed into law.

Marriner Eccles, the Chairman of the Board of Governors, suggested in 1942 that direct purchases may have been prohibited to prevent excessive government expenditures:

> The restriction forbidding Federal Reserve banks to buy Government obligations except on the open market was imposed . . . on the theory that forcing the Government to borrow on the open market would afford a check on excessive public expenditures . . .[62]

and further suggested in 1947 that the prohibition was aimed at preventing chronic deficits:

> Those who inserted this proviso were motivated by the mistaken theory that it would help to prevent deficit financing. According to the theory, Government borrowing should be subject to the "test of the market."[63]
>
> [T]here was a feeling that [the absence of a prohibition] left the door wide open to the Government to borrow directly from the Federal Reserve all that was necessary to finance the Government deficit, and that took off any restraint toward getting a balanced budget.[64]
>
> There was some feeling that [Congress] ought to give the money market more control and influence over what money the Government was going to be able to

59 Committee on Banking and Currency (April 19 to June 3, 1935, pp. 399, 403, and 409).

60 Letter from Coolidge to Carter Glass, July 30, 1935, Box 6D, Carter Glass papers at the University of Virginia.

61 Committee of Conference (1935, pp. 50–51).

62 Committee on the Judiciary (January 30 and February 2, 1942, pp. 44–45).

63 Committee on Banking and Currency (March 3, 4, and 5, 1947, p. 2).

64 Committee on Banking and Currency (March 3, 4, and 5, 1947, p. 8).

raise, and that if they stopped the open-market committee from purchasing directly from the Treasury they would thereby deter deficit financing.[65]

Since the Reserve Banks retained the authority to buy Treasury securities in the open market, the idea of limiting either expenditures or deficits by prohibiting direct purchases was clearly fallacious.

65 Committee on Banking and Currency (March 3, 4, and 5, 1947, p. 121).

3

Reserves, Reserve Requirements, and Reserves Management

A reserve requirement is a statutory or regulatory instruction that a bank must hold a designated fraction of specified liabilities in the form of a fundamental medium of exchange, such as gold or deposits at a central bank. Originally considered a device to enhance the liquidity of bank liabilities,[1] by the early 1930s, US monetary authorities had come to view reserve requirements as an instrument for controlling monetary aggregates. A System committee stated in 1932 that "it is no longer the primary function of legal reserve requirements to assure or preserve the liquidity of the individual member bank" and that one of the main functions of such requirements was to "operate in the direction of sound credit conditions by exerting an influence on changes in the volume of bank credit."[2]

[1] A 1938 history of reserve requirements ("The History of Reserve Requirements for Banks in the United States," *Federal Reserve Bulletin*, November 1938, pp. 953–72) states (p. 953) that "originally it was considered that the principal purpose of reserve requirements was to assure the convertibility into cash of bank notes and deposits . . ." Feinman (1993, p. 569) states that "before the establishment of the Federal Reserve System, reserve requirements were thought to help ensure the liquidity of bank notes and deposits . . ."

[2] 1932 Annual Report of the Federal Reserve Board, pp. 260–61. The 1938 history of reserve requirements cited in the preceding footnote states (p. 953) that "reserve requirements under the Federal Reserve System have served primarily . . . as a medium through which an influence can be exercised on the expansion and contraction of credit." Feinman (1993, p. 569) states that "since the creation of the Federal Reserve System as a lender of last resort, capable of meeting the liquidity needs of the entire banking system, . . . reserve requirements have evolved into a supplemental tool of monetary policy, a tool that reinforces the effects of open market operations and discount policy on overall monetary and credit conditions."

RESERVE REQUIREMENTS

Section 19 of the Federal Reserve Act imposed reserve requirements on two types of member bank liabilities:[3] demand deposits (defined as deposits payable on demand or within thirty days) and time deposits (deposits payable after thirty days, and all savings accounts and certificates of deposit subject to not less than thirty days' notice before payment.)

Demand Deposits

Reserve requirements for demand deposits were based on a bank's geographic location – a carryover from the National Banking System (Box 3.1). Prior to 1936, the requirements were fixed by statute and not subject to variation by either district Federal Reserve Banks or the Federal Reserve Board in Washington.

Following a 1917 amendment to the Federal Reserve Act,[4] demand deposits at member banks in "central reserve cities" – New York, Chicago, and St. Louis in 1917, but only New York and Chicago after 1922[5] – were subject to a 13 percent reserve requirement. Demand deposits at member banks in some fifty "reserve cities" were subject to a 10 percent requirement. Demand deposits at all other member banks, commonly known as "country banks," were subject to a 7 percent requirement. Reserves were assessed against deposits net of funds due from other banks (such as demand deposits with clearing center banks) and cash items (such as checks) in process of collection.

The original version of the Federal Reserve Act allowed banks to use specified forms of vault cash, including gold coins minted by the Treasury and Treasury gold certificates (but not Federal Reserve notes[6]), to satisfy

[3] Nonmember banks were subject to reserve requirements prescribed by state statutes or state banking regulations.

[4] Act of June 21, 1917.

[5] Section 11 of the Federal Reserve Act gave the Federal Reserve Board authority to designate and de-designate reserve cities and central reserve cities. "The History of Reserve Requirements for Banks in the United States," *Federal Reserve Bulletin*, November 1938, pp. 953–72, provides a summary of the Board's early exercise of that authority.

[6] Miller (1921, p. 182) states that "under the terms of the Federal Reserve act, federal reserve notes were not available as legal reserve money to member banks." Glass (1927, p. 334) observes that a provision "permitting Federal reserve notes to be used as reserves in the individual banks" was removed in the course of House-Senate conference committee negotiations prior to final passage of the Federal Reserve Act. Timberlake (1978, p. 203) states that the Federal Reserve Act "prohibited the use of Federal Reserve notes as eligible reserves for member banks."

Box 3.1 Reserve Requirements under the National Banking System

The National Banking System was created by Congress during the Civil War to facilitate war finance and modified from time to time thereafter to enhance the stability of the banking system.[1]

National banks were banks of deposit and issue. Bank notes issued by national banks and used as currency by the public were backed by Treasury bonds of equal value deposited with the Department of the Treasury.[2] In the event a national bank failed, Treasury officials would sell the bonds pledged by the failed bank and use the proceeds to redeem the notes issued by the bank. The scheme was so successful that Americans commonly treated national bank notes the same as "lawful" money such as gold coins and gold certificates.[3]

National bank deposit liabilities were subject to reserve requirements. Deposits, including both demand deposits and time deposits, at national banks in three large "central reserve cities" (New York, Chicago, and St. Louis) had a 25 percent reserve requirement that could only be satisfied with lawful money kept in the banks' vaults. Deposits at national banks in about fifty smaller "reserve cities" also had a 25 percent reserve requirement, but up to half of the required reserves could be kept in the form of deposits with central reserve city banks. Deposits at all other national banks had a 15 percent reserve requirement, two-thirds of which could be kept in the form of deposits with reserve and central reserve city banks. The tiered structure of reserve requirements was patterned on the historic practice of smaller banks keeping funds on deposit with larger "clearing" banks in regional and national financial centers to facilitate check collection and note redemption.[4]

1 See Timberlake (1978, ch. 7), Taus (1943, p. 61), Davis (1910), and Patterson (1954, pp. 27–29 and 151–52). The National Banking System was first authorized by the National Currency Act of February 25, 1863. That Act was repealed and reenacted in a modified form by the Act of June 3, 1864. The latter Act was renamed the National Bank Act by the Act of June 20, 1874. See also the Act of March 3, 1887.

2 The bonds were valued at the lesser of market value and principal value. Committee on Banking and Currency (1960, p. 32).

3 Friedman and Schwartz (1963, pp. 20–23). National bank notes were retired in 1935. Garbade (2012, ch. 22).

4 Garbade (2012, pp. 20–21).

reserve requirements; but the 1917 amendment limited reserves to funds on deposits at a Federal Reserve Bank. The change was intended to minimize the benefits from holding gold coins or gold certificates and thus to promote the concentration of the precious metal in Federal Reserve Banks.[7]

7 Miller (1921, p. 180) states that "the policy [of the act of June 21, 1917] was to impound as much of the stock of monetary gold in the country as possible in the federal reserve system." Warburg (1930, p. 157) states that the legislation "enabled the Reserve System to corral and mobilize the country's gold."

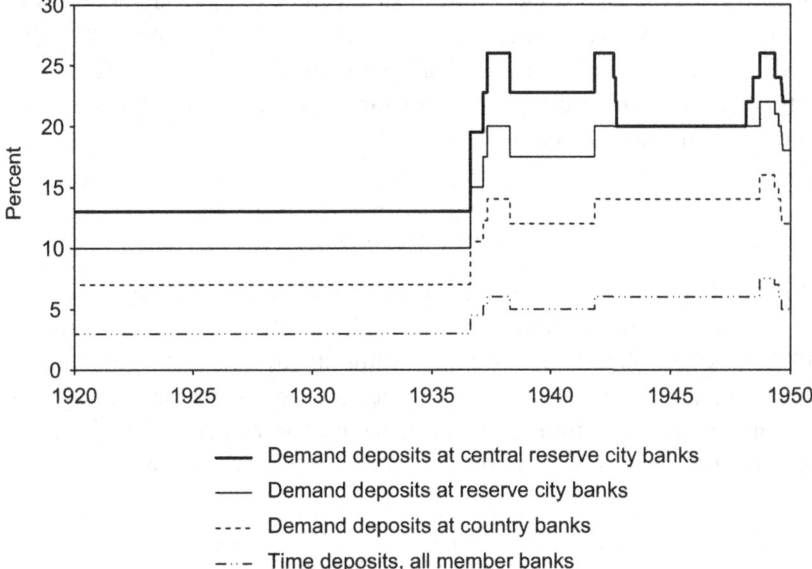

Chart 3.1 Reserve requirements.
Board of Governors of the Federal Reserve System (1976, table 10.4).

Consistent with the reframing of reserve requirements as an instrument of monetary control, the Banking Act of August 23, 1935, authorized the Board of Governors to as much as double member bank reserve requirements. Section 207 of the Act allowed the Board to vary reserve requirements on demand deposits within a band of 7 to 14 percent for country banks, 10 to 20 percent for reserve city banks, and 13 to 26 percent for central reserve city banks.

Acting on its new authority, the Board increased reserve requirements in 1936 and 1937, reduced them in 1938, increased them again following the US entry into World War II, and actively varied them in the late 1940s (Chart 3.1). At the end of 1949, the reserve requirement on demand deposits was 22 percent for central reserve city banks, 18 percent for reserve city banks, and 12 percent for country banks.

Federal government deposits at member banks were demand deposits and, at the end of 1949, were subject to the same reserve requirements as private demand deposits. Government deposits had, however, been exempted from reserve requirements during World War II to encourage member bank participation in the Treasury's War Loan Deposit Account program.[8] (As discussed more fully in an appendix to this chapter, the War Loan Deposit Account program was introduced during World War I to buffer US money markets from what would otherwise have been disruptive settlements of war bond sales. The program was renamed the Treasury Tax and Loan Account System in 1950.[9])

Time Deposits

Between 1917 and 1935, the reserve requirement for time deposits was fixed by statute at 3 percent, regardless of a bank's location. The Banking Act of 1935 gave the Board of Governors authority to vary the requirement. Beginning in mid-1936, the Board changed the requirement in parallel with changes in reserve requirements for demand deposits (Chart 3.1).[10] At the end of 1949, the reserve requirement on time deposits was 5 percent.

Computation Periods

Reserve requirements did not have to be satisfied each day, every day. Banks in reserve and central reserve cities averaged their close-of-business deposit liabilities and reserve balances each day over a reserve computation week that began on Thursday and ended on the following Wednesday. A bank was compliant if its *average* reserve balance exceeded the reserve requirement computed from its *average* deposit liabilities. Country banks averaged their deposit liabilities and reserve balances over semimonthly reserve computation periods that ran from the first to the fifteenth of a month, and from the sixteenth to the end of the month. The averaging provisions allowed a bank to make up deficiencies incurred early in a reserve period with later surpluses and to apply early surpluses against later deficiencies.[11]

[8] The exemption was mandated by the Act of April 13, 1943. See also Federal Reserve Bank of New York Circular no. 2608, April 13, 1943. The exemption was removed six months after the presidential proclamation of the cessation of hostilities. See Federal Reserve Bank of New York Circular no. 3224, July 1, 1947.

[9] Federal Reserve Bank of New York Circular no. 3518, December 2, 1949.

[10] Goodfriend and Hargraves (1983, p. 5) state that the substantial difference between reserve requirements on time deposits and reserve requirements on demand deposits "was apparently established to enable member banks to compete more effectively with state-chartered banks, who generally had a lower or zero reserve requirement on time deposits."

[11] Section 3 of Regulation D, enclosed in Federal Reserve Bank of New York Circular no. 3383, September 28, 1948.

Table 3.1 *Factors supplying and absorbing reserves, May 31, 1950. Millions of dollars.*

Factors supplying reserves	
US government securities	17,389
Loans, discounts, and advances	309
Float	236
Gold	24,231
Treasury currency	4,606
Total	46,771
Factors absorbing reserves	
Money in circulation	27,090
Treasury cash	1,309
Treasury deposits at Federal Reserve Banks	588
Other factors	1,972
Total	30,959
Member Bank Reserves	15,814

Federal Reserve Statistical Release H.4.1, June 1, 1950.

A bank was also allowed to make up a deficiency in one reserve computation period with a surplus in the following period as long as the earlier deficiency was not in excess of 2 percent of the bank's reserve requirement. The inter-period provision, however, was asymmetric: a bank could not use a surplus in one period to offset a deficiency in the next period.[12]

RESERVES IN AGGREGATE

The aggregate supply of reserves available to the banking system is conventionally constructed as the sum of factors that supply reserves, less the sum of factors that absorb reserves.

Table 3.1 shows the conventional construction for May 31, 1950. (An appendix to this chapter shows how the table was derived from the consolidated balance sheet of the twelve Reserve Banks, the Treasury Daily Statement, and the Circulation Statement of United States Money.) Factors supplying reserves include:

- US government securities held in the System Open Market Account;
- loans, discounts, and advances extended to member banks;

[12] Federal Reserve Bank of New York Circular no. 3503, October 18, 1949.

- float, the difference between cash items (mostly checks) in process of collection (an asset of the Federal Reserve Banks) and deferred availability cash items (a liability of the Banks);[13]
- gold, including nonnegotiable dollar-denominated gold certificates issued by the Treasury to the Reserve Banks (at the rate of $35 per ounce of gold pledged as security) in exchange for deposit balances at the Banks,[14] and gold held in the Treasury general fund; and
- Treasury currency, such as United States notes and silver certificates, silver dollars, and minor coin.

Factors absorbing reserves include:

- money in circulation, including Federal Reserve notes outstanding, less Federal Reserve notes held by a Reserve Bank other than the Bank of issue, less Federal Reserve notes held in the Treasury general fund, plus Treasury currency in circulation;
- Treasury cash, certain assets (including gold, Treasury currency, and Federal Reserve notes) held in the Treasury general fund; and
- Treasury deposits at Federal Reserve Banks.

Other things remaining the same, member bank reserves increase when the Federal Reserve Bank of New York buys securities for the System Open Market Account, when a Reserve Bank makes a discount window loan, when a storm delays check collection and float increases, and when the Treasury monetizes previously unpledged gold. Reserves decline when Americans choose to hold more cash (such as during holiday periods) and when tax payments lead to an increase in Treasury deposits at Federal Reserve Banks. Items that are not under the direct control of Federal Reserve officials, such as float, money in circulation, and Treasury deposits at Federal Reserve Banks, are commonly called "autonomous factors."

THE INTER-BANK MARKET FOR FEDERAL FUNDS

Every member bank had to hold at least the amount of reserves required but there was no benefit to holding more than what was required. Banks with excess reserves, or anticipating excess reserves, had an incentive to

[13] Float arises when a Federal Reserve Bank credits the reserve account of a bank that tendered a cash item for collection before the reserve account of the bank that will ultimately pay on the item has been debited.

[14] Garbade (2012, p. 245) explains the mechanics of this process.

lend reserves to banks with actual or anticipated deficiencies.[15] The result was a market in "Federal" funds – that is, funds on deposit with a Federal Reserve Bank.[16]

Large New York banks were at the center of the market for Federal funds, primarily because most transactions in negotiable financial instruments, including Treasury securities as well as money market instruments like commercial paper and bankers' acceptances,[17] involved payments from and to customers of the banks, including especially dealers who underwrote and made markets in the securities.[18] There were, consequently, significant flows of funds among the large New York banks (and between those banks and banks in the interior of the country) that sometimes left a bank with a reserve deficiency and sometimes with a surplus, either of which was liable to be reversed in a day or two. The Federal funds market offered a way to cure transient deficiencies and a way to earn interest on transient excesses.

The market in Federal funds was largely a market for overnight credit. A 1957 System study noted that "in recent years, most of the larger banks, in order to keep fully invested, have followed a policy of daily or at least very short-term adjustments in their reserve positions. Such a policy frequently requires quick turnarounds in the market: a bank may be a lender of excess reserves one day, a borrower to meet a deficiency the next."[19] Transaction costs made purchases and sales of securities, including even Treasury bills, unrewarding for adjustments that might be reversed in a day or two.[20] Garvin, Bantel & Co., a New York money broker, played a

[15] A 1957 study of the Federal funds market – the first System study of that market – stated that "most of the large banks strive to maintain an average reserve balance just sufficient to meet the legal minimum for the reserve computation period." Balles et al. (1959, pp. 13–14).

[16] Balles et al. (1959, pp. 22–39) reviews the origins of the Federal funds market in the 1920s and the development of the market after World War II. See also Turner (1931) and "Federal Funds," Federal Reserve Bank of New York *Monthly Review*, March 1950, pp. 28–30.

[17] Kreps (1952a, b) describes the postwar markets for commercial paper and bankers' acceptances.

[18] Roelse (1952, p. 4) states that "most money market transactions are cleared through [the books of the large New York City banks], and all inflows or outflows of funds between New York City and other parts of the country ... go through their reserve accounts on the books of the Federal Reserve Bank of New York."

[19] Balles et al. (1959, p. 8).

[20] McWhinney (1952, p. 8) states that "if a bank expects its money position to ease shortly ... it is likely first to try to buy (borrow) Federal funds. ... If a reserve deficiency is expected to be of some duration, the bank will probably sell securities ..." Balles et al. (1959, p. 10) states that "expectation as to the length of time a reserve excess or deficiency is likely to continue is [a] factor having a significant influence on choice of a reserve

major role in pairing off borrowers and lenders and establishing market-clearing interest rates.[21]

If a Federal funds transaction involved two New York banks, the bank "selling," or lending, funds would give the "purchasing" bank a draft on its account at the Federal Reserve Bank of New York and receive in return a conventional bank check.[22] The purchasing bank would forward the draft by messenger to the New York Fed, which, upon receipt, would debit the reserve account of the selling bank and credit the reserve account of the purchasing bank, thereby completing the contemplated transfer. The funds would be returned the following day when the bank check cleared. Interest was paid either by returning more than the amount borrowed or in a separate transfer. Transactions between New York banks and banks outside of the Second District were settled through transfers of funds on the Fed's leased wire system.[23]

The Federal funds market was important for two reasons: first, it facilitated an efficient distribution of reserves among member banks and reduced the need for banks to maintain buffer stocks of excess reserves, thus keeping aggregate reserves more closely aligned with aggregate reserve requirements and hence with monetary and credit aggregates.[24]

Second, the interest rate on purchases and sales of Federal funds provided a useful indicator of the availability of reserves relative to requirements.[25] If aggregate reserves expanded, perhaps because of an increase in

adjustment mechanism. The spread between bid and asked quotations and the risk of price change make the Treasury bill and other short-term securities unsuitable for very short-term reserve adjustments." See also Federal Reserve Bank of New York (1952, pp. 6–9).

21 See "Broker House Settles Loans Among Banks," *New York Herald Tribune*, February 25, 1951, p. A9, "Federal Funds Bank Deals Rise," *Journal of Commerce, N.Y.*, September 10, 1951, p. 3, "Along the Highways and Byways of Finance," *New York Times*, December 11, 1955, p. 185, and Balles et al. (1959, pp. 4–5, 11, 34, 35, 60, and 92–93).

22 Roelse (1952, p. 4) and Carr (1952, p. 13). Market participants universally used the terms "purchasing" and "selling" in lieu of "borrowing" and "lending." Balles et al. (1959, p. 16).

23 Carr (1952, p. 13) and Balles et al. (1959, pp. 6 and 52–53). See also Smith (1956).

24 Federal Reserve Bank of New York (1952, p. 6–9) noted that "the efficient utilization of 'available Federal funds' permits the money market to function on a minimum of excess reserves … and so keeps the banking system within the scope of the credit control measures of the Federal Reserve." However, a 1957 study of the Federal funds market observed that "many small banks … prefer to maintain cushions of excess reserves so that they need not be concerned about their reserve balances falling below the legal minimum." Balles et al. (1959, pp. 13–14).

25 Roelse (1952, pp. 6–7) states that rates on purchases and sales of Federal funds were "the most sensitive … interest rate in the money market." See also Balles et al. (1959, p. 105), stating that "the Federal funds rate is a useful indicator of conditions in a segment of the money market that has grown in importance. It reflects the demand for and supply of

float, the Federal funds rate would fall. Conversely, if aggregate reserves contracted, perhaps because of an increase in Treasury deposits at Federal Reserve Banks or an increase in public demand for currency, the rate would rise. However, because member banks had ready access to Reserve Bank credit at posted discount rates, the funds rate hardly ever rose above the discount rate.[26] Thus, the level of the Federal funds rate was not a particularly useful indicator of reserve availability when reserves were scarce.[27] Moreover, the funds rate was never a simple spot measure of reserve availability even when reserves were abundant, because

- reserve requirements and reserve balances were computed from *average* deposits over the course of a week (for banks in reserve and central reserve cities) or half a month (for country banks) so that *past* excesses and deficiencies and *expected future* excesses and deficiencies had a material effect on the current level of the funds rate,[28] and because
- the rate was liable to be disproportionately affected by reserve availability in New York, because New York banks were the largest market participants and because frictions like time zone differences and information costs limited full market integration.[29]

existing reserve balances for very short-term reserve adjustment purposes, and thus provides information of value in interpreting changing conditions in the money market."

26 A study by the Federal Reserve Bank of New York (1952) states (p. 6–8) that "the Federal Reserve Bank discount rate sets an upper limit on fluctuations in the Federal funds rate." Balles et al. (1959, p. 10) states that "The fact that the prevailing Federal funds rate does not rise above the discount rate ... is evidence that preferences for the Federal funds market are normally not strong enough to induce banks to pay more than the cost of borrowing from a Federal Reserve Bank" and (p. 98) that "it is clear that no member bank would normally pay a higher rate for Federal funds than the discount rate." Balles et al. further states (on p. 98) that "the purchase of Federal funds at a rate above the discount rate is likely to occur only when, because of some particular situation, a bank is unable or is extremely reluctant to borrow from a Reserve Bank."

27 Balles et al. (1959, p. 11) states that "the Federal funds rate is inherently a sensitive indicator of bank reserve positions," but notes that its significance is limited in periods of credit restraint, when the rate "tends to move up to the discount rate and remain there for extended periods."

28 Carr (1952, p. 15) notes that "excess reserves of certain banks may be immobilized to offset a previous (or anticipated) deficiency in the current reserve requirement period" and that "a bank may sell Federal funds even when its reserves are temporarily deficient if it is protected by 'overages' ... during the earlier part of the same reserve requirement period."

29 Rolse (1952, p. 6) notes that "even though banks in other areas may be experiencing an increase in their excess reserves, if the New York City banks are short of reserves, firm

RESERVES MANAGEMENT

At least on paper, Federal Reserve officials appeared to have more than enough tools to manage aggregate bank lending and the nation's money supply. If officials wanted to restrain lending, they could raise the discount rate and either contract the supply of reserves by selling securities from the System Open Market Account or expand the demand for reserves by raising reserve requirements. Either action could be expected to lead to higher rates on interbank loans and thus to higher commercial loan rates. Conversely, if officials wanted to stimulate lending, they could create excess reserves by buying securities for the Open Market Account or reducing reserve requirements.

During World War II and in the first few years after the war, the ability of Federal Reserve officials to implement a countercyclic monetary policy was limited by the System's commitment to ceilings on Treasury yields. An attempt to restrain loan demand and money supply growth was likely to put upward pressure on Treasury yields and force the System to enter the Treasury market as a buyer – providing the very reserves that it was trying to make scarce.

The fate of a 1947–48 policy initiative illustrates the adverse consequences of capping interest rates while trying to restrain inflation. Following the cessation of hostilities in August 1945, Federal Reserve officials began to focus on the problem of controlling inflationary pressures stemming from wartime debt monetization, demobilization, and reconversion to a peacetime economy. Increases in the consumer price index of 8.5 percent from 1945 to 1946 and 14.4 percent from 1946 to 1947 underscored the urgency of the problem.

In June 1947, Allan Sproul, the president of the Federal Reserve Bank of New York, plumped for an increase in short-term interest rates "for the purpose of preventing further increases in the already excessive money supply."[30] The Secretary of the Treasury, John Snyder, gave ground grudgingly, consenting at mid-year to ending the stabilization of bill yields

money market conditions are likely to prevail at least temporarily" and that "when New York City banks have substantial amounts of excess reserves, money market conditions are likely to be easy, and the most sensitive open market rates are likely to decline temporarily, even though banks in other areas may be losing reserve funds through Government tax collections, public demands for currency, or other factors."

30 Minutes of the Federal Open Market Committee, June 5, 1947, p. 10.

at ⅜ percent and announcing in the early fall an offering of one-year certificates at a yield of 1 percent, up ⅛ percent from wartime levels.[31]

In October 1947, the FOMC developed a comprehensive anti-inflation program. In a letter to Secretary Snyder outlining the program, the Committee observed that,

> Inflationary pressures have been strong in our economy during the past few months, and there is ample indication that these pressures will continue strong, and perhaps be accentuated, in the months immediately ahead. The basic causes of this situation are well known. A vast supply of money and other liquid assets was created during the war and there have been additions to this accumulation of purchasing power since the end of the war.[32]

The Committee expressed its belief that "further credit expansion would augment the existing forces of inflation" and that "the situation is now so critical as to warrant our taking every action, within the power of the Treasury and the Federal Reserve System, to eliminate or moderate excessive credit expansion."

The FOMC's anti-inflation program contemplated two forms of monetary restraint:

- an increase in reserve requirements (for banks in central reserve cities from 20 percent to the statutory maximum of 26 percent,[33] to be accomplished in three steps of 2 percent each), and
- an increase in the discount rate from 1 percent to 1¼ or 1½ percent.[34]

Additionally, the Committee proposed that Treasury drain reserves from the banking system by using some of its deposit balances at commercial banks to redeem Treasury debt held in the System Open Market Account. Finally, the Committee requested that Treasury further increase the yield on new certificates.

31 "Unpegs Interest on Treasury Bills," *New York Times*, July 3, 1947, p. 25, "Federal Reserve Announces the End of 'Pegged' ⅜% Interest Rate on Government Short Term Bills," *Wall Street Journal*, July 3, 1947, p. 8, Federal Reserve Bank of New York Circular no. 3262, September 22, 1947, Meltzer (2003, pp. 642–43), Thomas (1951, p. 626), and Sproul (1964, pp. 228–29).

32 Minutes of the Executive Committee of the Federal Open Market Committee, October 14, 1947, p. 3.

33 Reserve requirements for country banks and reserve city banks had been at their statutory maxima of 14 percent and 20 percent, respectively, since November 1941.

34 Minutes of the Federal Open Market Committee, October 6, 1947, pp. 6–13, and minutes of the Executive Committee of the Federal Open Market Committee, October 14, 1947, pp. 3–7.

By late November, the Treasury had agreed to a bump in the certificate rate – it issued certificates at 1⅛ percent on December 1 – and agreed to use some of its commercial bank deposit balances to retire securities held in the Open Market Account.[35] Concurrently, the Reserve Banks were preparing to raise their discount rates to 1¼ percent – they did so in early January 1948 – and the Board of Governors was preparing to increase reserve requirements on demand deposits at banks in central reserve cities to 22 percent – the increase was announced in late January and became effective on February 27.[36]

Federal Reserve officials continued to be concerned with inflation during the spring of 1948. The FOMC told Secretary Snyder, in March, that "inflationary pressures are still strong in our economy [and] there is as yet no convincing evidence that the need for restraint upon borrowers and lenders of credit has passed."[37] Two months later, Allan Sproul stated, in a letter to Snyder, that "there is nothing in the situation yet to warrant a relaxation of general pressure."[38] However, the ability of the Fed to restrain credit expansion was limited by its commitments to the Treasury. Market participants responded to the second 2 percent increase in reserve requirements, which became effective on June 11,[39] by selling $1 billion of securities to the System Open Market Account between June 9 and the end of the month.

In August, Congress authorized the Board of Governors to increase reserve requirements to as much as 18 percent on demand deposits at country banks, 24 percent on demand deposits at reserve city banks, 30 percent on demand deposits at central reserve city banks, and 7½ percent on time deposits.[40] A month later, the Board used its expanded authority to increase reserve requirements at country and reserve city banks to 16 percent and 22 percent, respectively, contemporaneously with the third 2 percent increase in reserve requirements on demand deposits at central reserve city banks.[41] Woodlief Thomas, the director of the Division of Research and Statistics at the Board of Governors, remarked that the

[35] Sproul (1964, pp. 228–29) and minutes of the Federal Open Market Committee, December 9, 1947, p. 11.

[36] Federal Reserve Bank of New York Circular no. 3303, January 23, 1948.

[37] Minutes of the Executive Committee of the Federal Open Market Committee, March 1, 1948, p. 4.

[38] Minutes of the Federal Open Market Committee, May 20, 1948, p. 10.

[39] Federal Reserve Bank of New York Circular no. 3340, June 2, 1948.

[40] Senate Joint Resolution of August 16, 1948.

[41] Federal Reserve Bank of New York Circular no. 3372, September 8, 1948.

increases "would put banks in a position where they would have to sell securities if they wished to expand loans further."[42] Thomas's conjecture that the need to sell securities "*might* make [banks] *somewhat* more reluctant to expand credit" [emphasis added] reflected the futility of the exercise.

Banks met their increased reserve requirements by selling Treasury securities and the System Open Market Account made good on its commitments to the Treasury by buying the securities to forestall an increase in interest rates. Between September 15 and September 29, total Account holdings of Treasury debt increased by $2.1 billion. By the end of October, member bank reserves were more than $3 billion higher than they had been a year earlier.

APPENDIX. TREASURY CASH MANAGEMENT

Section 15 of the Federal Reserve Act provided that federal government cash balances "may, upon the direction of the Secretary of the Treasury, be deposited in Federal Reserve banks, which banks, when required by the Secretary of the Treasury, shall act as fiscal agents of the United States; and the revenues of the Government or any part thereof may be deposited in such banks, and disbursements may be made by checks drawn against such deposits." On November 23, 1915, Treasury Secretary William McAdoo appointed the twelve Reserve Banks as government depositories and fiscal agents and authorized them to accept deposits of public funds and to pay checks written against those deposits, "as well as to perform any other services incident to or growing out of the duties and responsibilities of fiscal agents."[43]

From an administrative perspective, the simplest scheme would have been for the Treasury to credit all of its receipts to its Reserve Bank accounts, allowing those accounts to rise when receipts exceeded disbursements and to fall when the opposite was true. However, Treasury receipts attributable to tax collections and sales of securities during World War I arrived episodically, while expenditures were more evenly distributed though time. Reliance on Reserve Bank accounts alone would have drained reserves from the banking system when receipts exceeded

[42] Minutes of the Executive Committee of the Federal Open Market Committee, September 8, 1948, p. 3.

[43] "Federal Reserve Banks as Fiscal Agents," *Federal Reserve Bulletin*, December 1915, p. 395, and 1916 Treasury Annual Report, p. 6.

expenditures, tightening short-term credit markets and pushing up short-term interest rates.

Alternatively, the Treasury could have maintained accounts in a broad swath of commercial banks. An excess of receipts over expenditures would change the ownership of some deposit balances (from the public to the Treasury) but would not affect the aggregate supply of reserves available to the banking system. This approach might have been feasible if there had been only a small number of large, nationwide banks but was probably not realistic in light of the many thousands of banks in the United States.

Treasury officials solved their cash management problem with a hybrid scheme. Receipts from sales of Treasury securities were deposited in "War Loan Deposit Accounts" at designated commercial banks (thus leaving aggregate reserves undisturbed) and later transferred to the Treasury's Reserve Bank accounts to offset contemporaneous disbursements from those accounts, again leaving aggregate reserves undisturbed. The War Loan Deposit Account system was introduced in 1917[44] and continued in operation through the 1920s, the Great Depression, and World War II.

Securities sales were the only source of War Loan Deposit Account credits in 1947.[45] Withheld income tax payments were added in March 1948,[46] social security taxes in January 1950,[47] large quarterly corporate income and profit tax payments in March 1951,[48] and large individual nonwithheld income tax payments in June 1951.[49] The expansion "materially lessened the severity of the impact upon the money market of fluctuations in the Treasury's cash position."[50]

The Treasury distinguished between two classes of depositories in the late 1940s. Banks with government deposits of less than $100,000 were

44 Garbade (2012, ch. 8). 45 Cooke (1954, p. 8).

46 Cooke (1954, p. 8), Cooke and Straus (1954, p. 12), and Federal Reserve Bank of New York Operating Circular no. 18, December 8, 1947.

47 Cooke and Straus (1954, p. 13), and Federal Reserve Bank of New York Circular no. 3518, December 2, 1949.

48 Cooke and Straus (1954, pp. 13–14) and Federal Reserve Bank of New York Circular no. 3658, February 21, 1951. The latter circular stated that "the Treasury Department, in the interest of economy and efficiency in this operation, has authorized adoption of this procedure with respect to checks in the amount of $10,000 or over only, inasmuch as it is estimated that such checks represent approximately ninety per cent of the dollar value of these tax payments while comprising only approximately ten per cent of the total volume."

49 Cooke and Straus (1954, p. 13) and Federal Reserve Bank of New York Circular no. 3713, May 31, 1951.

50 Cooke (1954, p. 11).

designated Group A banks and were called upon to transfer a specified fraction of their government deposits once a month. Banks with government deposits in excess of $100,000 were designated Group B banks.[51] Calls for a specified fraction of the government deposits of Group B banks were typically announced on Monday (for transfer on Friday and the following Monday) and on Thursday (for transfer in the middle of the following week).[52]

APPENDIX. IDENTIFYING THE SOURCES AND USES OF RESERVES

Table 3.2 shows the consolidated balance sheet of the twelve Federal Reserve Banks at the close of business on Wednesday, May 31, 1950. Assets included

- gold certificates: nonnegotiable dollar-denominated gold certificates issued by the Treasury to the Reserve Banks (at the rate of $35 per ounce of gold pledged as security) in exchange for deposit balances at the Banks;
- other Federal Reserve cash: currency and coin issued by the Treasury and held by Reserve Banks;
- loans, discounts, and advances extended to member banks;
- US government securities held in the System Open Market Account;
- cash items in process of collection: checks and similar instruments received for collection by a Federal Reserve Bank but not yet paid by the banks liable on the instruments; and
- Federal Reserve notes of other Banks: Federal Reserve notes held by a Reserve Bank other than the Bank of issue.

[51] Cooke (1954, p. 8) and Federal Reserve Bank of New York Circular no. 3493, September 13, 1949. Treasury moved the boundary between the two classes from time to time. For example, the boundary was set at $300,000 in January 1946 and at $150,000 in March 1947 (Federal Reserve Bank of New York Circular no. 3055, January 22, 1946, and Circular no. 3197, March 22, 1947).

[52] Cooke (1954, p. 8). A description of the call process observed that "How much to 'call' from the commercial banks must be gauged in accordance with estimates of how large the needs of the Treasury are likely to be. This requires a calculation involving a forecast of daily receipts and expenditures which flow in and out of the Reserve Bank balance of the Treasury. In order to make these forecasts, detailed studies are made of many individual categories of receipts and expenditures by both Treasury and Federal Reserve staffs." Carr (1954, p. 5).

Table 3.2 *Consolidated balance sheet of the twelve district Federal Reserve Banks on May 31, 1950. Millions of dollars.*

Assets	
Gold certificates	22,998
Other Federal Reserve cash	182
Loans, discounts, and advances	309
US government securities	17,389
Cash items in process of collection	2,373
Federal Reserve notes of other banks	94
Other assets	179
Total	**43,525**
Liabilities	
Federal Reserve notes	22,836
Member bank reserve balances	15,814
Treasury deposits at Federal Reserve Banks	588
Other deposits at Federal Reserve Banks	1,254
Deferred availability cash items	2,137
Other liabilities	14
Capital accounts	
Capital and surplus	883
Total	**43,525**

Federal Reserve Statistical Release H.4.1, June 1, 1950.

Table 3.3 *Factors supplying reserves reconciled to the consolidated balance sheet of the twelve district Federal Reserve Banks for May 31, 1950. Millions of dollars.*

		Factors supplying reserves
17,389		US government securities in the System Open Market Account
309		Loans, discounts, and advances
	22,998	Gold pledged against certificates issued to Reserve Banks
	41	Gold pledged against certificates withdrawn from circulation but not yet recovered
	156	Gold held as a reserve against US notes and Treasury notes of 1890
	1,036	Gold held in the Treasury general fund
24,231	24,231	Gold
	2,373	Cash items in process of collection
	−2,137	Deferred availability cash items
236	236	Float
	69	Treasury currency held in Treasury general fund
	182	Treasury currency held by Reserve Banks
	4,354	Treasury currency in circulation
4,606	4,606	Treasury currency
46,771		Total factors supplying reserves

Items in boldface are taken from the consolidated balance sheet, items in *italics* are taken from the Circulation Statement of United States Money for May 31, 1950, items in ***boldface italics*** are taken from the Treasury Daily Statement for May 31, 1950.

Table 3.4 *Factors absorbing reserves reconciled to the consolidated balance sheet of the twelve district Federal Reserve Banks for May 31, 1950. Millions of dollars.*

			Factors absorbing reserves
588			Treasury deposits at Federal Reserve Banks
		22,836	Federal Reserve notes outstanding
		−94	Federal Reserve notes held by a Reserve Bank other than the bank of issue
		−48	Federal Reserve notes held in the Treasury general fund
	22,696	22,696	Federal Reserve notes in circulation
	4,354		Treasury currency in circulation
	41		Gold certificates withdrawn from circulation but not yet recovered
27,090	27,090		Money in circulation
	69		Treasury currency held in Treasury general fund
	48		Federal Reserve notes held in Treasury general fund
	156		Gold held as a reserve against US notes and Treasury notes of 1890
	1,036		Gold held in the Treasury general fund
1,309	1,309		Treasury cash
	1,254		Other deposits at Federal Reserve Banks
	883		Capital and surplus of Federal Reserve Banks
	14		Other liabilities of Federal Reserve Banks
	−179		Other assets of Federal Reserve Banks
1,972	1,972		Other factors
30,959			Total factors absorbing reserves

Items in boldface are taken from the consolidated balance sheet, items in *italics* are taken from the Circulation Statement of United States Money for May 31, 1950, items in boldface *italics* are taken from the Treasury Daily Statement for May 31, 1950.

Liabilities included

- outstanding Federal Reserve notes;
- member bank reserve deposit balances;
- Treasury deposits at Federal Reserve Banks;
- other deposits at Federal Reserve Banks; and
- deferred availability cash items: cash items in process of collection for which the tendering bank has not yet received credit to its reserve account.

Table 3.5 *Treasury currency, May 31, 1950. Millions of dollars.*

	Outstanding	Held in Treasury general fund	Held by Federal Reserve Banks	In circulation
Silver certificates	2,298	0	120	2,178
Standard silver dollars	213	40	3	170
Subsidiary silver	1,001	15	26	960
Minor coin	379	9	10	360
US notes	347	4	21	322
Treasury notes of 1890	1	0	0	1
National bank notes	88	0	1	87
Federal Reserve Bank notes	280	1	3	276
Total Treasury currency	4,606	69	182	4,354

Circulation Statement of United States Money, May 31, 1950.

Tables 3.3 and 3.4 reconcile the entries in Table 3.1 with the consolidated balance sheet, the Treasury Daily Statement, and the Circulation Statement of United States Money. Table 3.5 shows details from the Circulation Statement.

4

The Institutional Framework of Open Market Operations

Open market operations in US Treasury securities began in the early 1920s (Box 4.1), but they were not embedded in a robust statutory framework until the Banking Act of 1935. The 1935 Act renamed the Federal Reserve Board as the Board of Governors of the Federal Reserve System and created a new governance structure for US monetary policy: a Federal Open Market Committee, consisting of the seven governors and representatives of five Reserve Banks.[1] The five Bank members rotated between (or among)

- the Boston and New York Banks;
- the Philadelphia and Cleveland Banks;
- the Chicago and St. Louis Banks;
- the Richmond, Atlanta, and Dallas Banks; and
- the Minneapolis, Kansas City, and San Francisco Banks.[2]

The act directed that "no Federal Reserve bank shall engage or decline to engage in open-market operations ... except in accordance with the direction of and regulations adopted by the Committee."[3]

The new committee held its organizational meeting on March 18, 1936, with Presidents George Harrison (New York), Matthew Fleming

[1] The Banking Act of June 16, 1933, created the first Federal Open Market Committee, consisting of one representative from each of the twelve Reserve Banks but no Federal Reserve Board representatives.

[2] The Act of July 7, 1942, revised the structure of Bank representation so that New York had a permanent seat, with the other four seats shared between (or among) (1) the Boston, Philadelphia, and Richmond Banks; (2) the Cleveland and Chicago Banks; (3) the Atlanta, Dallas, and St. Louis Banks; and (4) the Minneapolis, Kansas City, and San Francisco Banks.

[3] Section 205 of the Banking Act of 1935.

Box 4.1 The Origins of Open Market Operations

Prior to World War I, the Reserve Banks used their section 14 authorities[1] primarily to acquire earning assets, including state and local government securities and bankers' acceptances.[2] After the war the Banks turned to more readily available Treasury securities to satisfy their need for income.[3] (Income was not an issue during the war because the Banks had ample earnings from discount window loans extended in support of the Liberty Loan drives.[4])

In the spring of 1922, the twelve Reserve Banks formed the Committee of Governors on Centralized Execution of Purchases and Sales of Government Securities by Federal Reserve Banks to coordinate their purchases. The committee consisted initially of the governors of the Boston, New York, Philadelphia, and Chicago Banks.[5] Chandler points out that, "as originally conceived, the function of the committee was to be only that of executing orders received from the various Reserve Banks. It was not to determine policy."[6]

Whatever the original intent, the new committee soon began to formulate recommendations to purchase and sell Treasury securities for the express purpose of making reserves more or less readily available to member banks. The Federal Reserve Board became alarmed at the growth of a policymaking body outside of its purview and, in March 1923, ordered the committee replaced by the Open Market Investment Committee (OMIC). OMIC membership was identical to that of the Committee on Centralized Execution but the new committee, unlike the committee that it replaced, operated under the Board's "general supervision."[7]

Defensive open market operations, directed at neutralizing fluctuations in autonomous factors affecting bank reserves and contributing to interest rate volatility, quickly became quite sophisticated. Chandler observes that,

> Before the end of 1924 the [Open Market Investment Committee] was engaging in open-market operations to offset disturbing effects of Treasury operations around tax-payment dates, selling securities to mop up excess funds resulting from net outpayments by the Treasury, and buying securities to offset net Treasury withdrawals of money from the market. In 1925 it began to buy and sell securities to offset net outflows of currency into circulation and net inflows of currency from circulation, especially around Christmas and other holiday periods.[8]

Chandler concludes that "in a period of only about three years, Federal Reserve officials [came] to understand open-market operations, to develop economically meaningful objectives for them, to centralize control of them, and to use them with force and skill."[9]

[1] Section 14 of the Federal Reserve Act set out the basic statutory authority for open market operations. The section authorized Reserve Banks to "purchase and sell in the open market at home and abroad . . . cable transfers and bankers' acceptances and bills of exchange of the kinds and maturities by this Act made eligible for rediscount," and to "buy and sell, at home or abroad, bonds and notes of the United States," as well as short-term state and local government securities.

[2] Chandler (1958, p. 76).

[3] Chandler (1958, p. 209). The 1923 Federal Reserve Board Annual Report states (p. 13) that "some of the reserve banks, in order to assure themselves of sufficient earnings to meet their

expenses and their dividend requirements, began to purchase considerable amounts of short-term Treasury securities" in early 1922.

4 Garbade (2012, ch. 9).

5 Chandler (1958, pp. 214–15). The governor of the Cleveland Bank was added in the fall of 1922.

6 Chandler (1958, p. 215).

7 Chandler (1958, pp. 217–19 and 227–28) and Meltzer (2003, pp. 149–50).

8 Chandler (1958, p. 234).

9 Chandler (1958, p. 234).

(Cleveland), George Hamilton (Kansas City), and Buckner McKinney (Dallas), filling four of the five Bank seats. (George Schaller, president of the Chicago Reserve Bank, filled the fifth seat two months later.) Marriner Eccles, chairman of the Board of Governors, was named chairman, Harrison became vice chairman, and Emanuel Goldenweiser, director of the Division of Research and Statistics at the Board of Governors, was designated Committee economist.[4]

Committee bylaws provided that "the Committee shall select a Federal Reserve bank to execute transactions for the System Open Market Account. Such bank shall select a Manager of the System Open Market Account who shall be satisfactory to the Committee." The Committee selected the Federal Reserve Bank of New York and Harrison appointed W. R. Burgess, a vice president of the Bank, as manager.[5]

The following day, the FOMC approved the formation of a five-member executive committee charged with directing "the execution of transactions in the open market in accordance with the open-market policies adopted by the Federal Open Market Committee."[6] Eccles, Harrison, Fleming, and Governors Menc Szymczak and Ronald Ransom were selected as members.[7]

4 Minutes of the Federal Open Market Committee, March 18, 1936, pp. 2–6, and May 25, 1936, p. 1.

5 Minutes of the Federal Open Market Committee, March 18, 1936, pp. 4 and 6. In April 1962, the Committee assumed responsibility for selecting the Manager, subject to the approval of the Reserve Bank selected to execute transactions for the System Open Market Account. Minutes of the Federal Open Market Committee, April 17, 1962, pp. 1–28.

6 Minutes of the Federal Open Market Committee, March 19, 1936, pp. 2–3. The FOMC abolished the Executive Committee in June 1955. Minutes of the Federal Open Market Committee, June 22, 1955, pp. 1–26.

7 Minutes of the Federal Open Market Committee, March 19, 1936, p. 5.

THE RECOGNIZED DEALER PROGRAM

The structure of the market for US Treasury securities – an over-the-counter dealer market – did not settle the question of how the Federal Reserve Bank of New York would execute transactions for the System Open Market Account. One possibility was to solicit bids from the general public when the Bank wanted to sell (just as the Treasury did in bill auctions) and offerings when the Bank wanted to buy (as the Treasury did in three "reverse auctions" in the 1920s[8]). Alternatively, the Bank could limit its solicitations to the core of the market, the dealers, and leave it to the dealers to distribute securities to, or gather securities from, the public.

Officials chose the latter course of action. A 1940 New York Bank study stated that "it has always been the policy of the Federal Reserve System not to deal directly with 'investment' holders of Government securities but only with . . . dealers and other merchandisers."[9] A 1952 Bank study noted similarly that because it was "in the public interest to have a strong dealer market and in the System's interest to have a strong private market, the System deals with, and does not attempt to step around, the over-the-counter dealer mechanism."[10] In practice, the Bank directed most of its business to a small group of "recognized" dealers, although it also executed transactions with other "responsible" dealers when those dealers volunteered attractive bids or offers.[11]

The concept of "recognized dealer" was somewhat amorphous. An October 1939 Bank memo observed that the term was "not an exact appellation" and noted that "the principal factors which we consider in extending such recognition are: (1) reputation for integrity, experience, and knowledge; (2) capital at risk of the business; (3) willingness to make

8 Garbade (2012, pp. 209–13 and Box 14.2).

9 Federal Reserve Bank of New York (1940, p. 15).

10 Federal Reserve Bank of New York (1952, p. 2-7).

11 Memo from Messrs. Rouse and Miller to Mr. Sproul, Federal Reserve Bank of New York, "Authorizations and procedure with respect to the purchase and sale of securities for System Account and others," July 21, 1939, pp. 4–5. See also memo from R. G. Rouse to Mr. Sproul, Federal Reserve Bank of New York, October 26, 1939, p. 8, urging that "we should reserve to ourselves the privilege of by-passing the dealer and going direct to banks in order to effectuate some System or Treasury policy when it clearly [is] in our interest to do so," but observing also that "there would not be occasion to pursue such a course frequently," and memo from Allan Sproul to Mr. Harrison, Federal Reserve Bank of New York, "Authorizations for the Purchase and Sale of Securities," October 30, 1939, p. 4, mentioning R.W. Pressprich & Co., Lazard Frères, and J.&W. Seligman & Co. as responsible, but nonrecognized, dealers with whom the Bank had done business.

markets under all ordinary conditions and to take positions both long and short; and (4) large volume [of business] of national scope, with the contacts which such trading provides."[12]

There were eight recognized dealers at the end of the 1930s:

- Bankers Trust Co.,
- C. F. Childs & Co.,
- C. J. Devine & Co.,
- Discount Corp.,
- First Boston Corp.,
- Guaranty Trust Co.,
- New York Hanseatic Corp., and
- Salomon Brothers & Hutzler.[13]

Continental Illinois National Bank and Trust Company was sometimes also characterized as a recognized dealer in Treasury bills.[14]

Formalization of the Recognized Dealer Program

Burgess resigned from the New York Fed in September 1938 and Allan Sproul, the Bank's first vice president, filled in as interim manager of the System Open Market Account.[15] The following summer, the Bank hired Robert Rouse, a manager in the government bond department at the Guaranty Trust Company, to be the next SOMA manager.[16]

In the course of familiarizing himself with the operations of the Securities Department, Rouse discovered that the Bank's board of directors

[12] Memo from Allan Sproul to Mr. Harrison, Federal Reserve Bank of New York, "Authorizations for the Purchase and Sale of Securities," October 30, 1939, p. 2.

[13] Memo from R. G. Rouse to Mr. Sproul, Federal Reserve Bank of New York, October 26, 1939, p. 9.

[14] Memo from R. G. Rouse to Mr. Sproul, Federal Reserve Bank of New York, October 26, 1939, p. 11; and memo from Mr. Sproul to Mr. Harrison, Federal Reserve Bank of New York, "Authorizations for the Purchase and Sale of Securities," October 30, 1939, p. 2.

[15] "W.R. Burgess Quits Reserve Bank Post," *New York Times*, September 14, 1938, p. 33; "New Task for Official of Reserve Bank Here," *New York Times*, September 23, 1938, p. 43, and minutes of the Federal Open Market Committee, September 21, 1938, p. 2.

[16] "Reserve Bank Aide to Retire June 30," *New York Times*, June 16, 1939, p. 43, and "Robert G. Rouse to Become Officer of N.Y. Reserve Bank," *Wall Street Journal*, June 16, 1939, p. 4. Rouse's designation as manager was announced on November 15, 1939, and approved by the FOMC on December 13, 1939. "Three Promoted by Reserve Bank," *New York Times*, November 16, 1939, p. 35; "R.G. Rouse Named Vice President of N.Y. Federal Reserve Bank," *Wall Street Journal*, November 16, 1939, p. 9, and minutes of the Federal Open Market Committee, December 13, 1939, p. 2.

had never specifically authorized transactions with dealers.[17] He suggested that formal authorization be obtained, and on November 2, 1939, the directors explicitly authorized the recognized dealer program, stating

> (1) that it is the policy of this bank, in executing purchases and sales of United States Government securities ... for account of the System Open Market Account, ... to effect such purchases and sales through ordinary market channels with ... recognized dealers, the term "recognized dealer" ... being defined to mean a firm or corporation (including a bank) which is a substantial dealer ... in United States Government securities, ... and which has furnished to this bank a recent statement of assets and liabilities, and such other information as this bank may have requested, showing to the satisfaction of this bank that such firm or corporation is a substantial dealer and has ... adequate capital and is otherwise in satisfactory financial condition;
>
> *provided, however*, that purchases and sales of United States Government securities ... for the System Open Market Account ... may also be effected with ... responsible concerns (including banks) other than recognized dealers ... when in the judgment of the president, the first vice president, or the vice president in charge of the open market function of this bank, this will properly aid in the execution of System open market policy ...; and
>
> (2) that the president and the first vice president are ... authorized to determine and designate the firms and corporations which are from time to time recognized dealers as defined in this resolution.[18]

The authorization had two notable features: first, transactions were to take place through "ordinary market channels." Bank officials were not authorized to introduce a public auction process in connection with either purchases or sales. Second, transactions were generally limited to recognized dealers that met prescribed standards, although officials could enter

[17] Memo from Messrs. Rouse and Miller to Mr. Sproul, Federal Reserve Bank of New York, "Authorizations and procedure with respect to the purchase and sale of securities for System Account and others," July 21, 1939, p. 7, noting that "no action was ever taken by our board of directors with respect to the selection of firms for the execution of ... purchase and sale orders for the System Open Market Account ..."

[18] Resolution of the Board of Directors of the Federal Reserve Bank of New York adopted November 2, 1939.

into transactions with other dealers when such transactions would "aid in the execution of System open market policy." Thus, the formal recognized dealer program, like its informal predecessor, had somewhat fuzzy boundaries. The standards for recognition indicated what was important – capital and scale of operations.[19]

Sproul submitted the names of nine dealers for designation as recognized dealers, including the eight that had been recognized informally in the late 1930s plus, for transactions in Treasury bills, Continental Illinois National Bank & Trust Co. Harrison "recognized" all nine dealers on November 15, 1939.[20]

In addition to satisfying the qualifying standards, a recognized dealer was required to report, on a daily basis, its position in Treasury securities, long or short, in prescribed maturity brackets; its trading volume in each bracket; and the amount of money and securities borrowed to finance its positions. The data allowed the New York Fed "to keep a continuous record of the activities of each of the dealers, and also of the activities of the dealer market as a whole."[21] Bank staff met regularly with dealer representatives and kept in telephone contact with the dealers during trading hours.[22]

ADVENT OF THE QUALIFIED DEALER PROGRAM

Following completion of the first war loan drive in December 1942, the FOMC began to discuss the role that government securities dealers might play in the war effort. Governor John McKee suggested a study "of the functions [dealers] should perform and how their operations should be fitted into the [war] financing program."[23] The Committee asked Emanuel Goldenweiser to prepare the report.

[19] Bank officials subsequently developed more detailed standards, including (1) a reputation for integrity, experience, and knowledge; (2) capital at risk in the dealer's business of not less than $2,500,000; (3) a willingness to "make" markets (except for very large transactions) under all ordinary circumstances, and to take moderate positions, both long and short; and (4) a large volume of business of national scope with the contacts which such trading provides. Federal Reserve Bank of New York (1940, p. 42). That these were the same as the earlier informal requirements indicates that the directors' resolution marked a formalization of, but not a new direction for, the recognized dealer program.

[20] Memo from Allan Sproul to Mr. Harrison, Federal Reserve Bank of New York, November 3, 1939; and memo from R. G. Rouse to Mr. S. A. Miller, Federal Reserve Bank of New York, November 20, 1939, citing the action by President Harrison on November 15.

[21] Federal Reserve Bank of New York (1940, p. 42).

[22] Federal Reserve Bank of New York (1940, p. 44).

[23] Minutes of the Federal Open Market Committee, January 26, 1943, pp. 3–4.

Goldenweiser's report emphasized three points:

1. dealer services were essential to financing the war, and they could be provided directly by the Federal Reserve only at great expense to the System;
2. dealers were willing to submit to regulation that advanced the war effort; and
3. dealers "stirred up" unnecessary trading and exacerbated market volatility.

As to need, Goldenweiser asserted that "in this war-time situation the dealers unquestionably serve an essential purpose. Through their widespread branch offices and their network of telegraphic and telephonic wires they cover the country and have numberless contacts with banks, corporations, and individuals on whom the Government must depend for absorbing its securities."

More pointedly, "if [the dealers] did not exist or were eliminated, the Federal Reserve System would be obliged to build up a similar mechanism, at great expense and with much costly delay."[24]

With respect to regulation, the report asserted that dealers wanted to "cooperate in promoting a smooth financing of the war" and that "their activities are, in practice, closely supervised and kept in line with System policy by constant contact with the management of the open-market account."[25]

The report did not, however, suggest that dealers were beyond criticism, observing that,

> Probably the least desirable thing that dealers do is one which is difficult to control, namely, suggestions and advice that they pass on to their customers in conversations, on the telephone and otherwise. It is clearly to the financial interest of dealers that the market should be lively with movements of prices and with a large volume of operations. That dealers sometimes suggest sales or purchases for the purpose of stirring up the market and that they sometimes jiggle their quotations for that purpose, it would be very hard to establish, and yet it is almost certainly done to some extent.[26]

The report had "no remedy to offer for this situation other than watchfulness by the System and warnings to dealers when such practices come to its attention."

[24] Goldenweiser et al. (1943, p. 2). [25] Goldenweiser et al. (1943, p. 2).
[26] Goldenweiser et al. (1943, pp. 4–5).

Goldenweiser's report also addressed "the desirability of having Federal Reserve Banks buy and sell securities for their own account . . . for the purpose of offering somewhat more direct [liquidity services] to banks and other investors outside of New York." The report concluded that "at this time it would not be advisable [for the Reserve Banks to provide liquidity services directly to investors], particularly in view of the shortage of personnel and the heavy volume of work at the Reserve Banks," but it allowed that the "question may well be reopened for further consideration at a later time."[27]

Eccles was not satisfied with Goldenweiser's report.[28] He asked Leroy Piser and David Kennedy, the chief and assistant chief, respectively, of the Government Securities Section of the Division of Research and Statistics, to prepare a memo addressing "certain questions in relation to the regulation of the Government security market."[29]

The memo prepared by Piser and Kennedy suggests that Eccles was contemplating a significant expansion of Federal Reserve supervision of the market. The memo observed that, as a result of prospective open market operations, "the System is in the position of adding between $500,000 and a million dollars a year to the profits of a group of dealers who perform a useful function but about whose activities the System has relatively little knowledge and over whom the System has relatively little control." The memo admitted ignorance of dealer operations – "It may well be that the net profits of dealers are excessive or they may be only sufficient for the maintenance of a necessary function. The undesirable activities of dealers and of other groups in the market may be of great or of little importance." –

[27] Goldenweiser et al. (1943, pp. 7–8). The idea that Federal Reserve Banks should provide a market for Treasury securities came up repeatedly during the war. See, for example, memo from Allan Sproul to Robert Rouse, Federal Reserve Bank of New York, August 27, 1945, noting that "because it is believed that the [government security] market as presently constituted has not always kept the national interest in mind, and because it is believed that better services might be given to all buyers and sellers of Government securities, it has been suggested from time to time that all of the Federal Reserve Banks deal directly with the public in Government securities instead of having the Federal Reserve Bank of New York carry out transactions for all of the Banks through the dealer market." A 1940 New York Bank study of the government securities market had cautioned against the idea (Federal Reserve Bank of New York, 1940, p. 48) and Bank officials never departed from that position.

[28] Minutes of the Federal Open Market Committee, June 28, 1943, p. 8, stating Eccles's belief that "the report did not appear to him to cover adequately certain aspects of the problem."

[29] Minutes of the Federal Open Market Committee, June 28, 1943, p. 8.

but nevertheless asserted that the System should be in a position to control those operations.[30]

The Piser–Kennedy memo suggested several regulations and requirements "that might be made applicable to all dealers and brokers in Government securities," including regular examination of dealer books and records and prohibition of (a) "the dissemination of information, whether true or false, to the effect that prices are likely to rise or fall because of the operations of [the Federal Open Market Committee]" and (b) "transactions in series [undertaken] for the immediate purpose of causing the market to be active or causing quotations to move with the ultimate purpose of inducing other persons to buy or sell."[31] The memo further suggested that "it would seem that the System should have knowledge of and control over the activities of the dealers and other elements in the Government securities market."

The FOMC met to discuss the Goldenweiser report and the Piser–Kennedy memo on June 28, 1943. Eccles opened the discussion by expressing his belief that "developments in the future might make the regulation of the activities of the dealers under a voluntary arrangement [such as the New York Bank's recognized dealer program] much more difficult." That being the case, the Committee should "develop with the Manager of the System Account something in the way of regulations which would govern the relationship with the dealers in somewhat the same manner as would be done under a statutory requirement." Eccles suggested that a panel of Committee members meet with Rouse "for the purpose of working out a program that would be approved by the Committee" but warned that if the dealers were unwilling to accept such regulation the Committee "should undertake to get the necessary statutory authority to handle the situation."[32]

Allan Sproul, president of the New York Fed since January 1943, agreed with the Goldenweiser report and stated that while he recognized the difficulties identified in the Piser–Kennedy memo, he "questioned the desirability and effectiveness of an attempt more formally to regulate dealers' activities." Sproul challenged the notion that dealer profits were out of line and observed that "the principle question raised by the [Piser–Kennedy memo] was whether the System needed to have more control

[30] Memo from Leroy Piser and David Kennedy to Chairman Eccles, Federal Open Market Committee, June 26, 1943, R&S 100-723.

[31] Memo from Leroy Piser and David Kennedy to Chairman Eccles, Federal Open Market Committee, June 26, 1943, R&S 100–723.

[32] Minutes of the Federal Open Market Committee, June 28, 1943, pp. 8–9.

over the activities not only of Government security dealers but of all other elements in the Government security market," a course of action, "which would mean that the System would have to control activities of practically everyone dealing in Government securities."[33]

Revising the Institutional Framework of Open Market Operations

Following the June meeting, Piser prepared a memo identifying possible requirements for dealers who wanted to participate in open market operations.[34] The memo suggested that,

(a) Recommendations to any client to buy, sell, or swap securities should be made only at the request of the client, should be made only by a senior member of the firm, and should be on an investment basis and not on a speculative basis.
(b) Dissemination of rumors as to future Treasury financings, as to amounts of subscriptions or allotment percentages, or as to other matters that might influence the market should be prohibited.
(c) Dissemination of information, whether true or false, to the effect that prices are likely to rise or fall because of the operations of some investor, such as the Federal Open Market Committee, should be prohibited.

[33] Minutes of the Federal Open Market Committee, June 28, 1943, pp. 9–10.
Two memos written by Robert Rouse in 1940 suggest what Sproul may have had in mind when he made reference to "all other elements in the Government security market." In the first memo Rouse noted "the presence in the market of many banking institutions, a number of non-dealer investment houses, corporate holders, and even some individuals who are trading holders, who are probably every bit as volatile as the dealers. The efforts of such holders towards small quick trading profits are not subject to control of any kind, and it seems to me, cannot be unless the whole government bond market is to be subject to legal control. The holders just described, I think, are those who, more than any single group, affect the market when any sudden news develops, and cause the market to be marked up or down without any substantial volume of business being transacted." Memo from R. G. Rouse to Mr. Sanford, Federal Reserve Bank of New York, "The Place of the Dealer in the Government Security Market," April 18, 1940.
In a later memo, Rouse observed that "if dealers' portfolios are eliminated or closely controlled, the activity would still be in the market but in different hands – the trading banks and other non-dealer traders. The next step would be to control them, and so on, until the whole market would have to be controlled, which, of course, would end up in substantially no market at all as we understand it." Memo from R. G. Rouse to Mr. Sanford, Federal Reserve Bank of New York, "The Place of the Dealer in the Government Security Market," April 26, 1940.

[34] "Relationship of the Federal Reserve System to Government Security Dealers," Leroy Piser, Board of Governors, October 6, 1943.

(d) The making of false or misleading statements as to any material fact should be prohibited.
(e) Quotations should not be changed when there are no buying or selling orders or only nominal orders, except after consultation with the Federal Reserve Bank of New York.
(f) No dealer should transmit false or misleading quotations.
(g) The amount of borrowings by a dealer should at no time exceed ten times the net worth of the dealer.

The FOMC discussed Piser's memo on October 18, 1943.[35] Eccles explained that the Executive Committee had, in prior discussions, identified three possible courses of action:

1. the Committee could give "formal approval to the continuation of the existing procedure and [dealer] relationships established by the New York Bank with the understanding that any proposed change in substance will be submitted to the Committee for approval";
2. the Committee could decide that "the procedure and relationships should be governed through formal rules and regulations to be adopted by the Committee under its existing powers"; or
3. the Committee could decide that "the whole problem should be reported to Congress with the recommendation that express statutory authority to regulate the operations of dealers in the Government security markets be granted."

Acting on the recommendation of the Executive Committee, the FOMC unanimously approved the second option and charged the Executive Committee with preparing a draft of terms and conditions governing the relationship between the New York Reserve Bank and government securities dealers. The Executive Committee in turn directed Rouse to prepare the draft.[36]

Pursuant to the instructions of the Executive Committee, Rouse prepared a white paper on the New York Bank's relationship with the dealers and a draft of terms and conditions that might govern that relationship.[37] He observed that the Bank did business with some seventeen dealers in the

[35] Minutes of the Federal Open Market Committee, October 18, 1943, pp. 3–6.
[36] Minutes of the Executive Committee of the Federal Open Market Committee, October 18, 1943, p. 2.
[37] "Report and Recommendations Regarding Relationship Between Federal Reserve Bank of New York and Dealers in United States Government Securities," Robert Rouse, Federal Reserve Bank of New York, February 1, 1944.

course of executing open market transactions. Most of the business was done with seven recognized dealers,[38] but some business had been done with Continental Illinois National Bank & Trust Co. (which was recognized for purposes of Treasury bill operations) and with nine other nonrecognized dealers,

- Blair & Co.;
- Briggs, Schaedle & Co.;
- First National Bank of Chicago;
- Harriman, Ripley & Co.;
- Harvey Fisk & Sons;
- R. W. Pressprich & Co.;
- Charles E. Quincey & Co.;
- D. W. Rich & Co.; and
- J. B. Roll & Co.

Rouse identified a variety of issues bearing on the nature of the terms and conditions that might govern the relationship of the New York Bank with the dealers. First, the Federal Reserve System had no statutory authority to regulate dealers, so the program would have to be on a voluntary basis. Second, the program had to steer clear of anything that might violate antitrust law. And third, for the purpose of protecting the System, including its reputation, transactions should be confined to dealers of "integrity, experience, and adequate capital."

Rouse also cautioned that while dealers were anxious to cooperate – because "the business of the Federal Reserve System represents to a dealer [a] large and desirable account [that] carries with it considerable prestige" – the members of the Committee should not assume that the dealers would comply with "practically any request." Doing business with the Fed involved "a considerable amount of work in the preparation and filing of reports."

Box 4.2 shows the terms and conditions suggested by Rouse. The most interesting features are those in italics, which echo the requirements of the Bank's recognized dealer program, and those in boldface, which reflect additional concerns voiced by Board staff and members of the FOMC. The latter include agreement to abstain from soliciting orders in anticipation of

[38] New York Hanseatic Corp., one of the eight dealers recognized by the New York Fed in November 1939, withdrew from the government securities business in 1940. "New Concern Here to Deal in Bills," *New York Times*, November 2, 1940, p. 25.

Box 4.2 Federal Reserve Bank of New York Draft of Terms and Conditions Governing the Relationship between the Federal Reserve Bank of New York and Dealers in Government Securities, February 1, 1944. Text in italics parallels existing Bank requirements for a recognized dealer. Text in boldface reflects additional concerns articulated by FOMC members.

The Federal Reserve Bank of New York, as agent for the Federal Open Market Committee of the Federal Reserve System is willing to transact business in United States Government securities, both direct and guaranteed, with reputable brokers and dealers in United States Government securities provided they agree in writing to the requirements set forth below.

In determining whether a person (individual, partnership or corporation, including a bank) is a reputable broker or dealer with whom the Federal Reserve Bank of New York, as such agent, will transact business, and the extent to which business will be transacted with such person, the following factors are taken into consideration by the Reserve Bank:

(a) *Integrity, knowledge, and capacity and experience of management*;
(b) *Willingness to make markets (over-the-counter) under all ordinary conditions, and to take positions*;
(c) *The volume and scope of business and the contacts such business provides*;
(d) **Cooperation in the maintenance of an orderly market**; and
(e) *Financial condition and capital at risk of business.*

The requirements of the Federal Reserve Bank of New York, as Agent, to which a broker or dealer must agree in writing, are as follows:

1. He shall promptly furnish the Agent with a statement showing as of the close of business each business day:
   a. the *total amount of money borrowed*;
   b. the *par value of all Government securities borrowed*;
   c. his *position, both long and short, in Government securities, classified by classes of securities and maturity groups* (or by issues, if so requested by the Agent);
   d. the *volume of transactions during the day in Government securities, classified by classes of securities and maturity groups* (or by issues, if so requested by the Agent); and
   e. such *other statistical data* as in the opinion of the Agent will aid in the execution of transactions for the System Open Market Account.
2. **At or before the completion of each transaction with the Agent, he shall furnish the Agent with a written notification disclosing whether he is acting as a broker for the Agent, as a dealer for his own account, as a broker for some other person, or as a broker for both the Agent and some other person. In the absence of a special agreement to the contrary with the Agent with respect to a particular transaction, he will not act as a broker for any other person in connection with any transaction with the Agent.**
3. In the absence of special arrangements with the Agent, delivery of securities shall be made at the office of the Bank before 2:15 p.m. on the next full business day following the day of the contract and all payments by the broker or dealer shall be in immediately available [i.e., Federal,] funds.

4. He shall furnish the Agent not less frequently than once during each calendar year with a *report of his financial condition* as of a date not more than 45 days prior to the delivery of the report to the Agent in form acceptable to the Agent and prepared or certified by a public accountant acceptable to the Agent.
5. **Unless the Agent shall have informed him of the Agent's desire to purchase or sell a particular issue of Government securities, he shall not solicit from any other person offerings of or bids for any issue of Government securities for the purpose of placing himself in a position to offer to sell to or buy from the Agent securities of such issue.**

"Report and Recommendations Regarding Relationship Between Federal Reserve Bank of New York and Dealers in United States Government Securities," Robert Rouse, Federal Reserve Bank of New York, February 1, 1944, Exhibit B.

open market operations and cooperation in maintenance of an orderly market. (The appendix to this chapter discusses the idea of an "orderly market.")

Rouse pointed out that many of the requirements itemized in the Piser memo were either already part of market practice or "'vows against sin,' practically impossible of enforcement by a formal or informal supervisory agency." He opined that "on the whole, it appears that the informal influence now exercised [by the New York Bank over the dealers], while not completely effective, is adequate for the System's purposes and does not entail responsibilities which the prescription of a definite rule might bring upon the System."

Executive Committee discussions on February 21 and 29, 1944, led to a revised draft that the Executive Committee recommended to the full FOMC (Box 4.3). The revised draft introduced the term "qualified dealer" and included a somewhat more explicit specification of what was expected of a dealer in connection with the maintenance of an orderly market.

The full Committee discussed the recommended terms and conditions on February 29, 1944.[39] Eccles explained that the Executive Committee had examined a variety of more extreme actions, including

(1) establishing an organization to handle purchases and sales of Government securities currently handled by dealers;

[39] Minutes of the Federal Open Market Committee, February 29, 1944, pp. 4–8.

Box 4.3 Statement of Terms and Conditions Governing the Relationship between the Federal Reserve Bank of New York and Dealers in Government Securities, Approved by the Executive Committee of the Federal Open Market Committee on February 29, 1944, and Recommended to the Full Committee. Text in italics parallels existing Bank requirements for a recognized dealer. Text in boldface reflects additional concerns articulated by FOMC members.

The Federal Open Market Committee has directed the Federal Reserve Bank of New York to transact business in United States Government securities on behalf of the open market account of the Federal Reserve System only with reputable brokers and dealers in such securities who qualify in the manner set forth below.

A. QUALIFICATIONS

In determining whether a person (individual, partnership, or corporation, including a bank) is a qualified broker or dealer with whom the Federal Reserve System will transact business, and the extent to which business will be transacted with such person, the following factors will be taken into consideration:

(a) *Integrity, knowledge, and capacity and experience of management*;
(b) **Observance of high standards of commercial honor, and just and equitable principles of trade**;
(c) *Willingness to make markets (over-the-counter) under all ordinary conditions*;
(d) *The volume and scope of business and the contacts such business provides*;
(e) *Financial condition and capital at risk of business*;
(f) **The reliance that can be placed on such broker or dealer to cooperate with the Bank and the Federal Open Market Committee in maintaining an orderly market for Government securities; to refrain from making any recommendations or statements or engaging in any activity which would encourage or stimulate undue activity in the market for Government securities; and to refrain from disclosing any confidential information which he obtains from the Bank or through his transactions with the Bank.**

B. AGREEMENT

In order to qualify further as a broker or dealer recognized as eligible to transact business with the Federal Reserve Bank of New York acting on behalf of the open market account of the Federal Reserve System (hereafter referred to in this capacity as "the Bank"), each such person must agree in writing to comply with the following terms and conditions:

1. He will promptly furnish the Bank with a statement as of the close of business each business day:
   a. The *total amount of money borrowed* (directly or indirectly);
   b. The *par value of all Government securities borrowed*;
   c. His *position, both long and short, in Government securities, classified by classes of securities and maturity groups* (or by issues, if so requested by the Bank);

   d. The *volume of transactions during the day in Government securities, classified by classes of securities and maturity groups* (or by issues, if so requested by the Bank); and
   e. Such *other statistical data* as in the opinion of the Bank will aid in the execution of transactions for the System open market account.
2. **At or before the completion of each transaction with the Bank, be will furnish the Bank with a written notification disclosing whether he is acting as a broker for the Bank, as a dealer for his own account, as a broker for some other person, or as a broker for both the Bank and some other person. In the absence of a special agreement to the contrary with the Bank with respect to a particular transaction, he will not act as a broker for any other person in connection with any transaction with the Bank.**
3. In the absence of special arrangements with the Bank, delivery of securities will be made at the office of the Bank before 2:15 p.m. on the next full business day following the day of the contract and all payments by the broker or dealer will be in immediately available funds.
4. He will furnish the Bank not less frequently than once during each calendar year with a *report of his financial condition* as of a date not more than 45 days prior to the delivery of the report to the Bank in form acceptable to the Bank and prepared or certified by a public accountant acceptable to the Bank and upon the request of the Bank he will furnish a statement of condition as of a stated recent date as shown by his books.
5. **Unless the Bank shall have informed him of the Bank's desire to purchase or sell a particular issue of Government securities, he will not solicit from any other person offerings of or bids for any issue of Government securities for the purpose of placing himself in a position to offer to sell to or buy from the Bank securities of such issue.**

In any case in which the Bank has concluded that a recognized broker or dealer no longer meets the qualifications set forth above or has willfully violated or failed to perform any of the terms and conditions set forth in the agreement, the Bank shall decline to transact any further business with such broker or dealer.

Minutes of the Executive Committee of the Federal Open Market Committee, February 29, 1944, pp. 5–8.

(2) requiring that transactions handled by dealers for the System Open Market Account be on a brokerage, i.e., agency, basis only; and
(3) going to Congress for additional statutory authority to regulate the dealers.

He reported that "the executive committee felt that the procedure recommended ... was the most satisfactory, at least for the present, that it might be necessary at a later date to consider modification of the procedure or adoption of one of the other available alternatives, but that it was felt that if the dealers cooperated in the proposed arrangement ... the procedure should work satisfactorily." The FOMC approved the recommended terms and conditions, and, after some further editorial tweaks, the Executive Committee adopted a final version.[40]

Implementing the Revised Framework

Following the FOMC action, Rouse set about conferring with the recognized and nonrecognized dealers, explaining the new rules, and deciding which dealers satisfied the FOMC's terms and conditions.[41]

Eleven dealers ultimately qualified, including

- Bankers Trust Co.;
- C. F. Childs & Co.;
- Continental Illinois National Bank and Trust Co.;
- C. J. Devine & Co.;
- Discount Corp.;
- First Boston Corp.;
- First National Bank of Chicago;
- Guaranty Trust Co.;
- Harriman, Ripley & Co.;
- D. W. Rich & Co.; and
- Salomon Brothers & Hutzler.[42]

In a statement to the Executive Committee, Sproul explained that five nonrecognized firms (Briggs, Schaedle & Co., Harvey Fisk & Sons, R. W. Pressprich & Co., Charles E. Quincey & Co., and J.B. Roll & Co.) that had done business with the New York Bank did not qualify "because of the relatively small volume and restricted scope of their business and the limited amount of capital at the risk of their business." The Bank chose to exclude dealers "with whom some business has been transacted at times

[40] Reprinted in 1944 Board of Governors of the Federal Reserve System Annual Report, pp. 49–51. See also "Reports Required of Bond Dealers," *New York Times*, May 17, 1944, p. 25, and "Reserve Board Sets Up New Policy for Dealers in Government Securities," *Wall Street Journal*, May 17, 1944, p. 9.

[41] Minutes of the Board of Directors of the Federal Reserve Bank of New York, May 18, 1944, pp. 164–69.

[42] Minutes of the Executive Committee of the Federal Open Market Committee, July 28, 1944, pp. 3–4.

in the past, if they do not clearly qualify under the written terms and conditions now effective. The line of demarcation must be as clearly defined as possible, if our practice is to be understood and defensible, and if future requests for qualification are to be capable of determination."[43]

In discussing the FOMC's qualified dealer program with the directors of the New York Bank, Rouse suggested that the program was not fundamentally different from the recognized dealer program approved by the directors in 1939.[44] In fact, however, the new program lacked the "fuzziness" of the recognized dealer program – firms were now either designated as eligible to participate in open market operations or excluded from such operations. The new program also imposed substantial new requirements for cooperation in the maintenance of an orderly market.

The Qualified Dealer Program at the End of the 1940s

At the end of the 1940s, ten dealers were qualified to do business with the Federal Reserve Bank of New York, a net loss of one dealer from May 1944. Since that time, Chemical Bank & Trust Cop. had qualified,[45] Harriman, Ripley & Co. had dropped out voluntarily,[46] and D. W. Rich & Co. was disqualified.[47]

[43] Minutes of the Executive Committee of the Federal Open Market Committee, July 28, 1944, pp. 4–5.

[44] Minutes of the Board of Directors of the Federal Reserve Bank of New York, May 18, 1944, pp. 164–69. See also Joint Committee on the Economic Report (1954, p. 315), reporting a Federal Reserve Bank of New York statement that the qualified dealer program "formalized and continued in operation a system of market contact that was originally set up at the Federal Reserve Bank of New York [in 1939] to serve the interest of credit policy."

[45] Minutes of the Executive Committee of the Federal Open Market Committee, February 26, 1948, p. 10, and memo from Edward J. Ozog to Dealer Surveillance Staff Files, Federal Reserve Bank of New York, "The Evolution of the Primary Dealer 'System,'" September 14, 1987, p. 4.

[46] Minutes of the Executive Committee of the Federal Open Market Committee, October 3, 1946, pp. 8–9.

[47] Memo from R. G. Rouse to Confidential Files, Federal Reserve Bank of New York, "D.W. Rich & Company, Incorporated," November 6, 1947. See also memo from S.A. Miller to Mr. Rouse, Federal Reserve Bank of New York, "Dealers' Positions," June 24, 1946, reporting a conversation with D.W. Rich & Co. concerning its excessive position in government securities; minutes of the Executive Committee of the Federal Open Market Committee, October 3, 1946, p. 7; and letter from Robert Rouse to Marriner Eccles, November 6, 1947, stating that the disqualification "has been handled as a continuation of the discussion which began" at the October 3, 1946, meeting.

APPENDIX. ORDERLY MARKETS

The idea that the Federal Reserve System had some responsibility for maintaining an orderly market for US Treasury securities was first discussed at the December 21, 1936, FOMC meeting. The minutes of that meeting state that, in the context of "a general discussion of the responsibilities of the Reserve System and the Treasury with respect to the market,"

> . . . it was brought out that, in addition to its operations to serve general credit policy, the Reserve System had some responsibility for the maintenance of an orderly money market, and that in recent years the government security market had become so large a part of the money market that the general responsibility for the money market involves some measure of responsibility for avoiding disorderly conditions in the government security market.[48]

By 1939, Federal Reserve officials generally accepted that the System had a responsibility for maintaining an orderly market for government securities. In an April memo to the president of the New York Reserve Bank, written in anticipation of a war in Europe, the first vice president, Allan Sproul, observed that "we have an obligation . . . to help prevent panic selling in the government security market, and to facilitate an orderly adjustment of that market to new conditions."[49]

The September 1939 Intervention

World War II began on Friday, September 1, 1939, when Germany invaded Poland. The onset of war was not unanticipated – Britain had suspended gold payments a week earlier and Treasury bond prices had fallen about 2 points since mid-August (Chart 4.1) – but nevertheless converted what had been a likely prospect into a concrete fact. Treasury

[48] Minutes of the Federal Open Market Committee, December 21, 1936, p. 4. See also Federal Reserve Bank of New York (1952, p. 11–19), stating that "the maintenance of orderliness in the market was announced as a System objective for the first time in 1937, in recognition of the growing importance of Government securities in the portfolios of the commercial banks and the role of those issues in money market adjustments," and Rouse (1952, p. 23), stating that "An orderly market is . . . a fairly recent *self-imposed* responsibility of the System. Orderly market operations have been undertaken by the System from time to time over the past fifteen years, both in the Treasury's interest and to prevent the undesirable developments in the credit situation that a lack of orderliness in the Government securities market might set off." Emphasis added.

[49] Memo from Allan Sproul to Mr. Harrison, Federal Reserve Bank of New York, "The Government Security Market," April 12, 1939.

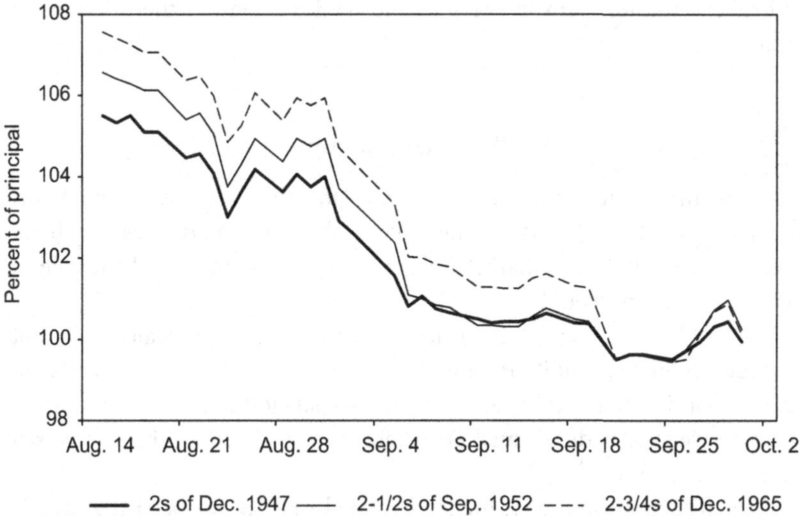

Chart 4.1 Treasury bond prices, August 15, 1939, to September 30, 1939. Average of dealer bid and offer prices.
New York Times.

bond prices fell another 4½ to 6½ points during the first three weeks of September.

In an effort to slow the price decline and maintain an orderly market, the Federal Reserve Bank of New York, acting at the direction of the Federal Open Market Committee and on behalf of the US Treasury, purchased $800 million of Treasury securities during the first two weeks of September.[50] The purchase program was the largest to date, exceeding both the $157 million of purchases (over a two-week period) in the fall of 1929 and the $640 million of purchases (over a seven-week period) in the spring of 1932.[51] The selling abated at the end of September and prices thereafter rose to the end of the year, recovering all but about a point of the losses incurred after mid-August.

The importance attached to the maintenance of an orderly market was evidenced by the unusual character of the September intervention: the Fed first "relieved" Treasury dealers of their positions and then used the dealers

[50] Federal Reserve Bank of New York (1940, p. 38), stating that the Federal Open Market Committee "was attempting to aid in the maintenance of an orderly market after the outbreak of war," and Meltzer (2003, p. 550).

[51] Meltzer (2003, p. 551).

as brokers, asking them to bring to the Bank's attention the offerings of their customers.[52]

A Reexamination

The September intervention led the FOMC to reassess its responsibility for orderly markets. As part of the review the New York Reserve Bank prepared a study of the market for government securities and the role of dealers in that market.[53]

The study addressed two principle complaints: that dealers did not provide adequate liquidity in large transactions, and that they exacerbated price volatility. The study also considered suggestions that the System should itself provide a market where investors could buy and sell Treasury securities.[54]

With respect to liquidity, the study stated that "it has been the experience of the Federal Reserve Bank of New York that, except under extraordinary conditions, the dealers execute all small to moderate size transactions (up to $250,000, which constitutes the bulk of the number of trades) on the basis of the markets they are 'making'" and that "at times, competition has led the dealers to make their quotations 'firm' for larger amounts, particularly in the active issues, and, except in recent months, $1,000,000 'markets' have been usual." The study further suggested that

52 Federal Reserve Bank of New York (1940, pp. 26, 38, and 45–46), noting that "the dealers were relieved by the Federal Reserve Bank of New York of the securities held in their portfolios on the outbreak of the war," that dealers "were relieved of their positions by the Federal Reserve Bank of New York ... after the outbreak of war," and that the New York Bank had "lightened the portfolios of the dealers and enlisted their services to submit to it all offerings made to them by customers." See also memo from Allan Sproul to files, Federal Reserve Bank of New York, September 1, 1939, noting that, at a dealer meeting at the New York Fed at 9:30 a.m. on September 1, Sproul stated that "it looked as if this might be the day," and that the Bank was "prepared to see that no disorder develops ... In order to make our program effective, ... we are willing to clean up the dealers' net positions at a price 1/8 below last night's late closing prices."

53 Federal Reserve Bank of New York (1940). Rouse played a prominent role in shaping the study. After receiving a copy, Emanuel Goldenweiser wrote to Rouse on June 3, 1940, to tell him "how much I appreciated the excellent thoroughgoing piece of work that you have done. A clear-cut statement like that of the way that the dealers actually function and of the problems involved should go a long way towards affording a basis for constructive consideration of the situation."

54 Federal Reserve Bank of New York (1940, p. 48). The study noted that "from time to time the suggestion has been made that the Reserve Banks or the Treasury should assume the duty of providing a market for Government securities, in the interest of the establishment of more stable Government security prices."

"dealers would seem to be justified . . . in making 'order markets' to clients who have larger orders to execute because of the risk, time, and expense involved in endeavoring to find a buyer or seller in a rapidly moving market." (The study characterized an "order market" as one in which dealers were only willing to act as the agent of a customer in searching for an acceptable counterparty.[55])

Dealers were said to exacerbate price volatility in two ways: when they recommended trades that did not serve a legitimate investment purpose and when they failed to make clear whether they were acting as a principal or as a broker in a transaction. The study stated that the first problem was "one of the . . . most questionable aspects of dealers' operations, from the standpoint of market stability." The study noted that "while able portfolio managers are not likely to be influenced by trading suggestions made by dealers or others, unless the recommendations possess merit, it is still true that many small banks . . . cannot afford to employ on their staffs able bond portfolio officers, and consequently constitute a 'fertile field' for recommendations and suggestions."[56]

The study conceded that principal–agent conflicts could be a problem but stated that the Bank had not been able to investigate the matter adequately. In the absence of any dispositive information it recommended that dealers be allowed to continue as in the past "because the ability of dealers to act in [a] dual capacity is of service to holders of large portfolios who cannot ordinarily expect to have actual markets quoted by the dealers for very large amounts of securities."[57]

The most controversial issue addressed in the study was whether the Fed should itself provide a market for Treasury securities. The study cautioned that "the establishment of such an arrangement would seem to constitute the abandonment of a free market for Government securities [, something that] has always been considered essential to the economic well-being of the country."[58]

[55] Federal Reserve Bank of New York (1940, pp. 39 and 58).

[56] Federal Reserve Bank of New York (1940, pp. 56–57). In October 1939, Rouse stated that "Undoubtedly the dealers, by reason of the frequency of their contacts and (in many cases) their short-term outlook, encourage activity, some of which is of a speculative nature. . . . Such activity accomplishes little for a particular portfolio and it accentuates market movements." Memo from R.G Rouse to Mr. Sproul, Federal Reserve Bank of New York, October 26, 1939, p. 4.

[57] Federal Reserve Bank of New York (1940, p. 41).

[58] Federal Reserve Bank of New York (1940, p. 48).

PART II

THE ACCORD AND ITS AFTERMATH

The Treasury-Federal Reserve Accord of March 3, 1951, is the Magna Carta of modern US monetary and debt management policy. Although obtuse, the Accord set the Federal Open Market Committee free to conduct monetary policy independent of Treasury arm-twisting and put the Treasury on notice that it would have to price its offerings in line with prevailing market conditions – but reassured the Treasury that if it did so the Fed would ensure the success of the offerings. Chapter 5 discusses the run-up to the Accord, its terms, and the initial implementation.

The relaxation of wartime constraints on monetary policy forced the Fed to rethink how it should conduct open market operations. The result was a pair of studies, discussed in Chapter 6, by the Federal Reserve Bank of New York and by a subcommittee of the FOMC. The reports covered matters pertaining to the qualified dealer program, Federal Reserve supervision of the government securities market, relations between the System and the Treasury, and whether transactions for the System Open Market Account should be limited to short-term securities.

Chapter 7 explains the policy choices made by the FOMC in March 1953, including a preference for conducting open market operations in the bill market and providing no more than indirect support for Treasury offerings. Chapter 8 describes a temporary relaxation of the restrictions on support of Treasury offerings in June 1953, when the Committee had to confront the consequences of a doctrinaire approach to a market driven as much by human emotion as economic theory. Three months later, with the crisis safely in the rearview mirror, the Committee reimposed the restrictions. Chapter 9 explains how the Committee further narrowed the scope of open market operations in December 1953.

Taken together, the five chapters in this part trace the conceptual reconstruction of open market operations following the termination of wartime controls. Part III below examines the implementation of the new construction.

5

The Accord

The first postwar recession ran from November 1948 to October 1949. Following the resumption of economic growth in the winter of 1949–50, the interest rate on Treasury issues in the one-year sector returned to the 1¼ percent ceiling rate. New issues included a twenty-month note in January 1950, a sixteen-month note in February, a fifteen-month note in March, and a thirteen-month note in May (Table 5.1).

In mid-June, the FOMC voted to raise the ceiling rate in the one-year sector to 1⅜ percent, effective following the conclusion of an offering of thirteen-month notes.[1] The increase was put on hold when, on June 25, North Korean soldiers crossed the 38th parallel into South Korea.[2]

Early North Korean successes fueled concerns that the United States might be on the verge of another major war.[3] For their part, Federal Reserve officials wanted to avoid repeating the mistakes of the preceding war. Allan Sproul suggested, during a July FOMC Executive Committee meeting, that "in the event of major military commitments a more nearly horizontal structure of rates than existed during the last war [would be] highly desirable."[4] The ensuing clash between the Treasury's desire for cheap money and the System's desire for a noninflationary monetary

[1] Minutes of the Federal Open Market Committee, June 13, 1950, p. 13.

[2] Minutes of the Executive Committee of the Federal Open Market Committee, July 10, 1950, p. 9, stating, in a letter sent to the Secretary of the Treasury on July 13, that "in view of the Korean situation, we have been holding in abeyance our previous decision . . ."

[3] Treasury Secretary Snyder stated, in the 1951 Treasury Annual Report (p. 263), that "when aggression broke out in Korea, the Treasury visualized the possibility of a third world war."

[4] Minutes of the Executive Committee of the Federal Open Market Committee, July 10, 1950, p. 6.

Table 5.1 *Exchange offerings of marketable coupon-bearing Treasury debt issued in 1950.*

Issue date	Term	Coupon rate (percent)	Amount issued ($ billions)
Jan. 3	1 yr.	1⅛	5.37
Feb. 1	20 mo.	1¼	1.92
Mar. 1	16 mo.	1¼	2.74
Mar. 15	5 yr.	1½	1.86
Apr. 1	15 mo.	1¼	0.89
Apr. 1	4 yr., 11½ mo.	1½	3.50
Jun. 1	13 mo.	1¼	4.82
Jul. 1	13 mo.	1¼	5.35
Sep. 15	13 mo.	1¼	5.94
Oct. 2	13 mo.	1¼	5.25
Dec. 15	5 yr.	1¾	6.85

Treasury annual reports and offering circulars.

policy led to the final dismantling of the interest rate ceilings that had been in place for almost a decade.

RUN-UP TO THE ACCORD[5]

In light of the rapidly expanding US combat commitment in Korea and the prospect for substantial increases in defense expenditures, the FOMC voted on August 18 to reinstate its earlier decision to raise the ceiling rate in the one-year sector to 1⅜ percent.[6] The increase was not disclosed to the public, but the concurrent, publicly announced decision of the Board of Governors to approve a request from the Federal Reserve Bank of New York to raise its discount rate from 1½ percent to 1¾ percent signaled that short-term rates were going up. A Board press release stated that the Board and the FOMC were "prepared to use all the means at their command to restrain further expansion of bank credit."[7]

[5] The narrative in the introduction to this chapter, this section, and the following section first appeared in Garbade (2012, pp. 345–49).

[6] Minutes of the Federal Open Market Committee, August 18, 1950, p. 23.

[7] "Federal Reserve Statement of Policy," *Federal Reserve Bulletin*, September 1950, p. 1110. See also "Reserve Board Hikes Discount Rate to Curb Credit; Treasury Still Backs Cheap Money on Refunding Bonds," *Wall Street Journal*, August 19, 1950, p. 2; and "Federal Reserve and U.S. Treasury Act Separately to Curb Inflation," *New York Times*, August 19, 1950, p. 26.

Treasury Secretary John Snyder did not accept the Fed's decision to raise interest rates and "reacted angrily" to what he interpreted as an ultimatum.[8] Shortly after being informed of the Board's discount rate action, he announced that the Treasury would offer 1¼ percent thirteen-month notes at par, in exchange for $7.3 billion of securities due to be redeemed on September 15 and $6.2 billion of securities scheduled to mature on Sunday, October 1.[9]

Since investors were unlikely to pay par for a 1¼ percent thirteen-month note if they could buy similar securities in the secondary market at or near a 1⅜ percent yield, Snyder's precipitous action risked a failed offering of Treasury securities in wartime. Market participants concluded that the Fed and the Treasury were in open conflict. The *Wall Street Journal* stated that the two agencies were "working at cross purposes."[10] A week later, the *Journal* remarked on "the break into the open of the feud between the Federal Reserve System and the Treasury on fiscal and monetary policy."[11]

The Fed responded to Snyder's challenge by bidding aggressively for the maturing securities and then exchanging its purchases for the new notes.[12] Largely as a result of its efforts, 81 percent of the securities due to be redeemed on September 15 and 84 percent of the securities scheduled to

[8] Hetzel and Leach (2001, p. 38) state that "when told that the Fed planned to raise short-term interest rates, Secretary Snyder reacted angrily." See also minutes of the Federal Open Market Committee, February 6–8, 1951, pp. 34 and 36 (summaries of statements of Chairman Thomas McCabe and Allan Sproul that Snyder interpreted the Fed's decision to raise interest rates as an ultimatum).

[9] "Federal Reserve and U.S. Treasury Act Separately to Curb Inflation," *New York Times*, August 19, 1950, p. 26. Meltzer (2003, p. 692) discusses the chronology of the Fed's decision to raise short-term interest rates and Snyder's announcement of the terms of the September refundings. See also "Fiscal Hatchet: Feuding Treasury and Federal Reserve Are Trying to Bury It," *Wall Street Journal*, September 30, 1950, p. 1, reporting that Snyder announced the terms of the refundings at about 5 p.m. on Friday, August 18.

[10] "Reserve Board Hikes Discount Rate to Curb Credit; Treasury Still Backs Cheap Money on Refunding Bonds," *Wall Street Journal*, August 19, 1950, p. 2.

[11] "Firm Money Apparently Wins First Round in Clash of Fiscal Policies," *Wall Street Journal*, August 28, 1950, p. 7.

[12] "Board Doesn't Like Terms of Treasury's New 13-Month Notes, But It's Still Expected to Be a Major Subscriber," *Wall Street Journal*, August 23, 1950, p. 2; and "Chapter is Added to Fiscal History," *New York Times*, September 10, 1950, p. 125. See also memo from R. G. Rouse to the Executive Committee of the Federal Open Market Committee, "Dealer Commissions on Transactions for System Open Market Account," January 23, 1952, stating that "purchases of rights in support of the Treasury's September 1950 Treasury financing" were made "in heavy volume largely against sales of other short term securities."

mature on October 1 were exchanged.[13] (The balance was redeemed for cash. The attrition rates of 19 percent and 16 percent, respectively, were unprecedented. In the late 1940s, cash redemptions in exchange offerings usually ran about 5 percent.[14])

In mid-October, the FOMC raised the ceiling rate in the one-year sector to 1½ percent.[15] Treasury officials accepted the increase. On November 22, they announced that they would refinance $8 billion of debt maturing in mid-December and early January with a five-year note bearing a 1¾ percent coupon that was in line with secondary market yields.[16] The offering nevertheless required substantial Federal Reserve support after units of the Chinese army crossed into North Korea on November 25 and began to engage American forces.[17] The Fed bought and exchanged $2.7 billion of the maturing debt; 14 percent of the debt was redeemed for cash.[18]

THE ACCORD

Some observers hoped the five-year note offering signaled that the Fed and the Treasury had settled their differences. The *New York Times* observed that "by choosing a 1¾ percent rate . . . the Treasury reversed its repeated publicly-avowed disagreement with the persistent moves of the central bank over the last year to raise short-term interest rates" and that the rate

[13] 1951 Treasury Annual Report, p. 156. See also "Treasury Reports 81% Response to Offer to Exchange Certificates," *New York Times*, September 15, 1950, p. 45; "New Notes Find Fewer Takers Than Any Issue in Recent Years: Reserve Buying Prevents a Serious Failure," *Wall Street Journal*, September 15, 1950, p. 3; and "Treasury Notes Only 85% Taken," *New York Times*, September 30, 1940, p. 27.

[14] 1951 Treasury Annual Report, p. 269.

[15] Minutes of the Federal Open Market Committee, October 11, 1950, p. 8, and minutes of the Executive Committee of the Federal Open Market Committee, October 11, 1950, p. 3.

[16] 1951 Treasury Annual Report, p. 269 (1¾ percent rate chosen "to price the new issue in line with the market"), Federal Reserve Bank of New York Circular no. 3619, November 24, 1950, and Circular no. 3622, December 4, 1950. See also "Treasury Gives in to Reserve Board Demands for Rise: to Offer 1¾%, Five-Year Notes for $8 Billion Issue," *Wall Street Journal*, November 24, 1950, p. 2, stating that the rate was important "in that it recognizes a situation that already exists."

[17] "China's Reds Stall U.N Push in Korea," *New York Times*, November 27, 1950, p. 1, and "Allies are Driven Back in Korea," *New York Times*, November 28, 1950, p. 1.

[18] 1951 Treasury Annual Report, p. 156; and "Treasury Offers Undersubscribed," *New York Times*, December 15, 1950, p. 54. See also minutes of the Federal Open Market Committee, January 31, 1951, p. 11, comment of Chairman Thomas McCabe that the Federal Reserve purchased "more than 2.5 billion dollars of the maturing issue in support of the Treasury refinancing."

"was taken in financial circles to reflect a full meeting of minds for the first time in a year between the Treasury and the Federal Reserve System"[19]

In fact, however, events moved in the opposite direction. Faced with the prospect of a much larger and much longer war, and concomitantly larger Treasury financings, Federal Reserve officials began, for the first time, to free themselves from their commitment to keep long-term Treasury yields below 2½ percent. In a late November FOMC meeting, Sproul suggested that the Committee should "look toward unfreezing the long end of the rate pattern."[20] Secretary Snyder and President Truman, on the other hand, sought reaffirmation of the Fed's commitment to the 2½ percent ceiling, a reaffirmation that the Fed declined to provide.[21] The impasse continued until mid-February 1951, when Snyder went into the hospital for eye surgery and left Assistant Secretary of the Treasury William McChesney Martin to negotiate what has since become known as "the Treasury-Federal Reserve Accord" or, more simply, "the Accord."[22]

Late on Saturday, March 3, 1951, Treasury and Federal Reserve officials announced that they had "... reached full accord with respect to debt-management and monetary policies to be pursued in furthering their common purpose to assure the successful financing of the Government's requirements and, at the same time, to minimize monetization of the public debt."[23]

Observers hoped that the announcement signaled the end of the dispute between the two agencies, but the *New York Times* remarked that the agreement "left more to the imagination than it actually revealed" and that it "might prove to have been only an 'armed truce.'" The *Wall Street Journal* suggested that the agencies "have thrown a smoke screen around their differences on debt management and interest rate policy" and that

[19] "Rapprochement is Seen," *New York Times*, November 23, 1950, p. 62.

[20] Minutes of the Federal Open Market Committee, November 27, 1950, p. 9. See also 1951 Treasury Annual Report, pp. 269–70, stating that, early in 1951, "officials of the Federal Reserve System outlined to the Treasury a program which would involve a reorientation of debt management policy. The program included proposals for further increases in interest rates, including increases in the long-term area."

[21] Hetzel and Leech (2001, p. 40) and Meltzer (2003, pp. 700 and 705).

[22] The Accord and the events leading up to it are recounted in 1951 Treasury Annual Report, pp. 263–73, Sproul (1964), Hetzel and Leach (2001), and Meltzer (2003, pp. 699–712). The negotiation of the terms of the Accord is recorded in the minutes of the Federal Open Market Committee, March 1–2, 1951 and minutes of the Executive Committee of the Federal Open Market Committee, March 3, 1951.

[23] Federal Reserve Bank of New York Circular no. 3665, March 5, 1951.

"the crux of the fight – whether the Reserve System should continue to support the bond market – has been left as much in the air as ever."[24]

The wording of the announcement did not give much reason for believing that the crisis was over. The actions of the Treasury and the Federal Reserve System were to be directed at *minimizing* debt monetization, subject to the *constraint* of assuring "the successful financing of the Government's requirements." In other words, the success of Treasury debt offerings would not be at risk in the fight against inflation. Meltzer provides a balanced assessment of the responsibilities of the respective parties:

> The March 1951 Accord freed the Federal Reserve from Treasury control of interest rates but gave it co-equal responsibility for debt management. The Treasury had to price its issues in the light of current market interest rates. The Federal Reserve's role was to prevent the market from failing to accept a Treasury issue.[25]

Separately, but relatedly, the Treasury announced that it would soon offer holders of the two largest long-term bonds then outstanding – the 2½ percent bonds of June 15, 1972 (sold in the Seventh War Loan, $8.0 billion outstanding), and the 2½ percent bonds of December 15, 1972 (sold in the Victory Loan, $11.7 billion outstanding) – an opportunity to exchange their bonds for a long-term *nonmarketable* bond with a 2¾ percent coupon.[26] A successful offering would shift a substantial amount of marketable long-term debt into nonmarketable form, limiting the pressure on long-term interest rates that might follow from further increases in short-term rates. Privately, the Fed agreed that it would,

(1) provide limited support for long-term bonds until the Treasury could complete the exchange offering;[27]
(2) maintain orderly conditions in the Treasury market, albeit without reference to any maximum rate of interest (other than as noted in the preceding item); and
(3) consult with the Treasury if it wanted to raise the discount rate above 1¾ percent before the end of 1951.[28]

[24] "Bond Agreement Viewed as 'Truce,'" *New York Times*, March 5, 1951, p. 16; and "Announced 'Accord' Doesn't Tell Whether Board will Continue Bond Market Support," *Wall Street Journal*, March 5, 1951, p. 3.

[25] Meltzer (2009, pp. 474–75).

[26] "Treasury Settles Rift with Reserve over Bond Policy," *New York Times*, March 4, 1951, p. 1.

[27] Treasury officials repeatedly stressed the importance of keeping secret the limitations on Federal Reserve support during the offering. Minutes of the Federal Open Market Committee, March 1–2, 1951, pp. 10, 15, 18, 19, and 38, and minutes of the Executive Committee of the Federal Open Market Committee, March 3, 1951, p. 8.

[28] The unannounced terms of the Accord are noted by Meltzer (2003, p. 711). See also 1951 Treasury Annual Report, p. 272.

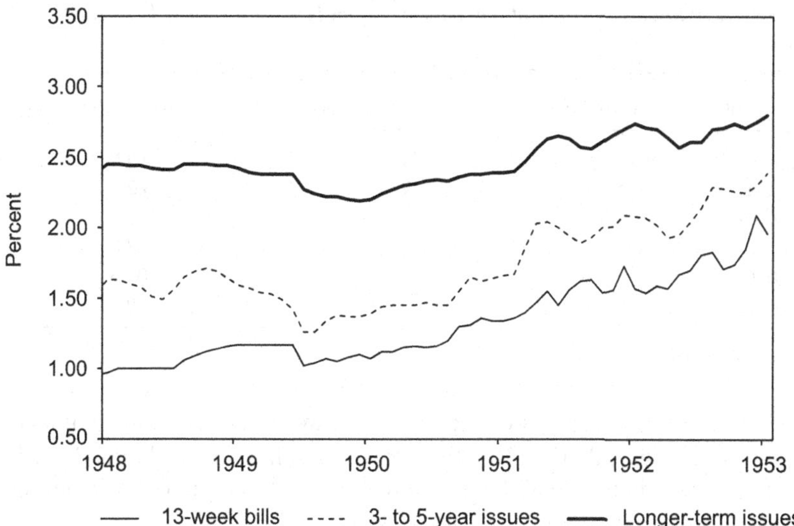

Chart 5.1 Treasury yields. Monthly averages.
Board of Governors of the Federal Reserve System (1976, tables 12.7A and 12.12A).

The Nomarketable Bond Offering

Treasury officials formally offered the long-term nonmarketable bond on March 19, 1951, in a par-for-par exchange for the 2½ percent bonds of June and December 1972.[29] The new bonds were dated April 1, 1951, and would mature on April 1, 1980.[30]

The lack of marketability of the new bonds was mitigated in two ways. First, the bonds could, at the option of a holder, be converted (on a par-for-par basis on any interest payment date) into *marketable* five-year notes paying a 1½ percent coupon. The conversion option provided an off-ramp for investors.

Second, the bonds could be tendered – by a representative of the estate of a deceased owner – in payment of federal estate taxes at par and accrued interest. This "estate tax privilege" had been used during World War I to enhance the attractiveness of long-term debt to investors worried that their heirs might one day be forced to sell at a loss to pay estate taxes.[31]

[29] Federal Reserve Bank of New York Circular no. 3671, March 19, 1951.

[30] They could also be redeemed by the Treasury in whole or in part at par on any interest payment date beginning April 1, 1975.

[31] Garbade (2012, p. 78).

Table 5.2 *Exchange offerings of marketable coupon-bearing Treasury debt issued in 1951.*

Issue date	Term	Coupon rate (percent)	Amount issued ($ billions)
Jun. 15	9½ mo.	1⅞	9.52
Aug. 1	11 mo.	1⅞	5.22
Sep. 15	11 mo.	1⅞	0.58
Oct. 1	11 mo.	1⅞	1.83
Oct. 15	11½ mo.	1⅞	10.86
Dec. 15	11½ mo.	1⅞	1.06

Treasury annual reports and offering circulars.

The subscription books opened on Monday, March 26, and reminded open until Friday, April 6.[32] A total of $13.6 billion of bonds was issued, including $6.0 billion in exchange for the June 1972 bonds and $7.6 billion in exchange for the December 1972 bonds.[33]

AFTER THE ACCORD

Long-term Treasury yields rose through the 2½ percent level in early April 1951 (Chart 5.1), but the Accord did not immediately free monetary policy from the constraints that had bound it since 1942. In his groundbreaking book on Treasury debt management, Tilford Gaines states that "adjustment to the new setting of freely moving interest rates and independent central bank policy was not an instantaneous process. Old ideas and practices died slowly, both among private market specialists and investors and among official authorities."[34] The Fed maintained the discount rate at 1¾ percent through the end of 1951 and continued to support Treasury financings until November 1952;[35] the Treasury continued to rely on offerings of short-term securities (Table 5.2).

32 Federal Reserve Bank of New York Circular no. 3685, April 3, 1951.

33 1951 Treasury Annual Report, p. 27.

34 Gaines (1962, p. 66).

35 The first unsupported offering was the November 1952 offering of 8½-month 2 percent certificates. Federal Reserve Bank of New York Circular no. 3919, November 17, 1952. Meltzer (2009, p. 56) states that "until November 1952 [the Federal Reserve] supported refunding of Treasury certificates, usually by purchasing rights to the new issue." See also "Treasury's Offer Undersubscribed," *New York Times*, November 29, 1952, p. 25, quoting a Treasury official as observing that "for the first time in many years there was no Federal Reserve participation"; and "Treasury Refinanced 82% of Certificates in Last 1952 Refunding," *Wall Street Journal*, November 29, 1952, p. 2, quoting a Treasury official as observing that "the Federal Reserve did not hold any [rights] and it didn't buy up any of them," and that "we were strictly on our own."

Although the transition was gradual, it was ultimately complete. Gaines states that the Accord marked the beginning of "the modern period of Treasury debt management."[36] Meltzer concludes that the Accord was "a major achievement for the country."[37]

[36] Gaines (1962, p. 65). [37] Meltzer (2003, p. 712).

6

Taking Stock

The ink was hardly dry on the Accord when Federal Reserve officials began discussing how open market operations should be conducted in the new era of a free market for Treasury debt. William McChesney Martin, chairman of the Board of Governors since April 2, 1951, became the chairman of the Federal Open Market Committee (FOMC) on May 17 and wasted no time taking control of the emerging debate. Martin suggested that the Committee should "authorize him to appoint a committee ... to make a study of the scope and adequacy of the Government securities market."[1] The Committee approved his suggestion for what became known as the "ad hoc subcommittee study."[2] Contemporaneously, but independently, the Federal Reserve Bank of New York initiated its own review of open market operations.

THE NEW YORK RESERVE BANK STUDY

The New York Reserve Bank study[3] was divided into four parts: a review of the existing framework for open market operations, an appraisal of the prospect for fundamental change, appraisals of several more modest changes, and some concluding remarks on relations between the System and the Treasury.

[1] Minutes of the Federal Open Market Committee, May 17, 1951, p. 7.

[2] The subcommittee was chaired by Martin and included Governor A. L. Mills and Malcolm Bryan, president of the Federal Reserve Bank of Atlanta. Minutes of the Executive Committee of the Federal Open Market Committee, May 9, 1952, p. 3.

[3] Federal Reserve Bank of New York (1952).

The Existing Framework

The study began by reciting the primary responsibility of a central bank: maintaining "general control over the quantity of money and the cost and availability of the credit that accompanies the process of money creation," and by noting that, in the United States, the principal control mechanism was open market operations in US Treasury securities.[4]

The study next observed that the government securities market was an over-the-counter market intermediated by dealers:

> As a general rule, relatively little trading occurs directly between the investor who wishes to sell and the investor who wishes to buy. . . . Instead, a number of highly specialized dealers have sprung up to fulfill an indicated need for intermediaries who are willing to act as principles. Although these dealers on occasion may act . . . as brokers, their main activity consists in buying Government securities outright from those who wish to sell, and in selling Government securities outright to those who wish to buy.[5]

The study noted that since almost every major dealer had its main office in New York, "it would probably be physically possible for the System Account to engage in transactions with most of the dealers." Nevertheless, "the System has limited its relationships to those dealers who . . . have broad national contacts, do a large volume of business in all segments of the maturity range and have adequate capital."[6] The study acknowledged that "few dealers have qualified under this procedure."[7]

Prospects for Fundamental Change

The Bank study examined three proposals for fundamental change. All three sprang from the complaint that the existing market did not meet the needs of investors, that the market was not sufficiently liquid, and that prices were too volatile.

An Exchange Market

The first proposal suggested that an exchange market, patterned after the New York Stock Exchange, might better meet the needs of investors, the Treasury, and the System.

[4] Federal Reserve Bank of New York (1952, p. 2-1).
[5] Federal Reserve Bank of New York (1952, pp. 2-4 to 2-5).
[6] Federal Reserve Bank of New York (1952, p. 2-8).
[7] Federal Reserve Bank of New York (1952, p. 11-4).

Proponents believed an exchange market would provide "the most direct expression of market forces affecting securities prices by bringing together all bids and offers on one trading floor where the closest approximation to a full knowledge of supply and demand can be achieved," that it would provide "a true continuous market at a fair price, through an impersonal mechanism," and that "changes in market quotations would be effected more smoothly and continuously and be freed from the influence of unregulated activities of professional operators."[8]

Bank officials did not agree. They pointed out that transactions in the government market, dominated as the market was by institutional investors, were larger but less frequent than transactions in the stock market. Liquidity depended on the willingness of market makers to commit capital to accommodate customer trading interests, rather than on the presence or imminent arrival of off-setting orders from other investors. They suggested that "the exchange type of market . . . does not provide . . . for the quick execution of transactions," while the over-the-counter market was "suited to facilitate immediate executions between principals by a single [telephone] call."[9]

The study also pointed out that over-the-counter trading in government securities had emerged during the 1920s in direct competition with Exchange trading of Treasury bonds and suggested that "the fact that the over-the-counter market . . . displaced the Exchange as a medium for transactions . . . seems to indicate that the former was better adapted to handle effectively the type and volume of business which developed."[10]

Direct Trading by Federal Reserve Banks

The second proposal suggested that the System should conduct transactions "directly with all types of investors, thereby cutting out the dealers as intermediaries as far as System activities are concerned."[11]

The Bank study warned that "if the System were to trade with all comers, it would face the difficult task of maintaining bid and offer quotations on all Government securities at all times" and that "by becoming . . . a dealer in its own right, the System might eventually crowd most of the private dealers out of business."[12] The study also pointed out that "in making a

[8] Federal Reserve Bank of New York (1952, p. 12-2).
[9] Federal Reserve Bank of New York (1952, pp. 12-3 to 12-4).
[10] Federal Reserve Bank of New York (1952, p. 12-6). See also Garbade (2012, pp. 196–98).
[11] Federal Reserve Bank of New York (1952, p. 3-3).
[12] Federal Reserve Bank of New York (1952, p. 3-3).

broad and complete market for Government securities, the Reserve Banks would [lose the buffer of dealer inventories and] have to deal directly with the full weight of supply and demand." The change could "leave the System with much less scope for initiative in controlling . . . bank reserves."[13]

Reliance on Nonmarketable Long-Term Debt

The third proposal for fundamental change would have the Treasury rely primarily, even exclusively, on *nonmarketable* securities when issuing long-term debt, in order "to escape the risks of wide price fluctuations in long-term marketable Treasury obligations which inevitably bring with them political pressures . . . to peg or support the market . . ."[14]

The study noted that investors would likely require a higher rate of interest to compensate for the illiquidity of nonmarketable securities and suggested that the rate might be more than what the Treasury could, "as a practical matter, afford to offer."[15] Relying on nonmarketable debt could also impair the System's efforts at credit control: "Effective credit policies may require operations in both the long- and the short-term sectors of the Government securities market in order to influence the relative attractiveness of Government securities as compared with private debt instruments. In these circumstances, the maintenance of a supply of long-term marketable Treasury obligations becomes essential for credit policy."[16]

Prospects for More Modest Changes

The New York Bank study also examined several more modest changes to the existing framework for open market operations, including expanding the number of qualified dealers and increasing System supervision of the Treasury market.

Expanding the Number of Qualified Dealers

The study recognized that "there is a reasonable presumption that dealers who are not qualified suffer at times a competitive disadvantage" relative to qualified dealers, and accepted as well the claim that "without access to the System, it would be virtually impossible to make primary markets in all

[13] Federal Reserve Bank of New York (1952, p. 12-9).
[14] Federal Reserve Bank of New York (1952, p. 12-10).
[15] Federal Reserve Bank of New York (1952, pp. 12-13 and 12-15).
[16] Federal Reserve Bank of New York (1952, p. 12-14).

classes of securities."[17] However, rather than examine whether there was any justification for continuing to maintain stringent qualification requirements, the Bank chose to examine whether there was any affirmative basis for relaxing those requirements.

The study concluded that "no significant gain, and some possible risks, would be involved . . . in any attempt to loosen present standards materially for the simple objective of increasing the number of qualified dealers."[18] In particular, "it might be unwise for the System to drop all the [terms and conditions for] qualification, for in that event there would be no privilege or prestige in qualification and it might prove difficult for the System to secure the necessary degree of cooperation from the dealers on those occasions when that might become necessary."[19]

The study reviewed the factors used to determine whether a dealer was qualified to participate in open market operations, including,

1. integrity, knowledge, and capacity and experience of management;
2. observance of high standards of commercial honor and just and equitable principles of trade;
3. willingness to make markets under all ordinary conditions;
4. the volume and scope of business and the contacts such business provides;
5. financial condition and capital at risk of business; and
6. the reliance that can be placed on such person to cooperate with the Bank and the Federal Open Market Committee in maintaining an orderly market for Government securities.[20]

The study suggested that the first and second factors were "those kinds of factors which any good businessman is likely to consider in determining with whom he will do business" and that the need for factor six was "apparent in light of the dealers' role in maintaining orderly markets."[21]

The study recognized that the third, fourth, and fifth factors attracted most of the criticism directed at the qualified dealer program. It argued that the third factor was "essential if the System is to stick to its conclusion that it wishes to encourage a private market and to deal with that portion of the market where the final effort at private purchase and sale takes

[17] Federal Reserve Bank of New York (1952, pp. 3-5 and 13-2).
[18] Federal Reserve Bank of New York (1952, p. 3–6).
[19] Federal Reserve Bank of New York (1952, p. 13-9).
[20] Federal Reserve Bank of New York (1952, p. 11-3). These are the factors set out by the FOMC Executive Committee in February 1944 and reproduced in Box 4.3 above.
[21] Federal Reserve Bank of New York (1952, p. 13-5).

place."[22] The study did not, however, defend the fourth and fifth factors. Instead, the study considered whether it might be useful to add a category of "limited qualification" and allow some nonqualified dealers to purchase Treasury bills from, and sell bills to, the System Open Market Account. The study did not come to a conclusion on the matter but did point out that the five qualified bank dealers did a disproportionate business in short-term securities and suggested that there was "some basis for the contention that [expanding the number of banks qualified for open market operations in bills] would be in line with the System's interest in broadening and extending market facilities in that area where . . . open market operations, intended to influence the availability of credit, would normally be concentrated."[23]

Expanding System Supervision of the Treasury Market

With respect to Federal Reserve supervision of the Treasury market, the study noted that "qualification primarily concerns the business relations between the Federal Reserve Bank of New York and the dealer." It acknowledged, however, that "because of the System's assumed public responsibility and the character of its role in the market, there is inherent in the qualification process a limited element of supervisory responsibility."[24] It further recognized that daily submission of detailed data on transactions, positions, and financing "does impose some restraint on a dealer's activities by providing an outside party with a close working knowledge and an insight into his operations."

However, in a clear warning against mission creep, the study concluded that "it would seem unwise for the Federal Reserve System to undertake an active supervisory influence over [the government securities market]. The System would be involved in an operation quite apart from its statutory responsibility and it might create an unwholesome mixture of credit control and market administration."[25]

Relations between the System and the Treasury

The New York Reserve Bank study took a balanced approach to the question of the relationship between the System and the Treasury, arguing

[22] Federal Reserve Bank of New York (1952, p. 13-5).
[23] Federal Reserve Bank of New York (1952, p. 13-7).
[24] Federal Reserve Bank of New York (1952, p. 13-17).
[25] Federal Reserve Bank of New York (1952, p. 13–18).

that "the Treasury cannot be concerned solely with debt management nor can the System be concerned solely with credit policy. The need is for coordination 'between equals;' it is not possible to effect a solution through subordination of one agency to the other."[26]

The crucial question was whether and how the Fed would support primary market Treasury offerings. The study argued that the Fed should determine "the general availability of credit in the light of national economic developments" and that the Treasury should then tailor its issues to "the conditions prevailing in the Government securities market." The study stated rather emphatically that the Treasury "should not . . . expect the System to 'tailor the market' to the types of securities that the Treasury might like to offer."[27]

On the other hand, the study conceded that the Fed could not operate independently of the Treasury and that it could not "uninterruptedly pursue policies of restraint or neutrality without occasionally standing aside in order to assist the Treasury during periods when it is offering new issues."[28] Once the terms of a new issue were announced, "the System may have to make some compromises with its current credit policy if that policy is in a phase of restraint or neutrality. . . . [T]he System may, depending upon existing circumstances, have to provide some assistance to the market temporarily, through the purchase of 'rights', or of 'when issueds', or of outstanding securities of nearby term if these should react unfavorably in the face of the given Treasury offering."[29] However, such occasions were not likely to be a problem, "as long as the Treasury does not regard the cost of debt service as the paramount objective to which all other considerations must be subordinated."[30]

Summing Up

The New York Reserve Bank study offered no support for fundamental change in the framework of open market operations and only guarded support for more modest change. The Bank was prepared to contemplate a limited expansion of the qualified dealer program but did not support a general relaxation of qualification standards. Additionally, the Bank was

[26] Federal Reserve Bank of New York (1952, p. 14-1).
[27] Federal Reserve Bank of New York (1952, pp. 14-1 to 14-2).
[28] Federal Reserve Bank of New York (1952, p. 14-2).
[29] Federal Reserve Bank of New York (1952, p. 14-6).
[30] Federal Reserve Bank of New York (1952, p. 14-2).

prepared to undertake, from time to time, open market operations in long-term debt and accepted that it would sometimes have to assist Treasury offerings.

THE AD HOC SUBCOMMITTEE STUDY

The recommendations of the New York Bank on the continuation of the qualified dealer program, open market operations in long-term Treasury debt, and occasional assistance to Treasury offerings were all rejected by the ad hoc subcommittee study.

After delaying the start of the study for a year (because he thought "we should have more experience with the unpegging of the market"),[31] Martin unveiled his plan of study at the April 21, 1952, meeting of the FOMC Executive Committee. The objectives included developing a better understanding of

- the organization and functioning of the market for government securities, with particular attention to its suitability as a medium for flexible open market operations directed toward economic stabilization,
- the organization and operation of the System Open Market Account, and
- the advantages and disadvantages of the System's relationships with qualified and nonqualified dealers.[32]

Martin believed that it was important to get market assessments of the Committee's existing practices[33] so the first step was preparation of a questionnaire to serve as the basis for interviews with dealers and others.[34] The questionnaire was sent to recipients at the end of May.[35] The

[31] Minutes of the Federal Open Market Committee, March 4–5, 1953, p. 26. Meltzer (2009), p. 56, n. 11, states that "Martin wanted to commission the report in May 1951 but delayed a year to await the report of the Joint Economic Committee chaired by Congressman Wright Patman in 1952."

[32] Outline of "Ad Hoc Subcommittee of the Open Market Committee to Study the Government Securities Market with Special Reference to the Organization and Operation of the Open Market Account," April 21, 1952.

[33] Minutes of the Federal Open Market Committee, March 4–5, 1953, p. 26.

[34] The questionnaire is reproduced in Joint Committee on the Economic Report (1954, pp. 287–89).

[35] Distribution of the questionnaire quickly led to press reports of the study. See "Reserve Reviews Its 'Unpegged' Price Plan for Government Bonds," *Wall Street Journal*, May 31, 1952, p. 2, and "Reserve Scanning Open-Market Data," *New York Times*, June 8, 1952, p. F1.

interviews commenced in mid-June and were substantially complete by the end of July.[36]

The ad hoc subcommittee finalized its report in November 1952.[37] The report began by asserting the centrality of open market operations:

> [O]pen-market operations are not simply another instrument of Federal Reserve policy, equivalent or alternative to changes in discount rates or in reserve requirements. They provide a continuously available and flexible instrument of monetary policy for which there is no substitute, an instrument which affects the liquidity of the whole economy. They permit the Federal Reserve System to maintain continuously a tone of restraint in the market when financial and economic conditions call for restraint, or a tone of ease when that is appropriate.[38]

The report pointed out the importance of a liquid secondary market for Treasury securities, stating that open market operations required a market "characterized by depth, breadth, and resiliency."[39] (The report stated that a market "possesses depth when there are orders, either actual orders or orders than can be readily uncovered, both above and below [current market prices]. The market has breadth when these orders are in volume and come from widely divergent investor groups. It is resilient when new orders pour promptly into the market to take advantage of sharp and unexpected fluctuations in prices."[40]) The report covered a variety of topics, including dealer qualification requirements, acquisition of market intelligence, and System intervention to maintain an orderly market and to assist in the successful placement of Treasury offerings.

System Intervention

The subcommittee directed its most withering comments at the System's past conduct of open market operations:

> It is the unanimous view of the subcommittee that the Federal Open Market Committee should keep its intervention in the market to such an absolute minimum as may be consistent with its credit policy. . . . The normal functioning of the market is inevitably weakened by the constant threat of intervention by the

[36] Minutes of the Federal Open Market Committee, June 19, 1952, p. 5; and minutes of the Executive Committee of the Federal Open Market Committee, July 22, 1952, p. 2.

[37] The subcommittee report is reproduced in Joint Committee on the Economic Report (1954, pp. 257–307).

[38] Joint Committee on the Economic Report (1954, p. 259).

[39] Joint Committee on the Economic Report (1954, p. 259).

[40] Joint Committee on the Economic Report (1954, p. 265).

Committee. In any market, the development of special institutions and arrangements that serve to protect the market with natural strength and resilience and to give it breadth and depth tend to be greatly inhibited by official "mothering." Private market institutions of this kind are repressed particularly by the constant possibility of official actions which, by the market's standards, will frequently seem – and be – capricious. Such actions constitute a risk that cannot be reasonably evaluated in advance and anticipated in the formulation of individual, private judgments of market prospects.

The subcommittee has come to the conclusion – fully supported by the testimony before it – that the Federal Open Market Committee bears a real measure of responsibility for part of the lack of depth, breadth, and resiliency in the Government securities market. . . . [I]n official publications, and in public speeches by its personnel, the [FOMC] has indicated that it contemplates operating in a free market from here on out, but at the same time the policy record of the Federal Open Market Committee, published in the 1951 annual report, shows that it is still committed to the "maintenance of orderly markets," which clearly implies intervention.

This inconsistency has not added to dealer or customer confidence. To take positions in volume and make markets, dealers must be confident that a really free market exists in fact, i.e., that the Federal Open Market Committee will permit prices to equal demand and supply without direct intervention other than such as would normally be made to release or absorb reserve funds.

They have no such assurance. To the dealers, and to professional buyers and sellers of Government securities, the pronouncements of the Federal Open Market Committee mean

(1) that it has dropped the [wartime] pegs,
(2) that it is willing to see fluctuations in the market, but
(3) that it is watching these fluctuations closely and is prepared to intervene on occasion whenever it considers intervention necessary.

From the dealer's point of view, this means that the Federal Open Market Committee desires a fluctuating market but will not necessarily permit one to develop that is free. Their conclusion is that they are operating in a fluctuating market subject to unpredictable, however reluctant, intervention by the Federal Open Market Committee.

. . .

It is easy to understand why dealers, with their lack of confidence in the Committee's intentions to restore a free market, would be reluctant to go very far in taking positions. To do so would not only involve the risk of being wrong in their evaluation of economic and market trends, but also of being wrong in guessing at what point the Federal Open Market Committee might feel it necessary to intervene. A difference of a few thirty-seconds in the level of prices of such intervention would not necessarily be of great moment to the Federal Open Market Committee, but it might be of real importance to a dealer's operations.[41]

[41] Joint Committee on the Economic Report (1954, pp. 266–67).

The subcommittee advanced two recommendations for limiting System intervention in the government securities market: (1) limiting, outside of truly exceptional cases, open market operations to very short maturity issues; and (2) abandoning the policy of assisting Treasury offerings.

Bills Preferably

The subcommittee believed that "when intervention by the Federal Open Market Committee is necessary to carry out the System's monetary policies, the market is least likely to be seriously disturbed if the intervention takes the form of purchases or sales of very short-term Government securities." Confidence that System intervention would be limited to such securities "would be reflected in greater depth, breadth, and resilience in all sectors of the market."[42] This soon became known as the "bills preferably" doctrine, which is more commonly, albeit inaccurately, known as the "bills only" doctrine.[43]

The subcommittee believed that limiting open market operations to short-term securities would not impede operations "designed either to put reserve funds into the market or to withdraw them to promote economic stability. It would simply guarantee that the first impact of such purchases and sales would fall on the prices of very short-term issues, where dollar prices react least in response to a change in yield, and where the asset value of a portfolio is least affected. A dealer organization, even though it operates on thin margins of capital, can live with impacts such as these and consider them a part of its normal market risks."[44]

The ad hoc subcommittee recognized one exceptional situation where intervention outside of the short-term sector was justified: when the government securities market became "disorderly." The subcommittee characterized a disorderly market as one where "selling feeds on itself so rapidly and so menacingly that it discourages both short covering and the placement of offsetting new orders by investors who ordinarily would seek to profit from purchases made in weak markets." It accepted that "there are

[42] Joint Committee on the Economic Report (1954, p. 267). Luckett (1960) later found the committee's assertions unfounded.

[43] In 1958, Winfield Riefler, Assistant to the Chairman of the Board of Governors, stated that the FOMC "generally confines itself to purchases and sales of short-term securities, preferably Treasury bills." Riefler (1958, p. 1260). Ten years later, Stephen Axilrod, an associate economist of the FOMC, observed that the ad hoc subcommittee study "led to the adoption of the 'bills preferably' policy." Minutes of the Joint Study Steering Committee, April 2, 1968, p. 3.

[44] Joint Committee on the Economic Report (1954, p. 267).

occasions when such really disorderly reactions occur in the market," that "they may lead, if left unchecked, to the development of panic conditions," and that they must be corrected. The subcommittee suggested that "it is in these circumstances, and these circumstances only, that the Federal Open Market Committee would be impelled, by its basic responsibilities for the maintenance of sound monetary conditions, to intervene, and intervene decisively, in other than the very short-term sector of the Government securities market."[45]

Treasury Financings

The subcommittee viewed System support for Treasury financings as emblematic of the FOMC's penchant for excessive intervention. The subcommittee noted that "the practice of supporting Treasury financings developed during the period of war finance, when the Treasury and the Federal Open Market Committee undertook jointly to see that lack of funds would not impede effective prosecution of the war." The continuation of the practice after the war worked to the detriment of an effective monetary policy because "when sales to the Federal Reserve are appreciable, they result in the injection of reserve funds into the market in amounts that are embarrassingly large."[46]

The subcommittee identified two polar positions regarding debt management and monetary policy. The first contemplated strict separation:

> If it is believed that the System's responsibilities are strictly limited to the formulation and execution of credit and monetary policy, logic would preclude the Federal Open Market Committee from purchasing rights or other issues to support Treasury financings. Under this view, the Treasury, being responsible for debt management, would be responsible also for naming such terms and coupons on new securities that [a positive value for exchange rights] would be established automatically. There would be no occasion, therefore, for intervention or support by the Federal Open Market Committee. . . .
>
> This view rests on the doctrine that the governmental structure must provide that responsibility for public decisions be clearly fixed and that public officials be held strictly accountable for their decisions. . . . In this view, the Federal Open Market Committee would buy no rights on a maturing issue, with the result that all attrition would fall on the Treasury if the issue were not attractively priced. . . . If attrition were large, the Treasury would be expected to replenish its cash balance with a second offering on terms more in tune with the market.[47]

45 Joint Committee on the Economic Report (1954, p. 268).
46 Joint Committee on the Economic Report (1954, p. 269).
47 Joint Committee on the Economic Report (1954, p. 270).

An alternative approach was predicated on the view that debt management and reserves management cannot be separated:

> While the Treasury is primarily responsible for debt-management decisions, that responsibility under this second view is shared in part by the Federal Reserve System, and while the Federal Reserve is primarily responsible for credit and monetary policy, that responsibility must also be shared by the Treasury.
>
> According to this position, the problems of debt management and monetary management are inextricably intermingled, partly in concept but inescapably so in execution. The two responsible agencies are thus considered to be like Siamese twins, each completely independent in arriving at its conclusions, and each independent to a considerable degree in its actions, yet each at some point subject to a veto by the other if its actions depart too far from a goal that must be sought as a team.[48]

The subcommittee remarked that "this view was perhaps unconsciously expressed by the two agencies in their announcement of the Accord in March 1951."[49]

The subcommittee recommended that, during periods of Treasury financing, the Committee abstain from purchasing,

(a) any maturing issues for which an exchange was being offered, i.e., any "rights";
(b) any when-issued securities; and
(c) any outstanding issues with maturities comparable to the maturity of an issue being offered for sale,

but allowed that the System should be prepared to support a floundering offering with injections of reserves from purchases of short-term securities.[50]

Dealer Qualification Requirements

The ad hoc subcommittee uncovered deep dissatisfaction with the qualified dealer program. Interviewees stated that "some of the presently qualified

[48] Joint Committee on the Economic Report (1954, p. 270). The blended approach was favored by the Federal Reserve Bank of New York. See minutes of Federal Open Market Committee, March 4–5, 1953, p. 28, quoting remarks of Allan Sproul that "With a Federal debt which is so large a part of all debts, public and private, which permeates and dominates to some extent the whole securities market, and which has become a principal medium for adjusting portfolios of financial institutions, and the reserves of banks and others, we are not and won't be wholly free to administer credit policy without regard to the government security market, and without regard to Treasury financing requirements. It won't be enough to say to the Treasury, here is the credit policy we are going to follow; now you manage the debt. These are areas of overlapping secondary responsibilities and opportunities."

[49] Joint Committee on the Economic Report (1954, p. 270).

[50] Joint Committee on the Economic Report (1954, p. 271).

firms do not appear to possess as many of the attributes for qualification as some of the nonqualified dealers."[51] The subcommittee report observed that "it would be hard for anyone sitting through all the hearings to reach the conclusion that [the] group of unrecognized dealers differed significantly [from] the recognized dealers with respect to training, integrity, professional capacity, or ability to analyze problems."[52]

Interviewees "supported the view that the distinction between qualified and non-qualified firms might have been necessary as a wartime expedient but that the need for this arrangement had long since expired."[53] There was "practically unanimous agreement ... that character, integrity, and professional grasp of the business are the essential prerequisites to effective operation as a Government securities dealer. All seemed to feel that capital, though important, is secondary."[54] Some interviewees believed that the manager of the System Open Market Account should be "free to transact business with those dealers who in the judgment of the management were best equipped to handle transactions for the account in the most efficient and least costly manner" and that "a more proper relationship between the open-market account and the dealer organization would be one that would conform as nearly as possible to that which exists between dealers and other customers."[55]

With respect to the consequences of the qualified dealer program for non-qualified dealers, the report suggested that,

> The lines drawn by the Federal Open Market Committee ... struck the unrecognized dealers in a most vulnerable spot, namely, in their ability to service their customers. It cut down the range of their customer potentialities and thus reduced their ability to attract or earn capital to meet the minimum capital requirements of the Federal Open Market Committee. It acted in the same way to impair the ability of a non-recognized dealer to earn recognition by developing customer relations that were nationwide in scope and that extended to all sectors of the list. In short, once the lines were drawn and recognition was accorded to some dealers and not others, a hurdle of some magnitude was imposed on the unrecognized dealers which impaired their ability to develop their business to the point where it would be able to meet the standards imposed by the committee.[56]

[51] Joint Committee on the Economic Report (1954, p. 295).
[52] Joint Committee on the Economic Report (1954, p. 277).
[53] Joint Committee on the Economic Report (1954, p. 295).
[54] Joint Committee on the Economic Report (1954, p. 277).
[55] Joint Committee on the Economic Report (1954, p. 296).
[56] Joint Committee on the Economic Report (1954, pp. 277–78).

The subcommittee concluded, in rather pungent language, that the distinction between qualified and nonqualified dealers was fraught with difficulties and that its continued existence had to be affirmatively justified:

> The Federal Open Market Committee cannot afford to be complacent about this situation. It has explosive potentialities. Privilege as such is repugnant to the spirit of American institutions. The privilege of dealer recognition, if it is to be continued, must be justified on grounds of high public policy as essential and necessary to the effective conduct of open market operations. It is not sufficient to aver that dealer recognition was once useful or that it should be maintained because it is already in existence, in the absence of a positive reason for change. The fact that privilege exists by virtue of actions of the Federal Open Market Committee is in itself a positive reason for its eradication unless there are necessary and compelling considerations to require its perpetuation.[57]

The subcommittee recommended that the FOMC drop the qualified dealer program "completely."[58]

Market Intelligence

In an effort to distance the System from individual dealers, the subcommittee recommended several changes in how the Federal Reserve Bank of New York went about acquiring market intelligence. It suggested abandoning meetings with individual dealers and replacing the existing system of dealer activity reports with data collection by an officer of the System not connected with the Federal Open Market Committee, that officer to furnish the Desk with aggregate summaries that did not reveal the activity of individual dealers.[59]

[57] Joint Committee on the Economic Report (1954, p. 278).
[58] Joint Committee on the Economic Report (1954, p. 278).
[59] Joint Committee on the Economic Report (1954, p. 280).

7

New Directions

On March 4–5, 1953, the Federal Open Market Committee (FOMC) met to discuss the recommendations of its ad hoc subcommittee. In prefatory remarks, Chairman Martin recalled what had prompted the formation of the subcommittee: a desire to examine "the operations of the [government securities] market and [the System's] relation to the market" in terms of whether "there was developing a market with depth, breadth, and resiliency." He emphasized a central conclusion of the subcommittee study: the "desirability of minimizing [market] intervention."[1]

MARKET INTERVENTION

The ad hoc subcommittee had found "a disconcerting degree of uncertainty . . . among professional dealers and investors . . . with respect both to the occasions which the FOMC might consider appropriate for intervention and to the sector of the market in which such intervention might occur." The uncertainty was "detrimental to the development of depth, breadth, and resiliency" but could be mitigated "by an assurance from the [FOMC] that henceforth it will intervene in the market . . . solely to effectuate the objectives of monetary and credit policy, and that it will confine such intervention to transactions in very short-term securities, preferably bills."[2]

The subcommittee acknowledged two commitments that could require intervention for reasons other than conventional monetary policy: the FOMC's commitment to maintaining orderly conditions and its support

[1] Minutes of the Federal Open Market Committee, March 4–5, 1953, pp. 25–26.
[2] Minutes of the Federal Open Market Committee, March 4–5, 1953, pp. 31–32.

of Treasury offerings.[3] With respect to the first, the subcommittee accepted the prospective need for intervention in the intermediate- and long-term sectors, but recommended that such intervention be limited to correcting disorderly conditions (rather than aimed more broadly at maintaining orderly conditions). The subcommittee further recommended that the System terminate its direct support of Treasury offerings in the form of purchases of rights, when-issued securities, and securities with maturities comparable to the maturity of a new issue, retaining only the option to support a troubled offering indirectly with purchases of short-term securities.

Allan Sproul objected to the idea of giving the market any assurance that, outside of the need to correct a disorderly market, it would deal only in short-term securities. He observed that "there might be times when the System would wish to intervene in other than the short-term area in order to get direct effects on the availability and cost of credit in the capital market or the mortgage market."[4] Sproul agreed that "at the present time . . . it was desirable to operate only in the short-term sector" but he could not say "what would be desirable next year or two years from now."

More fundamentally, Sproul objected to the idea of committing to policies that might not be appropriate in future circumstances not presently imaginable. He agreed that "at the present time there was no argument . . . that dealing in the short-term market met the needs of the Committee" but argued that "it was unnecessary and undesirable to try to give assurance . . . for all time to come on this or any other point having to do with credit policy."[5]

Martin responded vigorously to Sproul's remarks, stating that "the idea that the Open Market Committee should carry on operations having to do with the supply of reserves by operating in the long-term market was entirely inconsistent with having a good [i.e., liquid] Government securities market" and that "there must be a reasonably good Government securities market in order that the Committee might effectuate its credit policies."[6] Martin acknowledged that the Committee could not give a "contractual sort of assurance" to the market and would be free to change its credit policy at any time. Nevertheless, "it seemed to him to be an unnecessary, disturbing element for those in the . . . market to feel that

[3] Minutes of the Federal Open Market Committee, March 4–5, 1953, p. 32.
[4] Minutes of the Federal Open Market Committee, March 4–5, 1953, pp. 35–36.
[5] Minutes of the Federal Open Market Committee, March 4–5, 1953, p. 36.
[6] Minutes of the Federal Open Market Committee, March 4–5, 1953, p. 37.

such an important element as the open market account might step in and operate directly in long-term securities because it decided to do so."[7] No dealer, he claimed, could "be expected to stay in the business if he felt that the Federal Reserve ... would attempt to effectuate credit policy by intervening in the long-term market."[8]

Following further discussion, Governor A. L. Mills expressed the sense of the Committee that the current practice of operating in the short end of the market should be continued in the future unless there was a change in the market or in the policy of the Committee.[9] Martin and Sproul concurred and the Committee unanimously agreed that

1. under present conditions, operations for the System account should be confined to the short end of the market (not including correction of disorderly markets);
2. intervention in the Government securities market is solely to effectuate the objectives of monetary and credit policy (including correction of disorderly markets); and that
3. the System should refrain during a period of Treasury financing from purchasing
   (a) any maturing issues for which an exchange is being offered,
   (b) when-issued securities, and
   (c) any outstanding issue with a maturity comparable to the maturity of a security being offered for exchange.[10]

Unless advised to the contrary by the full Committee, the Executive Committee was bound by the new restrictions when giving instructions to the manager of the System Open Market Account and the manager was similarly bound when directing open market operations for the Account.

DEALER RELATIONS

The minutes of the March 1953 FOMC meeting express succinctly the subcommittee's recommendation regarding the qualified dealer program: "The subcommittee finds no present or prospective justification for continuing the present system of rigid qualifications for dealers with whom the

[7] Minutes of the Federal Open Market Committee, March 4–5, 1953, p. 40.
[8] Minutes of the Federal Open Market Committee, March 4–5, 1953, p. 37.
[9] Minutes of the Federal Open Market Committee, March 4–5, 1953, pp. 40–41.
[10] Minutes of the Federal Open Market Committee, March 4–5, 1953, pp. 41–42.

[System Open Market Account] will transact business, and recommends that the system be dropped."[11]

Martin remarked that the subcommittee "felt it would be desirable to eliminate the dealer qualification system as a means of removing any basis for the charge that the Open Market Committee favored certain dealers in Government securities in carrying on its transactions."

Sproul agreed that the "rigid qualification system" should be eliminated and suggested that the Manager be given "discretion to do business with whatever dealers seemed best suited to carry out the policy of the Committee." However, he pointed out that "as a matter of practical administration . . . it would not be possible for the account to do business with [everyone] who might offer to sell securities to or buy securities from it."[12]

With Martin and Sproul in agreement, the Committee had no trouble deciding that "the present system of rigid qualifications for dealers with whom the account will transact business [would] be abandoned, with the understanding that henceforth transactions would be carried on with any persons or firms actually engaged in the business of dealing in Government securities."[13]

Market Intelligence

The subcommittee recommendations regarding acquisition of market intelligence – eliminating regular face-to-face meetings and restricting Desk access to individual dealer data – were motivated by a desire to put some distance between the Desk and the major dealers.

Robert Rouse, the manager of the System Open Market Account, was distinctly unhappy with both recommendations. With respect to access to individual dealer data, Rouse remarked that information on dealer positions was "most helpful to the manager of the account" and that "to the best of his knowledge, the information received had never been used to the disadvantage of any dealer." When Sproul asked whether any dealers had complained, Martin admitted that the recommendations were "not based on the views of dealers so much as the feeling of the subcommittee that it would be a protection to the manager of the account against any charge of misuse of the information." (Rouse, obviously, did not feel the need for such protection.) Sproul observed that aggregate data sometimes concealed

[11] Minutes of the Federal Open Market Committee, March 4–5, 1953, p. 42.
[12] Minutes of the Federal Open Market Committee, March 4–5, 1953, p. 43.
[13] Minutes of the Federal Open Market Committee, March 4–5, 1953, p. 44.

substantial individual long and short positions. He suggested that data collection should continue unchanged on a voluntary basis and the Committee agreed.[14]

With respect to the meetings, Rouse noted that "the conferences had been useful to both the manager of the account and the dealers" and that "no dealer had to attend a conference." He stated that "while he found the conferences very useful, he would not want any dealer to feel that he was not being treated fairly, and that he would be glad to terminate the present arrangements and permit them to start over if the dealers wanted them on their own initiative." The Committee approved that course of action.[15]

SUBSEQUENT ACTIONS

Following the March meeting, Martin sent a letter of instruction to the Federal Reserve Bank of New York, giving formal advice of the decisions reached by the Committee.[16] The letter provided, in pertinent part, that,

1. under present conditions, operations for the System account were confined to short-term securities (not including correction of disorderly markets);
2. pending further study and further action by the Committee, the System would refrain during a period of Treasury financing from purchasing (a) any maturing issues for which an exchange is being offered, (b) when-issued securities, and (c) any outstanding issues of comparable maturity to those being offered for exchange; and that
3. the system of rigid qualifications for dealers with whom the Open Market Account will transact business should be abandoned, with the understanding that henceforth transactions would be carried on with persons or firms actually engaged in the business of dealing in Government securities.

The End of the Qualified Dealer Program

The FOMC announced the end of the qualified dealer program on April 14, 1953, stating that,

> The Federal Open Market Committee has discontinued ... its requirement that transactions with the Open Market Account be confined to dealers in Government securities who meet certain specified qualifications. The requirement, adopted by the Committee in 1944 to meet wartime conditions, is no longer deemed necessary

[14] Minutes of the Federal Open Market Committee, March 4–5, 1953, pp. 52–53.

[15] Minutes of the Federal Open Market Committee, March 4–5, 1953, p. 51.

[16] Minutes of the Executive Committee of the Federal Open Market Committee, April 8, 1953, pp. 9–12.

or desirable now that open market operations of the Federal Reserve Banks are divorced from support of any particular pattern of prices or yields in the Government securities market.[17]

Rouse later testified before the Joint Economic Committee that he would "do business with any firm or organization purporting to be a dealer who can demonstrate that he makes primary markets regularly in the securities of the United States."[18]

The termination of the qualified dealer program precipitated a rapid expansion of the primary dealer community to seventeen dealers.[19] The list included the ten dealers that were qualified at the end of the 1940s:

- Bankers Trust Co.,
- Chemical Corn Exchange Bank,[20]
- C. F. Childs & Co.,
- Continental Illinois National Bank and Trust Co.,
- C. J. Devine & Co.,
- Discount Corp.,
- First Boston Corp.,
- First National Bank of Chicago,
- Guaranty Trust Co.,
- Salomon Brothers & Hutzler,

and seven new counterparties:[21]

[17] "Books Close on 3¼% U.S. Bonds; Heavy Oversubscription Indicated," *New York Times*, April 15, 1953, p. 47; and "'Qualified' Dealers Only Rule Dropped by FRB's Open Market Group," *Wall Street Journal*, April 15, 1953, p. 15. See also minutes of the Executive Committee of the Federal Open Market Committee, April 8, 1953, pp. 12–13.

[18] Joint Economic Committee (1959, Part 6B, p. 1509).

[19] Joint Economic Committee (1959, Part 6B, pp. 1507–9); and Meltzer and von der Linde (1960, p. 2).

[20] So named following the merger of Chemical Bank & Trust Co. with Corn Exchange Bank in 1954.

[21] New York Hanseatic Corp. had been "recognized" by the New York Reserve Bank in October 1939 but withdrew as a recognized dealer in 1940. Briggs, Schaedle & Co., Charles E. Quincey & Co., and D.W. Rich & Co. had participated in open market operations on an occasional basis before the advent of the qualified dealer system. The three other dealers were relative newcomers. William E. Pollock & Co. was formed in late 1944 ("Bond Concern Organized," *New York Times*, December 20, 1944, p. 31), Bartow Leeds & Co. was formed in 1945 ("New Bond House Announced," *New York Times*, June 1, 1945, p. 27), and Aubrey G. Lanston & Co. was formed in 1949 ("New Lanston Concern to Deal in Federal, Municipal Issues," *New York Times*, September 8, 1949, p. 45; "Aubrey G. Lanston & Co.," *Wall Street Journal*, September 8, 1949, p. 4; and "Lanston Firm to Open Today," *Wall Street Journal*, September 20, 1949, p. 16).

- Bartow Leeds & Co.,
- Briggs, Schaedle & Co.,
- Aubrey G. Lanston & Co.,
- New York Hanseatic Corp.,
- William E. Pollack & Co.,
- Charles E. Quincey & Co., and
- D. W. Rich & Co.

All seven became primary dealers within a year of the termination of the qualified dealer program.[22]

The New York Reserve Bank received several inquiries, but no requests to do business, during the balance of the 1950s.[23] A highly regarded study of the Treasury market by Allan Meltzer and Gert von der Linde concluded that the most important barrier to entry was the profitability of the business, that "prior to 1957 the relative profitability of the present dealers in Government securities was not sufficient to attract sizable financial commitments to the business from dealers in corporate or municipal bonds."[24]

Publicizing the New Restrictions on Market Intervention

The FOMC did not similarly announce the new limits on market intervention. The first, tentative, recognition came in a speech by Chairman Martin to the Economic Club of Detroit on April 13, 1953.[25]

Martin began by reminding his listeners of the importance of the Accord: "In withdrawing from supporting fixed prices in the Government bond market, the Federal Reserve System regained its influence over the volume of money," and recited the conclusion of the ad hoc subcommittee that the government securities market "did not have the depth, breadth, and resiliency needed for the execution of effective and responsive market operations and for flexible debt management." He noted two reasons for the market's shortcomings: the System "continued to

[22] Two additional firms – Northern Trust Co. and J.G. White & Co. – were designated as primary dealers shortly after the termination of the qualified dealer program but were de-designated in 1956. 1956 Annual Report of Open Market Operations, p. 27.

[23] Joint Economic Committee (1959, Part 6B, p. 1509), testimony of Robert Rouse.

[24] Meltzer and von der Linde (1960, p. 26).

[25] Remarks of William McChesney Martin to the Economic Club of Detroit, "The Transition to Free Markets," April 13, 1953. Martin's speech was reported in "Non-Intervention Policy," *New York Times*, April 14, 1953, p. 40; and noted in "Free Money Bias Under Final Test," *New York Times*, April 19, 1953, p. F1.

support the market for short-term securities during periods of Treasury refunding" and "had a policy of maintaining an orderly market in all sectors of the Government securities market."

Martin then reviewed how the System had altered its behavior since the Accord: "Since the unpegging, we have endeavored to confine open market transactions to the effectuation of credit policy, that is, to maintain a volume of member bank reserves consistent with the needs of a growing and stable economy. We have tried to confine our operations to short-term securities, in practice largely Treasury bills."

He noted that the System had refrained from supporting a small refunding in November 1952 and a much larger refunding three months later.[26] The idea, he said, was to "develop methods of operation which, as they became known through practice, would give [market participants] a familiarity with how the Federal Reserve may intervene, when it may intervene, [and] for what purpose it may intervene."

[26] The November 1952 offering is described in footnote 35 in Chapter 5. In February 1953, the Treasury gave holders of $8.9 billion of maturing certificates the opportunity to exchange their certificates for either a new one-year certificate or a new five-year, ten-month bond. Federal Reserve Bank of New York Circular no. 3942, February 2, 1953. The bond was priced at market, but the certificate was priced attractively cheap to the market. See "Treasury Issues Refunding Terms," *New York Times*, January 30, 1953, p. 29, stating that the Treasury "offered little or no premium over average current market rates for the longer term bond, but offered more attractive terms on the one-year certificate." The generous terms on the certificate offering meant that the System did not have to support the dual-option refunding. See "Investors Watch Refunding Moves," New *York Times*, February 1, 1953, p. F1, stating that "the especially generous terms appointed for the shorter exchange indicates that support of the Federal Reserve System will not be necessary to hold [attrition] to a minimum," and "Refunding Success Pleases Treasury," *New York Times*, February 15, 1953, p. F1, stating that "in the exchange offering just finished the Federal Reserve played no part at all, so far as support purchases were concerned" and that the 1.5 percent rate of attrition was the lowest since 1944. Holders of the maturing certificates exchanged 91.5 percent of their securities for the new notes and 7 percent of their securities for the new bonds. 1953 Treasury Annual Report, pp. 32–33; and "New Refinancing Held Big Success," *New York Times*, February 10, 1953, p. 37.

8

Challenging the New Restrictions

The debate over bills preferably and Federal Reserve support of Treasury offerings did not end with the March 1953 Federal Open Market Committee (FOMC) meeting. When an unsettled market in late May deteriorated into what some observers characterized as a disorderly market, Allan Sproul sought to set aside the new restrictions.

THE APRIL 1953 BOND OFFERING

After successfully completing their first refunding in February 1953,[1] officials in the new Eisenhower administration – including Secretary of the Treasury George Humphrey and his deputy for debt management (and later Under Secretary for Monetary Affairs), W. R. Burgess – began to contemplate how to shift issuance away from what they viewed as an overreliance on short-term debt. A steady stream of certificates, notes, and short-term bonds between 1947 and 1952 had brought the average maturity of the debt down from ten years and five months in mid-1947 to five years and eight months in mid-1952.[2] (Treasury coupon offerings for 1947 to 1949 are shown in Table 2.4 above, for 1950 in Table 5.1, for 1951 in Table 5.2, and for 1952 in Table 8.1.) Paul Heffernan, a financial correspondent for the *New York Times*, reported that "the Treasury can be expected to press ahead toward the avowed objective of lengthening the maturity structure of the present heavy concentration of short-dated . . . debt."[3]

[1] "New Refinancing Held Big Success," *New York Times*, February 10, 1953, p. 37; and "Treasury Refunds $8.9 Billion But Few Take Bonds," *Wall Street Journal*, February 10, 1953, p. 15.

[2] *Treasury Bulletin*, February 1959, p. 25, and March 1995, p. 38.

[3] "Refunding Success Pleases Treasury," *New York Times*, February 15, 1953, p. F1.

Table 8.1 *Treasury offerings of coupon-bearing debt, 1952.*

Security offered	Issue date	Maturity	Amount issued ($ billions)
February exchange offering			
11½-month 1⅞% certificate	Mar. 1	Feb. 15, 1953	8.87
7-year 2⅜% bond	Mar. 1	Mar. 15, 1959	0.93
June exchange offering			
11-month 1⅞% certificate	Jul. 1	Jun. 1, 1953	4.96
June cash offering			
5-year 11½-month 2⅜% bond	Jul. 1	Jun. 15, 1958	4.25
August exchange offering			
1-year 2% certificate	Aug. 15	Aug. 15, 1953	2.88
September exchange offering			
14-month 2⅛% note	Oct. 1	Dec. 1, 1953	10.54
November exchange offering			
8½-month 2% certificate	Dec. 1	Aug. 15, 1953	0.87

Treasury annual reports and offering circulars.

On Wednesday, April 8, Secretary Humphrey announced preliminary terms for a $1 billion fixed-price cash subscription offering of thirty-year bonds, the first offering of long-term marketable debt since the Victory Loan in the fall of 1945. Heffernan wrote that "the new issue is adequate proof – even though demonstrated on only a modest scale – that the Eisenhower Administration [is] in earnest in its pledge to work for more balance in the public debt structure."[4] Sylvia Porter, author of a widely read money market newsletter, enthused that "the Treasury is proving its determination to pursue a fundamental program of reconstructing the national debt."[5]

Priced at par with a 3¼ percent coupon, the new offering was seen as a "sure thing" – contemporaneous yields on outstanding long-term Treasury bonds were about 3 percent – and likely to trade in the secondary market at a premium of a point or more after the close of the subscription books. (At

[4] "New U.S. Bond Seen of Major Import," *New York Times*, April 12, 1953, p. F1.
[5] Sylvia Porter, *Reporting on Governments*, April 11, 1953, p. 1.

the time, when-issued trading in a new certificate, note, or bond did not begin until after the subscription books for the security had closed, a convention grounded in a World War II agreement among major Treasury dealers.[6]) One observer thought the new bonds would "go over with a zip."[7]

The Treasury opened the subscription books on April 13.[8] Humphrey, concerned about demand from "free-riders" – speculators who subscribed with the intention of selling their awards quickly and pocketing the expected premium – asked banks and other creditors to abstain from making unsecured loans to finance subscriptions.[9]

As anticipated, the Treasury was swamped with some $6 billion of orders and closed the books the day after they opened. Officials weeded out about $750 million of tenders attributed to free-riders and allocated $1 billion of bonds among the remaining subscriptions. Subscriptions up to $5,000 were filled in full; larger subscriptions were awarded 20 percent of the amount subscribed, subject to a minimum of $5,000.[10]

In spite of the substantial oversubscription, the new bonds traded at only a modest quarter point premium when trading opened on April 15.[11] The *Wall Street Journal* pointed to the unexpectedly small premium as evidence that "the Treasury staff [had] judged the appetite of the government bond market expertly."[12] An alternative explanation was that a large quantity of bonds had gone to speculators who were either selling or poised to sell.

Less than two weeks later, the new bonds broke through par. The *New York Times* attributed the price slide to "the unloading of small aggregates of bonds by speculators disappointed at not having realized a quick profit on a would-be 'free ride.'"[13]

[6] Childs (1947, pp. 373 and 375).

[7] "Treasury's 30-Year 3¼% Bond Issue to Raise $1 Billion Goes on Sale," *Wall Street Journal*, April 13, 1953, p. 13.

[8] Federal Reserve Bank of New York Circular no. 3964, April 13, 1953.

[9] "New Issue Finds Bonds Unsettled," *New York Times*, April 14, 1953, p. 37. Treasury concern with free-riders in fixed-price cash offerings went back more than two decades. See Garbade (2012, pp. 303–10).

[10] "Books Closed on 3¼% U.S. Bonds; Heavy Oversubscription Indicated," *New York Times*, April 14, 1953, p. 47; "Treasury Awards $1,080,000,000 of 3.25% Issue on 20% Quota Basis," *New York Times*, April 23, 1953, p. 46, Federal Reserve Bank of New York, Circular no. 3967, April 17, 1953, Circular no. 3970, April 22, 1953, and Circular no. 3973, April 29, 1953.

[11] "New 30-Year Bond is Quoted at 100¼," *New York Times*, April 16, 1953, p. 8.

[12] "The Treasury Bond Offering," *Wall Street Journal*, April 16, 1953, p. 8.

[13] "Dip in Prices is Largest Since Support by Federal Reserve was Dropped in March,'51," *New York Times*, April 28, 1953, p. 37.

THE MID-MAY EXECUTIVE COMMITTEE MEETINGS

When the FOMC Executive Committee met on May 6 and again on May 13 to chart the course of monetary policy over the balance of the month and into early June, it did so in the context of a program of monetary restraint that had been adopted earlier by the full Committee and in light of a gradual rise in interest rates over the preceding four months. (Box 8.1 summarizes monetary policy in late 1952 and the first half of 1953.) Thirteen-week bill rates increased from 2 percent at the end of 1952 to 2.20 percent in early May; long-term Treasury yields experienced a similar increase.

The May 6 Meeting

The leading topic of discussion at the May 6 meeting was the unsettled state of the government securities market. Robert Rouse, the manager of the System Open Market Account, reported that "outside [of] Treasury bills, there was virtually no market for Government securities at the present time" and noted "the probable need for a minimum [Treasury] borrowing of $10 billion during the next six months."[14] Sproul warned the Executive Committee that its policy of restraint was in danger of becoming a "tight money" policy.[15]

Other committee members were reluctant to undermine the on-going program of restraint. Governor A. L. Mills argued that, going forward, monetary policy had to avoid "being misled by conditions in the long-term sector into taking actions in the short-term sector that would be detrimental to a necessary continuance of restraint against the over-all expansion of bank credit."[16] The long end of the market, he continued,

> ... is suffering from severe congestion with the demand for long-term capital running far ahead of the potential supply of genuine investment funds. It would ... be an error to believe the injection of new reserves into the money market will have more than a minor effect on the ability of the long-term sector of the market to absorb long-term security issues. On the contrary, an over-injection of new

[14] Minutes of the Executive Committee of the Federal Open Market Committee, May 6, 1953, p. 2.

[15] Minutes of the Executive Committee of the Federal Open Market Committee, May 6, 1953, p. 8.

[16] Minutes of the Executive Committee of the Federal Open Market Committee, May 6, 1953, p. 4.

Box 8.1 Extract of a Response from Chairman Martin to a Question from the Subcommittee on Economic Stabilization of the Joint Committee on the Economic Report Relating to the Role of Monetary Policy between 1952 and 1954.

Total national expenditures increased in the [year after the spring of 1952] as a result of growing private expenditures both for consumption and investment, including a building up of inventories. By late 1952 the economy generally was operating on an overtime basis. . . .

All major kinds of credit increased more sharply in the 12 months ending June 1953 than in the preceding 12 months . . . The biggest change was in consumer credit, which increased $5 billion as compared with only little change during most of the previous year. The United States Government became a net borrower of about $3 billion from the public, as compared with a reduction in its indebtedness in the previous year. . . .

. . .

The Federal Reserve occasionally bought Government securities in this period but the objective of monetary policy continued to be restraint on undue credit and monetary expansion. . . .

Over the whole period April 1952 to April 1953 . . . net purchases were less than enough to cover the drains on bank reserves resulting from gold outflow and larger currency demands. Banks had to borrow substantial amounts from the Federal Reserve to meet growing demands for credit. Discounts and advances at Federal Reserve banks generally exceeded a billion dollars from July 1952 to May 1953, and they averaged $1.6 billion in December 1952. . . . To make the policy of restraint more effective, the Federal Reserve discount rate was raised from 1¾ to 2 percent in January 1953.

. . .

The money market showed a marked response to the strong demand for credit and the restraints on its availability. Interest rates rose during the period, reflecting the pressures of credit demand in excess of the available supply. The rise in interest rates was particularly great in the spring of 1953 when yields on high-grade securities and loans generally reached the highest levels for 15 to 20 years. Treasury bill rates approached 2½ percent, the average yield on long-term Treasury bonds rose above 3 percent, and a small new issue of 30-year Treasury bonds bore a coupon rate of 3¼ percent. . . .

By May 1953 the market developed a condition of tension that threatened to become unduly severe. This reflected a number of converging factors. Apprehension rose regarding the ability of the credit market to meet borrowing demands of the State and local governments, consumers, home buyers, and business corporations, together with rising Treasury financing needs. The combination of a Government deficit and large private credit demands is exceptional for a period other than one of active war and it was difficult to gage the problems that it might present. At that time the Treasury made its offer on a $1 billion issue of 30-year 3¼ percent bonds to raise new money form nonbank investors. This offering gave probably the first tangible evidence of a striking nature, not only of the fact that the Treasury had to borrow substantial amounts, but also that it had to compete against large private borrowing

Box 8.1 (cont.)

demands for the available supply of savings at competitive rates if resort to the creation of an undue volume of new money through the banking system were to be avoided.

...

The continued high level of member bank borrowing from the Federal Reserve and the limited availability of reserve funds were keeping banks under pressure. The effect on the money market was a marked rise in interest rates, which exerted a considerable amount of restraint on private credit demands. ...

Early in May 1953 Federal Reserve officials recognized that as a result of a combination of circumstances, some of which were unexpected, undue tension was developing in the credit market. They concluded that steps should be taken to temper restraints currently imposed on member banks, particularly in view of prospective seasonal credit and currency demands.

The Open Market Committee began early in May to supply reserves by purchasing Government securities and by midyear about $1 billion of securities had been acquired. ...

Joint Committee on the Economic Report (1954, pp. 7–8).

reserves into the market, besides failing to relieve the long-term sector of the market, would seriously handicap all efforts to restrain the growth of bank credit.

...

This is seemingly a situation which the Treasury must recognize and in so doing make the terms of its new issues ... attractive enough to preempt the market. In so doing, certain prospective borrowers will be crowded out, but as they will be the least creditworthy and as their projects will presumably be postponable, this will be a desirable development.[17]

Mills nevertheless believed that "a minimum of new reserves should be provided promptly" to "ease the position of the central reserve city banks."

Sproul supported Mills's recommendation to add reserves, noting that the Treasury would have to raise about $1 billion of new money before the beginning of July, that "banks will have to underwrite some of this financing temporarily" and that "there will be financing through the banks, which will put a further strain on the banks' reserve position."[18] He concurred with Mills's observation regarding the need for the Treasury to crowd out other borrowers, warning that "there is no telling how high rates [will] go" and that "the market might become 'disorderly' before it

[17] Minutes of the Executive Committee of the Federal Open Market Committee, May 6, 1953, pp. 4–6.

[18] Minutes of the Executive Committee of the Federal Open Market Committee, May 6, 1953, pp. 6–7.

gets to the equilibrium point." Sproul recommended putting some reserves into the market immediately, and more following the announcement of Treasury's borrowing plans for June. "It is not right," he concluded, "that we should have deficit financing at the top of a boom, but that is what we have and I think we should adjust credit policy to the situation that exists and not to what we would like to have."

FOMC economist Woodlief Thomas summarized staff projections of some $14 billion of Treasury borrowings before the end of the calendar year. The Treasury's requirements, coupled with anticipated changes in public demand for currency and other autonomous factors, indicated a need for approximately $3 billion of additional reserves.[19] Thomas anticipated that the money market would be under "considerable additional pressure" by the end of the month. He recommended a program of moderate purchases, at a rate of about $50 million per week, "with generous allowance for the use of repurchase agreements to alleviate temporary tightness that would develop from time to time."

Chairman Martin concluded the meeting by summarizing his understanding that the Executive Committee was "in agreement ... regarding the injection of some reserves into the market, without, however, any understanding as to the amount of such reserves that might be needed." The quantity of purchases would be "left to the judgment of the Manager of the Account who would 'feel his way' in the market."[20]

The May 13 Meeting

At the May 13 Executive Committee meeting, Thomas reiterated staff projections that the market for bank reserves would tighten at the end of the month "as a result of increased demands for currency over the Memorial Day holiday and [a] month-end decline in float."[21] Rouse suggested that, in view of Thomas's projections, "some purchases of short-term securities for the System account would be advisable" but admitted that he did not have "any fixed amount" in mind.[22] At the end

[19] Minutes of the Executive Committee of the Federal Open Market Committee, May 6, 1953, pp. 9–10.

[20] Minutes of the Executive Committee of the Federal Open Market Committee, May 6, 1953, p. 19.

[21] Minutes of the Executive Committee of the Federal Open Market Committee, May 13, 1953, p. 5.

[22] Minutes of the Executive Committee of the Federal Open Market Committee, May 13, 1953, pp. 6–7. Rouse further remarked that there was a shortage of bills in the market and

of the meeting, Rouse summed up his understanding of the discussion, saying that the New York Fed "should put reserves into the market over a period of time which would be sufficient to avoid further tightening of the money market" but that "none of the members of the committee felt there should be a relaxation in the credit situation."[23]

System Open Market Account Activity and Reserve Availability in May

As shown in Table 8.2, the Desk purchased more than $150 million of bills for the System Open Market Account during the month of May – roughly at the rate suggested by Thomas. The Desk also entered into repurchase agreements, but it neither purchased nor sold any certificates, notes, or bonds.

Excess reserves increased by more than $300 million (from April 29 to May 27) as a result of a $220 million increase in reserves and a $100 million decrease in required reserves; borrowed reserves fell by $266 million. The interbank market in Federal funds remained steady at a bid rate equal to, or slightly less than, the 2 percent discount rate then in effect, although the rate dipped to 1⅜ at the end of the maintenance period on Wednesday, May 20, and to ⅜ percent at the end of the following period (Table 8.3).

BREAKDOWN AND INTERVENTION

In spite of the injection of reserves and the Executive Committee's stated desire to maintain existing money market conditions, the Treasury market

suggested that "the easiest procedure for getting reserve funds into the market would be for the System account to make purchases of 2 per cent Treasury bonds," a reference to three bonds issued during World War II and maturing later in 1953 and in 1954. Martin responded by stating that bond purchases would be a "mistake," that "it would be distinctly preferable for the System account to continue to operate in the bill market," and that he believed bills would be available. Rouse walked his comment back, saying that it was not a recommendation and that he had mentioned the purchases only as a way of getting reserves "into the market easily in the most helpful form." Minutes of the Executive Committee of the Federal Open Market Committee, May 13, 1953, p. 7.

23 Minutes of the Executive Committee of the Federal Open Market Committee, May 13, 1953, p. 14. The instructions of the Executive Committee to the Account Manager remained essentially unchanged at the May 26 Executive Committee meeting. Minutes of the Executive Committee of the Federal Open Market Committee, May 26, 1953, pp. 13–14.

Table 8.2 *US government securities in the System Open Market Account and bank reserves, 1953. Close of business, millions of dollars.*

	US government securities in the System Open Market Account			Bank reserves			
	On repurchase agreements	Bills	Special certificates	Member bank reserves	Required reserves (estimated)	Excess reserves (estimated)	Discounts and advances
Apr. 29	0	515	0	19,489	19,457	32	837
May 6	54	515	0	19,811	19,433	378	932
May 13	28	560	0	19,912	19,292	620	1,264
May 20	31	600	0	19,824	19,348	476	530
May 27	125	672	0	19,706	19,361	345	571
Jun. 3	50	780	0	19,729	19,261	468	507
Jun. 10	5	890	451	20,168	19,421	747	454
Jun. 17	0	1,040	823	20,958	19,712	1,246	286
Jun. 24	0	1,250	296	20,173	19,561	612	317
Jul. 1	0	1,475	0	19,828	19,163	665	245

Federal Reserve Statistical Release H.4.1.

Table 8.3 *Money market rates, 1953. Percent.*

	Federal funds		13-Week Treasury bills		
	Bid	Offer	Maturity	Bid	Offer
May 4	2		Jul. 30	2.28	2.22
May 5	1–15/16		Jul. 30	2.30	2.22
			Aug. 6	2.37	2.32
May 6	1–15/16	2	Aug. 6	2.33	2.28
May 7	2		Aug. 6	2.28	2.20
May 8	2		Aug. 6	2.26	2.18
May 11	2		Aug. 6	2.23	2.13
May 12	2		Aug. 6	2.20	2.12
			Aug. 13	2.23	2.17
May 13	2		Aug. 13	2.20	2.12
May 14	2		Aug. 13	2.15	2.07
May 15	2		Aug. 13	2.10	2.00
May 18	1–14/16	1–15/16	Aug. 13	2.05	1.92
May 19	1–7/8	1–7/8	Aug. 13	2.00	1.90
			Aug. 20	2.04	1.96
May 20		1–3/8	Aug. 20	2.06	2.00
May 21	1–3/4	1–15/16	Aug. 20	2.10	2.00
May 22	1–15/16	1–15/16	Aug. 20	2.10	2.00
May 25	1–3/8	1–1/2	Aug. 20	2.06	1.98
May 26			Aug. 20	2.10	2.00
			Aug. 27	2.12	2.06
May 27	3/8	1/2	Aug. 27	2.16	2.10
May 28	1–15/16	2	Aug. 27	2.20	2.14
May 29	1–15/16	2	Aug. 27	2.28	2.18
Jun. 1	1	1–1/4	Aug. 27	2.35	2.20
Jun. 2	2	3–1/4	Aug. 27	2.25	2.15
			Sep. 3	2.43	2.37
Jun. 3	2	3–1/4	Sep. 3	2.34	2.26
Jun. 4	2	3–1/4	Sep. 3	2.24	2.16
Jun. 5	2	3–1/4	Sep. 3	2.26	2.18

"Money Rates" column of the *Wall Street Journal* and "U.S. Government and Agency Bonds" column of the *New York Times.*

began to break down at the end of May. The on-the-run thirteen-week Treasury bill maturing on August 27 slid from a bid discount rate of 2.16 on May 27 to a bid rate of 2.28 percent on May 29 (Table 8.3), the 2½s of December 1972 (the long-term bond offered in the 1945 Victory Loan)

Table 8.4 *Bond prices, 1953. Percent and 32nds of a percent of principal.*

	2½s of Dec. 1972		3¼s of Jun. 1983	
	Bid	Offer	Bid	Offer
May 18	91^{20}	91^{28}	99^{29}	100^{1}
May 19	91^{14}	91^{22}	99^{26}	99^{30}
May 20	91^{14}	91^{22}	99^{26}	99^{30}
May 21	91^{18}	91^{26}	99^{28}	100
May 22	91^{18}	91^{26}	99^{28}	100
May 25	91^{16}	91^{22}	99^{26}	99^{30}
May 26	91^{12}	91^{18}	99^{25}	99^{29}
May 27	91^{2}	91^{10}	99^{22}	99^{26}
May 28	90^{28}	91^{4}	99^{18}	99^{22}
May 29	90^{20}	90^{28}	99^{6}	99^{10}
Jun. 1	90	90^{8}	98^{20}	98^{28}
Jun. 2	90^{6}	90^{14}	98^{24}	99
Jun. 3	90^{24}	91	99^{2}	99^{10}
Jun. 4	91^{4}	91^{12}	99^{4}	99^{12}
Jun. 5	91^{14}	91^{22}	99^{6}	99^{12}

"U.S. Government and Agency Bonds" column of the *New York Times*.

dropped almost a half point, and the new thirty-year bond, the 3¼s of June 1983, dropped a full half point (Table 8.4).

The market continued to drop on Monday, June 1. The August 27 bill fell another 7 basis points, to 2.35 percent, the auction for new thirteen-week bills averaged 2.42 percent (up from 2.08 percent at the beginning of the preceding week) and very nearly failed,[24] and the new thirty-year bond was down another half point.

Some market participants described the Monday retreat as disorderly and suggested that "there was nothing to indicate that the present downward phase of the market may be near an end." The *New York Times* reported that dealers were being asked by customers to bid on offerings of long-term bonds while finding "virtually no investment demand from institutional investors" and were forced to "lower [their] bids successively

[24] The Treasury received only $1.8 billion in tenders for the $1.5 billion of bills offered. "Treasury Bill Borrowing Cost at 20-Year High," *New York Times*, June 2, 1953, p. 15. Gaines (1962, p. 179) states that "there was some uncertainty for a time as to whether bids would be adequate to cover the auction."

to avoid becoming locked into involuntary inventories at unmarketable prices."[25]

On Tuesday, June 2, the August 27 bill rallied 10 basis points to close at a bid rate of 2.25 percent and the new thirty-year bond closed up one-eighth of a point. The *New York Times* reported that the turnaround "came during the morning trading when bids for large blocks of bills" appeared, including "substantial bids . . . from outside the [dealer] community."[26]

The improving market tone was a direct result of contemporaneous Desk purchases of $81.5 million of bills for the System account and $3.5 million of long-term bonds for government investment accounts.[27] The System purchased another $110 million of bills over the interval from June 3 to June 10, and by June 10 it was lending the Treasury an additional $450 million on special certificates of indebtedness issued directly to the Open Market Account (Table 8.2).[28] The System ultimately increased its bill holdings by $800 million during June, more than doubling what it had owned at the end of May. Excess reserves increased to $1.2 billion in the middle of June and remained north of $600 million at the end of the month.

REVISITING THE RESTRICTIONS ON INTERVENTION

In the wake of the June 1 turmoil and the June 2 intervention, Sproul asked the Open Market Committee to revisit its decision to limit System activity to short-term securities and its decision to abstain from directly supporting Treasury offerings. At the June 11 FOMC meeting, he argued that "the present situation and the likely situation during the next three months require that we remove these prohibitions and restore to ourselves greater freedom of action."[29]

Sproul challenged the basis for the prohibitions, reminding the Committee that "we were told that the market should be relieved of the threat of our intervention in the longer term areas so that it might develop breadth, depth, and resiliency" and pointing out that, although "we have

[25] "Sharp New Losses Occur in U.S. Bonds," *New York Times*, June 2, 1953, p. 43.

[26] "U.S. Bond Market Stages Good Gain," *New York Times*, June 3, 1953, p. 47.

[27] Minutes of the Federal Open Market Committee, June 11, 1953, pp. 3–4.

[28] Garbade (2014) describes direct issues of Treasury securities to the Federal Reserve. Details for direct issues in 1953 appear in the 1953 Board of Governors of the Federal Reserve System Annual Report, p. 65. All of the $450 million went into bank reserves because Treasury deposits at Federal Reserve Banks fell from $137 million on June 3 to $6 million on June 10. Federal Reserve Statistical Release H.4.1, June 4 and June 11, 1953.

[29] Minutes of the Federal Open Market Committee, June 11, 1953, p. 14.

not intervened in these areas for some months," "seldom has the market shown less breadth and depth."[30] Events had demonstrated that,

> ... if apprehension concerning our intervention in the market was once the cause of uncertainty, it was a transient phenomenon. Other factors have since been at work. Recently these have been our restrictive credit policy, continued heavy private demands for funds, and mounting Treasury cash needs. These have generated the expectation of a decline in Government security prices ... and a rise in interest rates of unknown extent and duration.
>
> Under such conditions a market of the size and present vulnerability of the Government security market doesn't develop real breadth, depth, and resiliency, and the Treasury's necessitous financing can be made unnecessarily difficult and onerous.
>
> In so far as credit policy is responsible for this, the problem is how to direct open market operations with sufficient flexibility and versatility to minimize the adverse effects of [that] policy without sacrificing the ... objective [of the policy].
>
> I don't think we can do it if we continue, as we have been doing, to confine ourselves at all times to operations in Treasury bills. We have been told that operations in bills would have prompt and pervasive effects throughout the market. ... I think historical records and current observation indicate that a prompt and invariable response between short and long markets can not always be expected. Under present conditions operations solely in bills may relieve the reserve position of the banks without giving timely relief from the complex pressures in the credit and capital markets created by large Treasury borrowing operations.[31]

Sproul asked why, "if the threat of our intervention isn't the source of lack of breadth, depth, and resiliency in the Government security market, ... we deprive ourselves of freedom of action?"

Sproul did not suggest a return to pegged prices but rather a flexible approach within the context of whatever credit policy the Committee deemed appropriate:

> No one here wants to return to pegging nor to try to substitute our judgment as to prices and yields for those of the market. But if our credit policy calls for putting funds into the market, as it does, and if at the same time we can assist the Treasury with its very difficult task of debt management, we should do it.
>
> We should be free, particularly at times of Treasury financing, to make purchases in whatever area of the market is under most pressure, so that there will not be an unnecessary erosion of rates, affecting adversely investor and banking psychology and intensifying the restrictive effects of our credit policy at the wrong time.
>
> We have made it clear to the market that we are not interested in pegging prices, and the Treasury has made it clear that it wants to price its obligations on the market, not on us. Within this framework, I think we should reserve for ourselves

[30] Minutes of the Federal Open Market Committee, June 11, 1953, p. 14.
[31] Minutes of the Federal Open Market Committee, June 11, 1953, pp. 14–15.

maximum freedom to operate in any way which, without sacrificing credit policy, will support the Treasury's program and the stability of the market.[32]

Sproul framed the restrictions on intervention as a matter of adherence to an "untried theory" that bordered on irresponsibility:

> To withhold the System portfolio from participation in the market, except for bill transactions, in the light of the present economic situation and the Treasury's needs, seems to me to be sacrificing credit policy to untried theory.
>
> To go further, and to withhold the System portfolio from participation in the tremendous redistribution and swapping process which takes place in the market during the short period of a Treasury financing is likely to prove irresponsible.[33]

He concluded with a plea for a more flexible policy:

> Even though our operations continue to be largely in bills, effective credit policy can best be achieved, in my opinion, by retaining flexibility of action to meet the unpredictable circumstances which are always arising,

and a warning of the dangers of inflexibility:

> To freeze the System into a pattern of behavior which involves not doing certain things could be just as harmful to the success of credit policy as a frozen commitment to do certain things. We can't afford a succession of black Mondays [a reference to the events of June 1] and Treasury near-failures over the next few months.[34]

Chairman Martin responded to Sproul's arguments with two reasons for not abandoning the restrictions that the Committee had imposed three months earlier. First, market sentiment had "improved markedly" following the $81.5 million of bill purchases on June 2, suggesting that limiting intervention to the bill market did not preclude effective intervention.[35] Second, Martin noted that the Committee had agreed in March to operate in intermediate- and long-term securities to correct a disorderly market but that Rouse had not notified the Executive Committee that the market was, in fact, disorderly.[36] In a statement illustrating the distinctly different views of the two men as to what had calmed the markets

[32] Minutes of the Federal Open Market Committee, June 11, 1953, p. 15.

[33] Minutes of the Federal Open Market Committee, June 11, 1953, p. 15.

[34] Minutes of the Federal Open Market Committee, June 11, 1953, p. 16.

[35] Minutes of the Federal Open Market Committee, June 11, 1953, p. 16. In a thinly veiled criticism of Rouse's management of the Open Market Account, Martin additionally stated his belief that "if the System account had made aggressive purchases of bills during the last several weeks there would have been a much sounder market."

[36] It became clear in the course of the discussions that the FOMC was not operating with a clear and unambiguous understanding of the characteristics of a disorderly market.

on June 2, Rouse replied that he had considered contacting the Executive Committee but did not do so when the purchase of $3.5 million of long-term bonds for Treasury investment accounts "took care of the situation."[37]

Whether to continue the restrictions on intervention came to a vote in the middle of the afternoon of June 11. Sproul's motion to set the restrictions aside passed on a close vote of 5 to 4.[38] The Record of Policy Actions published in the 1953 annual report of the Board of Governors states that "it was felt that, in carrying out the Committee's credit policy, the executive committee should have discretion, particularly at times of Treasury financing, to make purchases in whatever areas of the market were under pressure so that there would not be unnecessary erosion of rates, affecting adversely investor and banking psychology."[39] The Record of Policy Actions further states that "it was also believed that, so long as it was the policy of the Committee to put funds into the market, freedom to put them where the pressures were greatest might minimize the amount the Committee would have to put in and thus help to achieve the purposes of monetary policy most effectively."

Reimposition

Three months later, at its September 1953 meeting, the FOMC voted to reimpose the March restrictions.[40] The Committee's second about-face was the product of two considerations.

Sproul stated that "his impression of a disorderly market as discussed at the March meeting had been the situation that might exist in the event of an outbreak of war ... [as, for example, the situation that existed on September 1, 1939 – see the appendix to Chapter 4 above], whereas it now had been suggested that during the past two weeks there may have been a disorderly condition, or incipient disorder." Minutes of the Federal Open Market Committee, June 11, 1953, pp. 27–28.

Hugh Leach, president of the Federal Reserve Bank of Richmond, believed that "disorderly markets should be interpreted a little differently now than had been the case earlier" and confessed that "he was more concerned at present about the Treasury's financing problem than he had been." Minutes of the Federal Open Market Committee, June 11, 1953, p. 37.

Joseph Erickson, president of the Federal Reserve Bank of Boston, stated that "he had felt [a week ago] that the market was bordering on being 'disorderly'" and suggested that "a more precise definition might be helpful." Minutes of the Federal Open Market Committee, June 11, 1953, pp. 27–28.

[37] Minutes of the Federal Open Market Committee, June 11, 1953, p. 17.

[38] Minutes of the Federal Open Market Committee, June 11, 1953, p. 52.

[39] 1953 Board of Governors of the Federal Reserve System Annual Report, p. 96.

[40] Minutes of the Federal Open Market Committee, September 24, 1953, p. 29.

First, some Committee members had grown reluctant to delegate what they considered a policy issue to the Executive Committee. They felt that the full Committee, the body authorized by Congress to make open market policy, should decide whether and when to intervene in other than the bill market for purposes other than control of monetary and credit aggregates.[41] In the absence of an explicit directive by the full Committee, the Executive Committee would have to limit its instructions to the Account Manager to operations in short-term securities.

Second, and relatedly, some FOMC members felt that the Committee should be more knowledgeable about, and actively engaged with, market developments. Retention of the authority to intervene was one way to foster deeper engagement.[42]

Sproul pushed back against the effort to reimpose the restrictions, arguing that "the interpretation and direction of [the credit policy approved by the full Committee] under changing conditions is the job of the Executive Committee" and that "there was an implication of permanent policy" in the motion to reimpose the restrictions that "tended to inhibit the free and flexible consideration of the problem by either the full Committee or the executive committee."[43] In the event, Sproul lost on a vote of 9 to 2.

[41] Minutes of the Federal Open Market Committee, September 24, 1953, p. 19 (comments of Delos Johns, president of the Federal Reserve Bank of St. Louis), p. 23 (comments of Governor James Vardaman), and p. 24 (comments of H. Gavin Leedy, president of the Federal Reserve Bank of Kansas City). See also the Record of Policy Actions in the Board of Governors of the Federal Reserve System Annual Report, stating (p. 99) that proponents of reimposition believed the Committee "should have some general rules for the guidance of the management of the System open market account in conducting operations to carry out the general credit policy of the Committee," that such general rules "should not leave too much discretion to the executive committee," and that "if such rules relating to broad operating procedures were to be changed, any change should be authorized by the full Committee."

[42] Minutes of the Federal Open Market Committee, September 24, 1953, pp. 23–24 (comments of Governor M. S. Szymczak) and p. 28 (comments of Clifford Young, president of the Federal Reserve Bank of Chicago). This consideration ultimately led to the abolition of the Executive Committee in June 1955. Minutes of the Federal Open Market Committee, June 22, 1955, pp. 1–26.

[43] Minutes of the Federal Open Market Committee, September 24, 1953, pp. 17 and 25–26. See also the Record of Policy Actions in the 1953 Board of Governors of the Federal Reserve System Annual Report, p. 100, stating that opponents of reimposition believed that the Committee "was trying to write into a 'constitution of the Open Market Committee a prohibition against actions put in the form of a continuing directive at a particular time," and that it would be "preferable for the executive committee of the Federal Open Market Committee to be free to use its judgment, within the limits of the Committee's general credit policy, as to the best method of achieving the objectives of credit policy, in whatever circumstances might arise between meetings of the full Committee."

THE CONTROVERSY BECOMES PUBLIC

The wrangling between Martin and Sproul became public in early May 1954, when the FOMC's Record of Policy Actions for 1953 was published in the Board of Governors' annual report.[44]

The dispute attracted further attention following a speech by Sproul at the annual convention of the New Jersey Bankers Association in Atlantic City, New Jersey, in the same month. The *Wall Street Journal* reported that Sproul "took issue with the [FOMC's] present view that purchases or sales of Treasury securities should be limited to short-term issues and made solely to provide or absorb bank reserves."[45] The *New York Times* reported that,

> Mr. Sproul emphasized that he was not arguing against the proposition that the primary purpose of open market operations is to affect the volume of member bank reserves, nor that this might be best accomplished by purchases and sales of Treasury bills. However, he said, there are occasions when operations through the Treasury bill market may involve unnecessarily large purchases and sales, or may not find its best reflection in the credit and capital markets because of imperfect arbitrage within and between markets. Finally, he asserted, there have been and may be occasions when some direct assistance to Treasury operations . . ., through open market operations in securities other than Treasury bills, would be good economics and good central banking.[46]

The dispute attracted even more attention during hearings before the Subcommittee on Economic Stabilization of the Joint Committee on the Economic Report in December 1954. In a written response to questions from the subcommittee, Martin claimed that the restriction of open market operations to the front end of the yield curve was needed to address stability problems in the intermediate and long-term credit markets that had developed since the Accord.[47] He stated, in both written and oral testimony, that the restriction had improved market functions.[48] Sproul maintained precisely the opposite, that the restriction had narrowed, rather

[44] 1953 Board of Governors of the Federal Reserve System Annual Report, pp. 86–91. The annual report was released in early May 1954. "Reserve Explains 1953 Policy Shifts," *New York Times*, May 6, 1954, p. 22.

[45] "Some Federal Reserve Monetary 'Techniques' Are Criticized by Sproul," *Wall Street Journal*, May 7, 1954, p. 9.

[46] "Difference Aired on Reserve Role," *New York Times*, May 16, 1954, p. F1.

[47] "FRB, Treasury Credited With Big Role in Halting 'Boom-Bust,'" *Wall Street Journal*, December 3, 1954, p. 3; and Joint Committee on the Economic Report (1954, pp. 15–26).

[48] "Federal Reserve Wins Policy Fight," *New York Times*, December 8, 1954, p. 53; and Joint Committee on the Economic Report (1954, pp. 16, 24, and 228).

than broadened, the market.[49] The *Wall Street Journal* reported that the clashing testimonies brought the differences between the two men "into the open."[50] The highly visible differences led the subcommittee to publish what the *New York Times* described as the "long-suppressed" ad hoc subcommittee study, as well as rebuttal comments from the Federal Reserve Bank of New York.[51]

49 "Federal Reserve Wins Policy Fight," *New York Times*, December 8, 1954, p. 53; and Joint Committee on the Economic Report (1954, pp. 225–27).

50 "Humphrey Opposes 'Drastic' Steps to Aid Economy; Says Policies Checked Inflation, Cushioned Recession," *Wall Street Journal*, December 8, 1954, p. 3.

51 "Congressional Group Releases '52 Report that Split Two Federal Reserve Leaders," *New York Times*, December 20, 1954, p. 42. The ad hoc subcommittee report appears in Joint Committee on the Economic Report (1954, pp. 257–307). The rebuttal comments of the New York Reserve Bank appear in Joint Committee on the Economic Report (1954, pp. 307–31).

9

An Additional Limitation on the Conduct of Open Market Operations

The March 1953 Federal Open Market Committee (FOMC) meeting established three default principles for open market operations:

(1) operations for the System Open Market Account (other than to correct disorderly markets) would be confined to the front end of the yield curve;

(2) intervention in the Government securities market (other than to correct disorderly markets) would be solely to effectuate the objectives of monetary and credit policy; and

(3) during a period of Treasury financing the System would not purchase (a) maturing issues for which an exchange was being offered, (b) when-issued securities, and (c) outstanding issues with maturities comparable to the maturity of an issue being offered for exchange.

The three principles were default principles because they could be modified or eliminated by the FOMC at any time.

In an unexpected development in late 1953, the FOMC adopted a fourth operating principle: that transactions for the Open Market Account (other than to correct disorderly markets) were *solely for the purpose of providing or absorbing reserves.* Most prominently, the new principle precluded exchanges of securities with different maturities but equal value.

A SWAP AUTHORIZATION

In late November 1953, the Executive Committee discussed how to accommodate the usual seasonal surge in demand for currency over the coming holiday period, as well as the reabsorption of reserves once demand ebbed after the turn of the year. Robert Rouse, the manager of the Open Market

Account, suggested that the post-holiday reabsorption "would be facilitated if some of the short-term securities presently held in the account were to be swapped for Treasury bills [maturing in January] which could be permitted to run off."[1] Governor A. L. Mills stated that Rouse's proposal "seemed logical" and Chairman Martin agreed that "the more bills the account acquired, the better off it would be." The Executive Committee approved Rouse's suggestion unanimously.[2]

PUSHBACK

When the full FOMC assembled for its regular quarterly meeting three weeks later, Governor J. L. Robertson, who was not a member of the Executive Committee, unleashed a frontal assault on the swap authorization.

Robertson began by stating his understanding that "one of the chief purposes of our action at the September [1953 FOMC] meeting was to effectuate further the principle which permeated the ad hoc subcommittee report and underlay the policy decisions of the Committee throughout 1953 – that our intervention in the market should be *solely for the objective of providing or absorbing reserves* in accordance with the needs of the economy."[3] He then expressed his belief that "the possible advantages of participating in all sectors of the Government securities market, with a variety of objectives, are outweighed by the benefits of a *strictly limited participation*,"[4] including,

(1) the likelihood of increased effectiveness of market action designed to effectuate general credit policy when that action is not impeded, and its objectives are not obscured by the pursuit of other objectives;[5] and

(2) the development of greater depth, breadth, and resiliency in the Government securities market, as dealers and others become certain, as months go by, that (in the absence of very unusual

[1] Minutes of the Executive Committee of the Federal Open Market Committee, November 23, 1953, p. 14.

[2] Minutes of the Executive Committee of the Federal Open Market Committee, November 23, 1953, p. 15.

[3] Minutes of the Federal Open Market Committee, December 15, 1953, p. 8. Emphasis added.

[4] Minutes of the Federal Open Market Committee, December 15, 1953, p. 8. Emphasis added.

[5] Almost a half-century later, Under Secretary of the Treasury Peter Fisher similarly sought the clarity of a single objective. See Garbade (2015, pp. 112–13).

conditions) the Open Market Committee's transactions will be solely in the shortest-term sector.[6]

Robertson believed that the Committee's job was "to supply reserves and withdraw reserves in order to contribute to the maintenance of an economy that is both stable and highly productive" and that a policy of "rigorous self-limitation" would allow it to pursue single-mindedly that "most vital duty."[7] He proposed that the Committee adopt a fourth operating principle, that "[t]ransactions for the System account in the open market shall be entered into solely for the purpose of providing or absorbing reserves (except in the correction of disorderly markets), and shall not include offsetting purchases and sales of securities for the purpose of altering the maturity pattern of the System's portfolio."[8]

Chairman Martin and Allan Sproul had quite different reactions to Robertson's proposal. Martin cautioned against adopting a "doctrinaire" position, but felt that, "as a matter of principle, . . . the position suggested by [Robertson] would be a sound position in light of the general philosophy under which the Committee had been working for some time."[9]

Sproul, on the other hand, thought that requiring that the sole purpose of open market operations was to put reserves into the market, or to take them out, was "much too narrow an interpretation; much narrower than saying that the sole purpose is to effectuate the objectives of monetary and credit policy."[10] As in his campaign against bills preferably, Sproul argued for the retention of flexibility:

In Mr. Sproul's view, the emphasis in open market operations should be on putting reserves into or taking them out of the market, and the ad hoc subcommittee report indicated that to be the primary responsibility of the Committee, but the entire experience of the Committee's operations indicated that there might be times when money market factors (and therefore credit policy) suggested operations which were not solely for the purpose of putting in or taking out reserves. Mr. Sproul felt that if the Committee adopted the proposed prohibition, it would be moving further into a situation of freezing itself into a position from which it would be difficult to extricate itself; its adoption would be an attempt to put the Open Market Committee on record in such a way that the idea of resiliency or flexibility in its policy function would almost disappear.[11]

6 Minutes of the Federal Open Market Committee, December 15, 1953, p. 9.
7 Minutes of the Federal Open Market Committee, December 15, 1953, p. 9.
8 Minutes of the Federal Open Market Committee, December 15, 1953, p. 10.
9 Minutes of the Federal Open Market Committee, December 15, 1953, pp. 11–12.
10 Minutes of the Federal Open Market Committee, December 15, 1953, p. 12.
11 Minutes of the Federal Open Market Committee, December 15, 1953, pp. 18–19.

Martin denied any intent to limit flexibility but nevertheless thought that "it was more appropriate to develop a philosophy and make exceptions to that philosophy, rather than to take the view that there should be no philosophy."[12]

The Committee also debated whether Rouse's swaps might have confused market participants. In response to a question about exactly what was undesirable about the swaps, Governor Mills replied that the swaps had "clouded the pattern of the Government securities market." He argued that "dealers in Government securities were very alert to every influence injected into the market and that where that influence was in the form of entrance by the System open market account in a manner which was not clearly discernable in its objectives, the action might cause confusion among Government securities dealers in reaching their judgments."[13] Mills stated that "it was his view that to inject into the market *any* extraneous influence that was apart from the free market concept would result in throwing a haze over the market."[14] When Rouse stated that the swaps had had "no discernable effect on dealer positions or on the willingness of dealers to take positions," Mills replied that "while there may have been no observable effect ... the recent swaps had given the dealer fraternity some indication that the System open market account may, on occasion, enter the market for purposes other than providing or absorbing reserves or correcting disorderly markets, that this would cause uncertainty, and the sooner such uncertainties could be disabused, the better."[15]

Following the discussion (and ultimate rejection) of a more flexible version of Robertson's proposal, the Committee adopted the proposal by a vote of nine to two.[16] The Record of Policy Actions of the Federal Open Market Committee, published in the 1953 Board of Governors annual report, states the basis for the Committee's action:

> It was felt that if the System open market account were to engage in purchases and sales in the open market without altering total holdings of securities in the portfolio, the objective of such transactions would not be clearly discernable to the market, and thus might cause confusion and uncertainty as to credit policy and, in so doing, militate against the depth, breadth, and resiliency sought in the Government securities market.[17]

[12] Minutes of the Federal Open Market Committee, December 15, 1953, pp. 18–19.
[13] Minutes of the Federal Open Market Committee, December 15, 1953, p. 14.
[14] Minutes of the Federal Open Market Committee, December 15, 1934, p. 14.
[15] Minutes of the Federal Open Market Committee, December 15, 1953, p. 14.
[16] Minutes of the Federal Open Market Committee, December 15, 1953, p. 22.
[17] 1953 Board of Governors of the Federal Reserve System Annual Report, p. 104.

ROUND TWO

The FOMC revisited its operating principles during the March 1954 Committee meeting, when it had to decide whether to renew the principles for another year. Responding to a request from Chairman Martin for comments on the new fourth principle, Sproul suggested that it reflected a "fundamentalist view of central banking" and that it was "a statement not of operating policy but a capsule statement of a whole theory of central banking." He went on to argue that,

> We have been misled, I think, by our aversion to pegged or manipulated markets, and bemused by the ideal of a "free market." Such a market has been made and is being defined "as one in which the allocation of available funds among various uses is effected through competition in the market. Borrowers offer interest rates and other terms that enable them to obtain funds they require, and lenders bid for loans and securities in accordance with their appraisal of risks and yields and their portfolio needs. In such a market Federal Reserve purchases and sales would be solely for the purpose of influencing the supply of bank reserves in order to promote economic stability and growth.
>
> That may be fine classical economics and fine 19th and early 20th century central banking tradition, but I think the fact is that we can't and don't now have a "free market" as thus defined. We have a market in which lenders and borrowers have to and do take account of action and possible action by the Federal Reserve System to increase or decrease the supply, availability, and cost of funds; a market which has to and does take account of possible actions by the Treasury with respect to debt management, and by the Government with respect to fiscal policy.
>
> The proponents of the doctrine of solely putting in and taking out reserves go on to say that "changes in bank reserves necessarily affect the supply, availability, and cost of credit." That as I have said is sliding over a critical point. Changes in bank reserves not only affect the supply, availability, and cost of credit – they are for the purpose of influencing the supply, availability, and cost of credit. And I would go on to say that we cannot rely solely on the supply of reserves, at all times and in all circumstances, to achieve our objectives in all areas of credit policy in a mixed Government-private economy such as we have.[18]

Sproul concluded by saying that, "[T]he sooner we get back to the general statement of policy adopted unanimously when the Ad Hoc Committee report was prepared, that we shall intervene in the market solely to effectuate the objectives of credit policy, the better off we shall be, in terms of our record, in terms of objective thinking about the subject, and in terms of objective appraisal of the practices we are now following."

Robertson responded to Sproul's critique by observing that the new restriction was no more than a "policy that should be followed until

[18] Minutes of the Federal Open Market Committee, March 3, 1954, pp. 11–12.

Box 9.1 Operating Principles for Open Market Operations as Renewed at the March 3, 1954, Meeting of the Federal Open Market Committee

It is not now the policy of the Committee to support any pattern of prices and yields in the Government securities market and intervention in the Government securities market is solely to effectuate the objectives of monetary and credit policy (including correction of disorderly markets).

Operations for the System account in the open market shall be confined to short-term securities (expect in the correction of disorderly markets) and that during a period of Treasury financing there shall be no purchases of (1) maturing issues for which an exchange is being offered, (2) when-issued securities, or (3) outstanding issues of comparable maturity to those being offered for exchange; and that these policies be followed until such times as they may be superseded or modified by further action of the Federal Open Market Committee.

Transactions for the System account in the open market shall be entered into solely for the purpose of providing or absorbing reserves (except in the correction of disorderly markets), and shall not include offsetting purchases and sales of securities for the purpose of altering the maturity pattern of the System's portfolio; such policy to be followed until such time as it may be superseded or modified by further action of the Federal Open Market Committee.

Minutes of the Federal Open Market Committee, March 3, 1954, pp. 9 and 20

conditions warrant a deviation from it" and that it was "an operating policy designed for the present time and is not a 'capsule statement' designed to encompass the 'whole theory of central banking.'"[19] Sproul reiterated his belief that it was "undesirable for the Committee to have in its record such a statement of central banking policy which he thought tended to freeze thinking."[20]

The discussions at the March 1954 committee meeting illuminated two additional facets of the debate over the new operating principles: the appropriate locus of open market policymaking and lingering concern with relations with the Department of the Treasury.

With respect to the locus of policymaking, Martin stated that "he thought it important procedurally that the authority of arranging for transactions and determination of the purpose of such transactions be in the Open Market Committee," rather than in the hands of the Executive Committee or left to the discretion of the Manager. He claimed that, in adopting the fourth operating principle, the Committee was "aiming at . . . a means of having a shared responsibility" and not letting that

[19] Minutes of the Federal Open Market Committee, March 3, 1954, p. 14.
[20] Minutes of the Federal Open Market Committee, March 3, 1954, p. 15.

responsibility "get out of its hands." Martin acknowledged that "the wording of the action . . . might not be the best way of carrying out this objective" but nevertheless supported the new policy as a way of avoiding Committee meetings that were little more than "passing words around the table."[21]

With respect to the System's relationship with the Treasury, Governor Menc Szymczak observed that "it had taken the Committee a long time to extricate itself from the pegged market" of World War II. It was natural, he believed, for the System to "'lean over backwards' to keep from slipping back to a pegged market." Szymczak allowed that the Committee might have "gone too far in adopting the particular language in question" but nevertheless believed that "the more clearly the Committee could state the reasons for or purposes of its operations, the less likely it was to fall back into a pegged market."[22]

Following further discussion, the FOMC renewed the operating principles shown in Box 9.1. The principles were thereafter renewed annually for the balance of the 1950s.[23]

[21] Minutes of the Federal Open Market Committee, March 3, 1954, p. 18.

[22] Minutes of the Federal Open Market Committee, March 3, 1954, p. 19.

[23] Minutes of the Federal Open Market Committee, March 2, 1955, pp. 52–53 and 58–59; March 6, 1956, pp. 13 and 20; March 5, 1957, pp. 11–13; March 4, 1958, pp. 55–57; and March 3, 1959, pp. 11–14.

PART III

THE NEW REGIME

In 1954, the Federal Open Market Committee became fully engaged in implementing monetary policy within the framework of the operating principles established a year earlier. A survey of Committee deliberations and decisions from 1954 to 1957 supports three key observations:

1. Officials focused on managing reserves, rather than interest rates or the money supply. This was most clearly evident in 1954, when the Committee sought to promote recovery (from a recession that started in mid-1953) by keeping the banking system flush with free reserves, but reserves management continued to be the principal channel of monetary control even when the Committee began to look to other indicators and targets.
2. Officials were acutely aware of the importance of accommodating Treasury offerings. Accommodation was not a problem in 1954, when reserves were ample, but became a more vexing issue when the Committee began to tighten in 1955. By the end of that year, the Committee was forced to abandon rigid adherence to the principle of no direct support for Treasury offerings.
3. Officials identified repurchase agreements as a particularly useful instrument for injecting large quantities of reserves into the banking system quickly to alleviate actual or anticipated transient stringencies.

Repos were, however, limited by the size of dealer inventories and could not be used to drain reserves. Additionally, they were undertaken at a fixed rate (which vexed some Committee members when the rate was fixed below Reserve Bank discount rates) and were not undertaken with bank dealers.

10

Monetary Policy in 1954

Minutes of Federal Open Market Committee (FOMC) meetings in 1954 show that the Committee relied on free reserves – the difference between (a) member bank reserve deposits in excess of requirements and (b) borrowed reserves – as both an indicator of money market conditions and a policy target. *Ceteris paribus*, more free reserves were believed to foster an easier money market and promote member bank balance sheet expansion.

MONITORING ECONOMIC ACTIVITY

The first agenda item at every FOMC meeting was a briefing on the state of the economy. Board staff economists presented full-scale reviews at the full committee meetings; updates, usually by FOMC economist Ralph Young, launched the Executive Committee meetings.

The economy was contracting at a gradual pace at the beginning of 1954. In mid-January, Young reported "recent declines in output and employment" but noted that the overall level of activity "remained high." In early February, he observed that activity was "edging downward" and that unemployment had increased. Similar comments followed in mid-February ("few signs of a halt in the contraction"), mid-March ("the decline ... was continuing"), and late March (the recession "appeared to have continued at a moderate pace"). In mid-April, Young reported the decline was slowing. By May, activity had "leveled off."[1]

[1] Minutes of the Executive Committee of the Federal Open Market Committee, January 19, 1954, p. 3; February 2, p. 2; February 17, p. 2; March 16, p. 3; March 30, p. 9; April 13, p. 2; and May 26, p. 3. The National Bureau of Economic Research subsequently located a trough in economic activity in May.

The economy moved sideways during the summer, with no sign of either renewed decline or recovery,[2] but began to strengthen in the fall. Young reported in early November that the strengthening "was being widely interpreted as foreshadowing sustained, though possibly moderate, cyclical expansion." Four weeks later, "the big question with which business observers are now concerned is whether a recovery movement is definitely taking form." By the end of the year "a vigorous economic recovery" was "visible and tangible."[3]

MONETARY POLICY

There are two authoritative sources for identifying US monetary policy in 1954: directives issued by the Federal Open Market Committee to the Executive Committee and by the Executive Committee to the Federal Reserve Bank of New York, and minutes of the Committee and Executive Committee meetings.

The Directives

The directives of the full Committee and the Executive Committee are archetypes of opacity, virtually useless for understanding, more than sixty years later, what policymakers were thinking.[4]

At the beginning of 1954, the most recent FOMC directive (issued in December 1953) provided, in relevant part, that,

[2] Minutes of the Executive Committee of the Federal Open Market Committee, June 8, 1954, p. 2 (not clear whether the economy was at a turning point or whether the downturn would resume); July 7, p. 3 (mixed trends with no clear evidence that an upturn was underway) August 3, p. 2 (a revival in activity "not yet clearly evident"); and September 8, p. 3 (reports indicated continuing sideways movement).

[3] Minutes of the Executive Committee of the Federal Open Market Committee, November 9, 1954, p. 5; Minutes of the Federal Open Market Committee, December 7, 1954, p. 2; and Minutes of the Executive Committee of the Federal Open Market Committee, December 28, 1954, pp. 3–4.

[4] However, it is not clear that the directives were intended to be detailed instructions for the management of the System Open Market Account. Governor J. L. Robertson observed that "the Manager of the Account sits with the Open Market Committee and has the benefit of discussion around the table, for which reason it is not essential to pinpoint specific instructions to the Manager." Minutes of the Federal Open Market Committee, May 26, 1959, p. 60. See, similarly, Holmes (1970, p. 236), stating that "for the Manager, the full discussion of the Committee as it reaches a policy decision adds a great deal of flesh to the bare bones of the directive."

The executive committee is directed, until otherwise directed by the Federal Open Market Committee, to arrange for such transactions for the System open market account, either in the open market or directly with the Treasury (including purchases, sales, exchanges, replacement of maturing securities, and letting maturities run off without replacement), as may be necessary, in the light of current and prospective economic conditions and the general credit situation of the country, with a view

(a) to relating the supply of funds in the market to the needs of commerce and business,
(b) to promoting growth and stability in the economy *by actively maintaining a condition of ease in the money market,*
(c) to correcting a disorderly situation in the Government securities market, and
(d) to the practical administration of the account;

provided that the aggregate amount of securities held in the System account (including commitments for the purchase or sale of securities for the account) at the close of this date ... shall not be increased or decreased by more than \$2,000,000,000.[5]

The key phrase was clause (b): the admonition to actively maintain a condition of ease in the money market. There was, however, no indication of what that phrase meant and there were no quantitative targets – of interest rates, reserves, or monetary aggregates – that the executive committee was to aim for.[6]

The same can be said for the concurrently issued directive of the Executive Committee to the New York Reserve Bank. That directive authorized the Bank,

To make such purchases, sales, or exchanges (including replacement of maturing securities and allowing maturities to run off without replacement) for the System account in the open market or, in the case of maturing securities, by direct exchange with the Treasury, as may be necessary in the light of current and

[5] Minutes of the Federal Open Market Committee, December 15, 1953, p. 32. Emphasis added.

[6] Allan Sproul, the president of the Federal Reserve Bank of New York, subsequently recognized the need for greater specificity in characterizing open market policy. In January 1955, he stated that, for him, active ease meant "short-term money market rates ordinarily far below the discount rate so that access to reserve funds will be cheaper through the open market than through the discount window," ease was when "the more sensitive money market rates – Federal funds, dealer loans, and Treasury bills – move up toward the discount rate so that, at times, borrowing reserves through [the] discount window may be more advantageous than obtaining them through the open market," and restraint was when "sensitive money market rates would be close to or above the discount rate at all times." Minutes of the Federal Open Market Committee, January 11, 1955, pp. 10–12.

prospective economic conditions and the general credit situation of the country, with a view

(a) to relating the supply of funds in the market to the needs of commerce and business,
(b) to promoting growth and stability in the economy *by actively maintaining a condition of ease in the money market*, and
(c) to the practical administration of the account;

provided that the total amount of securities in the System account (including commitments for the purchase or sale of securities for the account) at the close of this date shall not be increased or decreased by more than $500 million.[7]

The wording of the directives changed infrequently. Reluctance to vary the wording may have stemmed from the practical difficulty of crafting more granular language, as well as concern that the Committee might appear to be getting ahead of the data or that its directives might be subject to misinterpretation. At the December 1954 Committee meeting, when change was clearly warranted, Governor C. Canby Balderston defended his resistance by declaring that "any change in the wording ... might be misinterpreted by the public" and that "it was better for any shifts to become evident as a result of actions rather than words."[8]

The Minutes

The minutes of the FOMC and Executive Committee meetings are far more informative sources of information. Even William McChesney Martin, the chairman of the Board of Governors, acknowledged, after one particularly opaque discussion, that "it was difficult to know just how to write an instruction regarding open market operations during the next two weeks other than to record in the minutes the views that had been expressed and to give the Manager of the System Account discretion to operate in accordance with these views."[9]

The minutes show that both the full Committee and the Executive Committee focused on free reserves as the touchstone of US monetary policy. Every meeting heard a presentation on the current state of financial

[7] Minutes of the Executive Committee of the Federal Open Market Committee, December 15, 1953, p. 5. Emphasis added.

[8] Minutes of the Federal Open Market Committee, December 7, 1954, p. 18.

[9] Minutes of the Executive Committee of the Federal Open Market Committee, November 23, 1954, p. 9.

markets, usually from FOMC economist Woodlief Thomas. Thomas typically reviewed the recent behavior of free reserves and presented staff projections of how free reserves were likely to evolve over the next few weeks in the absence of any open market initiatives. In mid-January 1954, he told the Executive Committee that a "return flow of currency [reversing the elevated demand associated with the Christmas holiday season], a sharp decline in Treasury balances at the Reserve Banks, and the usually large mid-month [level of] float supplied abundant reserves to the market. The net result of these changes was that an extremely easy condition currently was prevailing in the money market with excess reserves running around $1,300 million and member bank borrowings from the Federal Reserve Banks below $100 million."[10] In early May, Thomas observed that "the reserve position of banks continued fairly easy during April, … and although there was some temporary tightening last week it appeared … that daily average free reserves during the next two weeks would range around $500 to $700 million."[11] Similar remarks appear in the minutes of every other meeting in 1954.

The members of the FOMC not only kept appraised of the current state and expected future course of free reserves, they also expressed monetary policy in terms of target levels for free reserves.[12] At the February 2 meeting of the Executive Committee, Chairman Martin referred to $400 million of free reserves as "a possible guide to open market operations" and queried his colleagues whether they deemed that figure consistent with the contemporaneous objective of active ease.[13] A month later, Governor Robertson suggested that "free reserves should be somewhere between $300 and $500 million under present circumstances …, that anything below that would be too tight and that anything above would be too sloppy."[14] By the end of September, with recovery not yet in sight, the Executive Committee unanimously concluded that "operations for the System account … should be directed toward maintaining a level of free

[10] Minutes of the Executive Committee of the Federal Open Market Committee, January 19, 1954, p. 4.

[11] Minutes of the Executive Committee of the Federal Open Market Committee, May 11, 1954, p. 4.

[12] Meltzer (2009, p. 44) states that "the main target was free reserves."

[13] Minutes of the Executive Committee of the Federal Open Market Committee, February 2, 1954, p. 5.

[14] Minutes of the Executive Committee of the Federal Open Market Committee, March 16, 1954, p. 8.

reserves within the approximate range of $400-700 million."[15] Allan Sproul, the president of the Federal Reserve Bank of New York, summed up the importance of free reserves at the September meeting:

> All during 1954, in the face of a declining or sidewise movement of the general economy, we have followed a credit policy labeled a policy of 'active ease.' . . . [The objective of the policy] has been to encourage the free use of credit and an active capital and mortgage market. *Its main technical guide has been the maintenance of a substantial volume of 'free reserves' in the banking system.*[16]

When economic growth resumed at the end of the year, the FOMC responded by lowering the free reserves target. Martin observed in November that "operations had been carried on with the idea of providing free reserves nearer the upper limits of a range of $400–700 million" and suggested that "the committee consider whether operations should [now] be directed toward a volume of free reserves nearer the lower limits of that range." He recapitulated the ensuing discussion by stating that "a majority of the committee [believed] that for the immediate future there should be a minimum disturbance in the general tone of operations as carried out recently, with the understanding, however, that during the next two weeks it would be desirable to look toward a lower level of free reserves than currently existed."[17] Sproul summarized an Executive Committee meeting in late December as indicating that "operations should aim toward a level of free reserves near the lower part of the suggested range of $300–500 million, and that doubts should not be resolved on the side of ease."[18]

There was no significant discussion in 1954 of any alternative to free reserves as an indicator of money market conditions or as a target for monetary policy. Neither the full committee nor the Executive Committee paid any attention to interest rates or the money supply. An alternative measure of reserve availability was discussed on only one occasion. During the June 23 FOMC meeting, Malcolm Bryan, the president of the Federal Reserve Bank of Atlanta, stated that he was unsure "whether there was full understanding of the criteria being used in connection with open market

[15] Minutes of the Executive Committee of the Federal Open Market Committee, September 22, 1954, p. 2.

[16] Minutes of the Federal Open Market Committee, September 22, 1954, p. 12. Emphasis added.

[17] Minutes of the Executive Committee of the Federal Open Market Committee, November 9, 1954, pp. 7 and 19–20.

[18] Minutes of the Executive Committee of the Federal Open Market Committee, December 28, 1954, p. 12.

operations [and] questioned whether the concept of 'free reserves' was a better guide than total reserves."[19] Asked for his views, Woodlief Thomas acknowledged that "there could be a difference of opinion as to whether free reserves or total reserves or the volume of member bank borrowing offered the best guide to System policy," but the discussion did not go any further.

WHY FREE RESERVES?

Karl Brunner and Allan Meltzer trace[20] the origins of the Fed's interest in free reserves to studies of the US monetary system in the 1920s by Winfield Riefler at the Federal Reserve Board and W. R. Burgess at the Federal Reserve Bank of New York.[21] Focusing on bank borrowings from the Fed – which, in the 1920s, was essentially equivalent (with a change in sign) to free reserves (because excess reserves were small and stable[22]) – the two economists concluded that "banks were reluctant to borrow [from the Fed], borrowed only if reserves were deficient, and repaid promptly."[23]

As a result of banks' purported reluctance to borrow, open market sales of System securities that drained reserves and forced banks to borrow were believed to put upward pressure on money market rates as the banks contracted their loans and investments in order to repay their borrowings. The result was less monetary ease (or more restraint), slower credit creation, and slower growth of the money supply. Conversely, open market purchases that added reserves and allowed banks to reduce their indebtedness prompted them to expand their loans and investments and

[19] Minutes of the Federal Open Market Committee, June 23, 1954, pp. 7–8.

[20] Brunner and Meltzer (1964, pp. 2–10); and Meltzer (2003, pp. 161–65). See also Meigs (1962, ch. 2).

[21] See Riefler (1930) and Burgess (1936).

[22] Brunner and Meltzer (1964, p. 3) note that "excess reserves were small during the period and exhibited negligible variations."

[23] Meltzer (2003, p. 161). The idea that banks were reluctant to borrow from the Fed and that they restricted their loans and investments in order to repay promptly was remarkably durable. See Federal Reserve Bank of New York (November 1958, p. 162), describing borrowings as a "stopgap" and stating that "rather than resort too frequently or on too large a scale to the 'discount window,' a member bank must take other steps to maintain or restore its reserve position – perhaps through liquidating investments or restricting loan volume," Young (1958, p. 24), stating that "under normal conditions member banks will make a practice of limiting their resort to Reserve Bank borrowing to necessary contingencies" and that "once in debt, they will seek to repay promptly," and Young (1958, p. 35), stating that "after they have borrowed, [member bank] lending policies tend to become more stringent because they are under pressure to repay their indebtedness."

stimulated economic activity. "Reluctance to borrow" thus provided a framework for a proactive monetary policy conducted through open market operations.

Bank behavior changed dramatically after 1933. Concluding that the Fed had not been a reliable lender of last resort during the Great Contraction, banks began to accumulate extraordinary quantities of excess reserves. The change necessitated a revision of the Riefler-Burgess framework to one that recognized a role for excess as well as borrowed reserves. Brunner and Meltzer conclude that,

> In the new view excess reserves were treated as an extension of bank indebtedness, a magnitude offsetting the retarding influence of member bank borrowing. Free reserves assumed the position and role which originally had been assigned to bank indebtedness. The free reserve conception thus emanated as a result of an adjustment in the central building block of the Riefler-Burgess view of the monetary process.[24]

Open market sales of securities that reduced free reserves were viewed as putting upward pressure on money market rates, resulting in less ease (or more restraint). Conversely, open market purchases stimulated activity.

FOMC minutes from 1954 support Brunner and Meltzer's characterization of the Fed's interpretation of free reserves. When the Committee was keeping free reserves high in June, Sproul suggested that "the concept of free reserves as a guide to credit policy involved leaving the banks with a feeling of ability to meet credit demands without strain ... It *allows the banks to run without checkrein* and lets the capital markets know there is no present or prospective likelihood of credit restraint."[25] When the

[24] Brunner and Meltzer (1964, p. 10). Meltzer (2009, p. 44) states that "recognition that excess reserves could change, as they did in the 1930s, shifted attention to free reserves." The Federal Reserve Bank of New York (November 1958, pp. 162–63) explained the shift to free reserves similarly: "During most of the 1930's, ... member banks held large amounts of excess reserves, and did little or no borrowing at the Reserve Banks after the 'bank holiday' in 1933. Attention thus shifted to excess reserves as a measure of reserve availability and potential credit expansion. In more recent years, many member banks have again found it necessary to borrow frequently, even while excess reserves existed elsewhere in the banking system. ... Thus, taken alone, neither excess reserves nor borrowings can provide an adequate continuing measure of credit availability. To meet the need for such a measure, the concept of 'free reserves' – defined as excess reserves less member bank borrowings from the Reserve Banks – was developed." Brunner and Meltzer (1964, p. 10, fn. 34), state that "Irving Auerbach of the Federal Reserve Bank of New York is often given credit for the development of the free reserves concept."

[25] Minutes of the Federal Open Market Committee, June 23, 1954, p. 9. Emphasis added. A checkrein is a piece of tack used to prevent a horse from lowering its head.

economy began to grow in November, Sproul thought that an appropriate modification of credit policy "might be in the direction of reducing the volume of free reserves maintained in the banking system and placing greater reliance upon the discount window as a source of reserves."[26]

CAVEATS

The use of free reserves as an indicator of monetary policy was subject to several significant caveats. Because it was defined as the difference between excess reserves and borrowed reserves, a given level of free reserves could result from smaller excess reserves and smaller advances or larger excess reserves and larger advances. It was not clear whether all of the combinations of excess reserves and borrowings that produced a given level of free reserves also produced the same degree of restraint or ease.

The geographic distribution of reserves also mattered. Country banks had lower reserve requirements than reserve and central reserve city banks, so required reserves fell, and free reserves expanded, when commercial bank assets and deposit liabilities moved from city banks to country banks. However, country banks were more likely than city banks to allow excess reserves to lie idle, so a shift in free reserves from city banks to country banks could tighten, rather than ease, the interbank market for reserve balances.

Federal Reserve officials were well aware of the difference in the behavior of country banks and city banks. In early September Allan Sproul commented on "the slowness with which reserve funds flowed from country banks to the city banks."[27] Two weeks later, Oliver Powell, the president of the Federal Reserve Bank of Minneapolis, noted that "during the past few months there has been a 'stickiness' of excess reserves at country banks, and such reserves had not flowed into central money markets as rapidly as had been contemplated . . ."[28]

Officials were also cognizant of the policy implications of the difference in behaviors. The Federal Reserve Bank of New York observed that "the level of free reserves at which [stimulative] results may be expected is not fixed and immobile. The figure would have to be higher, for example, when

26 Minutes of the Executive Committee of the Federal Open Market Committee, November 9, 1954, pp. 9–10.

27 Minutes of the Executive Committee of the Federal Open Market Committee, September 8, 1954, p. 3.

28 Minutes of the Federal Open Market Committee, September 22, 1954, p. 4.

the national total of free reserves included a heavy concentration in those member banks that habitually maintain substantial excess reserves (usually "country" banks). Money market banks are generally more aggressive in seeking outlets for excess funds than are country banks, so that the significance of any national total of free reserves ... must depend in part upon the distribution of the total."[29]

Milton Friedman identified a third important caveat when he pointed out that what mattered was the difference between free reserves and *desired* free reserves.[30] Friedman suggested that the volume of free reserves that banks wanted to hold depended, among other things, on market rates of interest (such as Treasury bill rates) and the Fed's discount rate.[31] *Ceteris paribus*, a higher discount rate reduced the attractiveness of borrowed reserves, and increased the attractiveness of excess reserves, as a liquidity buffer. Similarly, lower money market rates reduced the implicit cost, and increased the attractiveness, of excess reserves. If reductions in the discount rate lagged behind the decline in market rates during a recession, as was the case during the recession that ran from July 1953 to May 1954 (see Chart 10.1), free reserves became more attractive and the degree of ease associated with a given level of free reserves declined.

Distributional considerations became a major issue in August 1954. The Board of Governors had reduced reserve requirement rates in late June[32] and Ralph Young anticipated a sharp reduction in required reserves, "perhaps as much as $800 million," in August. At the August 3 Executive Committee meeting, Martin suggested that "it would be preferable to aim at having a volume of free reserves on the low side" of the existing $400-700 million target range. The minutes state that "in an effort to hold down the level of free reserves ... maturing bills would be permitted to run off."[33]

However, August also saw a shift in reserves from city banks to country banks that left reserves in major money markets unexpectedly

[29] Federal Reserve Bank of New York (November 1958, p. 163).

[30] Friedman (1960, p. 42).

[31] Friedman (1960, p. 42), stating that the desired level of free reserves depends "on market rates of interest and their relation to the discount rate." See also Meigs (1962, p. 3), suggesting that "banks seek to maintain certain desired ratios of [free reserves] to total deposits and that these desired ratios are functionally related to market interest rates and the discount rate."

[32] Federal Reserve Bank of New York Circular no. 4117, June 21, 1954.

[33] Minutes of the Executive Committee of the Federal Open Market Committee, August 3, 1954, pp. 3, 5, and 6.

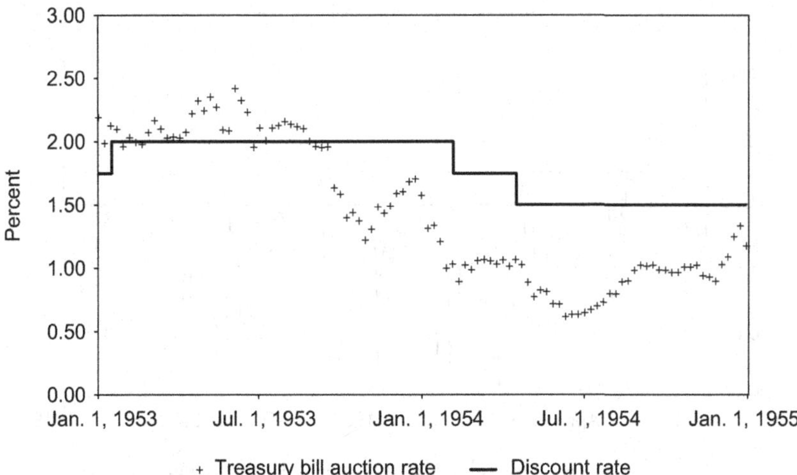

Chart 10.1 Weekly auction rate for thirteen-week Treasury bills and Federal Reserve Bank of New York discount rate.
Board of Governors of the Federal Reserve System (1976, tables 12.1A and 12.7B).

tight. (Chart 10.2 shows that the Federal funds rate pressed up against the discount rate during most of the month.) Malcolm Bryan, president of the Atlanta Fed, pointed out that:

> The distribution of free reserves, in combination with our policy [of allowing maturing bills to run off], has allowed a very considerable increase in short rates, which has at times carried over into longer rates. The result can be explained on many grounds; but the effect has been that we have permitted a policy of monetary ease to some extent to be contravened by the holders of free reserves, who have wanted liquidity.[34]

Some FOMC members complained that the policy of allowing maturing bills to run off should have been adjusted in light of the shift in reserves. Governor A. L. Mills suggested that "account should have been taken of [the distribution of reserves] in ways so as not to have penalized the money market as severely as has been the case."[35] In fact, the unexpected tightness in the reserves market *had* led Robert Rouse, the manager of the System Open Market Account, to act contrary to the policy consensus reached at the August 3 Executive Committee meeting. In spite of the agreement to move toward the lower end of the $400-700 million target range for free

34 Minutes of the Federal Open Market Committee, September 22, 1954, p. 9.
35 Minutes of the Executive Committee of the Federal Open Market Committee, August 24, 1954, p. 8.

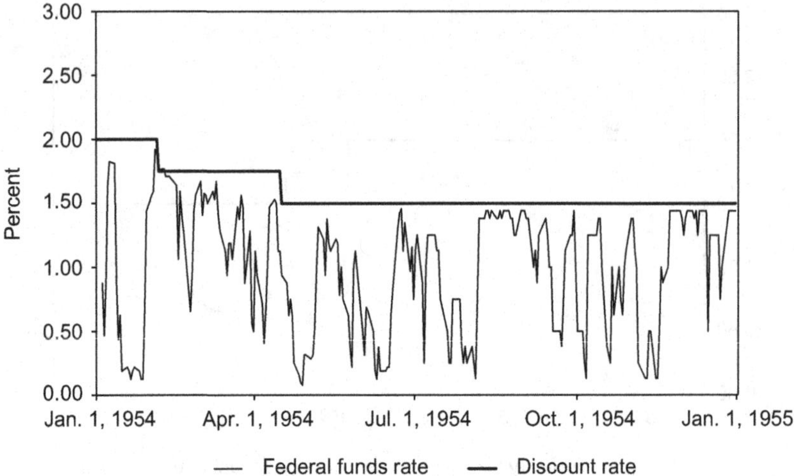

Chart 10.2 Federal funds rate and Federal Reserve Bank of New York discount rate. Daily figures.

Federal Reserve Statistical Release H.15 and Board of Governors of the Federal Reserve System (1976, table 12.1A).

reserves, Rouse kept free reserves "well above the maximum." He pointed out that "during most of the period [free reserves] were well above $800 million and in some weeks were $900 million."[36] Sproul explained that "the decision not to bring free reserves down to the level anticipated by the committee ... was taking account of the fact that reserves were less available in the money centers than they were elsewhere."[37]

Hitting a free reserves target was also not free from complications. Several autonomous factors affecting reserve availability, including Treasury balances at Federal Reserve Banks, float, and public demand for currency, were volatile – see Chart 10.3 – and difficult to forecast.[38] In the second half of January a combination of the usual post-holiday return flow of currency to bank deposit accounts, an increase in float, and

[36] Minutes of the Executive Committee of the Federal Open Market Committee, August 24, 1954, p. 10.

[37] Minutes of the Executive Committee of the Federal Open Market Committee, August 24, 1954, p. 11. See also Sproul's remark at the September 8 Executive Committee meeting, that "because of the maldistribution of free reserves and the slowness with which reserve funds flowed from country banks to the city banks it had not been possible to work down the level of free reserves as much as had been discussed." Minutes of the Executive Committee of the Federal Open Market Committee, September 8, 1954, p. 3.

[38] Carr (1959, pp. 506–10) addresses forecasting Treasury deposits, float, and currency.

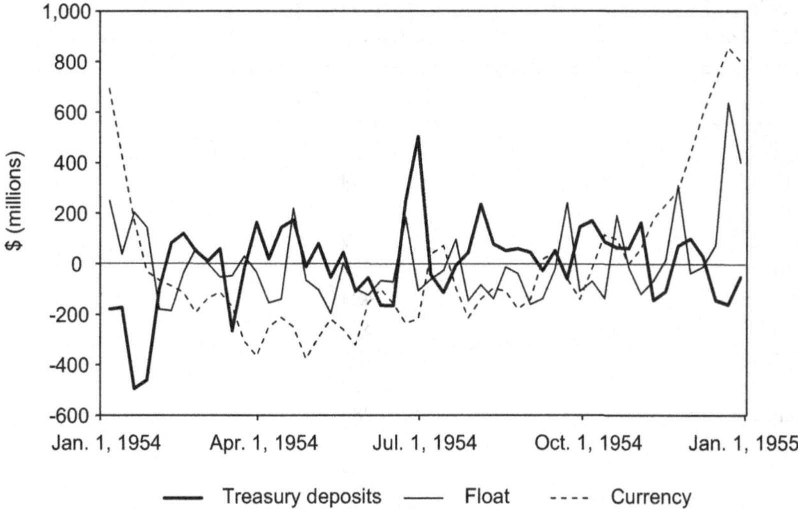

Chart 10.3 Treasury deposits at Federal Reserve Banks, float, and currency in circulation. Weekly averages of daily figures, plotted as deviation from average value over the year ($507 million for Treasury deposits, $737 million for float, and $30.029 billion for currency).
Board of Governors of the Federal Reserve System (1976, table 10.1C).

unexpectedly large federal cash disbursements – disbursements that depleted Treasury balances at Federal Reserve Banks and triggered the issuance of special certificates of indebtedness directly from the Treasury to the Reserve Banks (Table 10.1)[39] – led to more than $1.2 billion in excess reserves (Chart 10.4) that kept the funds rate below twenty-five basis points, a paydown of advances to less than $100 million (Chart 10.5), and a spike in free reserves (Chart 10.6).

The easy money market conditions in the second half of January led to an illuminating exchange between Martin and Rouse. During Executive Committee meetings in late January and early February, Martin was openly critical of the management of the Open Market Account, complaining that "the market had gotten too sloppy" and that the System "should have been more active in selling bills into the market earlier."[40] Rouse agreed that the

39 Garbade (2014) examines direct purchases of US Treasury securities by Federal Reserve Banks.

40 Minutes of the Executive Committee of the Federal Open Market Committee, January 19, 1954, p. 6; and February 2, 1954, p. 6.

Table 10.1 *Special one-day certificates of indebtedness issued directly to Federal Reserve Banks, January 1954.*

Date	Amount ($ millions)
Jan. 14	22
Jan. 15	169
Jan. 16	169
Jan. 17*	169
Jan. 18	323
Jan. 19	424
Jan. 20	323
Jan. 21	306
Jan. 22	283
Jan. 23	283
Jan. 24*	283
Jan. 25	203
Jan. 26	3

* Sunday.
1955 Annual Report of the Board of Governors of the Federal Reserve System, p. 65.

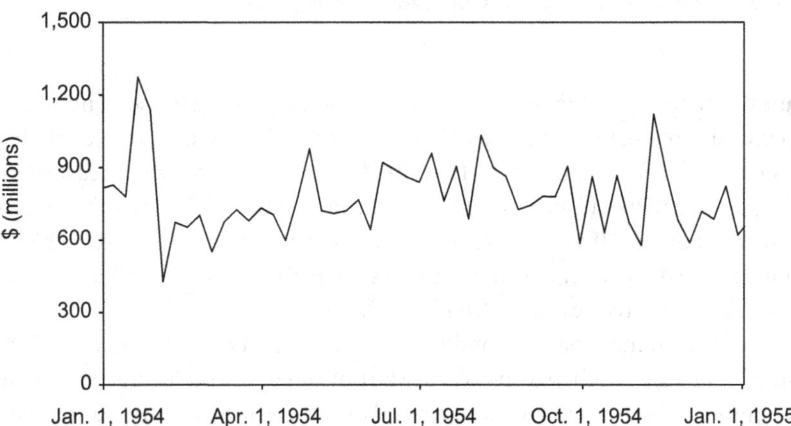

Chart 10.4 Excess reserves. Weekly averages of daily figures.
Board of Governors of the Federal Reserve System (1976, table 10.1C).

market "had gotten pretty sloppy" but explained that "in discussions of the situation at that time it had seemed that it might require sales of around $500-$600 million in order to take out the sloppiness" and that projections "indicated that the account would be faced with a problem of buying back securities in that amount a little later on." When Martin remarked that "it

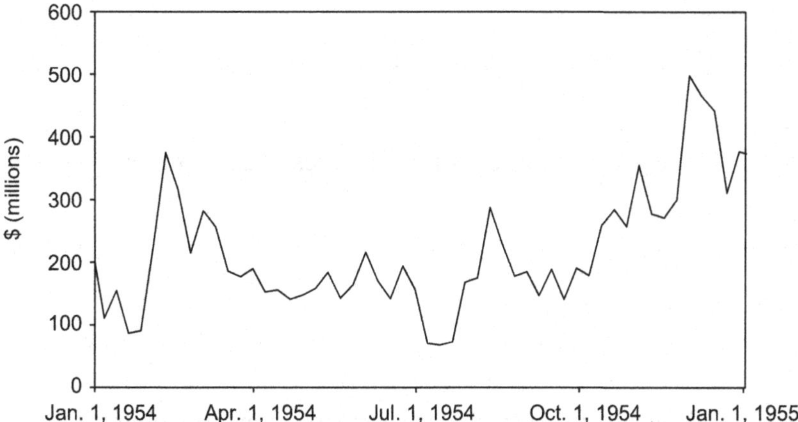

Chart 10.5 Borrowed reserves. Weekly averages of daily figures.
Board of Governors of the Federal Reserve System (1976, table 10.1C).

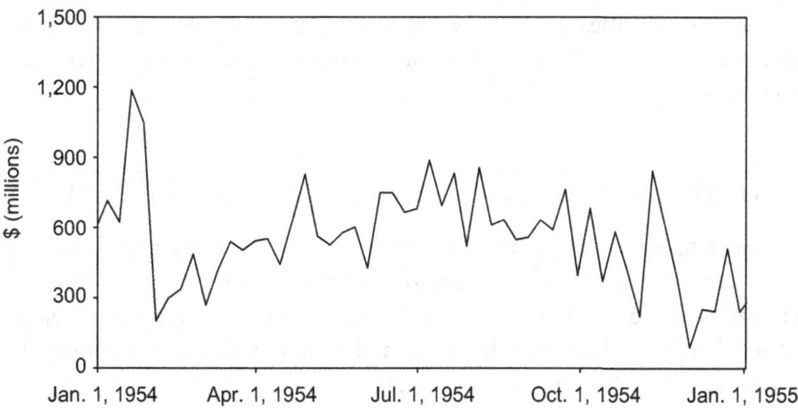

Chart 10.6 Free reserves. Weekly averages of daily figures.
Author's calculations.

would have been wiser to have been more flexible," Rouse responded that the System "could pursue a flexible course when transactions undertaken are of the order of $100-200 million" but that "an attempt to conduct flexible in-and-out operations in a volume substantially in excess of that would encounter difficulty."[41]

[41] Minutes of the Executive Committee of the Federal Open Market Committee, February 2, 1954, pp. 6–7.

11

Policy Instruments for Reserves Management

Rapid and quantitatively significant fluctuations in autonomous factors, such as Treasury balances at Federal Reserve Banks, float, and currency in the hands of the public, generated an interest in policy instruments that could inject and drain large quantities of reserves quickly with a minimal impact on securities prices. The two most important were outright purchases and sales of Treasury bills and repurchase agreements on Treasury securities.

OUTRIGHT PURCHASES AND SALES OF TREASURY BILLS

Treasury bills were attractive for System open market operations because they were the most liquid sector of the government securities market. However, while the bill market could accommodate operations as large as $200 million, two episodes suggest that it was not liquid enough to accommodate substantially larger operations.

As discussed at the end of the preceding chapter, mopping up the surfeit of reserves in the second half of January 1954 would have required the sale, and later repurchase, of upward of $500 to $600 million of bills. Robert Rouse, the manager of the System Open Market Account, did not believe that the bill market was liquid enough to absorb transactions of that size without difficulty.[1] And in early July 1954, Rouse decided to roll over, rather than redeem, a position in maturing bills when he learned that a foreign account was going to redeem $180 million of the same bills, fearing that "redemption of the System holdings in addition to the [foreign

[1] Minutes of the Executive Committee of the Federal Open Market Committee, February 2, 1954, pp. 6–7.

redemption], would place undue pressure on the money market and on dealers' positions."[2]

Settlement lags were a second drawback to outright transactions in bills. Purchases and sales typically settled on the business day after a trade – that is, the securities traded for "regular" settlement.[3] Thus, a sale of $50 million of bills on Wednesday would not drain reserves from bank balance sheets until Thursday. The delay meant that the Desk could not use outright transactions to quickly mitigate either a tight or sloppy reserves market.

In early June 1954, Governor J. L. Robertson asked Rouse whether the Desk could eliminate the delay. Rouse agreed that eliminating the lag "might be desirable" and said he would look into the matter.[4]

A month later, Rouse forwarded a generally favorable memo on the possibility of trading bills for "cash" settlement, and the Executive Committee agreed to a trial program.[5] The program got underway in August and in late November Rouse reported that the initiative was proceeding satisfactorily.[6] Fourteen months later, he reported "active use" of outright transactions for cash settlement and stated that the transactions had been of "definite assistance."[7]

REPURCHASE AGREEMENTS ON SHORT-TERM TREASURY SECURITIES

Repurchase agreements offered a second way of injecting (but not draining) large quantities of reserves. The liquidity of the repo market was at least as good as that of the bill market, and repos typically settled on

2 Minutes of Executive Committee of the Federal Open Market Committee, July 7, 1954, p. 2.

3 Minutes of the Executive Committee of the Federal Open Market Committee, March 30, 1954, p. 3, text of letter to Congressman Wright Patman stating that "'outright' transactions for the System Open Market Account are effected for regular delivery, that is for delivery and settlement on the next business day"; and July 20, 1954, p. 10, remark of George Vest, General Counsel of the FOMC, expressing his understanding that "transactions for the System account had almost always been on a 'regular' delivery basis."

4 Minutes of the Executive Committee of the Federal Open Market Committee, June 8, 1954, p. 12.

5 Minutes of the Executive Committee of the Federal Open Market Committee, July 20, 1954, pp. 8–9 and 9–11.

6 Minutes of the Executive Committee of the Federal Open Market Committee, November 23, 1954, p. 2.

7 Minutes of the Federal Open Market Committee, March 6, 1956, p. 12. See also Cooper (1967, pp. 9–10).

the same day they were negotiated,[8] so there was no delay in the effect on bank balance sheets. Repos were particularly well suited to providing reserves on a temporary basis to mitigate a stringency that was likely to recede within a couple of days, such as an elevated demand for currency over a holiday or a temporary shrinkage in float.

Repurchase Agreements before the Accord

Repos were not specifically authorized by the Federal Reserve Act and staff of the Federal Reserve Bank of New York and the Federal Reserve Board had sometimes disagreed, during World War I and in the early 1920s, about whether they were permitted transactions.[9] However, the Board put to rest any residual uncertainties in 1925, when it took "specific and definite action authorizing and approving . . . repurchase agreements."[10]

Section 205 of the Banking Act of August 23, 1935, provided that "no Federal Reserve bank shall engage or decline to engage in open-market operations . . . except in accordance with the direction of and regulations adopted by the [Federal Open Market] Committee." Repos were commonly construed by System officials as open market transactions, and their continued availability depended on the Committee's approval.

Shortly after the Federal Open Market Committee (FOMC) opened for business in 1936, George Hamilton, president of the Federal Reserve Bank of Kansas City, requested that the Committee authorize the Reserve Banks to undertake "temporary purchases of Government securities under resale agreements." The minutes of the May 25 Committee meeting state that "such purchases had been made from time to time in the past with the approval of the Federal Reserve Board" and that permission to continue the practice would "enable the Federal Reserve Banks to render a service"

[8] Minutes of the Executive Committee of the Federal Open Market Committee, March 30, 1954, p. 3, stating, in a letter to Congressman Wright Patman, that repurchase agreements "were executed with Government securities dealers . . . by the Federal Reserve Bank of New York for its own account as a matter of convenience in dealing with the money market on a 'cash' basis, that is immediate delivery and settlement of the transactions."

[9] Garbade (2012, pp. 192–95).

[10] Minutes of the Executive Committee of the Federal Open Market Committee, September 22, 1954, p. 4, statement of George Vest, general counsel to the FOMC, that "the question of the use of repurchase agreements was given extensive consideration many years ago" and that "in 1925 the Board took specific and definite action authorizing and approving the practice of repurchase agreements." The formal Board action appears in minutes of the Federal Reserve Board, March 19, 1925, pp. 8–9. See also minutes of the Federal Reserve Board, February 10, 1925, p. 7; February 17, 1925, pp. 7–8; March 5, pp. 1 and 5–6; and March 10, pp. 3–4.

to member banks. The Committee agreed unanimously to permit the practice for loan periods not in excess of fifteen days.[11]

As a result of the immense excess reserves accumulated by the banking system in the second half of the 1930s and the decision to cap interest rates during World War II, there were few instances of Reserve Bank repos prior to 1945. In March 1945, the FOMC revoked the 1936 authority for lack of use.[12]

Postwar Reinstatement

During a Committee meeting two and a half years later, Allan Sproul, the president of the New York Fed, presented a request from Rouse that the repo authority be reinstated.[13] Sproul explained (in a subsequent meeting of the Executive Committee) that Treasury dealers were reluctant to purchase a security if the yield on the security was less than the interest rate charged by the large New York banks on dealer loans. The Fed was still capping interest rates on coupon-bearing securities and was obliged to purchase, at the ceiling rate, what the dealers didn't want, expanding its balance sheet and adding to bank reserves. Sproul hoped that making repo credit available at the Fed's discount rate would leave dealers less reluctant to acquire and hold securities.[14]

Marriner Eccles, the chairman of the Board of Governors, was not enthusiastic but asked Rouse to prepare a memo summarizing the pros and cons of the proposal. He additionally suggested that the Executive Committee recommend to the full Committee that it be authorized to decide, on the basis of the requested memo, whether to approve Rouse's request. The Executive Committee adopted his suggestion and the full Committee concurred.[15]

Following receipt of Rouse's memo, the Executive Committee returned to the issue of dealer repos in early January 1948.[16] Although it was understood that repo credit would be provided at the discount rate,

[11] Minutes of the Federal Open Market Committee, May 25, 1936, p. 9.

[12] Minutes of the Federal Open Market Committee, March 1, 1945, p. 13, stating that repos had not been undertaken "for a long time."

[13] Minutes of the Federal Open Market Committee, October 6, 1947, p. 18.

[14] Minutes of the Executive Committee of the Federal Open Market Committee, December 9, 1947, pp. 3–6.

[15] Minutes of the Executive Committee of the Federal Open Market Committee, December 9, 1947, p. 5, and minutes of the Federal Open Market Committee, December 9, 1947, pp. 19–20.

[16] Minutes of the Executive Committee of the Federal Open Market Committee, January 20, 1948, pp. 7–10.

Box 11.1 Repo Authority of January 20, 1948.

Each Federal Reserve Bank was authorized "to enter into repurchase agreements with dealers in United States Government Securities who are qualified to transact business with the System open market account, provided that

(1) such agreements
  (a) are at rates not below the rate in effect at the Bank on discounts for and advances to member banks under sections 13 and 13a of the Federal Reserve Act,
  (b) are for period of not to exceed 15 calendar days,
  (c) cover only short-term Government securities selling at a yield of not more than the issuing rate for one-year Treasury obligations,
  (d) are used only in periods of strain, with care and discrimination, as a means of last resort in the special types of situations and conditions reviewed in Mr. Rouse's memorandum,[[1]] and
  (e) that reports of such transactions should be included in the weekly report of transactions furnished the Committee, and
(2) in the event Government securities covered by such an agreement are not repurchased by the dealer pursuant to the agreement or a renewal thereof, the securities will be sold in the market or transferred to the System open market account."

1 The referenced memorandum is noted on p. 7 of the minutes of the January 20, 1948, Executive Committee meeting.

Minutes of the Executive Committee of the Federal Open Market Committee, January 20, 1948, p. 10.

Sproul remarked that "if the present differential between the Treasury one year issuing rate [then 1⅛ percent] and the discount rate [then 1¼ percent] should widen beyond the present ⅛ per cent, consideration might be given to a [repo] rate below the discount rate."[17] The idea of pricing repo credit cheaper than advances would soon become a contentious feature of the repo program.

The key elements of the repo authority provided by the Executive Committee in January 1948 (Box 11.1) provided that,

- Repo credit would be extended only to "qualified" dealers, i.e., bank and nonbank dealers accepted by the Federal Reserve Bank of New York as counterparties in open market operations.

17 Minutes of the Executive Committee of the Federal Open Market Committee, January 20, 1948, p. 9.

- Repo credit would be extended directly by a Reserve Bank, and not through the System Open Market Account. However, since it was likely that the Federal Reserve Bank of New York would be the principal provider of repo credit and since the manager of the Open Market Account was a senior officer of that Bank, it was unlikely that extensions of repo credit would conflict with FOMC policy objectives.
- Repurchase agreements were limited to a maximum tenor of fifteen days.
- Repo credit could not be extended at less than the discount rate.
- Collateral was limited to short-term Treasury issues yielding no more than the issuing rate on one-year certificates.
- Repurchase agreements would be used "only in periods of strain, with care and discrimination."

Linking the Floor on Repo Rates to the Treasury Bill Rate Instead of the Discount Rate

In the spring of 1950, bill rates were at 1.15 percent and the discount rate was 1½ percent. The 35-basis-point spread limited dealer interest in bills financed with System repos.

In an attempt to mitigate dealer carrying costs, Rouse suggested tying the minimum repo rate to bill rates instead of the discount rate. He observed that repos "might be particularly helpful in a period like the present when the discount rate was considerably higher than short-term market rates" and justified the change in terms of the utility of repos for monetary policy, noting that repos were "one means of putting funds into the market in periods of strain to help in carrying out the policies of the Committee." Rouse suggested that the repo authority be revised to provide for a repo rate not less than ⅛ percent above the average auction rate on the most recent offering of Treasury bills and that the authority be used "as a means of providing the money market with sufficient Federal Reserve funds to avoid undue strain on a day-to-day basis."[18] FOMC economist Woodlief Thomas enthusiastically backed the proposal, saying that the repo facility "should be used more extensively than it had been as a means of helping to provide the market with additional bank reserves to meet shortages of a strictly temporary nature."[19]

To avoid appearing to favor dealer banks over nondealer banks (who could not participate in System repos and were limited to discount window

[18] Minutes of the Federal Open Market Committee, March 1, 1950, p. 6.
[19] Minutes of the Federal Open Market Committee, March 1, 1950, p. 7.

Box 11.2 Repo Authority of March 1, 1950.

Each Federal Reserve Bank was authorized, "in lieu of all previous authorizations, to enter into repurchase agreements with nonbank dealers in United States Government securities who are qualified to transact business with the System open market account, provided that:

(1) such agreements
  (a) are at a rate at least ⅛ per cent above the average issuing rate on the most recent issue of United States Treasury bills,
  (b) are for periods of not to exceed 15 calendar days,
  (c) cover only short-term Government securities selling at a yield of not more than the issuing rate for one-year Treasury obligations,
  (d) are used with care and discrimination as a means of providing the money market with sufficient Federal Reserve funds as to avoid undue strain on a day-to-day basis,
(2) reports of such transactions shall be made to the Manager of the System Open Market Account to be included in the weekly report of open market operations which is sent to the Federal Open Market Committee, and
(3) in the event Government securities covered by such an agreement are not repurchased by the dealer pursuant to the agreement or a renewal thereof, the securities thus acquired by the Federal Reserve Bank are sold in the market or transferred to the System open market account."

Minutes of the Federal Open Market Committee, March 1, 1950, p. 8.

credit), repos were limited to nonbank dealers (even though this favored those dealers over bank dealers). Eccles questioned whether Reserve Banks should be lending to nonbank dealers but allowed that "he would have no objection to continuance of the authority if it was clearly understood that it was to be used only in emergencies."[20] The Committee unanimously approved the authority reproduced in Box 11.2.

Consequences of the Accord

The Treasury-Federal Reserve Accord was announced on March 3, 1951. System officials quickly recognized that, regardless of the details of the post-Accord monetary policy framework, repurchase agreements were likely to become more important. Allan Sproul noted at the March 8 FOMC meeting that his Bank's repo authority had previously been used

[20] Minutes of the Federal Open Market Committee, March 1, 1950, p. 7.

"infrequently" but suggested that "it might be of greater use in a period such as that immediately ahead." Woodlief Thomas agreed, saying that "the authority might be very useful in helping to develop a freer market."[21]

Five months later, Rouse confirmed that the New York Fed had used repurchase agreements "much more frequently during the recent period than was contemplated when the authority was originally given." He concluded that repos had "demonstrated their usefulness as an effective instrument" of monetary policy.[22]

The FOMC tweaked its repo authority several times between the Accord and the end of 1953:

- In 1952, the FOMC modified the minimum repo rate to the *lesser* of (a) the discount rate and (b) the auction rate on thirteen-week bills.[23]
- Also, in 1952, the Committee authorized the manager of the System Open Market Account to set the repo rate for all twelve Reserve Banks.[24]
- In 1953, the FOMC changed the limitation on repo collateral to "short-term Government securities maturing within fifteen months" and eliminated the requirement that the yield to maturity on repo collateral had to be less than the offering rate on one-year certificates.[25]

The resulting authority is reproduced in Box 11.3.

Repurchase Agreements in 1954

By 1954, the members of the Open Market Committee and the Committee's senior staff had a shared appreciation for the utility of repurchase agreements. The minutes of the March 3 FOMC meeting noted that "in earlier years the [repo] authority was used infrequently but that during the past year or two it had been used upon frequent occasions to

[21] Minutes of the Federal Open Market Committee, March 8, 1951, pp. 4–5.

[22] Minutes of the Executive Committee of the Federal Open Market Committee, August 8, 1951, p. 2.

[23] Minutes of the Executive Committee of the Federal Open Market Committee, July 22, 1952, pp. 12–14; and minutes of the Federal Open Market Committee, September 25, 1952, p. 2.

[24] Minutes of the Executive Committee of the Federal Open Market Committee, July 22, 1952, pp. 12–14; and minutes of the Federal Open Market Committee, September 25, 1952, p. 2.

[25] Minutes of the Federal Open Market Committee, March 4, 1953, pp. 6–8.

Box 11.3 Repo Authority of March 4, 1953.

Each Federal Reserve Bank was authorized, "in lieu of all previous authorizations, to enter into repurchase agreements with nonbank dealers in United States Government securities under the following conditions:

(1) Such agreements
  (a) Are at a rate which will be specified from time to time by the Manager of the System open market account in the light of market conditions and developments and in accordance with any directive or limitations prescribed by the full Committee or the executive committee for the purpose of carrying out the current policies of the Federal Open Market Committee, but in no event shall the effective rate be below whichever is the lower of (1) the discount rate of the purchasing Federal Reserve Bank on eligible commercial paper, or (2) the average issuing rate on the most recent issue of three-month Treasury bills;
  (b) Are for periods of not to exceed 15 calendar days;
  (c) Cover only short-term Government securities maturing within 15 months; and
  (d) Are used with care and discrimination as a means of providing the money market with sufficient Federal Reserve funds as to avoid undue strain on a day-to-day basis.

(2) Reports of such transactions are made to the Manager of the System open market account to be included in the weekly report of open market operations which is sent to the members of the Federal Open Market Committee.

(3) In the event Government securities covered by any such agreement are not repurchased by the dealer pursuant to the agreement or a renewal thereof, the securities thus acquired by the Federal Reserve Bank are sold in the market or transferred to the System open market account."

Minutes of the Federal Open Market Committee, March 4, 1953, pp. 7–8.

help relieve tightness in the market."[26] Five months later, Rouse reported that he was countering a scarcity of reserves in the New York market by "making repurchase agreements freely available."[27]

Allan Sproul was outspoken in his support of repurchase agreements for in-and-out reserves management. In May 1954, he recommended "meeting temporary situations with repurchase agreements"[28] and in June suggested

[26] Minutes of the Federal Open Market Committee, March 3, 1954, p. 7.

[27] Minutes of the Executive Committee of the Federal Open Market Committee, August 24, 1954, p. 2. The scarcity of reserves in New York, and the abundance of reserves at country banks, in August 1954 was discussed in Chapter 10 above, text at footnotes 32–37.

[28] Minutes of the Executive Committee of the Federal Open Market Committee, May 11, 1954, p. 5.

that an expected end-of-quarter scarcity "would be an appropriate time to use the repurchase method of applying some reserves."[29] In early October, Sproul remarked that "this might ... be a period for use of repurchase agreements as a means of putting funds into the market on a temporary basis in a manner that would result in their being withdrawn automatically."[30]

But in order for repos to function effectively, it was important that the repo rate be kept in line with other money market rates. A repo rate substantially in excess of market rates was comparable to keeping a room air conditioner set at 100°: relief would come only after the room had become uncomfortably hot.

Officials were aware of the problem. Woodlief Thomas stated in May 1954 that

> with the discount rate and the repurchase rate as far above the market rate for bills as they are now [see Chart 10.1], changes in the market result in wide gyrations in rates. If the System was going to maintain a situation which resulted in a bill rate below 1 per cent, this called for a discount rate or a repurchase rate close to that level.[31]

A month later Rouse complained that "there had been such a decline in short-term money rates that the money market had lost the use of both the discount and the repurchase facilities at their existing rates."[32] In September, Thomas remarked that for the discount window and repo facility to operate smoothly in relieving money market pressures, "it was essential that [the discount and repo] rates be not too far above the market rate."[33] Accepting that the Board of Governors sometimes left the discount rate well in excess of short-term market rates for policy reasons, the question was whether the FOMC was prepared to fix a repo rate *below* the discount rate in order to keep the repo rate in line with market rates.

In late November 1953, Winfield Riefler, the secretary of the FOMC, anticipated substantial seasonal reserve needs associated with the coming holiday season and asked whether the repo rate should be set below the existing 2 percent discount rate. He admitted that "the question of a rate

[29] Minutes of the Executive Committee of the Federal Open Market Committee, June 8, 1954, p. 7.

[30] Minutes of the Executive Committee of the Federal Open Market Committee, October 5, 1954, p. 5.

[31] Minutes of the Executive Committee of the Federal Open Market Committee, May 26, 1954, p. 7.

[32] Minutes of the Federal Open Market Committee, June 23, 1954, p. 4.

[33] Minutes of the Federal Open Market Committee, September 22, 1954, p. 23.

for [nonbank] dealers which was lower than that offered to banks presented something of a problem." Governor Mills doubted the propriety of such an action "since it might provoke a charge of preference to nonbank borrowers."[34]

Nevertheless, Rouse lowered the repo rate to 1¾ percent on December 8, 1953, and kept it there until early January.[35] Repos added between $120 million and $735 million of reserves per day, on average over the course of a maintenance week, between the week ending on December 9, 1953, and the week ending on January 13, 1954.[36]

The FOMC debated the merits of Rouse's action at its quarterly meeting in mid-December 1953. Sproul suggested that a repurchase rate lower than the discount rate was "peculiarly adopted to relieving temporary situations in the money market":

> We have an example in the recent situation. . . . [W]e had a relatively easy reserve position in most of the country and relative tightness in New York. It was a money market phenomenon of temporary character.
>
> Our job was to smooth it out, without actual or apparent major or significant changes in general credit policy. A reduction in the repurchase rate and an increased use of repurchase facilities avoided a temporary undue run-up of rates and a temporary undue tightening of credit due to increased bank borrowing [at the discount window], and also avoided the substantially more permanent commitment of a reduction in the discount rate, and the slightly more permanent commitment of larger outright purchases of Government securities. It emphasized the money market aspect of the situation as distinguished from the overall business and credit aspect.[37]

Sproul's remarks reflected the growing appreciation for repurchase agreements as a tactical instrument of monetary policy. However, Governor Robertson, Delos Johns (president of the Federal Reserve Bank of St. Louis), and Malcolm Bryan (president of the Federal Reserve Bank of Atlanta) all expressed "some doubts."[38]

Robertson's Resistance to System Repurchase Agreements

Governor Robertson was the FOMC member most discomforted by the use of repurchase agreements. He was particularly uncomfortable with

[34] Minutes of the Executive Committee of the Federal Open Market Committee, November 23, 1953, pp. 4–5.

[35] "New York and Chicago Reserve Banks Cut Rate of Repurchase Pacts," *Wall Street Journal*, December 9, 1953, p. 3; and minutes of the Executive Committee of the Federal Open Market Committee, January 5, 1954, p. 5.

[36] Board of Governors of the Federal Reserve System (1976, table 10.1C).

[37] Minutes of the Federal Open Market Committee, December 15, 1953, pp. 26–27.

[38] Minutes of the Federal Open Market Committee, December 15, 1953, p. 28.

setting the repo rate below the discount rate, expressing "serious doubts" about the practice at the March 1954 FOMC meeting.[39] Three months later he won unanimous consent to charge the Executive Committee, rather than the manager of the Open Market Account, with responsibility for setting repo rates, saying that "it seemed undesirable to give [the manager] the authority [to set the repo rate] and then not expect him to use it freely, as has been the case in recent months."[40]

The Opening Round

At the September 22, 1954, Executive Committee meeting, Robertson objected to Sproul's proposal that the committee authorize the Manager to enter into repurchase agreements at rates between 1¼ percent and 1½ percent (the discount rate was 1½ percent at the time), saying that "the repurchase arrangement constituted a loan, that it was not consistent with the purpose of the [Federal Reserve Act], and that it benefited nonbank dealers in Government securities in a manner which did not apply to dealers who were banks or to member banks in general." Robertson believed that "[nonbank] dealers in Government securities should not be given an advantage which was not given to member banks."[41]

Governor Szymczak responded vigorously to Robertson's objections, focusing on the utility of repos and noting that they were "the most effective instrument which the System could use for meeting certain market situations which would exist for short periods of time." He suggested that "the provision of funds to the market through [repurchase agreements] at a rate below the discount rate was no more inequitable to member banks than was the provision of funds to the market through outright purchases of Government securities . . . at a rate below the discount rate."[42]

Robertson's rejoinder, as recorded in the minutes of the Executive Committee meeting, left no doubt about the true nature of his objections to System repurchase agreements:

> Mr. Robertson stated that notwithstanding the use of the repurchase arrangement for many years, he felt that originally it was an *illegal arrangement*. The fact that it

[39] Minutes of the Federal Open Market Committee, March 3, 1954, p. 7.

[40] Minutes of the Federal Open Market Committee, June 23, 1954, pp. 15–16.

[41] Minutes of the Executive Committee of the Federal Open Market Committee, September 22, 1954, pp. 2–3.

[42] Minutes of the Executive Committee of the Federal Open Market Committee, September 22, 1954, p. 3.

had been an administrative practice for many years gave some legal support to its present use, however, and he did not wish to have a decision on its future use based on the question of legality. He did wish, nevertheless, to raise the question of its use on the basis of *equity*, to which he had already referred, and *need.*[43]

Robertson further asserted that

> there was no necessity for the repurchase agreement, and that any needs of the market which have been met by this means could be met by outright purchases and sales of securities for the System account, or at most by making advances to Government securities dealers under repurchase agreements at rates no less than the rates charged to member banks on discounts.

Chairman Martin suggested that the matter be explored in more detail at a later meeting. In the meantime, the Executive Committee, by a vote of 4 to 1 (with Robertson dissenting), approved Sproul's proposal to authorize a repo rate below the discount rate.[44]

Robertson's Critique

Robertson read a lengthy critique of System repurchase agreements at the October 20, 1954, Executive Committee meeting.[45] The statement made several significant points:

- Repos were loans. They were not bona fide "open market" transactions because they were not available to other than nonbank dealers.
- Entering into repos on Treasury securities with nonbank dealers opened the door to entering into similar agreements with, for example, nonmember banks, corporations, and individuals, and with respect to any instrument described in section 14 of the Federal Reserve Act, all at rates below the discount rate.
- The intent of Congress was that loans would be extended by the Reserve Banks, subject to the supervision of the Board of Governors, pursuant to section 13 and that open market operations would be undertaken at the direction of the Federal Open Market Committee, pursuant to sections 12A and 14.
- The doubtfulness of the FOMC's legal position, with respect to repurchase agreements with nonbank dealers, was a strong reason

[43] Minutes of the Executive Committee of the Federal Open Market Committee, September 22, 1954, p. 3. Emphasis added.

[44] Minutes of the Executive Committee of the Federal Open Market Committee, September 22, 1954, pp. 4 and 5.

[45] Minutes of the Executive Committee of the Federal Open Market Committee, October 20, 1954, pp. 11–15.

to limit the use of such agreements and to limit repo rates to not less than the discount rate.

- Extending repo credit to nonbank dealers at rates below the discount rate gave a competitive advantage to those dealers relative to bank dealers that was difficult to justify.
- The recent advent of outright transactions for cash settlement invalidated the argument that repos were needed to get reserves into the market quickly.

Martin suggested that copies of Robertson's "stimulating and provocative" memo be circulated to the members of the committee "for study and consideration at a later meeting."[46]

A Proposal

At the March 1955 FOMC meeting, Robertson proposed an "open window" lending facility, based on repurchase agreements and available to *all* dealers in Treasury securities at a rate not less than the discount rate. The facility would be for the specific purpose of "enabling dealers in Governments to maintain broad and ready markets." Robertson suggested that "dealers should feel assurance that the facility is always available to them within reasonable limits ... as the discount window is open to banks."[47] In discussing the proposal three months later, Robertson argued that repos should be "for the purpose of aiding dealers in making markets in Government securities," an activity that could be undertaken "much more efficiently if the Federal Reserve Banks made a completely impersonal arrangement similar to that followed in discount policy."[48]

Governor Mills objected to Robertson's characterization of the use of repos, arguing instead that repos were intended to "supply reserves to the market." It followed that "the initiative [for a repo] should lie with the System, ... rather than with individual dealers whose reasons for seeking repurchase agreements might not necessarily coincide with the objectives of System policy."[49]

Allan Sproul reacted particularly strongly to Robertson's proposal, stating that "what [dealers] would like to have is assured access to funds at lower rates so they would always, or nearly always, have a profit on the

[46] Minutes of the Executive Committee of the Federal Open Market Committee, October 20, 1954, p. 15.
[47] Minutes of the Federal Open Market Committee, March 2, 1955, p. 44.
[48] Minutes of the Federal Open Market Committee, June 22, 1955, p. 32.
[49] Minutes of the Federal Open Market Committee, June 22, 1955, p. 33.

"carry" of their securities in position." He suggested that "no central bank can give such assurance without also giving up its initiative in credit control" and disparaged the analogy between Robertson's proposal and the discount window: "The discount window is open as a privilege not a right, there are no credit lines to be drawn on at will, and the suggestion that member banks should borrow freely and continuously has usually been frowned upon."[50]

Robertson's proposal went down to defeat on a vote of 9 to 1.[51]

Reconciliation

Following the defeat of Robertson's proposal, the Open Market Committee turned to the business of setting the repo rate. (The FOMC had abolished the Executive Committee in June 1955 and assumed for itself the responsibility for setting repo rates.)

Sproul suggested leaving it up to the manager of the Open Market Account to set a rate not less than the smaller of (1) the discount rate and (2) the average auction rate on the most recent offering of three-month Treasury bills, noting that "there have been situations in the past and will be in the future when a repurchase rate below the discount rate can make possible a desirable temporary release of credit to meet an unusual and concentrated need for immediate bank reserves."[52]

Robertson agreed to abstain from objecting "if it was understood that a rate below the discount rate would be used only if such procedure seemed essential as a means of carrying out Committee policy." Sproul stated that "this was the way in which the [authority] has been used in the past" and Martin said that "his sentiment was in accordance with Mr. Robertson's suggestion."[53]

Hugh Leach, the president of the Federal Reserve Bank of Richmond, provided a concise coda to the FOMC's efforts to reframe repurchase agreements, observing that "repurchase agreements had a very useful purpose in keeping the Federal Reserve from having to make frequent outright purchases and sales of securities" and that "such frequent purchases and sales were undesirable . . . because they had an effect upon the securities market itself and because they might confuse the public as to

[50] Minutes of the Federal Open Market Committee, June 22, 1955, pp. 34 and 35.
[51] Minutes of the Federal Open Market Committee, July 12, 1955, p. 11.
[52] Minutes of the Federal Open Market Committee, July 12, 1955, p. 14.
[53] Minutes of the Federal Open Market Committee, July 12, 1955, p. 17.

Box 11.4 Repo Authority of August 2, 1955.

The Federal Reserve Bank of New York was authorized "to enter into repurchase agreements with nonbank dealers in United States Government securities subject to the following conditions:

1. Such agreements
   (a) In no event shall be at a rate below whichever is the lower of (1) the discount rate of the Federal Reserve Bank on eligible commercial paper, or (2) the average issuing rate on the most recent issue of three-month Treasury bills;
   (b) Shall be for periods not to exceed 15 calendar days;
   (c) Shall cover only Government securities maturing within 15 months; and
   (d) Shall be used as a means of providing the money market with sufficient Federal Reserve funds as to avoid undue strain on a day-to-day basis.
2. Reports of such transactions shall be included in the weekly report of open market operations which is sent to the members of the Federal Open Market Committee.
3. In the event Government securities covered by any such agreement are not repurchased by the dealer pursuant to the agreement or a renewal thereof, the securities thus acquired by a Federal Reserve Bank are sold in the market or transferred to the System Open Market Account."

Minutes of the Federal Open Market Committee, August 2, 1955, pp. 3–4.

what the Committee was trying to attain." Leach concluded that "in the absence of repurchase agreements, the only way to [control free reserves] more precisely ... would be to make more frequent purchases and sales in the open market." Since that was undesirable, "it was his view that there was much to be said for authorizing repurchase agreements in a manner which would permit the Committee to carry out its policy objectives more effectively."[54]

Subsequent Events

The Committee made several additional changes to the repo authority at its July and August 1955 meetings:

- The Committee deleted the words "with care and discrimination" from clause 1(d) so the clause stated only that repos would be used "as a means of providing the money market with sufficient Federal Reserve funds as to avoid undue strain on a day-to-day basis."[55]

[54] Minutes of the Federal Open Market Committee, July 12, 1955, p. 19.
[55] Minutes of the Federal Open Market Committee, July 12, 1955, pp. 19–20.

- The Committee limited repurchase agreements to the Federal Reserve Bank of New York, on the grounds that there was little likelihood that the authority would be used by any other Reserve Bank.[56]

Box 11.4 shows the form of the Committee's repo authority as of August 2, 1955.

[56] Minutes of the Federal Open Market Committee, August 2, 1955, pp. 3–4.

12

Monetary Policy in 1955

Nineteen fifty-five was a year of recovery and expansion and a year that raised new concerns for the Federal Open Market Committee (FOMC) regarding how to accommodate Treasury offerings while tightening monetary policy, as well as how to avoid confusing market participants with short-term "in-and-out" operations.

ECONOMIC ACTIVITY

The recovery that had become evident at the end of 1954 continued into early 1955. A Board staff memorandum observed in late January that "consumer and business demands in early January were maintained or increased further from December levels" and that "some further rise in industrial activity was indicated."[1] A staff review in March disclosed that the recovery "had carried activity almost back to [the] previous peak." Nominal gross national product (GNP) during the first quarter was estimated at an annual rate of $369 billion, compared with a peak of $370 billion in the spring of 1953.[2]

Recovery soon blossomed into expansion. In mid-April, FOMC economist Ralph Young observed that "the recovery phase of this business cycle now seemed to be in process of being succeeded by a high-level expansion phase."[3] In late June, Board economists reported that second-quarter GNP was expected to come in at $377 billion per annum.[4]

[1] Minutes of the Executive Committee of the Federal Open Market Committee, January 25, 1955, p. 8.

[2] Minutes of the Federal Open Market Committee, March 2, 1955, p. 6.

[3] Minutes of the Executive Committee of the Federal Open Market Committee, April 12, 1955, p. 2.

[4] Minutes of the Federal Open Market Committee, June 22, 1955, p. 40.

Continued expansion during the summer aroused concern that production was approaching capacity limits. At the end of August, Young noted that "after the general rise in activity which has already taken place, more industrial groups seem to be producing close to apparent capacity."[5] Two months later he suggested that "the economic situation is still one of advance but with the pace of advance in terms of physical output slowing down with the approach of capacity operations."[6] By the end of November, the economy was "at a stage of bulging, even inflationary, industrial prosperity." Production continued to advance, but at a pace "slower than earlier as capacity output is being approached in more and more lines."[7]

FOMC DIRECTIVES

FOMC directives, to the Executive Committee in the first half of the year, and directly to the Federal Reserve Bank of New York following the abolition of the Executive Committee in June, reflected the accelerating pace of economic activity.

The directive in force at the beginning of the year provided, in relevant part, that,

> The executive committee is directed, until otherwise directed by the Federal Open Market Committee, to arrange for such transactions for the System open market account, either in the open market or directly with the Treasury (including purchases, sales, exchanges, replacement of maturing securities, and letting maturities run off without replacement), as may be necessary, in the light of current and prospective economic conditions and the general credit situation of the country, with a view
>
> (a) to relating the supply of funds in the market to the needs of commerce and business,
> (b) to promoting growth and stability in the economy by maintaining a condition of ease in the money market,
> (c) to correcting a disorderly situation in the Government securities market, and
> (d) to the practical administration of the account;

[5] Minutes of the Federal Open Market Committee, August 23, 1955, p. 3.
[6] Minutes of the Federal Open Market Committee, October 25, 1955, p. 3.
[7] Minutes of the Federal Open Market Committee, November 16, 1955, p. 2.

> provided that the aggregate amount of securities held in the System account (including commitments for the purchase or sale of securities for the account) at the close of this date ... shall not be increased or decreased by more than $2,000,000,000.[8]

The key phrase, clause (b), mandated operations aimed at "promoting growth and stability" by "maintaining a condition of ease."

At the January 11 FOMC meeting, with recovery manifestly underway, Chairman Martin suggested that "to continue to use ... the word "promote" in speaking of ease seems to me to be uncalled for at this time. We ought not to be 'promoting' ease now. ... It seems to me that in place of the word promote' we ought to substitute the word 'foster.'"[9] The Committee agreed and revised clause (b) to "fostering growth and stability in the economy by maintaining conditions in the money market that would encourage recovery and avoid the development of unsustainable expansion."[10]

Allan Sproul chaired the April 26 meeting of the Executive Committee in Martin's absence. Agreeing that "we are now out of the recovery phase and in the expansion or growth phase" of the business cycle, Sproul recommended deleting the reference to recovery in clause (b).[11] The full Committee acted on his recommendation in early May, amending the clause to "fostering growth and stability in the economy by maintaining conditions in the money market that would avoid the development of unsustainable expansion."[12]

Three months later Martin expressed growing anxiety over the inflationary implications of economic activity that was approaching capacity limits, saying that "we can not always wait for statistics" to act.[13] He suggested placing greater emphasis on restraining inflation and the Committee revised clause (b) to "restraining inflationary developments in the interest of sustainable economic growth."[14] The directive thereafter remained unchanged through year end.

MONEY MARKET INDICATORS

Consistent with the need to restrain a rapidly expanding economy, free reserves trended lower over the year (Chart 12.1) and short-term interest

[8] Minutes of the Federal Open Market Committee, December 7, 1954, p. 25.

[9] Minutes of the Federal Open Market Committee, January 11, 1955, p. 8.

[10] Minutes of the Federal Open Market Committee, January 11, 1955, p. 27.

[11] Minutes of the Executive Committee of the Federal Open Market Committee, April 26, 1955, p. 12.

[12] Minutes of the Federal Open Market Committee, May 10, 1955, p. 27.

[13] Minutes of the Federal Open Market Committee, August 2, 1955, pp. 13 and 14.

[14] Minutes of the Federal Open Market Committee, August 2, 1955, p. 49.

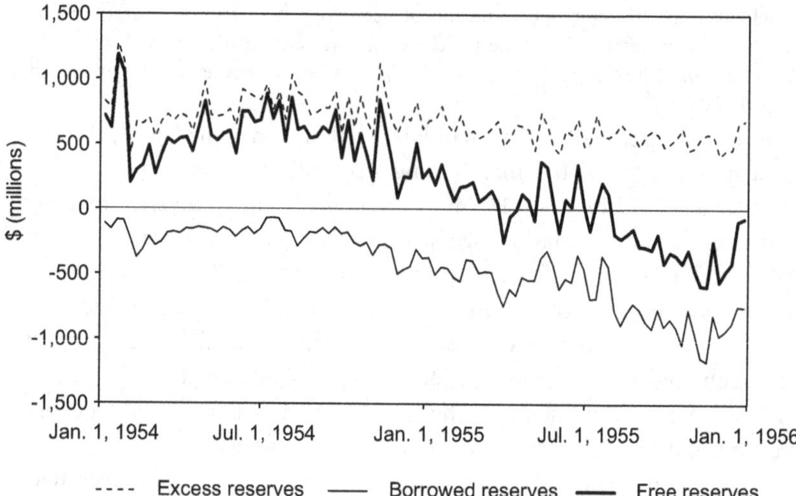

Chart 12.1 Excess reserves, borrowed reserves, and free reserves. Weekly averages of daily figures.
Board of Governors of the Federal Reserve System (1976, table 10.1C).

rates ratcheted upward (Chart 12.2). However, the role of free reserves as the principle indicator of money market conditions and objective of monetary policy began to recede. Unlike 1954, when free reserves had hardly any competition, Federal Reserve officials began to look to other indicators and objectives in 1955.

Robert Rouse, the manager of the System Open Market Account, started 1955 much as he had ended 1954, referencing the level of free reserves in discussing the basis for open market operations. On January 11 he said that he planned to let some bills run off and to sell some bills to offset currency reflow, holding free reserves to no more than $300 million.[15] Two weeks later he observed that "a negative free reserve position might possibly develop during the next day or two and it might be necessary to replace some of the bills that had been sold or permitted to run off recently."[16]

In early March, C. E. Earhart, president of the Federal Reserve Bank of San Francisco, took a different tack, arguing for the use of interest rates "as

[15] Minutes of the Federal Open Market Committee, January 11, 1955, p. 2.
[16] Minutes of the Federal Open Market Committee, January 25, 1955, p. 2.

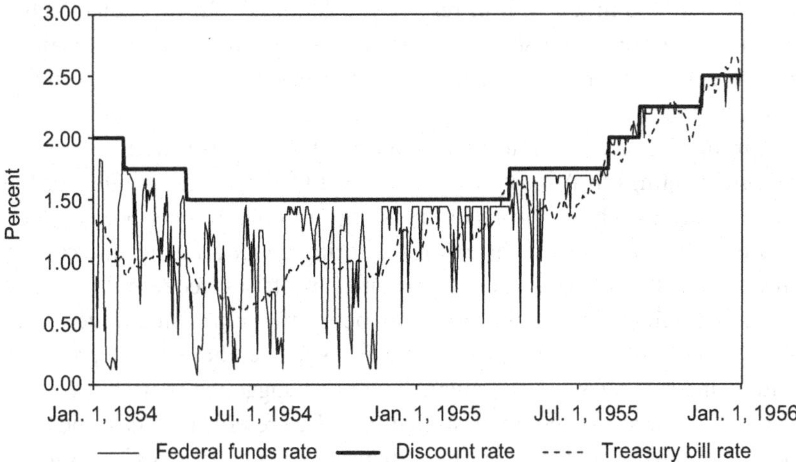

Chart 12.2 Federal funds rate, thirteen-week Treasury bill rate, and Federal Reserve Bank of New York discount rate. Daily figures.
Federal Reserve Statistical Release H.15 and Board of Governors of the Federal Reserve System (1976, table 12.1A).

a guide to credit policy" because "it was not possible to know exactly what the results would be if a given level of free reserves were put into the market. Rates on Treasury bills or other securities were something that could be seen in specific terms and something which could be definitely understood."[17] Hugh Leach, the president of the Federal Reserve Bank of Richmond, suggested that "in addition to watching free reserves [the Committee] should watch borrowings at Federal Reserve Banks, rates on Federal funds and Treasury bills, and yields on the 2½ per cent Treasury bonds."[18]

Sproul also looked to new indicators of money market conditions. Posing a hypothetical choice between (1) a program of controlling free reserves based on "more or less rigid projections" of what was needed "to permit and promote sustainable expansion of the private economy" and (2) "paying relatively more attention to interest rates and to member bank borrowings, and relatively less attention to a free reserve target, as signals of the possible economic effects of our policy," he suggested that the

[17] Minutes of the Federal Open Market Committee, March 2, 1955, p. 32.
[18] Minutes of the Executive Committee of the Federal Open Market Committee, March 15, 1955, p. 6.

former put "too much faith in reserve projections."[19] In particular, "a too rapid and continuous rise in interest rates or a too rapid and sustained increase in member bank borrowing ... would be a signal for reconsideration of policy."[20]

Sproul continued to reference interest rates and borrowed reserves at FOMC meetings in August, September, and October. The minutes of the August meeting show him recommending "an open market policy which will develop conditions tight enough to bring about a further increase in member bank borrowing and interest rates. Insofar as free reserves are still used as a guide, they would ordinarily be on the minus side of zero, but they would be less a guide than fluctuations in member bank borrowings and in interest rates."[21] In September, Sproul suggested that "during this period ... our sights should be shifted from free reserve targets to member bank borrowing and the entire structure of interest rates."[22] And in October, he remarked that "the Committee should be paying more attention to ... interest rates and credit extension," that "too much attention had been paid to 'free' reserves and that more attention should be paid to member bank borrowings, the level of reserves, ... and changes in interest rates"[23]

Other System officials believed similarly. Malcolm Bryan, president of the Atlanta Fed, was inclined to "use as our chief present guide to policy, not free reserves, not total reserves, but money rates, relying upon our knowledge that increases in those rates, particularly as they are transmitted into the long markets, will have a pervasive and powerful, though lagged, effect on the real economy."[24] Governor J. L. Robertson believed that "too much attention was being given to the volume of free reserves and not enough to money rates."[25]

[19] Minutes of the Executive Committee of the Federal Open Market Committee, May 24, 1955, pp. 7–8.

[20] Minutes of the Executive Committee of the Federal Open Market Committee, May 24, 1955, pp. 7–8.

[21] Minutes of the Federal Open Market Committee, August 2, 1955, p. 21.

[22] Minutes of the Federal Open Market Committee, September 14, 1955, p. 14.

[23] Minutes of the Federal Open Market Committee, October 25, 1955, pp. 23–24.

[24] Minutes of the Federal Open Market Committee, August 2, 1955, p. 31. Bryan reiterated the same view in October, stating that "the Committee would do better if it would watch the short-term rate rather than the volume of negative free reserves." Minutes of the Federal Open Market Committee, October 4, 1955, p. 21.

[25] Minutes of the Federal Open Market Committee, September 14, 1955, p. 9.

Table 12.1 *Treasury offerings of coupon-bearing debt in 1955.*

Security offered	Issue date	Maturity	Amount issued ($ billions)
February exchange offering			
13-month 1⅝% note	Feb. 15	Mar. 15, 1956	8.45
2½-year 2% note	Feb. 15	Aug. 15, 1957	3.78
40-year 3% bond	Feb. 15	Feb. 15, 1995	1.92
March cash offering			
2¾-month 1⅜% tax anticipation certificate	Apr. 1	Jun. 22, 1955	3.21
May cash offering			
15-month 2% note	May 17	Aug. 15, 1956	2.53
May exchange offering			
15-month 2% note	May 17	Aug. 15, 1956	3.18
July cash offering			
8-month 1⅞% tax anticipation certificate	Jul. 18	Mar. 22, 1956	2.20
39½-year 3% bond (reopening)	Jul. 20	Feb. 15, 1995	0.82
July exchange offering			
11-month 2% tax anticipation certificate	Aug. 1	Jun. 22, 1956	1.49
12½-month 2% note (reopening)	Aug. 1	Aug. 15, 1956	6.84
October cash offering			
8-month 2¼% tax anticipation certificate	Oct. 11	Jun. 22, 1956	2.97
November exchange offering			
1-year 2⅝% certificate	Dec. 8	Dec. 1, 1956	9.08
2½-year 2⅞% note	Dec. 8	Jun. 15, 1958	2.28

Treasury annual reports and offering circulars.

TREASURY OFFERINGS OF COUPON-BEARING DEBT

Treasury officials brought thirteen offerings of coupon-bearing securities in 1955 (Table 12.1), including eight exchange offerings and five cash offerings.

In each of the five cash offerings, Treasury officials announced that they would sell, at a fixed price of par, a specified amount of a security with a specified maturity date and coupon rate (Table 12.2). Interested parties were invited to submit subscriptions for desired amounts, directly or

Table 12.2 *Treasury cash offerings of coupon-bearing debt in 1955.*

Offering announced	Subscription books opened	Security offered	Amount offered ($ billions)	Amount subscribed ($ billions)	Amount issued ($ billions)
March cash offering					
Mar. 18	Mar. 22	2¾-month 1⅝% tax anticipation certificate maturing Jun. 22, 1955	3.00	7.94	3.21
May cash offering					
Apr. 28	May 3	15-month 2% note maturing Aug. 15, 1956	2.50	3.99	2.53
July cash offering					
Jul. 5	Jul. 8	8-month 1⅞% tax anticipation certificate maturing Mar. 22, 1956	2.00	10.60	2.20
	Jul. 11	39½-year 3% bond maturing Feb. 15, 1995 (reopening)	0.75	1.72	0.82
October cash offering					
Sep. 29	Oct. 3	8-month 2¼% tax anticipation certificate maturing Jun. 22, 1956	2.75	8.78	2.97

Treasury annual reports and offering circulars.

through a bank,[26] to a Federal Reserve Bank or branch. System officials collated the subscriptions and informed the Treasury of the results. Treasury officials then decided how much they would actually sell – usually an amount somewhat greater than the originally proposed amount – and how securities would be allocated among the subscribers.

In most cases, all subscribers received the same fraction of what they had subscribed for, subject to a specified minimum. For example, subscribers to the March offering of 2¾-month tax anticipation certificates[27] received 40 percent of the amount subscribed, subject to a minimum of the lesser of $50,000 and the amount subscribed.[28]

In some cases, Treasury officials opted for a more complicated allocation scheme. Subscriptions for more than $25,000 of the July offering of 39½-year bonds from "savings-type" institutions[29] received 65 percent of the amount subscribed (subject to a minimum of $25,000), while subscriptions for more than $25,000 from other market participants received only 30 percent of the amount subscribed (subject to the same minimum).[30] The differential allotments reflected Treasury's desire to place long-term bonds with investors with long investment horizons.

Attrition on Exchange Offerings

The attrition rate on an exchange offering, the ratio of the amount redeemed to the amount maturing, was commonly interpreted as a measure of the success of the offering. A high attrition rate, such as the 18.5 percent in the May refunding (Table 12.3), indicated a less successful

[26] Only banks were permitted to submit subscriptions on behalf of others. Market participants other than banks, including nonbank primary dealers, were limited to submitting subscriptions for their own account. Nonbank primary dealers were not allowed to act on behalf of customers until 1974. Compare, for bill auctions, Federal Reserve Bank of New York Circular no. 7384, April 30, 1974, with Circular no. 7389, May 7, 1974, and, for auctions of coupon-bearing securities, Circular no. 7385, May 1, 1974, with Circular no. 7429, July 31, 1974.

[27] A tax anticipation certificate was a certificate of indebtedness scheduled to mature about a week after corporate tax payments were due, but which could be presented in payment of tax liabilities at principal value plus accrued interest to the maturity date. See, for example, Federal Reserve Bank of New York Circular no. 4211, March 18, 1955.

[28] Federal Reserve Bank of New York Circular no. 4214, March 25, 1955.

[29] Savings-type institutions included public and private pension and retirement funds, endowment funds, insurance companies, mutual savings banks, savings and loan associations, and credit unions. Federal Reserve Bank of New York Circular no. 4244, July 5, 1955.

[30] Federal Reserve Bank of New York Circular no. 4249, July 14, 1955.

Table 12.3 *Treasury exchange offerings of coupon-bearing debt in 1955.*

Offering announced	Subscription books opened	Security eligible for exchange	Quantity eligible for exchange ($ billions)	Quantity exchanged into . . . . . . the shorter security offered ($ billions)	. . . the longer security offered (if any) ($ billions)	Attrition ($ millions)
February exchange offering						
					13-month 1⅝% note	**2½-year 2% note**
Jan. 27	Feb. 1	1⅝% certificate maturing Feb. 15	7.01	5.74	1.18	85 (1.2%)
	Feb. 1	1½ % note maturing Mar. 15	5.37	2.39	2.61	372 (6.9%)
					13-month 1⅝% note	**40-year 3% bond**
	Feb. 1	2⅞% bond to be redeemed Mar. 15	2.61	0.32	1.92	375 (14.4%)
May exchange offering						
				15-month 2% note		
Apr. 28	May 3	1⅛% certificate maturing May 17	3.90	3.18		723 (18.5%)

July exchange offering						
				11-month 2% certificate	**12½-month 2% note (reopening)**	
Jul. 18	Jul. 20	1⅛% certificate maturing Aug. 15	8.48	1.49	6.84	150 (1.8%)
November exchange offering						
				1-year 2⅝% certificate	**2½-year 2⅞% note**	
Nov. 25	Nov. 28	1¼% certificate maturing Dec. 15	5.36	1.16	0.81	388 (7.2%)
	Nov. 28	1¾% note maturing Dec. 15	6.85	4.93	1.47	460 (6.7%)

Treasury annual reports and offering circulars.

offering; either because interest rates rose after the terms of the offering were announced or because the securities had too low a coupon rate to begin with. Very low attrition – such as the 1.8 percent in the July refunding – indicated that the new securities had an overly generous coupon rate or that market yields had declined after terms were announced.

Maintaining an Even Keel

Treasury offerings of coupon-bearing debt, whether to raise new cash or to refinance maturing debt, presented the Federal Open Market Committee with the challenge of accommodating the offerings in an environment of increasing monetary restraint.[31] Although the Committee had adopted, in 1953, an operating policy that precluded direct support of Treasury offerings, the Committee remained keenly aware that an ill-timed move to tighten during an offering could lead to a failed offering – that is, a cash offering that failed to attract subscriptions in excess of the amount offered or an exchange offering that resulted in an extraordinary level of attrition.

During the run-up to the $15 billion February exchange offering, Chairman Martin informed the members of the Committee that Treasury officials were considering a long-term bond and suggested that "we certainly don't want a weak market while they are doing their financing. I think we ought to show, during the time the Treasury is doing its financing, that we are on the constructive side."[32] When asked what sort of open market operations would provide "a minimum disturbance to the market," Rouse suggested keeping free reserves at about $200 to $250 million. He further remarked that "under the circumstances it probably would be desirable for the System to put some reserves – perhaps $100 million – into the market through outright purchases [of Treasury bills] and to be reasonably free with repurchase facilities in order to assist dealers in fulfilling their [underwriting] function during the Treasury financing." Martin reiterated that "whatever the course the [Open Market Account] had been pursuing in the market lately, at the moment it should serve as a stabilizing influence. . . . The account should not do anything in its current

[31] The 1955 Annual Report of Open Market Operations noted (p. 4) that "the meshing of a restrictive credit policy with [the Treasury's "heavy refunding and borrowing program"] imposed particularly difficult problems on the System Account management in attaining the Committee's objectives."

[32] Minutes of the Federal Open Market Committee, January 11, 1955, p. 8.

operations that would appear to interfere with the success of the Treasury's forthcoming financing."[33]

Martin could be seen as seeking unusually accommodative money market conditions, but he retreated a bit by stating that open market operations should aim at keeping an "even keel." "The Treasury's offering," he said, "should not appear either to be floated by the Federal Reserve or hindered by the Federal Reserve."[34]

The idea of maintaining an even keel during Treasury financings (and beyond, extending into a post-settlement "underwriting" period) was a recurring topic of FOMC deliberations in 1955. Prior to the May refunding and cash offering, Sproul noted that "for the immediate future, open market operations, if they become necessary, should be used to ... maintain an even keel for Treasury financing."[35] Prior to the July refunding, Martin summed up a Committee discussion by stating that "whatever action or emphasis was necessary to 'keep the situation on an even keel' would be the goal of the Committee for the next three weeks."[36]

Martin was not reluctant to complain when things did not go as planned. Bill auction rates and one-year certificate yields rose a quarter of a percentage point during the month prior to the May offerings, markedly trimming investor appetites. The $3.9 billion exchange offering suffered an 18.5 percent attrition rate and the $2.5 billion cash offering of fifteen-month notes attracted only $4 billion of subscriptions.[37] Following the completion of the offerings Martin suggested that there should be "further discussion of the desirability and practicality of 'keeping the keel a little more even' than it had been lately." He "did not intend to be critical of the management of the System account" but "felt the committee should try to keep as even a keel as possible before, during, and immediately after

[33] Minutes of the Executive Committee of the Federal Open Market Committee, January 25, 1955, pp. 8–10.

[34] Minutes of the Executive Committee of the Federal Open Market Committee, January 25, 1955, p. 13.

[35] Minutes of the Executive Committee of the Federal Open Market Committee, April 26, 1955, p. 14.

[36] Minutes of the Federal Open Market Committee, July 12, 1955, p. 31.

[37] "Treasury's New Notes Get Coolish Greeting in Financial Circles," *Wall Street Journal*, May 5, 1955, p. 15, "Treasury Announces $4 Billion Subscriptions for $2.5 Billion Notes," *Wall Street Journal*, May 6, 1955, p. 15; and Federal Reserve Bank of New York Circular no. 4230, May 12, 1955.

a Treasury financing. . . . [I]t does not help the committee and it does not help the Treasury to have a Treasury financing failure."[38]

The close call in the May financings made an impression on the members of the Committee. During the run-up to the July financing, Governor A. L. Mills stated that, unless there was an adequate volume of free reserves, "there would be a distinct possibility of another refunding with heavy attrition, and the impression might be created that the Federal Reserve was so intent on its own policy that it was indifferent to the needs of the Treasury." Rouse responded that he anticipated buying bills to satisfy the bulk of a $500 to $700 million reserve need and observed that "buying by the Federal Reserve in advance of the announcement would be reassuring to the market, . . . even though the volume of free reserves did not make for a 'flush' situation: the mere addition of such reserves would be taken as an indication that the System was going to 'see the Treasury through.'"[39] In the event, a cash offering of $2 billion of eight-month tax anticipation certificates attracted over $10 billion of subscriptions. An exchange offering of eleven-month tax anticipation certificates and 12½-month notes to refinance $8.5 billion of maturing certificates resulted in a rock bottom 1.8 percent attrition rate.[40]

Increases in the Discount Rate

Decisions to increase the discount rate as economic activity continued to expand in 1955 were particularly difficult because the discount rate was a highly visible object of intense speculation and discussion. Federal Reserve officials could hardly increase the discount rate while they were doing their best to keep the money markets on an "even keel" during a Treasury offering.

There were four discount rate increases in 1955. The New York Reserve Bank's rate for eligible collateral was 1½ percent at the start of the year, moved to 1¾ percent on April 15, 2 percent on August 5, 2¼ percent on September 9, and 2½ percent on November 18. Officials strained to increase discount rates either well before or shortly after an offering. Chart 12.3 shows the timing of the four increases relative to the intervals

38 Minutes of the Executive Committee of the Federal Open Market Committee, May 24, 1955, pp. 6 and 17.

39 Minutes of the Federal Open Market Committee, June 22, 1955, p. 50.

40 Federal Reserve Bank of New York Circular no. 4250, July 18, 1955; Circular no. 4252, July 19, 1955; and Circular no. 4259, July 29, 1955.

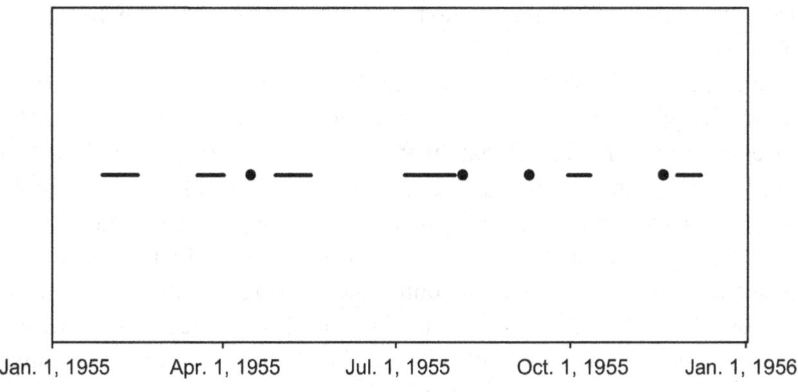

Chart 12.3 Intervals of Treasury offerings and increases in the Federal Reserve Bank of New York discount rate during 1955.
Board of Governors of the Federal Reserve System (1976, table 12.1A), and Treasury annual reports and offering circulars.

during which the Treasury offered coupon-bearing debt for sale.[41] None of the increases occurred in the midst of an offering and only the last occurred in close proximity to the beginning of an offering.

In mid-April, Chairman Martin observed, in reference to the offerings subsequently announced on April 28, that,

> We have to 'fish or cut bait' in the next ten days or two weeks, in considering the problem of what to do with the discount rate. I understand that the Treasury hopes to make an announcement of its financing around May 1, which means that we don't have too much time if we are going to do anything about changing the discount rate. . . . If we are going to make any move on the discount rate, my feeling is that it will have to be done not later than April 21. The more time we give the Treasury the better, if we are to make a move.[42]

One Reserve Bank increased its discount rate from 1½ percent to 1¾ percent on April 14. Seven Banks, including New York, increased their

[41] An offering interval starts with the announcement of the offering and ends on the issue date of the offered securities.

[42] Minutes of the Executive Committee of the Federal Open Market Committee, April 12, 1955, pp. 5–6.

rates on April 15. Three more followed on April 22. The last Bank increased its rate on May 1.[43]

When a higher discount rate was indicated but not urgent, officials could defer taking action until after an offering. During the June 22 FOMC meeting, Sproul remarked that "if the [economic] situation continued to need restraint, as now seemed likely, an increase in the discount rate could again be considered when the Treasury financing [announced on July 5 and concluded on August 1] is out of the way."[44] In fact, all twelve Reserve Banks raised their discount rates during the interval between August 4 and August 12. Eleven Banks moved to 2 percent and one, the Federal Reserve Bank of Cleveland, moved to 2¼ percent. All twelve Banks were at 2¼ percent by mid-September.[45]

Pressure to bump the discount rate to 2½ percent began to build in late September, but the cash offering announced on September 29 precluded any action until the offering settled on October 11. During the October 4 FOMC meeting, Governor C. Canby Balderston stated that he favored an increase in the discount rate after October 11 but before mid-November.[46] In mid-November, Sproul recommended an immediate increase in the rate, noting that "the way had been somewhat prepared" by the Committee's decision on November 10 to raise the repo rate from 2¼ percent to 2⅜ percent. Martin added that "if the discount rate were not increased at this time, he seriously doubted that a change could be made until some time after the turn of the year."[47] All twelve Banks moved to 2½ percent during the interval from November 18 to 23.[48]

DEFENSIVE OPERATIONS

Defensive open market operations, aimed at neutralizing short-run fluctuations in autonomous factors, such as float and currency in the hands of the public, grew in importance during 1955. Repurchase agreements continued to find favor as the preferred instrument for those operations.

[43] Board of Governors of the Federal Reserve System (1976, Table 12.1). The chronological dispersion of the rate increases was due to differences in scheduling meetings of the boards of directors of the respective Banks.

[44] Minutes of the Federal Open Market Committee, June 22, 1955, p. 55.

[45] Board of Governors of the Federal Reserve System (1976, Table 12.1).

[46] Minutes of the Federal Open Market Committee, October 4, 1955, pp. 5 and 6.

[47] Minutes of the Federal Open Market Committee, November 16, 1955, pp. 10 and 23.

[48] Board of Governors of the Federal Reserve System (1976, Table 12.1).

Sproul expressed the view that "repurchase agreements were better than in-and-out purchases and sales of securities"[49] and Hugh Leach stated that he preferred repos for short-term operations "because they have less effect on the market."[50] The 1955 Annual Report of Open Market Operations – hereafter, the "Markets annual report – observed that "repurchase agreements are well suited to dealing with temporary 'knots' in the money market that threaten to arise from time to time when reserve positions are subjected to mounting pressure, since they avoid whipsawing the market, as outright purchases and sales in quick succession might do."[51]

Repo Rates

Repurchase agreements sometimes had to be offered at interest rates below the prevailing discount rate to attract dealer interest – a practice that continued to vex some Committee members.

Challenged on the decision of the Desk to lower the repo rate to 1.65 percent between May 4 and May 6, at a time when the New York Bank's discount rate was 1¾ percent, Robert Roosa[52] stated that it was based on "the feeling of the New York Bank, in the light of the executive committee's general instruction, that as far as possible the account should avoid intervention on an outright basis." Roosa recalled, in particular, "the indication at the meeting of the executive committee on April 26 that it would be preferable to do as much as possible in adjusting market conditions through the use of repurchase agreements." He stated that "making funds available through repurchase agreements meant that the funds furnished to the market would automatically be taken out through the repayment of the ... agreements" and expressed his opinion that "this was a case in which the use of the lower rate repurchase agreements had avoided or minimized [outright] intervention by the System account.[53]

[49] Minutes of the Executive Committee of the Federal Open Market Committee, February 8, 1955, p. 14.

[50] Minutes of the Executive Committee of the Federal Open Market Committee, March 29, 1955, p. 8.

[51] 1955 Annual Report of Open Market Operations, p. 20.

[52] Roosa was, at the time, an assistant vice president in the Securities Function of the Federal Reserve Bank of New York. He sometimes represented the management of the Open Market Account at FOMC meetings.

[53] Minutes of the Federal Open Market Committee, May 10, 1955, pp. 17–18.

When Reserves Needed to Be Drained

Although widely appreciated for their utility in injecting reserves on a short-term basis, repurchase agreements were useless for draining reserves.[54] To reduce the availability of reserves in the banking system, the Open Market Desk had to rely on outright sales and consequently had to weigh the benefit of a drain against the cost of roiling the market.

Martin initiated an illuminating discussion of the problem during a meeting of the Open Market Committee on Tuesday, May 10, when he commented that "he wished the swings in the actual volume of free reserves were not so great, and inquired of Mr. Roosa as to the possibility of trying to smooth out some of [those] swings."[55]

Roosa responded by citing a recent case in which the Desk had abstained from removing a transient bulge in reserves in order to avoid confusing market participants as to Federal Reserve policy intentions:

> Yesterday … it was decided to roll over the System account's holdings of bills in the amount of $74 million even though it was realized that at this time free reserves were higher than the Committee wished them to be. This was a difficult decision to make …, for the reason that the Committee previously had indicated that System account operations might confuse the market as to System policy if the account were to be in and out of the market too frequently. Consequently, since the projections made it appear that the System account would be back in the market making outright purchases by the end of May, it was felt that it would be confusing if the account showed a runoff in bills and a reduction in holdings during the current week, when market conditions had not changed broadly, to be followed later on this month by purchases of bills.[56]

Roosa stated that the choice was, "on the one hand, whether the account should be in and out and risk the confusion and the possibility of seeming to buffet the market from side to side; or whether, on the other hand, it should not attempt to avoid swings such as had taken and were taking place." He put the matter back in Martin's court when he observed that "the System account could have run off bills yesterday or it could now sell bills … with the knowledge that it would be necessary to buy bills back toward the end of this month" and inquired "whether the smoothing of

[54] Minutes of the Federal Open Market Committee, May 10, 1955, p. 16, reporting the statement of Robert Roosa that "one of the difficulties in using repurchase agreements is that they cannot be used to take up slack unless there previously had been a purchase. Otherwise it would be necessary to make an outright sale."

[55] Minutes of the Federal Open Market Committee, May 10, 1955, p. 15.

[56] Minutes of the Federal Open Market Committee, May 10, 1955, pp. 15–16.

operations was of enough importance to warrant the System account being in and out of the market on an outright basis at the risk of confusing the market as to System policy."[57] Martin replied, in effect, that he would like to have his cake and eat it too: that he "favored minimum intervention in the market but that he also thought the System should try to minimize the sweeping moves indicated by the projections of free reserves."

The trade-off between neutralizing a transient bulge in reserves and limiting outright operations came up again in early October, when Governor J. L. Robertson criticized account managers for leaving too many reserves in the banking system during the first two days of the statement week ending Wednesday, September 21. Rouse responded that reserve projections at the time indicated there would be a large reserve deficiency on the last three days of the week and that "if an attempt had been made to sell securities from the account to reduce the volume of free reserves on the Thursday and Friday in question, it would have become necessary to reverse that operation on the following Monday because of the expected very tight situation." He noted his understanding that such "in-and-out operations . . . were generally not desired by the Committee."[58]

Two Work-Arounds

System interest in draining reserves without resorting to outright sales of securities led to the development of two work-arounds in 1955.

On an ad hoc basis, Treasury officials sometimes cooperated with the Desk in announcing an accelerated call for funds from Treasury Tax and Loan depositories.[59] The resulting transfers drained reserves from the banking system into Treasury accounts at the Reserve Banks.

The second work-around was more elaborate. In January 1955, the FOMC Executive Committee wrote to the Fiscal Assistant Secretary of the Treasury, complaining that erratic fluctuations in Treasury balances at Federal Reserve Banks were creating problems for FOMC efforts to control reserve balances:

57 Minutes of the Federal Open Market Committee, May 10, 1955, pp. 16–17.

58 Minutes of the Federal Open Market Committee, October 4, 1955, p. 15. Robertson thought Rouse was "overestimating the criticism to be put on in-and-out transactions" and that he "did not understand the Committee to be clearly opposed to 'in-and-out' transactions for the System account if they were not confusing to the market." Minutes of the Federal Open Market Committee, October 4, 1955, p. 16.

59 An ad hoc TT&L call is noted in the minutes of the Federal Open Market Committee, for October 4, 1955, at p. 15. The Treasury Tax and Loan program is described in the appendix to Chapter 3 above.

As you know, one of the most disturbing factors influencing the supply of member bank reserve balances from day to day is the fluctuation of the Treasury's deposit balance at the Federal Reserve Banks. Various staff members within the Federal Reserve System, as well as within the Treasury, have been studying the techniques through which the funds are being called from its depositary banks by the Treasury, in the hope of finding some means for moderating the extremes of this fluctuation.

The executive committee of the Federal Open Market Committee feels that this subject is of sufficient importance to warrant the suggestion from this committee that your staff investigate the possibility of developing techniques that might result in practical improvement. Our people both at the Board and at the Reserve Banks would be glad to work with your staff to that end, i.e., toward developing some means of reducing the frequency and extent of the disturbances to bank reserves and the money market that have been characteristic results of the daily swings in the Treasury's balance over recent years.[60]

Federal Reserve and Treasury officials subsequently worked together to expand the Treasury Tax and Loan program by creating a new class of depositories whose balances could be called on a *same-day* basis. Banks with total deposits of more than $500 million were designated Group C banks and required to be prepared to satisfy Monday and Thursday calls on the day of the call. When apprised of the new facility, Chairman Martin responded that it was "a very desirable development which represented real progress toward helping to carry out credit policy."[61]

[60] Minutes of the Executive Committee of the Federal Open Market Committee, January 11, 1955, pp. 6–7.

[61] Minutes of the Executive Committee of the Federal Open Market Committee, June 6, 1955, p. 16.

13

Pragmatism in the Accommodation of Treasury Offerings

One of the three operating principles adopted by the Federal Open Market Committee (FOMC) in March 1953 stated that the System would refrain, during Treasury offerings, from purchasing (a) any maturing issue for which an exchange was being offered, (b) when-issued securities, and (c) any outstanding issue with a maturity comparable to the maturity of a security being offered for exchange. The Committee softened that principle in 1955 when it decided to allow repurchase agreements on "rights" – maturing securities for which the Treasury was offering an exchange – and when it bailed out a floundering offering. The two events suggest that FOMC members were pragmatic in their interpretation of, and adherence to, the principle of no direct support for Treasury offerings.

REPURCHASE AGREEMENTS ON RIGHTS

Treasury officials offered three new securities in the February 1955 financing, including a thirteen-month note and a 2½-year note in exchange for maturing certificates and notes, and the thirteen-month note and a forty-year bond in exchange for maturing bonds (Table 12.3). Following the announcement of the offerings, officials at the Federal Reserve Bank of New York informed the dealers with whom they did business that the Bank would provide credit on repurchase agreements for the purpose of enabling the dealers to carry positions in the maturing securities up to February 15, when the exchanges would settle.[1]

[1] Minutes of the Executive Committee of the Federal Open Market Committee, February 8, 1955, p. 2.

At the February 8 Executive Committee meeting, Governor J. L. Robertson asked the manager of the System Open Market Account whether "there was any real difference between purchasing maturing issues during a period of Treasury financing and executing repurchase agreements covering such securities."[2] Rouse replied that "he felt there was a substantial difference":

> Both were for the purpose of putting reserves into the market, but in the case of repurchase agreements there was no thought of influencing any phase of the market except to facilitate dealer operations. Funds put into the market through repurchase agreements were like a 'loan' and would automatically come out of the market within a short time.[3]

Robertson questioned "whether the full Committee's understanding on this point was clear" and suggested that "it would be desirable to clarify the Committee's intent."[4]

The ensuing discussion focused on the effect of repurchase agreements on securities prices but additionally illuminated the ambiguous nature of the contracts. Governor Menc Szymczak felt that repurchase agreements were open market purchases and sales – he did not agree that they were loans – and concurred in a comment by FOMC economist Woodlief Thomas that "one of the differences between outright purchases and repurchase agreements was in price: outright purchases may be made at definite prices, which influence market prices, whereas repurchase operations involve both purchase and sale at an agreed price which may have little relation to the market price and thus entail no price support."[5] Governor James Vardaman stated that, "he would not consider that repurchase agreements covering maturing Treasury securities would be inconsistent with the general policy of the Federal Open Market Committee . . . That policy had been concerned with action that might be taken to influence price, and there was no support where price was not involved. He did not see how repurchase agreements could be construed as being for the purpose of supporting any pattern of prices."[6]

[2] Minutes of the Executive Committee of the Federal Open Market Committee, February 8, 1955, pp. 3–4.

[3] Minutes of the Executive Committee of the Federal Open Market Committee, February 8, 1955, p. 4.

[4] Minutes of the Executive Committee of the Federal Open Market Committee, February 8, 1955, p. 4.

[5] Minutes of the Executive Committee of the Federal Open Market Committee, February 8, 1955, pp. 4–5.

[6] Minutes of the Executive Committee of the Federal Open Market Committee, February 8, 1955, p. 5.

The matter was resolved a month later when the Committee, during its annual review of the operating principles, adopted Martin's suggestion of an explicit exception for repurchase agreements.[7]

INTERVENTION

During a hastily arranged telephone meeting of the FOMC at 9:30 a.m. on Wednesday, November 30, 1955, Rouse disclosed that the Treasury's $12 billion financing then under way (see Table 12.3) was in trouble. He stated that the exchange offering had been "extremely well received" when it was announced on the preceding Friday but that it had since become clear that "a number of large holders of the maturing issues who needed funds for tax payments, dividends, or other year-end purposes would not exchange their holdings into the new securities." The Desk had made repos "freely available," had made outright purchases of about $130 million of bills, and had executed orders for Treasury and foreign accounts for "substantial amounts of Treasury securities, including securities of the new offering on a when-issued basis," but it looked as though there would be "substantial attrition" on the offering. Martin informed the Committee that the Treasury had made a formal request for assistance.[8]

Allan Sproul, the president of the New York Fed, urged the Committee to intervene to bail out the floundering offering by lengthening the maximum term of a System repo to thirty-five days (so that dealers could be confident of financing over the year's end) and by purchasing the new securities offered by the Treasury on a when-issued (w.i.) basis. (The w.i. purchases would settle on December 8 and add reserves at about the time that the Fed's reserve projections indicated a need to add.) Sproul observed that "we have here a Treasury issue which was by all counts properly priced on the market" at the time it was announced so that "if the Committee should take action it would not be in the position of trying to peg what would seem to be a wrongly-priced issue." He suggested instead that "this is a situation in which credit policy and debt management can aid one another." Sproul admitted that he could not claim that "the results will be disastrous if we do not step in and do what I am now suggesting. But I do think it would be helpful and appropriate in the circumstances from the standpoint of credit policy and debt management."[9]

[7] Minutes of the Federal Open Market Committee, March 2, 1955, pp. 53–59.
[8] Minutes of the Federal Open Market Committee, November 30, 1955, pp. 2–3.
[9] Minutes of the Federal Open Market Committee, November 30, 1955, pp. 3–4.

The Committee was divided on how to respond and was stressed by the need to act quickly; trading would open at 10:00 a.m., and the subscription books were due to close at the end of the day. Governor A. L. Mills remarked that, should the Committee approve the purchase of the when-issued securities, it "would be abandoning a position that was taken after very mature consideration and without, in my own opinion, being confronted with an issue of a seriousness that would justify such deviation." He went on to argue that,

> [t]here are no indications of what the amount of attrition would be if we stayed aside from purchasing when-issued securities. If there is substantial attrition, ... that attrition can be corrected within a matter of some days when the Treasury comes back for new money and the System can then, in an orthodox and conventional manner, provide the reserve base for the tax anticipation certificates that presumably will be offered.[10]

He indicated that he would support an extension of repo maturities to thirty-five days, but nothing more than that.

Sproul was supported by C. E. Earhart, president of the Federal Reserve Bank of San Francisco; Hugh Leach, president of the Richmond Fed; and W. D. Fulton, president of the Cleveland Bank. Earhart noted that the System might have to furnish "a smaller amount of reserves than would be necessary if it tried to help the Treasury indirectly entirely through the purchase of bills, and there would be less doubt as to the effectiveness of the assistance." Leach observed that "the Treasury had tried to price the issue correctly" and suggested that, with the offering now in trouble, "he would dislike anything which made it appear that the System was 'running out' on the Treasury." Fulton stated that "under the circumstances, where the Treasury's issue was priced with the market, ... the Committee was justified in ... buying the when-issued securities."[11]

Martin voiced the Committee's fundamental conundrum: How could it support the refunding without abandoning its operating principle of not directly supporting Treasury offerings? Martin understood that the Committee was in "a difficult situation." On the one hand, he said, "the Committee's relations with the Treasury are important," and he believed that "it would be unwise ... for the Committee to ignore the position in which it had been placed by [Treasury's] request ... for assistance." On the other hand, providing assistance would create the moral hazard that

[10] Minutes of the Federal Open Market Committee, November 30, 1955, p. 5.

[11] Minutes of the Federal Open Market Committee, November 30, 1955, pp. 7–8 and 10.

Treasury officials would price their offerings closer to the market in the future. Martin asserted that "if we do make an exception to our general policy, we should make it clear that it is only an exception . . . It would be very unwise for the Treasury to think that at any time it gets into trouble on an issue the Federal Reserve will bail it out."[12]

In the event, the Committee approved, by a vote of nine to three, the purchase, on a when-issued basis, of up to $400 million of the one-year certificates included in the offering.[13] Sproul agreed that the w.i. purchase authority was adequate and that there no need to also extend the maximum term of a repurchase agreement to thirty-five days.[14] The Open Market Desk ended up acquiring $167 million of the certificates and kept attrition on the $12 billion exchange offering to a comfortable 7 percent.[15]

INTERVENTION BY ANOTHER NAME

The issue of bailing out a faltering Treasury offering resurfaced barely a week later. In a second hastily arranged telephone meeting on the morning of Thursday, December 8, Rouse informed the Committee that there had been "a psychological deterioration in the market in the last three-quarters of an hour which apparently was feeding upon itself." Bidding on an auction offering of $1.5 billion of ninety-nine-day tax anticipation bills[16] was due to close at 1:30 p.m.[17] and investor interest appeared quite limited. Rouse reported that "the auction price for the new bills was estimated at about 2.35 per cent on Tuesday; yesterday the talk was in terms of 2½ percent; and in the 'moonlight' discussions late yesterday there was talk of the possibility of 2¾ percent, or even 2⅞ per cent." He informed the Committee that the Desk had purchased $85½ million of bills on Wednesday and anticipated buying another $125 million before the close of bidding but that "he did not think buying bills would necessarily be the

[12] Minutes of the Federal Open Market Committee, November 30, 1955, pp. 4 and 6.

[13] Minutes of the Federal Open Market Committee, November 30, 1955, p. 12.

[14] Minutes of the Federal Open Market Committee, November 30, 1955, p. 13.

[15] That the Fed had, in spite of its operating principles, bailed out a floundering Treasury offering became evident upon the release of the H.4.1 report of member bank reserves and statement of condition of the Federal Reserve Banks dated December 15, 1955. "Reserve's Buying Propped U.S. Issue," *New York Times*, December 16, 1955, p. 45.

[16] A tax anticipation bill was a Treasury bill scheduled to mature about a week after corporate tax payments were due which could be presented in payment of tax liabilities at full face value. See, for example, Federal Reserve Bank of New York circular no. 4290, December 6, 1955.

[17] Federal Reserve Bank of New York Circular no. 4290, December 6, 1955.

answer to the situation."[18] Rouse suggested that there was a prospect of "incipient disorder."

The Committee was not thrilled with the prospect of another bailout and looked around for an alternative. Governor Mills recalled that,

> [t]here had been a precedent in the past on occasions where there has been a 'stickiness' in a Treasury financing offering where the Federal Reserve Banks had communicated with the more important member banks in their districts to *encourage participation* in a particular offering. In the present case, where the central reserve city banks were feeling the pinch of tight money more than the out-of-town banks, there could be a good reason for the Federal Reserve Banks, depending on developments during the day, to contact the out-of-town banks by way of suggesting *reasonable participation* in the tax anticipation bill offering and stating that where the discount window is used to support that participation, it would not under present circumstances be regarded as a violation of the general understanding against continuous borrowing.[19]

Sproul said that he was "getting in touch with the banks in New York and reminding them of their *responsibility as underwriters* in connection with a Treasury ... offering such as this."[20] The allusions to "encouraging participation," "reasonable participation," and banks' "responsibility as underwriters" were, of course, little more than euphemisms.

In the event, the Committee took no specific actions. Martin chose instead to be guided by "the judgment of Mr. Sproul and of Mr. Rouse and others on the desk."[21] The Desk bought a total of $141 million of bills before the close of bidding and "granted repo credit liberally at maximum [fifteen-day] maturities."[22] The auction was covered; the Treasury received bids for $4.1 billion of the bills and sold the $1.5 billion offering at an average discount rate of 2.47 percent.[23]

The incident, however, was not forgotten. At the December 13 FOMC meeting, Governor Robertson expressed his opinion that assuring access to the discount window for the purpose of financing an auction award of Treasury securities "was a perversion of the discount function as well as a perversion of the auction market mechanism. It amounted to getting the

[18] Minutes of the Federal Open Market Committee, December 8, 1955, pp. 2–3.

[19] Minutes of the Federal Open Market Committee, December 8, 1955, pp. 4–5. Emphasis added.

[20] Minutes of the Federal Open Market Committee, December 8, 1955, p. 5. Emphasis added.

[21] Minutes of the Federal Open Market Committee, December 8, 1955, p. 6.

[22] 1955 Annual Report of Open Market Operations, p. 11.

[23] Federal Reserve Bank of New York Circular no. 4293, December 9, 1955.

Federal Reserve Banks into the position of being security salesmen in connection with a Treasury financing."[24]

Committee members who had supported pressuring the banks were subdued in their responses. Mills stated that "in an atmosphere such as had existed," assuring banks that they would have access to discount window credit to carry a position in the tax anticipation bills was "appropriate and desirable, if it could be accomplished without sacrifice of some other authority or some other policy which was essential to the System." In the instant case, he said, "he could see no way in which there was a sacrifice of policy or a loss of control." Governor Szymczak admitted that "he did not think any of the members of the Committee liked the situation but that it had existed and the time in which to try to meet it had been very short. . . . He thought it was the right thing for the Committee to have done under those circumstances."[25]

The November refunding and the subsequent auction offering of tax anticipation bills demonstrated that the Committee faced a fundamental contradiction between what it said it wanted to do and what it felt compelled to do in the heat of the moment. Martin wrestled with the problem:

> My view is that, the Treasury having appealed to us for assistance and the refunding issue having been priced correctly, we could be open to the charge of being 'doctrinaire' if in this particular instance we had wanted to assert and to stick rigidly with those principles which we have enunciated . . . Nevertheless, every time we give way in those principles we encourage the market to think that the System has been 'panicked' into taking a position to bail the Treasury out. Ultimately if we do that enough and pick up the Treasury issues, the charge can be made that it is becoming necessary for the Fed to pick up and establish the going rate on the securities. We have been through all of that before.
>
> However, I don't think we have enough perspective on the market at the moment to be rigid in this principle. . . .[26]

Robertson was more emphatic, arguing that "an essential for the success of the [Committee's operating principles], recognized and observed by the Treasury, has been the setting of terms on new Treasury issues attractive enough to elicit adequate market reception without Federal Reserve support" and that "the current experience indicates the need for further consideration of these procedures to avoid requests for emergency support

[24] Minutes of the Federal Open Market Committee, December 13, 1955, p. 19.
[25] Minutes of the Federal Open Market Committee, December 13, 1955, pp. 19–20.
[26] Minutes of the Federal Open Market Committee, December 13, 1955, pp. 24–25.

action by the System." He wanted Treasury officials to "recognize and openly acknowledge the risk of substantial attrition and [to] be prepared to meet it by contemporaneous or subsequent sales of securities for cash, rather than rely upon Federal Reserve efforts to produce an adequate exchange."[27]

Sproul, for his part, recalled his earlier concern that explicit operating principles, even if not more than default principles that the Committee could change at any time, ran the risk of hardening into barriers to action. He stated that he had "detected in some of the comments which have been made a seeming reversion to the idea that the directives which the Committee has adopted from time to time are a form of Mosaic law" and that "the longer we went without deviation from the general principle adopted by the Committee, the more likely it would be that when we did have to deviate it would be taken as a sign that a situation had developed which was more dangerous and critical than actually was the case, and that this would mislead the market."[28] He accepted what he viewed as inevitable in light of the Treasury's debt management burden:

> [T]hat under conditions of credit restriction when the Treasury has to come to market for large refundings, and when it is also faced with the necessity for some cash borrowing, it is unlikely that the market will always be able to make the massive readjustments which are necessary within the short period of the Treasury's offering; some form of underwriting of part of the transaction is likely to be necessary.[29]

[27] Minutes of the Federal Open Market Committee, December 13, 1955, pp. 27 and 28.
[28] Minutes of the Federal Open Market Committee, December 13, 1955, p. 31.
[29] Minutes of the Federal Open Market Committee, December 13, 1955, p. 32.

14

1956 and 1957

The Federal Open Market Committee sought, in 1956 and most of 1957, to restrain inflation while sustaining the economic expansion that began in the latter part of 1954. Box 14.1 shows the policy-relevant portion of the directives issued by the Committee to the Federal Reserve Bank of New York during those two years. Until the last two months of 1957, the directives focused on "restraining inflationary developments in the interest of sustainable economic growth."

In the spring and summer of 1957, FOMC deliberations characterized the economy as having leveled out at a high level of activity, with little indication of whether it was more likely to resume growing or contract. In April, FOMC economist Ralph Young characterized the economy as moving "on a high plateau ... marked ... by divers surface irregularities. Whether upward or downward tilt is to predominate next is the question everybody asks and nobody can answer."[1] In July, Albert Koch, the assistant director of the Division of Research and Statistics at the Board of Governors, stated that "over-all economic activity is being maintained at about the high level of the past winter. Downward adjustments have been going on in a number of lines but the areas of weakness have not widened significantly and upward adjustments have been taking place in other areas."[2] In September, Alfred Hayes, the president of the Federal Reserve Bank of New York since August 1956, observed that "there has been no material change in over-all business activity since the last meeting, or, in fact, for the past several months. The economy is still characterized by stability of production and employment and by well-sustained consumer demand."[3]

[1] Minutes of the Federal Open Market Committee, April 16, 1957, p. 5.
[2] Minutes of the Federal Open Market Committee, July 9, 1957, pp. 6–7.
[3] Minutes of the Federal Open Market Committee, September 10, 1957, p. 11.

Box 14.1 Federal Open Market Committee Directives in 1956 and 1957.

At the beginning of 1956, the most recent directive of the FOMC to the Federal Reserve Bank of New York directed the Bank

> [t]o make such purchases, sales, or exchanges (including replacement of maturing securities, and allowing maturities to run off without replacement) for the System open market account in the open market, or in the case of maturing securities, by direct exchange with the Treasury, as may be necessary in the light of current and prospective economic conditions and the general credit situation of the country, with a view

(a) to relating the supply of funds in the market to the needs of commerce and business,
(b) to restraining inflationary developments in the interest of sustainable economic growth, and
(c) to the practical administration of the account; . . .[1]

Clause (b) was the key policy instruction.

The members of the Committee revised clause (b) a total of nine times in 1956 and 1957:[2]

- *January 24, 1956*: "to restraining inflationary developments in the interest of sustainable economic growth while taking into account any deflationary tendencies in the economy";
- *March 27, 1956*: "to restraining inflationary developments in the interest of sustainable economic growth";
- *May 23, 1956*: "to restraining inflationary developments in the interest of sustainable economic growth while taking into account any deflationary tendencies in the economy";
- *August 7, 1956*: "to restraining inflationary developments in the interest of sustainable economic growth";
- *November 27, 1956*: "to restraining inflationary developments in the interest of sustainable economic growth while recognizing additional pressures in the money, credit, and capital markets resulting from seasonal factors and international conditions";
- *January 8, 1957*: "to restraining inflationary developments in the interest of sustainable economic growth while recognizing unsettled conditions in the money, credit, and capital markets, and in the international situation";
- *March 5, 1957*: "to restraining inflationary developments in the interest of sustainable economic growth, while recognizing uncertainties in the business outlook, the financial markets, and the international situation";
- *November 12, 1957*: "to fostering sustainable growth in the economy without inflation, by moderating the pressures on bank reserves";
- *December 17, 1957*: "to cushioning adjustments and mitigating recessionary tendencies in the economy."

The last two revisions reflect the onset of the recession that began in August 1957.

[1] 1956 Board of Governors of the Federal Reserve System Annual Report, p. 17.
[2] 1956 Board of Governors of the Federal Reserve System Annual Report, pp. 17–47; and 1957 Board of Governors of the Federal Reserve System Annual Report, pp. 33–62.

The Committee's assessment of economic activity began to change in the fall. Young remarked in October that "an increasing number of business observers are disposed to the view that the momentum of major expansive factors on the demand side has now been spent, [that] the pressure of inflationary forces is in process of lessening and even dispersing, and that the prospective movement of activity and prices is to be downward."[4] Three weeks later a staff review pointed out that recent declines in equity prices and in the prices of industrial commodities had been "of sufficient magnitude to bring into question continued dominance of inflationary forces."[5] By mid-November Young was reporting that "the most recently available data confirm that moderate downward adjustment has ... been occurring" and Hayes concluded that "there is no longer much doubt that at least a mild downturn in business activity is under way."[6] The revision was complete when Chairman Martin concluded, in early December, that the country was in recession.[7]

Consistent with the Committee's focus on restraining inflation, free reserves were generally negative in 1956 and 1957 (Chart 14.1). Free reserves turned positive briefly during the winter of 1956–57 – partly as a result of accommodating a Treasury financing in the second half of November and partly as a result of forecasting errors in several autonomous factors.[8] Most of the variation in free reserves was attributable to fluctuations in borrowed reserves; excess reserves were at stable around $500–600 million.

Reserve Banks raised their discount rates three times in 1956–57 and lowered them once (Chart 14.2). Consistent with the FOMC's even keel policy, none of the increases came immediately before or during a Treasury offering (Chart 14.3).

The rate on thirteen-week Treasury bills varied more or less in parallel with the discount rate (Chart 14.2). Federal funds traded at the discount rate – albeit with deviations that were generally sporadic but included a smattering of low rates between November 1956 and January 1957.

[4] Minutes of the Federal Open Market Committee, October 1, 1957, p 3.
[5] Minutes of the Federal Open Market Committee, October 22, 1957, p. 7.
[6] Minutes of the Federal Open Market Committee, November 12, 1957, pp. 6 and 17.
[7] Minutes of the Federal Open Market Committee, December 3, 1957, p. 47.
[8] 1956 Annual Report of Open Market Operations, p. 14, and 1957 Annual Report of Open Market Operations, p. 10.

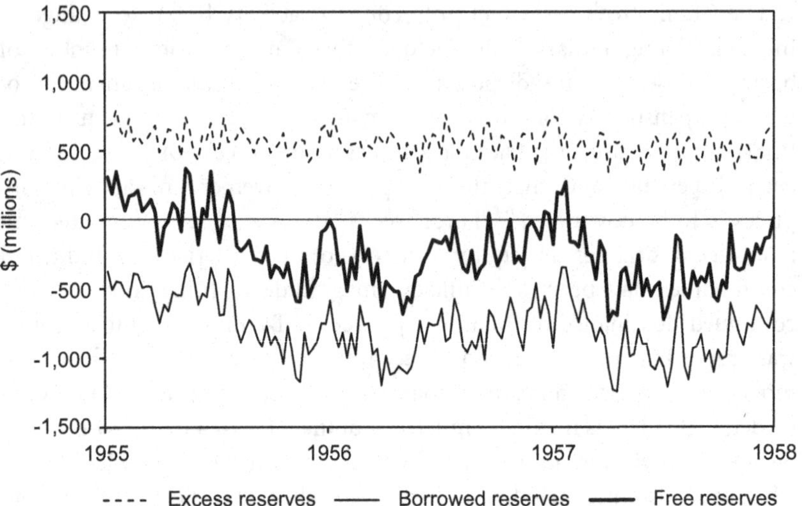

Chart 14.1 Excess reserves, borrowed reserves, and free reserves. Weekly averages of daily figures.
Board of Governors of the Federal Reserve System (1976, table 10.1C).

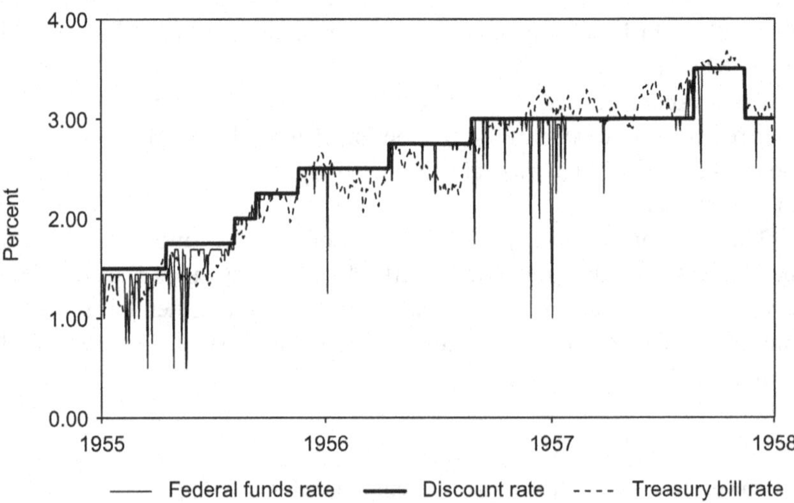

Chart 14.2 Federal funds rate, thirteen-week Treasury bill rate, and Federal Reserve Bank of New York discount rate. Daily figures.
Federal Reserve Statistical Release H.15 and Board of Governors of the Federal Reserve System (1976, table 12.1A).

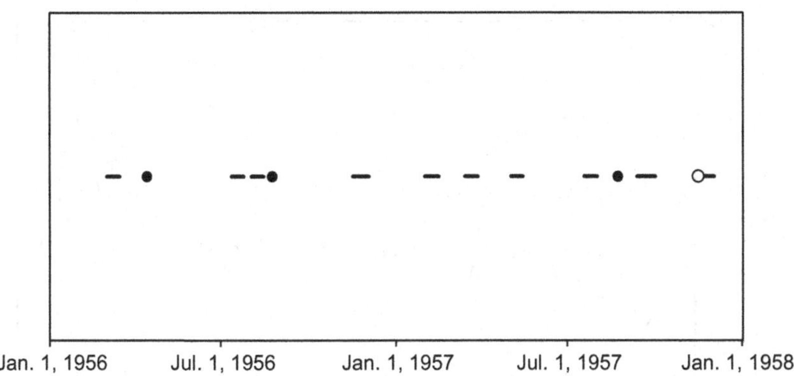

Chart 14.3 Intervals of Treasury coupon offerings and changes in the Federal Reserve Bank of New York discount rate during 1956 and 1957.
Board of Governors of the Federal Reserve System (1976, table 12.1A) and Treasury annual reports and offering circulars.

DEFENSIVE OPERATIONS

In the interest of stabilizing the quantity of reserves available to the banking system, Desk officials regularly sought to offset transient fluctuations in three particularly significant autonomous factors: currency in the hands of the public, float, and Treasury balances at Federal Reserve Banks.

Currency

Chart 14.4 shows large spikes in public demand for currency every December. (Smaller spikes around the July 4 holiday are also evident.) To stabilize bank reserves, the Desk regularly bought Treasury securities in outright transactions and on repurchase agreements in the second half of November and through December and then sold securities and let the repos run off in January (Charts 14.5 and 14.6).

The January operations were quite large and took place over a relatively short interval of time. In early 1956, for example, the Desk allowed $393 million of repos and $577 million of maturing Treasury bills to run off and sold an additional $548 million of bills on an outright basis.[9]

[9] 1956 Annual Report of Open Market Operations, p. 6.

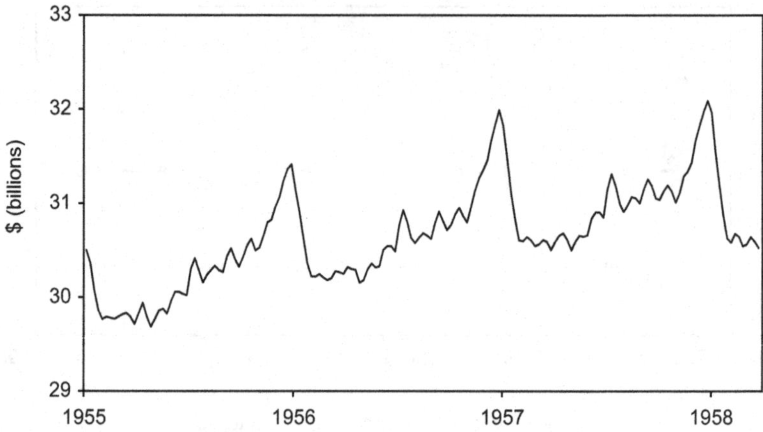

Chart 14.4 Currency in circulation. Weekly averages of daily figures.
Board of Governors of the Federal Reserve System (1976, table 10.1C).

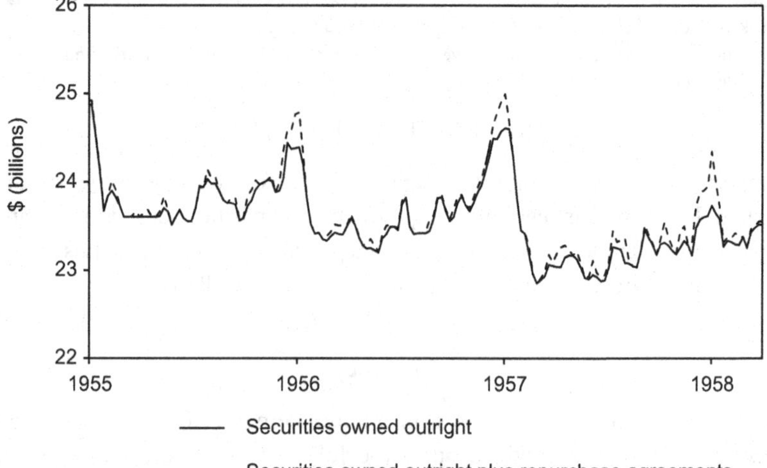

Chart 14.5 Treasury securities and repurchase agreements in the System Open Market Account. Weekly averages of daily figures.
Board of Governors of the Federal Reserve System (1976, table 10.1C).

The 1957 Markets annual report states that, at the beginning of 1957, the Desk "was engaged in absorbing a record return flow of reserves after the year end ... Year-end repurchase agreements were quickly liquidated and Treasury bills were sold aggressively or redeemed at maturity."[10]

[10] 1957 Annual Report of Open Market Operations, p. 1.

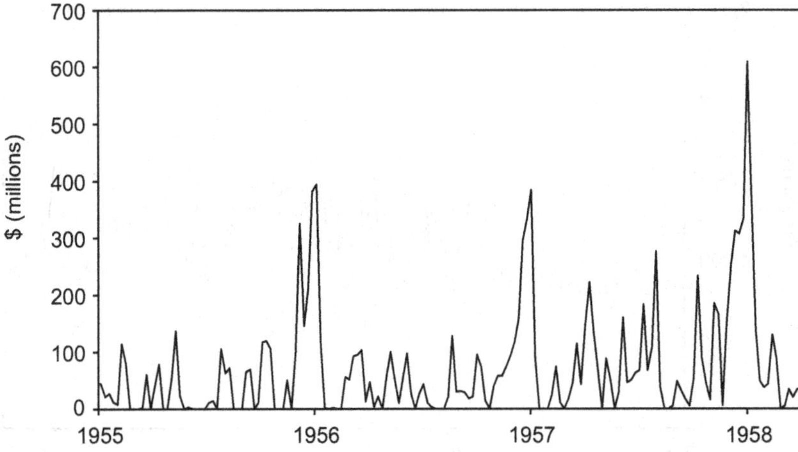

Chart 14.6 Repurchase agreements in the System Open Market Account. Weekly averages of daily figures.
Board of Governors of the Federal Reserve System (1976, table 10.1C).

Smaller spikes in currency demand, also associated with holiday periods but not readily apparent in Chart 14.4, were well known to market participants. The 1956 Markets annual report noted that "during the latter part of August and early September, the System Account engaged in a large-scale buying program. The purchases, aggregating more than $400 million, were designed to supply the banks with the reserves needed to carry the Treasury's new issue sold for cash in mid-August, and to offset the outflow of currency over the Labor Day week end."[11]

Float

Chart 14.7 shows a regular year-end spike in float that supplied reserves to the banking system and dampened (but did not eliminate) the need to expand the Open Market Account in December and to contract the Account in January. Smaller mid-month spikes are also evident. The latter were well known to System officials. Rouse, for example, noted at the July 9, 1957, FOMC meeting that he was likely to sell bills "to counter the usual [mid-month] float expansion."[12]

11 1956 Annual Report of Open Market Operations, p. 12.
12 Minutes of the Federal Open Market Committee, July 9, 1957, p. 6.

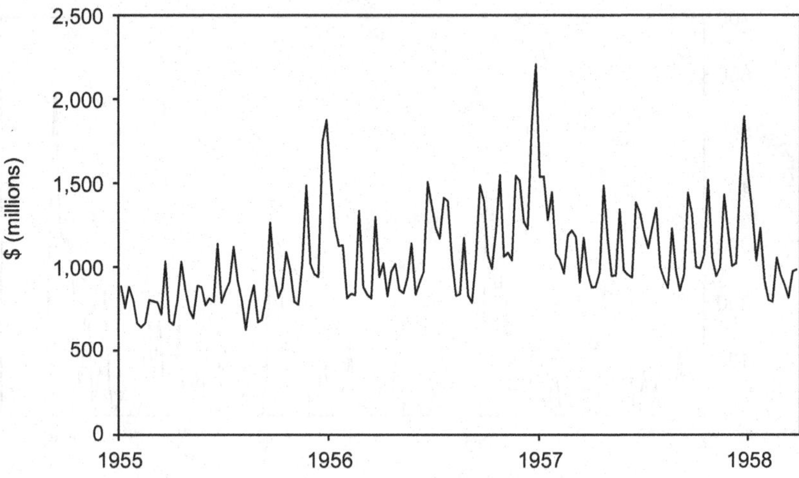

Chart 14.7 Float. Weekly averages of daily figures.
Board of Governors of the Federal Reserve System (1976, table 10.1C).

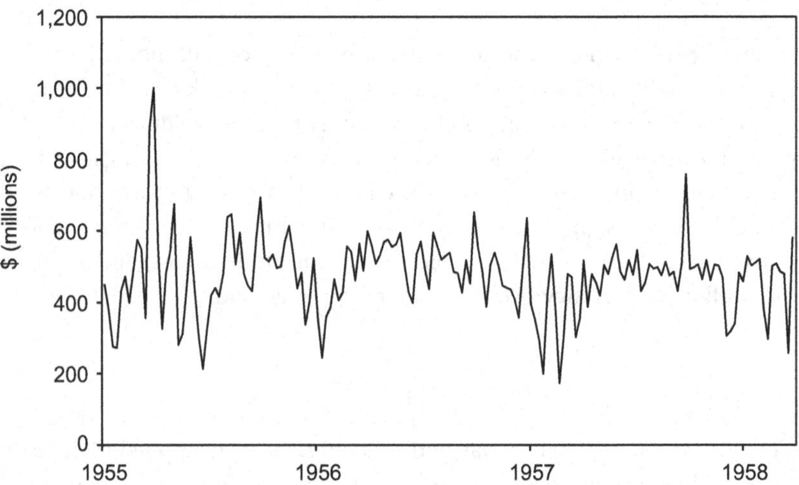

Chart 14.8 Treasury deposits at Federal Reserve Banks. Weekly averages of daily figures.
Board of Governors of the Federal Reserve System (1976, table 10.1C).

Treasury Balances at Federal Reserve Banks

Chart 14.8 shows the variation in Treasury balances at Federal Reserve Banks. The range of variation was smaller than the ranges for currency and float, but the variation was nevertheless consequential because it did not follow any regular pattern.

Forecasting Errors

Errors in forecasting short-run fluctuations in autonomous factors were distressingly common. The scale of the January 1957 reserves absorption program (noted in the text at footnote 10 above) was attributed to a variety of autonomous factors, "all of which supplied reserves in amounts that were not anticipated in the projections."[13]

Float was particularly difficult to forecast. The 1956 Markets annual report observed that purchases for the Open Market Account undertaken at the end of June had "overshot the mark, owing to an unexpectedly early and steep rise in float."[14] The 1957 report noted that "float declined less rapidly than expected during January, and, in general, its behavior was at substantial variance with the projections throughout a good part of the [first quarter of the year]."[15] In October 1957, Rouse explained to FOMC members that "the period around Columbus Day was always a difficult one for forecasting float. This year, open market operations were conducted on the expectation that float would rise immediately after the holiday. When it did not, the money market turned tighter ... than the Committee had intended."[16]

ACCOMMODATING TREASURY OFFERINGS

Tables 14.1 and 14.2 show Treasury offerings of coupon-bearing debt in 1956 and 1957, respectively. Nineteen fifty-six was much the lighter year, with five exchange offerings and one cash offering for a total of $25.9 billion. In contrast, 1957 saw eight exchange offerings and seven cash offerings for a total of $54.6 billion. Only one of the six issues sold in 1956 had a maturity materially more than one year, while seven of the fifteen issues sold in 1957 had maturities in excess of three years, including two bonds maturing in more than ten years.

For the FOMC, the most significant aspect of Treasury offerings in 1956 and most of 1957 was how to balance its tight monetary policy with the need to provide an accommodative environment when Treasury came to market. The 1956 Markets annual report observed that "the recurrent problem posed by Treasury financing operations in a generally unreceptive

[13] 1957 Annual Report of Open Market Operations, p. 9.

[14] 1956 Annual Report of Open Market Operations, p. 11.

[15] 1957 Annual Report of Open Market Operations, p. 10.

[16] Minutes of the Federal Open Market Committee, October 22, 1957, p. 5.

Table 14.1 *Treasury offerings of coupon-bearing debt in 1956.*

Security offered	Issue date	Maturity	Amount issued ($ billions)
March exchange offering			
11-month 2⅝% certificate	Mar. 15	Feb. 15, 1957	7.23
2¼-year 2⅞% note (reopening)	Mar. 15	Jun. 15, 1958	2.11
July exchange offering			
12-month 2¾% note	Jul. 25	Aug. 1, 1957	12.06
August cash offering			
7-month 2¾% tax anticipation certificate	Aug. 15	Mar. 22, 1957	3.22
November exchange offering			
7½-month 3¼% tax anticipation certificate	Dec. 3	Jun. 24, 1957	1.31
10-month 3¼% certificate	Dec. 3	Oct. 1, 1957	7.27

Treasury annual reports and offering circulars.

market environment of rising interest rates and growing money tightness" was an "important influence on the conduct of open market operations." The report further remarked that "the need to assure that [the Treasury's] financing program was successfully absorbed necessarily modified System open market operations."[17] When the Desk realized that it had over-shot the target level of reserves with its end-of-June purchases (noted earlier in the text at footnote 14), it undertook a large-scale program of bill sales and redemptions in July. The program ultimately drained some $536 million of reserves and would have been larger but for the need to maintain an even keel during the July financing.[18] In November and December 1956, the Desk bought more than $700 million of bills on an outright basis and, at times, lent more than $400 million on repurchase agreements to maintain an even keel during and following the November refunding, as well as to accomodate seasonal demands for currency.[19] Follow-on operations to drain reserves at the end of January 1957 were "impeded by the approach of a large refunding."[20]

[17] 1956 Annual Report of Open Market Operations, p. 4.
[18] 1956 Annual Report of Open Market Operations, p. 11.
[19] 1956 Annual Report of Open Market Operations, p. 14.
[20] 1957 Annual Report of Open Market Operations, p. 9.

Table 14.2 *Treasury offerings of coupon-bearing debt in 1957.*

Security offered	Issue date	Maturity	Amount issued ($ billions)
February exchange offering			
1-year 3⅜% certificate	Feb. 15	Feb. 14, 1958	8.42
3¼-year 3½% note	Feb. 15	May 15, 1960	1.45
March cash offering			
10½-month 3⅜% certificate	Mar. 28	Feb. 14, 1958	2.44
3-year 1½-month 3½% note	Mar. 28	May 15, 1960	0.94
May exchange offering			
11-month 3½% certificate	May 15	Apr. 15, 1958	2.35
4¾-year 3⅝% note	May 15	Feb. 15, 1962	0.65
July exchange offering			
4-month 3⅝% certificate	Aug. 1	Dec. 1, 1957	9.87
1-year 4% certificate	Aug. 1	Aug. 1, 1958	10.50
4-year 4% note	Aug. 1	Aug. 1, 1961	2.49
September cash offering			
10-month 4% certificate	Sep. 26	Aug. 1, 1958	0.93
4-year 11-month 4% note	Sep. 26	Aug. 15, 1962	2.00
12-year 4% bond	Oct. 1	Oct. 1, 1969	0.66
November exchange offering			
1-year 3¾% certificate	Dec. 2	Dec. 1, 1958	9.83
November cash offering			
5-year 3¾% note	Nov. 29	Nov. 15, 1962	1.14
17-year 3⅞% bond	Dec. 2	Nov. 15, 1974	0.65

Treasury annual reports and offering circulars.

The May 1957 Refunding

The tension between maintaining a restrictive monetary policy and the practical necessity of accommodating Treasury offerings came to a dramatic head in May 1957, when Treasury officials offered investors a choice between an eleven-month certificate and a 4¾-year note in exchange for $4.2 billion of a maturing note.[21] In what the *New York Times* described as a failed offering, the exchange suffered a 28 percent attrition rate and Treasury had to pay out $1.2 billion in cash to holders of the maturing note.[22]

[21] Federal Reserve Bank of New York Circular no. 4456, May 6, 1957.

[22] "28% Insist on Cash in U.S. Refunding," *New York Times*, May 11, 1957, p. 27.

The roots of the May debacle can be traced to a cash offering of $2.25 billion of 10½-month certificates and $750 million of 3-year 1½-month notes two months earlier.[23] At an FOMC meeting on March 26, Governor J. L. Robertson expressed his unhappiness with Rouse's management of the Open Market Account during the offering (which had closed on March 18), believing that Rouse failed to maintain an appropriate level of reserve stringency.[24] Rouse defended himself by claiming that "there were pressures in the market that were not apparent from the [reserves] figures presented," that Treasury faced a "serious situation" in the financing, that "there was a good deal of doubt in some quarters as to whether the offering would prove acceptable," and that "the situation had been 'touch and go' for several days."[25] Hayes thought the offering had succeeded only because money center banks had been willing to act as underwriters, purchasing the offered securities with a view to distribution at a later date. He cautioned that it was incumbent upon the Fed "to provide sufficient reserves to enable the banks to take up their subscriptions on March 28 without creating undue money market strains."[26]

Ignoring Hayes's advice, the Committee instructed Rouse to increase the level of restraint in advance of the March 28 issue date. As a result, banks were forced to borrow at the discount window to pay for the new securities. On April 16, Hayes observed that "there is no question that the market is a great deal tighter than it was three weeks ago."[27]

It was clear that the May refunding was in trouble a week before the Treasury announced the terms of the offering. In a telephone meeting on April 24, Martin informed the members of the Open Market Committee that Under Secretary of the Treasury W. R. Burgess had expressed "considerable alarm."[28] Rouse informed the Committee that Burgess was contemplating an extraordinary action: shifting $150 million to $200 million of Treasury balances at Federal Reserve Banks to depository commercial banks in an effort to ease money market conditions. He related Burgess's belief that "the Treasury could not have a successful refunding when a considerable portion of the securities to be refunded were held by commercial banks if these banks were heavily in debt and under pressure by the

[23] Federal Reserve Bank of New York Circular no. 4436, March 18, 1957.
[24] Minutes of the Federal Open Market Committee, March 26, 1957, pp. 3–7.
[25] Minutes of the Federal Open Market Committee, March 26, 1957, p. 6.
[26] Minutes of the Federal Open Market Committee, March 26, 1957, p. 21.
[27] Minutes of the Federal Open Market Committee, April 16, 1957, p. 11.
[28] Minutes of the Federal Open Market Committee, April 24, 1957, pp. 1–2.

System to get out of debt."[29] (At the time, member banks were borrowing about $950 million a day from the twelve Reserve Banks, down from $1.2 billion a day in the two preceding statement weeks.[30])

Burgess, the first manager of the System Open Market Account, could hardly have failed to appreciate that he was threatening to open a second, Treasury-controlled channel of reserves management. He tried to paper over the challenge to the System by suggesting "it might be unwise for the System to take overt action to reduce . . . net borrowed reserves . . . [but that] if the Treasury balances were reduced it would be taken in stride." Rouse stated that he had "made it clear [to Treasury officials] that I thought that the Treasury should not engage in such an open market operation."[31] Federal Reserve officials threatened to make offsetting sales of Treasury securities from the System Open Market Account, Burgess backed off, and the May financing proceeded without further incident, albeit also without great success.[32] Rouse characterized the episode as "an unhappy experience for the Treasury."[33]

The FOMC was left to ponder two questions in the wake of the failed offering: how to respond to the Treasury's threat to meddle in reserves management, and how to accommodate future Treasury offerings.

Some Committee members were furious with the Treasury's threat. Governor Robertson said it "represented an obvious and unjustifiable attempt to interfere with Federal Reserve credit policy." H. G. Leedy, the president of the Federal Reserve Bank of Kansas City, described it as "an act that was intended to circumvent the program being followed by the Committee."[34] However, Watrous Irons, president of the Federal Reserve Bank of Dallas, "doubted the wisdom of making it a major issue." He agreed the matter was important but noted also that "handling of the Treasury balance was within the province of the Treasury."[35] Irons suggested that Chairman Martin meet with Treasury Secretary Humphrey to

[29] Minutes of the Federal Open Market Committee, April 24, 1957, pp. 3–4.

[30] Board of Governors of the Federal Reserve System (1976, table 10.1C).

[31] Minutes of the Federal Open Market Committee, April 24, 1957, p. 4.

[32] 1957 Annual Report of Open Market Operations, p. 5, stating that "Another delicate situation developed late in April, when the Treasury began to run down its balances at the Reserve Banks in a deliberate attempt to ease the money market in advance of its May refunding. The balances were rebuilt, however, when it appeared that System sales might be undertaken as an offset."

[33] Minutes of the Federal Open Market Committee, May 28, 1957, p. 2.

[34] Minutes of the Federal Open Market Committee, May 7, 1957, pp. 22 and 28.

[35] Minutes of the Federal Open Market Committee, May 7, 1957, p. 34.

clear the air. The matter was quietly buried at a meeting of the two principals on May 23.[36]

The question of how to accommodate future Treasury offerings was not so easily resolved. Sitting in for Hayes at the May 7 FOMC meeting, William Treiber, the first vice president of the New York Bank, argued that "we cannot administer credit policy without regard to the Government securities market and to the financing requirements of the Treasury." He agreed that the Treasury "should price its securities in line with market rates," but that "when it does so – when it submits ... to the discipline of the market – the System has a responsibility to avoid action that may jeopardize the financing. We should then, as we have consistently since the accord, recognize that the initial impact of an operation as large as a Treasury financing may create temporary digestive disturbances with which we need be concerned."[37]

Treiber, like other Committee members, insisted that the predicate for System accommodation was Treasury's willingness to price its offerings in line with market prices. However, it was not always clear, even in retrospect, whether an offering was, in fact, priced in line with the market. When Chairman Martin stated in July that "it was clear that the Treasury underpriced the rate on its offering in May," Rouse responded that "the Treasury and the market felt that the [May] refunding ... was priced on the market."[38]

Subsequent Offerings in 1957

Treasury offerings in the second half of 1957 went more smoothly. Following Committee instructions to consider the large July financing a "critical operation," Rouse supported the financing with repurchase agreements on rights.[39] The offering of $11.9 billion of soon-to-mature certificates and notes suffered only a 6.3 percent attrition and $12.1 billion of maturing notes suffered an even lower 2.8 percent attrition.[40]

Market receptivity to Treasury offerings improved dramatically in the fall as economic activity weakened. In mid-September, the Treasury offered, for cash, $750 million of a ten-month certificate, $1.75 billion of a four-year eleven-month note, and $500 million of a twelve-year bond. The cover ratios were 4.1 on the certificate, 3.5 on the note, and a

[36] Minutes of the Federal Open Market Committee, May 28, 1957, pp. 8–9.
[37] Minutes of the Federal Open Market Committee, May 7, 1957, pp. 11–12.
[38] Minutes of the Federal Open Market Committee, July 9, 1957, p. 41.
[39] Minutes of the Federal Open Market Committee, July 30, 1957, p. 35.
[40] Federal Reserve Bank of New York Circular no. 4493, July 31, 1957.

remarkable 9.3 on the bond. An "elated" Treasury official observed that "there was much more interest in the long bonds than we anticipated, and much more than we were led to believe by our advisers."[41]

A combined cash and exchange offering in November did almost as well in the wake of a reduction in the discount rate at four Federal Reserve Banks just three days before the offerings were announced.[42] The Treasury received $7.8 billion of subscriptions for a $1.0 billion cash offering of five-year notes and $3.8 billion of subscriptions for a $500 million cash offering of seventeen-year bonds. A concurrent exchange offering of one-year certificates for $10 billion of maturing certificates suffered only a 1.4 percent attrition.[43] At the end of the year, the problem of accommodating Treasury offerings was in abeyance, albeit unresolved.

THE CONTINUING IMPORTANCE OF REPURCHASE AGREEMENTS

The annual reports of System open market operations for 1956 and 1957 show that the Desk continued to rely on repurchase agreements as an important instrument of monetary policy. The 1956 report, for example, noted a rebalancing of operations away from large outright transactions toward smaller, more frequent transactions and "heavy reliance on the repurchase agreement mechanism."[44] The rebalancing was consistent with the decline in liquidity typical of a period of rising interest rates (Chart 14.9).

[41] "Treasury Flooded with Orders for 12-Year 4% Bond, Suggesting Greater Availability of Investment Funds," *Wall Street Journal*, September 19, 1957, p. 3.

[42] Treasury delayed the announcement of the offering until after the discount rate reductions had been announced. "Treasury Plans $1 Billion Offering, $10 Billion Refinancing Today," *Wall Street Journal*, November 18, 1957, p. 16; "U.S. Trims Costs in Big Financing," *New York Times*, November 19, 1957, p. 49; and Meltzer (2009, p. 163).

[43] Federal Reserve Bank of New York Circular no. 4537, November 27, 1957.

[44] 1956 Annual Report of Open Market Operations, p. 2. See also p. 8 of the report, stating that

> "[f]ollowing mid-February, and until the increase in the discount rate two months later, open market operations were confined largely to smoothing out the seasonally changing availability of bank reserves, while maintaining net borrowed reserves in a broad range around the levels attained earlier in the year. Emphasis generally was placed on the repurchase agreement facility and there were relatively few outright transactions in the open market."

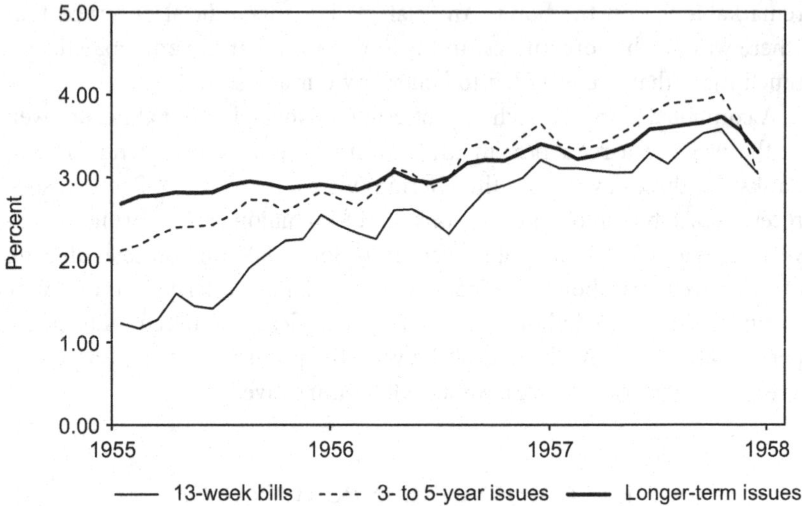

Chart 14.9 Treasury yields. Monthly averages.
Board of Governors of the Federal Reserve System (1976, tables 12.7A and 12.12A).

Repos proved particularly useful in providing relief when monetary restraint brought markets to the edge of orderly functioning. The 1957 report observed that "during the ... period from the end of March to mid-October, System open market operations were directed first toward creating an intensified degree of restraint and then, having done this, toward maintaining this tight rein on the money and securities markets. Repurchase agreements were generally relied upon to supply whatever relief was necessary whenever the biting effect of restraint threatened to produce serious maladjustments."[45] The report further noted that

> In maintaining the degree of restraint desired by the Committee from April to October, the Account Management faced the problem of achieving maximum effective tightness short of a point where orderly functioning of the money and securities markets would be impeded. Repurchase agreements were an ideal tool for the accomplishment of this objective, since they could be used to inject reserves, many times merely on an overnight basis, at the precise point where the market machinery was grating. ... During the twenty-nine statement weeks from the end of March to mid-October, there were only seven weekly statement weeks when there were not some new repurchase agreements written.[46]

[45] 1957 Annual Report of Open Market Operations, p. 1.
[46] 1957 Annual Report of Open Market Operations, p. 4.

Repos were not, however, without some limitations. Most importantly, they could not be used when dealers chose to limit their exposure to falling securities prices or when the Desk had to compete with other market participants actively seeking to lend on a short-term basis. The 1956 Markets annual report observed that

> [i]n the period from late May to the completion of the Treasury summer financing program in mid-August, there was some relaxation of the pressure on bank reserve positions. The Account Management would have preferred to use repurchase agreements to inject a part of these reserves, but dealers were able to finance their portfolios more conveniently in other ways.[47]

The 1957 report stated that,

> [r]eliance upon repurchase agreements as a principal instrument of open market operations when the money and securities markets are under severe pressure, however, is limited by the fact that dealer positions at such times frequently are so small that there is little opportunity to extend repurchase agreements, even when the System is willing and anxious to do so. Dealers naturally reduce their positions to minimum operating levels at times when interest rates are rising and are expected to go higher. Therefore, on frequent occasions during 1957 when the Management wished to supply funds to the market to meet a temporary need for reserves indicated by the projections, dealers' needs for funds were so small that it was not possible to put the reserves out in this fashion.[48]

The report concluded that while "the repurchase agreement is a valuable instrument in open market operations aimed at maintaining maximum restraint through releasing only minimum amounts of reserves," it nevertheless had "rather finite limits."[49]

[47] 1956 Annual Report of Open Market Operations, p. 11.
[48] 1957 Annual Report of Open Market Operations, p. 35.
[49] 1957 Annual Report of Open Market Operations, p. 35.

PART IV

SUMMER 1958 AND ITS CONSEQUENCES

The summer of 1958 was a turning point in Treasury debt management and Federal Reserve relations with the government securities market. The key events, described in Chapter 15, included a shake-out of speculative activity that triggered $600 million of Treasury purchases of its own debt to stabilize bond prices and a second sell-off that led the Federal Open Market Committee to declare a disorderly market and intervene with an additional $1.3 billion of purchases to avert a failed offering.

The events of summer 1958 led to several important innovations in Treasury debt management, including, as described in Chapter 16, the extension of regular and predictable bill auctions to the twenty-six-week and one-year sectors and the regularization of note and bond issuance to the mid-quarter refunding dates of February 15, May 15, August 15, and November 15.

The events of summer 1958 also triggered a study of the Treasury market by the Department of the Treasury and the Federal Reserve System (Chapter 17).[1] The study is important for its explicitly-stated

[1] U.S. Treasury and Federal Reserve System (1959, 1960a, and 1960b). Anderson and Martin (1959, p. 860) state that "developments in the Government securities market [in 1958] led the Treasury and the Federal Reserve System to undertake a joint study of current techniques and organization in that market." Friedman (1960, p. 60) states that the 1958 episode "stimulated the recent joint Treasury-Reserve study of the government security markets." The events of summer 1958 also led to the Meltzer and von der Linde (1960) study.

premise that the secondary market for government securities is affected by a public interest. Acceptance of that public interest led to the introduction of the reporting dealer program and the continuous public identification of dealers designated by the Federal Reserve Bank of New York as counterparties in open market operations.

15

The Summer 1958 Treasury Financings

A New York Reserve Bank study of the 1958 government securities market states that from mid-June to mid-August, the market "went through one of the most disorganized periods in its history . . . Price declines were exceedingly rapid and extensive, and trading at times was at a virtual standstill, leading to complaints that there was no market."[1] Market turmoil following a refunding in early June led the Treasury to repurchase $590 million of its own debt, including $456 million of a bond that it had just issued. A second price slide in mid-July prompted the FOMC to declare a "disorderly market" and authorize, for the first time since 1953, the purchase of notes and bonds for the System Open Market Account.

AN OVERVIEW OF 1958

After peaking in mid-1957 – the National Bureau of Economic Research locates a peak of economic activity in August of that year – the US economy slid off into a recession that, in its early stages, appeared quite ominous. A sharp deterioration of economic conditions in the beginning of 1958 seemed to confirm earlier predictions of a deep and prolonged contraction.[2] However, personal income and consumer spending held up better than expected and output bottomed out in April. By the end of the year aggregate production had recovered to the level reached in late 1957.[3]

Paralleling the trajectory of economic activity, monetary policy in 1958 passed through three distinct phases. From January to early March

[1] Federal Reserve Bank of New York (September 1958, p. 22).

[2] 1958 Annual Report of Open Market Operations, p. 1, and U.S. Treasury and Federal Reserve System (1960a, p. 7).

[3] 1958 Annual Report of Open Market Operations, p. 1.

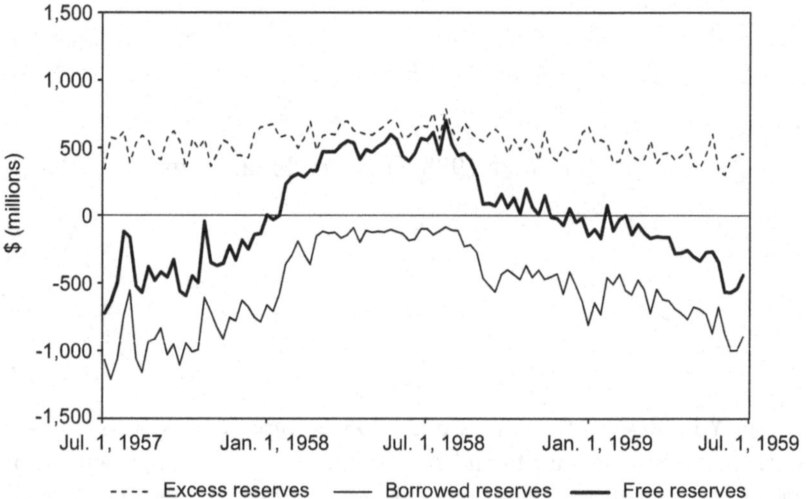

Chart 15.1 Excess reserves, borrowed reserves, and free reserves. Weekly averages of daily figures.
Board of Governors of the Federal Reserve System (1976, table 10.1C).

Federal Reserve officials focused on cushioning the ongoing contraction. Free reserves rose from zero at the beginning of the year to about $500 million in early March (Chart 15.1), the New York Fed lowered its discount rate from 3 percent to 2¼ percent (in two steps, on January 24 and March 7), and the Board of Governors reduced reserve requirement rates for demand deposits by ½ percent (at the end of February, Table 15.1).

Free reserves fluctuated between $400 million and $500 million from early March to early August as officials worked to maintain an ample supply of reserves. The Board of Governors reduced reserve requirements on demand deposits at country banks by another ½ percent, at reserve city banks by 1 percent, and at central reserve city banks by 1½ percent. On April 18, the New York Fed reduced its discount rate to 1¾ percent.

The third phase, from early August to the end of the year, saw officials tightening reserve availability as the economy began to recover. The New York Reserve Bank raised its discount rate to 2 percent on September 12 and to 2½ percent on November 7. Free reserves were back to zero by the end of the year.

Money market rates (Chart 15.2) and longer-term Treasury yields (Chart 15.3) followed a broadly similar pattern: declining during the first half of the year and rising with the onset of recovery in the second half.

Table 15.1 *Federal Reserve Bank of New York discount rates and reserve requirement rates for net demand deposits, 1958.*

Date of change	FRBNY discount rate (percent)	Reserve requirement rates: Central reserve city banks (percent)	Reserve requirement rates: Reserve city banks (percent)	Reserve requirement rates: Country banks (percent)
Effective beginning of year	3	20	18	12
Jan. 24	2¾			
Feb. 27 and Mar. 1		19½	17½	11½
Mar. 7	2¼			
Mar. 20 and Apr. 1		19	17	11
Apr. 17		18½		
Apr. 18	1¾			
Apr. 24		18	16½	
Sep. 12	2			
Nov. 7	2½			

Board of Governors of the Federal Reserve System (1976, tables 10.4 and 12.1A).

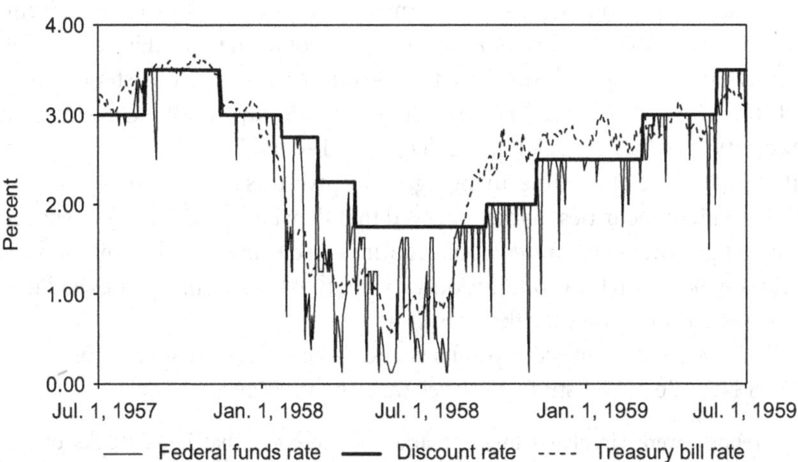

Chart 15.2 Federal funds rate, thirteen-week Treasury bill rate, and Federal Reserve Bank of New York discount rate. Daily figures.

Federal Reserve Statistical Release H.15 and Board of Governors of the Federal Reserve System (1976, table 12.1A).

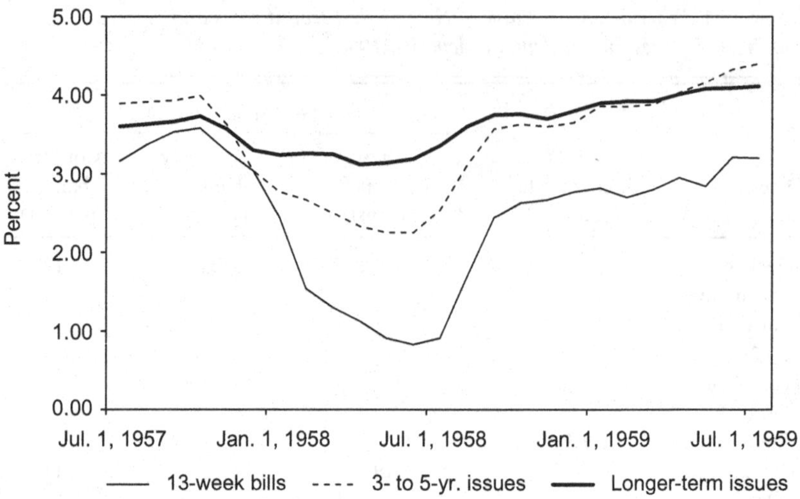

Chart 15.3 Treasury yields. Monthly averages.
Board of Governors of the Federal Reserve System (1976, tables 12.7A and 12.12A).

RUN-UP TO THE JUNE FINANCING

The June Treasury financing was preceded by nine months of falling interest rates and rising note and bond prices. (Table 14.2 shows the Treasury's offerings of coupon-bearing debt in 1957, Table 15.2 shows the 1958 offerings.) Yields on intermediate-term Treasury debt fell from 3.93 percent in September 1957 to a low of 2.25 percent the following May. Five rounds of Treasury offerings during that interval produced consistent gains (Table 15.3). The Treasury-Federal Reserve Study of the Government Securities Market – hereafter, the "Treasury-Federal Reserve Study" – states that "on the eve of the June financing, many investors in and observers of the Government securities market believed that they had good reason to expect that long-term interest rates would continue to decline. . . . The opinion was widespread, given the economic outlook . . ., that long-term . . . rates had not yet reached their lows for the year."[4]

The record of consistent profits sparked the interest of speculators. The 1958 New York Fed study observes that, in late May,

> . . . reports were circulated in the market to the effect that large blocks of . . . securities maturing in June were being purchased as "rights" by speculators. . . .

[4] U.S. Treasury and Federal Reserve System (1960a, p. 21).

Table 15.2 *Treasury offerings of coupon-bearing debt in 1958.*

Security offered	Issued	Maturity	Amount issued ($ billions)
February exchange offering			
1-year 2½% certificate	Feb. 14	Feb. 14, 1959	9.77
6-year 3% bond	Feb. 14	Feb. 15, 1964	3.83
32-year 3½% bond	Feb. 14	Feb. 15, 1990	1.73
February cash offering			
8½-year 3% bond	Mar. 10	Aug. 15, 1966	1.48
April cash offering			
4-year 10-month 2⅝% note	Apr. 15	Feb. 15, 1963	3.97
June cash offering			
27-year 3¼% bond	Jun. 18	May 15, 1985	1.13
June exchange offering			
11-month 1¼% certificate	Jun. 16	May 15, 1959	1.82
6⅔-year 2⅝% bond	Jun. 16	Feb. 15, 1965	7.38
July exchange offering			
1-year 1⅝% certificate	Aug. 1	Aug. 1, 1959	13.50
July cash offering			
7½-month 1½% tax anticipation certificate	Aug. 6	Mar. 24, 1959	3.57
September cash offering			
13-month 3½% note	Oct. 10	Nov. 15, 1959	1.18
November exchange offering			
11½-month 3⅜% certificate	Dec. 1	Nov. 15, 1959	7.71
2½-year 3⅝% note	Dec. 1	May 15, 1961	4.08

Treasury annual reports and offering circulars.

The success of the preceding ... offerings, and the sizable premiums on the resulting new issues, inspired visions of even greater profits on the new issues arising out of the June refunding, which was expected to include a long-term issue as a means of ... extending the maturity of the public debt.[5]

The Treasury-Federal Reserve Study states similarly that,

In light of the widespread knowledge that subscribers in the ... February refunding had profited handsomely on exchanges into the new intermediate- and long-term bonds issued in that operation, advance rumors that similar securities might be offered in the June refunding stimulated active interest in the maturing June "rights."

[5] Federal Reserve Bank of New York (September 1958, p. 4).

Table 15.3 *Price appreciation on Treasury notes and bonds issued between September 1957 and April 1958. All of the notes and bonds were originally offered at par for cash or in a par-for-par exchange for securities due to be redeemed.*

Security	Issue date	Price twenty days after issue	Price on May 23, 1958
September 1957 cash offering			
4% note maturing 8/15/1962	Sep. 26, 1957	100	106^{28}
4% bond maturing 10/1/1969	Oct. 1, 1957	100^{2}	109^{14}
November 1957 cash offering			
3¾% note maturing 11/15/1962	Nov. 29, 1957	103^{4}	106^{6}
3⅞% bond maturing 11/15/1974	Dec. 2, 1957	106^{16}	109^{10}
February 1958 exchange offering			
3% bond maturing 2/15/1964	Feb. 14, 1958	101^{5}	103^{4}
3½% bond maturing 2/15/1990	Feb. 14, 1958	102^{16}	105^{24}
February 1958 cash offering			
3% bond maturing 8/15/1966	Mar 10, 1958	101^{11}	102^{26}
April 1958 cash offering			
2⅝% note maturing 2/15/1963	Apr. 15, 1958	101	101^{4}

"U.S. Government and Agency Bonds" column of *New York Times.*

> On the basis of these rumors, prices of the "rights" were bid to premiums of about ⅜ of a point late in April and remained close to that level through all of May and the refunding exchange period which occurred from June 4-6. Occasionally in April and through virtually all of May and early June, yields on "rights" were at negative levels, reflecting speculative appraisal of acquiring whatever longer term issues might be offered in the exchange.[6]
>
> As the refunding grew closer, market rumors indicated a steady build-up of speculative positions in "rights," particularly on the part of investors not normally active in the market who were allegedly financing the bulk of their acquisitions on credit.[7]

Two days before the announcement of the June financing, John Larkin, an assistant vice president at the Federal Reserve Bank of New York responsible for supervising the execution of open market operations, remarked on the "continuing wave of speculation in the Government securities market."[8]

6 Cecchetti (1988) examines the phenomenon of rights trading at negative yields.
7 U.S. Treasury and Federal Reserve System (1960a, pp. 23–24).
8 Minutes of the Federal Open Market Committee, May 27, 1958, p.3.

THE JUNE FINANCING

On Thursday, May 29, Treasury officials announced the terms of the June refunding:[9]

- A cash subscription offering of $1 billion of twenty-seven-year, 3¼ percent bonds at 100½ for settlement on Wednesday, June 18. The subscription books would be open on Tuesday, June 3, for one day only. Subscribers had to make a down-payment of twenty percent of the amount subscribed.
- A par-for-par exchange offering of 11-month, 1¼ percent certificates and 6⅔-year, 2⅝ percent bonds to refinance $9.6 billion of debt maturing or called for redemption on June 15, for settlement on Monday, June 16. The subscription books would open on Wednesday, June 4, and remain open for three days.

The requirement for a 20 percent down-payment shifted speculative interest from the 27-year bonds to the 6⅔-year bonds. Interest came from investors who had held the rights for some time as well as from speculators who purchased the rights more recently. With respect to the former group of investors, Girard Spencer, a senior partner at Salomon Brothers & Hutzler, later explained to the Joint Economic Committee that "banks held the maturing security. They wanted to keep in short-term securities, but they felt they could make a profit by turning in their maturing rights [for the intermediate-term bonds]. There was no cash involved in this in any way and no margin. They just felt they could take in the exchange the longer of these two securities and, in turn, [sell] it in the market at a profit to themselves to buy in their place the short-run securities."[10]

Speculators who bought rights with borrowed funds planned to exchange the rights for the 6⅔-year bonds and sell the bonds at a profit. The strategy looked especially attractive because the virtually risk-free rights could be financed at low interest on little margin. (However, creditors were certain to call for additional margin following completion of the

[9] Federal Reserve Bank of New York Circular no. 4605, May 29, 1958.

[10] Joint Economic Committee (1959, Part 6B, p. 1561). Spencer further observed that "You had a 1-year 1¼ percent maturity, and you had this 6-year-odd-month, 2⅝. The 1¼ percent rate was fairly unattractive at the time. So a number of corporations and a great many banks, too, that eventually wanted to move into the 1¼, and wanted to stay in the short-term area, decided that because of this great spread in yield and because of the outlook for the market as they saw it at that time, they could afford [to] take the longer issue and retrade it in the market later to get into the position they wanted to get into."

exchange offering in light of the greater risk of the longer-term bonds acquired in exchange for the rights.[11])

Results of the Financing

On Tuesday, June 3, Treasury officials received subscriptions for $2.6 billion of the 27-year bonds. They allotted savings-type investors (including mutual savings banks, savings and loan associations, credit unions, insurance companies, and pension funds) 60 percent of their subscriptions; commercial banks received 40 percent; all others received 25 percent.[12] The *Wall Street Journal* reported that Treasury officials were "well-pleased with the outcome of the ... offering," that "the amount of subscriptions was about in line with their expectations," and that "speculation in the issue had been held to a minimum."[13]

Speculative interest was clearly evident in the exchange offering. Following the close of the subscription books on June 6, officials announced that investors had agreed to exchange 96.3 percent of the maturing debt, leaving attrition at an unusually low 3.7 percent. Investors opted to take $7.4 billion of the 6⅔-year bond and $1.8 billion of the eleven-month certificate.[14] The *New York Times* called the demand for the bond "a surprise."[15] Treasury and Federal Reserve officials later stated that the disproportionate take-down, "more than double what had been estimated by the financial community or by Government agencies as

[11] Federal Reserve Bank of New York (September 1958, pp. 12–13), stating that

> "one of the complications connected with the financing of 'rights' in the June refunding arose from the fact that many lenders required only small margins against the June 'rights' – as would be expected on such a very short-term obligation. However, when borrowers exchanged the 'rights' for the new [6⅔-year] bonds on June 16, the lenders immediately called for more margin."

[12] Federal Reserve Bank of New York Circular no. 4607, June 5, 1958; and Circular no. 4609, June 10, 1958. No subscriber received less than the lesser of $5,000 of bonds and the amount of bonds subscribed.

[13] "Treasury's $1 Billion Long-Term Issue is 2½ Times Oversubscribed," *Wall Street Journal*, June 6, 1958, p. 13.

[14] Federal Reserve Bank of New York Circular no. 4608, June 10, 1958, and Circular no. 4612, June 13, 1958; and "Attrition Down to 3.7% in Treasury Financing," *New York Times*, June 14, 1958, p. 26.

[15] "U.S. Notes Further Stretching For Maturity of National Debt," *New York Times*, June 11, 1958, p. 49. See also U.S. Treasury and Federal Reserve System (1959, pp. 11–12), stating that "announcement of the size of the exchange into [6⅔-year] bonds represented a distinct surprise to the market."

true investor demand," indicated that "a sizable amount of the newly acquired securities were speculatively held."[16]

THE AFTERMATH OF THE JUNE FINANCING

Around the time of the settlement of the exchange offering on Monday, June 16, information began to appear that, contrary to expectations, the economy was strengthening. FOMC economist Ralph Young told the Committee on June 17 that the most recent information confirmed that "bottoming out of the recession is in fact occurring."[17]

On Thursday, June 19, the *New York Herald Tribune* headlined an article on the first page of its business section with the claim that "Fed Sees Turning Point at Hand." The article stated that "the Federal Reserve System has reached a major turning point in its anti-recession drive and is slowing the pace at which it has been pressing toward easy money." It went on to say that "the shift in credit policy suggests that the end of the recession decline in interest rates is in sight and perhaps is at hand. This would mean that the prices of bonds and other fixed income obligations will go little if any higher."[18]

As shown in Chart 15.4, the price of the new 6⅔-year bond fell eleven thirty-seconds, to 99^{22}, on June 19, and the price of the new 27-year bond fell fourteen thirty-seconds, to 100^{8}, in what the *Wall Street Journal* characterized as "heavy trading." Both closing prices were below the original offering prices. The *Journal* reported that "observers described the heaviest selling pressure as coming from speculative interests which had taken on large blocks of securities from the Treasury's recent financing."[19]

Beginning Friday, June 20, significant numbers of leveraged market participants were forced to liquidate their positions. The Treasury-Federal Reserve Study observed that

16 Anderson and Martin (1959, p. 864). See also Federal Reserve Bank of New York (September 1958, p. 6), stating that "the market had previously estimated that about $4 billion of [the 6⅔-year bonds] would be issued," and that "it was evident that excessive amounts had been taken by speculators, and also, very surprisingly, by corporations which normally would have exchanged for the one-year 1¼ percent certificates."

17 Minutes of the Federal Open Market Committee, June 17, 1958, p. 4.

18 "Fed Sees Turning Point at Hand," *New York Herald Tribune*, June 19, 1958, p. B4.

19 "Long-Term Treasurys, Top Corporates Lower in Active Trading," *Wall Street Journal*, June 20, 1958, p. 11. See also "The Speculators Get Squeezed," *New York Times*, June 20, 1958, p. 32.

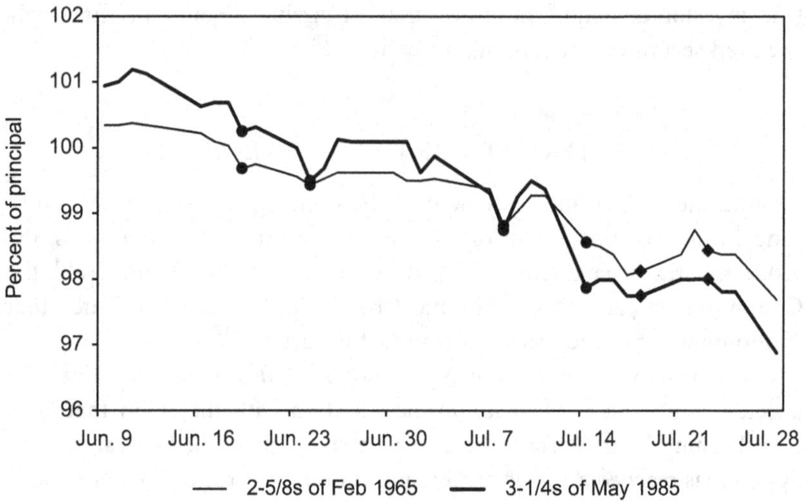

Chart 15.4 Treasury bond prices, June 9, 1958, to July 28, 1958. Average of dealer bid and offer prices. The balls mark days of unusual market turbulence: June 19, June 24, July 8, and July 14. The diamonds mark the beginning and end of the special purchase authority approved by the FOMC on July 18, 1958.
New York Times

> [b]ecause the narrow margins on some credit financing of the [6⅔-year] bonds were ... quickly wiped out, lenders were forced to make margin calls almost immediately to keep the value of collateral backing their financing from falling below loan value.... Although many had the financial resources to meet the calls – and many did so in the hope of recouping their potential losses in a subsequent market rally – others were unwilling to put up more margin and moved quickly to sell out.... Each significant new drop in prices elicited new margin calls which, in turn, prompted further liquidation and led to further decline.[20]

Liquidity broke down as dealers were unable to identify market-clearing prices. In a later statement to the Joint Economic Committee, Treasury Secretary Robert Anderson and Board of Governors Chairman William McChesney Martin observed that "there were times in [the second half of June] when dealers in order to protect their own capital positions would accept large-size orders to sell only on an agency basis, promising to make the best effort possible to carry out the customers' requests."[21]

[20] U.S. Treasury and Federal Reserve System (1960a, pp. 79–80).
[21] Anderson and Martin (1959, p. 866).

The Treasury Enters the Market

In an attempt to cushion the consequences of investor efforts to delever,[22] Treasury officials began to buy the 6⅔-year bond for government trust funds and (even though they had just issued the bond) for retirement.[23] The 1958 New York Fed study states that the Treasury "set out aggressively to purchase the [6⅔-year bond] on a declining price scale in an effort to cushion the downward price movement and to achieve more stability in the market." By June 25 officials had purchased "a substantial amount of [the] issue, as well as smaller amounts of other issues which were pressing on the market."[24] Thereafter, the price of the bond declined more slowly, to 99^{12}, on July 7.

Trading on July 8

The bond market hit another air pocket on Tuesday, July 8. With little selling pressure but "an almost total absence of buying"[25] the price of both the 6⅔-year bond and the 27-year bond fell eighteen thirty-seconds of a percent, to 98^{26} and 98^{24}, respectively. Dealers attributed the decline to continuing liquidation of speculative positions.[26]

[22] See "Long-Term Treasurys Fall Sharply," *Wall Street Journal*, June 24, 1958, p. 17, stating that "most of the recent steep decline in Treasury mart had been attributed to sales by speculators of securities acquired in the recent Federal financing," and "Speculator Liquidation Continues to Depress Long-Term Treasurys," *Wall Street Journal*, June 25, 1958, p. 16, reporting that "liquidation [of] speculative holdings of securities obtained in the Treasury's recent financing continued to press hard upon the market."

[23] "Treasury Lessens Squeeze on Bonds," *New York Times*, July 10, 1958, p. 37, reporting that Secretary Anderson "authorized purchase of [the 6⅔-year bond] for retirement so as to reduce it to an amount which can be more readily absorbed by the market"; and "Treasury Buys Back $589.5 Million of 2⅝% Bond Issue Sold in June," *Wall Street Journal*, July 10, 1958, p. 5, noting that Treasury purchases "to retire a specific issue were on the unusual side."

[24] Federal Reserve Bank of New York (September 1958, p. 7). The Daily Statement of the United States Treasury for June 30, 1958, shows (p. 7) that the Treasury issued $7,356 million of the 6⅔-year bond and retired $86 million of the bond by June 30. The July 31 statement shows (p. 7) $7,386 million issued and $491 million retired. The differences from June 30 can be attributed to reporting and settlement delays as well as to additional purchases in July. The August 29 statement shows substantially the same figures as July 31: $7,387 million issued and $491 million retired.

[25] "Treasury Bonds Fall Sharply," *New York Times*, July 9, 1958, p. 36.

[26] "Long-Term Treasurys Drop Again on Further Selling by Speculators," *Wall Street Journal*, July 9, 1958, p. 16; and "Treasury Bonds Fall Sharply," *New York Times*, July 9, 1958, p. 36.

During a regularly scheduled FOMC meeting that convened just as trading was getting under way, Robert Rouse, the manager of the Open Market Account, observed that "the Government securities market has been in a poor state in recent weeks." He took note of the "heavy volume of speculation" in the 6⅔-year bond but attributed rising yields "more fundamentally [to] the feeling of investors that economic conditions are improving and that recovery is in the making."[27]

Treasury Reveals Its Purchases

The next day, July 9, Treasury officials announced that since the settlement of the exchange offerings they had purchased $589.5 million of the 6⅔-year bonds, including $133.5 million for government trust funds and the balance for retirement. They justified the purchases by noting that the disproportionate demand for the bond in the refunding had contributed to fundamental market imbalances:

> The weight of an issue of [the size of the 6⅔-year bond], which was primarily adapted to commercial bank investors, together with large acquisitions of this issue by temporary holders [i.e., speculators], exerted a disturbing effect on the price structure in the market for outstanding public debt issues. Under these circumstances ... Secretary Anderson authorized the purchase of this issue for retirement so as to reduce it to an amount which can be more readily absorbed by the market."[28]

The *Wall Street Journal* reported that Treasury officials "did not think the bond market had gotten to the disorderly stage" but were concerned that it "would have become disorderly had they not stepped in and 'removed the overhang of speculative issues.'"[29] The 6⅔-year bonds closed at 99^{1}, up seven thirty-seconds, rose another eight thirty-seconds on July 10, and held steady at that level on Friday, July 11. The market appeared to have stabilized in advance of the next Treasury financing, due to be announced on July 17.

IRAQ AND LEBANON

During the early morning hours of Monday, July 14, US news outlets began reporting that the pro-Western king of Iraq had been overthrown

[27] Minutes of the Federal Open Market Committee, July 8, 1958, p. 3.

[28] "Treasury Lessens Squeeze on Bonds," *New York Times*, July 10, 1958, p. 37.

[29] "Treasury's New Exchange Offering May be Mostly Short-Term Issues," *Wall Street Journal*, July 11, 1958, p. 18.

in a coup.[30] The news, and the prospect of US military intervention, led to a sharp sell-off in the Treasury market. The 6⅔-year bond fell twenty-three thirty-seconds to close at 98^{18}; the 27-year bond fell 1½ points to close at 97^{28}.

At 9 a.m. on Tuesday, July 15, President Dwight Eisenhower announced that he had ordered a contingent of US Marines into Lebanon.[31] Thirty minutes later, Chairman Martin convened an emergency telephone meeting of the Federal Open Market Committee. Rouse informed the Committee that price declines had continued in after-hours trading on Monday and that there was little evidence of any buying interest. He expressed concern that developments in the Middle East might lead to a "total bear market," one characterized by a "virtual absence of buyers." Referring to the landing of Marines in Lebanon just then being reported on the Dow Jones "broad tape" (the quickest source of news at the time), Rouse asked whether he should intervene in the market.

Following a brief conversation with Treasury officials on another line, Rouse informed the Committee that the Department had authorized the Open Market Desk to purchase up to $85 million of Treasury securities for departmental purposes if needed "to avoid a sheer drop in prices without any market activity." Rouse suggested that the Committee wait and see what developed before acting.[32]

When the Committee reconvened at 11 a.m., Rouse reported that the market was holding its own, that trading was not disorderly, and that the Desk had purchased only $15 million of securities pursuant to the Treasury's authorization. The Committee refrained from taking any action on its own.[33]

THE JULY REFUNDING

On Thursday, July 17, Treasury officials announced the terms of the July refunding.[34] To refinance $11.5 billion of certificates maturing on August

[30] "President Bids U.N. Act Today on Mideast After Pro-Nasser Coup Outs Iraq's King; U.S. May Intervene; Britain Alerts Troops," *New York Times*, July 15, 1958, p. 1, noting that "the overthrow of King Faisal [of Iraq] was reported in late editions of Monday's *New York Times*."

[31] Shulimson (1966, p. 12), and "Eisenhower Sends Marines into Lebanon; Calls for a U.N. Force to Replace Them; Soviet Charges Move Threatens New War," *New York Times*, July 16, 1958, p. 1.

[32] Minutes of the Federal Open Market Committee, July 15, 1958, pp. 1–5.

[33] Minutes of the Federal Open Market Committee, July 15, 1958, pp. 5–8.

[34] Federal Reserve Bank of New York Circular no. 4620, July 17, 1958.

1 and $4.7 billion of two bonds called for early redemption on September 15,[35] the Treasury offered a one-year, 1⅝ percent certificate, for settlement on August 1. The *New York Times* reported that officials limited the offering to a one-year certificate because the bond market "needed a rest."[36]

Friday, July 18

At about noon on Friday, July 18, Rouse received a call from Under Secretary of the Treasury Julian Baird. Prices in the Treasury market were "drifting lower," Baird said, and "a condition was developing which the Treasury could not, in its opinion, hope to deal with." As Rouse subsequently related to the FOMC during a 1 p.m. conference call, Baird thought the problem "was a responsibility of the Federal Reserve System." More particularly, "while the Treasury felt that it had some justification in helping the market for the [6⅔-year bonds], it did not feel justified in easing the market down in other issues. The Treasury felt that this meant going into the market on a broad basis and that the Federal Reserve had a responsibility."[37]

Rouse told the Committee that trading was not disorderly, although it was heading in that direction. He saw a "threat to the impending Treasury financing," urged the Committee to "think in terms of a national emergency involving international affairs as against a purely domestic situation," and suggested that the Committee "authorize purchases of bonds for the [System Open Market] Account ... in order to steady the market."[38] Rouse further suggested that the Committee defer until Monday any decision on whether to support the refunding.

Al Hayes, the president of the Federal Reserve Bank of New York, admitted that "he had never quite understood what a disorderly market was" but nevertheless thought the market was pretty close to disorderly. In view of the "international situation" and Treasury's concern with the "incipient failure of its financing," he backed Rouse's recommended course of action.[39]

35 The redemption notice is reproduced in Federal Reserve Bank of New York Circular no. 4600, May 14, 1958.

36 "Treasury Offers a Big 1-Year Issue," *New York Times*, July 18, 1958, p. 29.

37 Minutes of the Federal Open Market Committee, July 18, 1958, 1:00 p.m., pp. 1–2.

38 Minutes of the Federal Open Market Committee, July 18, 1958, 1:00 p.m., pp. 2–5.

39 Minutes of the Federal Open Market Committee, July 18, 1958, 1:00 p.m., pp. 4 and 5.

Governors A. L. Mills and J. L. Robertson felt otherwise. Mills thought that Rouse's plan "would merely constitute temporizing" and "would do very little to restore confidence in the market. When it became known publicly – as it certainly would – that the Federal Reserve was buying other than bills for its own account, he feared that if there should be a disorderly market by Monday, the correction of it would have been seriously handicapped by temporizing and fluttering around the edges ... with minor purchases." On the other hand, Mills was "entirely willing to proclaim a disorderly market and to intervene vigorously in all areas of the market." (In the absence of a declaration of a disorderly market, note and bond purchases, as opposed to purchases of bills and short-term certificates, would breach the "bills preferably" doctrine. However, if the Committee concluded that a disorderly market existed it could authorize bond purchases without breaching that doctrine under the clause permitting such purchases when needed to correct a disorderly market.[40]) Robertson likewise declined to support a bond purchase program "on the strength of a merely incipient disorderly market," but "would not substitute his judgment for that of Mr. Rouse regarding the existence of a disorderly market; if Mr. Rouse should conclude that the market was disorderly, he would go along with the suggestion of Mr. Mills."[41]

Chairman Martin voted for Rouse's proposal "reluctantly"[42] and the other Committee members went along as well. With Mills and Robertson dissenting, and without declaring a disorderly market, the Committee authorized the purchase of up to $50 million "of Government securities at the discretion of the Manager of the System Open Market Account ... wherever the Manager deemed it appropriate in order to stabilize the market."[43] In so doing the Committee explicitly breached its "bills preferably" operating principle.

Barely an hour later the Committee was back in session. Rouse explained that "selling in the Government securities market was increasing and spreading through the list. Bids were disappearing and about the only bids were those put in by the System. Indications were that volume was getting to be considerable."[44] John Larkin elaborated on the deteriorating situation:

[40] See text at footnote 10 in Chapter 7 above.
[41] Minutes of the Federal Open Market Committee, July 18, 1958, 1:00 p.m., pp. 6–7 and 10.
[42] Minutes of the Federal Open Market Committee, July 18, 1958, 1:00 p.m., p. 9.
[43] Minutes of the Federal Open Market Committee, July 18, 1958, 1:00 p.m., pp. 10–11.
[44] Minutes of the Federal Open Market Committee, July 18, 1958, 2:30 p.m., pp. 1–2.

> At the conclusion of the last Committee meeting the [Desk] was informed by several leaders in the business that there were almost no bids, particularly on Treasury issues in the critical list, including the [6⅔-year bonds] . . . Until recently, the selling seemed to be mostly speculative-type selling. However, with prices falling and dealers withdrawing their bids, there were reports of increasing institutional selling. . . . Dealers were reporting that the market was tending to feed on itself, and holders, including institutional investors, were interested in selling.[45]

Larkin went on to say that "if the present atmosphere were to continue and prices moved downward . . . the supply of securities overhanging the market would increase substantially. There was the danger of a snowballing movement."

Rouse told the Committee that "he would now have to call the market disorderly," that the $50 million authorized earlier in the afternoon was no longer adequate, and that he "would like to have the views of Messrs. Mills and Robertson [for vigorous intervention] considered by the Committee."[46] (Box 15.1 describes the characterization of a disorderly market provided in the 1958 Markets annual report.)

Individual committee members voiced their support. Hayes agreed with Rouse's assessment of a disorderly market.[47] Watrous Irons, president of the Federal Reserve Bank of Dallas, stated that the existence of a disorderly market meant that "means must be taken by the System to restore stability," that the System "could not stand by and let the market move on its own." He pronounced himself ready "to take aggressive measures."[48] Martin proposed that the Committee give Rouse "maximum discretion to handle the situation in the way he thought best."[49]

Following a unanimous vote to authorize "purchase for the System Open Market Account in the open market, *without limitation*, Government securities in addition to short-term Government Securities,"[50] the Committee released, at 3 p.m.,[51] a public announcement that "[i]n view of the conditions in the U.S. Government securities market, the Federal Open Market Committee has instructed the Manager of the Open Market

[45] Minutes of the Federal Open Market Committee, July 18, 1958, 2:30 p.m., p. 2.

[46] Minutes of the Federal Open Market Committee, July 18, 1958, 2:30 p.m., p. 3.

[47] Minutes of the Federal Open Market Committee, July 18, 1958, 2:30 p.m., pp. 3–4.

[48] Minutes of the Federal Open Market Committee, July 18, 1958, 2:30 p.m., p. 4.

[49] Minutes of the Federal Open Market Committee, July 18, 1958, 2:30 p.m., p. 7.

[50] Minutes of the Federal Open Market Committee, July 18, 1958, 2:30 p.m., p. 8. Emphasis added.

[51] "Federal Reserve to Buy Longer-Term Issues in Move to Bolster Sagging Government Bond Market," *Wall Street Journal*, July 21, 1958, p. 3.

Box 15.1 Identifying a Disorderly Market.

The 1958 Annual Report of Open Market Operations included an illuminating discussion of how Bank officials identified a disorderly market.[1] The discussion began by noting that

> [t]he generally accepted definition of disorderly market conditions envisions a situation in which selling 'feeds on itself,' that is, a situation in which a fall in prices, instead of eliciting an increase in the amount of securities demanded and a decrease in the amount supplied, elicits the reverse, a falling away of bids and a rise in the number and size of offerings. Temporarily there is no price level which will clear the market.

The report agreed that such conditions were "unquestionably present" on the afternoon of Friday, July 18.

The report cautioned that "the presence of . . . technical conditions is not always enough to warrant a finding of 'disorderly conditions' and that other factors which accompany them or cause them must be considered." More specifically, the FOMC, "in arriving at its finding of 'disorderly conditions' last July was influenced not only by the rapid falling away of prices in the face of a multiplication of offerings but also by the threat of almost certain failure in a major Treasury refunding operation and by the emergence of a highly precarious international political and military situation." The report concluded that "price movement alone would not ordinarily justify a finding that a disorderly market exists (although such a movement would nevertheless require careful consideration of its causes and possible consequences)" and that "even rapid price change accompanied by minimal trading might not constitute a disorderly market condition if increased offerings were not being pressed on the market and, most important, if the price adjustment [was] occurring in an atmosphere free of panic."

The report suggested that three conditions would "ordinarily have to exist to justify a finding of disorder:

1. spiraling price changes that tend to 'feed upon themselves,'
2. a trading vacuum accompanied by a build-up in the number and size of offerings, and
3. a disorganized market psychology."

[1] 1958 Annual Report of Open Market Operations, pp. 37–39. The report also discussed the character of open market operations following a declaration of a disorderly market and the problem of disengaging once order had been restored. The definition of a disorderly market is also discussed in U.S. Treasury and Federal Reserve System (1959, p. 15) and was earlier discussed by the ad hoc subcommittee in 1952 (see text at fn. 45 in Chapter 6) and by the FOMC in 1953 (see fn. 36 in Chapter 8).

Account to purchase Government securities in addition to short-term Government securities."[52]

In the limited time remaining before the close of trading at 3:30 p.m., the Desk bought $32 million of five different issues.[53] The intervention reversed the earlier price decline and the market closed unchanged on the day.

The Subscription Period (Monday, July 21 to Wednesday, July 23)

Subscription books for the July exchange offering opened on Monday, July 21. Although secondary market prices were generally firm, large offerings of the two bonds eligible for exchange soon appeared. Observers pointed out that the sellers were turning down the opportunity to exchange their bonds for the one-year, 1⅝ percent certificates that the Treasury was offering and choosing instead to reinvest in outstanding intermediate-term issues, where yields were around 2 percent. Attrition on the exchange offering seemed likely to be quite high.[54]

During an 11 a.m. FOMC conference call, Larkin pointed out that "the situation was not one which would encourage the exchange of maturing securities." He said the Desk intended to support the offering and that it would purchase, on a when-issued basis, the certificates that Treasury was offering rather than the rights exchangeable into the certificates. (Buying certificates for when-issued settlement was preferable to buying rights for regular settlement on the next business day because it postponed the release of reserves until the August 1 settlement date of the exchange offer and thus gave the Desk time to arrange off-setting sales from the Open Market Account.) When Watrous Irons questioned whether purchasing either the rights or the when-issued certificates would gain much in the long run, Larkin replied that, in the absence of System support, the refunding "could turn out to be the worst failure in the history of Treasury financing." Irons cautioned that System support "would be a precedent suggesting that whenever a Treasury issue looked doubtful the Federal Reserve should step in" and that "the Committee should realize what it might be building itself up for in the future." Larkin responded that "this was a most unusual situation, particularly in view of the international situation."[55]

52 Minutes of the Federal Open Market Committee, July 18, 1958, 2:30 p.m., p. 9.
53 Minutes of the Federal Open Market Committee, July 21, 1958, p. 2.
54 "U.S. Bonds Rally; Conversion Lags," *New York Times*, July 22, 1958, p. 37.
55 Minutes of the Federal Open Market Committee, July 21, 1958, pp. 3–5.

The Open Market Desk began buying certificates on a when-issued basis on Monday afternoon when, in Larkin's estimation, "the atmosphere got worse." By the time the Committee met by telephone at 11 a.m. on Tuesday the Desk had purchased more than $78 million of the certificates.[56] Purchases exceeded $100 million before the meeting was over[57] and exceeded $500 million on the day.[58]

The Desk continued buying through Wednesday, July 23, the last day the subscription books were open. By the end of the day the Desk had bought, in aggregate, more than $1 billion of the when-issued certificates, $110 million of the bonds called for redemption in September, and $65 million of other notes and bonds.[59] On Thursday, July 24, the FOMC terminated the special purchase authority granted on July 18.[60]

Denouement

Treasury officials announced preliminary results for the exchange offering on Friday, July 25, and final figures one week later.[61] Attrition amounted to $2.8 billion, 17 percent of the total amount of securities eligible for exchange and 29 percent of the amount in private hands. To replace the cash drained by the unusually high attrition, Treasury announced that it would offer $3.5 billion of a 7½-month, 1½ percent tax anticipation certificate for settlement on August 6.[62] The Fed avoided a spike in reserves stemming from its support of the July refunding by redeeming and selling Treasury bills from the System Open Market Account.[63]

AFTERMATH TO THE JULY REFUNDING

The Committee faced two key issues in the wake of the July refunding: What was the status of the "bills preferably" doctrine, and what was the

56 Minutes of the Federal Open Market Committee, July 22, 1958, p. 2.
57 Minutes of the Federal Open Market Committee, July 22, 1958, p. 8.
58 Minutes of the Federal Open Market Committee, July 23, 1958, p. 2.
59 Minutes of the Federal Open Market Committee, July 29, 1958, p. 2.
60 Minutes of the Federal Open Market Committee, July 24, 1958, p. 5.
61 Federal Reserve Bank of New York Circular no. 4623, July 25, 1958, Circular no. 4627, August 1, 1958; and "U.S. Offer Meets Heavy Rejection," *New York Times*, July 26, 1958, p. 18.
62 Federal Reserve Bank of New York Circular no. 4624, July 25, 1958.
63 Minutes of the Federal Open Market Committee, August 19, 1958, pp. 2–3.

status of the related policy that the System did not directly support Treasury offerings?

Writing in the *New York Times* on July 21, financial reporter Paul Heffernan claimed that bills preferably had come to an end. He conjectured that it would "continue to be influential in Federal Reserve market policy but as a formal limitation it is now a dead letter and probably will not be revived."[64]

Writing in the same paper three days later, Edwin Dale more astutely observed that the bills preferably doctrine had an "escape clause" that allowed purchases of other than short-term securities if needed to correct a disorderly market. He reported that "the Federal Reserve is still opposed to efforts to manipulate long-term interest rates and bond yields" and that "the intention of the Federal Reserve remains that of allowing the free play of market forces."[65] (On March 3, 1959, the FOMC reaffirmed its "bills preferably" policy.[66])

Following the completion of the July refunding, the FOMC vigorously debated the wisdom of its actions. Malcolm Bryan, the president of the Federal Reserve Bank of Atlanta, was unhappy with the decision of New York Bank officials to rely on the Committee's July 18 authorization to purchase, without limitation, government securities other than short-term securities – an authority clearly limited to the restoration of an orderly market – in supporting the faltering exchange offering of one-year certificates. He suggested that "the sophisticated investment public has been shocked by an ill-considered Treasury support operation" and "even more shocked by the System's operation that began on the presumption of correcting disorder but that turned promptly into one of the most massive support operations ever undertaken."[67] Governor Robertson made a similar point, stating that "the experience indicates the need for being more explicit in our directions to the Manager of the Account so that we cannot be so easily maneuvered from an action 'to correct a disorderly market' to one designed to 'support a Treasury issue.'"[68]

Chairman Martin did not try to defend the intervention – indeed, he observed that "the Federal Reserve System, like others, can occasionally

64 "U.S. Bond Market Regaining Course," *New York Times*, July 27, 1958, p. F1.

65 "It's 'Bills Only' but . . .," *New York Times*, July 30, 1958, p. 35. Dale was unaware of the bond purchase authority approved by the FOMC, in the absence of a declaration of a disorderly market, at its 1 p.m. meeting on July 18.

66 Minutes of the Federal Open Market Committee, March 3, 1959, pp. 12–13.

67 Minutes of the Federal Open Market Committee, July 29, 1958, p. 18.

68 Minutes of the Federal Open Market Committee, July 29, 1958, p. 24.

make mistakes" – but rather reminded the Committee that "the Treasury and the Federal Reserve are working toward a common objective" and that Secretary Anderson and Under Secretary Baird "were dealing with a very difficult problem." He suggested that "the Committee should not throw up its hands the first time circumstances developed which made the Committee realize that some flexibility was required." Martin further reminded the Committee that "regardless of theories, when certain things are involved the public will not sit by and let the situation go unheeded."[69]

The volatility experienced between mid-June and late July, the visibility of the Fed's support of the July refunding, and the unusually high attrition in that refunding caught the attention of government officials, members of Congress, and others.[70] Representative Wright Patman of Texas complained about the "jungle like activities being carried on by gamblers and speculators which are causing a loss of confidence in bonds of the United States and a distaste and a disrespect for our Government's obligations on the part of conservative investors."[71] The uproar led the Treasury to introduce several innovations to its debt management program, described in the next chapter, and prompted the Treasury-Federal Reserve Study described in Chapter 17.

[69] Minutes of the Federal Open Market Committee, July 29, 1958, pp. 48–51.

[70] U.S. Treasury and Federal Reserve System (1960a, p. 1), noting that the episode "aroused considerable concern among the general public and the financial community as well as among officials of the Government and members of Congress."

[71] Telegram from Wright Patman to William McChesney Martin, July 9, 1958. See also "Patman Queries Martin," *New York Times*, July 10, 1958, p. 37, and "Treasury Buys Back $589.5 Million of 2⅝% Bond Issue Sold in June," *Wall Street Journal*, July 10, 1958, p. 5.

16

Innovations in Treasury Debt Management

Nothing limns the need for change quite as sharply as failure, so it is hardly surprising that the summer of 1958 focused attention on several dysfunctional aspects of Treasury debt management, prompting officials to adapt some of their policies to the reality of fluctuating interest rates and a permanent federal debt.

A NEED FOR CHANGE

Tilford Gaines produced the sharpest and best-informed critique of 1950s Treasury debt management. A former officer of the Federal Reserve Bank of New York assigned to the Open Market Desk, Gaines pointed out that the "management of the huge public debt created by the depression of the 1930's and the Second World War has been a dominant, sometimes the dominant, influence in the financial markets since the end of the war." The need to refinance maturing debt "brought the Treasury into the market several times each year in immense financing operations which often . . . had a jolting impact upon the smooth functioning of all securities markets." Gaines saw the absence of any regularity or predictability in certificate, note, and bond offerings as "a massive source of [capital market] instability."[1]

Treasury Issuance of Coupon-Bearing Debt from 1953 to 1958

Chart 16.1 illustrates the basis for Gaines's critique: offerings of coupon-bearing debt came on a more or less as-needed basis.

[1] Gaines (1962, pp. 1 and 266).

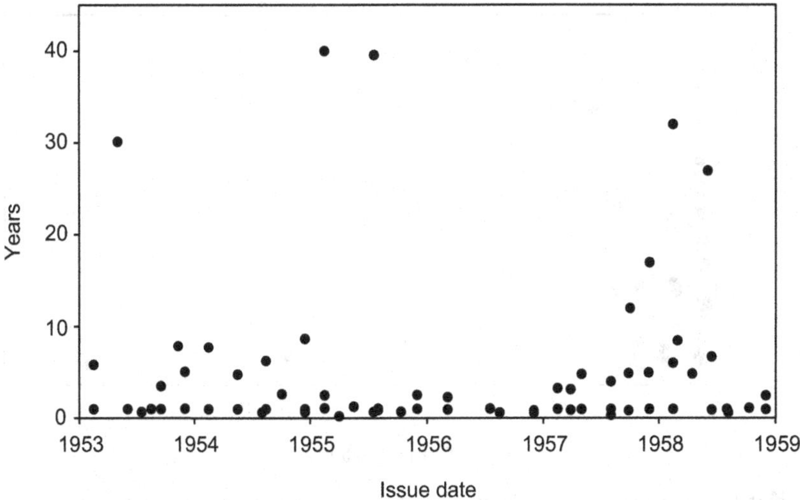

Chart 16.1 Maturities of coupon-bearing Treasury offerings.
Treasury annual reports and offering circulars.

Offerings of long-term debt were especially irregular and unpredictable. A new issue would sometimes be followed by another issue before the first issue had been fully distributed, and would other times become relatively scarce and illiquid before the Treasury chose to bring another offering of a similar maturity. More generally, offerings from 1953 to 1958 did not evidence any systematic plan or program of debt management.

Chart 16.2 shows that there was virtually no relationship between term to maturity and issue size. Short-term issues (under fifteen months to maturity) ranged widely between $500 million and $14 billion. Long-term issues (over ten years to maturity) were uniformly less than $2 billion but had terms ranging from twelve to forty years. Intermediate-term issues varied between $500 million and $11 billion but exhibited little systematic variation of size with term. Chart 16.3 shows that there was little consistency (of issue amounts) from offering to offering even within the eleven- to fifteen-month bracket where a preponderance of issuance took place.

Gaines's Critique

The starting point for Gaines's critique was the lack of a clearly stated objective and the absence of a program designed to achieve that objective. Since the beginning of the Eisenhower administration, "the closest thing to a firm policy objective that has been visible has been the desire to 'lengthen

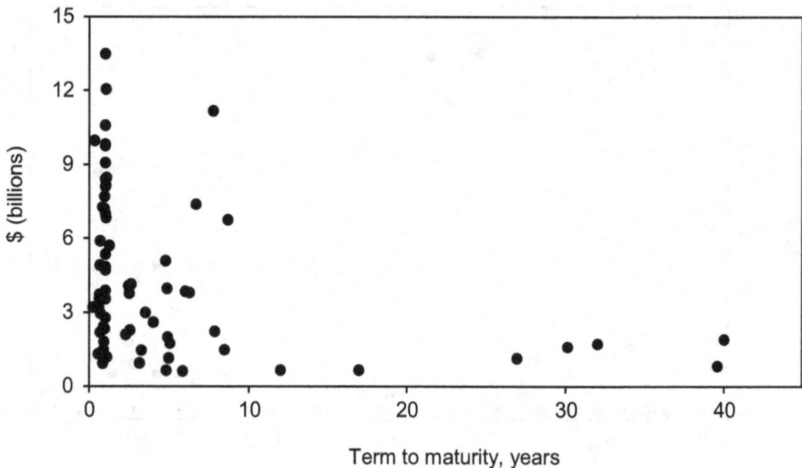

Chart 16.2 Issue amounts of coupon-bearing Treasury securities issued between 1953 and 1958 versus term to maturity.
Treasury annual reports and offering circulars.

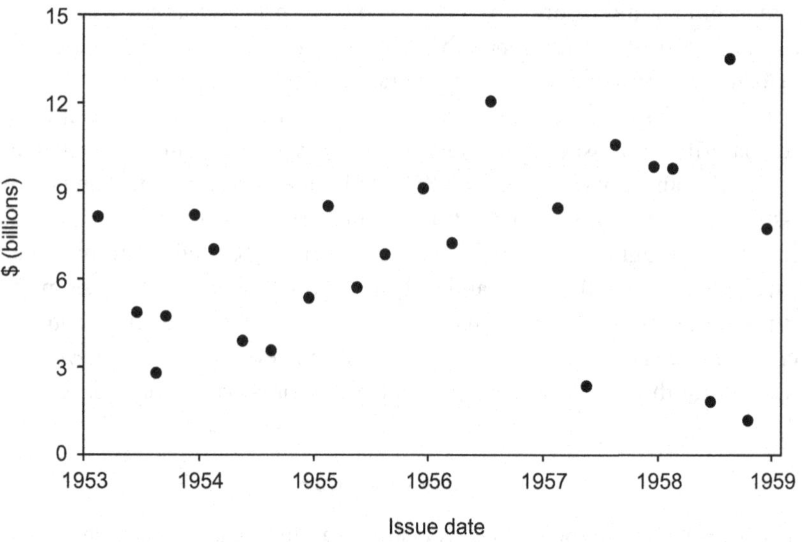

Chart 16.3 Issue amounts of coupon-bearing Treasury securities issued between 1953 and 1958 with maturities between eleven and fifteen months.
Treasury annual reports and offering circulars.

the average maturity of the debt' by selling as many securities at as long a term as possible," but "there has been no fully articulated program toward this or any other policy objective."[2]

Gaines suggested that the "key problem" of the postwar era was "the maintenance through refunding of a huge public debt."[3] Refunding operations ran through exchange offerings, where the holder of a maturing issue was given the right to exchange the issue for a new security. Gaines noted that many holders of maturing debt had correspondingly short investment horizons and were unlikely to be interested in rolling over into appreciably longer-term debt.[4] In the absence of significant interest on the part of existing holders in exercising their exchange rights, securities dealers bought the rights and either resold them to investors with longer horizons (for exchange into the new longer-term securities) or sold the longer-term issue that the Treasury was offering for when-issued settlement (obtaining the securities they sold by exercising the exchange option on the rights they purchased).

Exchange offerings were fixed-price offerings and attrition was liable to be unacceptably high if a new issue was not priced at an attractive level – a risk graphically illustrated by the July 1958 exchange offering of one-year certificates, where attrition ran to 17 percent (in spite of a massive Federal Reserve support operation) and triggered an emergency follow-on cash offering of 7½-month tax anticipation certificates. In late 1951, Robert Roosa, then a manager in the Research Department at the Federal Reserve Bank of New York, suggested that the Treasury could reduce the risk of unexpected attrition by giving investors a choice of *several* new issues.[5] The Eisenhower administration adopted Roosa's suggestion and in February 1953 offered holders of $8.9 billion of maturing certificates a choice between a one-year certificate and a five-year, ten-month bond.[6] Attrition amounted to a negligible 1.5 percent. The *New York Times* reported an "authoritative source" as saying that "this first experience of the new Administration with [an exchange that offered] alternative types of investment had been satisfactory enough to warrant use again."[7]

[2] Gaines (1962, pp. 156–58). [3] Gaines (1962, pp. 297–98). [4] Gaines (1962, p. 272).

[5] Roosa (1952, p. 234) observed that "the Treasury might also be able to vary its offering arrangements, and perhaps minimize the risks of miscalculating investor response in some situations, by using a package offering of several issues, thereby spreading the impact of a given operation over several sectors of the market."

[6] Federal Reserve Bank of New York Circular no. 3940, January 27, 1953; and Circular no. 3942, February 2, 1953.

[7] "New Refinancing Held Big Success," *New York Times*, February 10, 1953, p. 37.

Thirty-eight of forty-five exchange offerings between 1953 and 1958 were multiple-option offers.

Multiple-option exchange offers mitigated the risk of a cash flow emergency but created the new problem of shifting control of the maturity structure of the debt from government officials to private investors. In some cases (as in February 1953[8]) investors opted for a short-term certificate and in other cases (as in June 1958[9]) they preferred a longer security, but in all cases they were the ones deciding what Treasury would issue.

Gaines also found fault with several more specific Treasury financing practices. First and foremost, the size of individual offerings was frequently in excess of what the market could readily absorb. As a result, many offerings required some sort of underwriting support – that is, purchases by government securities dealers, banks, and others with a view to distribution at a later date. The putative underwriters bore risk because they had investment horizons far shorter than the term of the debt they were underwriting. The result was a market vulnerable to price declines that could force rapid liquidation of underwriting positions.[10]

Gaines further observed that Treasury offerings of coupon-bearing debt were neither regular nor predictable.[11] Every financing triggered a zero-based review of what to offer, with every maturity from six months to thirty years given active consideration. The result, Gaines concluded, "was a nearly continuous state of crisis in the Government securities market."[12]

Treasury Bills – A Bright Spot

Remarkably, none of the dysfunctionalities of certificate, note, and bond offerings carried over to bills. Prior to December 1958, most bills were auctioned on a regular and predictable weekly basis, on Monday for settlement Thursday to mature thirteen weeks later. (There were also sporadic auctions of tax anticipation bills, scheduled to mature shortly after tax payment dates that could be presented in payment of federal taxes at full face value, and occasional auctions of longer-term "special bills.") Offering amounts varied from time to time, but typically in relatively small increments of $100 million or $200 million (Chart 16.4).

[8] "New Refinancing Held Big Success," *New York Times*, February 10, 1953, p. 37; and "Treasury Refunds $8.9 Billion But Few Take Bonds," *Wall Street Journal*, February 10, 1953, p. 15.

[9] Federal Reserve Bank of New York Circular no. 4612, June 13, 1958.

[10] Gaines (1962, p. 269). [11] Gaines (1962, p. 89). [12] Gaines (1962, p. 79).

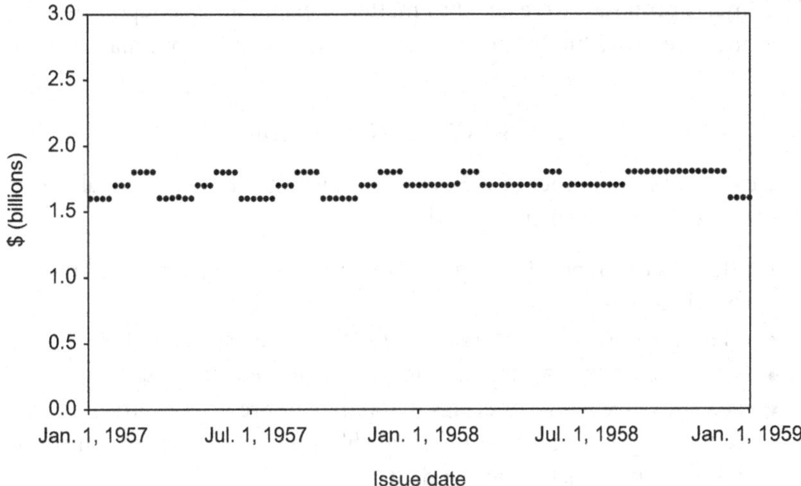

Chart 16.4 Thirteen-week Treasury bill issuance.
Treasury Bulletin.

Friedman's Recommendations

In the course of a series of lectures at Fordham University in 1959, Milton Friedman outlined his thoughts on how Treasury debt management policies could be improved. Friedman recommended eliminating the "lumpiness and discontinuity in debt operations" characterized by relatively few, sporadic offerings of unpredictable magnitude, timed to fit into "slack periods in the money market."[13] He proposed that the Treasury

- issue at standardized maturities (he suggested just two: thirteen weeks and ten years),
- issue frequently, in readily digestible amounts that vary smoothly over time, and
- issue via auction rather than fixed-price offerings, avoiding mispricing by Treasury officials and what Friedman described as "extensive consultation, crystal gazing, and plain guesswork."[14]

[13] Friedman (1960, p. 60).

[14] Friedman (1960, pp. 63–65). Roosa (1952, p. 232) also suggested the use of auctions to price new issues of coupon-bearing debt: "Setting a coupon which will be attractive to the market without unduly disturbing the holdings of outstanding securities is a challenging assignment. The successful development of the auction method in connection with Treasury bills suggests that an extension of this technique to obligations of somewhat

Friedman's proposals were largely a matter of extending to coupon-bearing securities the procedures employed so successfully in the bill market.

TREASURY'S INNOVATIONS

The events of the summer of 1958 exposed a variety of dysfunctionalities in Treasury debt management, including:

- offerings of coupon-bearing debt that were too large for the market to absorb comfortably,
- offerings at irregular intervals and with unpredictable maturities,
- fixed-price cash offerings that produced unpredictable allotments,
- fixed-price exchange offerings marked by unpredictable attrition, and
- multiple-option exchange offerings that impaired Treasury control of the maturity structure of the debt.

Change was clearly called for.

In the aftermath of the summer debacle, Treasury officials undertook four major debt management initiatives:

1. they further regularized short-term issuance by introducing a twenty-six-week bill series and a one-year bill series;
2. they partially regularized issuance of intermediate- and long-term debt by limiting issuance to four "refunding dates" each year: February 15, May 15, August 15, and November 15;
3. they introduced cash (as opposed to exchange) refundings; and
4. they introduced advance refundings – that is offers to exchange new debt for outstanding debt that was not yet close to maturity.

They did not, however, introduce any standard series of intermediate- or long-term debt (such as a regularly issued series of two-year notes or ten-year bonds) and they did not extend the auction process to coupon-bearing securities. (Both would ultimately transpire in the early 1970s – see Chapter 28.)

Issuing and Redeeming Coupon-Bearing Debt on a Regular Schedule

On November 18, 1958, the Treasury announced that it was offering holders of $12.2 billion of maturing certificates and bonds the option to

longer-term might provide the Treasury with a means of letting the market decide the precisely suitable yield, in relation to alternative uses of funds."

exchange their securities for an 11½-month certificate, to mature on November 15, 1959, or a two-year 5½-month note, to mature on May 15, 1961.[15] The choice of maturity dates was not accidental. The offering announcement stated that,

> [w]ith the completion of this financing, over 80 percent of outstanding Treasury marketable securities maturing within the next ten years (excluding Treasury bills and tax anticipation securities) will fall due in February, May, August, or November.
>
> For some time, the Treasury has been working toward scheduling its maturities on these quarterly dates to reduce the number of times each year its financing will interfere with other borrowers such as corporations, states, municipalities, etc.; to minimize the "churning" in the money markets on the major quarterly corporate income tax dates; and to facilitate the effective execution by the Federal Reserve of its monetary policy.

Table 15.2 shows that eleven of the thirteen coupon-bearing Treasury securities issued in 1958 were scheduled to mature in the middle of the second month of a quarter.[16] That pattern continued in 1959 and 1960, when eleven of twelve and nine of ten coupon-bearing securities, respectively, were issued with mid-quarter maturity dates (Tables 16.1 and 16.2).[17]

The adoption of regular refunding dates was an improvement, but it did not fully regularize issuance of coupon-bearing debt. Treasury retained discretion over how maturing securities would be refinanced – whether with short-term certificates, intermediate-term notes, or long-term bonds – and it did not introduce anything like a quarterly two-year or four-year series, and hence did not make the issuance of coupon-bearing debt nearly as regular and predictable as the issuance of thirteen-week bills.

[15] Federal Reserve Bank of New York Circular no. 4663, November 18, 1958.

[16] The first exception in Table 15.2, the 1⅝ percent certificate maturing on August 1, 1959, offered in the July exchange offering, had to be issued on August 1, 1958, to refinance $11.5 billion of securities maturing that day. Federal Reserve Bank of New York Circular no. 4620, July 17, 1958. Certificates had a maximum term to maturity of one year, so the new certificates had to mature before August 2, 1959.
The second exception, the 1½ percent certificate maturing on March 24, 1959, offered in the July cash offering, was a tax anticipation certificate receivable at par plus accrued interest to maturity in payment of income and profits taxes due on March 15, 1959. Federal Reserve Bank of New York Circular no. 4624, July 25, 1958.

[17] The 4 percent bond maturing on October 1, 1969, offered in the March 1959 cash offering reopened a security sold earlier in September 1957 – see Table 14.2. The 3⅛ percent certificate maturing on August 1, 1961, offered in the August 1960 cash offering added to the 4 percent note maturing on the same date included in the July 1957 cash offering – see Table 14.2. Neither security opened a new maturity date.

Table 16.1 *Treasury offerings of coupon-bearing debt in 1959.*

Security offered	Issued	Maturity	Amount issued ($ billions)
January cash offering			
16-month 3¼% note	Jan. 21	May 15, 1960	2.74
21-year 4% bond	Jan. 23	Feb. 15, 1980	0.88
February exchange offering			
1-year 3¾% certificate	Feb. 16	Feb. 15, 1960	11.36
3-year 4% note	Feb. 16	Feb. 15, 1962	1.44
March cash offering			
4-year 1½-month 4% note	Apr. 1	May 15, 1963	1.74
10½-year 4% bond (reopening)	Apr. 1	Oct. 1, 1969	0.62
May exchange offering			
1-year 4% certificate	May 15	May 15, 1960	1.27
July exchange offering			
12½-month 4¾% note	Aug. 3	Aug. 15, 1960	9.56
4-year 10-month 4¾% note	Aug. 3	May 15, 1964	4.18
October cash offering			
4-year 10-month 5% note	Oct. 15	Aug. 15, 1964	2.33
November exchange offering			
1-year 4¾% certificate	Nov. 16	Nov. 15, 1960	7.04
4-year 4⅞% note	Nov. 16	Nov. 15, 1963	3.01

Treasury annual reports and offering circulars.

Twenty-Six-Week Bills

In the fall of 1958, Treasury officials became increasingly anxious about prospects for funding the deficit over the coming year.[18] In view of the recent market turmoil, they planned to meet about half of their funding needs through bill issuance. However, simply expanding the weekly auctions of thriteen-week bills ran the risk of swamping investor interest in the three-month sector.

The solution, officials decided, was a new series of twenty-six-week bills. (They considered, but ultimately declined to adopt, a proposal to extend bill maturities from thirteen to seventeen weeks.[19]) At the same time that

[18] Banyas (1973, p. 5).

[19] Minutes of the Federal Open Market Committee, November 10, 1958, pp. 3–4, comment of Robert Rouse that "one method under consideration was a program that would

Table 16.2 *Treasury offerings of coupon-bearing debt in 1960 (other than advance refundings).*

Security offered	Issued	Maturity	Amount issued ($ billions)
February exchange offering			
1-year 4⅞% certificate	Feb. 15	Feb. 15, 1961	6.94
4¾-year 4⅞% note	Feb. 15	Nov. 15, 1964	4.19
April cash offering			
2-year 1-month 4% note	Apr. 14	May 15, 1962	2.21
25-year 4¼% bond	Apr. 14	May 15, 1985	0.47
May exchange offering			
1-year 4⅜% certificate	May 16	May 15, 1961	3.67
5-year 4⅝% note	May 16	May 15, 1965	2.11
August cash offering			
11½-month 3⅛% certificate	Aug. 15	Aug. 1, 1961	7.83
7¾-year 3⅞% bond (reopening)	Aug. 15	May 15, 1968	1.07
November exchange offering			
1¼-year 3¼% note	Nov. 15	Feb. 15, 1962	9.10
5½-year 3¾% bond	Nov. 15	May 15, 1966	1.21

Treasury annual reports and offering circulars.

they announced the terms of the November exchange offering, Treasury officials advised market participants that they would soon begin regular weekly auctions of twenty-six-week bills. They noted that "the rolling-over of bills does not create the disturbance in the money market that the refinancing of longer-term issues sometimes does."[20]

The new series was expected to allow a reduction in issuance of both thirteen-week bills and one-year certificates. The Treasury noted that "the shift of part of the volume of Treasury bills outstanding to a 26-week cycle will enable certain corporations and other investors to meet their requirements for a regular bill which is longer than the present 13-week maturity."[21] The *Wall Street Journal* reported that "policymakers figure the new bills will draw some money that previously has gone into Treasury

gradually convert regular Treasury bills to a 17-week cycle after the next three or four months."

[20] "Treasury Offers 2½-Year Note at 3.68%, 11½-Month Certificate at 3.43% to Refund $12.2 Billion Securities," *Wall Street Journal*, November 19, 1958, p. 2.

[21] Federal Reserve Bank of New York Circular no. 4663, November 18, 1958.

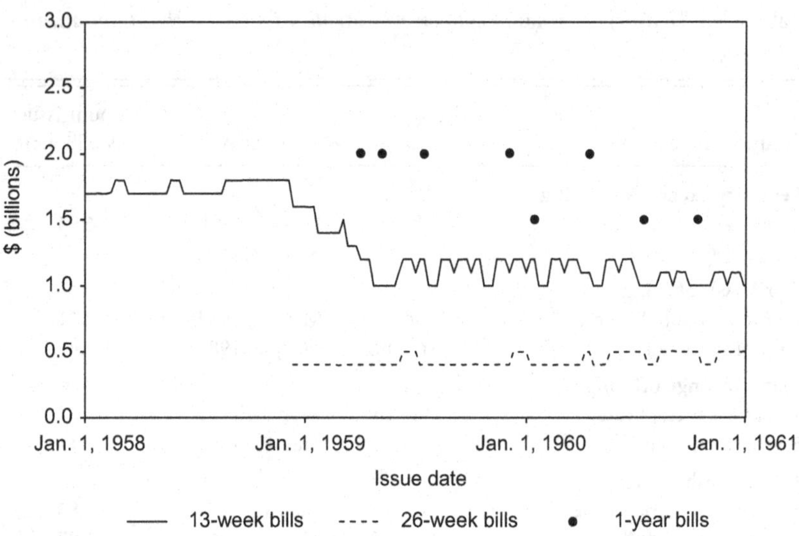

Chart 16.5 Treasury bill issuance.
Treasury Bulletin.

offerings of certificates and may also pull in some investors who are now putting their money into the short-term bills."[22]

The first twenty-six-week bill was auctioned on Monday, December 8, 1958, and issued on Thursday, December 11, to mature on Thursday, June 11, 1959. Thirteen weeks later the June 11 maturity date was reopened with a thirteen-week bill. The offering statement provided that the thirteen-week bills to be issued on March 13 would be "freely interchangeable" with the twenty-six-week bills issued on December 11 since it was "desirable that all bills maturing on the same date be the same issue."[23]

By mid-1959 the Treasury was issuing about \$1.1 billion of thirteen-week bills and \$400 million of twenty-six-week bills every week (Chart 16.5), funding in total about \$24.70 billion of debt (\$24.70 billion = 13 weeks × \$1.1 billion per week, plus 26 weeks × \$400 million per week), an increase of \$2 billion over the \$22.75 billion of debt funded by the \$1.75 billion average weekly issuance of thirteen-week bills in the first

[22] "Treasury Offers 2½-Year Note at 3.68%, 11½-Month Certificate at 3.43% to Refund \$12.2 Billion Securities," *Wall Street Journal*, November 19, 1958, p. 2.

[23] Federal Reserve Bank of New York Circular no. 4711, March 5, 1959.

eleven months of 1958 ($22.75 billion = 13 weeks × $1.75 billion per week). However, the relatively small auction sizes of the twenty-six-week bills meant that those bills had limited liquidity until they were reopened as thirteen-week bills.[24]

Year Bills

The Treasury needed more than $2 billion of new money in the first half of 1959 and it needed the money sooner than what would become available from the twenty-six-week bill program.[25] In mid-March Treasury officials announced that they would shortly begin to offer a third bill series: quarterly auction sales of one-year bills, with new bills scheduled to mature on the fifteenth day of the *first* month of a quarter (or the first business day thereafter).[26] The maturity dates for the new year bills were chosen specifically to avoid interfering with the mid-quarter refunding dates for coupon-bearing securities.[27]

Since year bills were scheduled to mature on the fifteenth day of a month (or the first business day thereafter if the fifteenth was not a business day), they were not fungible with subsequent issues of thriteen- and twenty-six-week bills, which were scheduled to mature on a Thursday (or Friday if Thursday was a holiday). Thus, the new one-year bills were separate and apart from the thirteen- and twenty-six-week bill series. Three of the first four tranches of the new bill series had irregular issue dates and terms shorter than a full year but, as shown in Table 16.3, succeeding tranches were regularly issued on the fifteenth day of the first month of a quarter (or the first business day thereafter).

[24] The 1959 Annual Report of Open Market Operations noted (p. 11) that "the relatively small size of the three- to six-month maturities outstanding made them difficult to trade in the market at times" and that "in most of the weekly auctions bidding was not particularly strong and spreads between average and stop out rates were generally quite wide."

[25] Banyas (1973, p. 5).

[26] Federal Reserve Bank of New York Circular no. 4715, March 19, 1959.

[27] "Treasury Plans New Debt Device," *New York Times*, March 20, 1959, p. 41, stating that Treasury officials explained the new plan "as partly stemming from the dilemma involved in the bunching of maturities in four months of the year. This has resulted, they noted, in the need for refunding large amounts." See also "Treasury to Offer $500 Million of 10-Year, 4% Bonds," *Wall Street Journal*, March 20, 1959, p. 2, stating that the limitation to four refunding dates had made "the amounts coming due in these months 'rather top-heavy.'"

Table 16.3 *One-year Treasury bill issuance.*

Auction	Amount ($ billions)	Issue	Maturity	Term (days)
Auctioned and issued in 1959, to mature in 1960				
Mar. 26	2.0	Apr. 1	Jan. 15	289
May 6	2.0	May 11	Apr. 15	340
Jul. 8	2.0	Jul. 15	Jul. 15	366
Nov. 24	2.0	Dec. 2	Oct. 17	320
Auctioned and issued in 1960, to mature in 1961				
Jan. 12	1.5	Jan. 15	Jan. 15	366
Apr. 12	2.0	Apr. 15	Apr. 15	365
Jul. 12	1.5	Jul. 15	Jul. 15	365
Oct. 11	1.5	Oct. 17	Oct. 16	365

Treasury Bulletin.

Cash Refundings

In March 1960, Treasury officials surprised the market by giving notice that they might terminate the practice of giving holders of maturing debt pre-emptive rights to refunding issues, instead offering the new securities to all investors on a cash basis. The change was prompted by four objectives:

1. eliminating attrition,
2. simplifying the refunding process by eliminating the need to rely on securities dealers to transfer rights from holders of maturing debt that wanted cash to investors interested in acquiring longer-term securities,
3. regaining full control over the maturity structure of the debt by eliminating multiple-option exchange offers, and
4. controlling speculative demand for longer-term securities by preferentially allotting longer-term securities to investors with longer-term horizons.[28]

The first cash refunding was announced in July 1960, when officials offered $7¾ billion of 11½-month certificates and $1 billion of 7¾-year bonds to refinance $9.6 billion of Treasury notes due to mature on

[28] "Treasury Offers 25-Year 4¼% Bond, 25-Month 4% Note: Terms are Surprise, But Chance for Success Called Good," *Wall Street Journal*, April 1, 1960, p. 3, and "Treasury to Sell a 25-Year Bond," *New York Times*, April 1, 1960, p. 1.

August 15.[29] The new securities could be paid for with cash or maturing notes but subscriptions tendering maturing notes would rank pari passu with cash subscriptions.

The Treasury received subscriptions for $17.4 billion of the certificates and awarded $7.8 billion, including $6.3 billion on 100 percent allotments to Federal Reserve Banks, foreign central banks, government investment accounts, state and local governments, and public pension funds and $1.5 billion on 13 percent allotments to all other investors.[30] The Treasury received subscriptions for $5.2 billion of the bonds and awarded $1.1 billion, including $314 million on 25 percent allotments to savings-type investors (such as pension and retirement funds, endowment funds, insurance companies, and mutual savings banks), $543 million on 20 percent allotments to commercial banks, and $188 million on 15 percent allotments to all other investors.[31] Officials were reported to be pleased with the results and likely to continue using the new technique.[32]

However, cash refundings were not without their own drawbacks. In particular, they replaced the assured reinvestments associated with exchange offerings with the prospect of uncertain allotments and the need to pad subscriptions to obtain a desired allocation.[33] Smaller banks and institutional investors were viewed as less likely to participate in cash offerings than exchange offerings, thus creating a larger underwriting role for dealers.[34] When Treasury officials faced the next, November 1960, refunding, they chose to return to a conventional exchange format.[35] Whether the Department would continue with cash refundings was left up to the incoming Kennedy Administration.

[29] Federal Reserve Bank of New York Circular no. 4918, July 28, 1960.

[30] The disparate treatment of Federal Reserve Banks, foreign central banks, etc. compared to other investors, the history of which is discussed below, triggered "a good number of complaints." Minutes of the Federal Open Market Committee, August 16, 1960, p. 4.

[31] Federal Reserve Bank of New York Circular no. 4921, August 5, 1960; and Circular no. 4926, August 12, 1960.

[32] "Treasury Pleased With Public Response to Refunding of Nearly $9 Billion Debt," *Wall Street Journal*, August 8, 1960, p. 2.

[33] The 1960 Annual Report of Open Market Operations states (p. 11) that "there was considerable dissatisfaction among corporates and other investors who, in order to replace fully their holdings of maturing securities were forced to engage in 'padding' their subscriptions – a procedure with which they were generally unfamiliar and which met with some resistance."

[34] Banyas (1973, p. 9).

[35] Federal Reserve Bank of New York Circular no. 4948, October 13, 1960, and Circular no, 4953, October 27, 1960.

The Problem of SOMA Reinvestments

The introduction of cash refundings created a problem for Federal Reserve officials. As explained in Chapter 2, the System Open Market Account was generally prohibited from acquiring Treasury securities other than in open market transactions. However, System officials had concluded that the prohibition did not extend to *exchanging*, directly with Treasury, maturing securities for new securities as long as the exchange did not provide the Treasury with new money and was on terms available to the general public. The Open Market Account could, therefore, participate in exchange offerings of coupon-bearing debt and, up to the amount of maturing bills that it held, in bill auctions, but it could not participate in cash offerings of coupon-bearing securities.

Treasury officials proposed two ways for the Open Market Account to participate in cash refundings.[36] Under what they called "Alternative A" they would offer to the public – for example, \$2 billion of notes with a specified term and coupon rate for cash settlement at par, and they would offer an additional amount of the same securities to the Open Market Account in exchange for whatever maturing securities the Treasury was seeking to refinance. Awards to public subscribers would be subject to pro rata reduction in the event subscriptions exceeded the amount offered. The amount offered to the Open Market Account would be identical to what Account managers wanted to roll over and the Account's subscription would be filled in full. Under "Alternative B" the Treasury made the same offers to the public and the Open Market Account, but would allow members of the public and the Account to tender maturing securities in lieu of cash and stipulated that it would fill all such subscriptions in full.

Howard Hackley, the General Counsel to the FOMC, opined that the Open Market Account could participate in either type of offering, reasoning that both alternatives were intended to meet the "test of the open market."[37] However, both alternatives had drawbacks.

Alternative B was hardly different from the existing method of exchange offerings, was unlikely to eliminate speculation in rights, and was therefore unappealing to the Treasury. Alternative A, on the other hand, would treat the Open Market Account differently than other subscribers. The difference discomforted some FOMC members. Carl Allen, the president of the Federal Reserve Bank of Cleveland, thought that Reserve Banks "should be treated and should seek to be treated exactly like any other purchaser."

[36] Minutes of the Federal Open Market Committee, October 21, 1958, pp. 4–6.
[37] Minutes of the Federal Open Market Committee, October 21, 1958, pp. 5–6.

William Treiber, the first vice president of the Federal Reserve Bank of New York and the alternate for the Bank's president, felt "there was a question of policy as to whether the Federal Reserve should concur in a proposal calling for special treatment for the Reserve Banks as compared with other holders of the same maturing securities."[38] In the event, the Committee decided that it would be "unwise" for the Treasury to proceed with Alternative A.[39]

The problem of facilitating Federal Reserve *exchange* participation in *cash* refundings was resolved when Treasury proposed a third alternative: it would fill in full all subscriptions to be settled with maturing securities tendered by a specified group of market participants, including state and local governments, foreign governments, international institutions, public pension funds, and – of course – the System Open Market Account.[40] All other participants, who could pay with cash or in maturing securities, would be subject to pro-rata allotment. The privileged class of subscribers was small enough to eliminate most of the Treasury's practical concern with speculation and attrition[41] but large enough that the Federal Reserve was not a conspicuous exception.

Advance Refundings

An advance refunding is an invitation to exchange securities that are *not* close to maturity for longer-term securities, thereby extending the maturity structure of the debt.

Advance refundings were intended to get around several problems associated with conventional exchange offers: that many holders of maturing securities were unlikely to want to exchange their securities for new

[38] Minutes of the Federal Open Market Committee, October 21, p. 7.

[39] Minutes of the Federal Open Market Committee, October 21, p. 12.

[40] Minutes of the Federal Open Market Committee, May 3, 1960, pp. 46–49. See also Federal Reserve Bank of New York Circular no. 4918, July 28, 1960, announcing the terms of an offering of \$7¾ billion of 11½-month certificates at par, for payment in cash or maturing securities, and noting that "all subscriptions from States, political subdivisions or instrumentalities thereof, public ... funds, international organizations in which the United States holds membership, foreign central banks and foreign States, Government Investment Accounts, and the Federal Reserve Banks, will be allotted in full."

[41] Nevertheless, beginning with the November 1963 cash refunding, a subscriber that tendered maturing securities eligible for a 100 percent allotment had to certify in writing that its subscription did not exceed the quantity of such securities that it held immediately prior to the offering announcement. Banyas (1973, p. 9) and Federal Reserve Bank of New York Circular no. 5407, October 25, 1963.

issues of longer-term debt and that the transfer of exchange rights from holders that wanted cash to prospective investors was complicated and costly. The Treasury sought to provide a way for investors with intermediate-term horizons to keep invested in intermediate-term debt, and for investors with long-term horizons to keep invested in long-term debt, without engaging in secondary market transactions.[42]

Treasury officials started with a modest trial offering in June 1960, giving holders of $11.2 billion of 2½ percent bonds maturing seventeen months later (in November 1961) an opportunity to exchange their bonds, on a par-for-par basis, for either a three-year eleven-month, 3¾ percent note or a seven-year eleven-month, 3⅞ percent bond.[43] Unsure of the reception likely to be accorded the offering and desirous of limiting speculative exchanges, they capped the note offering at $3.5 billion and the bond offering at $1.5 billion, saying that it was sufficient, in this initial foray, to "whittle down" the quantity of 2½ percent bonds that would have to be refinanced at maturity.[44]

Subscription books opened on Wednesday, June 8 and remained open until the close of business on Monday, June 13. The Treasury received subscriptions for $4.6 billion of the notes and issued $3.9 billion on 85 percent allocations; it received subscriptions for $322 million of the bonds and filled all of the subscriptions in full.[45]

Following the success of the June offering, officials proceeded with plans for larger advance refundings. In a speech at the University of Wisconsin on August 18, 1960, Under Secretary Baird outlined the conceptual framework of the program. Treasury would first refinance five- to ten-year debt with longer maturities in a "senior advance refunding" and then refinance one- to five-year debt into the five- to ten-year sector in a "junior advance

[42] "Treasury May Broaden Scope of Its Advance Refunding Plan," *New York Times*, August 19, 1960, p. 29, quoting Under Secretary of the Treasury Julian Baird as saying that "we are seeking to keep typical long-term investors in long bonds, typical intermediate holders in intermediates, and typical short-term holders in relatively short maturities."

[43] Federal Reserve Bank of New York Circular no. 4896, June 6, 1960. See also "Treasury to Offer 4-Year Notes and 8-Year Bonds in Advance Refunding: Short-Term Rates Fall Again," *Wall Street Journal*, June 7, 1960, p. 3.

[44] Minutes of the Federal Open Market Committee, June 14, 1960, p. 3, remark of Robert Rouse that "the limitations on amount were considered necessary to keep the offering from being vulnerable to what seemed … to be a possibility of speculation and at the same time not to discourage exchanges by reason of possible [small] size of new issues." "Whittling down" a large issue prior to maturity was also employed in the 1920s. Garbade (2012, ch. 12 and fn. 33 on p. 174).

[45] Federal Reserve Bank of New York Circular no. 4900, June 15, 1960; and Circular no. 4902, June 22, 1960.

refunding," thereby making room for new cash issues of one- to five-year debt.[46]

Treasury announced its first senior advance refunding on September 9, 1960: a three-part, par-for-par, offering of

- 3½ percent bonds maturing on November 15, 1980, for 2½ percent bonds of June 15, 1967, $2.1 billion of which had been issued in May and August 1942;
- 3½ percent bonds maturing on February 15, 1990, for 2½ percent bonds of December 15, 1968, $2.8 billion of which had been issued in December 1942; and
- 3½ percent bonds maturing on November 15, 1998, for 2½ percent bonds of June 15, 1969, $3.7 billion of which had been issued in April 1943, and for 2½ percent bonds of December 15, 1969, $3.8 billion of which had been issued in September 1943.[47]

All subscriptions for the bonds maturing in 1980 would be filled in full, but no more than a total of $4.5 billion of the 1990 and 1998 bonds would be issued. Officials stated that they were hoping to issue a total of between $3 billion and $5 billion of new bonds.[48]

In conjunction with the new operation, the Treasury launched its first marketing effort since World War II, meeting with investors at the Federal Reserve Banks of New York, Chicago, and San Francisco. Under Secretary Baird spoke in New York to "more than two hundred bond specialists from commercial and savings banks, insurance companies, bond houses, and other financial institutions."[49] Assistant to the Secretary of the Treasury Charls Walker spoke in Chicago and Assistant Secretary J. Dewey Daane spoke in San Francisco.[50]

Following the close of the subscription books on September 20, Treasury announced that it had received subscriptions for $4 billion of new bonds, including $644 million of the 3½s of 1980, $993 million of the 3½s of 1990, and $2.3 billion of the 3½s of 1998.[51] All subscriptions were filled in full.

[46] "Treasury May Broaden Scope of Its Advance Refunding Plan," *New York Times*, August 19, 1960, p. 29; and "Treasury Mulls Offer of Long-Term Bonds in Advance Refunding of Wartime 2½s," *Wall Street Journal*, August 19, 1960, p. 3.

[47] Federal Reserve Bank of New York Circular no. 4934, September 9, 1960.

[48] "U.S. Offers Trade in Wartime Bonds," *New York Times*, September 10, 1960, p. 1.

[49] "Backing Sought for Debt Plan," *New York Times*, September 15, 1960, p. 53.

[50] "Treasury Pleased with Response So Far to $10.8 Billion Advance Refunding Plan," *Wall Street Journal*, September 15, 1960, p. 5.

[51] Federal Reserve Bank of New York Circular no. 4937, September 22, 1960; and Circular no. 4940, September 30, 1960.

Officials pronounced themselves "pleased" with the results, taking special note of the "minimum market impact," the "relatively small changes in the price of the affected issues," and the "small amount of market churning."[52]

WHY THE TREASURY DECLINED TO EXTEND THE AUCTION PROCESS TO COUPON-BEARING SECURITIES

Treasury officials introduced a variety of innovations in debt management between the fall of 1958 and the end of 1960, but they declined to extend the auction process beyond bills. Testifying before the Joint Economic Committee on July 24, 1959, Secretary of the Treasury Robert Anderson acknowledged that auctions were "an efficient mechanism" for pricing bills and that auction sales of notes and bonds would "relieve [the Treasury] of a major responsibility in pricing and selling coupon issues."[53] But Anderson nevertheless claimed that fixed-priced offerings of coupon-bearing debt were preferable to auction offerings.[54]

Anderson based his claim on the observation that many of the small banks, corporations, and individuals who subscribed to fixed-price offerings did not have the "professional capacity" to bid in auctions.[55] Lacking the requisite expertise, they were liable to either bid too high and pay too much or bid too low and be shut out, and were therefore likely to avoid bidding altogether,[56] choosing instead to buy new securities in the post-auction dealer market.

Anderson suggested that the withdrawal of small institutional and individual investors from the primary market would have adverse consequences, including reducing Treasury's ability to distribute its debt broadly (an objective dating back to the nineteenth century) and increasing the risk

52 Federal Reserve Bank of New York Circular no. 4937, September 22, 1960, "Early Refunding Termed Success," *New York Times*, September 23, 1960, p. 41, and "Treasury Says Non-Government Holders Swapped $3.4 Billion Bonds in Refunding," *Wall Street Journal*, September 23, 1960, p. 3.

53 Joint Economic Committee (1959, Part 6A, pp. 1148 and 1150).

54 Joint Economic Committee (1959, Part 6A, pp. 1148–53).

55 Joint Economic Committee (1959, Part 6A, p. 1149).

56 This is exactly what happened when Treasury Secretary Henry Morgenthau tried to auction bonds in 1935. Garbade (2012, p. 292).

that pricing might not be competitive and that Treasury might fail to cover its financing requirements. He concluded that "the present practice of offering Treasury certificates, notes, and bonds at prices and interest rates determined by the Treasury . . . result[s] in an effective distribution of new Treasury issues at minimum cost to the taxpayer."[57]

[57] Joint Economic Committee (1959, Part 6A, p. 1153). Friedman responded to Anderson's defense of fixed-price offerings by suggesting that the Treasury adopt a *single-price* auction format, where all successful auction participants pay the lowest accepted price, instead of the multiple-price format used for bill auctions, where each accepted tender is invoiced at the price proposed in the tender. Joint Economic Committee (1959, Part 9A, p. 3024). See also Friedman (1960, p. 65). The idea of single-price auctions has a long history. See, for example, Adams (1887, pp. 168–69). Friedman's suggestion went unappreciated for more than a decade.

17

The Treasury-Federal Reserve Study of the Government Securities Market

The turmoil that marked the summer of 1958 prompted Treasury and Federal Reserve officials to examine in detail what had happened. Their efforts resulted in the three-part Treasury-Federal Reserve Study of the Government Securities Market.[1]

The study focused broadly on market "processes and mechanisms."[2] Part I summarized the views of market participants regarding the events of the summer and, more broadly, the functioning of the government securities market – including dealer finance, the adequacy of statistical information, Treasury debt management policies, and Federal Reserve open market operations. Part II described what happened in the summer of 1958. Part III presented supplementary studies of selected topics, including the adequacy of market statistics, margin requirements for government securities, repurchase agreements, and the need for an association of government securities dealers.

The Treasury-Federal Reserve Study is notable for the premise, sometimes stated explicitly and other times only implied, that the secondary market for government securities is affected by a public interest, that dealers have responsibilities to the public, and that the Treasury and Federal Reserve bear some measure of responsibility for supervising the market, at least at an informal level.[3] (Neither agency had any statutory authority to regulate or supervise the market.)

[1] U.S. Treasury and Federal Reserve System (1959 and 1960a, b). See also "Federal Investigation Set on Deals in U.S. Securities," *New York Times*, March 9, 1959, p. 1; "Treasury Spurs Government Bond Market Study," *Wall Street Journal*, March 9, 1959; p. 19, and "U.S. Bond Study Called Overdue," *New York Times*, March 15, 1959, p. F1.

[2] Anderson and Martin (1959, p. 861).

[3] See, in addition to the material discussed in this chapter, the remark of Governor C. Canby Balderston that "the Government securities market is affected by the public interest" and that "the System, including particularly the Open Market Committee, has a special

Treasury Secretary Robert Anderson and Board of Governors Chairman William McChesney Martin summarized the principle findings of the study in a written submission to the Joint Economic Committee in July 1959. Anderson and Martin described the purpose of the study as identifying "how organization and techniques in the Government securities market might be improved" and "by what means the danger of future speculative excesses . . . might be lessened."[4] They noted the "widespread speculation" in the June 1958 financing and observed that "many speculatively motivated exchanges" in that refunding were "apparently based on investor judgments that recession would continue for some time, and that long-term interest yields would decline further."[5] They suggested that "one key to [the] widespread speculation may have been the absence of adequate information about current tendencies in the Government securities market."[6] In particular,

> [t]he availability of regularly issued statistical information about the market itself might have succeeded to some extent in forewarning market participants and interested public agencies of potential speculative dangers around mid-1958. The fact of the matter, however, is that no such objective information was available to either group to gauge the extent of the speculative forces that were present in the market.[7]

In view of the locus of speculation during the run-up to the June financing, including (1) banks and others that exchanged their unlevered holdings of maturing debt for bonds that were longer than customary for those investors and (2) investors who purchased maturing debt on margin with the intention of exchanging it, one might think that Anderson and Martin were referring to information about investors generally. Such was not the case. They were instead referring to information about government securities dealers – market participants who had not played any significant role in the debacle. They noted several "defects attributed by some critics to the dealer market in U.S. Government securities," including that "the market is concentrated in a relatively small group of primary dealers," that "there is little information about its operations," and that it was "without supervision or formal rules governing its practices, despite its special public interest."[8]

Anderson and Martin dismissed the idea that the market was less than fully competitive: "[T]here is no question that the primary dealer market is very highly competitive, even though it comprises only twelve nonbank

responsibility toward that market and the public interest in it." Minutes of the Federal Open Market Committee, October 13, 1959, p. 50.

4 Anderson and Martin (1959, p. 860).
5 Anderson and Martin (1959, p. 865).
6 Anderson and Martin (1959, p. 865).
7 Anderson and Martin (1959, p. 869).
8 Anderson and Martin (1959, p. 871).

firms and five bank dealers."[9] They did not, however, dismiss the complaint that the market was opaque: "the dealer market makes available to the public practically no information on its operations other than market bid and offer quotations." They concluded that "the lack of formal rules, supervision, and adequate information leaves the market open on occasion to suspicion that it may not always be operating in the public interest."[10]

Three key topics examined in the Treasury-Federal Reserve Study related to market functioning:

(1) *public* disclosure of dealer positions and transactions,[11]
(2) dealer finance, and
(3) prospects for a dealer organization.

The first topic was of contemporaneous interest; the second and third were more important as harbingers of later initiatives.

MARKET STATISTICS

Anderson and Martin stated that "openly competitive and efficient markets are characterized by informed buyers and sellers" and that "a broad range of objective information needs to be available to serve effectively the interests of all market participants." They suggested that "the present flow of information relating to the [Treasury] market is inadequate" but believed that "a reporting program can be worked out by the Federal Reserve and Treasury staffs to put an adequate information program into active operation in the not too distant future."[12]

Consonant with their suggestions, the Treasury-Federal Reserve Study included a supplementary report on market statistics.[13] The report stressed

[9] The seventeen dealers are identified at the end of chapter 7. See also Joint Economic Committee (1959, Part 6B, pp. 1507–9) and Meltzer and von der Linde (1960, p. 2).

[10] Anderson and Martin (1959, p. 872).

[11] The Federal Reserve Bank of New York already received, for use by Federal Reserve officials, information on dealer positions and activity on a daily basis. The information was provided voluntarily by most of the dealers that participated in open market operations. Joint Economic Committee (1959, Part 6B, p. 1541–43), statement of Robert Rouse that position data was submitted daily by about three-quarters of the participating dealers and that dealer conferences were held daily on a rotating basis. See also Joint Economic Committee (1959, Part 6B, p. 1572), statement of Girard Spencer, Salomon Brothers & Hutzler, that his firm made its data available to the New York Bank "because I feel it is vital for them to know the picture in the market, and the amount of activity in the various maturity categories."

[12] Anderson and Martin (1959, p. 874).

[13] U.S. Treasury and Federal Reserve System (1960b, pp. 1–44).

the need for more, and more public, statistics reflecting market activity, dealer financing, and the financial condition of dealers. It asserted that investors "want to know as much as they can about the prices and price changes for all issues; about the volume of trading underlying these price movements; about the possible influence of overhanging long or short positions; and about all other significant influences affecting both the actual supply and demand conditions and expectations concerning those conditions."[14]

With respect to information on prices and interest rates, the report concluded that "prices quoted for specific issues are readily available from dealers all of the time. There is no shortage of basic information, nor of processed composites of prices and rates, in terms of the quotations in effect at the close of each business day."[15]

With respect to trading activity, the report noted that stock exchanges regularly disclosed aggregate trading volumes, sometimes as often as hourly during the day, and that the volume of trading in individual issues was made public soon after the close of trading.[16] The report concluded that "fully adequate data [on trading activity] should be obtainable through direct reports from the dealers on their own transactions, possibly supplemented by reports from large city banks that maintain trading relations with their own or correspondent customers."[17]

With respect to dealer positions, the supplementary report broached the idea of publishing position data on an aggregate basis, "by groups of issues, and perhaps including totals for ... gross long and gross short positions." Such data, the report claimed, could alert the market "at times of rapid change to the magnitude of the inventory being carried." The report recognized, however, that "the details of a given dealer's position and holdings are ... the equivalent of essential trade secrets" and concluded that the rationale for publication was not "sufficiently clear cut or compelling to support an early decision."[18]

With respect to financing, the report observed that

> [b]ecause Government securities dealers have to carry inventories of some size, the availability and price of borrowed funds to them is one important determinant of their ability and readiness to position or sell securities. It is thus through dealer

[14] U.S. Treasury and Federal Reserve System (1960b, p. 7).
[15] U.S. Treasury and Federal Reserve System (1960b, p. 8).
[16] U.S. Treasury and Federal Reserve System (1960b, p. 8).
[17] U.S. Treasury and Federal Reserve System (1960b, p. 9).
[18] U.S. Treasury and Federal Reserve System (1960b, p. 11).

borrowing that one of the important conduits is formed between the money market and the whole array of Government securities, from the shortest to the longest. This is why information on the sources and amounts of dealer financing, and the rates that they pay, is important not only for investors ... but also for Treasury and Federal Reserve policy and operations.[19]

The report concluded that "there is surely a public interest to be served by the regular, frequent, and prompt publication of aggregate data on dealer borrowing."[20]

Finally, with respect to the financial condition of dealers, the report noted that "the Federal Reserve does business with the dealers for itself and on behalf of the Treasury, and is familiar with their financial standing and ability to perform." The report suggested that such familiarity might be enough "to lead to the conclusion that no regular publication of financial statements should be required." However, "the very special nature of the quasi-public responsibility exercised by the dealers, in making markets for the Government's own credit instruments, raises a question as to whether the public is not entitled to some open periodic disclosure."[21]

Advent of the Reporting Dealer Program

Between the fall of 1959 and the spring of 1961, Federal Reserve officials crafted a program for collecting and publishing information on dealer activity in the government securities market. A later report of the Comptroller General states that the program was intended to provide "current information on the functioning of the market ... to the public, to students of the market, and to market participants, including the Federal Reserve System and the Treasury Department."[22]

Initial Discussions

At the October 13, 1959, meeting of the Federal Open Market Committee, FOMC economist Ralph Young presented a staff study[23] setting forth "an inventory of areas for possible administrative action growing out the recent Treasury-Federal Reserve study of the Government securities market."[24]

[19] U.S. Treasury and Federal Reserve System (1960b, p. 13).
[20] U.S. Treasury and Federal Reserve System (1960b, p. 14).
[21] U.S. Treasury and Federal Reserve System (1960b, pp. 16–17).
[22] Comptroller General of the United States (1971, p. 6).
[23] Staff study dated September 28, 1959, attached to a memo dated October 5, 1959, from Winfield Riefler, FOMC Secretary, to members of the FOMC.
[24] Minutes of the Federal Open Market Committee, October 13, 1959, pp. 44–45.

One area of particular interest was a series of suggestions to provide "more adequate information about the Government securities market" based on "a new program of statistics collection from all Government securities dealers." The program would cover trading, positioning, and financing. Following a trial period, the study anticipated "public release [of the data] on an aggregate basis as might be deemed appropriate by the Treasury and the Federal Reserve System jointly."[25]

The general nature of the statistics to be collected was not an issue during the ensuing discussion, but a recommendation that the Committee consider the "appropriate assignment of responsibility for . . . collection and analysis, for example, to the Open Market Trading Desk, to the Research Department of the New York Reserve Bank, or to the Research Division of the Board of Governors" triggered intense debate.[26] Young noted that the managing partner of Aubrey Lanston & Co. objected to supplying information because of "the possibility that such information might be used by the Desk to trade against him."[27] When Winfield Riefler, the secretary of the FOMC, remarked that "there was an indication that the Lanston firm would furnish current data if they were collected by the Research Department and only aggregate figures were released outside that department," Frederick Deming, the president of the Federal Reserve Bank of Minneapolis, asked "whether this contemplated the possibility that information collected by the System from the dealers might be kept from the Desk."[28] It was one thing for a single dealer to decline to submit information to the Desk; it was quite another for the Desk to lose access to the individual data of *all* of the dealers.

Following the conclusion of the October 13 meeting, the New York Reserve Bank prepared a memorandum that set out the Bank's views on data collection.[29] The memo concluded that "we do not see that it matters very much who collects the data," provided that individual dealer data should be available to the Desk "as expeditiously as they are now available, i.e., by the time each day's approach to operations is formulated."[30]

25 Minutes of the Federal Open Market Committee, October 13, 1959, p. 46.

26 Minutes of the Federal Open Market Committee, October 13, 1959, p. 51.

27 Minutes of the Federal Open Market Committee, October 13, 1959, p. 52.

28 Minutes of the Federal Open Market Committee, October 13, 1959, p. 52.

29 Federal Reserve Bank of New York (1959). The memorandum, dated November 18, 1959, was intended as an *aide memoire* for Young. Minutes of the Federal Open Market Committee, January 12, 1960, p. 63.

30 Federal Reserve Bank of New York (1959, p. 14).

The memo justified the Desk's need for individual dealer data in light of its responsibility for executing open market operations, for "supplying information on and interpretations of market developments to the FOMC," and for "keeping the Treasury informed concerning market developments – a responsibility that assumes especially large dimensions prior to and during Treasury financing operations and during special occurrences such as the events of the summer of 1958."[31] The memo noted that "there are numerous occasions on which an aggregative change reflects in large part a change in the figures of one or two dealers, and there are other occasions in which an aggregative change reflects the net effect of sizable shifts in opposite directions by only a few dealers. The interpretation placed by the Desk upon the aggregative change in these cases is quite different than if the aggregative change were distributed widely among the dealers."[32]

A Joint Staff Proposal

Efforts to design a data collection program culminated in a January 1960 report jointly authored by staff of the Board of Governors, the Federal Reserve Bank of New York, and the Department of the Treasury – hereafter, the "joint staff report."[33]

The joint staff report proposed that data be collected each business day on transactions, positions, and sources of financing from "all Government securities dealers with whom the Securities Department of the Federal Reserve Bank of New York engages in transactions pursuant to the directions of the Federal Open Market Committee."[34] The data would be collected and collated by a new Department of Statistics on Market Operations within the Research and Statistics Function of the New York Bank. The manager of the System Open Market Account and his staff would receive summaries of the data but, subject to several exceptions, would not have access to data on individual dealers.[35] The exceptions

[31] Federal Reserve Bank of New York (1959, p. 3).

[32] Federal Reserve Bank of New York (1959, p. 4).

[33] Young et al. (1960). The authors of the report included Ralph Young, Albert Koch, and Peter Keir from the Board of Governors, John Larkin and Robert Roosa from the New York Reserve Bank, and Robert Mayo and R. Duane Saunders from the Treasury Department. Memo from Ralph Young to Federal Open Market Committee, "Information Program for the Government Securities Market," January 7, 1960.

[34] Young et al. (1960, p. 1).

[35] The ad hoc subcommittee made a similar recommendation in 1952. See Joint Committee on the Economic Report (1954, p. 280). The FOMC ultimately rejected that recommendation. Minutes of the Federal Open Market Committee, March 4-5, 1953, pp. 52–53.

included data necessary for entering into repurchase agreements, episodes of disorderly markets, other instances of an exceptional nature at the direction of the president of the Bank, and in connection with any Treasury financing.

A sample reporting schedule provided for reports of transactions with a variety of counterparties, including "other dealers in Government securities" and "other dealers and brokers." The distinction between the two dealer categories required that each reporting dealer be appraised of the identity of every other reporting dealer – in order to determine whether transactions with a particular dealer were to be included with "other dealers in Government securities" or with "other dealers and brokers." More particularly, it would require, for the first time, *continuous public* identification of the dealers designated as counterparties in open market operations.[36]

Chairman Martin initiated discussion of the joint staff report at the January 12, 1960, meeting of the Federal Open Market Committee. Martin observed that the proposed program had four objectives:

(1) to enlarge the factual base available daily for System open market operations and Treasury debt management,
(2) to provide adequate information to meet potential Congressional requests,
(3) to provide a flow of current information for public use, and
(4) to do these things in such a way as to protect the confidentiality of individual dealer reports and at the same time avoid any market criticism of System operating officers.[37]

Martin opined that while it "had not come out with all of the answers," the report "appeared on the whole to be one that should be carried forward."[38]

[36] In 1985, E. Gerald Corrigan, then president of the Federal Reserve Bank of New York, stated that "the emergence of the list of primary dealers as a public document occurred in 1960 as an adjunct to an effort to receive more information from the primary dealers about their transaction volume. In 1960, the New York Fed instituted a formal reporting system in which primary dealers were requested to provide information on their transaction volume according to type of customer. In order to distinguish the amount of "professional" trading from the distribution of securities to customers, dealers were asked to report separately their transactions with other reporting dealers and their transactions with all other customers. The list of reporting dealers was distributed so that dealers could know the identities of the other reporting dealers, and, so, categorize their transaction volume appropriately." Committee on Banking, Housing, and Urban Affairs (1985, p. 135).

[37] Minutes of the Federal Open Market Committee, January 12, 1960, p. 60.

[38] Minutes of the Federal Open Market Committee, January 12, 1960, p. 61.

President Hayes of the New York Fed agreed that the proposed program was "constructive and needed." However, he expressed reservations about severing the Desk's access to individual dealer data, believing as he did that "the more the Desk knew, the more effective a job it could do."[39] Robert Rouse was also uncomfortable with the prospect of being denied access to individual dealer data. Rouse acknowledged that "ordinarily, . . . aggregate data would be sufficient to form an over-all appraisal of market conditions,"[40] but noted that "there are, and have been, many occasions when it has been necessary to go beyond the data covering all dealers as a group and to review the operations of individual dealers for the purpose of interpreting and evaluating the significance of the aggregative data."[41] Despite the reservations of Hayes and Rouse, no objections were heard when Martin proposed that the Committee adopt the recommendations of the joint staff report. As a result, the Desk lost regular access to individual dealer data for seven years.[42]

Implementation

Implementation of the joint staff report proceeded in three stages. First, the dealers had to agree to submit the requested data on a voluntary basis, there being no statutory basis to require submission. Second, a trial period of data collection was needed to identify and remediate unanticipated problems. Finally, the System had to proceed with publication.

[39] Minutes of the Federal Open Market Committee, January 12, 1960, p. 61.

[40] Minutes of the Federal Open Market Committee, January 12, 1960, p. 61.

[41] Minutes of the Federal Open Market Committee, January 12, 1960, p. 62.

[42] Minutes of the Federal Open Market Committee, January 12, 1960, p. 64. The lack of access contributed to a deterioration in the Desk's ability to acquire and interpret market intelligence. "Policy Issue #6, Availability of Individual Dealer Statistics to Trading Desk," unpublished paper of the Joint Treasury-Federal Reserve Study of the U.S. Government Securities Market, October 6, 1967, p. 2. In a 1967 letter to government securities dealers, Martin and Treasury Secretary Henry Fowler stated that Desk staff had had access to individual dealer data "only on a few unusual occasions" and that it had "become apparent that the quality of information available to the Trading Desk for interpreting the state of the market [had] deteriorated considerably because of the lack of access." Minutes of the Federal Open Market Committee, October 24, 1967, p. 71.

In 1967, a second Treasury-Federal Reserve study of the government securities market revisited the access question and recommended that the restriction be lifted. "Policy Issue #6, Availability of Individual Dealer Statistics to Trading Desk," unpublished paper of the Joint Treasury-Federal Reserve Study of the U.S. Government Securities Market, October 6, 1967, p. 3. Consultation with the primary dealers did not reveal any deep antipathy to the recommendation and the FOMC accepted the recommendation. Minutes of the Federal Open Market Committee, October 24, 1967, pp. 69–72.

At the May 3, 1960, FOMC meeting, Young advised the Committee that the program was moving ahead and that dealers would begin submitting data later in the month.[43] Data collection commenced, as anticipated, in late May.

The FOMC addressed the matter of regular public disclosure of aggregate summaries of the data at its March 7, 1961, meeting. Martin believed that "more public information on the Government securities market was required and that it was necessary to take steps to arrange to have such information supplied in some way."[44] The Committee concurred.

A week later, Martin and the new Secretary of the Treasury, C. Douglas Dillon, advised the reporting dealers of their decision to proceed with publication.[45] Two weeks after that the Federal Reserve Bank of New York issued a press release announcing the publication program. The Bank noted that comparatively little information had been available to the public concerning the operation of the government securities market and suggested that "the new program represents a constructive advance in the public interest. It should make possible a wider and better understanding of the operations of this market and the relations between it and other financial markets. This better understanding may contribute to the effective functioning of all our financial mechanisms."[46]

Details of the published data were set out in the April 1961 *Federal Reserve Bulletin*.[47] The data included

- weekly averages of daily aggregate reporting dealer *transactions* in Treasury securities, classified by maturity (under one year, one to five years, five to ten years, and over ten years) and by counterparty (other reporting dealers, other dealers, commercial banks, and all others);
- weekly averages of daily aggregate reporting dealer *positions* in Treasury securities, on a committed basis as of the close of business, classified by maturity (under one year, one to five years, and over five years); and
- weekly averages of daily aggregate reporting dealer *financings* of Treasury securities, classified by source (commercial banks in New York City, all other commercial banks, corporations other than commercial banks and insurance companies, and all others).

43 Minutes of the Federal Open Market Committee, May 3, 1960, p. 49.

44 Minutes of the Federal Open Market Committee, March 7, 1961, pp. 68–69.

45 Minutes of the Federal Open Market Committee, March 7, 1961, pp. 69–70.

46 "Data Expanding for U.S. Issues" *New York Times*, March 29, 1961, p. 45. See also "N.Y. Reserve Bank to Issue 4 New Reports on Federal Securities," *Wall Street Journal*, March 29, 1961, p. 13.

47 "Statistics on the Government Securities Market," *Federal Reserve Bulletin*, April 1961, pp. 397–404.

DEALER FINANCE

In the late 1950s, government securities dealers financed their long positions through three channels: loans from large New York banks, repurchase agreements with out-of-town banks and nonbank institutions (such as corporate treasurers, state and local governments, and pension and investment funds) and – in the case of nonbank dealers – repurchase agreements with the Federal Reserve. Dealers financed their short positions with security loans from large New York banks (against pledge of other securities and payment of a fee of ½ percent per annum) and reverse repurchase agreements with out-of-town banks.[48]

The Treasury-Federal Reserve Study observed that two large New York banks made dealer loans available on a regular basis and that several other large banks did so when it suited their interests. Dealers were able to access cheaper credit through repurchase agreements with out-of-town institutions but were willing to pay anywhere from 25 to 50 basis points over the repo rate for New York bank credit in light of the lower cost of delivering collateral within the city.

Dealers suggested that the government securities market would function more smoothly if they could access cheaper and more reliably available credit. In particular, they suggested that the Fed could be more lenient in lending on System repos and could provide discount window credit on more favorable terms to banks that were lending to dealers.[49]

Whether the Fed should, directly or indirectly, extend credit to government securities dealers on preferential terms was a topic that arose from time to time, usually following a poorly received Treasury offering or a sharp fall in bond prices. A complaint from Under Secretary of the Treasury Julian Baird to Chairman Martin about a lack of dealer support in the July 1959 auction of one-year Treasury bills sparked a lengthy discussion by the Federal Open Market Committee about whether the System should be more supportive of dealer underwriting activities.[50]

Dealers also pointed out that better access to securities to finance short positions would further promote market functioning. They observed that short selling was "essential to the effective maintenance of continuous markets," that without short selling "arbitraging ... and hedging of risk exposure on long positions" was problematic, but that short sales had been

[48] U.S. Treasury and Federal Reserve System (1959, pp. 23 and 38).
[49] U.S. Treasury and Federal Reserve System (1959, p. 36).
[50] Minutes of the Federal Open Market Committee, August 18, 1959, pp. 33–45.

"seriously hampered by the relatively limited facilities to borrow securities."[51] Treasury securities had become more difficult to borrow in part because pension funds, trusts, and state and local governments had been increasing their holdings but frequently lacked authority to lend.[52]

PROSPECTS FOR A DEALER ASSOCIATION

The Treasury-Federal Reserve Study also examined whether "an organization of Government Securities dealers might improve the functioning of the market."[53] Possible activities included:

- standardizing trading practices, such as trading for when-issued and deferred settlement, treatment of settlement fails, quotation conventions, and trading hours;
- developing a code of conduct addressing, *inter alia*, the fair and equitable treatment of customer orders that conflicted with the execution of proprietary purchases and sales;
- promulgating regulations aimed at curbing speculative abuses;
- sponsoring an interdealer brokerage facility;
- improving dealer access to credit and developing new sources for borrowing securities;
- promulgating minimum capital requirements;
- advising the Treasury on its offerings; and
- encouraging the underwriting of Treasury offerings.[54]

However, the report warned that a dealer organization was liable to "rigidify market practices" and that it was not certain that "innovations and adjustments in the market to changing conditions would develop as rapidly as under the present unregulated setup."[55] The study also noted that "Federal Reserve conduct of open market operations and Treasury management of the public debt require an impersonal approach to the

[51] U.S. Treasury and Federal Reserve System (1959, pp. 23–24). See also Roosa (1956, p. 29), stating that "few banks will lend securities," and Meltzer and von der Linde (1960, p. 95), stating that "the absence of an ability to borrow [securities] reduces the opportunities for dealers to arbitrage or to supply securities to the market."

[52] Meltzer and von der Linde (1960, p. 95).

[53] U.S. Treasury and Federal Reserve System (1960b, p. 96). Garbade and Keane (2017) describe a World War II–era dealer association, the Government Security Dealer Group.

[54] U.S. Treasury and Federal Reserve System (1960b, pp. 97–104). The report noted (p. 98) that "the participation of individual dealers in [Treasury] financings varies and on occasion has been limited."

[55] U.S. Treasury and Federal Reserve System (1960b, pp. 110–11).

market" and cautioned that "neither [agency] should be entangled with a supervisory relationship to this market."[56]

The report suggested that "if a voluntary organization were to exercise even mild disciplinary influence over its members, it would have to offer its members significant privileges as an inducement for joining," possibly including

- the privilege of trading with the Federal Reserve,
- preferential allotments of new securities,
- exemption from standard or required margins on loans collateralized with government securities, and
- improved access to financing.[57]

Alternatively, the Federal Reserve or the Treasury could affirmatively designate member dealers.

[56] U.S. Treasury and Federal Reserve System (1960b, p. 107).
[57] U.S. Treasury and Federal Reserve System (1960b, p. 106).

PART V

THE END OF BILLS PREFERABLY

Valued at the official price of $35 per ounce, the US gold stock fell from $22.9 billion at the end of 1957 to $17.8 billion at the end of 1960. The 22 percent, three-year decline was the largest and longest since World War II and included losses of $2.3 billion in 1958, $1.1 billion in 1959, and $1.6 billion in the second half of 1960.[1] The outflow provoked an important shift in U.S. monetary policy, the first time since the Great Contraction of 1929–33 that international economic developments impinged on the formation of monetary policy.[2] Chapter 18 describes the gold drain and the reaction of US monetary authorities.

The gold outflow occurred simultaneously with a recession in aggregate economic activity. The concurrent phenomena appeared to require choosing between higher short-term interest rates (to staunch the gold drain) and lower long-term rates (to promote recovery). Some Federal Reserve officials, and some officials of the incoming Kennedy administration, suggested that the System could achieve *both* objectives by replacing intermediate- and long-term debt in the hands of the public with short-term debt. Chapter 19 examines how, in 1960, economists understood the determinants of the term structure of interest rates and describes how the desire to keep yields on short-term debt relatively high and yields on long-term debt relatively low led to the abandonment of bills preferably.

[1] Board of Governors of the Federal Reserve System (1976, table 14.1).

[2] The 1960 Annual Report of Open Market Operations observed (p. 1) that the gold drain in the second half of 1960 "made it necessary, for the first time in several decades, for the System to give particularly close attention to the international implication of its credit policies, especially as these policies were reflected in short term interest rates."

18

The 1958–1960 Gold Drain

Since 1933, all gold (including gold bullion and gold coin) physically located in the United States – other than what was owned by foreign official institutions, included in numismatic collections, or used for commercial purposes – was owned by the Department of the Treasury.[1] President Franklin Roosevelt fixed the price of gold at $35 per ounce in 1934 and the Treasury Department thereafter stood ready to buy at that price, less ¼ percent for handling, and to sell to foreign central banks at the same price, plus ¼ percent.[2] Chart 18.1 shows that most of the Treasury's gold was pledged against dollar-denominated gold certificates issued, at the rate of $35 per ounce of gold pledged, to Federal Reserve Banks in return for book-entry credits to Treasury accounts at the Banks – commonly and collectively referred to as the Treasury General Account (TGA).

The Treasury paid for its gold purchases with checks drawn on the TGA. Upon receipt, the gold could be pledged against the issuance of new certificates, thereby "monetizing" the gold and restoring the TGA balance. Payments to sellers added to commercial bank reserves and, unless

[1] The Executive Order of April 5, 1933, reprinted in 1933 Treasury Annual Report, pp. 197–98, ordered all persons (including individuals, partnerships, and corporations) within the United States to surrender their gold to a Federal Reserve Bank against payment in "any other form of coin or currency coined or issued under the laws of the United States." Section 2 of the Gold Reserve Act of January 30, 1934, transferred ownership of Federal Reserve gold to the U.S. Treasury.

[2] Presidential Proclamation, January 31, 1934, reprinted in *Federal Reserve Bulletin*, February 1934, pp. 68–69; Statement to the Press by the President on January 31, 1934, reprinted in *Federal Reserve Bulletin*, February 1934, pp. 67–68; Statement to the Press by the Secretary of the Treasury on January 31, 1934, reprinted in *Federal Reserve Bulletin*, February 1934, p. 69; and Statement to the Press by the Secretary of the Treasury on February 1, 1934, reprinted in *Federal Reserve Bulletin*, February 1934, pp. 69–70.

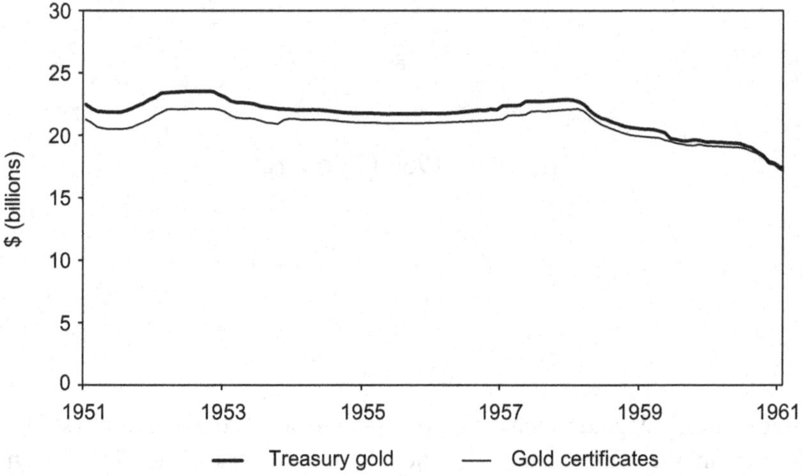

Chart 18.1 Treasury gold (end of month) and gold certificates issued by the Treasury to Federal Reserve Banks (monthly averages of daily figures).
Board of Governors of the Federal Reserve System (1976, tables 9.7 and 14.1).

sterilized with sales of securities from the System Open Market Account, made for easier money market conditions.[3]

Conversely, if the Treasury needed gold to satisfy demands from foreign central banks, it could direct the Federal Reserve to debit the TGA and return a corresponding quantity of gold certificates, releasing the gold pledged against the certificates and making it available for sale. Payments received from buyers were credited to the TGA (again restoring the balance in that account) and reduced bank reserves. Unless sterilized with purchases for the Open Market Account, the payments would lead to tighter money market conditions.

Federal Reserve Banks were required by statute to maintain a gold certificate reserve of at least 25 percent of their note and deposit liabilities.[4] At the end of 1957 the Reserve Banks had $27.5 billion of note liabilities

[3] Garbade (2012, pp. 243–45) discusses the flood of unsterilized gold that came into the United States after January 1934. Garbade (2012, p. 312, fn. 28) discusses how the Treasury sterilized gold inflows between December 1936 and March 1938. Garbade (2016) describes how the Treasury avoided a debt ceiling crisis in November 1953 by monetizing $500 million of free gold.

[4] Section 16 of the Federal Reserve Act specified gold reserve requirements of 40 percent of note liabilities and 35 percent of deposit liabilities. The Gold Reserve Act of January 30, 1934, recast the requirement in the form of gold certificates. The Act of June 12, 1945, reduced the reserve requirement to 25 percent for both notes and deposits.

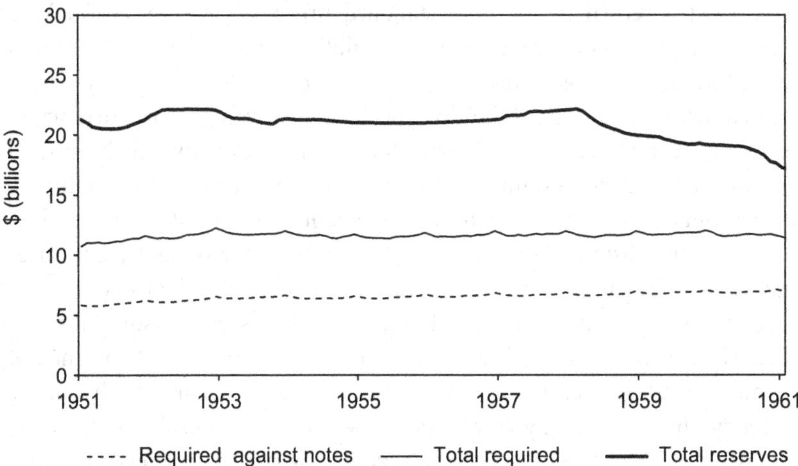

Chart 18.2 Required and total Federal Reserve gold certificate reserves. Monthly averages of daily figures.
Board of Governors of the Federal Reserve System (1976, table 9.7).

and $20.1 billion of deposit liabilities[5] and thus had an $11.9 billion gold certificate reserve requirement. They held $22.1 billion of gold certificates, leaving them with $10.2 billion of excess reserves. Chart 18.2 shows the behavior of the Fed's gold certificate reserves and reserve requirements during the 1950s.

GOLD IN THE INTERNATIONAL PAYMENTS SYSTEM

The international payments system was, in the late 1950s, based on fixed exchange rates that referenced US dollars as the numeraire. Policymakers had met in Bretton Woods, New Hampshire, in the summer of 1944 to map out a fixed-rate system intended to facilitate international trade that would nevertheless permit the pursuit of domestic macroeconomic agendas.[6] The world gold stock was too small and too unevenly distributed

[5] Board of Governors of the Federal Reserve System (1976, table 9.1B).

[6] See Steil (2013) and Conway (2014). Bordo, Humpage, and Schwartz (2015) state (p. 120) that "The Bretton Woods fixed-exchange-rate system attempted to maintain par values and promoted free cross-border financial flows while still allowing countries to promote domestic macroeconomic objectives, notably full employment," and (p. 121) that "The officials who signed the ... Articles of Agreement at Bretton Woods ... envisioned an international financial system based on close cooperation that would foster stability, promote full employment, and prevent a return to the beggar-thy-neighbor policies of the early 1930s."

to support a return to the gold standard prevailing before World War I. The policymakers chose instead to use dollars as the reference asset and created the International Monetary Fund to administer the new system.

Each member country of the IMF specified a par value for its currency in terms of US dollars.[7] Great Britain, for example, initially set the pound sterling at $4.03 per pound.[8] A country was expected to maintain the market value of its currency within one percent of the stipulated par value.[9]

To buffer seasonal and cyclical fluctuations in payments, countries maintained dollar-denominated reserves, including deposits at the Federal Reserve Bank of New York and investments in Treasury bills and other similar instruments. If a country enjoyed a surplus in its balance of payments and residents wanted to convert more dollars to the home currency than conversely, the country was obliged to sell its currency (against buying dollars) to keep the currency below 101 percent of its par value, thereby adding to its dollar reserves. Conversely, if a country had a balance of payments deficit and residents wanted to convert more of the home currency to dollars than the other way around, the country was obliged to buy its currency (against selling dollars) to keep the home currency above 99 percent of its par value, thereby reducing its dollar reserves.

A country with depleted dollar reserves was expected to attract fresh foreign funds (and, therefore, dollars) by raising interest rates and increasing exports. Conversely, a country with a balance of payments surplus and a dollar reserve larger than necessary was expected to run off its surplus reserves by reducing interest rates and expanding imports. To limit the disruptive impact of necessitous policy changes, a country with depleted reserves could borrow dollars from the IMF, albeit on terms that gave it reason to address expeditiously its underlying balance of payments deficit.

Foreign governments accepted dollars, in lieu of gold, as the basis for the post-war international payments system because of the credibility of the US commitment to buy and sell gold at $35 per ounce. As long as that commitment went unquestioned, it made little difference whether a country held dollars or gold as a reserve asset.

[7] de Vries (1969b) describes the process of setting par values. See also de Vries (1969a).

[8] de Vries (1969b, table 1).

[9] Policymakers understood that the relative productivities of different national economies could change over time and they empowered the IMF to oversee changes in par values to address "fundamental disequilibria" in exchange rates. Great Britain, for example, reduced the par value of the pound to $2.80 in September 1949. de Vries (1969c, table 4).

THE LONDON GOLD MARKET

In addition to its role as a reserve asset against the dollar, gold was in demand for industrial purposes and for fabrication into jewelry. Commercial gold markets began to reappear as soon as European and Asian economies began recovering from the ravages of World War II. The most important market was in London.

In March 1954, five bullion dealers – N.M. Rothschild & Sons; Johnson, Matthey & Co.; Samuel Montagu & Co., Ltd.; Sharps, Pixley & Co.; and Mocatta & Goldsmid Ltd. – reestablished the pre-war London "fixing" market.[10] Representatives of the five dealers met each business day at 10:30 a.m. in the offices of N. M. Rothschild & Sons to "fix," or identify, a market-clearing price. The fixing price balanced the aggregate purchase and sale interests of the five dealers and their customers and was widely accepted as the best measure of gold's value at the moment of the fixing.[11] Following a fixing the five dealers were free to trade with each other and with customers at whatever prices best reflected their respective assessments of market conditions.

Trading on the London gold market was relatively limited in the mid-1950s and prices were always close to the Treasury price of $35 per ounce. The price couldn't fall much below $35 because the Treasury would pay $34.9125 per ounce ($35 less ¼ percent for handling) for essentially unlimited quantities, and it couldn't rise much above $35 as long as the Treasury was prepared to sell at $35.0875. Nevertheless, the existence of a free market for gold had the potential to cause trouble. If commercial, industrial, and speculative demand threatened to outstrip supply and the London price rose much above $35, the Treasury could face a difficult choice between selling gold in sufficient volume to keep the market price near $35 or seeing the market price rise substantially above the official price – something that was likely to lead foreign central banks to question the US commitment that was at the heart of the Bretton Woods system.[12]

THE PLACE OF GOLD IN FOMC DELIBERATIONS

Yields on thirteen-week Treasury bills over the interval from 1958 to 1960 played a crucial role in determining the timing and magnitude of gold

10 "London to Reopen Gold Market," *New York Times*, March 20, 1954, p. 22, and "London Gold Market Reopened for First Day's Trading Since 1939," *New York Times*, March 23, 1954, p. 35.

11 See Jarecki (1976) and "The London Gold Market," Federal Reserve Bank of New York *Monthly Review*, March 1964, pp. 34–36.

12 See Combs (1976, p. 45).

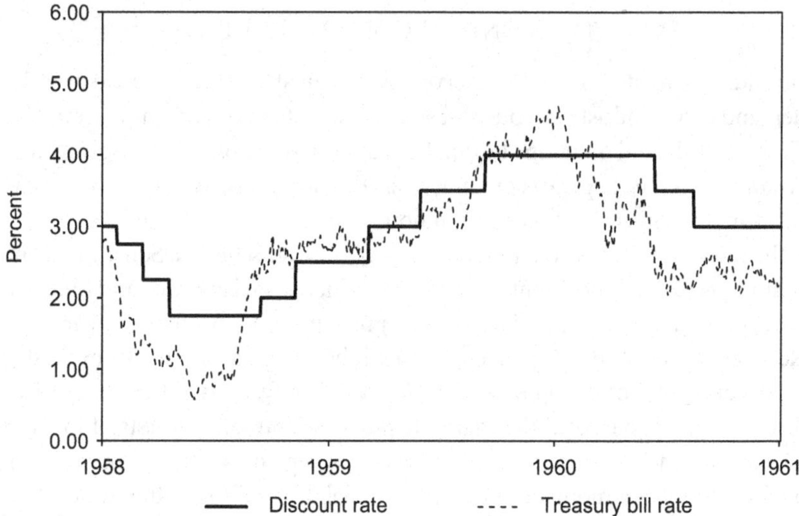

Chart 18.3 Thirteen-week Treasury bill rate and Federal Reserve Bank of New York discount rate. Daily figures.
Federal Reserve Statistical Release H.15 and Board of Governors of the Federal Reserve System (1976, table 12.1A).

outflows from the United States. As shown in Chart 18.3, bill yields hit a low of about ⅝ percent in late May 1958, approximately coincident with the April trough in economic activity. Rates rose as the economy recovered over the next two years, peaking at 4⅝ percent in early January 1960, but then slid off again with the onset of another recession, averaging about 2¼ percent in the second half of 1960.

Yields on Treasury bills in mid-1958 gave foreign central banks little incentive to hold bills in lieu of gold and some chose to convert part of their dollar balances to gold at the Treasury's gold window.[13] Staff reviews of financial market developments at the beginning of every FOMC meeting remarked on the gold drain, primarily in the context of the concomitant reserve drain that had to be sterilized with open market purchases of Treasury bills.[14]

[13] The 1958 Annual Report of Open Market Operations noted (p. 4) that "the heavy outflow of gold reflected not only the stronger financial position of European countries and the deficits in the United States balance of payments, but the sharp decline in domestic short-term money rates as well."

[14] The 1958 Annual Report of Open Market Operations stated (p. 4) that open market operations "to supply funds to the market to maintain the money market conditions and

There was virtually no discussion among Committee members, and little mention by staff economists, of whether the gold drain had implications for monetary policy beyond the technical issue of sterilizing open market purchases. Exceptionally, on two occasions FOMC economist Woodlief Thomas sought to broaden the discussion. At the October 17, 1958, meeting Thomas observed that,

> [t]he drain on bank reserves resulting from foreign gold acquisitions ... has amounted to about half a billion dollars in the past three months. ... This is largely the result of fundamental forces in our international economic position, that can be changed only through the operation of market forces and competitive factors. While the effects of the drain on bank reserves may be offset by System open market operations, *this situation is one that calls for a generally restrictive credit policy in this country.*[15]

At the November 10 meeting Thomas pointed to the gold outflow as an "aspect of the current situation that might call for more restrictive policies." He noted that the outflow "reflects basically increased productive capacity aboard and the movement of capital" but added, more ominously, that "it also reflects what might be called a flight from the dollar."[16]

Gold losses declined from $2¼ billion in 1958 to $1 billion in 1959 as bill yields rose but nevertheless became increasingly important for monetary policy. Some FOMC members began to look beyond the technical issue of sterilization, seeking to identify linkages between gold outflows, financial market conditions, and Federal Reserve policy.

In January 1959, Governor A. L. Mills asserted that "the Federal Reserve ... has international financial responsibilities" and questioned whether the gold outflow should be fully sterilized:

> An increase in the discount rate ... might be regarded by the domestic and international financial communities as an action on the part of the System to recognize the outflow of gold during the past eighteen months, and through such recognition to state tacitly that the System proposed to subject the private economy to the discipline that is implicit in a gold outflow by *terminating a policy of acquiring U.S. Government securities to offset gold withdrawals.*[17]

the levels of reserve availability sought by the Committee" required "almost constant System action."

15 Minutes of the Federal Open Market Committee, October 21, 1958, pp. 17–18. Emphasis added.

16 Minutes of the Federal Open Market Committee, November 10, 1958, pp. 10 and 11.

17 Minutes of the Federal Open Market Committee, January 6, 1959, p. 18. Emphasis added.

Mills noted that higher Treasury bill yields "would tend to stem the outflow of gold" and "might draw gold back to this country because of the more attractive investment opportunities offered in the U.S. Government securities market."[18]

Two months later, at a time when the discount rate was 2½ percent, Mills asserted that "a 3 per cent discount rate as an alignment with a corresponding structure of market interest rates is to be desired, especially for its influence toward making the Unites States money market more attractive for the investment of foreign funds and thus acting as check against the future outflow of gold."[19] Two days later the Board of Governors approved an increase in the discount rate to 3 percent.

In May 1959, Woodlief Thomas observed that "projections based on customary seasonal changes, together with moderate gold outflow, indicate a further substantial tightening of bank reserve positions in the absence of System operations." He suggested that while "it would seem appropriate to provide reserves to cover customary seasonal needs, some question may be raised about offsetting the gold outflow, which reflects influences with respect to competitive pricing of goods and to money market developments that might call for a tightening of credit restraints."[20]

In November, Delos Johns, the president of the Federal Reserve Bank of St. Louis, expressed the view that "the Committee might gear its sights to supplying the reserves needed to offset [a seasonal increase in public demand for currency]" but questioned "whether the System should supply reserves to offset any drain accompanying an outflow of gold."[21]

Gold outflows in the first six months of 1960 fell sharply, to a total of about $140 million, but began to recover following a reduction in the discount rate in early June and a concurrent fall in the thirteen-week bill rate from 2.70 percent to 2.30 percent.

Data available at the July 6 FOMC meeting indicated renewed deterioration in the US balance of payments. Alfred Hayes, the president of the Federal Reserve Bank of New York, suggested giving "some weight" to balance of payments concerns in the absence of any clear need for lower interest rates. (A recession had started in April but was not yet visible in the data.) He recommended giving the manager of the Open Market Account discretion "to operate freely throughout the short-term area,

[18] Minutes of the Federal Open Market Committee, January 6, 1959, p. 19.
[19] Minutes of the Federal Open Market Committee, March 3, 1959, p. 43.
[20] Minutes of the Federal Open Market Committee, May 5, 1959, p. 11.
[21] Minutes of the Federal Open Market Committee, November 24, 1959, p. 15.

instead of confining his attention to bills," with the objective of minimizing the impact on bill rates of any actions aimed at sterilizing gold outflows. Governor C. Canby Balderston believed otherwise, that "for the System to monkey around with rates through its own actions seemed . . . to assume a burden that properly belonged to the Treasury." Balderston stated that, in lieu of any System action, he would like to see the Treasury increase its bill offerings.[22]

Gold outflows strengthened further after mid-July. In late July Woodlief Thomas remarked on staff projections that "allow for a gold drain of about $100 million a month, which would build up to a substantial amount by the end of the year."[23] In mid-September Robert Rouse, the manager of the System Open Market Account, noted an "accelerated gold outflow" and Arthur Marget, director of the Division of International Finance at the Board of Governors, pointed out an article in the *Financial Times* that identified "growing mistrust of the dollar" as "the root of the recent resumption of the gold outflow."[24] Chairman Martin attributed international concerns about the value of the dollar to the June reduction in the discount rate and "the appearance that the country might be embarking on a cheap money policy."[25]

By early October, the conflict between keeping foreign accounts interested in bills and countering the deepening recession was clear to all. Substituting for Hayes at the October 4 FOMC meeting, William Treiber, the first vice president of the Federal Reserve Bank of New York, suggested that a reduction in long-term interest rates would "contribute to economic activity" but that "it may no longer be practicable for the Federal Reserve to seek to bring about a substantial reduction in long-term rates by helping to produce a very low Treasury bill rate."[26]

THE BREAK-OUT OF LONDON GOLD PRICES

On Thursday, October 20, the price of gold in London was fixed at $36.40 in the morning meeting of the five bullion dealers. Later in the day gold traded above $40 in the over-the-counter market. The break-out damaged the credibility of the US commitment to $35 gold.[27]

[22] Minutes of the Federal Open Market Committee, July 6, 1960, pp. 14 and 36.

[23] Minutes of the Federal Open Market Committee, July 26, 1960, p. 9.

[24] Minutes of the Federal Open Market Committee, September 13, 1960, pp. 3 and 10.

[25] Minutes of the Federal Open Market Committee, September 13, 1960, p. 42.

[26] Minutes of the Federal Open Market Committee, October 4, 1960, p. 16.

[27] "Free Gold Prices Spurt in Europe," *New York Times*, October 21, 1960, p.1, stating that "a free-market gold price well above the official rate cast a serious psychological reflection on the dollar"; "Bullion Rate Hits $40.60 in London," *New York Times*, October 21, 1960,

Pressure on gold prices had been evident for several days. Prices rose from $35.26 on Monday to $35.33 on Tuesday and $35.60 on Wednesday. The asserted willingness of the US Treasury to sell gold to foreign central banks at $35.0875 per ounce, coupled with the $0.12 per ounce cost of shipping gold from New York to London,[28] suggested an arbitrage threshold of about $35.21. Adding a few cents for profit and compensation for the risk of shipping delays gave the commonly accepted "trigger point" of $35.25, above which foreign central banks had an economic incentive to sell gold in London and to cover their sales with purchases from the Treasury.[29] That gold traded above the trigger point on Tuesday and Wednesday suggested the Treasury might not be willing to sell all the gold demanded.

The October 20 break-out provoked an immediate denial from Treasury officials that there was any softening of the Department's commitment to $35 gold:

> The United States will continue its policy of buying gold from and selling gold to foreign governments, central banks and, under certain conditions, international institutions, for the settlement of international balances or for other legitimate purposes, at the established rate of $35 per fine troy ounce, exclusive of handling charges. As Secretary [of the Treasury Robert] Anderson has stated many times in the past, it is our firm position to maintain the dollar at its existing gold parity.[30]

Following Treasury gold sales through the Bank of England (undertaken because the Treasury could not sell gold directly on the London market),[31] prices settled back towards $35. The damage, however, had been done. Market participants now had concrete reason to question the permanence of $35 gold.[32]

p. 54; and "Washington Concedes Damage Gold Boom Has Done to Dollar," *New York Times*, October 22, 1960, p. 35, stating that U.S. officials "were willing to concede that even a one-day spectacle hurts the dollar, by raising doubts," and that "the simple fact of the price increase reflected some nervousness . . . and presumably will cause some other holders of dollars to think twice."

28 Coombs (1976, p. 47).

29 "Free Gold Prices Spurt in Europe," *New York Times*, October 21, 1960, p.1, and Meltzer (2009, p. 359), stating that "an opportunity opened for central banks to buy gold at the U.S. Treasury and resell it at a profit in the London market."

30 "Treasury Says Gold Price Jump in Europe Won't Change Policy," *New York Times*, October 21, 1960, p. 54.

31 Yeager (1966, p. 447).

32 Coombs (1976, p. 57) states that the break-out left "worldwide confidence in the heretofore sacrosanct dollar . . . badly jolted."

THE PLACE OF GOLD IN FOMC DELIBERATIONS AFTER THE BREAK-OUT

When the FOMC met on the Tuesday after the Thursday break-out, it faced two problems: supporting an economy that was continuing to weaken and doing what it could to staunch the gold drain. Addressing the first problem required more reserves and lower interest rates; addressing the second problem required no lower, and preferably higher, short-term rates. Rouse observed that the two objectives were "not entirely compatible."[33]

Committee members agreed that the benchmark thirteen-week bill rate should be kept above 2 percent – the first time since the Accord that monetary policy was phrased so specifically in terms of an interest rate.[34] Hayes wanted to set a floor under the bill rate, arguing that "one of the causes of the gold speculation has been fear that this country might resort to unduly loose monetary and fiscal policies in an effort to combat recessionary tendencies."[35] H. Gavin Leedy, the president of the Federal Reserve Bank of Kansas City, thought the System "should be sensitive to the problem of the short-term rate and should attempt to do what it could to keep bill rates from drifting lower."[36] Chairman Martin stated that he too "would like to see the short-term rate stay at 2 per cent or above."[37]

There was also agreement on the importance of maintaining an ample supply of free reserves. Toward the end of the meeting Rouse expressed his understanding that "there should be free reserves at all times." The minutes of the meeting state that "there was no indication of views to the contrary."[38]

The Committee sought to achieve the two incompatible objectives – Woodlief Thomas remarked that "there had never been a time in history when there were free reserves for any extended period and the bill rate remained above 2 per cent"[39] – by proceeding along two tracks.

[33] Minutes of the Federal Open Market Committee, October 25, 1960, p. 2.

[34] Cooper (1967, p. 19) states that, prior to the fourth quarter of 1960, the FOMC "scrupulously [avoided] any specific interest rate objectives."

[35] Minutes of the Federal Open Market Committee, October 25, 1960, pp. 16 and 17.

[36] Minutes of the Federal Open Market Committee, October 25, 1960, pp. 32–33.

[37] Minutes of the Federal Open Market Committee, October 25, 1960, p. 50.

[38] Minutes of the Federal Open Market Committee, October 25, 1960, p. 55. Rouse further stated that he "interpreted the discussion as meaning that although no specific target was being suggested, the Committee would have in mind somewhere between \$300 to \$500 million of free reserves."

[39] Minutes of the Federal Open Market Committee, October 25, 1960, p. 50.

First, the Committee instructed Rouse to take "current international developments into account" in directing open market operations[40] – a euphemism for initiating operations in short-term securities other than bills, including notes and bonds under fifteen months to maturity as well as certificates. (The bills preferably doctrine precluded operations in longer-term Treasury debt but allowed – although it did not encourage – operations in short-term coupon-bearing securities.) The 1960 Markets annual report states that,

> While the System policy during the final few months of the year was designed to provide the reserves needed to stimulate business expansion, care was taken to meet this objective with minimum impact on short-term rates, so as to avoid aggravation of the outflow of short-term funds. This qualification was formally acknowledged at the meeting on October 25, when the New York Bank was directed to take international developments into consideration in the conduct of open market operations.[41]

Second, the Board of Governors released $1.3 billion of reserves by allowing member banks to count, beginning November 24, all of their vault cash towards their reserve requirements and by reducing the reserve requirement rate for central reserve city banks from 17½ percent to 16½ percent (Table 18.1).[42] (As explained in Box 18.1, Congress had authorized the Board to count vault cash toward reserve requirements in mid-1959 and the Board had been gradually expanding the allowance since November 1959.) The two initiatives served to increase free reserves without draining bills from the market.

The *Wall Street Journal* reported that the Board of Governors justified the expanded allowance for vault cash and the reduction in reserve requirements for central reserve city banks in terms of "meeting peak cash and credit needs during the holiday season."[43] The *Journal* went on to explain that the usual method for supplying reserves was to buy Treasury bills and suggested that the new approach was intended to avoid adding to the demand for bills and to keep the bill rate above 2 percent.

[40] Minutes of the Federal Open Market Committee, October 25, 1960, pp. 57–58.

[41] 1960 Annual Report of Open Market Operations, p. 6.

[42] Federal Reserve Bank of New York Circular no. 4952, October 26, 1960. The reduction in reserve requirements brought requirements for central reserve city banks down to the level of reserve requirements for reserve city banks, as mandated by Congress in the Act of July 28, 1959.

[43] "Reserve Board Acts to Expand Bank Lending Power, Step Called Bid to Aid Holiday Credit, Avoid Gold Loss," *Wall Street Journal*, October 27, 1960, p. 3.

Table 18.1 *Federal Reserve Bank of New York discount rates and reserve requirement rates for net demand deposits, 1960.*

		Reserve requirement rates		
Date of change	FRBNY discount rate (percent)	Central reserve city banks (percent)	Reserve city banks (percent)	Country banks (percent)
Effective beginning of year	4	18	16½	11
Jun. 10	3½			
Aug. 12	3			
Sep. 1		17½		
Nov. 24				12
Dec. 1		16½		

Board of Governors of the Federal Reserve System (1976, tables 10.4 and 12.1A).

Box 18.1 Reintroduction of Vault Cash as a Legal Reserve.

The Act of July 28, 1959, authorized, but did not require, the Board of Governors to count vault cash toward member bank reserve requirements, thereby reversing the 1917 exclusion of vault cash as a legal reserve.[1]

On November 30, 1959, the Board announced that, effective December 1, vault cash at a country bank in excess of 4 percent of the bank's net demand deposits could be counted toward the bank's reserve requirements and that, effective December 3, vault cash at a reserve or central reserve city bank in excess of 2 percent of the bank's net demand deposits could be counted toward the bank's reserve requirements.[2]

On August 8, 1960, the Board announced lower thresholds of 2½ percent of net demand deposits for country banks and 1 percent of net demand deposits for reserve and central reserve city banks.[3] On October 26, 1960, the Board announced that, effective November 24, all vault cash could be counted toward a bank's reserve requirements.[4]

[1] The 1917 exclusion is discussed in Chapter 3 above. See also "Banks May Rewin a Lost Privilege," *New York Times*, July 19, 1959, p. F1.

[2] Federal Reserve Bank of New York Circular no. 4817, November 30, 1959. See also "Banks May Count Some Vault Cash," *New York Times*, December 1, 1959, p. 55; and "Reserve Board Moves to Make More Funds Available for Banks to Lend," *Wall Street Journal*, December 1, 1959, p. 3.

[3] Federal Reserve Bank of New York Circular no. 4923, August 9, 1960.

[4] Federal Reserve Bank of New York Circular no. 4952, October 26, 1960.

The expansion of open market operations to short-term coupon-bearing securities did not receive as much attention as the expanded allowance for vault cash but was just as important. During the month before the vault cash allowance became effective, the Desk added about $1 billion of reserves to the banking system, three-quarters of which did not involve bill purchases. $500 million was added with repurchase agreements[44] and $250 million with purchases of short-term securities other than bills.[45] (Box 18.2 discusses the initiation of regular open market operations in short-term coupon-bearing securities.) Following the November 24 effective date of the expanded vault cash allowance, the Desk ran the bill position in the Open Market Account down from $3.37 billion to $2.86 billion at year end,[46] releasing $500 million of bills into the market.

The FOMC was remarkably successful in achieving the incompatible objectives of keeping the bill rate elevated and keeping free reserves in ample supply. The rate on thirteen-week bills did not go below 2 percent before the end of 1960 and generally exceeded 2¼ percent (Chart 18.3). Free reserves averaged about $560 million between October 26 and the end of the year.

CONTEMPLATING THE FUTURE

As 1960 drew to a close, FOMC members continued to contemplate the problem of how to promote economic recovery without reducing the attractiveness of Treasury bills for foreign investors. At the November 22 meeting, William Treiber asked whether the Committee shouldn't abandon its bills preferably operating principle and begin to conduct open market operations in longer-term securities, suggesting that "the dilemma between domestic and international objectives could become seriously aggravated over the coming months, if recessionary tendencies here should gain strength and if our balance of payments problem should prove recalcitrant."[47]

[44] The 1960 Annual Report of Open Market Operations states (p. 6) that "in order to make the repurchase agreements at times when other sources of credit were available to dealers at relatively low rates, ... the System made the agreements at 2¾ percent on some occasions instead of the discount rate of 3 per cent." See also Cooper (1967, pp. 36–37). The reappearance of System repo rates below the discount rate provoked a strong reaction from Governor J. L. Robertson. See minutes of the Federal Open Market Committee, November 22, 1960, pp. 4–9.

[45] Minutes of the Federal Open Market Committee, November 22, 1960, p. 16,

[46] Federal Reserve Statistical Release H.4.1, November 25, 1960, and December 29, 1960.

[47] Minutes of the Federal Open Market Committee, November 22, 1960, pp. 22–23.

Box 18.2 Open Market Operations in Short-Term, Coupon-Bearing, Treasury Securities

Prior to the decision of the Federal Open Market Committee to undertake open market operations in short-term securities other than bills as well as in bills, the usual procedure for arranging outright purchases or sales was a "go-around."

In a bills-only go-around, Desk staff would contact each of the primary dealers, informing them whether the Desk was a buyer or seller and stating whether it wanted cash or regular settlement. Dealers interested in transacting replied with lists of bids or offers, including discount rates and sizes. Desk staff would then assess the propositions, generally looking to sell at the lowest discount rates or buy at the highest rates.[1] Once they had decided which propositions to accept, Desk staff would inform each dealer whether its propositions had been accepted. The whole process took about thirty minutes.[2]

The Desk first began to operate in short-term coupon-bearing securities by responding to dealer initiatives rather than conducting go-arounds. However, within just a few days Desk staff was able to integrate certificates and short-term notes and bonds with bills and to use go-arounds to purchase the securities. Rouse reported at the November 22, 1960, FOMC meeting that "System purchases of short-term securities outside the bill area were generally taken in stride by the market," and that "several of the dealers commented on the smoothness with which the operation was carried out even though it took longer than a go-around in Treasury bills alone."[3]

Albert Koch, an adviser in the Division of Research and Statistics at the Board of Governors, agreed that the market had taken the expanded scope of open market operations in stride, but was not enthusiastic about operating in short-term coupon-bearing debt: "Short-term Government securities other than bills have been available only in relatively limited quantities and it has apparently been more difficult to buy them on a 'go-around' basis, thus raising the questions not only of equity in doing business with the various dealers but also of being sure of getting the best price."[4]

Koch also noted the greater analytical complexity of operating in a more heterogeneous market: "The question of buying on a best price basis also becomes difficult to accomplish when it is necessary to compare prices of what are in effect two different commodities, say a 3-month bill and a 13-month bond. In such a case, the determination of best price necessitates a judgment about the appropriateness of a given yield curve."[5]

He agreed that it did "seem possible, by buying different types and maturities of securities, even those concentrated in the short-term area, to achieve some differential effects on their interest rates, at least in the short run," but added that "the differential effects on rates, if they have in fact occurred, probably have been small, indicating that private arbitrage in the short-term area has been quite effective."[6]

[1] However, if bill positions in the Open Market Account were not evenly distributed across maturities, Desk staff might choose to fill in particularly deficient maturities and/or avoid buying more of a maturity that the Account already owned in abundance. Roosa (1956, p. 81).

[2] Roosa (1956, pp. 80–83), Meek (1963, pp. 1–2), and Cooper (1967, pp. 5–7).

[3] Minutes of the Federal Open Market Committee, November 22, 1960, pp. 2–3.

[4] Minutes of the Federal Open Market Committee, November 22, 1960, p. 17.

[5] Minutes of the Federal Open Market Committee, November 22, 1960, p. 17.

Box 18.2 (cont.)

[6] Minutes of the Federal Open Market Committee, November 22, 1960, p. 17. The term "arbitrage," more properly called "spread trading," refers to virtually simultaneous purchases and sales of securities with similar maturities with the intent of profiting from the subsequent erosion of transient yield spreads. For example, a purchase of certificates by the Desk might be reflected in a fall in certificate yields, both absolutely and in relation to yields on Treasury bills, that induces dealers and others to sell certificates and buy bills. Their transactions accelerate the erosion of the transient spreads that attracted them in the first place. Riefler (1958, p. 1265) noted that "at any point in time . . . the operations of professionals, though they do not determine its shape, are primary in accounting for the smoothness of the yield curve."

Chairman Martin felt the pressure for change, complaining that "more and more he got the impression that there was a conviction on the part of a good many people that all our problems . . . could be solved if the System would just raise short-term interest rates and lower long-term interest rates." He questioned "whether the System could operate in longer maturities for more than a very brief period of time without running into difficulties" and warned of the risk of falling "back into a pattern of [fixed] rates."[48]

Hayes expanded on Treiber's proposal at the December 13 Committee meeting, suggesting sales of bills *against* bond purchases, as well as outright bond purchases:

I am wondering if it is not incumbent on the System to demonstrate its willingness to explore all reasonable possibilities at its disposal to encourage domestic expansion without taking undue risks on the international front. I have an uneasy feeling that long-term rates are somewhat higher than they should be to be as helpful as possible in present economic circumstances, although I can't prove this or set any quantitative measure on it. Also, I have some fear that with bank liquidity still rather low, the banks may not be seeking expansion of their lending and investing as actively as we would wish.

Faced with this kind of problem, together with the even more serious problem of avoiding substantially lower bill rates, we may be approaching a time when a departure from our usual policy of confining open market operations to short-term securities may be justified. *It might turn out to be desirable to place reserves in the market by means of any maturity which seemed to be currently in supply – and even the possibility of useful swaps of shorts against longs should not be overlooked.* Probably we need not face up to these problems today; I am not sure that I would advocate operations in long-term securities even during the early months of next year. But I hope the members of the Committee will be considering these questions over the coming weeks with an open mind; for if ever there was a time when we

[48] Minutes of the Federal Open Market Committee, November 22, 1960, p. 42.

should demonstrate our flexibility, and our willingness to explore all alternatives, that time is the present.[49]

Martin acknowledged that "there was a need to look into the question of operations in long-term . . . securities" but cautioned that the Committee "should be very careful in its moves or it would get back to pegged interest rates before this was realized."[50]

49 Minutes of the Federal Open Market Committee, December 13, 1960, pp. 6–7. Emphasis added.

50 Minutes of the Federal Open Market Committee, December 13, 1960, p. 40.

19

Operation Twist

In early 1961, the US economy was still contracting and the gold outflow that had reached flood stage a few months earlier was continuing. Arthur Marget, the director of the Division of International Finance at the Board of Governors, observed that a "flight from the dollar" was in progress.[1] The gold drain could be staunched by an increase in short-term interest rates but that would work against the need for ample free reserves to promote recovery from the on-going recession.

Most senior Federal Reserve officials saw the situation as a dilemma that required choosing between two unappealing alternatives. Robert Rouse, the manager of the System Open Market Account, allowed that a choice might have to be made "between a bill rate below two per cent [and] lower levels of free reserves."[2] Some members of the FOMC focused on the international aspect of the dilemma. Governor A. L. Mills argued that it was the Committee's responsibility "to take into account first the international situation."[3] Others focused on the domestic aspect. Malcolm Bryan, the president of the Federal Reserve Bank of Atlanta, recalled that "the last time the System reacted in its policy decisions primarily because of foreign developments was when England went off the gold standard in 1931. At that time, with unemployment constantly increasing and with every element in the domestic

[1] Minutes of the Federal Open Market Committee, January 10, 1961, p. 10. Marget further stated that "a number of foreign monetary authorities which up to now have refrained even . . . from converting into gold new accretions of dollars, are not only converting . . . such new accretions . . . but have been converting, or are planning to convert, a considerable portion of their existing dollar holdings."

[2] Minutes of the Federal Open Market Committee, January 24, 1961, p. 3.

[3] Minutes of the Federal Open Market Committee, January 10, 1961, p. 29.

economy calling for ease, the System responded by tightening in order to protect the gold supply." Bryan added the hardly needed reminder that "every student of that action has concluded that it was a catastrophic mistake."[4]

Virtually alone, officials of the Federal Reserve Bank of New York suggested that the two horns of the dilemma could be addressed simultaneously by selling short-term Treasury securities and purchasing longer-term notes and bonds. William Treiber, the Bank's first vice president, observed that

> [l]ong-term rates are most important for investment spending; short-term rates are most important for foreign balances. We must continually strive for a flexible policy that will best serve our various interrelated goals. To this end, it may become desirable for the System to sell short-term securities and to buy securities of other maturities that are in supply in the market.[5]

Alfred Hayes, the Bank's president, urged the Committee to give "careful attention to some of the broader questions … concerning the role of the central bank in influencing the entire interest rate structure."[6]

The incoming Kennedy administration was also interested in addressing both facets of the dilemma. Speaking to Congress on February 2, the new President hinted that a solution might be at hand:

> Both full recovery and economic growth require expansion of expenditures for business plant and equipment, for state and local government facilities, and for residential construction. To increase the flow of credit for these purposes, long-term interest rates should decline. However, further declines in short-term interest rates, under present conditions, would lead to a further outflow of funds abroad, adding to the deficit in our balance of payments. …
>
> In these circumstances, monetary policy and debt management must serve two apparently contradictory objectives: checking declines in the short-term rates that directly affect the balance of payments, and increasing the flow of credit into the capital markets at declining long-term rates of interest to promote domestic recovery.
>
> These two objectives can be achieved concurrently, but only with close cooperation among all governmental agencies concerned. …
>
> The Treasury and the Federal Reserve System already are working together to further the complimentary effectiveness of debt management and monetary policy.[7]

4 Minutes of the Federal Open Market Committee, January 10, 1961, p. 44.

5 Minutes of the Federal Open Market Committee, January 10, 1961, p. 15.

6 Minutes of the Federal Open Market Committee, January 24, 1961, p. 9.

7 "Text of the President's Message to Congress on Economic Recovery and Growth," *New York Times*, February 3, 1961, p. 10.

On the same day, Robert Roosa, the new Under Secretary of the Treasury for Monetary Affairs, announced the February mid-quarter refunding: a cash offering of $6.9 billion of eighteen-month notes. The *Wall Street Journal* reported Roosa as indicating that "the decision to confine the [new] issue to a relatively short maturity was influenced by current market conditions, the economic situation and the nation's balance-of-payments deficit."[8]

HOW ECONOMISTS VIEWED THE TERM STRUCTURE OF INTEREST RATES

Economists had only recently begun to examine the determinants of the shape of the yield curve. Friedrich Lutz, an economist at Princeton University, wrote in 1940 that

> [i]t has long been customary in works on the theory of interest to talk about *the* interest rate, and to deal with the problem of the difference between rates on different maturities by adding a footnote to the effect that the author understands by *the* interest rate the whole "family" of interest rates. Although the incompleteness of this kind of treatment was generally recognized, it was not regarded as an essential defect of the theory, because it was assumed that the whole "family" of interest rates moved up and down together, and that furthermore there was a tendency towards equalization of the different rates.[9]

Contradictory empirical evidence – the failure of long-term rates to move in parallel with short-term rates in the 1930s – directed attention to the determinants of the term structure of interest rates. Lutz observed that "the wide discrepancy between long and short rates . . . which has existed ever since the middle of 1932 . . . has shown once again that [the assumptions of parallel movements and ultimate convergence] are not always borne out by the facts. The last few years have therefore seen new attempts to find out what determines the relationship between long and short interest rates."[10]

In 1939, John R. Hicks, an economist at Cambridge University and the University of Manchester, set out the first "expectations" model of the yield curve. The model was based on the idea that yields on long-term debt might usefully be thought of as an average of the current and expected future yields on short-term debt.[11]

8 "Treasury to Offer $6.9 Billion 3¼% 18-Month Notes," *Wall Street Journal*, February 3, 1961, p. 6.

9 Lutz (1940, p. 36). 10 Lutz (1940, p. 36).

11 Culbertson (1957, p. 487) states that "the doctrine on the term structure of rates most influential recently among English and American theorists, which we will term the expectational theory, was based upon the theoretical considerations of the implications

Hicks began his analysis[12] by expressing the n-period term rate R_n as a function of the current 1-period rate, R_1, and a sequence of 1-period forward rates, denoted $f_2, f_3, \ldots, f_n$, where f_k is the current rate on a loan due to start in k − 1 periods and mature in k periods:

$$(1 + R_n)^n = (1 + R_1) \bullet (1 + f_2) \bullet (1 + f_3) \bullet \ldots \bullet (1 + f_n)$$

He suggested that while most creditors "would prefer to lend short," some borrowers have "a strong propensity to borrow long." As a result, "the forward short rate will . . . exceed the expected [future] short rate by a risk premium" needed to attract some creditors into lending longer than they otherwise would and to dissuade some borrowers from borrowing as long as they would like. In algebraic terms,

$$f_k = r_k + L_k, \text{ with } L_k > 0,$$

where r_k is the rate currently expected on a one-period loan starting in k − 1 periods and maturing in k periods and L_k is a risk premium. The n-period term rate can then be written as

$$(1 + R_n)^n = (1 + R_1) \bullet (1 + r_2 + L_2) \bullet (1 + r_3 + L_3) \bullet \ldots \bullet (1 + r_n + L_n).$$

If the short rate is expected to remain unchanged ($R_1 = r_2 = r_3 = \ldots$) and the risk premia are monotonically increasing ($L_2 < L_3 < \ldots$), the yield curve will have a positive slope ($R_1 < R_2 < R_3 < \ldots$).

Lutz modified Hicks's model in an important way: he did not assume a chronic imbalance between shorter-horizon creditors and longer-horizon borrowers. Instead, he suggested only that risk aversion partitions the credit markets into different maturity segments and that different segments could exhibit different imbalances. Lutz further observed that the barriers between different segments are permeable and liable to be breached if there are sufficiently attractive lending or borrowing opportunities in nearby segments. More particularly, he suggested that "the essence of the matter is that an investor may ask for a risk premium whenever he moves out of his 'original' market, no matter whether he moves into a shorter or longer market, because in either case the return

of confidently held expectations and was made credible by the experience of the 1930's." Irving Fisher (1930, p. 70) had earlier suggested that the "rate on a five year contract may be considered as a sort of average of five theoretically existing rates, one for each of the five years covered." Riefler (1930, p. 121) argued similarly that yields on long-term bonds were not "directly comparable with the current yield on short-term loans, but rather with the average expected return on short-term loans over a similar period of years."

12 Hicks (1939, pp. 144–47).

which he will obtain in the market to which he moves is uncertain."[13] Lutz's model contemplates movement up and down the yield curve in response to the structure of risk premia, so that variations in those premia play a key role in balancing supplies and demands for credit across the curve.

Markets for debt of different maturities were linked together by the willingness of creditors and debtors to shift out of their preferred habitats and into shorter or longer maturities. The linkages would be tighter the greater the willingness of market participants to bear risk. Winfield Riefler, for example, spoke of "factors of broad substitutability on both sides of the money and capital markets" as "accounting for the fluidity, homogeneity, and responsiveness of the securities markets. This flexibility links the various sectors of the money and capital markets into a somewhat loosely integrated whole in which yield changes tend to move together in the various sectors."[14] Conversely, John Culbertson, an economist at the Board of Governors, suggested that substitutability between short-term and long-term debt on the part of both borrowers and lenders is "limited in extent, and when the maturity structure of debt supplied to the economy undergoes a substantial short-run change, either because of Treasury debt management operations or actions of private borrowers, this is reflected in the term structure."[15]

Term structure theory at the end of the 1950s supported at least the idea of a role for open market operations in affecting the term structure of interest rates. In particular, selling short-term securities from the Open Market Account and purchasing longer-term securities could reduce longer-term risk premia and longer-term interest rates without affecting the quantity of reserves in the banking system.

THE FEBRUARY 7 EXECUTIVE SESSION OF THE FEDERAL OPEN MARKET COMMITTEE

Initiating open market operations in longer-term securities meant reconsidering the bills preferably operating principle adopted in 1953 and renewed annually thereafter. (Box 19.1 shows the most recent reaffirmation.)

[13] Lutz (1940, p. 48). The Preferred Habitat Theory of Modigliani and Sutch (1966, pp. 183–84) was similarly based on the idea that a risk-averse investor with a long-term horizon would require a risk premium to hold a short-term security.

[14] Riefler (1958, pp. 1265 and 1268).

[15] Culbertson (1957, p. 488).

Box 19.1 Operating Principles Reaffirmed at the March 22, 1960, Meeting of the Federal Open Market Committee.

a. It is not now the policy of the Committee to support any pattern of prices and yields in the Government securities market, and intervention in the Government securities market is solely to effectuate the objective of monetary and credit policy (including correction of disorderly markets).

b. Operations for the System Account in the open market other than repurchase agreements, shall be confined to short-term securities (except in the correction of disorderly markets), and during a period of Treasury financing there shall be no purchases of
   (1) maturing issues for which an exchange is being offered,
   (2) when-issued securities, or
   (3) outstanding issues of comparable maturities to those being offered fro exchange;

   these policies to be followed until such time as they may be superseded or modified by further action of the Federal Open Market Committee.

c. Transactions for the System Account in the open Market shall be entered into solely for the purpose of providing or absorbing reserves (except in the correction of disorderly markets), and shall not include offsetting purchases and sales of securities for the purpose of altering the maturity pattern of the System's portfolio; such policy to be followed until such time as it may be superseded or modified by further action of the Federal Open Market Committee.

Minutes of the Federal Open Market Committee, March 22, 1960, p. 60.

On February 7, 1961, the Federal Open Market Committee met in executive session to decide the fate of bills preferably. Chairman Martin opened the discussion by noting "the very heavy barrage both from within and outside Government against the System" for the System's tenacious attachment to bills preferably.[16] He suggested that the System had to give some "tangible indication of open-mindedness and willingness to experiment," that "there had to be [empirical] evidence accumulated from actual experiment or testing to enable the System to escape from the charge of doctrinaire commitment to ... short-term securities."[17] Governor Mills

[16] See, example, the letter from twenty-one United States Senators to Chairman Martin urging the abandonment of bills preferably, reported in "Reserve is Urged to Change Policy," *New York Times*, March 15, 1960, p. 55.

[17] Minutes of the Federal Open Market Committee, February 7, 1961, p. 45. The second half of the 1950s saw a steady stream of articles by economists examining the pros and cons of bills preferably, including Carson (1955), Wood (1955), Fand and Scott (1958), Riefler (1958), Young and Yager (1960), and Luckett (1960).

commented that "while he had consistently supported the limitation of Federal Open Market Committee operations to short securities, he now felt that experiment to move long relative to short rates had to be made."[18]

Rouse proposed a plan of action. "The program," he said, "is based on the conviction that at this time the interest rate structure in relation to the balance of payments is paramount and that current short-term interest rates must be maintained and, preferably, allowed to rise somewhat." Appreciating the need to supply reserves to promote economic recovery, he proposed to undertake open market purchases of intermediate and long-term securities, launching the new program with purchases of one- to five-year issues, then expanding to longer securities and ultimately including swaps – sales of short-term securities coupled with purchases of longer-term issues. The swaps were intended "to affect the rate structure rather than to provide reserves," a material departure from the narrow post-Accord focus on reserves. He proposed an initial purchase program of $400 million of fifteen-month to five-year issues and $100 million of five- to ten-year issues.[19]

The FOMC approved Rouse's proposal with minimal discussion and the Desk launched the purchase program on February 20, announcing that "the System Open Market Account is purchasing in the open market U.S. Government notes and bonds of varying maturities, some of which will exceed 5 years."[20] The announcement marked the practical end of the struggle over bills preferably, a struggle that Martin characterized as "more marked and more contentious than . . . any other that I can recall in my ten years in the Federal Reserve."[21]

In 2011, Eric Swanson, a staff economist at the Federal Reserve Bank of San Francisco, examined the market impact of the February 2 speech by President Kennedy, Roosa's announcement that the February mid-quarter refunding would offer only a short-term note, and the Desk's announcement of the launch of the new program. As shown in Table 19.1, Swanson reported a cumulative 27-basis-point flattening of the yield curve, the consequence of a 12-basis-point increase in the yield on thirteen-week bills and a 15-basis-point decrease in the yield on ten-year notes. The

[18] Minutes of the Federal Open Market Committee, February 7, 1961, pp. 46 and 47.
[19] Minutes of the Federal Open Market Committee, February 7, 1961, pp. 49–50.
[20] Minutes of the Federal Open Market Committee, February 7, 1961, p. 62.
[21] "Reserve Bank Here Had an Ally in War on 'Bills Only' Policy," *New York Times*, March 10, 1961, p. 37.

Table 19.1 *Estimated market impact of three announcements in February 1961 regarding Operation Twist.*

	Sector					
	3m (bp)	1y (bp)	2y (bp)	5y (bp)	10y (bp)	30y (bp)
Kennedy speech on Feb. 2	1.0	−0.7	−4.3	−3.5	−3.7	−4.0
Roosa announcement on Feb. 2	−0.2	3.0	3.7	−2.0	−3.3	−1.5
Desk announcement on Feb. 20	11.0	6.0	−2.7	−9.0	−8.0	−6.0
Total	11.8	8.3	−3.3	−14.5	−15.0	−11.5

Swanson (2011, table 3).

market clearly expected that "Operation Twist," as it came to be called, would have a material impact on Treasury yields.

CONDUCTING OPEN MARKET OPERATIONS IN LONGER-TERM SECURITIES

Initial purchases of longer-term securities were modest. The Desk repoted a net increase of $7 million in one- to five-year securities, and $6 million in five- to ten-year securities, over the three business days from February 20 to the end of the statement week on Wednesday, February 22.[22] It recorded further increases of $77 million in one- to five-year debt, and $4 million in five- to ten-year debt during the following statement week.[23]

On March 7 Rouse reported to the FOMC that the initial purchases "have been carried out with reasonable success from the standpoint of market repercussions, which have been remarkably mild so far ... Dealers responded to the first purchases in a routine manner and appear to have accepted the fact of System operations in longer-term issues as something they can learn to live with." However, he also hinted at difficulties, noting that there had been, and still remained, "a great deal of confusion and misunderstanding." Dealers and investors needed "a better understanding

22 "Federal Reserve in Longer Issues," *New York Times*, February 24, 1961, p. 37.

23 "FRB Increased Buying of Longer U.S. Securities," *Wall Street Journal*, March 3, 1961, p. 3.

of what the System is trying to accomplish in its operations outside the short-term area. . . . Some progress [has] been made . . ., especially among the dealers, but only with time, patient explanation, and further experience can the market arrive at a proper evaluation of the newly created operating conditions."[24]

Three weeks later, Rouse reported that uncertainty about the Committee's objectives continued to hamper operations and that liquidity had been adversely affected. During operations on Thursday, March 23, "we found that our attempts to acquire a moderate amount of [intermediate-term] securities on a go-around basis [[25]] met with only $54 million of offers, and led to a significant withdrawal of offers and bids that were in the market prior to our operations, as potential buyers and sellers moved to the sidelines to see what the result of our activity would be."[26] More broadly,

> We have found that the go-around, and the publicity that goes with it, tends to . . . dry up other bids and offerings. As a result, the go-around has not been generally successful.
>
> A major difficulty is that it is well nigh impossible to prevent word of our go-arounds from spreading widely and rapidly throughout the investment community. The consequence is that potential sellers tend to withdraw from the market in hopes of getting higher prices and potential buyers tend to withdraw because they are reluctant to follow any upward price movement that might develop in the wake of our operation.[27]

Rouse suggested that the relatively short time frame of a go-around, about thirty minutes from start to finish,[28] did not afford dealers enough time to solicit sale interests in longer-term securities from customers and that the practice (carried over from bill operations) of relying on the liquidity provided by dealer inventories was impractical for operations in longer-term securities: "The second major difficulty is that dealers normally carry only modest positions in the area in which we are now working, and in the time interval within which go-arounds must be conducted, they rarely could develop the offers or bids that are desired

[24] Minutes of the Federal Open Market Committee, March 7, 1961, p. 21. Rouse complained (p. 22) that "the lack of dealer position figures for individual dealers has been a real handicap." The decision to withhold individual dealer data from the Desk was made in the course of structuring the reporting dealer program in 1960 – see Chapter 17 above.

[25] "Go-arounds" are described in Box 18.2.

[26] Minutes of the Federal Open Market Committee, March 28, 1961, p. 7.

[27] Minutes of the Federal Open Market Committee, March 28, 1961, p. 7.

[28] Roosa (1956, p. 82) and Meek (1963, p. 2).

even if there were no knowledge of our activity available to the investing public."[29]

Reacting to the limited liquidity of the note and bond markets, Rouse began to rely on unsolicited offerings from dealers and on operations limited to primary dealers active in longer-term markets. "These methods have," he said, "proved more effective and far less disturbing to the market."[30]

WHAT, EXACTLY, WERE THE OBJECTIVES OF THE NEW PROGRAM?

The most surprising aspect of the February 20 initiative was the absence of clarity about the objectives of the initiative. Although perhaps inevitable in view of Martin's long history of championing bills preferably, and the equally long history of resistance by senior officials of the Federal Reserve Bank of New York, the lack of clarity left investors confused and undermined liquidity.

The public understanding of the new program was best summarized by its sobriquet: "Operation Twist" – an attempt to maintain, and possibly raise, short-term interest rates while lowering long-term rates. Virtually all Committee members did indeed want to avoid a decline in short-term rates. The public understanding with respect to long-term rates was, however, an over-statement. While some Committee members wanted to "nudge" long-term rates lower, others viewed lower long-term rates as little more than a possible by-product of the Committee's policy of maintaining an ample quantity of free reserves through purchases of longer-term securities. A 1967 Federal Reserve staff study stated that, in 1961, "the Federal Open Market Committee did not publicly espouse any formal policy regarding long-term rates, largely because of the divergent and shifting opinions of the members and staff" and that "there never was any clear-cut or formal agreement as to whether a reduction in long-term rates should be a deliberate aim of policy or should be passively accepted, if it occurred, merely as a desirable outcome of shifting some System buying into coupon issues." The study observed that "there was considerable

[29] Minutes of the Federal Open Market Committee, March 28, 1961, p. 7. Cooper (1967, p. 5) states that, during the bills preferably period from 1953 to 1960, "the time allowed for dealer responses in 'go-arounds' was kept as short as possible in order to ... avoid immobilizing the bill market for an unduly long period."

[30] Minutes of the Federal Open Market Committee, March 28, 1961, p. 7.

confusion in the market regarding possible System objectives with respect to long-term interest rates."[31]

Hayes best articulated the consensus view within the Committee. He believed that the primary objective was a policy of "moderate ease" that involved maintaining a "reasonable kind of reserve position for the commercial banking system." However, "he saw no reason why the Committee could not have at the same time ... the objective of not permitting the short-term rate to go too low," and also "the objective of trying to exert some positive effect on longer-term rates." Hayes thought that "the most important objective was the maintenance of a moderate degree of ease" but acknowledged that "the short-term rate probably was regarded by at least some of the members of the Committee as having as much importance." Lowering the long-term rate was "of least importance," although "there was no reason not to push down longer-term rates in the course of Account operations," even if "operations were designed more specifically with a view to their effect on the short-term than the long-term area."[32]

George Clay, the president of the Federal Reserve Bank of Kansas City, expressed a similar view. Clay believed that the Fed's primary task was "conducting monetary policy with a view to encouraging economic expansion" and that "this objective called for a continuation of the policy of monetary ease." However,

> in view of the international flow-of-funds problem, it appeared ... essential that open market operations be so conducted that the Treasury bill rate would remain within the range of recent weeks [about 2¼ percent]. But it also appeared that, with resource utilization at low levels and with interest rates high in comparison with other recessions, appropriate policy involved more than supplying some given volume of reserve funds without depressing the Treasury bill rate. It called for an added endeavor to bring about lower interest rates in the intermediate and longer term sectors.[33]

Martin was uncomfortable with the new program and conflicted about its objectives. Shortly after the program's launch he expressed regret that the System could no longer "limit its operations to supplying and absorbing reserves and say that its operations had nothing to do with interest rates" but he accepted that "it was not possible to do that."[34] He suggested that the FOMC "did not intend to change monetary policy by

[31] Cooper (1967, p. 20).
[32] Minutes of the Federal Open Market Committee, March 28, pp. 64–65.
[33] Minutes of the Federal Open Market Committee, April 18, 1961, pp. 36–37.
[34] Minutes of the Federal Open Market Committee, March 7, 1961, p. 26.

authorizing a change in operating techniques" and "did not intend to shift the whole fulcrum of monetary policy from the providing and absorbing of reserves to interest rates." Nevertheless, he recognized that "in providing or absorbing reserves the System does exert an effect on interest rates" and he agreed that "to let the bill rate go down to 1½ per cent would invite disaster."[35]

DISENGAGEMENT?

An upturn in economic activity and a decline in the gold drain in the spring of 1961 led some FOMC members to question the need for continuing System operations in longer-term securities.

At the March 7 Committee meeting, Guy Noyes, director of the Division of Research and Statistics at the Board of Governors, observed that, "while it is still with us, the downturn seems to have lost momentum."[36] Three weeks later, Hayes stated that "we are at or close to a bottoming out of the recession"[37] and three weeks after that Noyes remarked that recovery was "clearly underway."[38] The National Bureau of Economic Research subsequently located a trough in economic activity in February 1961.

The gold outflow tapered off at about the same time (Chart 19.1). At the April 18 FOMC meeting, Woodlief Thomas, an adviser to the Board of Governors, observed that "gold movements in or out of U.S. monetary stocks have been negligible." Karl Bopp, the president of the Federal Reserve Bank of Philadelphia, also noted the "cessation of the gold outflow."[39]

The idea of disengaging first surfaced during the June 6 FOMC meeting. Martin thought he detected "a growing number [of Committee members] who would like to see a gradual disengagement from operations in the longer-term area" and expressed his opinion that "under present circumstances the so-called nudging effort was getting to be a matter of flying into the wind." Nevertheless, he questioned whether disengagement was the right approach, "particularly in light of all of the misunderstandings and public discussion." In what can only be described as a remarkable delegation of the Committee's responsibility for charting the course of monetary

[35] Minutes of the Federal Open Market Committee, March 28, pp. 49 and 61–62.
[36] Minutes of the Federal Open Market Committee, March 7, 1961, p. 27.
[37] Minutes of the Federal Open Market Committee, March 28, 1961, p. 16.
[38] Minutes of the Federal Open Market Committee, April 18, 1961, pp. 10–11.
[39] Minutes of the Federal Open Market Committee, April 18, 1961, pp. 13 and 25.

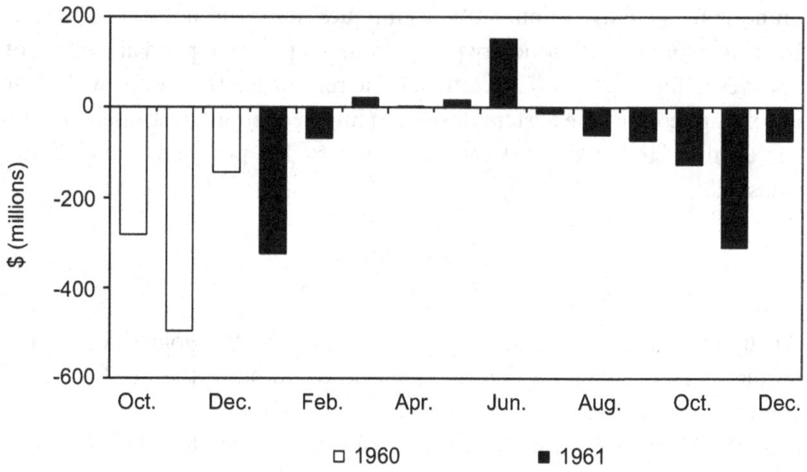

Chart 19.1 Monthly changes in Treasury gold.
Board of Governors of the Federal Reserve System (1976, table 14.1).

policy, Martin opted to leave continued System participation in longer-term markets up to Rouse.[40]

Twenty-one years as manager of the System Open Market Account had left Rouse well practiced in intuiting the policy preferences of the Committee. Two weeks later, on June 20, he told the Committee that

> [t]here has been no occasion to operate in long-term issues since Monday, June 5 … Since then operations have been confined entirely to sales of short-term issues. The longer-term market continues to be pretty much on its own at this point. Activity is light and dealer markets are generally quite thin, with relatively few offerings being made to the Trading Desk.[41]

While making clear his own preferences, Martin continued to delegate responsibility for deciding whether to operate in longer-term markets. At the June 20 meeting he expressed his hope for a "gradual disengagement," but felt that the Committee "ought to … rely on the judgment of the Account Manager …" In his opinion, "the Desk had conducted things well during the past several weeks, and he thought the Committee could afford to rely on the Manager's judgment."[42] The Desk continued to absent itself from the longer-term markets during late June and early July, confirming

[40] Minutes of the Federal Open Market Committee, June 6, 1961, pp. 58 and 60–61.
[41] Minutes of the Federal Open Market Committee, June 20, 1961, p. 5.
[42] Minutes of the Federal Open Market Committee, June 20, 1961, p. 35.

"the feeling of many observers that the System had no intention of pushing longer-term rates down."[43]

The FOMC continued to grapple with its commitment to the February 7 initiative during the summer and fall of 1961. Some members wanted to disengage immediately,[44] some wanted to continue[45] and even expand,[46] and some, apparently willing to accept a remarkable degree of opacity in an important area of public policy, wanted to terminate operations but leave the public announcement of February 20 undisturbed.[47]

THE SCALE OF OPEN MARKET OPERATIONS IN LONGER-TERM SECURITIES

In view of the limited liquidity of the markets for longer-term government securities, the concern with pegging, the lack of clarity about program objectives, the turn in the economy, and the decline in gold outflows, the character and scale of the Desk's operations in 1961 is a matter of some interest.

Chart 19.2 shows the cumulative change in Treasury bills held in the System Open Market Account from February 15, 1961, to the end of the year. The chart shows that bills were neither accumulated nor run off before the fourth quarter seasonal purchases. Thus, if Operation Twist did anything, it must have worked through the composition of System holdings of coupon-bearing debt.

Chart 19.3 shows the variation in System Open Market Account holdings of certificates, notes, and bonds during 1961. The discontinuous jumps in certificates and notes in February, May, and July are attributable to mid-quarter refundings (Table 19.2). In some refundings the Treasury offered notes to refinance maturing certificates and in other refundings it

43 Minutes of the Federal Open Market Committee, July 11, 1961, p. 3. Statement of Spencer Marsh, filling in for Rouse.

44 See the remarks of Governor J. L. Robertson, Minutes of the Federal Open Market Committee, July 11, 1961, pp. 31–35.

45 See the remarks of Edward Wayne, the president of the Federal Reserve Bank of Richmond, and George Clay of the Kansas City Bank, in minutes of the Federal Open Market Committee, July 11, 1961, pp. 40 and 41–42.

46 See the proposal of the Federal Reserve Bank of New York for expanded operations in longer-term debt described in minutes of the Federal Open Market Committee, July 11, 1961, pp. 5–6.

47 Minutes of the Federal Open Market Committee, July 11, 1961, pp. 36–37, where Governor Mills states that "he would renew the special authorization covering operations in longer-term securities" but "implement the authorization by abstaining from operations outside the bill sector."

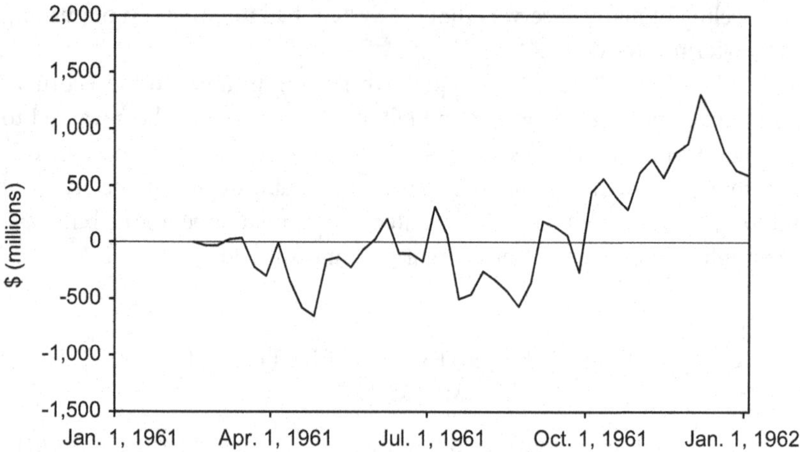

Chart 19.2 Cumulative change from February 15, 1961, in Treasury bills in the System Open Market Account. End of statement week.
Author's calculations.

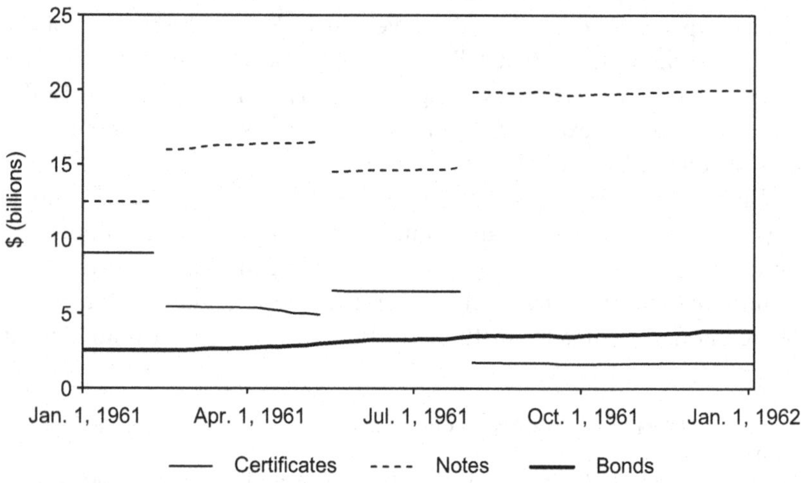

Chart 19.3 Coupon-bearing Treasury securities in the System Open Market Account. End of statement week.
Federal Reserve Statistical Release H.4.1.

offered certificates to refinance maturing notes. For example, in the February 1961 cash refunding the Treasury offered $6.9 billion of eighteen-month notes to refinance a like amount of maturing certificates.[48]

[48] Federal Reserve Bank of New York Circular no. 4994, February 2, 1961; and Circular no. 4995, February 6, 1961.

Table 19.2 *Treasury offerings of coupon-bearing debt in 1961 (other than advance refundings).*

Security offered	Issued	Maturity	Amount issued ($ billions)
February cash offering			
1½-year 3¼% note	Feb. 15	Aug. 15, 1962	7.32
May cash offering			
1-year 3% certificate	May 15	May 15, 1962	5.51
2-year 3¼% note	May 15	May 15, 1963	2.75
July exchange offering[1]			
15½-month 3¼% note	Aug. 1	Nov. 15, 1962	6.08
3-year 3¾ % note	Aug. 1	Aug. 15, 1964	5.02
6¾-year 3⅞% bond (reopening)	Aug. 1	May 15, 1968	0.75
October cash offering			
1-year 7-month 3¼% note	Oct. 11	May 15, 1963	2.30
November exchange offering			
15-month 3¼% note	Nov. 15	Feb. 15, 1963	3.64
4½-year 3¾% bond (reopening)	Nov. 15	May 15, 1966	2.38
13-year 3⅞% bond (reopening)	Nov. 15	Nov. 15, 1974	0.52

[1] Offering accelerated to mid-July because maturing securities were due to be redeemed on August 1, 1961.
Treasury annual reports and offering circulars.

The Account held $3.6 billion of the certificates and reinvested the entire amount in the new notes.[49] As a result, the quantity of certificates held in the Account fell by about $3.6 billion and the quantity of notes rose by about the same amount on the February 15 settlement date of the refunding.[50]

Over the interval from February 15, 1961, shortly before the launch of Operation Twist, to the end of 1961, certificates in the Open Market Account fell by $3.8 billion, notes rose by $4.0 billion, and bonds increased by $1.3 billion. However, the certificate and note changes reflect Account participation in Treasury refundings as well as open market transactions (Table 19.3). Exchanges (with Treasury) of maturing debt for new debt are extraneous to an assessment of Operation Twist because they do not reflect System activity that resulted in a change in the public's holdings of government securities. Notes in the Account fell by $2.0 billion during

[49] Minutes of the Federal Open Market Committee, February 7, 1961, p. 3.

[50] There are no discontinuous jumps when the November 1961 refunding settled because the Account did not participate in that refunding. Minutes of the Federal Open Market Committee, October 24, 1961, p. 4, statement of Robert Rouse that the System did not own any securities eligible for exchange in the November refunding.

Table 19.3 *Decomposition of change in the quantities of certificates and notes held in the System Open Market Account over the interval from February 15, 1961, to the end of 1961.*

	Certificates ($ millions)	Notes ($ millions)
Held at the close of business on February 15, 1961	5,462	15,994
Held at the close of business on December 27, 1961	1,699	19,984
Change from February 15 to December 27, 1961	−3,763	+3,990
Change over the week of May 11 to May 17, 1961	+1,644	−2,017
Change over the week of July 27 to August 2, 1961	−4,789	+5,004
Cumulative change over other weeks	−618	+1,003

Federal Reserve Bulletin.

the week the May 1961 refunding settled and rose by $5.0 billion during the week the July refunding settled. Subtracting the net increase of $3.0 billion attributable to the refundings from the $4.0 billion total increase leaves an increase of $1.0 billion that can be attributed to secondary market purchases. A similar calculation for certificates gives a decrease of $0.6 billion of certificates that can be attributed to secondary market sales over the interval from February 15, 1961 to the end of 1961.

Summing up, from February 15, 1961, weekly changes in certificate, note, and bond holdings *other than* those attributable to the settlement of a refunding provides insights into trends in System open market operations during 1961. Chart 19.4 shows that the Desk steadily sold certificates after the beginning of April 1961 but that the selling slowed around the end of May. The chart further shows that the Desk bought notes and bonds at a fairly steady pace from the beginning of March and that the buying continued through the end of the year.

Account holdings can also be classified by time remaining to maturity: under one year, one to five years, five to ten years, and over ten years. In this case a series can change discontinuously because of a refunding *or* because an issue rolls down from one maturity category to the next shorter category.[51] Summing up, from February 15, 1961, weekly changes in

[51] For example, on August 14, 1961, the System held $3.6 billion of the notes acquired in the February 1961 refunding. 1961 Annual Report of Open Market Operations, p. A-8. The

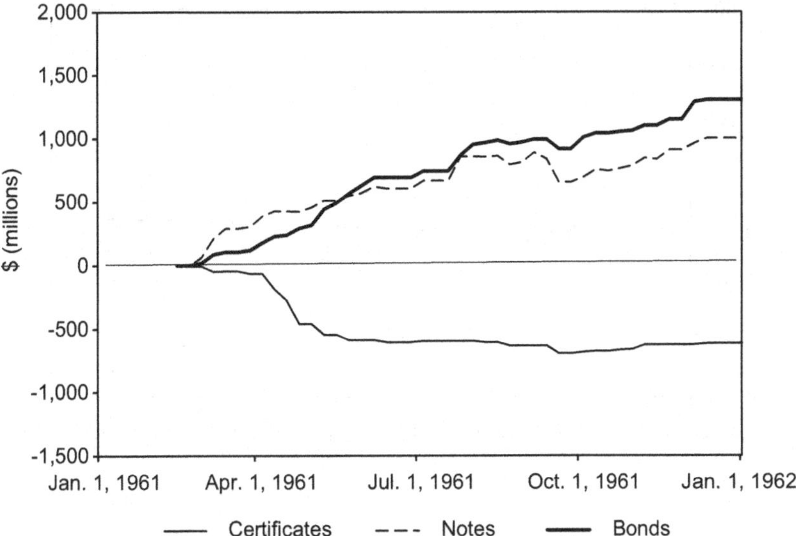

Chart 19.4 Cumulative change from February 15, 1961, in coupon-bearing Treasury securities held in the System Open Market Account, excluding weeks when holdings changed as a result of a refunding.
Author's calculations.

holdings in a given maturity category *other than* those attributable to the settlement of a refunding or a category roll-down provides additional information on trends in System activity. As shown in Chart 19.5, between February 15 and the end of 1961 the System sold about $800 million of coupon-bearing securities in the under-one-year category, purchased about $1.6 billion in the one-to-five-year category, $540 million in the five-to-ten-year category, and $113 million in the over-ten-years category. The chart is consistent with the proposition that after the beginning of April the Account mostly followed a sell strategy with respect to short-term coupon-bearing debt, that sales slowed in late May, accelerated briefly in September, and then reversed direction through the end of the year. The chart further suggests that the Desk continued buying securities in the one-to-five-year category through the end of the year, but slowed purchases of securities with more than five years to maturity in late May or early June.

notes matured on August 15, 1962, and were classified in the one-to-five-year category. On August 16, 1961, the notes rolled down to the under-one-year category. As a result, Account holdings of 1-to-5-year securities fell by $3.6 billion and holdings of under-one-year securities increased by $3.6 billion.

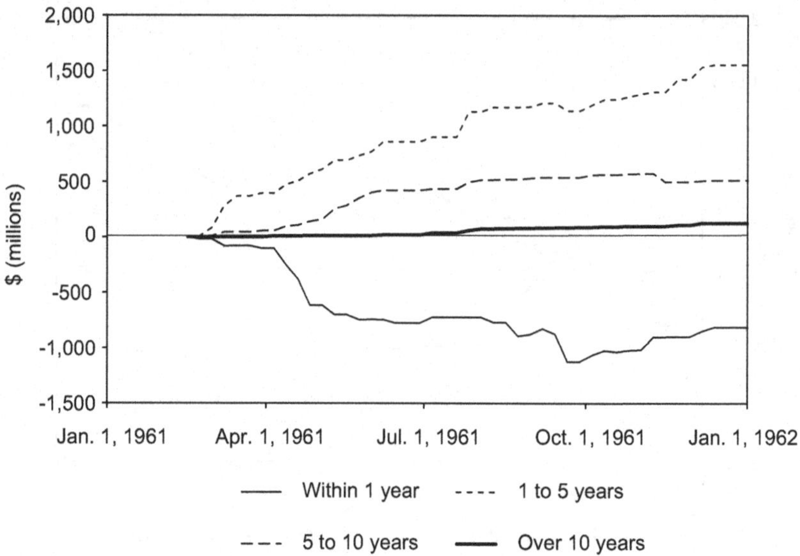

Chart 19.5 Cumulative change from February 15, 1961, in coupon-bearing Treasury securities held in the System Open Market Account, excluding weeks when holdings moved from one maturity category to another as a result of a refunding or the passage of time.
Author's calculations.

Taken together, Charts 19.4 and 19.5 are consistent with the proposition that Operation Twist, in its original conception of open market sales of short-term securities and purchases of longer-term securities, lasted until late May 1961 and involved sales of $750 million of the former and purchases of $1.2 billion of the latter. Open market purchases (but not sales) of coupon-bearing debt continued over the balance of the year but were limited to securities maturing in from one to five years.

In broad terms, the FOMC accomplished both of its primary objectives through the end of 1961. It provided the banking system with an ample supply of free reserves (Chart 19.6) without depressing the interest rate on thirteen-week Treasury bills below 2¼ percent (Chart 19.7). Yields on long-term Treasury issues remained at about 4 percent in spite of the onset of economic recovery. These results are particularly remarkable in light of concurrent Treasury efforts to *extend* debt maturities through advance refundings – a topic examined in the next chapter.

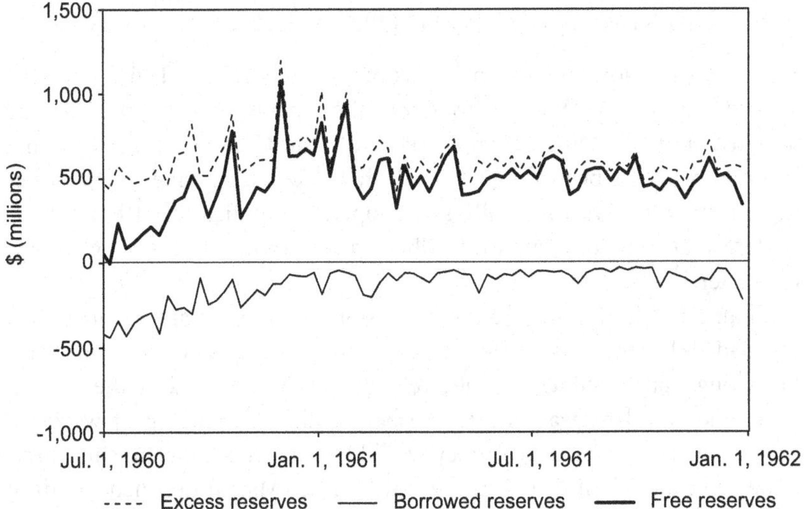

Chart 19.6 Excess reserves, borrowed reserves, and free reserves. Weekly averages of daily figures.
Board of Governors of the Federal Reserve System (1976, table 10.1C).

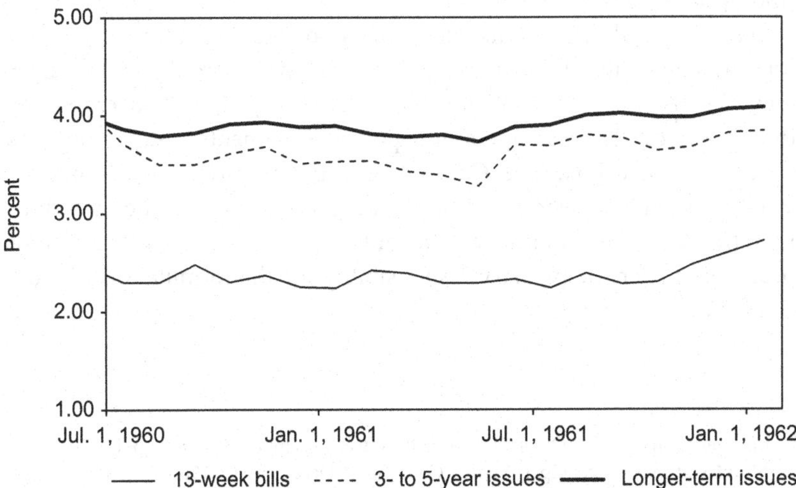

Chart 19.7 Treasury yields. Monthly averages.
Board of Governors of the Federal Reserve System (1976, tables 12.7A and 12.12A).

ABANDONING THE 1953 OPERATING PRINCIPLES

Perhaps the most important outcome of Operation Twist was the decision of the FOMC to abandon the operating principles it had adopted in 1953. On December 19, 1961, the Committee decided that Allan Sproul had been right after all, that it was a mistake to encumber monetary policy with formally stated operating policies that limited the System's ability to respond flexibly to emerging problems of novel character.[52]

Chairman Martin initiated the discussion. He was, he said, "more or less persuaded by the position of those who had suggested termination," observing that "a difficult public relations climate existed at the present time, and [that] he was inclined to believe that a changing of words in the statements of operating policy would be subject to more misinterpretation than abandonment of those statements." Martin declined to admit original error, saying that "a case could be made that the operating policy statement had been virtually essential in the transition from a pegged market to a free market in Government securities." More recently, however, "there may have been a real question whether the depth, breadth, and resiliency of the market was being furthered or not by the existence of [those] provisions."[53]

Hayes agreed with "the desirability of getting away from the formal statements of operating policy." Echoing Sproul's earlier argument for the importance of flexibility, he said he was "concerned that the existence of the operating policy statements might put the Committee in a box. The Committee ought to have a concern for a well-functioning Government securities market, but he did not think that this concern should ever be built up to a point where it took precedence over the primary responsibility for the formulation of monetary policy."[54]

[52] Minutes of the Federal Open Market Committee, December 19, 1961, pp. 68–70.

[53] Minutes of the Federal Open Market Committee, December 19, 1961, pp. 31–33. When, in 1959, the Joint Economic Committee questioned Martin on whether bills preferably had strengthened the government securities market, Martin acknowledged that the market had not "fully achieved the depth, breadth, and resiliency that is desirable and that was held out as a feasible goal in the [1952 report of the ad hoc subcommittee]. The market had not been wholly satisfactory in these respects at any time in the postwar period." Joint Economic Committee (1959, part 6C, p. 1813).

[54] Minutes of the Federal Open Market Committee, December 19, 1961, pp. 35–39.

Governor Mills and Governor Robertson opposed termination, on the grounds that the February 20 initiative had done significant damage to the market for longer-term government securities. Mills argued that,

> [t]he market has come to regard operations in bonds and other longer-term U.S. Government securities as patent efforts to support the market rather than as a means of influencing interest rates. The obvious fact that long-term securities acquired by the System Open Market Account have been very largely retained sustain the market's belief and give rise to the complaint that abstention from supporting purchases is allowing the market to drift uncontrollably. All in all, the System's longer-term securities transactions have set the stage for a full-fledged pegging operation that will ultimately burst from its chrysalis full-grown, unless discontinued promptly[;]

and that,

> [t]he great objection to System open market operations in both long- and short-term U.S. Government securities, other than Treasury bills, is that they have the effect of impairing the usefulness of the U.S. Government securities market as a sounding board for recording economic and financial movements that should be recognized by appropriate monetary and credit policy treatment. Operations confined to Treasury bills previously permitted the market to reflect the economic response that monetary and credit policy formulation must take into account.[55]

Robertson expressed concern with whether the Fed would be able to restore the Open Market Account to its previous condition, with whether the sale of long-term securities would "present real problems": "Such selling action on our part would not only absorb long-term funds from the limited supply, but would also aggravate the uncertainties which already plague the long-term market, weakening its supporting structure and attenuating its appeal to investors."[56]

Malcolm Bryan of the Atlanta Fed also opposed abandoning the operating policies, believing that they served as a reminder of "one of the classical canons of central banking," that "a central bank should deal only in paper of short term and of unquestioned goodness."[57]

Following the decision to terminate the 1953 operating policies, the Committee adopted a "continuing authority directive" that established the broad framework within which the Federal Reserve Bank of New York was

[55] Minutes of the Federal Open Market Committee, December 19, 1961, pp. 49–50.

[56] Minutes of the Federal Open Market Committee, December 19, 1961, pp. 57–58.

[57] Minutes of the Federal Open Market Committee, December 19, 1961, pp. 65–66.

to conduct open market operations. (The continuing authority directive was supplemented by a "current economic policy directive" that changed from time to time and that provided more detailed instructions to the Bank.) The continuing authority provided, in relevant part, that

> [t]he Federal Open Market Committee authorizes and directs the Federal Reserve Bank of New York to the extent necessary to carry out the current economic policy directive adopted at the most recent meeting of the Committee:
>
> (a) To buy and sell United States Government securities in the open market for the System Open Market Account at market prices and, for such Account, to exchange maturing United States Government securities with the Treasury or allow them to mature without replacement . . .
>
> (c) To buy United States Government securities with maturities of 24 months [[58]] or less at the time of purchase . . . from nonbank dealers for the account of the Federal Reserve Bank of New York under agreements for repurchase of such securities . . . in 15 calendar days or less, at rates not less than (a) the discount rate of the Federal Reserve Bank of New York at the time such agreement is entered into, or (b) the average issuing rate on the most recent issue of 3-month Treasury bills, whichever is lower.[59]

OPERATION TWIST AFTER 1961

Available evidence suggests that Operation Twist faded away in 1963. (Unlike bills preferably, Operation Twist did not end with a formal public announcement.) The return of economic expansion led to rising bill yields (Chart 19.8) and reduced pressure to limit bill purchases. Beginning in 1963 and continuing for the balance of the decade, bill purchases visibly outstripped coupon purchases (Chart 19.9). A 1967 Federal Reserve staff study states that "after 1963, the size and frequency of official operations in coupon issues, particularly those undertaken for the System [Open Market Account], were greatly reduced compared with the early 1960's."[60] Bordo and Eichengreen cite two 1963 FOMC meetings, on May 7 and July 30, where decisions to raise short-term interest rates were "part of Operation Twist."[61] They do not cite any subsequent Committee actions as being similarly motivated. Finally, a 1963 termination date is consistent with the introduction, in 1961 and 1962, of new policy instruments intended to

[58] The extension of the maturity limit for repo collateral to twenty-four months was added at Hayes' suggestion and did not provoke any opposition.

[59] Minutes of the Federal Open Market Committee, December 19, 1961, p. 71.

[60] Cooper (1967, p. 28).

[61] Bordo and Eichengreen (1976, p. 457).

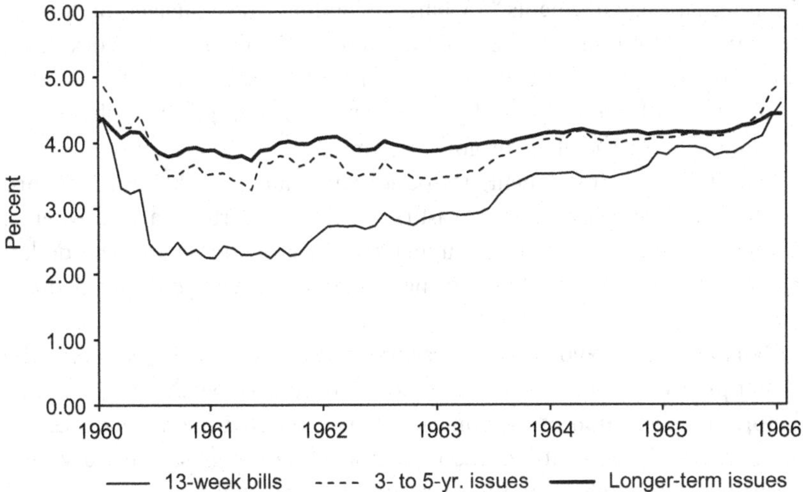

Chart 19.8 Treasury yields. Monthly averages.
Board of Governors of the Federal Reserve System (1976, tables 12.7A and 12.12A).

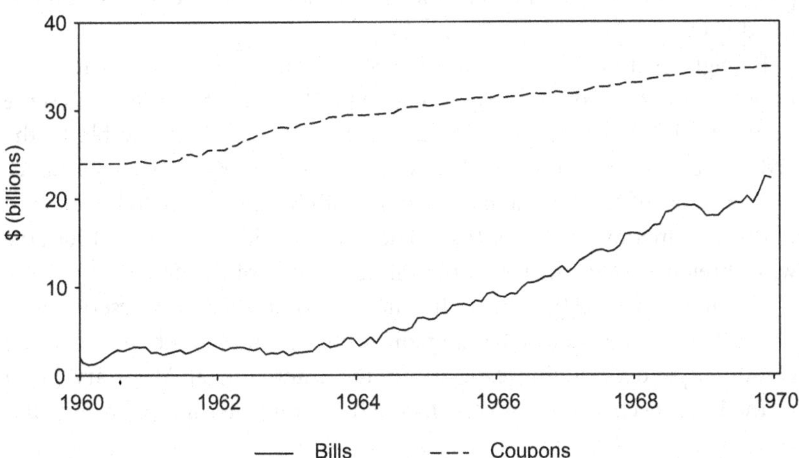

Chart 19.9 Treasury bills and coupon-bearing Treasury securities in the System Open Market Account. End of month.
Board of Governors of the Federal Reserve System (1976, table 9.5A).

replace gold flows as the primary means of accommodating transient imbalances in international payments.

New Policy Instruments

Beginning in the spring of 1961, the Treasury and the Fed introduced a variety of new policy instruments to buffer large but transient imbalances in international payments.[62] Charles Coombs, the manager of foreign exchange operations at the Federal Reserve Bank of New York from 1961 to 1975, states that the new instruments "transformed the financial machinery of Bretton Woods by . . . encouraging a progressive substitution of mutual credit facilities for gold settlements."[63]

The first new instrument, introduced in March 1961,[64] was forward sales of foreign currencies. Treasury officials undertook a sale when a foreign currency was near the upper end of its band against the dollar, intending to cover the sale when the foreign currency had declined closer to parity.

Forward sales exposed the Treasury to a risk of loss in the event the dollar price of the foreign currency did not decline below the contract price before the expiration of the contract. This prompted the introduction, in August 1961,[65] of what became known as "Roosa bonds," Treasury debt securities denominated in a foreign currency and sold to a foreign central bank. The proceeds could be used to settle a maturing forward sale of the currency – allowing time for a loss to turn into a gain. Alternatively, the proceeds could be sold in independent spot market transactions to support the dollar.

Foreign currency swaps, introduced in early 1962, were the most important new credit facility.[66] In a typical swap, the Federal Reserve Bank of New York created a dollar balance on its books payable to the order of a foreign central bank in exchange for a foreign currency balance on the books of that central bank, where both balances were to be reversed in three (sometimes six) months.[67] The swap provided the Federal Reserve with foreign currency that it could sell in defense of the dollar.

Coombs observed that "[b]y the end of 1964 the Federal Reserve swap network and other central bank credit facilities, the Roosa bonds, and the greatly expanded lending capacity of the International Monetary Fund formed a spectrum of short- through medium-term credit facilities

[62] See generally Coombs (1976) and Bordo, Humpage, and Schwartz (2015, ch. 4).

[63] Coombs (1976, pp. 195–96).

[64] Coombs (1976, pp. 33–35) and Bordo, Humpage, and Schwartz (2015, pp. 133–34).

[65] Coombs (1976, pp. 37–40) and Bordo, Humpage, and Schwartz (2015, p. 135).

[66] Bordo, Humpage, and Schwartz (2015) state (p. 148) that "the swap network . . . was the United States' first line of defense during Bretton Woods" and (p. 149) that "from 1962 until the closing of the US gold window in August 1971, the reciprocal currency arrangements, or swap lines, were the Federal Reserve System's key mechanism for defending the US gold stock."

[67] Coombs (1976, ch. 5) and Bordo, Humpage, and Schwartz (2015, pp. 137–48).

available to all the major trading countries for financing temporary deficits in their foreign payments."[68]

He characterized the new instruments as forming "concentric defense lines shielding the dollar":

> On the perimeter was the Federal Reserve swap network, reinforced as needed by Federal [Reserve] and Treasury operations in the forward exchange markets as well as by spot and forward operations conducted by our foreign central bank partners. When pressures on the dollar at any point could not be contained by such temporary holding actions, we could fall back to a second line of defense in the form of Roosa bonds. The final defense line protecting our gold stock was the IMF, through which the United States could borrow at medium term foreign currencies up to $5.2 billion equivalent as determined by its quota.[69]

New Empirical Evidence

The development of new policy instruments was not the only reason for the FOMC to terminate Operation Twist. In the second half of the 1960s, an emerging body of empirical evidence questioned whether shifts in the maturity structure of Treasury indebtedness had had anything more than a modest effect on the term structure of interest rates. Scott (1965) found that lengthening the average maturity of the debt by one month coincided with an increase in the spread between long-term Treasury yields and short-term yields of only about 3½ basis points. In a 1965 paper, Modigliani and Sutch concluded that "neither the maturity structure of the government debt nor changes in the maturity structure exert any significant, lasting or transient, influence on the relation between the [long rate and the short rate]."[70] In a follow-up paper a year later they concluded that "the responsiveness of the rate structure to variations in the age composition of the national debt outstanding was at best very weak."[71] And at the beginning of the 1970s, Bierwag and Grove (1971) reported that that Operation Twist had "a very temporary effect if any at all." Hamburger and Silber (1971) reported "an insignificant or token debt management effect" over monthly intervals and no effect over quarterly intervals.

THE END OF $35 GOLD

Maintaining the price of gold at $35 per ounce was a leading policy objective of Treasury and Federal Reserve officials through the end of

[68] Coombs (1976, p. 188). [69] Coombs (1976, p. 90).
[70] Modigliani and Sutch (1966, p. 191). [71] Modigliani and Sutch (1967, p. 587).

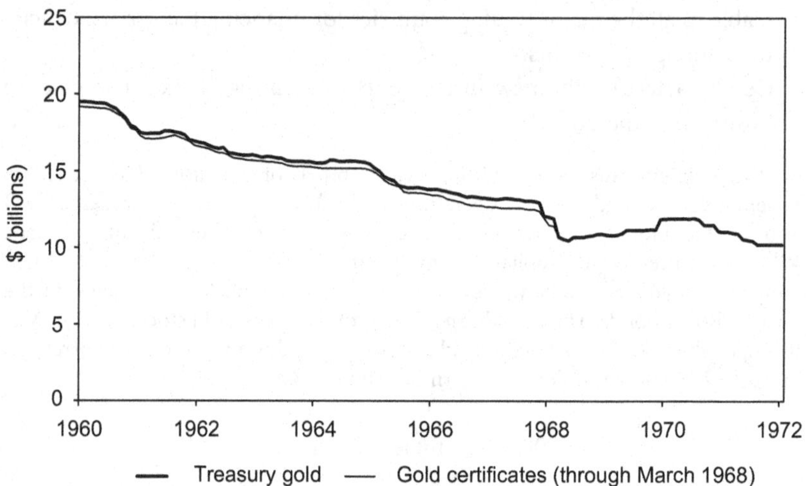

Chart 19.10 Treasury gold (end of month) and gold certificates issued by the Treasury to Federal Reserve Banks (monthly averages of daily figures).
Board of Governors of the Federal Reserve System (1976, tables 9.7 and 14.1).

1968. Coombs called it the "lynch-pin of Bretton Woods" and Bordo, Humpage, and Schwartz describe it as the "keystone of the entire Bretton Woods structure."[72] Paul Volcker, the Deputy Under Secretary of the Treasury for Monetary Affairs from November 1963 to November 1965 and a protégé of Roosa, remarks in his memoirs that

> [t]o Roosa, [$35 gold] was as much a moral issue, an obligation taken on by the United States as the leader of the free world, as a matter of economic policy. In his office any consideration of devaluing the dollar or ending the convertibility of the dollar [into gold] was taboo. The possibility that the dollar was chronically overvalued and that our gold stock might be depleted was simply not recognized in Treasury circles. American honor was at stake.[73]

Nevertheless, US gold reserves declined steadily until 1968 (Chart 19.10).

Satisfying foreign demand for US gold had to overcome two institutional impediments. First, almost all of the Treasury's gold was pledged against gold certificates issued to Federal Reserve Banks and was not, therefore, immediately available for sale to a foreign central bank. However, Treasury could lift the pledge on a specified amount of gold by redeeming certificates. Sale of the newly released gold would restore the Treasury's cash

[72] Coombs (1976, p. 5) and Bordo, Humpage, and Schwartz (2015, p. 122).
[73] Volcker (2018, p. 48).

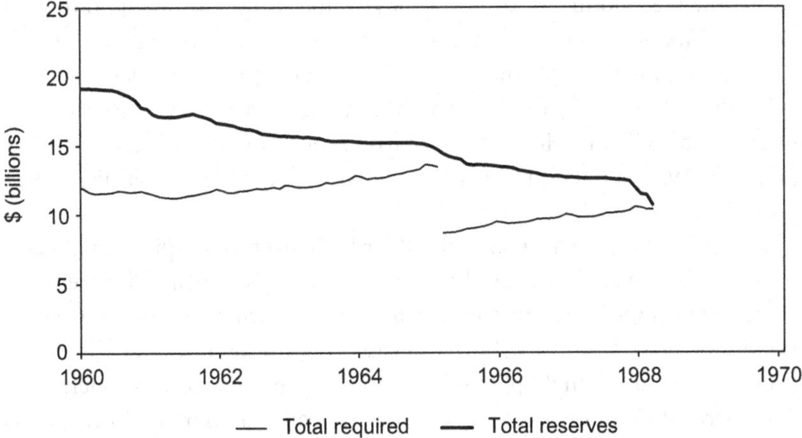

Chart 19.11 Required and total Federal Reserve gold certificate reserves. Monthly averages of daily figures.
Board of Governors of the Federal Reserve System (1976, table 9.7).

balance with the Fed; Desk purchases of Treasury securities would sterilize the concomitant reduction in reserves.

The statutory requirement for a 25 percent gold reserve on Federal Reserve note and deposit liabilities was a potentially more significant problem. However, Congress removed that impediment by eliminating the reserve requirement on the Fed's deposit liabilities in March 1965 and on its note liabilities in March 1968 (Chart 19.11).[74]

In March 1968, the United States and its major trading partners entered into an agreement to abstain from purchasing or selling gold in the public market and to limit their gold transactions to transactions with other countries undertaken to offset an imbalance of payments.[75] The result was a two-tier gold market, with a competitively determined price for public transactions and an administratively set price of $35 per ounce for transactions between countries. The agreement, coupled with high short-term US interest rates (see Chart 21.5 below), shut off the gold drain – and even prompted an increase in Treasury's gold stock – through mid-1970.

[74] Act of March 3, 1965, and act of March 18, 1968.

[75] Coombs (1976, ch. 9), "7 Nations Back Dual Gold Price, Bar Selling to Private Buyers; Pledge Support of the Dollar," *New York Times*, March 18, 1968, p. 1, "The Gold Crisis Forces Administration to Alter Its Stand on Key Issues," *Wall Street Journal*, March 18, 1968, p. 1, and "'Gold Pool,' an Informal Venture of Nations in West, Is Main Casualty in Latest Crisis," *Wall Street Journal*, March 18, 1968, p. 6.

National economic priorities changed following the inauguration of Richard Nixon in January 1969. The new administration was more interested in keeping unemployment low than worrying about budget deficits or inflation.[76] (Nixon famously attributed his loss in the 1960 Presidential election to William McChesney Martin's decision to tighten monetary policy in 1959, an action that precipitated the April 1960–February 1961 recession.[77])

Martin's term as chairman of the Board of Governors expired in January 1970 and Nixon appointed Arthur Burns as his replacement. The president concluded his introductory remarks at Burns' swearing-in ceremony with a none-too-subtle plea: "Dr. Burns, please give us some money.'"[78] Burns proved to be gratifyingly pliant: The yield on thirteen-week bills fell from 7.87 percent in January 1970 to 3.38 percent in March 1971. In his memoirs, Volcker remarks that "the new Fed leadership seemed almost perversely willing to ease policy, reducing money market interest rates, even when the dollar was under pressure."[79] The decline in rates reversed the gold flow and exacerbated a cascading series of problems that culminated in Nixon's decision to close the Treasury's gold window on August 15, 1971, putting an end to United States gold sales to foreign central banks at $35 per ounce. Within two years, the Bretton Woods system of fixed exchange rates was gone as well, replaced with floating rates.[80]

[76] Silber (2012, p. 73). [77] Volcker (2018, p. 66). [78] Coombs (1976, p. 206).

[79] Volcker (2018, p. 66).

[80] The closing of the gold window and the end of the Bretton Woods system is recounted in Coombs (1976, chapter 12), Solomon (1982, chapters 11–13), Silber (2012, part II), and Volcker (2018, chapters 5 and 6).

PART VI

THE 1960S

The second half of the 1960s witnessed a striking change in the needs of monetary policy and, consequently, in the relationship between the Federal Reserve System and the market. For reasons explained in Chapter 21 and the first half of Chapter 22, the System was obliged to undertake open market operations on a larger scale, more frequently, and to reverse direction more rapidly than had previously been the case. As a result, the System made increasing demands on market liquidity. At the same time, higher and more volatile interest rates sometimes left dealers unwilling to hold substantial inventories and reluctant to provide adequate liquidity to the Desk.

The System responded by expanding the scale and scope of its repo operations. As discussed in the second half of Chapter 22, the System first relaxed and then abandoned maturity limits on repo collateral, permitted back-to-back repos (where dealers acted as intermediaries between the Desk and their customers), initiated repos on agency securities, introduced matched sale-purchase agreements (functionally equivalent to a dealer's reverse repo), and tried (but failed) to introduce greater flexibility in repo pricing.

20

Treasury Debt Management in the 1960s

By the beginning of the Kennedy Administration in January 1961 Treasury officials had identified, for the first time since the end of World War II, a coherent debt management strategy, one reasonably calculated to sustain $185 billion of marketable debt and to fund modest annual additions. The Treasury auctioned thriteen- and twenty-six-week bills on a regular weekly basis and year bills on a quarterly basis. Certificates, notes, and bonds were sold in fixed-price mid-quarter refundings (introduced in 1958 to regularize offerings of coupon-bearing debt), as well as in advance refundings (introduced in 1960 to lengthen the maturity structure of the debt) and occasional "stand-alone" offerings (to raise new money). Tax anticipation bills were sold on an as-needed basis to bridge seasonal gaps between when cash was needed (typically in the second half of a calendar year) and when it would become available (usually the following spring).

This chapter reviews the subsequent evolution of Treasury debt management in the 1960s, beginning with several broad characteristics of marketable debt and then focusing more narrowly on bills and coupon-bearing securities, respectively. The chapter concludes with a discussion of the difference between financing operations in the bill and coupon markets.

SECULAR VARIATION OF MARKETABLE DEBT

Excluding tax anticipation bills, marketable Treasury debt grew at an average rate of $4.6 billion per year during the 1960s, from $182 billion at the end of 1959 to $228 billion at the end of 1969. (Tax anticipation bills are excluded from the present discussion because they were relatively minor in magnitude and varied seasonally.) There were no sharp jumps or dramatic reversals (Chart 20.1). Marketable debt grew faster than

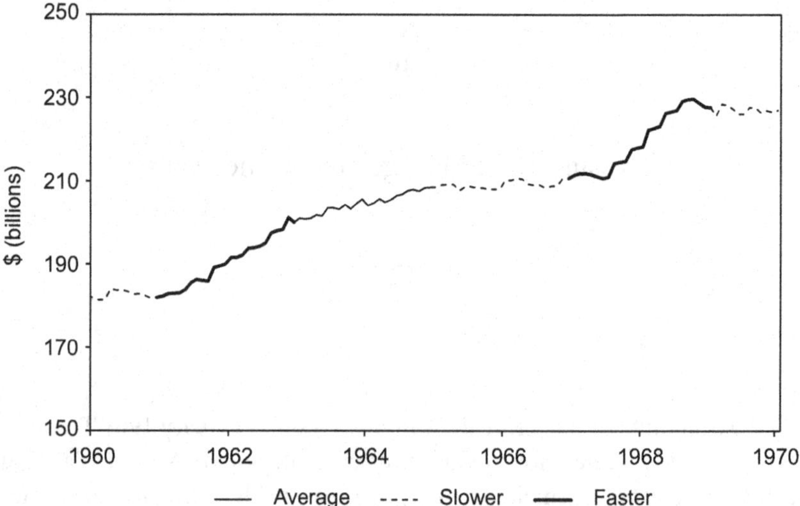

Chart 20.1 Marketable Treasury debt (exclusive of tax anticipation bills). End of month. The dashed lines denote years of slow or no growth (1960, 1965–66, and 1969); the heavy lines denote years of relatively rapid growth (1961–62 and 1967–68). Board of Governors of the Federal Reserve System (1976, table 13.2).

average in 1961–62 ($9.0 billion per year) and 1967–68 ($8.6 billion per year), slower than average in 1965–66 ($1.1 billion per year), and approximately on-trend in 1963–64 ($4.3 billion per year).

The average maturity of marketable debt increased from 4.2 years at the beginning of 1960 to 5.4 years in January 1965 (Chart 20.2), primarily as a result of the advance refunding program.[1] Average maturity then began declining when (as discussed in the next chapter) bond yields in the secondary market rose above a 4¼ percent statutory ceiling on bond coupon rates,[2] preventing the Treasury from issuing any additional bonds. It reached a decade low of 3.7 years at the end of 1969.

The composition of marketable Treasury debt exhibited three important features in the 1960s. In the second quarter of the decade, with economic

[1] Several authors, including Modigliani and Sutch (1966, pp. 191–92, and 1967, p. 578); Swanson (2011, pp. 165–66), and Greenwood, Hanson, Rudolph, and Summers (2014, p. 19, fn. 14), have noted that the Treasury debt extension program ran exactly opposite to the objectives of Operation Twist.

[2] The 4¼ percent ceiling was established by the Third Liberty Bond Act of April 4, 1918. See Garbade (2012, ch. 5 and especially p. 75).

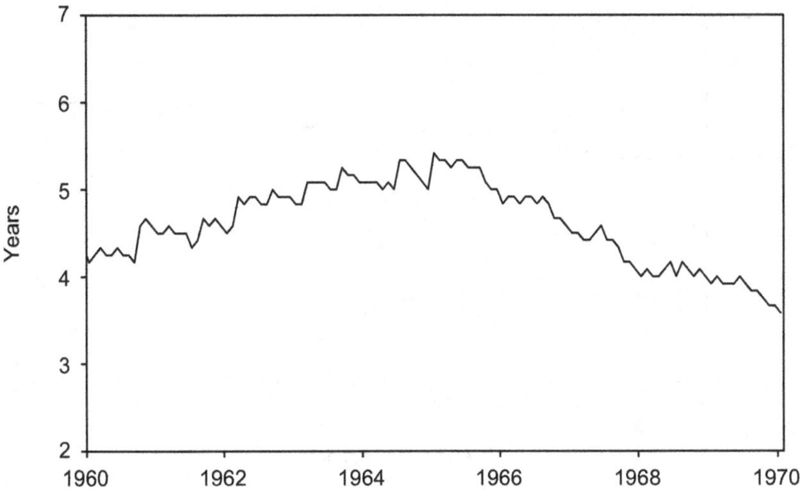

Chart 20.2 Average maturity of marketable Treasury debt.
Treasury Bulletin.

recovery well under way, officials throttled back on issuing certificates and notes and pumped up bond issuance to shift indebtedness away from what they considered an over-worked intermediate-term market.[3] A $27.5 billion increase in bonds outstanding from mid-1962 to mid-1965 offset a $26.5 billion decrease in certificates and notes (Chart 20.3). The variation reversed when the Treasury was disabled from issuing bonds after 1965: a $23.7 billion run-off in bonds from mid-1965 to mid-1969 was offset by a $26.4 billion increase in certificates and notes. The $31.8 billion increase in total marketable debt (exclusive of tax anticipation bills) over the combined interval from mid-1962 to mid-1969 was largely funded by a $28.2 billion increase in regular bills.

TREASURY BILLS

Treasury bills were issued in three functional categories in the 1960s: regular bills, bill strips, and tax anticipation bills.

[3] A 1960 Treasury white paper stated that the maturity structure of the debt was "far too heavily concentrated in the under-5-year area" and that "the real problem is the excessive amount of securities maturing between 1 and 5 years." U.S. Treasury Department (1960, p. 3). See also Beard (1966, p. 6).

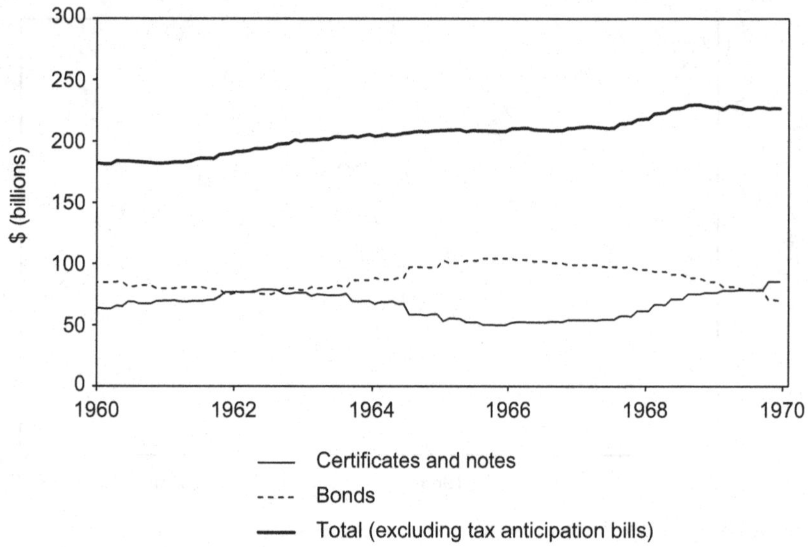

Chart 20.3 Treasury certificates and notes, Treasury bonds, and total marketable debt (exclusive of tax anticipation bills). End of month.
Board of Governors of the Federal Reserve System (1976, table 13.2).

Regular Bills

Regular bills, including thirteen- and twenty-six-week bills, one-year bills and (beginning in 1966) nine-month bills, accounted for the bulk of bill issuance. The decade-long expansion in bills outstanding was supported by

(1) steadily increasing auction offerings of thirteen- and twenty-six-week bills (Chart 20.4);
(2) more frequent offerings of one-year bills, shifting from quarterly to monthly in August 1963 (Chart 20.5); and
(3) the introduction of monthly nine-month bills, as reopenings of old year bills, in September 1966.

The 1966 Markets annual report remarked that one-year bills "became quite scarce and somewhat untradeable" a few months after issue. Nine-month bills were intended to mitigate the problem.[4]

[4] 1966 Annual Report of Open Market Operations, p. 64.

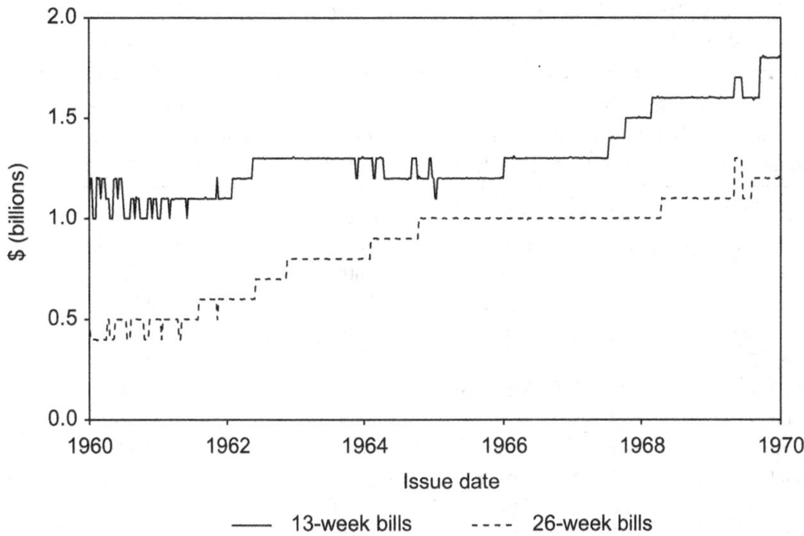

Chart 20.4 Treasury bill issuance.
Treasury Bulletin.

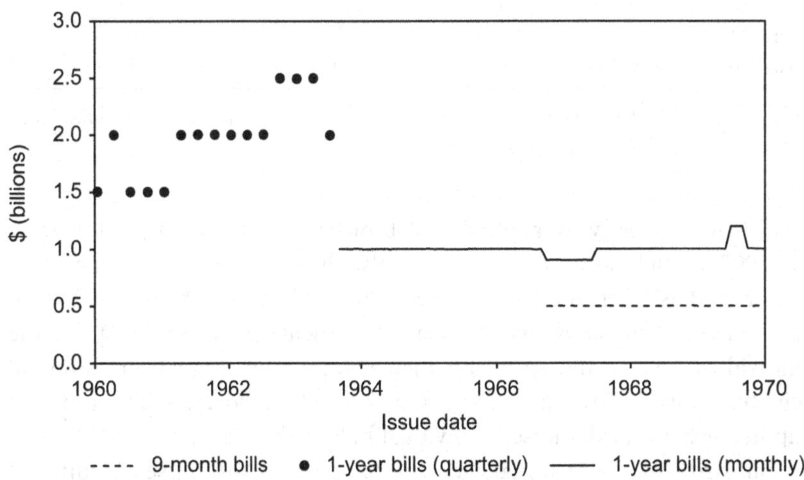

Chart 20.5 Treasury bill issuance.
Treasury Bulletin.

Bill Strips

Treasury officials auctioned the first bill strip in June 1961, an offering of $1.8 billion of eighteen different bills maturing weekly from Thursday, August 3 to Thursday, November 30 (Table 20.1). An auction tender had to specify the quantity of bills sought as an integer multiple of $18,000 and

Table 20.1 *Treasury offering of a $1.8 billion strip of Treasury bills for settlement on June 14, 1961.*

Bill maturity date	Days from settlement to maturity	Original issue date	Amount outstanding ($ millions)	Discount rate in secondary market trading on June 1, 1961 (percent)
Aug. 3	50	Feb. 2	1,601	2.33
Aug. 10	57	Feb. 9	1,601	2.33
Aug. 17	64	Feb. 16	1,600	2.33
Aug. 24	71	Feb. 23	1,600	2.35
Aug. 31	78	Mar. 2	1,501	2.35
Sep. 7	85	Mar. 9	500	2.31
Sep. 14	92	Mar. 16	500	2.31
Sep. 21	99	Mar. 23	500	2.37
Sep. 28	106	Mar. 30	500	2.39
Oct. 5	113	Apr. 6	500	2.47
Oct. 13	121	Apr. 13	500	2.47
Oct. 19	127	Apr. 20	400	2.51
Oct. 26	134	Apr. 27	400	2.51
Nov. 2	141	May 4	500	2.54
Nov. 9	148	May 11	500	2.54
Nov. 16	155	May 18	501	2.54
Nov. 24	163	May 25	500	2.54
Nov. 30	169	Jun. 1	500	2.57

Federal Reserve Bank of New York Circular no. 5043, June 2, 1961, and "U.S. Government and Agency Bonds," *New York Times*, June 2, 1961, p. 46.

successful tenders were allotted $1,000 of bills of each maturity for every $18,000 of bills awarded. A tender also had to specify a single price (expressed as a percent of par value) to be applied to each of the eighteen bills in the strip, so an auction market participant had to first price the individual bills in the strip and then compute an average price for all eighteen bills. Following settlement, a successful bidder was free to break up his or her award and sell individual bills at different prices.

Bill strips were a cash management device – a way to raise a significant amount of cash quickly by selling relatively small amounts of a variety of maturities in lieu of selling a large amount of a single maturity. They were a mirror image of the "tax date" bills offered in the second half of the 1930s.[5]

[5] Tax date bills were a series of bills that shared a common maturity date (on or shortly after a scheduled tax payment date) sold in small tranches over a period of five to ten weeks. Garbade (2012, pp. 293–96).

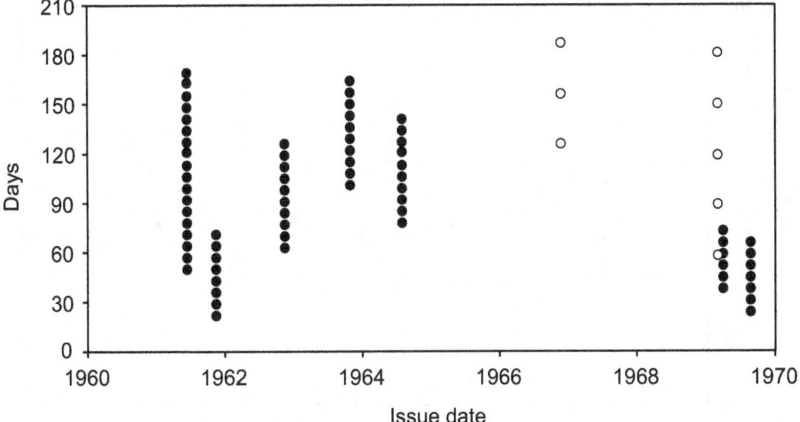

Chart 20.6 Maturities of bills offered in bill strips.
Federal Reserve Bank of New York circulars.

The Treasury sold bill strips nine times in the 1960s (Chart 20.6). Seven strips reopened Thursday maturities originally opened with twenty-six-week bills and two reopened end-of-month maturities originally opened with one-year bills.[6] The first five strips offered $100 million at each maturity date; the last two offered $300 million per maturity date. The two strips that reopened end-of-month maturities offered $400 million and $300 million per maturity date, respectively.

Tax Anticipation Bills

Tax anticipation bills were also a cash management device, issued when Treasury needed funds and timed to mature shortly after tax payment dates.

[6] Prior to the introduction of monthly year bill auctions in 1963, year bills were issued on the fifteenth of the first month of a quarter and scheduled to mature on the fifteenth of the same month a year later. It would have been natural to retain that convention following the move to monthly auctions, issuing and redeeming year bills on the ffiteenth of every month. Instead, Treasury officials moved the issue and maturity dates to the last day of a month to avoid issuing year bills at the same time they were issuing coupon-bearing securities in mid-quarter refundings (usually the fifteenth of the second month of a quarter).

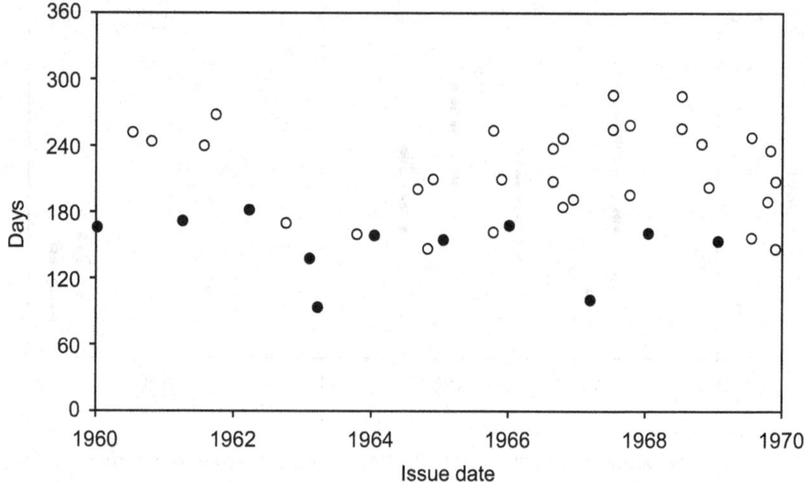

Chart 20.7 Maturities of tax anticipation bills.
Federal Reserve Bank of New York circulars.

The Treasury issued forty-two tax anticipation bills in the 1960s (Chart 20.7). Most were issued in the second half of a calendar year (when tax receipts were seasonally low) and scheduled to mature on or about the following March 22 (11 of the 42), April 22 (7 of the 42), or June 22 (21 of the 42).[7] Issue sizes ranged from $1 billion to $3½ billion. Tax anticipation bills added a seasonal component to the secular growth of marketable debt (Chart 20.8).

CERTIFICATES, NOTES, AND BONDS

Coupon-bearing debt was issued in three major programs: mid-quarter refundings, stand-alone offerings for new money, and advance refundings.

[7] One tax anticipation bill was issued on July 18, 1969, and scheduled to mature later in the *same* calendar year (December 22, 1969). Two other bills were issued in the *first* half of a calendar year (on April 3, 1961, and March 23, 1962) and scheduled to mature in the *second* half of the same year (September 21, 1961, and September 22, 1962, respectively).

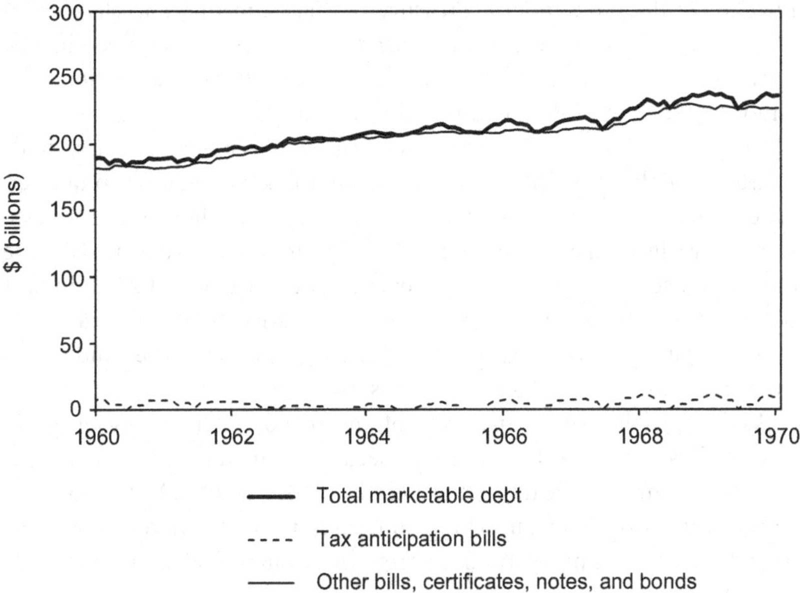

Chart 20.8 Tax anticipation bills and total marketable Treasury debt. End of month. Board of Governors of the Federal Reserve System (1976, table 13.2).

Mid-Quarter Refundings

In terms of dollar volume, mid-quarter refundings were the most important platform for issuing coupon-bearing debt. Offerings typically settled on the fifteenth of the second month of a calendar quarter and were usually limited to refinancing debt maturing on the settlement date or due to mature *before* the next mid-quarter refunding. For example, the February 1962 refunding refinanced three issues maturing on February 15, 1962, and one issue scheduled to mature six weeks later.[8] However, some refundings refinanced securities scheduled to mature *on* the next mid-quarter refunding – the August 1966 refunding refinanced three issues maturing on November 15, 1966, as well as two issues maturing on August 15, 1966 – and some were structured to raise new money as well as to refinance maturing debt. The August 1962 refunding raised more than $1 billion of new money in addition to refinancing $7.5 billion of maturing debt.[9]

Although most mid-quarter refundings were announced at the beginning of the second month of a quarter and scheduled to settle on the

[8] Federal Reserve Bank of New York Circular no. 5144, February 1, 1962; and Circular no. 5146, February 5, 1962.

[9] Federal Reserve Bank of New York Circular no. 5206, July 26, 1962; and Circular no. 5844, July 27, 1966.

fifteenth of the same month, Treasury officials sometimes accelerated an offering to refinance securities maturing shortly before the fifteenth. The third quarter 1961 refunding settled on August 1 to facilitate refinancing almost $10 billion of debt maturing on that day.[10]

Apart from the regular announcement and settlement times, mid-quarter refundings exhibited substantial variation from quarter to quarter. As described in more detail in Box 20.1, some refundings were for cash, some were in exchange for maturing debt, and some were mixed. The quantity of securities offered varied over a wide range (Chart 20.9), in part because the quantity of maturing securities varied but also because, as noted above, later-maturing securities were sometimes included and sometimes not and because some refundings raised new cash.

Aside from the regular inclusion of an "anchor" issue maturing in 1½ years or less, the maturities of offered securities varied irregularly, particularly in the first six years of the decade (Chart 20.10). After 1965, the Treasury was disabled from selling bonds and regularly offered notes at or near the maximum maturity (five years prior to June 1967 and seven years thereafter[11]).

Stand-Alone Offerings for New Money

Treasury officials choose to raise new money by selling coupon-bearing securities in stand-alone offerings on eight occasions in the 1960s. The offerings were "as needed" and unrelated to the regular mid-quarter refundings. There was no evident regularity in either the timing or the maturities of the offerings (Chart 20.11). Except for the April 1960 offering, officials sold a single security in each offering. All seven single-issue offerings matured in less than nine years and ranged between $1 billion and $2½ billion.

Officials offered two securities in April 1960: $2 billion of a two-year, one-month note and "up to" $1½ billion of a 4¼ percent twenty-five-year bond. It was the first time in more than a year that officials had been able to offer a bond at or under the 4¼ percent statutory ceiling on bond coupon rates.[12]

[10] Federal Reserve Bank of New York Circular no. 5059, July 13, 1961; and Circular no. 5060, July 17, 1961.

[11] The Act of June 30, 1967, redefined the maximum maturity of a note from five years (as originally provided in the Victory Liberty Loan Act of March 3, 1919) to seven years.

[12] The 1959 Annual Report of Open Market Operations states (p. 7) that "after March [1959, the Treasury] was unable to do any further financing outside the 5 year area because the rate it would have had to pay exceeded the 4¼ per cent maximum the Treasury is permitted to pay on new [bond] issues under existing legislation."

Box 20.1 Cash and Exchange Offerings in Mid-Quarter Refundings.

The Treasury sold securities two different ways in its mid-quarter refundings: in fixed-price offerings for cash and in fixed-price offerings in exchange for maturing or soon-to-mature debt.

CASH REFUNDINGS

In a cash refunding the Treasury offered one or more securities at fixed prices and allocated over-subscriptions on a pro-rata basis.

For example, the February 1961 refunding offered $6.9 billion of 1½-year notes at par to finance the redemption of a comparable amount of maturing certificates. Market participants subscribed for $19.0 billion of the notes and the Treasury issued $7.3 billion, giving larger subscribers 20 percent of what they requested.[1]

The November 1966 refunding offered two securities for cash, $2.5 billion of 1¼-year notes at par and $1.6 billion of 5-year notes at par, to finance the redemption of $4 billion of maturing securities. Market participants subscribed for $5.9 billion of the shorter notes (receiving $2.6 billion on 30 percent allocations to larger subscribers) and $14.0 billion of the longer notes (receiving $1.7 billion on 10 percent allocations).[2]

EXCHANGE REFUNDINGS

In an exchange refunding the Treasury offered one or more securities in par-for-par exchanges for maturing or soon-to-mature securities. Holders of exchange-eligible securities could choose which securities best suited their needs.[3] Subscriptions, limited as they were by the quantity of exchange-eligible debt outstanding, were filled in full.

For example, the August 1963 refunding offered 1¼-year notes in a par-for-par exchange for $6.6 billion of securities maturing on August 15. Investors exchanged $6.4 billion of the maturing debt, resulting in 4.0 percent attrition.[4]

The February 1963 refunding gave investors a choice between two securities, a 1-year certificate and a 5½-year bond, in exchange for $9.5 billion of securities maturing on February 15. Investors exchanged $9.2 billion of the maturing debt, choosing to take $6.8 billion of the certificates and $2.5 billion of the bonds, resulting in 2.4 percent attrition.[5]

The November 1962 refunding gave investors a choice of *three* securities, a 1-year certificate, a 3-year note, and a 9¼-year bond, in exchange for $11.0 billion of maturing and soon-to-mature securities. Investors exchanged $10.4 billion of the exchange-eligible debt, choosing to take $4.8 billion of the certificates, $3.3 billion of the notes, and $2.3 billion of the bonds, resulting in 5.2 percent attrition.[6]

MIXED REFUNDINGS

In a couple of cases the Treasury combined cash and exchange offerings in a single mid-quarter refunding. The May 1968 refunding, for example, gave holders of $8.0 billion of maturing securities the option to exchange their securities for 7-year notes and also offered $3 billion of a 1¼-year note for cash. Investors exchanged $6.7 billion of the exchange-eligible securities, resulting in 16.4 percent attrition, and subscribed for $10.2 billion of the 1¼-year notes (receiving $3.3 billion on a 28 percent allocation to larger subscribers).[7]

Box 20.1 (cont.)

1 Federal Reserve Bank of New York Circular no. 4994, February 2, 1961; Circular no. 4995, February 6, 1961; and Circular no. 4999, February 9, 1961.

2 Federal Reserve Bank of New York Circular no. 5889, October 27, 1966; Circular no. 5890, October 28, 1966; and Circular no. 5893, November 4, 1966.

3 As noted by Gaines (1962, p. 79), the Treasury could not control how much debt of each maturity was ultimately issued in a multiple-security exchange offering.

4 Federal Reserve Bank of New Circular no. 5361, July 24, 1963; Circular no. 5362, July 26, 1963; and Circular no. 5365, August 2, 1963.

5 Federal Reserve Bank of New York Circular no. 5293, January 30, 1963; Circular no. 5295, February 4, 1963; and Circular no. 5299, February 8, 1963.

6 Federal Reserve Bank of New York Circular no. 5245, October 25, 1962; Circular no. 5246, October 29, 1962; and Circular no. 5251, November 2, 1962.

7 Federal Reserve Bank of New York Circular no. 6159, May 1, 1968; Circular no. 6160, May 3, 1968; and Circular no. 6166, May 10, 1968.

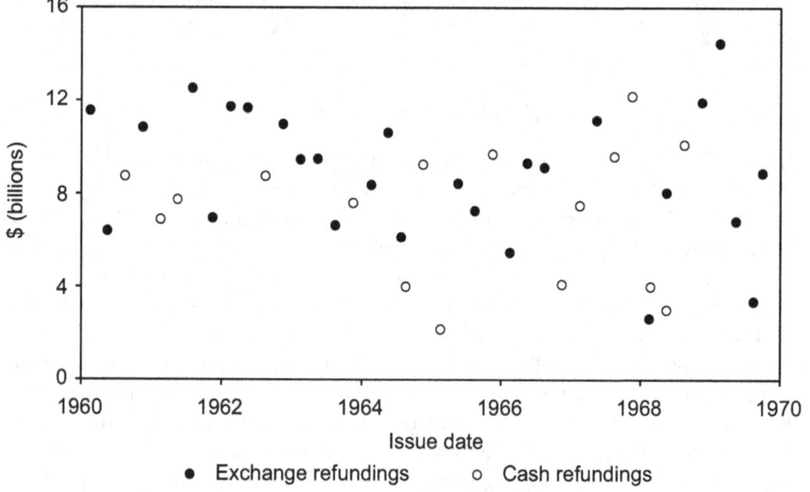

Chart 20.9 Offering amounts in mid-quarter refundings.
Federal Reserve Bank of New York circulars.

The "up to" language reflected their uncertainty about the breadth of investor demand for long-term debt.[13] (In the event, investors subscribed for only $470 million of the bond.)

13 "Treasury to Sell a 25-Year Bond," *New York Times*, April 1, 1960, p. 1, reporting that the Treasury "left the amount of the offering open – an unusual device – although it imposed a maximum of $1,500,000,000. In effect, the Treasury wants to test the market and see how much it will take in the way of long-term bonds at 4¼ per cent."

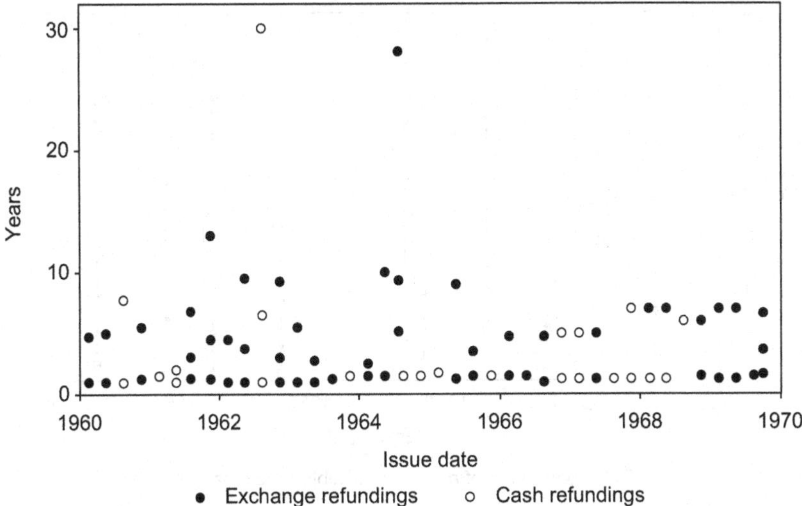

Chart 20.10 Maturities of offerings in mid-quarter refundings.
Federal Reserve Bank of New York circulars.

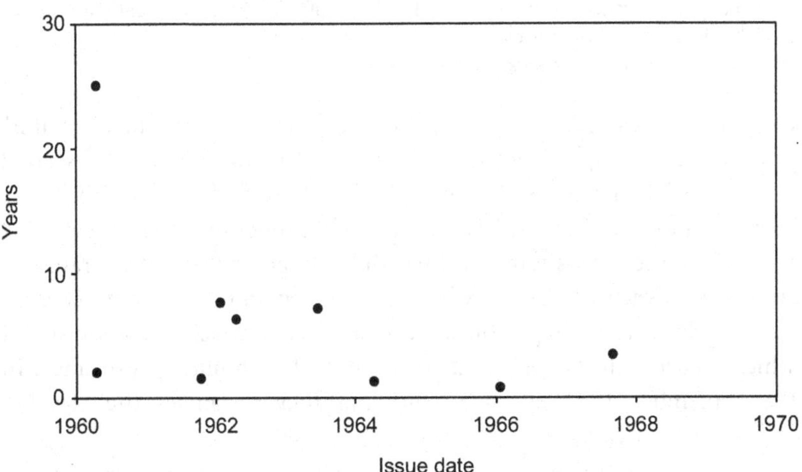

Chart 20.11 Maturities of stand-alone offerings. All of the offerings were fixed-price cash offerings.
Federal Reserve Bank of New York circulars.

Advance Refundings

Twice a year from 1960 to 1964, and once in 1965, officials offered new debt in exchange for outstanding debt of shorter maturities. The initial strategy was to first refinance outstanding five- to ten-year debt in a "senior" advance refunding and then to refinance debt in the overloaded

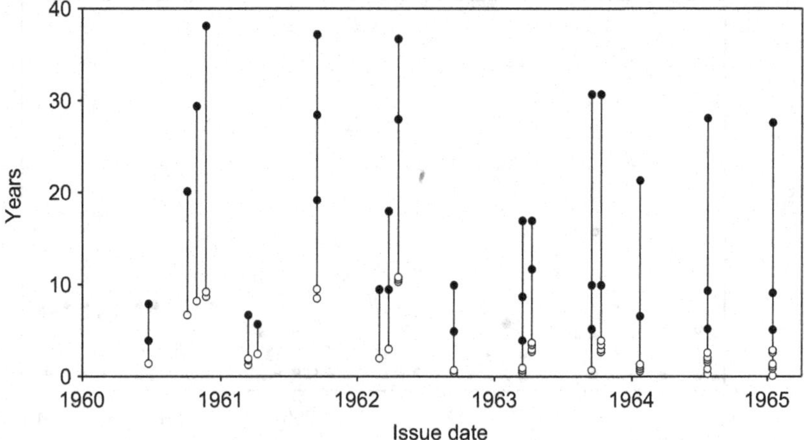

Chart 20.12 Term to maturity of securities eligible for exchange and securities offered in exchange in advance refundings. Unrelated offerings in a single operation are shown slightly displaced in time for clarity.
Federal Reserve Bank of New York circulars.

one- to five-year sector into the five- to ten-year sector in a "junior" advance refunding.[14] Officials adhered to that strategy in the second advance refunding in 1960 (the first advance refunding was little more than a test drive) and in the two advance refundings in 1961, but switched in 1962 to a less constrained format that contemplated a wider range of securities in each operation (Chart 20.12). Beginning with the February 1962 advance refunding, officials exercised substantial discretion about which securities to target for exchange and what to offer in exchange. In the September 1962 advance refunding they expanded the class of

[14] "Treasury May Broaden Scope of Its Advance Refunding Plan," *New York Times*, August 19, 1960, p. 29; and "Treasury Mulls Offer of Long-Term Bonds in Advance Refunding of Wartime 2½s," *Wall Street Journal*, August 19, 1960, p. 3. See also Beard (1966, p. 7), stating that Treasury officials "originally thought that debt extension could be achieved best by a 'leap frog' technique involving both junior and senior advance refundings. First, the senior operations could be used to shift 5- to 12-year maturities into long-term bonds. Then the stretching-out process could be completed by using junior operations to shift an even larger volume of 1- to 5-year issues into the 5- to 10-year range. Thus, debt extension could be achieved through a series of exchanges, each exchange involving new securities that are at least moderately substitutable for the outstanding eligible issues."

securities eligible for exchange by including "pre-refunding" issues due in less than a year.

In a speech on November 19, 1964, Robert Roosa, the Under Secretary of the Treasury for Monetary Affairs, explained why advance refundings were attractive to Treasury officials:

> The *Treasury has complete initiative with respect to timing and amounts.* Instead of being bound to act on a maturity date established many years earlier, the Treasury can choose when to enter the market, in the light of prevailing market conditions – accomplishing more, disturbing less.
>
> Moreover, *should the response be comparatively poor* [[15]] – either because new events intervened while the books were open or because the design of the offering was not adequately attractive – *the Treasury suffers no significant consequences.* It still will have other opportunities to handle the remaining holdings of securities eligible for the advance exchange, and there will be no impact at all upon its cash position. Low response to a refunding of actually matured issues, on the other hand, raises innuendoes of 'failure' and leads to a possible short-fall of cash as the Treasury pays out heavy amounts for redemptions.
>
> By combining many issues in a single operation, often taking maturities scattered over a range of several years, the Treasury can reduce the total number, or the scale, or both, of its subsequent operations. The effect can be to reduce the weight of Treasury operations in the market, particularly important in periods when the market itself is under strain.[16]

Advance refundings were the primary vehicle for long-term bond issuance in the first half of the 1960s. The eleven operations undertaken between 1960 and 1965 resulted in the sale of $4 billion of bonds maturing in from ten to twenty years and $13.8 billion of bonds maturing in more than twenty years. In contrast, all of the mid-quarter refundings and all of the stand-alone offerings between 1960 and 1965 sold only $2 billion of bonds maturing in from ten to twenty years and only $1.4 billion of bonds maturing in more than twenty years.

Advance Refundings after Mid-1965

When bond yields rose above the 4¼ percent statutory ceiling rate in mid-1965, the Treasury could not issue securities longer than the maximum maturity of a note. Advance refundings, as originally conceived, were no longer feasible. For the balance of the decade, and continuing into the early 1970s, Treasury officials limited their forward refunding operations to

15 Bryan (1972) examined the determinants of the success of an advance refunding.

16 Remarks by Under Secretary of the Treasury for Monetary Affairs Roosa, November 19, 1964, before the Bankers Club of Chicago. Reprinted 1965 Treasury Annual Report, pp. 324–29. Emphasis added. See also Beard (1966, p. 20).

Table 20.2 *Pre-refundings offered between mid-1965 and the end of 1969.*

Settlement date	Offer to issue . . .	In exchange for . . .
Feb. 15, 1966	4¾-year notes	\$11.2 billion of securities maturing in 3 months, and \$12.0 billion of securities maturing in 6 months
Aug. 15, 1966	4¾-year notes	\$5.8 billion of securities maturing in 3 months
May 15, 1967	5-year notes	\$11.0 billion of securities maturing in 3 months
Feb. 15, 1968	7-year notes	\$10.2 billion of securities maturing in 6 months, and \$11.5 billion of securities maturing in 9 months

Federal Reserve Bank of New York circulars.

pre-refundings, offering notes with a maturity equal to or just short of the maximum in exchange for coupon-bearing securities due to mature within a year. Table 20.2 shows the four pre-refundings offered between mid-1965 and the end of the decade.

THE TWO WORLDS OF TREASURY FINANCE

Treasury finance took place in two different worlds in the 1960s: bills on the one hand and certificates, notes, and bonds on the other.

Bills were sold by auction and mostly offered on a "regular and predictable" basis – the exceptions being tax anticipation bills and bill strips. Regular bills were offered at fixed maturities, auctioned weekly, monthly, or quarterly, and in amounts that varied incrementally from offering to offering. The regularity and predictability of the offerings facilitated dealer underwriting and market-making activities. Dealers knew when the Treasury would come to market, at what maturities, and in approximately what amounts. They did not risk being surprised with unexpectedly large offerings when they were holding long positions and they expected to be able to roll short positions into new, more liquid, bills of the same series.

The picture was quite different for certificates, notes, and bonds. Mid-quarter refundings were (mostly) regular, but less predictable as to maturity (except for the anchor issue), amount, and form (cash versus exchange). Stand-alone offerings and advance refundings were neither regular nor predictable. The lack of regularity and predictability increased the risks associated with making markets in coupon-bearing securities and with underwriting offerings of that debt. As noted in Chapter 16 above, several commentators urged greater regularity and predictability in coupon offerings, smaller and more frequent offerings, and wider use of auctions.

An Experiment in Auctioning Bonds

Treasury officials at the end of the Eisenhower administration defended their continued reliance on fixed-price offerings of coupon-bearing debt in terms of efficiency as well as equitable treatment of small investors who were said to lack the "professional capacity" to bid in auctions.[17] Under Secretary Roosa proved more willing to experiment.

In 1963, Roosa tried to combine the benefits of auctions with the fixed-price format favored by small investors. Emulating contemporary practice in the sale of municipal and utility company bonds, Treasury officials twice offered long-term bonds on an all-or-none auction basis to competing syndicates of securities dealers, where the winning syndicate was required to reoffer the bonds to public investors at a fixed price.[18] Officials hoped that the scheme would enhance the efficiency of the primary market while preserving the access of small investors to new issues at fixed prices. They characterized the initiative as a "trial" intended to "explore the practicality" of syndicate auctions for selling bonds "at the lowest possible interest cost."[19]

The first auction of $250 million of thirty-year bonds on January 8, 1963,[20] attracted bids from four syndicates. Less than a basis point separated the yield on the winning bid from the yield on the third best bid. The Treasury indicated that the results were "highly satisfactory" and "provided the base for the potential development of an important new instrument for debt management."[21] The offering was also a success for the members of

[17] Joint Economic Committee (1959, Part 6A, pp. 1148 and 1149–61).

[18] See Federal Reserve Bank of New York Circular no. 5224, September 14, 1962, "Treasury to Try Auction of Bonds," *New York Times*, September 14, 1962, p. 41, "Treasury Trying New Psychology," *New York Times*, September 23, 1962, Section III, p. 1, "Sale Date Fixed on U.S. Bond Issue," *New York Times*, October 18, 1962, p. 57, "Treasury Lists Proposed Rules for Competitive Bond Bidding," *New York Times*, November 16, 1962, p. 47, "Treasury Releases Regulations on the Sale of Bonds at Competitive Bidding," Treasury Department press release, December 17, 1962, and attachment to Federal Reserve Bank of New York Circular no. 5271, December 17, 1962.

[19] Federal Reserve Bank of New York Circular no. 5224, September 14, 1962.

[20] See Federal Reserve Bank of New York Circular no. 5273, December 20, 1992, "U.S. Plans to Sell Bonds Privately," *New York Times*, December 21, 1962, p. 9, and Federal Reserve Bank of New York Circular no. 5280, January 2, 1963.

[21] Federal Reserve Bank of New York Circular no. 5282, January 8, 1963.

the syndicate: the public reoffering sold out at a profit within a matter of hours.[22]

The second offering – $300 million of thirty-year bonds on April 9, 1963[23] – resulted in comparably tight bidding[24] but the reoffering was not well received. Less than half of the issue was sold by the close of trading on April 9 and few, if any, additional bonds were sold before the winning syndicate disbanded in late April.[25] Market participants suggested that a third offering would produce a more dispersed distribution of bids and that participating syndicates were certain to try to protect themselves by building larger underwriting spreads into their bids.[26] Roosa remarked that the next auction offering was "a long time" off.[27] Officials thereafter sold coupon-bearing debt in fixed-price offerings through the end of the 1960s.

22 "Treasury Experiment," *New York Times*, January 11, 1963, p. 6.

23 Federal Reserve Bank of New York Circular no. 5317, March 20, 1963, "Treasury to Sell 300-Million Issue," *New York Times*, March 21, 1963, p. 9, and Federal Reserve Bank of New York Circular no 5321, April 3, 1961.

24 Federal Reserve Bank of New York Circular no. 5322, April 9, 1963.

25 "Treasury Raises 300 Million in Auction of Long-Term Bonds," *New York Times*, April 10, 1963, p. 51, "Bonds: Market Unsettled by $300,000,000 Long-Term Offering by U.S. Treasury," *New York Times*, April 10, 1963, p. 56, "Bond Syndicate Being Broken Up," *New York Times*, April 26, 1963, p. 47, and "Bonds: Treasury's New Issue Declines After Restrictions End," *New York Times*, April 27, 1963, p. 32.

26 "Reception is Cool to U.S. Bond Issue," *New York Times*, April 14, 1963, section III, p. 1, and "U.S. to Try Again on Underwriting," *New York Times*, April 21, 1963, section III, p. 1.

27 "Bond Syndicate Being Broken Up," *New York Times*, April 26, 1963, p. 47.

21

Monetary Policy in the 1960s

The National Bureau of Economic Research locates a peak in economic activity in April 1960, a tough in February 1961, and the following peak in December 1969. During the decade between the two peaks, Federal Reserve officials had to contend first with an economy that recovered only gradually from the recession that opened the decade and then with the initial appearance of what would become, in the 1970s, a virulent inflation. Their efforts to restrain an overheated economy produced historically high interest rates in 1966 and again in 1968 and 1969.

1961 TO 1965

In his encyclopedic history of the Federal Reserve System, Allan Meltzer waxes ecstatic about US economic performance in the first half of the 1960s, observing that "the economy grew 17 percent [between 1961 and 1965]; inflation . . . rose at a 1.6 percent average [annual] rate and, as late into the expansion as January 1965, the reported annual rise in the consumer price index was only 1 percent. After its usual slow decline, the unemployment rate fell below 5 percent in 1964 and reached 4 percent by the end of 1965."[1] Meltzer concludes that "the two and one half years ending in mid-1965 are probably the best years under the Federal Reserve Act to that time and for many years to follow."[2]

The recovery that began in early 1961 was marked by a gradual tightening of reserve availability, reflected in the shift from $500 million

[1] Meltzer (2009, p. 367). [2] Meltzer (2009, p. 399).

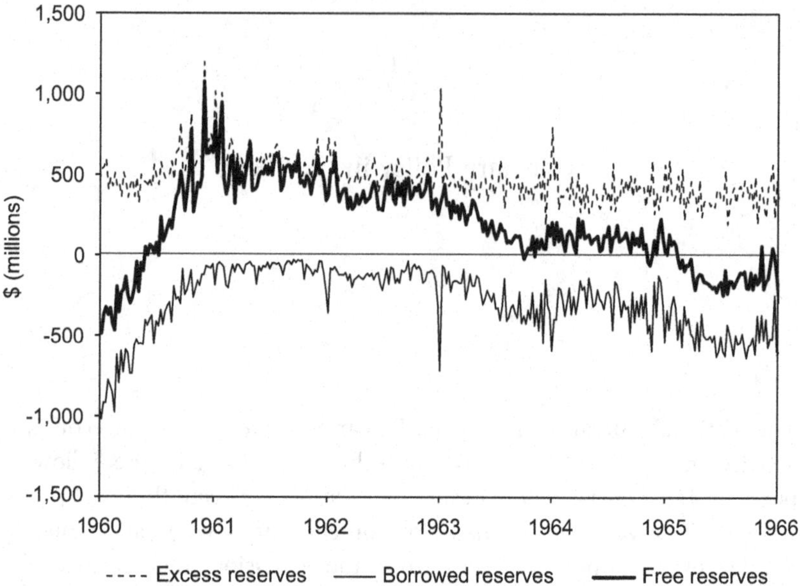

Chart 21.1 Excess reserves, borrowed reserves, and free reserves. Weekly averages of daily figures.
Board of Governors of the Federal Reserve System (1976, table 10.1C).

of net free reserves to almost $200 million of net borrowed reserves in mid-1965 (Chart 21.1). Short-term interest rates rose at a comparably measured pace (Chart 19.8).

Meltzer identifies 1965 as the year when the economy transitioned from steady, noninflationary growth to an erratic, start-stop dynamic marked by a seemingly irrepressible inflationary bias.[3] The year ended with the Reserve Banks raising their discount rates to 4½ percent over the fierce opposition of President Lyndon Johnson.[4] The balance of the decade was marked by alternating bursts of restraint – in 1966, the first half of 1968, and 1969 – and ease (Charts 21.2 and 21.3) as the System struggled to contain inflation while promoting growth.

[3] Meltzer (2009, p. 441), stating that 1965 "was the transition from one of the best four-year periods in U.S. experience to years of inflation and slow growth. It was the last year of strong productivity growth and the first year of rising inflation."
[4] See Meltzer (2009, pp. 452–59) and Bremner (2004, pp. 205–11).

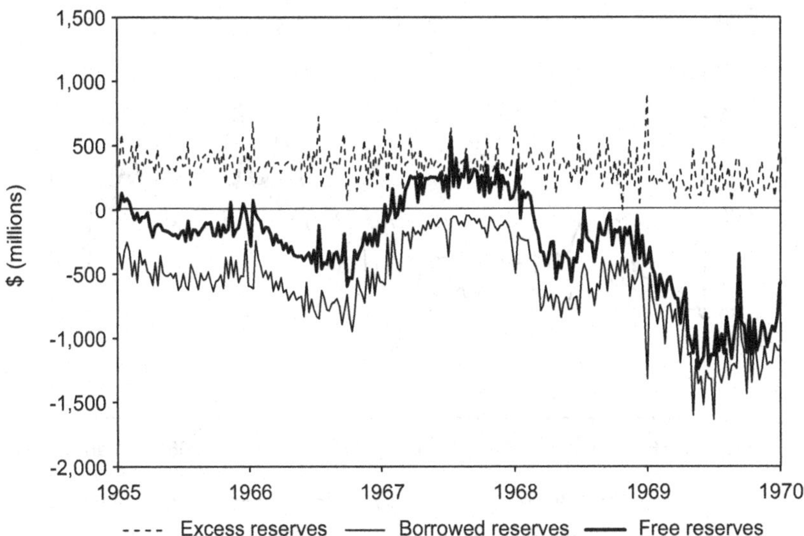

Chart 21.2 Excess reserves, borrowed reserves, and free reserves. Weekly averages of daily figures.
Board of Governors of the Federal Reserve System (1976, table 10.1C).

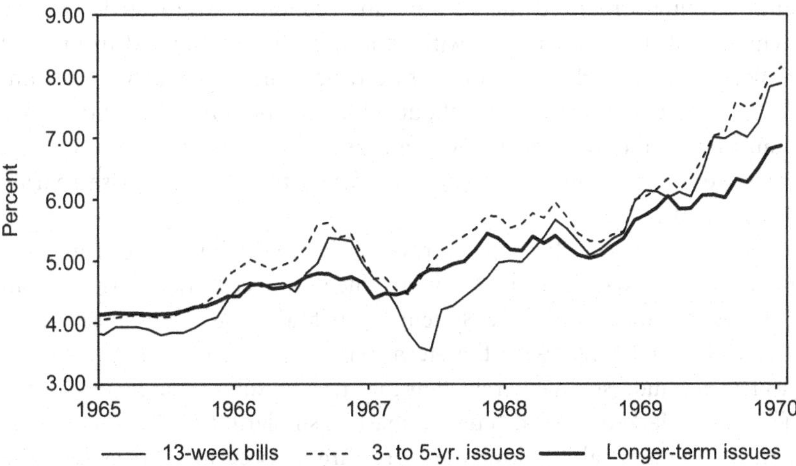

Chart 21.3 Treasury yields. Monthly averages.
Board of Governors of the Federal Reserve System (1976, tables 12.7A and 12.12A).

1966

Nineteen ninety-six demonstrated how difficult it can be to conduct an effective monetary policy in the absence of supportive fiscal policies. The 1966 Markets annual report states that "monetary policy and open market operations were put to a considerable test in 1966. For a good part of the

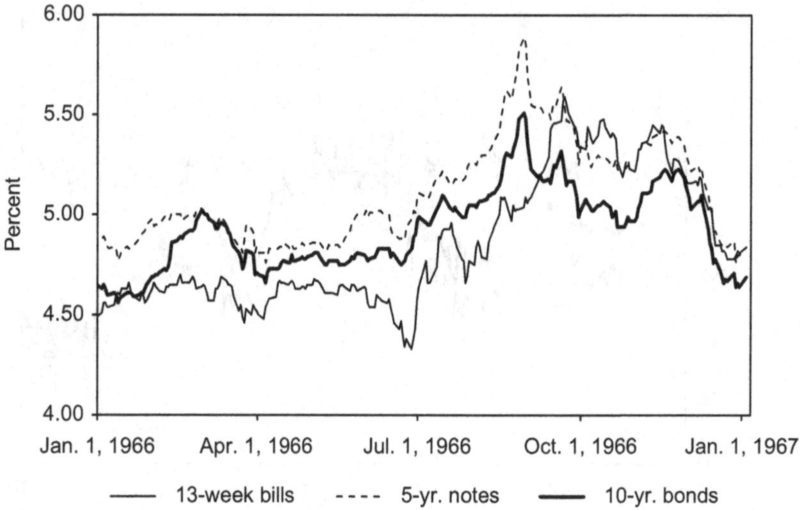

Chart 21.4 Treasury yields. Daily figures.
Federal Reserve Statistical Release H.15.

year, the Federal Reserve had to deal with inflationary pressures and surging credit demands in an economy overheated by the demands of the Vietnam war with insufficient restraining aid from fiscal policy."[5] Open market operations forced net borrowed reserves up from $100 million in February to about $400 million in early June.[6] After adjusting to the December 1965 increase in the discount rate, interest rates were fairly stable until late June, when they began to rise sharply (Chart 21.4).

Government securities dealers responded predictably to the rising cost of short-term credit and the eroding value of longer-term securities. Alan Holmes, the manager of the System Open Market Account since March 1965, observed that, "with the stern reality of high financing costs, … dealers are understandably reluctant to carry any substantial inventories."[7] The 1966 Markets annual report remarked similarly that "market uncertainties, the general … downward pressure on securities prices, and the persistently high cost and limited availability of dealer financing all combined to make dealers reluctant over much of the year to maintain

5 1966 Annual Report of Open Market Operations, p. 1.
6 1966 Annual Report of Open Market Operations, p. 3.
7 Minutes of the Federal Open Market Committee, July 26, 1966, p. 23.

significant trading positions in securities."[8] Shrinking inventories limited the ability of dealers to participate in open market operations.[9]

Dealers also grew reluctant to underwrite Treasury offerings. The 1966 Markets report recalled a number of difficult bill auctions:

> In several auctions ... it appeared that total tenders from investors might not fully cover the amount of the new issues being sold – in some cases even at considerably higher rates than were prevailing on outstanding bills. To ensure coverage ... at some reasonable rate levels, the Treasury on several occasions submitted tenders of $100 million or more for special investment accounts. The bills won in these auctions were subsequently sold into the market after the general atmosphere had improved.[10]

In a late August review of recent market activity, Holmes observed that the most recent mid-quarter refunding had started out in good shape but subsequently fell apart:

> The initial reactions to the Treasury's offer of a 5¼ per cent note and a 5¼ per cent certificate were quite favorable, with Government securities dealers generally adopting a more constructive attitude than in recent Treasury operations. But as time went on the atmosphere soured, and when the books closed on August 3 both new issues were quoted at par bid, down 5/64 from their peaks. They have since declined almost uninterruptedly.[11]

Holmes added that "those dealers who stood up to their function of underwriting Treasury financing operations have suffered substantial losses as a result of their participation."

An offering of two tax anticipation bills at the end of August received an especially poor reception. Holmes stated that "there was considerable caution in the bidding, with some banks withdrawing altogether and others cutting back their participation. While both issues were covered, bidding was lighter than in any similar auction in recent history [and] the range of bids was wide." He suggested that "the Treasury's experience with its latest financing raises some fundamental questions about the possibility of carrying out an effective debt management policy in a period when rates are constantly on the rise and the market's ability and willingness to perform an underwriting function are weak."[12]

[8] 1966 Annual Report of Open Market Operations, p. 8.

[9] 1966 Annual Report of Open Market Operations, pp. 8–12, stating that "the System often had difficulty in injecting reserves to meet developing or anticipated reserve needs" because of "the low level of dealer inventories."

[10] 1966 Annual Report of Open Market Operations, p. 23.

[11] Minutes of the Federal Open Market Committee, August 23, 1966, pp. 33–34.

[12] Minutes of the Federal Open Market Committee, August 23, 1966, p. 34.

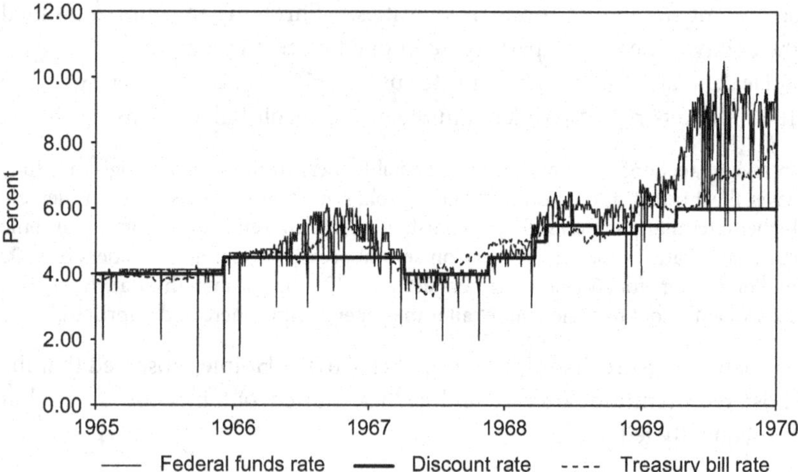

Chart 21.5 Federal funds rate, thirteen-week Treasury bill rate, and Federal Reserve Bank of New York discount rate. Daily figures.
Federal Reserve Statistical Release H.15 and Board of Governors of the Federal Reserve System (1976, table 12.1A).

Further problems emerged when, for the first time, the Federal funds rate rose significantly above the discount rate (Chart 21.5). Interbank lending at rates over the discount rate had been seen before, briefly in 1964 and more persistently in 1965 (Box 21.1), but the spread widened appreciably in 1966. Albert Burger, an economist at the Federal Reserve Bank of St. Louis, suggested that Reserve Banks had restricted access to the discount window:

> Although the Federal Reserve banks did not explicitly refuse credit to any member banks in 1966, there are strong indications that, as the level of member bank borrowing approached the $750-$800 million range, rather than raising the cost of such borrowing to ration potential borrowers out of the market, the result of some Federal Reserve banks' tighter administration of the discount window was, in effect, to "close the window" to further increases in the level of member bank borrowing.
>
> Beginning in about June, the Federal Reserve may have used tighter administration of the discount window to force member banks to reduce their borrowings, or member banks may have felt that the Reserve banks would show great reluctance to extend additional accommodation. Also, some member banks may have decided to husband their "goodwill" at the discount window to meet expected future emergency cash demands.[13]

[13] Burger (1969, p. 25). Two years later, during a second episode of historically high interest rates, the Markets annual report noted a "growing desire" by money center banks to

Box 21.1 Trading in Federal Funds at Rates above the Discount Rate in 1964 and 1965.

The 1964 Markets annual report provides a concise overview of the first instance of trading in Federal funds at a rate above the discount rate:

> In the firmer money market of early October [1964], a major New York City bank began to bid 3⅝ per cent for Federal funds on occasion – ⅛ per cent above the [3½ percent] Federal Reserve discount rate – in an effort to introduce greater flexibility into the Federal funds market and to attract additional excess reserves beyond the market's current reach.
>
> At first, the practice attracted little following, particularly as the money market became very easy after the Columbus Day weekend. For a time there appeared to be little point in bidding aggressively for funds. In early November, however, when a surge in deposit expansion in country banks limited the flow of Federal funds to the central money market, a larger number of banks bid 3⅝ per cent for Federal funds in competition with those already bidding at that rate, and funds traded predominantly at 3⅝ per cent on a number of days.
>
> The full implications of the experience had not really emerged by the time the Federal Reserve discount rate was increased [to 4 percent] in late November. (After the increase, there was little or no use of premium bids.)[1]

Trading in Federal funds at rates above the discount rate became more persistent in 1965:

> Firm conditions prevailed in the money market throughout the February 4 – March 24 period, as Federal funds traded at or above the 4 per cent discount rate on most days. Indeed, a "premium" for Federal funds . . . became fairly common as the firm environment in the money market persisted and as banks with persistent basic reserve deficiencies sought to avoid excessive use of the discount window.[2]

[1] 1964 Annual Report of Open Market Operations, p. 31.
[2] 1965 Annual Report of Open Market Operations, p. 25.

The appearance of trading in Federal funds at rates substantially in excess of the discount rate created a novel problem. If Federal Reserve officials continued to price repos at the discount rate, they could be accused of giving nonbank dealers a benefit not available to bank dealers (who were not allowed to participate in System repo operations). On the other hand, officials were reluctant to move the repo rate above the

"reserve recourse to the Federal Reserve discount window." 1968 Annual Report of Open Market Operations, pp. 38–39. Goodfriend (1983, p. 344) similarly pointed out the non-price administration of access to the discount window: "Since 1965, the Federal funds rate has, on numerous occasions, risen above the discount rate. . . . This indicates that an effective form of non-price rationing is being administered at the discount window."

discount rate out of fear that the move would be interpreted as a harbinger of further monetary restraint. Alfred Hayes, the president of the Federal Reserve Bank of New York, later recalled that

> "the spread between the RP rate and money market rates grew so large that the former could not be increased to restore a desirable relation without attracting a good deal of attention and affecting expectations [of further rate increases]. Under those circumstances the Committee [was] reluctant to have the RP rate raised, even though it was clear that Federal Reserve credit was being provided through repurchase agreements at much too low an interest rate."[14]

Chary of appearing to finance nonbank dealers at bargain interest rates, the Desk limited its use of repurchase agreements; Holmes subsequently recalled that the repo rate had gotten so badly out of line that the Desk "hesitated to use RP's at all."[15]

The August Money Panic

The 1966 Markets annual report leaves no doubt about the severity of the crisis that broke over US financial markets in August. The report speaks of "stresses and strains unprecedented in over a generation" and "fears of an almost complete breakdown of the market mechanism."[16]

The crisis was largely of the Fed's own making. Burger provides a concise explanation:

> In three previous periods in the sixties, July 1963, November 1964, and December 1965, when the secondary market interest rate on outstanding certificates of deposit issued by commercial banks [[17]] moved above the Regulation Q limit on

[14] Minutes of the Federal Open Market Committee, April 2, 1968, pp. 34–35. Chairman Martin agreed (p. 35) that "the Committee had discouraged the Manager [of the System Open Market Account] from setting an RP rate above the discount rate when the possibility was considered in 1966.

[15] Minutes of the Federal Open Market Committee, April 2, 1968, p. 31. See also 1966 Annual Report of Open Market Operations, p. 12, noting "reluctance on the part of the Account Management to use repurchase agreements after market rates had risen far above the 4½ per cent discount rate."

[16] 1966 Annual Report of Open Market Operations, pp. 25 and 46.

[17] Negotiable certificates of deposit were introduced in 1961 by First National City Bank. Discount Corporation, a primary dealer in government securities, made a market in the new instruments. See "Interest on Time Deposits Paid by the First National City Bank," *New York Times*, February 21, 1961, p. 49; "Rates Increased for Short Debt," *New York Times*, February 22, 1961, p. 36; and "Bonds: Yields on Long-Term Issues Fall to a Two-Year Low," *New York Times*, February 22, 1961, p. 40.

> newly issued CD's,[[18]] the Federal Reserve System raised the Regulation Q ceiling. This policy action allowed commercial banks, by offering yields on time deposits competitive with other available market assets, to compete effectively with other borrowers.
>
> However, when the market rate on outstanding CD's moved above the Regulation Q ceiling in the summer of 1966, the Federal Reserve System refused to raise Regulation Q ceilings. . . .
>
> With the market yield on CD's rising above the ceiling rate on new issue CD's, and the Board of Governors refusing to raise Regulation Q ceilings . . ., banks now realized they could no longer rely on time deposits to acquire funds to expand their flow of credit to the business sector. Further, the banks now expected a reversal of the flow of time deposits.
>
> In August over $3.7 billion of outstanding negotiable certificates of deposit matured at large commercial banks, and $6.7 billion in negotiable CD's were scheduled to mature in the September-October period. By middle and late August there were expectations of a large loan demand converging on the commercial banking system just as the expected heavy runoff of certificates of deposit occurred. Large offerings of Treasury tax-anticipation bills were expected in late August . . . There were growing fears in the capital and money markets that the major suppliers of funds would be unwilling to continue to supply funds at currently existing interest rates.[19]

Yields on coupon-bearing Treasury debt spiked on Monday, August 29, with the five-year rate reaching a postwar high of 5.89 percent.

[18] Section 11(b) of the Banking Act of June 16, 1933, prohibited the payment of interest on demand deposits by member banks of the Federal Reserve System and gave the Federal Reserve Board authority to regulate maximum rates of interest payable by member banks on time and savings deposits. Gilbert (1986, pp. 22 and 23) notes that "One important congressional objective was to encourage country banks to lend more in their local communities rather than hold [interest-earning] balances with larger banks in financial centers" and that "another objective was to increase bank profits [and restrain bank risk-taking] by limiting the competition for deposits." The Board promulgated Regulation Q pursuant to the latter authority. "Early observations suggest that the Federal Reserve interpreted its mandate for administering Regulation Q to restrain the especially aggressive banks from offering such high interest rates on deposits that they might get into financial trouble." Gilbert (1986, pp. 25–26). See also Ruebling (1970). Linke (1966) and Cox (1967) discuss the evolution of interest rate regulation prior to 1933.

[19] Burger (1969, p. 25). The 1966 Markets annual report similarly located the source of the crisis in the prospective inability of commercial banks to fund the loan demands of their business customers: "[T]he major immediate cause of the near panic in late August was a growing apprehension over the ability of the markets to accommodate the pressures that seemed to be building up for September. In particular, it was expected that large fall loan demands would at that time be converging on a banking system that faced heavy maturities of negotiable certificates of deposit, which could not be replaced under the constraints imposed by existing Regulation Q ceilings." 1966 Annual Report of Open Market Operations, p. 46.

The crisis quickly abated in the wake of administration and Federal Reserve actions taken in response to the August 29 rate spike. Testifying before the House Rules Committee on August 30, Under Secretary of the Treasury Joseph Barr stated that the administration was "distressed" by the high level of interest rates: "We can't rely on monetary policy much more. ... If we have to do more, we will have to do it by taxing or [lowering] spending. There is no other way."[20] Credit markets cheered the prospect of actions that would take some of the steam out of the economy.[21] Two days later, Federal Reserve officials reassured member banks that "Federal Reserve credit assistance to meet appropriate seasonal or emergency needs, *including those resulting from shrinkages of deposits or of other sources of funds*, will continue to be available as in the past."[22] And on Thursday, September 8, President Johnson announced a package of fiscal actions – including suspension of investment tax credits and a cutback in expenditures – aimed at restraining aggregate economic activity.[23] Intermediate-term Treasury yields receded to where they had been at the beginning of the year.

1967–1969

Federal Reserve officials spent the first few months of 1967 dialing back the restraints imposed during 1966: pushing free reserves up to about $250 million by mid-year, reversing the December 1965 increase in the discount rate, and otherwise relaxing access to the discount window and allowing the Federal funds rate to fall to approximately the level of the discount rate. The 1967 Markets annual report observed that "prospects for renewed business expansion seemed to be improving toward the end of April."[24]

Concern with an overheating economy resurfaced when price increases became "more numerous" by late July.[25] On August 3, President Johnson asked Congress for a 10 percent income tax surcharge.[26] By December, the

[20] "Treasury Hints a Tax Rise Move at this Session," *New York Times*, August 31, 1966, p. 1.

[21] "Bonds Struggle to Higher Level," *New York Times*, August 31, 1966, p. 57.

[22] Federal Reserve Bank of New York Circular no. 5865, September 1, 1966. Emphasis added.

[23] "Johnson Acts Against Inflation by Asking Congress to Suspend Tax Credit Granted to Business," *New York Times*, September 9, 1966, p. 1.

[24] 1967 Annual Report of Open Market Operations, p. 40.

[25] 1967 Annual Report of Open Market Operations, p. 40.

[26] "Johnson Asks for 10% Surcharge on Personal and Business Taxes; 45,000 More Men to Go to Vietnam," *New York Times*, August 4, 1967, p. 1.

FOMC was once again moving toward monetary restraint "to resist inflationary pressures and protect the dollar."[27] 1968 opened with economic activity "expanding at a rapid rate and inflationary pressures . . . strong and expected to persist."[28] The Fed raised the discount rate to 5 percent in mid-March and 5½ percent in mid-April. The Federal funds rate hit 6¼ percent at the end of April. Net borrowed reserves increased to more than $550 million by early June.

In late June, Congress passed the tax surcharge that President Johnson had requested nine months earlier. Passage raised concerns that the added tax burden might produce more of an economic slowdown than desired and System officials began "facilitating the development of somewhat less firm conditions in the money market."[29] They allowed net borrowed reserves to decline to about $200 million and, in late August, lowered the discount rate to 5¼ percent. When the anticipated slowdown failed to materialize, the System shifted back to restraint, restoring the discount rate to 5½ percent and tightening reserve availability.

The Fed continued its efforts to restrain inflation in 1969, raising the discount rate to 6 percent in April and forcing the Federal funds rate to more than 9 percent. Yields on Treasury bills and notes rose to 8 percent. Economic activity peaked in December and the ensuing recession bottomed out in November 1970.

EVEN KEEL

Even keel continued to be a problematic feature of monetary policy in the 1960s because while it facilitated Treasury financing operations, it sometimes delayed the System's response to changing economic conditions. The 1967 Markets annual report states as follows: "Even keel considerations of one form or another appeared in eight of the 15 current policy directives voted by the Committee during the year. The frequency of such occasions called for by the numerous Treasury financing operations undertaken during the year tended to lock the System into an unchanged policy posture for extended periods of time."[30]

[27] 1967 Annual Report of Open Market Operations, p. 24.

[28] 1968 Annual Report of Open Market Operations, p. 26.

[29] 1968 Annual Report of Open Market Operations, p. 40, stating (p. 41) that "for a time, there was even talk of economic 'overkill.'"

[30] 1967 Annual Report of Open Market Operations, p. 10.

The 1968 report observed similarly that "the Treasury's large scale financing operations precluded abrupt changes in System policy for significant intervals in 1968 during which the financings were in progress."[31] Meltzer states that even keel "delayed ... policy action, sometimes for months."[32]

Identifying the consequences of even keel is complicated by the absence of a clear, widely accepted definition of the policy. In his 1971 PhD dissertation, John Markese observed that "there is no consensus on what an 'even keel' action of the Federal Reserve consists of, nor is there any overall agreement as to its purpose."[33]

Meltzer traces the policy to the Fed's 1951 bargain with the Treasury and emphasizes interest rate stabilization:

> The ... Accord freed the Federal Reserve from Treasury control of interest rate levels but gave it co-equal responsibility for debt management. The Treasury had to price its issues in the light of current market interest rates. The Federal Reserve's role was to prevent the market from failing to accept a Treasury issue; in practice, that meant it supplied enough reserves to *keep interest rates from rising* around the time the Treasury sold its offering.[34]

Stephen Axilrod, a senior economist at the Board of Governors, had a different conception of the policy:

> In practical terms even keel has meant that, for a period encompassing the announcement and settlement dates of a large new security offering or refunding by the Treasury, the Federal Reserve has not made new monetary policy decisions ... that would impede the orderly marketing of Treasury securities and significantly increase the risks of market disruption from sharp changes in market attitudes in the course of a financing.[35]

In Axilrod's view, the Fed simply *abstained* from actions that would *impede* an offering. He did not believe that even keel involved interest rate

[31] 1968 Annual Report of Open Market Operations, p. 14.

[32] Meltzer (2009, p. 478). Humpage and Mukherjee (2013, p. 3) state similarly that "the FOMC systematically delayed monetary-policy adjustments."

[33] Markese (1971, p. 18). Markese (p. 49) cites the 1959 complaint of Malcolm Bryan, the president of the Federal Reserve Bank of Atlanta, that "he did not know precisely what was meant by an even keel policy. Should it be measured by net free reserves, net borrowed reserves, the feel of the market, or the intuition of the Account Manager?" Robert Rouse, the manager of the System Open Market Account, replied that it was a mixture of all of those things. Minutes of the Federal Open Market Committee, May 5, 1959, p. 45.

[34] Meltzer (2009, pp. 474–75). Emphasis added.

[35] Axilrod (1971, p. 28). See also Struble and Axilrod (1973).

stabilization, noting that it "provides those who help underwrite Treasury issues ... with a short period of time in which market forces rather than new monetary policy decisions are the main factors affecting interest rates."[36]

Identifying intervals during which even keel was in effect sheds some light on the nature of the policy. When William McChesney Martin was asked about how long he thought the System should maintain an even keel in connection with the February 1958 mid-quarter refunding, he responded that "he thought it would be necessary to consider the period from the time of the Treasury's announcement of the refunding to several days after payment for the securities." Robert Rouse, the manager of the System Open Market Account, "thought it would be necessary to allow a week or 10 days after the payment date. There was a certain amount of underwriting that would have to be done, and this should be the minimum period to allow for distribution of these securities to be completed."[37]

Even keel not only extended beyond the settlement of an offering, it began before an offering was announced. Axilrod, for example, asserted that the policy typically started a week before an announcement.[38] The earlier start reflected the desire of System officials to give the market time to digest any significant policy changes before the Treasury began surveying participants about prospective terms. Delimiting an even keel period as beginning a week before the announcement of an offering and ending a week after settlement reflected the System's recognition of the significance of private sector underwriting activities to the success of Treasury offerings.

What the Fed did and did not do during even keel periods further illuminates the nature of even keel. Markese reports that between 1951 and 1970 the System almost never raised the discount rate or reserve requirements while a Treasury offering was in progress: "On 80 per cent of the dates when a change in the discount rate was made, no Treasury financings were in progress. In the six instances when a discount rate change was made during a financing period, five of the changes involved a decrease in the rate." He further notes that only one of fourteen changes in reserve requirement rates occurred during a Treasury offering.[39] Markese also reports that, for the period from January 1955 to December 1970, the size of the System Open Market Account showed statistically

[36] Axilrod (1971, p. 28).

[37] Minutes of the Federal Open Market Committee, January 7, 1958, pp. 51–52.

[38] Axilrod (1971, p. 29). [39] Markese (1971, pp. 73 and 74).

significant increases during even keel periods relative to other times.[40] His findings suggest that the Desk undertook to supply enough reserves to satisfy the elevated dealer financing requirements associated with Treasury offerings and, in the process, stabilized the Federal funds rate and free reserves.

[40] Markese (1971, pp. 99–110). Meltzer (2009, p. 478) notes that "during even keel periods, usually lasting up to four weeks, the Federal Reserve often added large increments to reserve growth." Humpage and Mukherjee (2013, p. 3) conclude that the FOMC "added reserves to the banking system to facilitate the U.S. Treasury's debt-funding operations."

22

Repurchase Agreements in the 1960s

The Open Market Trading Desk supplied reserves with outright purchases of Treasury securities and repurchase agreements in the early 1960s, but it did not view the two instruments as close substitutes. It used outright purchases to satisfy intermediate- and long-run requirements – such as neutralizing gold outflows and accommodating secular increases in the demand for currency – and repos to meet shorter-run needs: neutralizing transient reserve drains such as reductions in float and increases in Treasury balances at Federal Reserve Banks.

Repurchase agreements assumed increasing importance in the second half of the decade, when Reserve Banks began to administer access to discount window credit and commercial banks responded by exercising greater caution in managing their reserve positions. The 1965 Markets annual report remarked on "the appearance of some trading of Federal funds at a 4¼ per cent premium rate [¼ percent over the contemporaneous 4 percent discount rate], apparently reflecting purchases by banks that had come to rely heavily on the regular use of borrowed funds to finance growing credit demands. Some of these banks were willing to pay a higher premium on funds in order to avoid the discount window. . . . In general, a feeling developed that it would be prudent to play safe with reserve positions."[1] The report went on to describe how open market operations were structured to provide additional reserves in response to strong precautionary demands early in a statement week, noting that "while this procedure often moderated the variations in money market conditions, it was sometimes necessary to reverse direction toward the end of the statement week when reserve availability

[1] 1965 Annual Report of Open Market Operations, pp. 37–38.

turned out unexpectedly high."[2] Repurchase agreements were particularly well-suited for such short-lived reserve injections.

Intraweek variation in the demand for reserves intensified in 1966. The Markets annual report for that year describes how Desk officials "generally sought to counter ... intra-weekly swings in [money market] conditions ... to head off extreme tightness [early in a statement week] that might generate instability in financing markets. This approach involved considerable short-run reversibility in System operations – *on a scale not attempted or necessary in earlier years* – mostly involving injections of reserves early in a week, followed by a mopping up of redundant reserves after the weekend."[3]

Commenting on open market operations between early February and early March 1966, the report observed that banks "were fairly aggressive bidders in the Federal funds market on the opening days – Thursday and Friday – of each of the five statement weeks" during that period. It went on to describe the consequences:

> With nationwide net reserve availability at generally low levels on such days, conditions in the money market became rather taut and virtually all Federal funds trading on each Thursday and Friday was at either 4⅝ or 4¾ per cent [while the discount rate was 4½ percent].
>
> To meet some of the indicated reserve needs and head off undue tightness in the money market, the Federal Reserve injected roughly $200 - $450 million of reserves at the beginning of each of the weeks in question ...
>
> Money market pressures tended to subside ... following the weekends ... Undue easing was headed off, however, as the System reversed direction in each of the five statement weeks and absorbed about $150 - $550 million of reserves ...[4]

Revised reserve requirements, introduced in September 1968,[5] added an overlay of interweek oscillations in bank demand for reserves. The new requirements provided that both reserve excesses and reserve deficiencies (up to two percent of required reserves) could be carried over from one statement week to the next. (The old requirements did not allow excesses to be carried over.) The 1968 Markets annual report states that,

> Given the privilege of carrying over reserve excesses, as well as deficits, ... reserve city banks fell into a pronounced cycle of alternating deficits and surpluses. Money

[2] 1965 Annual Report of Open Market Operations, p. 38.
[3] 1966 Annual Report of Open Market Operations, p. 14. Emphasis added.
[4] 1966 Annual Report of Open Market Operations, p. 40.
[5] See Federal Reserve Bank of New York Circular no. 6157, April 29, 1968; and Circular no. 6213, September 17, 1968.

market conditions often tended to be taut early in the statement weeks in which large banks started with sizable reserve deficiencies and tended to be relatively comfortable early in alternate weeks when they began with large surpluses.[6]

The report goes on to describe a representative oscillation:

In the week ended October 16 the System injected reserves in large volume to counter undue firmness in the money market that resulted from the caution of the banks that had carried over deficiencies that had to be covered in that week. When easy conditions finally emerged at the end of the statement week, the System absorbed reserves in volume . . . Nevertheless, these actions did not match fully the extent of excess reserves accumulated so that the large banks carried sizable reserve excesses into the next statement week.

In consequence, bidding for Federal funds was quite relaxed early in the October 23 statement period, and the Account Management absorbed a substantial volume of reserves in an effort to promote money market firmness and induce an appropriate volume of bank borrowing over the weekend. However, the banks were content to accumulate deficits and borrowing was quite light through Tuesday. Partly because of the low borrowing early in the week, reserves available in the Federal funds market were insufficient to meet the insistent demands of deficit banks so that Federal funds were bid up to as high as 6½ per cent in the scramble for funds. [The discount rate was 5¼ percent at the time.] The System then reversed direction, moderating the tightness by injecting reserves.[7]

Even as evolving discount window policies and reserve requirements were creating a need for larger and more frequent operations, higher and more volatile interest rates were leading government securities dealers to trim their inventories. The 1966 Markets annual report observed that "markets in Government securities tended to be quite thin" during the year:

Dealers were reluctant to hold sizable positions in the face of the uncertain environment, the rapid upward movement of interest rates, and the high cost and limited availability of dealer financing. Over the first two months of the period [from early June to early August], until the Treasury auctioned $3 billion of tax-anticipation bills in mid-August, the total amount of Treasury bills held in dealers' trading positions averaged only $1.1 billion, compared with an average of $3 billion in the comparable months of 1965. On occasion, such as around the end of June and again in early August, dealers' trading positions in bills dropped to around $250 million. In this environment, outright System operations of major size in either direction persistently faced the potential problem of contributing to exaggerated movements in bill rates.[8]

[6] 1968 Annual Report of Open Market Operations, p. 51.
[7] 1968 Annual Report of Open Market Operations, p. 54.
[8] 1966 Annual Report of Open Market Operations, pp. 51–52.

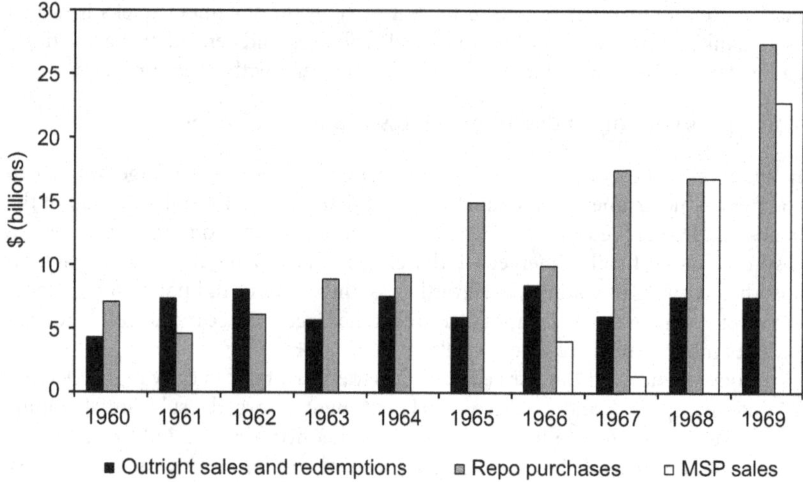

Chart 22.1 Outright sales and redemptions of Treasury securities, repo purchases, and MSP sales in the 1960s.
Annual reports of open market operations.

Repurchase agreements were an obvious and economical alternative to outright operations in less liquid markets. Repos were deemed especially desirable as a way of injecting reserves at "the point of greatest pressure in the money market" – dealer financing needs.[9] For example, "early in the month [of August 1966], when dealers were concerned about the high cost of financing positions swollen by acquisitions of rights to the Treasury's August refunding, the System confined its reserve injections to the purchase of rights and other Treasury issues under repurchase agreements."[10] Similarly, "repurchase agreements were . . . used heavily during a period of accommodation in the first half of August [1968] when sharply rising costs of financing dealers' positions were putting upward pressure on Government securities yields."[11]

Chart 22.1 shows three measures of System open market activity in the 1960s: outright sales and redemptions of Treasury securities, purchases on repurchase agreements, and sales on matched sale-purchase agreements (MSPs), a form of reverse repurchase agreement used to drain reserves from the banking system. In view of the trend increase in the quantity of

[9] 1966 Annual Report of Open Market Operations, p. 68.
[10] 1966 Annual Report of Open Market Operations, p. 54.
[11] 1968 Annual Report of Open Market Operations, p. 22.

Treasury securities held in the System Open Market Account during the 1960s (Chart 19.9), outright sales and redemptions are roughly comparable to repos and MSPs as transactions undertaken for reasons of short-run reserves management (because they were ultimately offset with purchases). Outright purchases, on the other hand, are clearly not comparable to repos and MSPs because a large fraction of purchases in the second half of the 1960s supported the secular increase in System holdings. The chart shows a rising volume of repos and MSPs in the second half of the decade, compared to a steady level of outright sales and redemptions.[12] The contrast reflects the System's increasing reliance on short-term injections and withdrawals of reserves as intra- and interweekly fluctuations in bank demand for reserves grew larger. The next two sections of this chapter examine how Federal Reserve officials engineered the expanding volume of short-term operations.

SYSTEM ACCESS TO REPO COLLATERAL

At mid-decade, a two-year maturity limit on repo collateral loomed as a significant constraint on the fullest possible use of repos for reserves management.[13] The growing reliance on repurchase agreements triggered efforts to expand the boundaries of acceptable collateral.

Relaxing the Two-Year Maturity Limit

In early March 1965, Robert Stone, the manager of the System Open Market Account,[14] suggested relaxing the maturity limit on repo collateral. He observed that the Desk commonly supported Treasury exchange offerings by financing dealer positions in rights with repurchase agreements.[15] However, if the rights were designated for exchange they became (as a practical matter following the close of the subscription books) the offered securities and could not continue to back System repo credit if the offered

[12] The anomalous contraction in repos in 1966 may be attributable to the reluctance (discussed in the preceding chapter) of the Desk to use repos during part of that year.

[13] The maturity limit had been fifteen months at the beginning of the decade but was bumped out to two years in December 1961. Minutes of the Federal Open Market Committee, December 19, 1961, pp. 71–72.

[14] Stone became Manager in May 1962 and resigned in late March 1965.

[15] The FOMC approved repos on rights in March 1955. Minutes of the Federal Open Market Committee, March 2, 1955, pp. 53–59.

securities were scheduled to mature in more than two years.[16] This sometimes led to terminations of System repo credit that were "burdensome to the market and inconvenient to the System."[17] Stone recommended that the Desk be allowed to finance dealer positions in rights up to the settlement date of an exchange, at which time when-issued sales of the offered securities were due to be settled. Stone thought the simplest procedure would be to eliminate the maturity limit on repo collateral altogether but allowed that it would be sufficient to suspend the limit during exchange offerings.[18]

Governor George Mitchell was reluctant to eliminate the maturity limit, believing that elimination "might encourage dealers to hold larger amounts of longer-term securities and to speculate in them, thereby hampering operations of the Committee."[19] Governor Dewey Daane concurred, and asked whether "it would be feasible to take the more limited step of authorizing repurchase agreements only against rights due to be exchanged for longer-term securities which dealers had already sold on a when-issued basis."[20] Stone acknowledged that the latter course of action was feasible but expressed reluctance to undertake the requisite monitoring of dealer positions.

Following Chairman Martin's expression of support for suspending the maturity limit during Treasury offerings, the Committee approved a change in the repo directive to the Federal Reserve Bank of New York. The revised directive provided that,

> U.S. Government securities bought under the provisions of this section shall have maturities of 24 months or less at the time of purchase, except that, during any period beginning with the day after the Treasury has announced a refunding operation and ending on the day designated as the settlement date for the exchange, the U.S. Government securities bought may be of any maturity.[21]

The expanded limits on repo collateral during Treasury financings quickly proved their usefulness. The 1965 Markets annual report observed that,

[16] Minutes of the Federal Open Market Committee, March 2, 1965, p. 5, stating that the two-year maturity limit had at times "caused the Management [of the System Open Market Account] to terminate repurchase agreements against 'rights' in refundings the day after the subscription books closed . . . The rights in question were those that dealers had committed for exchange for new securities of longer than two years to maturity."

[17] Minutes of the Federal Open Market Committee, March 2, 1965, p. 5.

[18] Minutes of the Federal Open Market Committee, March 2, 1965, p. 5.

[19] Minutes of the Federal Open Market Committee, March 2, 1965, p. 5.

[20] Minutes of the Federal Open Market Committee, March 2, 1965, p. 6.

[21] Minutes of the Federal Open Market Committee, March 2, 1965, p. 13.

During the week ended May 5 the Trading Desk purchased $860 million of Treasury issues under new repurchase contracts, meeting a portion of the huge dealer financing needs stemming from purchases of the maturing May issues which served as rights to the Treasury's May refunding program then in progress. These rights had to be financed by the dealers until May 15 when delivery was made of the new securities sold to customers on a when-issued basis. An earlier revision in the Open Market Committee's standing instructions – which permitted the Account Management to waive, at times of Treasury financing, the maturity limitation on Treasury issues purchased under repurchase agreements – was especially helpful in the conduct of operations during this period.[22]

Eliminating the Two-Year Maturity Limit and Permitting Back-to-Back Repos

The restrictive monetary policy adopted in 1966 produced "a very basic operational problem" for System repurchase agreements: a "generally low level of dealer positions in Treasury bills and coupon issues."[23]

The issue of collateral scarcity came to a head in late June 1966 as the Desk was preparing to accommodate the large currency drains occasioned by the Fourth of July holiday weekend. Alan Holmes, the manager of the System Open Market Account since March 1965, reported to the FOMC that the Desk was estimating a $1 billion temporary reserve need and observed that dealer inventories in thirteen-week bills had dropped to less than $100 million. He thought the System could scrape by with purchases of other, less actively traded bills and coupon-bearing debt, repurchase agreements, and some runoff of Treasury balances at the Reserve Banks, but suggested that an additional instrument for injecting reserves would provide a welcome backstop.[24]

Holmes recommended that the Committee authorize "back-to-back" repos, where the Desk would finance repo collateral that dealers sourced from customers. He reminded the Committee that "dealer financing needs lately have been minimal because of the heavy demand for Treasury bills and high dealer financing costs, and the repurchase agreement has not therefore been a feasible means of reserve supply":

22 1965 Annual Report of Open Market Operations, p. 31.

23 1966 Annual Report of Open Market Operations, p. 8. The report went on to note that "market uncertainties, the general upward pressure on interest rates and downward pressure on securities prices, and the persistently high cost and limited availability of dealer financing all combined to make dealers reluctant over much of the year to maintain significant trading positions in securities."

24 Minutes of the Federal Open Market Committee, June 28, 1966, pp. 27 and 29.

> However, we are quite certain if dealers were told in advance that repurchase agreements were available, they would be able to find the necessary collateral by arranging back-to-back repurchase agreements with either banks or other holders of Government securities who were looking for cash over a period of expected monetary stringency. This approach would not involve any change in the repurchase instrument. It would involve a change from our usual practice of relating repurchase agreements to dealer inventories to a use of the dealers as a channel to those holders of Government securities who have temporary cash needs and who would prefer not to sell Treasury bills or other Government securities outright.[25]

Holmes further recommended eliminating the two-year collateral maturity limit "in order to give maximum flexibility to such a repurchase agreement approach."[26] In response to a question from Hugh Galusha, the president of the Federal Reserve Bank of Minneapolis, about the prospective spread between the repo rate charged to dealers and the repo rate that dealers might charge their customers, Holmes replied that he contemplated lending to dealers at the customary discount rate and letting "market competition set the rates at which dealers made RP's with others."

In response to a question from Governor Andrew Brimmer about whether back-to-back repos would be limited to nonbank dealers, as was the case with conventional repos, Holmes replied in the affirmative. However, he noted that banks would, presumably, "be among those that the nonbank dealers would get in touch with immediately regarding their RP's, so that the funds would be available to the bank dealers indirectly."[27]

Following the conclusion of discussions, Chairman Martin voiced his support of Holmes's recommendations and both recommendations received the Committee's unanimous approval.[28]

In the immediate aftermath of the expansion in its repo authority, the Desk arranged only a limited volume of repos on collateral longer than two years and did not arrange any back-to-back repos. However, the expanded authority remained in place and proved "helpful in meeting reserve needs on other occasions."[29] The 1967 Markets annual report states that "on July 5, when readily available securities in dealers' positions were at a particularly low level, dealers were offered repurchase agreements against any

[25] Minutes of the Federal Open Market Committee, June 28, 1966, pp. 29–30.
[26] Minutes of the Federal Open Market Committee, June 28, 1966, p. 30.
[27] Minutes of the Federal Open Market Committee, June 28, 1966, p. 32.
[28] Minutes of the Federal Open Market Committee, June 28, 1966, p. 33.
[29] 1966 Annual Report of Open Market Operations, p. 52.

Government securities that were either already in position or could be acquired from others."[30] The 1969 annual report states similarly that "the scarcity of bills in the market . . . tended to complicate reserve provision through repurchase agreements since nonbank dealers did not always have sufficient collateral to match System needs to supply reserves. Thus, on occasion, the Desk departed from its normal practice of dealing only with nonbank dealer financing needs and permitted these dealers to round up additional securities from customers to place under repurchase contract with the System."[31]

System Repos on Agency Collateral

In September 1966, Congress amended the Federal Reserve Act to allow Reserve Banks to purchase and sell debt issued or guaranteed by federal agencies, including the Federal National Mortgage Association, the Federal Home Loan Banks, and the Federal Farm Credit Banks.[32] (Box 22.1 discusses the amendment.) Shortly thereafter, Chairman Martin took note of the Banks' new powers and suggested that the FOMC discuss whether to authorize open market operations in federal agency debt.[33] Governor Robert Holland led the discussion at the November 1, 1966, Committee meeting.

Holland began by observing that Holmes had indicated his willingness to undertake repurchase agreements on agency collateral but was not prepared to recommend outright transactions in agency debt. Holland did not think the matter was of pressing importance but noted that dealer inventories in agency issues had been rising and were approaching $500 million. He suggested that agency repos "might be an appropriate means of making some necessary reserve injections" at times when dealers had financing needs in connection with their holdings, and that "such RP's

[30] 1967 Annual Report of Open Market Operations, p. 47.

[31] 1969 Annual Report of Open Market Operations, p. 32.

[32] Section 6 of the Act of September 21, 1966. The 1966 act was aimed broadly at reducing interest rates and primarily addressed interest rate ceilings on bank deposits and bank reserve requirements. Haltom and Sharp (2014, p. 2) state that section 6 "received relatively little emphasis in hearings and public statements." The original authority to purchase and sell federal agency debt was limited to one year but the authority was extended for a second year (by the Act of September 21, 1967) and subsequently made permanent (by the Act of September 21, 1968).

[33] Minutes of the Federal Open Market Committee, October 4, 1966, pp. 14–15.

Box 22.1 Statutory Authority to Purchase and Sell Federal Agency Debt.

Section 6 of the Act of September 21, 1966, added a new subsection to section 14(b) of the Federal Reserve Act, authorizing Federal Reserve Banks "to buy and sell in the open market, under the direction and regulations of the Federal Open Market Committee, any obligation which is a direct obligation of, or fully guaranteed as to principal and interest by, an agency of the United States." The new authority was understood to apply to debt issued by the Federal National Mortgage Association, the Federal Home Loan Banks, and the Federal Farm Credit Banks, including the twelve Federal Intermediate Credit Banks, the thirteen Banks for Cooperatives, and the twelve Federal Land Banks.

The most nuanced explanation of the new authority appeared in the report of the Senate Banking Committee on H.R. 14026, the bill that was ultimately signed into law:

> The principal agency issues in terms of aggregate size and market activity are Federal intermediate credit bank debentures, Federal home loan bank notes and bonds, Federal land bank bonds, bank for cooperatives debentures, and Federal National Mortgage Association debentures and certificates of participation. Aside from short-term (6 months or less) Federal intermediate credit bank obligations, none of these issues are eligible for System transactions, even though from a "market" point of view there is little to distinguish them from those issues that are either explicitly guaranteed or covered [by an opinion of the Attorney General that they are backed by the full faith and credit of the United States]. In fact, these currently ineligible issues could probably be bought and sold by the System in substantial volume with less risk of disrupting market conditions than could the currently eligible issues.
>
> Making all agency issues eligible for System purchase or sale would increase the potential flexibility of open market transactions and could also serve to make these securities somewhat more attractive to investors. While public acceptance and understanding of these issues has grown, there may still be a lingering public hesitation in some cases to acquire and hold some of these issues because of diverse and complex legal and administrative factors. If all the issues were eligible for System operations, this could act as something of a common denominator of market acceptability and would tend to establish a more uniform market background for the various agency issues.
>
> By authorizing System transactions in agency issues, [H.R. 14026] would place them on the same footing as direct obligations of the U.S. Government so far as System open market operations are concerned. As with direct Treasury debt, System decisions as to whether, when, and how much to buy or sell of agency issues would have to be made a with a view to the need for supplying or absorbing reserves as indicated by the stance of monetary policy and in light of developments in the markets, including the need to cope with disorderly markets, should they emerge. In any event, it would be important, as at present, to avoid any semblance of 'rigging' the markets or 'pegging' the interest rates for any particular issues, for such actions would give rise to official dominance of the markets that would run counter to many of the broader objectives of Federal financial policies and might in fact harm rather than aid the propitious functioning of the market for such securities.[1]

[1] Committee on Banking and Currency (1966, pp. 8–9).

might also facilitate flotations of agency issues."[34] Holmes agreed, adding that "repurchase agreements against agency issues would have been useful in the recent past on occasion when there was a shortage of bills in the market."

Governor Mitchell was more aggressive, stating that "it would be desirable to . . . authorize outright transactions" immediately, in anticipation of pressures on the agency market that he expected to appear in the spring. Governor Brimmer agreed with Mitchell's forecast of renewed pressure but stated that it would be enough to start with repos, giving the Desk an opportunity to get comfortable dealing in a new market. He thought the Committee should not ignore Congress and "should take some action in response to the enactment of [the] enabling legislation."

Martin thought "it would be desirable for the Committee to authorize RP's against agency issues" but that it should defer consideration of outright transactions for the time being.[35] The Committee voted unanimously to authorize repurchase agreements on "obligations that are direct obligations of, or fully guaranteed as to principal and interest by, any agency of the United States,"[36] and the Desk initiated its first repurchase agreements on agency debt a month later.[37]

MATCHED SALE-PURCHASE AGREEMENTS

Expanding access to repo collateral – by first relaxing and later eliminating the collateral maturity limit, permitting back-to-back repos, and accepting federal agency debt as collateral – enhanced the scale of System repo operations. Matched sale-purchase agreements, on the other hand, were introduced to effect reserve drains, a matter of expanding the scope, rather than the scale, of repurchase agreements.

The need for a policy instrument to drain reserves on a temporary basis first came to prominence in the early 1960s. Allan Meltzer writes that in about 1963, "the staff of the New York [Reserve] bank considered several ways of offsetting large temporary changes in float," and ultimately settled on "a new instrument – reverse repurchase agreements, with government securities dealers." However, Board staff "opposed [reverse repos] on

[34] Minutes of the Federal Open Market Committee, November 1, 1966, p. 15.

[35] Minutes of the Federal Open Market Committee, November 1, 1966, pp. 15, 16, and 17.

[36] Minutes of the Federal Open Market Committee, November 1, 1966, p. 19.

[37] "Reserve System Makes First Use of Authority to Buy Certain Issues," *Wall Street Journal*, December 6, 1966, p. 24; and "Monetary Policy Easing Slightly," *New York Times*, December 9, 1966, p. 73.

grounds that the transaction constituted a loan to the Federal Reserve from dealers that might be illegal and would be embarrassing." Nothing came of the Bank's proposal.[38]

Interest in an instrument to drain reserves on a temporary basis resurfaced in the summer of 1966, when a major airline strike slowed check collection and led to a bulge in float. The 1966 Markets annual report observed that float was $1 billion greater than normal four days after the strike started on July 8 and that it remained $800 million or more above normal until after the strike ended on August 19.[39] In the absence of some action to drain reserves, the interbank market for reserve balances would not be as restrictive as the FOMC intended. (Net borrowed reserves fell to $125 million during the first week of the strike – they had been about $480 million immediately prior to the strike – and the Federal funds rate dropped from 5½ percent on July 7 to 4½ percent on July 13.)

One way to deal with the problem would have been to sell Treasury securities outright and, in a separate and independent operation, repurchase them when the strike was over – a strategy complicated by the prospective need to vary the size of the reduction in the Open Market Account in parallel with variations in strike-related float, which was likely to exhibit "large and erratic day-to-day fluctuations."[40] During a hastily scheduled telephone meeting of the FOMC on July 11, Holmes observed that "given current market conditions, such operations may be difficult to accomplish, heavily taxing the facilities of the market and possibly causing sudden, large, and undesirable [interest] rate fluctuations." He noted that "outright sales of Treasury bills on the scale needed do not appear feasible" because dealers were "naturally reluctant to carry any substantial inventories at current rate levels."[41]

Holmes proposed implementing matched sale-purchase agreements in lieu of outright sales. The Desk would sell a Treasury bill to a dealer for cash settlement and simultaneously agree to buy the bill back at a higher price on a later date – effectively entering into what the dealer would view as a reverse repurchase agreement. The Desk would fix the original sale price of the bill and supervise a multiple-price auction in which participating dealers would tender repurchase prices, with the lowest prices winning the auction. (Accounting for the sale and repurchase prices separately

[38] Meltzer (2009, pp. 374 and 464).
[39] 1966 Annual Report of Open Market Operations, p. 53.
[40] Minutes of the Federal Open Market Committee, July 11, 1966, p. 4.
[41] Minutes of the Federal Open Market Committee, July 11, 1966, pp. 2 and 4.

bolstered the appearance that the System was not paying interest on borrowed money – something that would have been more evident if bidding was in terms of a repo rate.) Drawing on the recent Committee approval of back-to-back repos, Holmes proposed to allow dealers to source funds from their customers and to use the securities sold by the Desk as collateral in repo transactions with those customers, effectively allowing back-to-back MSPs. Back-to-back transactions were expected to provide "a broader base for operations since the dealers would be able to reverse the transactions with other investors, particularly banks which acquired reserves from the float bulge and would, therefore, be in a position to acquire such short-term investments."[42]

The Committee ultimately approved Holmes proposal, with several members expressing the hope that MSPs would be used only if the situation worsened considerably.[43]

The Desk began executing MSPs on Tuesday, July 12. Within a week net borrowed reserves were back up above $400 million. By the end of the month the Desk had transacted a cumulative total of $1.9 billion of MSPs, with the amount outstanding exceeding $800 million on at least one occasion.[44] Holmes reported to the Committee that the new instrument worked "even better than we had expected."[45] Although originally viewed as a temporary response to an unusual situation, Chart 22.1 shows that MSPs became as important as repos by the end of the decade.

AN UNSUCCESSFUL EFFORT TO INTRODUCE MORE FLEXIBLE REPO PRICING

The convention of setting the System repo rate equal to the discount rate, regardless of whether open market repo rates were higher or lower, also

[42] Minutes of the Federal Open Market Committee, July 11, 1966, p. 3. See also 1968 Annual Report of Open Market Operations, p. 20:

> "Since the dealers incurred no market risk when entering into these transactions, they were generally willing to do a large volume of business with the System so long as they could find customers (generally banks) who would take on the bills under repurchase agreements even at a time when a nervous market atmosphere made them reluctant to take bills into position on an outright basis except at sharply higher rates. Since the Account Management usually offered matched sale-purchase transactions when the banking system had sizable excess reserves, it was usually possible to accomplish tremendous short-run reserve absorption by this means with little or no impact on the securities markets."

[43] Minutes of the Federal Open Market Committee, July 11, 1966, pp. 18–20.

[44] 1966 Annual Report of Open Market Operations, p. 53.

[45] Minutes of the Federal Open Market Committee, July 26, 1966, p. 23.

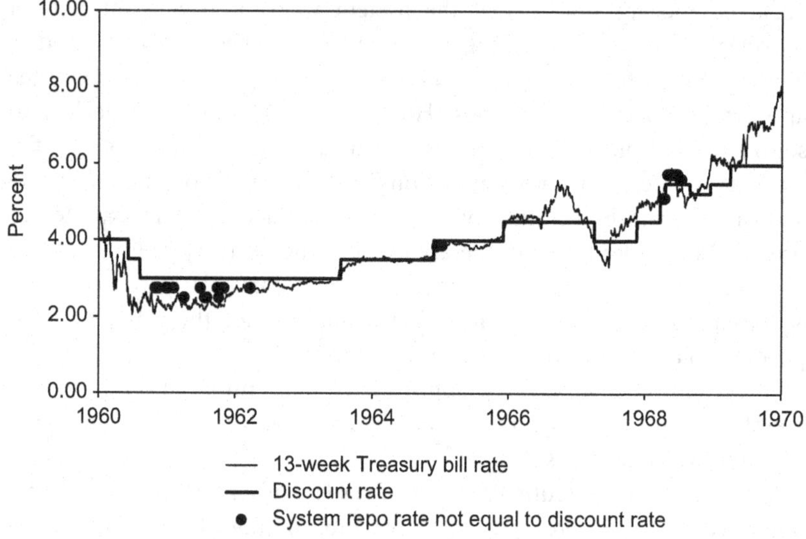

Chart 22.2 Rates on System repurchase agreements that were not equal to the Federal Reserve Bank of New York discount rate. Daily figures.
Federal Reserve Statistical Release H.15, Board of Governors of the Federal Reserve System (1976, table 12.1A), and annual reports of open market operations.

imposed a significant restraint on the fullest use of repos. Desk officials had found it "impracticable to use any rate other than the discount rate" in the second half of the 1950s because "to go above the discount rate would create a feeling on the part of the nonbank dealers that they were being imposed upon, while to go below the discount rate would mean that bank dealers would feel imposed upon."[46] The Desk set the System repo rate at a rate other than the discount rate of the Federal Reserve Bank of New York on eight days in 1955. The two rates differed by no more than ⅛ percent on any of the eight days.[47] The Desk otherwise kept the repo rate at the discount rate during the 1950s.

Chart 22.2 and Table 22.1 show that the Desk entered into repurchase agreements at rates different from the contemporaneous discount rate during three intervals in the 1960s. Differences between the System repo rate and the discount rate were small in all three episodes. The first interval ran from late 1960 to early 1962, when Federal Reserve officials were

[46] Minutes of the Federal Open Market Committee, March 1, 1960, p. 11. Bank dealers were not allowed to borrow on Federal Reserve repos.

[47] 1955 Annual Report of Open Market Operations, p. A-5.

Table 22.1 *System repurchase agreements at rates less than, equal to, and greater than the Federal Reserve Bank of New York discount rate.*

	Total value of repo contracts entered into ($ billions)	Percent of contracts at rates . . .		
		. . . Less than discount rate	. . . Equal to discount rate	. . . Greater than discount rate
1960	7.1	22	78	0
1961	4.6	26	74	0
1962	6.1	5	95	0
1963	8.9	0	100	0
1964	9.3	24	76	0
1965	14.9	7	93	0
1966	10.0	0	100	0
1967	17.5	0	100	0
1968	16.8	0	62	38
1969	27.4	0	100	0

Annual reports of open market operations.

seeking to keep short-term interest rates high in defense of the dollar, were reluctant to cut the discount rate, and were reluctant to buy bills on an outright basis. When the Desk needed to inject reserves on a short-term basis it had little alternative but to price repos closer to market levels. The second interval ran from mid-December 1964 to early January 1965, satisfied a transient demand for currency, and resulted in repos no more than fifteen basis points below the discount rate. The third interval, discussed in more detail below, occurred in the spring of 1968 and resulted in repos no more than twenty-five basis points above the discount rate.

The members of the FOMC and the staff of the Open Market Desk understood that fixing the price of System repo credit at the discount rate limited, from time to time, the utility of repos for managing the supply of reserves available to the banking system. Committee members had debated for years whether to set the repo rate below the discount rate when the Reserve Banks were slow to cut their discount rates in parallel with a decline in open market rates. Failure to lower the repo rate to market levels limited the Desk's ability to inject reserves on a short-term basis. Conversely, failure to set the repo rate *above* the discount rate in 1966, when open market rates, including the Federal funds rate, had moved well above the discount rate, left the Desk hesitant to provide reserves with repurchase agreements.[48]

The repo rate conundrum faded in the fall of 1966 in the wake of Administration actions taken in response to the August 29 money panic and disappeared when the FOMC began easing, but it was not forgotten. Money market rates rebounded in the second half of 1967 and by the spring of 1968 it was clear that the problem with repo pricing had reappeared.

At the April 2, 1968, FOMC meeting, Holmes observed that "with Federal funds now trading about ½ per cent above the [5 percent] discount rate and New York dealer loan rates higher than that, our 5 per cent repurchase agreement rate is already getting out of line – and the disparity could increase under the pressure of future Treasury financing, or if the Committee decides to push further towards restraint." He suggested that "it would be desirable to break away from our tradition of a repurchase rate no higher than the discount rate now, rather than waiting until pressures increase." Holmes said he would like to "introduce flexibility in the RP rate, adjusting it in light of market developments," and allowed that "under certain circumstances the RP rate might well be one-fourth of a point or more above the discount rate."[49]

Governor Brimmer reacted strongly and negatively to the idea that the rate on System repurchase agreements should be left up to the manager of the Open Market Account. "If that were done," he said, "the market might mistakenly begin to interpret changes in the RP rate as conveying messages about System views on appropriate rate levels in general." However, he allowed, "the risk of such mistaken interpretation would be reduced if the RP rate were tied to some market rate, so that changes in it would be purely mechanical."[50]

Chairman Martin adopted a more pragmatic stance, stating that it was "desirable to experiment occasionally with operating techniques." His suggestion that the Committee authorize the manager to "experiment in a mild way with a higher RP rate" encountered no opposition.[51]

48 See Chapter 21, text at footnote 15, and footnote 12 in this chapter.

49 Minutes of the Federal Open Market Committee, April 2, 1968, p. 32.

50 Minutes of the Federal Open Market Committee, April 2, 1968, pp. 32–33. Alfred Hayes, the president of the Federal Reserve Bank of New York, expressed doubt that "it would be feasible to link the [repo] rate mechanically to some market rate." Minutes of the Federal Open Market Committee, April 2, 1968, p. 35.

51 Minutes of the Federal Open Market Committee, April 2, 1968, pp. 35 and 38.

Holmes outlined his preliminary thinking on a flexible repo rate at the April 30 FOMC meeting. He proposed setting the rate about ¼ percent below the Federal funds rate but noted that the spread might change from time to time. He further proposed basing the repo rate on an average of recent past Federal funds rates, leaving out of the averaging any rates "that deviated significantly from the norm."[52]

W. Braddock Hickman, the president of the Federal Reserve Bank of Cleveland, asked whether Holmes had considered using the dealer loan rate posted by large New York banks as an alternative base rate, "a procedure that would appear logical because, at times when the System was making RP's, dealers had the alternatives of securing financing from banks or from the System." Holmes responded that the "major New York banks acted as lenders of last resort to dealers, and their rates on [collateral] loans tended to be substantially higher than those at which dealers could borrow elsewhere." The Desk, on the other hand, had to set a rate that was "competitive with the general level of rates at which dealers could borrow."[53]

Governor Robertson expressed his belief that "the discount rate established by the System represents the ultimate cost of liquidity to the economy, and in that sense is the anchor rate in the market." Like Brimmer, he was unwilling to leave the repo rate to the discretion of the Account manager and suggested auctioning repo credit.[54]

Martin suggested that the Committee authorize the manager "to continue experimenting with flexible RP rates in the manner he had outlined [and] that a study of Mr. Robertson's proposal be undertaken." The minutes state that "[n]o disagreement was expressed with the Chairman's suggestions."[55]

Following the April 30 meeting the Desk set the System repo rate at 5¾ percent, ¼ percent over the 5½ percent discount rate.[56] At the time the Federal funds rate varied between 6 and 6¼ percent.

On July 5, following a decline in longer-term money market rates, the Desk moved the System repo rate down to 5⅝ percent, even though the discount rate remained unchanged at 5½ percent and the funds rate was still around 6 percent. The reduction "was generally interpreted as

[52] Minutes of the Federal Open Market Committee, April 30, 1968, pp. 29–30.
[53] Minutes of the Federal Open Market Committee, April 30, 1968, pp. 30–31.
[54] Minutes of the Federal Open Market Committee, April 30, 1968, p. 32.
[55] Minutes of the Federal Open Market Committee, April 30, 1968, pp. 36–37.
[56] 1968 Annual Report of Open Market Operations, pp. 22–23.

meaning that the System was favorably disposed to the lower level of [longer-term] interest rates that had developed" following passage of the tax surcharge.[57] The interpretation of the reduction as a signal of Committee intentions was exactly what some members of the Committee had wanted to avoid.

The market's interpretation of the July 5 change in the repo rate did not pass unnoticed. Governors Mitchell, Daane, and Brimmer all expressed concern that since the repo rate functioned as a "device for transmitting subtle changes in System policy," and since "the market tended to look at the RP rate as a proxy for the discount rate," changes in the repo rate should be a matter for the Committee.[58] Desk officials set the repo rate back to the discount rate and kept it equal to that rate for the balance of the decade.[59]

[57] Minutes of the Federal Open Market Committee, July 16, 1968, p. 18, statement of Alan Holmes.

[58] Minutes of the Federal Open Market Committee, July 16, 1968, pp. 27–29.

[59] 1968 Annual Report of Open Market Operations, pp. 22 and B-8, and 1969 Annual Report of Open Market Operations, p. B-8.

PART VII

UPDATING MARKET INFRASTRUCTURES
The Joint Study

Prior to the second half of the 1960s the Federal Reserve System maintained a laissez faire attitude in its dealings with the Treasury market. The Fed certainly had objectives when it interacted with the market – it wanted to be able to access liquidity sufficient for open market operations of the desired size in the contemplated time frame and to be confident that Treasury offerings would be adequately supported – but it did not seek to influence the evolution of the market's infrastructure or promote or discourage particular market structures or practices.

After 1965, the System, and the Federal Reserve Bank of New York in particular, began to intervene actively in discussions and initiatives aimed at reshaping the structure of the market. It more or less demanded the formation of a dealer association (through which it could convey informal guidance regarding market practices), it contemplated providing primary dealers with preferential access to Federal Reserve credit (to bolster their market making and underwriting efforts), it sponsored the development of a novel netting arrangement for settling transactions in Treasury securities (to reduce its own operating expenses and the operating expenses of the large New York clearing banks), it began to lend securities from the System Open Market Account (to mitigate settlement fails), and it introduced a book-entry system for Treasury securities (to further reduce operating costs and risks).

The Fed's new-found interest in market infrastructure was clearly expressed in the Joint Treasury-Federal Reserve Study of the U.S.

Government Securities Market – hereafter, the "Joint Study."[1] In announcing the study, the Board of Governors stated that "the broad purpose of the review is to ascertain how the dealer market for U.S. Government securities has evolved and performed during the 1960's in light of economic developments during the period, of innovations affecting financial processes, and of operating techniques utilized by the Treasury and the Federal Reserve."[2] The study was conducted under the guidance of a steering committee chaired by William McChesney Martin that included Under Secretary of the Treasury Joseph Barr, Under Secretary of the Treasury for Monetary Affairs Frederick Deming, Governors George Mitchell and J. Dewey Daane, and Reserve Bank presidents Alfred Hayes (New York) and George Ellis (Boston). The Secretary of the Treasury, Henry Fowler, participated as an ex officio member. Meetings of the steering committee provided a forum for discussing the initiatives examined in the following five chapters.

[1] The final report of the Joint Study appears in U.S. Treasury and Federal Reserve System (1969). Staff studies appear in U.S. Treasury and Federal Reserve System (1970, 1971, and 1973).

[2] "U.S. Studies Trade in Its Securities," *New York Times*, March 9, 1966, p. 51; and "Study of the Government Securities Market of60s Set by Federal Reserve, Treasury," *Wall Street Journal*, March 9, 1966, p. 8.

23

The Association of Primary Dealers

In April 1969, the primary dealer community came together to form the Association of Primary Dealers in United States Government Securities – hereafter, "the Primary Dealers Association," or, more simply, "the Association." The Association is most important for its pivotal role in a 1982 revision of contracting conventions for repurchase agreements.[1] More broadly, the Association provided an important channel of communication between the Desk and the government securities market.

This chapter examines the circumstances that prompted the formation of the Primary Dealers Association. The discussion begins with a brief summary of changes in the primary dealer community in the 1960s, continues with a review of Treasury and Federal Reserve thinking about a dealer association, and then describes the episode that triggered the formation of the Association.

ARRIVALS AND DEPARTURES

During the 1960s, the Federal Reserve Bank of New York designated six new primary dealers; three dealers withdrew from participation, leaving twenty primary dealers at the end of the decade.

The first two additions, Second District Securities Co., and First National City Bank, were designated in mid-1961.[2] Second District Securities was a subsidiary of M.A. Shapiro & Co., a brokerage firm specializing in bank stocks, and was staffed with personnel who had previously worked at First Boston and C. F. Childs.[3]

[1] Garbade (2006, pp. 32–33). [2] 1961 Annual Report of Open Market Operations, p. 43.
[3] "Search for U.S. Bond Experts Starts Game of Musical Chairs," *New York Times*, April 1, 1962, p. 143.

Blyth & Co., a large New York–based investment bank, was the third new dealer. Blyth staffed its trading desk with personnel from Second District Securities (itself only a year old), C. F. Childs, Aubrey G. Lanston, Bankers Trust, Morgan Guaranty Trust, and Chemical Bank. The *New York Times* took note of the "scramble to hire the few financiers around who are steeped in [the] highly specialized" market for Treasury securities and described the personnel changes as "a game of musical chairs."[4] Blyth was designated a primary dealer in mid-July 1962.[5] Three more primary dealers were added later in the decade: United California Bank in mid-1964,[6] Harris Trust and Savings Bank in mid-1965,[7] and Francis I. duPont & Co. at the end of 1968.[8]

There were three withdrawals from, and one important change of control in, the primary dealer community in the 1960s.

Francis Bartow, the managing partner of Bartow, Leeds & Co., died in mid-March 1962. The firm was forced to liquidate when Bartow's partners were unable to replace the capital owed to his estate.[9]

A year later Christopher Devine, the managing partner at C. J. Devine & Co., passed away. His partners faced the same problem as Bartow's partners when two-thirds of the firm's $18 million of capital went to Devine's estate. However, Devine's partners had enough of their own money in the business to forestall outright liquidation. In May 1964, Merrill Lynch, Pierce, Fenner & Smith, Inc., acquired the dealership. The C. J. Devine partners exchanged their partnership interests for Merrill Lynch common stock and became officers of the far larger and rapidly expanding broker-dealer.[10] The transaction catapulted Merrill, a firm that was not previously active in the government securities market, into the first rank of primary dealers.[11]

[4] "Search for U.S. Bond Experts Starts Game of Musical Chairs," *New York Times*, April 1, 1962, p. 143.

[5] 1962 Annual Report of Open Market Operations, p. 49.

[6] 1964 Annual Report of Open Market Operations, p. 58.

[7] 1965 Annual Report of Open Market Operations, p. 63.

[8] 1968 Annual Report of Open Market Operations, p. B-2.

[9] "Francis D. Bartow, Jr.," *New York Times*, March 17, 1962, p. 25; and minutes of the July 10, 1962, meeting of the Federal Open Market Committee, p. 4.

[10] "Christopher J. Devine, 58, Dies; A Dealer in Government Bonds," *New York Times*, May 11, 1963, p. 25; "Merrill Lynch Today Takes Over Business of C.J. Devine & Co.; No Cash is Involved," *Wall Street Journal*, May 13, 1964, p. 4; and "Wall Street: A Sweet Deal," *Time*, May 22, 1964.

[11] "Wall Street: A Sweet Deal," *Time*, May 22, 1964; and "U.S. Bond Business Found Changing," *New York Times*, May 17, 1964, p. F1.

Table 23.1 *Primary dealers at the end of the 1960s.*

At the end of 1969 the primary dealer community consisted of twenty firms
Bankers Trust Co.
Blyth & Co.
Briggs, Schaedle & Co.
Chemical Bank
Continental Illinois National Bank & Trust Co.
Discount Corp.
Francis I. duPont & Co.
First Boston Corp.
First National Bank of Chicago
First National City Bank
Harris Trust and Savings Bank
Aubrey G. Lanston & Co.
Merrill, Lynch, Pierce, Fenner & Smith (formerly C.J. Devine & Co.)
Morgan Guaranty Trust Co.
New York Hanseatic Corp.
William E. Pollack & Co.
Charles E. Quincey & Co.
Salomon Brothers & Hutzler
Second District Securities
United California Bank

1969 Annual Report of Open Market Operations, p. B-2.

C. F. Childs & Co. withdrew as a primary dealer in 1965,[12] reportedly in the wake of financial difficulties,[13] and D. W. Rich & Co. withdrew in 1969.[14] Table 23.1 identifies the twenty members of the primary dealer community at the end of the 1960s.

FEDERAL RESERVE AND TREASURY THINKING ABOUT A DEALER ASSOCIATION

The idea of a regular channel of communication with the government securities market was never far from the thinking of System officials. The

[12] 1965 Annual Report of Open Market Operations, p. 63.

[13] "C.F. Childs & Co. Quits Securities Business, Plans New Activities," *Wall Street Journal*, July 1, 1965, p. 2, stating that "the abrupt decision [to withdraw] was believed to have been triggered by the breakoff Monday of merger talks between Childs and Cantor, Fitzgerald & Co., an over-the-counter broker-dealer based in Beverly Hills" and noting "reports that the firm had been having financial difficulties."

[14] 1969 Annual Report of Open Market Operations, p. B-2.

question of a formal dealer association had been discussed in the 1960 Treasury-Federal Reserve study of the government securities market and received renewed attention in the Joint Study.

In July 1967, the Joint Study steering committee convened to discuss a staff memo on the "official relationship" with the market. The memo proposed the formation of a committee of senior Federal Reserve and Treasury staff that would consult with members of the dealer community from time to time. Albert Koch, the deputy director of the Division of Research and Statistics at the Board of Governors, stated that "there was a need for better communications between [Treasury and Federal Reserve] officials and [government securities] dealers" and that the proposal "was intended to steer a middle course between the present informal contacts between officials and the dealer community and a somewhat more organized formal surveillance of the market." Alan Holmes, the manager of the System Open Market Account, thought that the proposed committee "should prove far less upsetting to the dealers than a committee formally charged with the task of market surveillance."[15]

There was immediate pushback from the steering committee. Governor Dewey Daane thought the existing system of informal contacts "worked satisfactorily" and Chairman Martin was "skeptical that any net gain could be derived from the proposed committee." Treasury Secretary Fowler though it would be better to have the dealers take the initiative, observing that "it seemed preferable to encourage the dealers to form their own formal group which could designate a committee to meet with appropriate Government officials."[16]

A revised staff memo focusing on the formation of a voluntary association began by reciting the importance of public confidence in the government securities market: "a diminution of confidence ... as a result of undesirable market practices, speculative excesses or financial difficulties would have widespread repercussions on all financial markets and would seriously inhibit the effectuation of Treasury and Federal Reserve policy." In view of the importance of public confidence, the memo proposed that the Treasury and the Federal Reserve System *officially* promote "the formation of a dealer association to encourage more self-regulation."[17]

[15] Minutes of the Steering Committee for the Joint Treasury-Federal Reserve Study of the U.S. Government Securities Market, July 5, 1967, pp. 6–7.

[16] Minutes of the Steering Committee for the Joint Treasury-Federal Reserve Study of the U.S. Government Securities Market, July 5, 1967, pp. 7–8.

[17] U.S. Government Securities Market Study, "Official Relationship to the Market," Policy Issues # 7, no date. Emphasis added.

The need for additional regulation was far from evident. The revised memo acknowledged that "no major problems of undesirable market practices or dealer financial difficulties have developed in recent years" and that "the present informal surveillance and at times moral suasion exercised by Treasury and System officials has thus far worked reasonably well." Nevertheless, the memo complained, "the responsibilities for and access to the various bits of information are now diffused throughout the Treasury and the System." The memo recommended that the Treasury and Federal Reserve encourage "some form of dealer organization – to concern itself with such matters as quotation and trading practices, trading agreements, hours of trading, and the like."

Taken at face value, the recommendation of the revised memo addressed little more than market plumbing – important matters to be sure, but hardly matters of high policy. However, the memo went on to point out that "such an organization could provide a basis for self-regulation in the industry and could become a principle source of contact between the market and the Treasury-Federal Reserve" – functionalities that went well beyond market plumbing.

The steering committee convened to discuss the revised memo on April 2, 1968. Holmes acknowledged that the memo recommended an "*official* indication to the market that Treasury and Federal Reserve authorities would welcome the formation of an association of U.S. Government securities dealers" but noted also that "it was fully intended that the dealers themselves would take the initiative in organizing such an association." He reiterated the expectation that the association "could provide a basis for self-regulation . . . and could become a principal source of contact between the market and the authorities."[18]

Even the limited proposal for official encouragement met with significant pushback. R. Duane Saunders, the Special Assistant to the Secretary of the Treasury for Debt Management, observed that "an official endorsement would imply a commitment to establish a working relationship with, and to assume some responsibility for, any dealer association that was formed." Governor Daane stated that he was in favor of a dealer association but shared Saunders' reservations about official sponsorship. He wondered "if the Treasury and Federal Reserve could simply make their view known that such an association might be useful while stopping short of actual endorsement." Chairman Martin and Reserve Bank President Hayes concurred

[18] Minutes of the Steering Committee for the Joint Treasury-Federal Reserve Study of the U.S. Government Securities Market, April 2, 1968, p. 4. Emphasis added.

with that approach. The discussion ended with the suggestion of Secretary Fowler that "the Treasury and Federal Reserve not actively endorse a dealer association while still indicating the view that it could be useful."[19]

PRECIPITATING EVENTS

A flood tide of embarrassing revelations in 1968 and 1969 swept away the reluctance of System officials to press for the formation of a dealer association.

In March 1968, the Treasury announced that Federal Reserve Banks would no longer receive advance notice of the terms of Treasury debt offerings.[20] Officials had previously released offering information to the twelve Reserve Banks at about 1 p.m. on the day of an announcement, and followed up with a public announcement at 3:30 p.m.

The change in policy stemmed from indications of anomalous trading shortly before public announcement of an August 1967 note offering. Market participants had been expecting a 5- to 7-year note but the Treasury surprised them by offering 3½-year notes maturing in February 1971. In the hour before the public announcement, outstanding notes maturing between November 1970 and May 1972 declined and notes maturing around August 1973 rallied.[21] The price action suggested that someone had leaked the terms of the offering. Subsequent investigation identified the head of the government bond and custody department at the Federal Reserve Bank of Philadelphia as the source of the leak.[22]

Ten months later, the Securities and Exchange Commission announced that Blyth & Co. had agreed to close its government securities trading desk for fifteen days to settle charges of abuse of nonpublic information on

[19] Minutes of the Steering Committee for the Joint Treasury-Federal Reserve Study of the U.S. Government Securities Market, April 2, 1968, pp. 4–7.

[20] "Treasury to Delay Telling Federal Reserve Its Bond Terms Due to Recent News Leak," *Wall Street Journal*, March 6, 1968, p. 8; "News of Borrowing Leaked, U.S. Finds," *New York Times*, March 6, 1968, p. 61L; "Washington Attracts Many Seeking to Profit from Inside Information," *Wall Street Journal*, March 14, 1968, p. 1; and "S.E.C. Commences New Enforcement, Disciplines Blyth," *Wall Street Journal*, January 20, 1969, p. 2.

[21] Federal Reserve Bank of New York Circular no. 6020, August 17, 1967, and Circular no. 6021, August 18, 1967; "U.S. Bond Issue Set for Tuesday," *New York Times*, August 18, 1967, p. F43; and "Treasury to Delay Telling Federal Reserve Its Bond Terms Due to Recent News Leak," *Wall Street Journal*, March 6, 1968, p. 8.

[22] "Treasury to Delay Telling Federal Reserve Its Bond Terms Due to Recent News Leak," *Wall Street Journal*, March 6, 1968, p. 8; and "S.E.C. Commences New Enforcement, Disciplines Blyth," *Wall Street Journal*, January 20, 1969, p. 2.

Treasury offerings. The head of the desk was suspended for five days for his failure to supervise other desk employees.[23] A month later, in February 1969, the SEC announced that it had uncovered a separate scheme involving "secret" trading in US Treasury securities by employees on the government trading desks at Morgan Guaranty Trust Co., Blyth & Co., and Second District Securities.[24]

The discovery of abuses of nonpublic information and secret trading by employees of several primary dealers alarmed New York Reserve Bank officials. In a memo to senior Bank officers in March 1968, during an early stage of the investigation, Peter Sternlight, an officer in the Bank's Securities Department, wrote that,

> The injection of the Securities and Exchange Commission into this investigation is not necessarily the happiest development because we would not like to see this incident become a first step in a broader SEC role in the Government securities market. A self-policing Government securities market, with unobtrusive leadership exercised by the Treasury and Federal Reserve, would seem to be a preferable state of affairs in order to promote a broad, healthy market.[25]

Supervisory issues continued to be of concern to the New York Bank as the SEC investigation continued to unfold in 1968. Notes prepared for a December presentation by Alan Holmes to the Board of Governors observed that, with respect to market supervision:

> There is ... the longer run problem of the continuing surveillance or supervision of the market in which both the Treasury and the Federal Reserve have a stake. The SEC representatives did not appear anxious to take over supervision of trading in exempt securities. In fact they tentatively put forward a suggestion that the Federal Reserve might use its trading relationship with dealers to set up standards of dealer conduct. It would seem logical that whatever eventual course of action is to be taken – whether informal supervision rising out of trading relationships, the seeking of legislation for more formal supervision of the market, or the establishment of a dealer organization to exercise self-discipline – that action should be undertaken jointly with the Treasury.[26]

[23] "S.E.C. Closes Bond Unit of Blyth & Co. 15 Days," *New York Times*, January 18, 1969, p. 41; and "S.E.C. Commences New Enforcement, Disciplines Blyth," *Wall Street Journal*, January 20, 1969, p. 2.

[24] "S.E.C. Acts to End Traders' Scheme in Federal Bonds," *New York Times*, February 14, 1969, p. 1; and "SEC Acts to End Alleged Schemes by Government-Securities Traders," *Wall Street Journal*, February 14, 1969, p. 3.

[25] Memo from P.D. Sternlight to Messrs. Hayes, Treiber, Bilby, Guy, and Debs, Federal Reserve Bank of New York, March 19, 1968.

[26] Alan R. Holmes's Notes for Meeting with Federal Reserve Board on SEC Investigation of Government Securities Market, December 2, 1968.

FORMATION OF THE ASSOCIATION OF PRIMARY DEALERS

In a February 1969 letter to primary dealers, Holmes stated that the disclosures of insider and secret trading "raise a serious question about the adequacy of procedures used by dealer firms to guard against the possibility of improper activity on the part of any employee. More broadly, the situation requires a review as to whether or not something more than the informal watch over the market that has been exercised by the Federal Reserve and the Treasury may be desirable."[27]

Holmes's letter and the disclosure of secret trading in Treasury securities spurred the dealers to action. The day after the disclosure the *New York Times* reported that "the Government securities industry does not want any more regulation, and it fears the S.E.C. cases this year may result in stiffer controls." As a result, "there may be some drive to form a self-regulating group to police the Treasury market."[28]

Between mid-February and mid-April 1969, the primary dealers, led by Salomon Brothers & Hutzler, Discount Corp., First Boston Corp., and Aubrey G. Lanston & Co., agreed to form the Association of Primary Dealers.[29] The articles of association that memorialized their agreement expressed the purposes of the new group:

1. To foster high standards of commercial honor and business conduct among its members and to promote just and equitable principles of trade.
2. To promote practices conducive to efficient conduct of the business of its members.
3. To provide a medium through which its members may be enabled to confer, consult and cooperate with the Federal Reserve Bank of

[27] Letter from Alan Holmes, Senior Vice President, Federal Reserve Bank of New York, to senior officers of each of the primary dealers, February 13, 1969.

[28] "U.S. Bond Market is Troubled," *New York Times*, February 16, 1969, p. F1.

[29] "Dealers Weigh Forming Group," *New York Times*, April 16, 1969, p. 25, "Dealers in Securities of U.S. Government Form an Association," *Wall Street Journal*, April 24, 1969, p. 25; and "Officers Elected by Primary Dealers," *New York Times*, April 24, 1969, p. 77. William Simon of Solomon Brothers & Hutzler was elected president of the new association. Other officers included C. Richard Youngdahl of Aubrey G. Lanston & Co., vice president, Carl Cooke of First Boston Corp., treasurer, and Herman Frenzel of Bankers Trust Co., secretary. Other members of the executive committee included Charles Dunbar of Discount Corp., Carl Kreitler of Merrill Lynch, Pierce, Fenner & Smith, Donald Stoddard of Morgan Guaranty Trust Co., David Taylor of Continental Illinois National Bank & Trust Co., and Paul Uhl of United California Bank.

New York, the Federal Reserve Open Market Committee, the United States Treasury Department and other United States Government agencies with respect to matters affecting the market for United States Government and Agency securities.[30]

The new Association played an important role in facilitating communication between market participants and the Federal Reserve on matters of market infrastructure. Beginning in mid-1969 and continuing through most of the 1970s, the Federal Reserve worked to replace definitive bills, notes, and bonds with book-entry securities and to integrate the book-entry system with its existing wire transfer system – see Chapters 25, 27, and 32. The effort required close coordination among investors, dealers, clearing banks, and other securities custodians – coordination materially enhanced by the Association. As early as September 1969, officials of the Federal Reserve Bank of New York met with Association representatives to discuss the introduction of a new computer message switch at the New York Bank and the expansion of an early book-entry system to include securities of bank dealers and non-bank dealers held at custodian banks.[31] The Association was also important in discussions of who should have access to the inter-dealer broker market[32] and in focusing the attention of Federal Reserve officials on the importance of upgrading the book-entry system to mitigate delays in securities transfers and extensions of operating hours – see Chapter 31.[33] However, the most memorable achievement of the Association was its role in revising contract conventions for repurchase agreements following the failure of Drysdale Government Securities in 1982.[34]

[30] Articles of Association of the Association of Primary Dealers in United States Government Securities.

[31] Memo from Matthew J. Hoey to files, Federal Reserve Bank of New York, "Meeting with William Chisolm – First Boston," September 12, 1969.

[32] See Chapter 31 below.

[33] See also minutes of the quarterly meeting of the Association of Primary Dealers in U.S. Government Securities, September 22, 1980, and letter from Paul Cieurzo, Charles E. Quincey & Co., to Thomas Strauss, Salomon Brothers, "Changes in Federal Reserve Policy," March 10, 1981.

[34] Garbade (2006, pp. 32–33).

24

Dealer Finance

Dealer finance became a matter of concern to Federal Reserve officials following the appearance, in the mid-1960s, of dealer reluctance to carry inventories of Treasury securities large enough to accommodate System open market operations. A 1968 Joint Study policy memorandum states that "at times, and rather frequently in recent years, the dealers have faced great difficulty and high cost in financing their positions" and that "financing difficulties have tended to reduce dealer willingness to take on positions and make markets." Reduced commitments "threatened the healthy functioning of the market" and from time to time impaired the Desk's ability to execute open market operations and inhibited dealer underwriting of Treasury offerings.[1]

The memorandum attributed the contraction in dealer inventories to increased interest rate volatility, reduced carry when the yield curve flattened, and reduced confidence among dealers that they would always be able to finance their inventories.[2] Given their dual concerns with promoting economic growth and restraining inflation, there was little that Federal Reserve officials could do to ameliorate the first two concerns, but they did contemplate how they might enhance dealer confidence in the continuing availability of short-term credit.

DEALER FINANCE AND THE ROLE OF MONEY MARKET BANKS AS RESIDUAL LENDERS

As short-term interest rates rose in the first half of the 1960s, government securities dealers worked assiduously to expand and diversify their funding

[1] U.S. Government Securities Market Study, "Use of Federal Reserve Resources to Finance Dealers," Policy Issues # 8, July 22, 1968, p. 1. Federal Reserve Bank of New York (1964) describes dealer finance in the early 1960s.

[2] U.S. Government Securities Market Study, "Use of Federal Reserve Resources to Finance Dealers," Policy Issues # 8, July 22, 1968, pp. 3–4.

sources, seeking new sources of credit on repurchase agreements with regional banks, corporations, and state and local governments, but they continued to rely on money center banks, especially the large New York banks, for residual financing.[3]

For both dealers and money center banks, dealer loans were a matter of convenience, negotiated on a day-to-day basis rather than part of a long-term relationship such as commonly characterized bank lending to industrial corporations. Dealers did not seek funding from money market banks if, as was usually the case, they could get cheaper money elsewhere. Similarly, if a money center bank that normally lent to dealers found itself in need of reserves, it did not hesitate to raise its loan rate to a level that forced dealers to find alternative sources of credit. The Joint Study stated that,

> The changing terms on which [money center banks] lend to dealers are one of the most important means by which banks make continuous adjustments to daily, and often unpredictable, inflows and outflows of funds. Day-to-day swings in money position can be especially large at the major money market banks, which have large corporate depositors and which have the most volatile portions of Treasury [TT&L] deposits.
>
> As their money positions become stringent, banks would tend to raise interest rates on new loans to dealers, often by individual banks to levels that would discourage any borrowing by dealers. Interest rates on renewal loans would also be raised at times to levels that might force borrowers to seek funds elsewhere. Some major money market banks have from time to time simply posted no new loan rate.[4]

The practice of looking to money center banks for residual, albeit high-cost, financing worked well as long as at least some of the banks were in a position to lend. It became more problematic in the second half of the 1960s when, in an effort to rein in inflation, the FOMC squeezed reserves across a wide swath of banks. The Joint Study found that,

> Erosion in the willingness of [money center banks] banks to provide residual financing, even at temporarily very high interest rates, can lead to excessive pressures in the securities market as dealers are forced to liquidate inventories at an overly rapidly pace, or become unwilling – because of uncertainties as to sources of financing – to position securities in order to, say, help in the secondary market distribution of a Treasury financing.[5]

[3] U.S. Treasury and Federal Reserve System (1969, p. 43), stating that "the [Treasury securities] market has come to rely on a relatively few major money market banks for 'last resort'-type financing."

[4] U.S. Treasury and Federal Reserve System (1969, p. 43).

[5] U.S. Treasury and Federal Reserve System (1969, p. 43).

RECOMMENDATIONS OF THE JOINT STUDY STEERING COMMITTEE

The Joint Study steering committee accepted the claim that "the financing problems encountered by dealers under tight money conditions have had adverse effects on dealer performance and on the functioning of the market,"[6] stating that,

> Dealer financing has been a recurrent problem, especially in periods of tight money, although it is recognized that a restrictive monetary policy unavoidably involves pressures on dealer financing as part of the process of achieving monetary restraint. Granted that such pressures are unavoidable, it is also recognized that a persistent financing burden can sap the vitality of the market, reducing the willingness of dealers to make broad markets and hence impairing the usefulness of the market as a vehicle for Treasury financing, for Federal Reserve open market operations, and for adjustments in the private financial markets.[7]

The Committee examined two proposals aimed at mitigating instances of exceptionally costly and barely adequate dealer financing. The first contemplated more liberal access to the discount window for dealer banks and banks that financed nonbank dealers. The second contemplated making repo credit available to nonbank dealers at their own initiative, under standing lines of credit.[8]

The committee recognized that "financing of dealers by the Federal Reserve at dealer initiative ... might create problems for the System open market operations ... if the Trading Desk considered it necessary to offset, through open market operations, the reserves supplied by dealer-initiated loans in order to keep reserve measures in line with System policy objectives." Sterilization of the loans through matched sale-purchase agreements or outright sales "could impose additional financing needs on the dealers ...which, if not met, would tend to generate the same undesirable effects on dealer operations and market performance which it was designed to avoid."[9]

[6] U.S. Government Securities Market Study, "Use of Federal Reserve Resources to Finance Dealers," Policy Issues # 8, July 22, 1968, p. 4.

[7] U.S. Government Securities Market Study, "Use of Federal Reserve Resources to Finance Dealers," Policy Issues # 8, July 22, 1968, p. 9.

[8] U.S. Government Securities Market Study, "Use of Federal Reserve Resources to Finance Dealers," Policy Issues # 8, July 22, 1968, pp. 2–3. The Committee also contemplated (pp. 2–3) making discount window credit available to all dealers pursuant to Section 13(13) of the Federal Reserve Act and making repo credit available to bank as well as nonbank dealers, but did not pursue either possibility in any detail.

[9] U.S. Government Securities Market Study, "Use of Federal Reserve Resources to Finance Dealers," Policy Issues #8, July 22, 1968, p. 5.

However, the steering committee thought the problem "might be minimized or avoided . . . if the reserves created as a result of dealer-initiated loans . . . were considered to represent very temporary accommodation, with the dealers expected to make adjustments to reduce this indebtedness, in somewhat the same sense as banks do when their borrowing from the Federal Reserve is too large or sustained." In particular, "it may be possible to develop a means for dealers to take the initiative in obtaining Federal Reserve financing . . . under conditions whereby the dealers will be under a certain amount of pressure to pay down those special borrowings or repurchase accommodations fairly promptly."[10]

The Committee discussion of how the System might establish lines of credit and set interest rates on dealer loans at the discount window or on repurchase agreements suggests how difficult it would be to ameliorate the problems with dealer finance. The Committee observed that lines of credit "would present a number of problems of equity among dealers and judgments as to the strength and market performance of individual firms":

> A number of criteria, including measures of capital strength and market activity, could be used by the manager [of the System Open Market Account] in developing appropriate lines. The problem would be somewhat similar to that faced by the Treasury, with advice from the Trading Desk, when it sets maximum subscription lines for the primary nonbank dealers in Treasury financing operations. The problems would be difficult, but should not be insurmountable, although there may be some degree of arbitrariness in the final results.[11]

With respect to interest rates, the Committee observed that,

> The interest rate charged on any dealer loan or repurchase agreement at dealer initiative, should bear a realistic relationship to market interest rates – including bill rates, Federal funds rates, and rates on other forms of dealer financing such as corporate repurchase agreements or the daily dealer lending rates of money market banks. This would not mean that the rate on official accommodation would necessarily be as high as certain of those market rates – since this could defeat the whole purpose of providing some assistance to the functioning of the market. But neither should the rate be tied by regulation or tradition to something like the discount rate which may sometimes be out of line with market rates. There should be sufficient flexibility in the official rate so that the Account Manager would not

[10] U.S. Government Securities Market Study, "Use of Federal Reserve Resources to Finance Dealers," Policy Issues # 8, July 22, 1968, pp. 5–6.

[11] U.S. Government Securities Market Study, "Use of Federal Reserve Resources to Finance Dealers," Policy Issues # 8, July 22, 1968, p. 7.

feel constrained from arranging credit assistance merely because to do so would tend to involve the provision of funds at unrealistically low rates.[12]

The Committee suggested alternatively that the problem of dealer finance might be resolved if discount window officers at district Reserve Banks adopted a more "sympathetic" attitude toward requests for advances intended to support dealer activities:

Part of the problem of dealer financing could be solved . . . if money market banks around the country were prepared to take a more constructive role in this area. In turn, that more constructive role might be much more readily undertaken if the money market banks felt that they could turn, with some moderate degree of assurance, to the Federal Reserve's discount window for temporary assistance when maintenance of a dealer lending posture puts them in a tight reserve position. Similarly, a dealer bank that borrows from the Federal Reserve to help maintain its own dealer department position may also merit special consideration at the discount window . . .[13]

The Committee further observed that "loans to dealers tend to be regarded by some [money center] banks as highly flexible investments, to be encouraged when there is a temporary availability of funds and to be sharply discouraged when that availability is lacking" and suggested that,

What might be sought instead is the cultivation of an attitude among the lending banks that there is some responsibility for continuity in dealer lending even if the maintenance of that continuity would oblige the bank to turn to the Federal Reserve's discount window and in turn there would be a need for the Reserve Banks to view the resultant borrowing requirements sympathetically.[14]

The committee concluded by recommending a combination of an expanded repo program for nonbank dealers in "near-emergency periods" and, in more routine periods, a program of "special consideration" for banks seeking to borrow at the discount window to finance nonbank dealers or to fund their own dealer operations.[15]

[12] U.S. Government Securities Market Study, "Use of Federal Reserve Resources to Finance Dealers," Policy Issues #8, July 22, 1968, p. 7.

[13] U.S. Government Securities Market Study, "Use of Federal Reserve Resources to Finance Dealers," Policy Issues # 8, July 22, 1968, p. 8.

[14] U.S. Government Securities Market Study, "Use of Federal Reserve Resources to Finance Dealers," Policy Issues # 8, July 22, 1968, pp. 8–9.

[15] U.S. Government Securities Market Study, "Use of Federal Reserve Resources to Finance Dealers," Policy Issues # 8, July 22, 1968, pp. 10–11.

RESPONSE OF THE FEDERAL OPEN MARKET COMMITTEE

The FOMC discussed the recommendations of the steering committee at its regularly scheduled meeting on October 8, 1968. Committee members pushed back against both the suggestion of a "near-emergency" repo facility and the suggestion of "special consideration" at the discount window. Karl Bopp, the president of the Federal Reserve Bank of Philadelphia, thought there was "considerable question about the appropriateness of implementing the Steering Committee's suggestions [for special consideration at the discount window] under current circumstances, especially at a time when dealer positions were at historically high levels."[16] Governors Sherman Maisel and Andrew Brimmer expressed concern that such "special consideration" was contrary to representations made by the Board of Governors to members of Congress concerning the equitable availability of discount window credit.[17]

Holmes tried to smooth over the reactions of Committee members by claiming that the recommendations did not actually contemplate any real change in policy and that "the Steering Committee was addressing itself mainly to a practical problem of a type that sometimes arose, rather than to a basic matter of policy."

> For example, if the reserve position of a major bank suddenly tightened in the middle of a Treasury financing, the bank might borrow at the discount window instead of sharply cutting back its loans to dealers. However, not all large banks regarded borrowing for that purpose as appropriate and the attitudes of System discount officers toward such borrowing were not necessarily uniform. The Steering Committee felt it would be helpful to have an official statement to the effect that it was appropriate on occasion for banks performing a residual dealer lending function to engage in limited short-term borrowing at the discount window. No real policy change would be involved in such a statement.
>
> Similarly, on occasion when dealer financing was unavailable elsewhere and dealer financing costs were under substantial upward pressure, the Desk had found it necessary to make repurchase agreements with the dealers in order to carry out the Committee's instructions concerning money market conditions. In his judgment, to make RP's at the dealers' initiative under near-emergency conditions would not involve a fundamental change.[18]

In spite of Holmes's efforts, it was clear that the FOMC was not inclined to promulgate any sort of "official statement" that might be interpreted as

[16] Minutes of the Federal Open Market Committee, October 8, 1968, p. 86.
[17] Minutes of the Federal Open Market Committee, October 8, 1968, pp. 86–88.
[18] Minutes of the Federal Open Market Committee, October 8, 1968, p. 88.

giving dealers preferential access to System credit. Chairman Martin ended the discussion by concurring with a staff suggestion that the published report of the Joint Study include a simple statement that "some official assistance in dealer financing can help to assure the satisfactory performance of the market without impeding the market's role in transmitting monetary policy," as well as an indication that the official assistance "might involve flexible use of the discount window and of RP's," but that the report should not describe "the manner or circumstances in which such assistance would be provided."[19] Consistent with Martin's decision, the final report of the Joint Study did no more than note the prospective utility of System assistance to dealer financing.[20]

[19] Minutes of the Federal Open Market Committee, October 8, 1968, p. 89.

[20] U.S. Treasury and Federal Reserve System (1969, p. 44).

25

The Government Securities Clearing Arrangement

In the second half of the 1960s, the Federal Reserve Bank of New York sponsored the development of a novel architecture for settling transactions in US Treasury securities. The Government Securities Clearing Arrangement contemplated the substantial elimination of trade-by-trade bilateral settlement in favor of a multi-lateral netting process. The Bank's sponsorship reflected the importance of a liquid Treasury market to the Federal Reserve System and the growing intertwining of the System and the market.[1]

SETTLING TRANSACTIONS IN TREASURY SECURITIES BEFORE 1965

Prior to 1968, marketable Treasury securities came in two forms: bearer and registered. Both were paper instruments, so-called "definitive" securities, inscribed with the government's promise of future payments. Notes and bonds came in both forms and could be converted from one to the other; bills and certificates were issued only in bearer form.

A Treasury bill promised to pay a specified sum of money on a single specified future date. When the payment date of a bill drew near, a holder would send the bill through the banking system for collection.

Certificates, bearer notes, and bearer bonds consisted of a "corpus" reciting the government's promise to pay interest periodically and principal at maturity and a series of detachable coupons, each of which was a

[1] The Joint Study did not play a decisive role in the evolution of either the Government Securities Clearing Arrangement or the book-entry system described in chapter 27, but the steering committee was kept abreast of progress in both. Davis (1966) was prepared as a staff study. See also Davis and Hoey (1973).

claim to a specified interest payment on a specified future date. To obtain an interest payment, an investor detached the appropriate coupon and sent it for collection. When the security matured the investor asserted his or her claim to the principal payment by sending the corpus for collection. Since the government's promises to pay on a bearer security ran to whoever held the security, that is, to the *bearer*, a holder could transfer ownership simply by delivering the instrument.

A note or bond was said to be *registered* if the government's promise to pay principal and interest ran to a person whose name and address were recorded with the Treasury Department. There was an engraved instrument associated with a registered security, on the face of which the name of the owner appeared, but the instrument served primarily as a device for effecting a change in ownership. An investor who wanted to convey a registered security to a new owner inscribed the re-registration instructions on the back of the instrument and sent it to the Treasury. Upon receipt, the Treasury would change its records and issue a new instrument to the new owner. The Treasury sent interest checks to owners of registered notes and bonds on its own initiative. It could have done the same with principal payments, but instead required tender at maturity as a way of recovering matured securities.

Active traders, and investors facing a likely need to sell before maturity, preferred bearer instruments for the lower cost and greater convenience of settling purchases and sales. Institutional investors and securities dealers commonly employed banks in New York, Chicago, and other money centers to act as custodians for their bearer securities. Seven large New York banks, including Bankers Trust Co., Chase Manhattan Bank, Chemical Bank New York Trust Co., First National City Bank, Irving Trust Co., Manufactures Hanover Trust Co., and Morgan Guaranty Trust Co., were particularly important custodians.

Intracity Settlements

As illustrated in Exhibit 25.1, if a seller's custodial bank and a buyer's custodial bank were located in the same city, settlement with a bearer security was straightforward. The first step was for the seller to authorize delivery to the buyer against payment and for the buyer to authorize payment to the seller against receipt of the securities.

Following receipt of the seller's authorization, the seller's bank would withdraw the specified bearer securities from the seller's custodial account, package the securities, and send them by messenger to the buyer's bank,

Exhibit 25.1 Settlement of a Transaction When the Buyer's Custodial Bank and the Seller's Custodial Bank are in the Same City. Heavy line indicates physical movement of bearer securities by messenger.

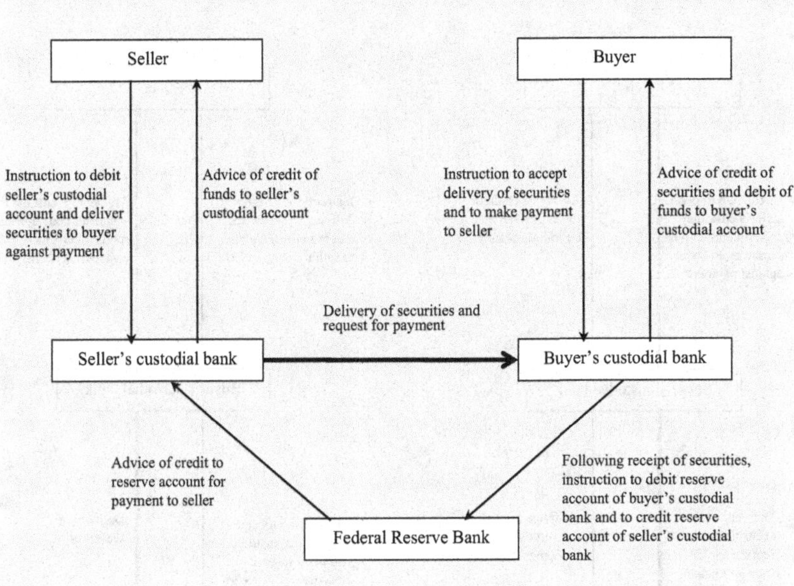

along with an advice that the securities were for the buyer's account and a request for payment.

The buyer's bank would verify that the securities were of the type and quantity specified by the buyer and that the requested payment was for the authorized amount.[2] The bank would then place the securities in the buyer's custodial account and make payment to the seller's bank (most commonly by a transfer of funds from its reserve account to the reserve account of the seller's bank), advising the seller's bank that the funds were for the seller's account. The last step would be for the seller's bank to credit the seller's account with the payment and for the buyer's bank to debit the buyer's account.

[2] In the event of a mismatch, the buyer's bank would "DK" the delivery, returning the securities with a statement that it "did not know" the proposed terms of settlement.

Exhibit 25.2 Settlement of a Transaction When the Buyer's Custodial Bank and the Seller's Custodial Bank are in Different Cities. Heavy lines indicate physical movement of bearer securities by messenger; dashed line indicates movement of virtual securities over Federal Reserve private wire system.

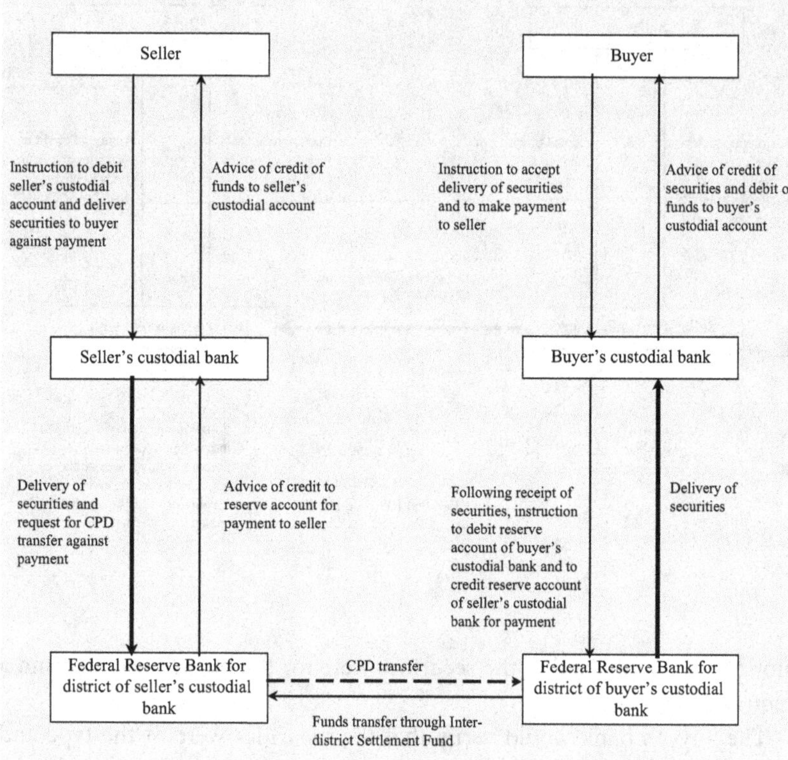

CPD Settlement

Settlement was more complicated if, as in Exhibit 25.2, the custodial banks were in different cities. Upon receipt of the seller's authorization, the seller's bank would withdraw the specified bearer securities from the seller's account, package the securities, and transport them to the local Federal Reserve Bank, requesting that the securities be transmitted to the Federal Reserve Bank serving the buyer's bank, for delivery to the buyer's

Box 25.1 Federal Reserve Banks as Fiscal Agents of the United States

Prior to the establishment of the Federal Reserve System, the US Treasury received, carried, and dispersed funds through a network of subtreasuries and national bank depositories. Section 15 of the Federal Reserve Act provided an alternative: that government cash balances "may, upon direction of the Secretary of the Treasury, be deposited in Federal reserve banks, which banks, when required by the Secretary of the Treasury, shall act as fiscal agents of the United States; and the revenues of the Government or any part thereof may be deposited in such banks, and disbursements may be made by checks drawn against such deposits."

On November 23, 1915, Treasury Secretary William McAdoo appointed the Reserve Banks as government depositories and fiscal agents and authorized them to accept deposits of public funds, "as well as [to perform] any other services incident to or growing out of the duties and responsibilities of fiscal agents."[1]

Following McAdoo's action, Federal Reserve Banks became actively involved in processing subscriptions to Treasury offerings, administering the issuance of new securities, making interest payments, redeeming maturing securities, and effecting denominational exchanges. They also held securities pledged to the Treasury as collateral against deposits of public funds. In 1921, the Banks began to transfer Treasury certificates and notes by wire. They extended the service to bills in 1930 and bonds in 1948.[2]

1 "Federal Reserve Banks as Fiscal Agents," *Federal Reserve Bulletin*, December 1915, p. 395; and 1916 Treasury Annual Report, p. 6.

2 Smith (1956, pp. 86–92).

bank against payment along with an advice that the securities were for the buyer's account.

The former Reserve Bank would add the securities that it received from the seller's bank to the inventory of *unissued* Treasury securities that it maintained as a fiscal agent of the Treasury and instruct (by wire) the latter Reserve Bank to deliver identical securities, against payment, to the buyer's bank. (Box 25.1 describes the role of Federal Reserve Banks as fiscal agents of the United States; Box 25.2 describes the Federal Reserve's private wire system.) Upon receipt of the instructions the latter Reserve Bank would withdraw bearer securities of the specified type and quantity from *its* fiscal agency inventory and advise the buyer's bank that the securities were available for pick-up against payment. Interdistrict wire transfers of Treasury securities were commonly known as "CPD transfers" because, in earlier decades, the Commissioner of Public Debt had to approve each individual transfer.[3]

3 Smith (1956, p. 93).

Box 25.2 The Federal Reserve Private Wire System.

The Federal Reserve private wire system was inaugurated on June 7, 1918, to facilitate telegraphic communication among the twelve Reserve Banks, the Federal Reserve Board, and the Department of the Treasury. The new system accommodated the expansion in System messages that followed the initiation of Federal Reserve clearing and collection of commercial bank checks in mid-1915 and the growth in Treasury financing operations during World War I. (System messages had previously been sent by commercial telegraph.) Message volume was expected to increase further in July 1918, when the frequency of interdistrict settlements was set to change from weekly to daily.[1]

The private wire system was upgraded several times as a result of technological developments and growth in message volume. A scarcity of telegraph operators in the late 1920s led to the introduction of teletype machines and the replacement of telegraphers with less expensive typists.[2] In July 1953, the system underwent a major upgrade when the manual teletype system was replaced with a perforated tape system configured around a semi-automatic switching center in Richmond, Virginia.[3] The paper tape system lasted until 1970, when continued growth in the volume of money and securities transfers prompted the Fed to upgrade again, this time to a fully automatic computer-based system built around a switching center in Culpepper, Virginia.[4] In early 1971, the Federal Reserve Bank of New York installed a new computer, the Sigma-5, to interface with the Culpepper switch and to maintain the cash and securities accounts of member banks in the Second District.[5]

[1] Smith (1956, pp. 11–24).
[2] Smith (1956, pp. 32–35).
[3] Smith (1956, pp. 44–47), Federal Reserve Bank of Richmond (1960), and Vollkommer (1970, pp. 23–25).
[4] Vollkommer (1970, pp. 26–28), Hoey and Vollkommer (1971, pp. 23–24), and Federal Reserve System (1975).
[5] Federal Reserve Bank of New York (March 1972, April 1972, and 1984).

Upon receipt of notice from its Reserve Bank, the buyer's bank would verify that the securities were of the type and quantity specified by the buyer and that the requested payment was for the authorized amount.[4] It would then pick up the securities, make payment by authorizing a debit to its reserve account, debit the buyer's account for the payment, and place the securities in the buyer's custodial account. The Reserve Bank serving the buyer's bank would advise the Reserve Bank serving the seller's bank to

[4] In the event of a mismatch, the buyer's bank would "DK" the delivery. Its Reserve Bank would then replace the securities in its fiscal agency inventory and wire the Reserve Bank serving the seller's bank to return identical securities to the seller's bank along with an advice that the putative buyer "did not know" the proposed terms of the settlement.

credit the reserve account of the seller's bank with the payment.[5] The seller's bank would, in turn, credit the seller's account.

ORIGINS OF THE CLEARING ARRANGEMENT

Prior to 1965, settling a transaction in Treasury securities was time consuming – a minimum of two hours from start to finish was the norm – and labor-intensive – bearer securities had to be withdrawn from the seller's inventory, counted, transported, counted again, and placed in the buyer's inventory, a process that had to be completed twice in the case of an interdistrict settlement. There was an ever-present risk of clerical error and a nontrivial risk of loss or theft. Officials at the Federal Reserve Bank of New York had good reason to contemplate alternative settlement structures, particularly structures that might reduce the cost of CPD settlements in which the Bank played a prominent role.[6]

A white paper issued by the Bank in early 1965 noted that "one of the more promising suggestions ... contemplates the establishment of a clearing arrangement for Government securities, which arrangement would involve most of the larger New York City member banks, and would be operated by the Federal Reserve Bank." As the white paper described it,

> Such an arrangement would largely eliminate the need for the costly and time-consuming operations now being performed ... in counting, examining, and making physical delivery of securities incident to their withdrawal from one institution and deposit in another.
>
> Under the proposed clearing arrangement, Government securities to be transferred by wire to out-of-district points would not be physically delivered to us by the initiating bank but would be offset against securities of the same issue owed by this Bank in fulfillment of incoming transfers, with settlement of the net balances being made at a stated time in the afternoon of each day.[7]

The clearing arrangement contemplated in the white paper was relatively limited. During each business day the New York Bank would record, on an issue-by-issue basis, each bank's requests to deliver securities to

[5] The movement of reserve balances between the two Federal Reserve Banks was settled through the Interdistrict Settlement Fund.

[6] Federal Reserve Bank of New York (1965, p. 1), stating that "the Federal Reserve Bank of New York has from time to time considered various suggestions aimed at reducing the volume of United States Government securities handled by this Bank in connection with telegraphic transfer ... transactions. The rate of activity in these transactions frequently entails more than 1,500 separate receipts and deliveries of securities by us in a single day."

[7] Federal Reserve Bank of New York (1965, p. 1).

other Federal Reserve Banks and its receipt of securities from other Reserve Banks.[8] "Prior to the established settlement hour the [Bank] would inform each participating bank of the amounts of each issue of securities owing to or from such participant ... Preliminary information would be communicated to the participating banks by telephone at approximately 3:00 p.m., with final figures available at 3:15 p.m. Settlement would be made at 3:45 p.m. the same day at the Federal Reserve Bank, which would deliver or receive the net amounts of each security issue owing to or from the various participating banks."[9] The white paper suggested that the arrangement "would eliminate up to 80 per cent of the physical deliveries presently being made by or to this Bank in connection with telegraphic transfers of Government securities" and noted that the underlying concept could go much further:

> In addition to the normal telegraphic transactions, it would appear practicable to include within the clearing arrangement any Government securities to be transferred between two of the participating member banks, whether as a result of 'secondary' transfers arising out of incoming [CPD] transfers, or as original transactions negotiated between the banks concerned or their [customers].[10]

The clearing arrangement did not contemplate the complete elimination of definitive securities but rather sought to limit deliveries to the New York Reserve Bank associated with outbound CPD transfers to other Reserve Banks and to limit deliveries by the Bank engendered by inbound CPD transfers. The difference remained to be settled with bearer securities at the end of the day. Bearer securities would continue to be used in bilateral intracity settlements.

Two ancillary features of the proposed clearing arrangement illustrate the difficulties that could arise in the course of introducing a net settlement scheme into a market that continued to settle a large volume of transactions on a trade-by-trade basis with bearer securities. The white paper recognized that dealers who bought securities from sellers using geographically remote custodial banks might need bearer securities during the day

8 Federal Reserve Bank of New York (1965, p. 2), stating that "the Federal Reserve Bank of New York would maintain daily securities clearing accounts, by issues, for each participating bank and, in lieu of receiving or delivering securities for each individual transaction, would debit or credit the appropriate securities accounts of the banks concerned with the amounts and issues of all Government securities dispatched or received for its account that day."

9 Federal Reserve Bank of New York (1965, pp. 2–3 and 5).

10 Federal Reserve Bank of New York (1965, p. 2).

to deliver to buyers using local custodial banks. Thus, the paper proposed that "whenever it became necessary to do so, any New York City bank participating in the clearing arrangement would have the privilege of requesting the delivery of actual [bearer] securities . . . in fulfillment of a transfer order received by us for account of that bank."[11]

The white paper also recognized that a dealer who bought securities from a seller using a local custodial bank and sold them to a buyer using a remote custodial bank for settlement on the same day might fail to receive the securities it had purchased and be unable to meet its settlement obligation to the New York Reserve Bank at the end of the day. The paper proposed that "in the event of nondelivery of certain securities to us at the settlement hour, an equivalent sum [of money] owing to the . . . bank on account of the related transfer transactions would not be credited to that bank's reserve account but would be withheld pending such settlement."[12]

Securing the approval of the Treasury Department was a key hurdle in implementing the clearing arrangement. Historically, a Reserve Bank could not undertake an outbound CPD transfer of Treasury securities without first taking in bearer securities from the bank requesting the transfer, thereby ensuring that there would never be more Treasury securities outstanding than what the Treasury had issued. The proposed clearing arrangement would breach that safeguard by allowing participating banks to request CPD transfers without simultaneously tendering bearer securities. In addition, as two Bank officials later explained,

> The ability to implement the clearing arrangement concept hinged on obtaining approval from the Treasury Department to employ the stock of unissued U.S. Government securities, held at the Federal Reserve Bank of New York for various fiscal purposes, to effect the end-of-day settlements. This procedure was essential to the efficient conduct of the clearing concept so that securities 'due to' participants at the settlement could be paid out without awaiting receipt of the same issue 'due from' other participants.[13]

In late February 1965, Harold Bilby, a senior officer of the New York Fed, sent the Bank's white paper to John Carlock, the Fiscal Assistant Secretary of the Treasury, and requested Carlock's thoughts on the merits of the proposed arrangement. Bilby noted that Morgan Guaranty Trust was prepared to enter into a pilot program designed to explore "the mechanical and other aspects of the clearing arrangement" but that New

[11] Federal Reserve Bank of New York (1965, p. 3).
[12] Federal Reserve Bank of New York (1965, p. 3).
[13] Hoey and Vollkommer (1971, p. 24).

York Bank officials hesitated "until we were assured that the necessary changes ... would be practicable from the point of view of the Treasury Department."[14] Carlock replied that he had no objection to the pilot study and had "no reason to believe the entire clearing arrangement operation [would] offer any significant problems from the viewpoint of the Department."[15]

THE PILOT PROGRAM

Having secured the approval of Treasury officials, the New York Fed proceeded with the pilot program. On July 19, 1965, the Bank announced that it had begun testing "a clearing system to simplify telegraphic transfers of U.S. Government securities to and from Morgan Guaranty Trust Company."[16] Irving Trust joined the pilot program a month later.

After the pilot program had been running successfully for about a year, Bank officials felt confident enough to begin including some intracity transfers. In August 1966, the Bank announced a facility for "re-directing" inbound CPD transfers from the original recipient to another participating bank.[17] This was an important step because it eliminated physical deliveries beyond the initial inbound transfer. The cost savings made possible by re-directs induced the five remaining large New York clearing banks to join the pilot program before mid-1967.[18]

INTRACITY TRANSFERS

The next step in the evolution of the clearing arrangement was providing for a wider range of intracity transfers. A revised agreement, approved by the seven participating banks in early August 1967,[19] replaced redirected

14 Letter dated February 23, 1965, from Harold Bilby, Vice President, Federal Reserve Bank of New York, to John Carlock, Fiscal Assistant Secretary of the Treasury.

15 Letter dated April 8, 1965, from John Carlock to Harold Bilby. Hoey and Vollkommer (1971, pp. 24) state that "the Treasury concurred in the view that the new procedure promised benefits to all concerned."

16 Federal Reserve Bank of New York press release, July 19, 1965.

17 Government Securities Clearing Arrangement Participant Memo no. 2, August 4, 1966.

18 Government Securities Clearing Arrangement Participant Memo no. 4, November 14, 1966; Participant Memo no. 6, March 22, 1966; and Participant Memo no. 8, April 26, 1967.

19 Clearing Agreement Providing for Transfers of U.S. Government and U.S. Agency Securities, August 4, 1967. Three smaller banks (Bank of New York, Marine Midland Grace Trust Co., and United States Trust Co.) also signed the August 1967 clearing

transfers with a new facility that allowed a participating bank to order ab initio transfers of Treasury securities to other participating banks as well as CPD transfers. To keep message traffic within the capacity of a still largely manual system, intracity transfers were limited to not less than $3 million par value. The limit was lowered as participants became more familiar with the transfers and finally eliminated, in June 1971, following the introduction of automated accounting and message switching equipment.[20]

The August 1967 agreement provided that intracity transfers could not be requested after 2:30 p.m., that the New York Reserve Bank would advise participants of the net balances in their clearing accounts at about 3:00 p.m., and that settlement with bearer securities would follow at 3:30 p.m. at the Bank. In the event of a settlement fail,

(1) the New York Reserve Bank could withhold funds from the participating bank's reserve account in an amount equal to the value of the securities that the Bank failed to receive,
(2) the Reserve Bank could "buy in" the failed securities, and
(3) any remaining loss to the Reserve Bank would be made good by the other banks participating in the agreement.

BALANCING THE DEMANDS OF COMPETING SETTLEMENT SYSTEMS

Beginning in August 1967, New York clearing banks could settle transactions in Treasury securities in either of two ways: through the net

agreement but remained "inactive" for the time being. Bank of New York became an active participant in December 1967 (Government Securities Clearing Agreement Participant Memo no. 18, December 12, 1967), Marine Midland in June 1970 (Participant Memo no. 33, June 26, 1970), and United States Trust Co. in June 1971 (Participant Memo no. 38, June 17, 1971). Franklin National Bank joined as an active participant in July 1969 (Participant Memo no. 32, July 18, 1969), and National Bank of North America became an active participant in November 1971 (Participant Memo no. 40, November 8, 1971). Franklin was replaced by European-American Bank and Trust Co. in October 1974 (Amendment to Revised Clearing Agreement Providing for Transfers of U.S. Government and U.S. Agency Securities, October 30, 1974).

20 See Government Securities Clearing Arrangement Participant Memo no. 13, August 16, 1967 (reducing the minimum to $1 million); Participant Memo no. 21, March 27, 1968 (reducing the minimum to $500 thousand); Revised Clearing Agreement Providing for Transfers of U.S. Government and U.S. Agency Securities, November 20, 1968 (reducing the minimum to $250 thousand); Participant Memo no. 35, February 19, 1971 (reducing the minimum to $100 thousand); and Participant Memo no. 38, June 17, 1971 (eliminating the minimum following the introduction of the Sigma-5 computer at the New York Reserve Bank).

settlement system of the Government Securities Clearing Arrangement or bilaterally with bearer securities. Unsurprisingly, there were some frictions between the two systems.

The August 1967 clearing agreement provided that the recipient of an inbound CPD transfer could obtain intraday settlement of the transfer with bearer securities, but that similar intraday settlement of an inbound intracity transfer was not available. (In the former case Federal Reserve officials already had definitive securities in hand (from the out-of-city transferor), whereas in the latter case the transferor may not have had appropriate securities either in its possession or in its clearing account at the time of the request.) If the recipient of an intracity transfer wanted bearer securities, it had to "reverse" the transfer and request "street" delivery by the transferor.[21]

In an effort to enhance the availability of bearer securities without simultaneously draining the clearing arrangement, the clearing agreement was revised in February 1968 to allow intraday settlement of "relayed" intracity transfers.[22] (A relayed intracity transfer was similar to a redirect: an intracity transfer that matched, with respect to the type and quantity of securities, a transfer received by the transferor earlier in the same day – either as a CPD transfer or as an intracity transfer from another bank.) Requests for intraday settlement of relayed intracity transfers were satisfied from the New York Reserve Bank's fiscal agency stock of unissued Treasury securities and thus added to the supply of immediately available bearer securities.

The February 1968 revision of the clearing agreement provided that a request for intraday settlement of a relayed intracity transfer had to be received by the New York Reserve Bank before 1 p.m. Three months later, the Bank changed the threshold to 1:45 p.m. to further increase the availability of definitive securities.[23] Additionally, to limit the drain of securities from the clearing accounts of participating banks earlier in the

[21] The August 1967 agreement did not contain any specific provision for reversing intracity transfers but a contemporaneous memo to participants in the clearing arrangement did refer to such reversals and provided detailed instructions for effecting reversals. Government Securities Clearing Arrangement Participant Memo no. 12, August 1, 1967. Specific contractual provision for reversals first appeared in late 1968. See paragraph 20 of Revised Clearing Agreement for Transfers of U.S. Government and U.S. Agency Securities, November 20, 1968.

[22] Government Securities Clearing Arrangement Participant Memo no. 20, February 6, 1968.

[23] Government Securities Clearing Arrangement Participant Memo no. 23, May 23, 1968.

day, the Bank stipulated that a transferee could not reverse a relayed intracity transfer before 1:45 p.m. (The Bank did not limit participants' rights to reverse other intracity transfers.) The restriction on reversals of relayed transfers served to reduce the incidence of participants accessing bearer securities by reversing a relayed transaction, which commonly precipitated a chain of reversals, and requests for bearer securities, back along the relay chain to its origin.

In March 1969 the Bank undertook a two-day test of a prohibition on *all* reversals of intracity transfers before 11:00 a.m.[24] In early April it initiated a second test, with the time limit set later, to 11:30 a.m.[25] The prohibition was subsequently made permanent and the time limit moved first to 12:30 p.m. and then to 1:45 p.m.[26] In February 1971 the participating banks agreed to eliminate the right of a transferee to reverse *any* intracity transfer.[27]

REMARKS

The Government Securities Clearing Arrangement introduced significant efficiencies into the settlement process for US Treasury securities by substituting a net settlement scheme for trade-by-trade settlement. However, full realization of the benefits of the scheme was blocked by the retention of end-of-day settlement of clearing account balances with bearer securities. Further economies depended on replacing those securities with book-entry securities.

[24] Government Securities Clearing Arrangement Participant Memo no. 29, March 11, 1969.
[25] Government Securities Clearing Arrangement Participant Memo no. 30, April 1, 1969.
[26] Government Securities Clearing Arrangement Participant Memo no. 32, July 18, 1969; and Participant Memo no. 33, June 26, 1970.
[27] Government Securities Clearing Arrangement Participant Memo no. 35, February 19, 1971.

26

Securities Lending

Settlement of a transaction in Treasury securities – regardless of whether it is an outright sale and purchase, or a repurchase agreement, or a matched sale-purchase agreement – is initiated by the seller in return for payment. (See, for example, the discussion of Exhibits 25.1 and 25.2 in the preceding chapter.) Absent a tender of securities, the buyer has no obligation to make payment. A seller who fails to tender a security on a timely basis foregoes payment until it completes delivery, thereby losing the time value of the proceeds – conventionally computed with an overnight interest rate.[1]

Dealers borrow Treasury securities to avoid failing on settlement commitments to buyers; more particularly, to avoid losing the time value of the proceeds due. A dealer has an economic incentive to borrow securities to make a delivery as long as the cost of borrowing is less than the overnight rate. In the 1950s and 1960s, dealers could borrow Treasury securities by pledging other securities of comparable value and paying the lender a fee of ½ percent per annum.[2]

A dealer can fail on a delivery commitment for either of two reasons. First, securities purchased earlier and scheduled for redelivery might fail to arrive. Borrowed securities can bridge the temporal gap between the settlement of the sale and the ultimate receipt of the earlier purchase. Second, a dealer can fail on a delivery commitment if it sells securities that it does not own and has not contracted to buy, i.e., if it sells short. Short sales can occur in the course of satisfying a customer's demand for a particular security, when a dealer is hedging the risk of price fluctuations

[1] Since 2009 there is also the possibility of an added "fails charge." See Garbade, Keane, Logan, Stokes, and Wolgemuth (2010).

[2] U.S. Treasury and Federal Reserve System (1959, p. 23) and Federal Reserve Bank of New York (1962).

on a similar security held long, or when a dealer anticipates a rise in interest rates. In all three cases the dealer can avoid failing by "financing" – for days, weeks, and sometimes even months – its short position with borrowed securities.

THE INPETUS FOR A FEDERAL RESERVE SECURITIES LENDING PROGRAM

Commercial banks held a significant fraction of all marketable Treasury debt at the time of the Accord. New York and Chicago-based dealers could almost always borrow what they needed from banks in the two cities. However, banks gradually reduced their Treasury investments as the decade wore on and pension funds, trusts, and state and local governments began to take their place.[3] The rising investor classes commonly lacked authority to lend securities and dealers began to experience difficulty satisfying their borrowing requirements. Three studies took note of the problem.

The 1959–60 Treasury-Federal Reserve Study of the Government Securities Market observed that short sales were "essential to the effective maintenance of continuous markets" but had been "seriously hampered by the relatively limited facilities to borrow securities." Without short selling, arbitrage and hedging were problematic.[4]

A second study of the government securities market, undertaken (at the request of the Joint Economic Committee), by Allan Meltzer and Gert von der Linde, remarked similarly that "the absence of an ability to borrow [securities] reduces the opportunities for dealers to arbitrage or to supply securities to the market."[5] Both studies suggested that market functioning would improve if securities were more readily available.

In a 1962 study, the Federal Reserve Bank of New York examined "whether System lending [from the System Open Market Account] would be helpful in improving the market [for Treasury securities] and whether and how the System should engage in lending activities."[6] The study noted that opportunities for dealers to borrow securities had not improved since the late 1950s and that while the problem was more significant for longer-term securities – because "insurance companies, pension funds and other large holders of intermediate and longer term Government securities will

[3] Meltzer and von der Linde (1960, p. 95).
[4] U.S. Treasury and Federal Reserve System (1959, pp. 23–24).
[5] Meltzer and von der Linde (1960, p. 95). [6] Federal Reserve Bank of New York (1962).

generally not lend . . . to dealers" – it was not unknown in the front end of the market.

With respect to Treasury bills, the New York bank study observed that dealers "buy and sell bills quite frequently without excessive concern over the availability of the actual bills to make delivery. They . . . count on borrowing the bills to make delivery, which is ordinarily quite feasible. . . . The normally small price spreads and fluctuations in Treasury bills tend to minimize the risks in this procedure and bills ordinarily can be repurchased within a reasonable time . . . Partly for this reason, trading in the bill market is ordinarily quite broad and flexible."

The study reported that, further out the yield curve, "dealers are often called upon to sell issues they do not own, and are not sure they can buy quickly." In addition to outright sales, the study noted the importance of swaps, simultaneous sales and purchases "undertaken by commercial banks to shorten or lengthen the maturities of their investment portfolios . . . Such 'swaps' are fairly continuous in the market and can result in chains of related transactions . . . This type of trading adds greatly to the breadth and fluidity of the market. In many instances the ability to execute these 'swaps' will depend on [the dealer] making the sale on a short basis, borrowing the securities to make delivery."

The study concluded that "from the standpoint of improving market performance, System ability to lend when the demand arises should be beneficial." The study recognized that lending securities would be a novel activity for Federal Reserve Banks and recommended only a limited program. In particular, the study suggested:

- lending at a fee "somewhat higher" than the conventional ½ percent per annum, to limit the System's role to that of lender of last resort;
- limits on the volume of lending, based on "the size of [an] issue, the amount and character of trading normally taking place in the issue, and the type of ownership of the issue"; and
- a limit on the duration of a loan, to avoid encouraging "'sloppy' market practices."

THE JOINT STUDY PROPOSAL

In 1967 the Joint Study began to examine the possibility of System lending of government securities. The topic was scrutinized first in a Reserve Bank staff study, then by the Joint Study steering committee, and finally by the FOMC.

The Staff Study

A 1967 staff study by the Federal Reserve Bank of New York suggested that securities lending "would improve the functioning of the Government securities market and, accordingly, could be expected to facilitate the [execution] of open market operations and to aid the System in achieving the objectives of monetary policy."[7]

The study looked at two types of lending:

1. lending to enable a dealer to avoid a redelivery fail, where the dealer sold, but was unable to deliver, securities purchased from another customer because that customer failed to deliver the securities in a timely fashion; and
2. lending to enable a dealer to settle a short sale.[8]

The study recommended implementation of the first type of lending "as soon as feasible" and postponing the second type pending an assessment of the initial program.

With respect to loans to avoid redelivery fails, the staff study followed the suggestion of the 1962 New York Reserve Bank study and recommended a loan fee of ⅝ percent per annum, as well as a series of additional restrictions:

- A dealer would have to certify that (a) it was unable to deliver securities on a previously negotiated sale, (b) the securities had not been sold short, and (c) it could not borrow the securities elsewhere.
- Loans would be for three business days and would be renewed only in unusual circumstances.
- Loans would be limited to $5 million par value per security per dealer, with caps of $25 million for total loans to a single dealer and $200 million for total loans to all dealers.

Lending to avoid redelivery fails was little more than good market hygiene, a bilaterally negotiated borrowing of securities against a pledge of other securities being preferable to a unilateral fail to deliver. Lending to facilitate short sales was an entirely different matter. The staff study distinguished three types of short sales:

[7] Federal Reserve Bank of New York (1967).

[8] The study also examined lending to large New York clearing banks to facilitate end-of-day settlements in the Government Securities Clearing Arrangement.

1. hedged short sales in connection with swap transactions,
2. unhedged short sales to accommodate customers, and
3. unhedged short sales in anticipation of a rise in interest rates.

The study suggested that hedged short sales did not involve "any substantial market or speculative risk," that unhedged short sales executed to satisfy customer demands were beneficial, albeit speculative, because they allowed dealers to "accommodate customers within reasonable price ranges," but that it did not "appear prudent for the System . . . to assist the market in establishing" short positions taken purely for speculative reasons.

Discussion by the Steering Committee

The Joint Study steering committee met on July 5, 1967, to discuss the recommendations of the staff study.[9] There was no resistance to the idea of lending to mitigate redelivery fails – in fact, there was interest in expanding the quantities of securities that could be lent – but there was also no enthusiasm for lending to facilitate short sales. Chairman Martin requested a revised proposal with more relaxed loan limits.

A year later, on July 16, 1968, the steering committee met to consider a revised staff proposal. A supplementary memo from Howard Hackley, the general counsel to the FOMC and Board of Governors, questioned whether the FOMC was authorized to lend securities from the System Open Market Account.[10]

Hackley began by noting that Federal Reserve Banks did not have express statutory authority to lend securities, so the question was whether such loans fell within the ambit of the "incidental powers" of a Reserve Bank.[11] In his opinion, the Banks could exercise "only such incidental powers as were *necessary* or *required* for the accomplishment of their

[9] Minutes of the Steering Committee for the Joint Treasury-Federal Reserve Study of the U.S. Government Securities Market, July 5, 1967, pp. 3–6.

[10] Memo from Mr. Hackley to Federal Open Market Committee, "Legality of Plan for Lending of Government Securities by Federal Reserve Banks," July 10, 1968. See also draft memo from Thomas Sloane, Assistant General Counsel, Federal Reserve Bank of New York "Authority of Federal Reserve Banks to 'Lend' Government Securities," May 6, 1968.

[11] Section 4 of the Federal Reserve Act authorizes Federal Reserve Banks to exercise "all powers specifically granted by the provisions of this Act and such *incidental powers* as shall be necessary to carry on the business of banking within the limitations prescribed by this Act." Emphasis added.

specifically granted powers" and that "mere desirability or convenience did not provide sufficient grounds for assuming the existence of such a power."[12] Whether securities lending was "necessary" or "required" was a question of fact for the FOMC to decide.[13] Treasury Secretary Fowler observed that "a question of fact seemed to be the main issue" and suggested that the issue "be resolved in favor of initiating System loans of securities."[14]

In the wake of Fowler's expression of support, Martin proposed that the committee "recommend loans of securities along the lines outlined." The other members of the committee concurred, and the matter moved to the FOMC.[15]

The FOMC Response

Following the July 1968 meeting of the Joint Study steering committee, Holmes prepared a decision memo for the FOMC that recommended lending to enable dealers to avoid redelivery fails. Holmes suggested limiting loans to $50 million per Treasury bill per dealer and $10 million per note or bond per dealer and capping total loans to a single dealer at $75 million. He suggested three business day loans and a loan fee of ⅝ percent per annum. Dealers would be required to certify that they were not seeking to borrow securities that they had sold short and that the securities could not be borrowed elsewhere.[16]

The FOMC began discussing the matter of securities lending at its August 13, 1968, meeting.[17] Discussion quickly focused on Hackley's contention that the Committee could authorize such lending only if it was required for the exercise of the System's specifically enumerated powers.

Holmes declined to address the legal question but noted that the steering committee had "unanimously concluded that the legal questions were not sufficiently serious to make undesirable [FOMC] consideration of the proposal on its merits." Hackley responded that "it was quite obvious that

[12] Minutes of the Steering Committee for the Joint Treasury-Federal Reserve Study of the U.S. Government Securities Market, July 16, 1968, p. 12. Emphasis in the original.

[13] Minutes of the Federal Open Market Committee, July 16, 1968, p. 14.

[14] Minutes of the Federal Open Market Committee, July 16, 1968, pp. 16 and 18.

[15] Minutes of the Federal Open Market Committee, July 16, 1968, p. 18.

[16] Memo from Alan Holmes to Federal Open Market Committee, "System Lending of U.S. Government Securities," August 6, 1968.

[17] Minutes of the Federal Open Market Committee, August 13, 1968, pp. 95–99.

the legal questions were debatable" and that "it did not seem at all clear to him that [lending securities] was reasonably necessary" for the conduct of open market operations.

Committee members expressed a variety of reactions to Hackley's position. Some agreed, some disagreed, some wanted to discuss the matter further, and some wanted to seek express authority from Congress. The committee agreed to discuss the matter further at a later date.

The FOMC revisited the issue of securities lending on September 10, 1968.[18] Holmes was absent, and Peter Sternlight represented the management of the Open Market Account. Discussion once again focused on the Committee's authority to authorize loans from the Account. Governor Andrew Brimmer observed that "the legal question ... seemed to turn on the importance, from the point of view of System open market operations, that was attached to reducing the frequency of delivery failures." Asked to comment, Sternlight replied that he "did not want to overstate the case; obviously, it had been possible for the System to conduct operations up to this point without benefit of the proposed lending arrangements." The Committee decided to postpone a decision.

THE 1969 FAILS CRISIS

Had there not been a change in the facts on the ground, the FOMC might have continued to put off deciding whether to lend securities from the System Open Market Account. There was, however, a dramatic change in circumstances.

During the winter of 1968–69, the Treasury market began to experience what the *Wall Street Journal* described as a "mounting problem of 'fails' to deliver."[19] The *Journal* reported that the problem was "of relatively recent origin," that "there wasn't any problem as recently as the middle of [1968]," but that since then "Government bond dealers, the New York Clearing House and the Federal Reserve Bank of New York have had many meetings to discuss what should be done to correct the problem."[20]

The New York Reserve Bank was quick to relate the fails problem to the difficulties dealers had borrowing securities and to the prospective

[18] Minutes of the Federal Open Market Committee, September 10, 1968, pp. 70–80.

[19] "Dealers in Treasurys Take Steps to Attack Rising 'Fails' Now Afflicting their Trading," *Wall Street Journal*, April 21, 1969, p. 31.

[20] The Federal Reserve Bank of New York expressed its concern in Federal Reserve Bank of New York Circular no. 6321, April 17, 1969. See also "Odd-Lot Purchases of Treasurys Climb, New York Banks Say," *Wall Street Journal*, January 27, 1969, p. 24.

consequences for open market operations. In the spring of 1969, Bank staff prepared a memo documenting the fails problem, its sources, and possible consequences.[21] Based on data collected from primary dealers and interviews with nearly a dozen large dealers and clearing banks,[22] the memo reported that fails had risen sharply, "far faster than the rise in trading volume." The memo suggested that while fails were costly, "the most serious aspect of the ... situation ... is that no one can really know what other problems may be masked by the backlog of uncompleted transactions. ... One does not have to be an alarmist to conclude that the prudent course would be to take every reasonable step to cut down the volume of failures."

The memo explained that borrowing securities was "an important means of avoiding delivery failures," that the large New York banks were the principal lenders of securities (because they had large, diversified portfolios and were located in the heart of the Treasury market), and that the universe of alternative lenders was limited (because other lenders had smaller portfolios or were unfamiliar with the mechanics of securities lending). Lending had contracted over the winter of 1968–69 because, "under the pressure of a restrictive monetary policy, the banks now need more of their securities to adjust reserves either by selling or by borrowing against them in one way or another." The memo reported that "dealers have been actively seeking to develop new sources of securities to borrow ..., but with little success," in part because many corporate treasurers "apparently do not have permission from their boards of directors to lend their securities."

The Bank memo further reported that, to cope with the rising tide of settlement fails, dealers had begun to stretch out the time between trade and settlement. "Many dealers have already stretched out delivery time on [small] transactions to five days, and have been unwilling to effect same-day trades for any but a few select customers – thus pushing most of their business on a next-day delivery basis." The memo noted that "some major dealers have ... talked about the need to go to a two-day delivery basis for typical trades."

[21] Memo from Trading Desk Officers to Alan Holmes, "The Need for System Lending of Securities," Federal Reserve Bank of New York, May 14, 1969.

[22] Interviews were conducted with Discount Corp., Salomon Brothers & Hutzler, William E. Pollack & Company, The First Boston Corp., Chemical Bank, First National City Bank, Manufacturers Hanover Trust Company, Bankers Trust, Irving Trust, and Merrill Lynch, Pierce, Fenner & Smith.

Stretchouts were worrisome because they threatened to delay the impact of the Desk's outright purchase and sale transactions on bank reserves. And even if dealers remained willing to accommodate the Fed's requests for same-day settlement, migration of the bulk of the market to next-day or skip-day settlement would leave the Fed operating in a thinner, less liquid market. The memo observed that, "on occasions when the Desk has [had] to execute purchase orders for both same-day and next-day delivery, there is typically a much greater availability of securities – and hence broader competition – when dealers have the additional day to produce the securities." The Bank memo concluded by urging the FOMC to revisit the issue of securities lending:

> In appraising the need for System lending of securities in order to carry out open market operations, it might have been reasonably concluded as recently as a few months ago that strict necessity did not require this facility. . . . Today, a different conclusion is warranted.[23]

A follow-up memo, prepared three months later, reiterated "the need for prompt remedies of some sort, especially System lending of its securities holdings."[24] After reviewing recent developments, the authors expressed their belief that "the dealer market will be increasingly unable to function properly unless there is some sort of improvement in the [fails] situation." The memo emphasized that while settlement problems were not new, they appeared to be "widespread and increasing in severity" and "interfering with the System's ability to carry out its own operations." System lending, the authors concluded, "would enable the dealers to complete more of their transactions, . . . thereby increasing their trading flexibility, and ability to make good markets."

THE FOMC REVISITS SECURITIES LENDING

Following distribution of the follow-up memo, Holmes again recommended that the FOMC implement a securities lending program. He noted that "there has been a material change for the worse in the 'fail' situation" and that current circumstances indicated an "urgent" need for the

[23] Memo from Trading Desk Officers to Alan Holmes, "The Need for System Lending of Securities," Federal Reserve Bank of New York, May 14, 1969, p. 9.

[24] Memo from Spencer Marsh and Peter Sternlight to Alan Homes, "'Fails' in the Government Securities Market," Federal Reserve Bank of New York, August 15, 1969.

program. In particular, he pointed out that "on at least one recent occasion, in making repurchase agreements to relieve excessive money market tautness . . ., the prospect of having numerous delivery problems was a factor inducing the Account Management to arrange somewhat fewer repurchase agreements than would have been undertaken otherwise."[25]

The FOMC discussed Holmes' recommendation on September 9 and again on October 7, 1969.[26] At the September 9 meeting, Holmes reviewed the worsening fails problem and remarked that Hackley, who was not present, recognized the changed circumstances.[27] The discussions concluded on October 7 with a unanimous vote to add a new paragraph to the Committee's directive to the Reserve Banks:

> In order to insure the effective conduct of open market operations, the Federal Open Market Committee authorizes and directs the Federal Reserve Banks to lend U.S. Government securities held in the System Open Market Account to Government securities dealers . . . under such instructions as the Committee may specify from time to time.[28]

An announcement in the *Federal Reserve Bulletin* states that the action was taken "after the Manger had advised that the problem of delivery failures in the Government securities market had worsened significantly over the past year, partly because private facilities for lending such securities had become inadequate; that delivery failures were markedly impairing the performance of the market; and that the functioning of the market would be improved if securities held in the System Open Market Account could be lent, for the express purpose of avoiding delivery failures, to Government securities dealers doing business with the Federal Reserve Bank of New York."[29]

Following consultation with the primary dealers and determination of the detailed terms of lending (summarized in Box 26.1), Federal Reserve Banks began lending securities on November 20, 1969.

[25] Memo from Alan Homes to Federal Open Market Committee and Presidents not now serving on the Committee, "System Lending of Securities," August 22, 1969.

[26] Minutes of the Federal Open Market Committee, September 9, 1969, pp. 79–85; and October 7, 1969, pp. 94–97.

[27] The meeting minutes state that Hackley "now believed that under current circumstances [securities lending] might properly be regarded as authorized under the incidental powers of the Reserve Banks." Minutes of the Federal Open Market Committee, September 9, 1969, p. 81.

[28] Minutes of the Federal Open Market Committee, October 7, 1969, p. 97.

[29] *Federal Reserve Bulletin*, January 1970, p. 32.

Box 26.1 Terms of the Federal Reserve Securities Lending Program at Its Inception on November 20, 1969.

- Initial term of a loan: 3 business days
- Basic loan fee: ¾ percent per annum
- Penalty fee for extensions beyond 3 days: 6 percent per annum
- Borrowings limited to not more than:
  - o $10 million per note or bond per dealer,
  - o $50 million per bill per dealer, and
  - o $75 million of total securities per dealer.
- Contingent on certification by the dealer that it was borrowing securities to fulfill its obligations under a contract to sell and deliver securities, that it had expected the securities sold to be available for delivery, that the securities to be borrowed would not be used in connection with a short sale, and that it was unable to borrow the securities elsewhere.

Memo from Alan Holmes to Federal Open Market Committee and Presidents not now serving on the Committee, "System Lending of Securities," August 22, 1969, and *Federal Reserve Bulletin*, January 1970, pp. 31–33.

WHETHER TO LEND AGAINST SHORT SALES

In 1972, after the lending program had been in operation for more than two years, the Association of Primary Dealers raised the question of whether it was time to extend the program to include lending to facilitate settlement of short sales.[30]

A New York Reserve Bank staff memo, written in response to the Association's inquiry, distinguished three types of short sales: hedges of long positions, accommodations of customer purchase interests, and outright speculations.[31] The memo observed that the first two types of short sales contributed to market liquidity and smoothed out "price and yield distortions that occur between similar maturities simply because a particular issue is not currently held in dealer positions or is not readily available from other holders." It concluded that both "would seem to be the kind of market activity that the System should be encouraging and a good way to

[30] A copy of the Association's proposal was attached to a memo from R. L. Cooper to Alan Holmes, "Dealer Association Proposal on System Lending of Securities," Federal Reserve Bank of New York, August 24, 1973.

[31] Memo from R. L. Cooper to Alan Holmes, "Dealer Association Proposal on System Lending of Securities," Federal Reserve Bank of New York, August 24, 1973, p. 3.

do it would be to lend the securities needed by the dealers for these purposes if they cannot be borrowed elsewhere." The memo further noted that "such loans would contribute toward the preservation of the kind of a market needed by ... the System, for its open market operations ..." The memo did not recommend that the Fed lend to facilitate speculative short sales.

The staff of the Board of Governors agreed that lending against short sales would enhance liquidity, limit price distortions, and facilitate open market operations.[32] However, Board staff also suggested that the magnitude of the benefits was not clear and that, because lending was limited to primary dealers, extension of the program could create "some equity problems among different types of market participants." They noted that "if instances of inequity were then to be highlighted by the press, they could pose troublesome political questions for the System" and that "it might be made to appear that the Federal Reserve had elected to help a select group of dealers 'bear' the U.S. Government securities market."[33] Board staff concluded that "evidence on the likely advantages to be obtained from a broadened program of System security lending does not appear to be sufficiently compelling to justify the political risks inherent in the change."

Holmes recommended that the FOMC extend the securities lending program to include lending to facilitate settlement of dealer short sales.[34] He placed special emphasis on "the belief that one of the problems of the coming decade is to rebuild a more viable long-term market in Government securities in order to provide greater scope for Treasury financing in all maturity areas of the market. [[35]] ... The dealer proposal would, I am convinced, contribute to that end by providing for a more stable and fluid market."

[32] Memo from Board Staff to Federal Open Market Committee, "Dealer association request for a broadening of System security lending," October 3, 1973, p. 3.

[33] System concern with short selling has a long history. See, for example, "'Short' Bond Sales Traced by Reserve," *New York Times*, November 23, 1933, p. 1; and "Federal Bonds Up On News of Inquiry," *New York Times*, November 23, 1933, p. 31.

[34] Memo from Alan R. Holmes to Federal Open Market Committee, "Proposed expansion of authority to lend securities from System Open Market Account," February 5, 1974.

[35] This is a reference to the absence of any Treasury bond offerings between mid-1965 and mid-1971 as a result of the statutory restriction on issuing bonds with interest rates above 4¼ percent per annum. Treasury began to re-establish a presence in the long-term market following Congressional provision of limited exemptive relief in the Act of March 17, 1971. Garbade (2007, p. 61) and Garbade (2017, text at fns. 98 to 101).

The FOMC considered Holmes' recommendation at its meeting on March 18, 1974.[36] Arthur Burns, chairman of the Board of Governors since February 1970, suggested that "since the opportunities for misunderstanding were so great, very clear advantages would have to be demonstrated before the proposal was considered seriously by the Committee." In his opinion, "a decisive case in its favor had not been made." Discussion ended with Burns' observation that "it appeared that the Committee did not favor the proposed expansion of the lending authority."

[36] Minutes of the Federal Open Market Committee, March 18, 1974, pp. 23–31.

27

The Book-Entry System, Part I

By the middle of the 1960s, market participants and Treasury and Federal Reserve officials understood that a book-entry and electronic transfer system for Treasury securities was highly desirable, but the route to that end was far from clear. Moving to book-entry securities would affect thousands of institutional investors and tens of thousands of retail investors, require significant regulatory and legal changes and the adoption of new technologies, and likely take years, perhaps decades. However daunting, the task was taken on and, eventually, accomplished.

ORIGINS OF THE BOOK-ENTRY SYSTEM

The most significant factor in the genesis of the book-entry system was the familiarity of the Reserve Banks with safekeeping securities, a familiarity grounded in their holding securities pledged by member banks as collateral on discount window loans and against deposits of public funds, such as Treasury Tax and Loan account balances. Additionally, the Banks safekept unpledged securities owned by geographically remote member banks.[1] The Federal Reserve Bank of New York had particularly deep experience with safekeeping practices because it also safekept securities owned by the System Open Market Account and by foreign central banks.[2] Safekeeping securities gave the Reserve Banks experience running vault facilities and

[1] Bureau of the Public Debt (1984, p. I–8) and Ringsmuth and Rice (1984, pp. 10–11). The service, provided free to those banks (Bureau of the Public Debt, 1984, p. I–8), kept the securities readily accessible in the event a bank needed to pledge them against a discount window loan or a deposit of public funds.

[2] Debs and Guy (1965, pp. 7–8).

hiring and retaining a trustworthy labor force, both of which made Bank officials well aware of the costs of providing custodial services.

Despite the care and attention devoted to the provision of safekeeping services, accidents happened from time to time. In early 1963, the Federal Reserve Bank of San Francisco reported the disappearance of $7.5 million of bearer Treasury securities held as collateral against a deposit of public funds at a member bank.[3] Following a Congressional investigation of the loss,[4] the Board of Governors asked the Conference of Presidents of the Federal Reserve Banks to consider whether Treasury securities safekept at the Banks might be converted to book-entry form. The Board was primarily interested in reducing the risk of lost or stolen securities, but additionally in reducing Bank operating costs.[5] A Conference subcommittee investigated the matter and concluded that a book-entry system was both "practical and desirable."[6]

ISSUES IN CREATING A BOOK-ENTRY SYSTEM

During the mid-1960s, System officials focused on developing institutional arrangements that would support the conversion of definitive securities already safekept at Reserve Banks to book-entry form. Implementing even a limited, internal, book-entry system proved to be extraordinarily difficult.

The threshold issue was whether the Reserve Banks would operate the system in their individual capacities or as fiscal agents of the Untied States. (Box 25.1 describes the role of Federal Reserve Banks as fiscal agents of the United States. A Reserve Bank acted as a fiscal agent when it held securities pledged against Treasury Tax and Loan balances; it acted in an individual capacity when it held securities pledged against discount window loans.) If

[3] "$7,500,000 Bonds Disappear at Bank," *New York Times*, March 28, 1963, p. 1. See also "If Lost Securities Were Stolen, Theft was Biggest in History," *New York Times*, May 28, 1963, p. 75; and "Loss of Securities Remains a Mystery," *New York Times*, May 30, 1963, p. 17. Earlier losses included the loss of $101 thousand of certificates at the Federal Reserve Bank of Atlanta in 1953 and the loss of a $100 thousand certificate at the Federal Reserve Bank of Richmond in 1962. Committee on Banking and Currency (April 1963, p. 14, and May 1963, pp. 47–48).

[4] Committee on Banking and Currency (April 1963 and May 1963).

[5] Letter from Merritt Sherman, Secretary, Board of Governors of the Federal Reserve System, to Watrous Irons, Chairman, Conference of Presidents, June 11, 1963, and memo from Harold Bilby and Edward Guy to Secretary's Office, Federal Reserve Bank of New York, "Topic II.B.1, Conference of Presidents – September 27, 1965," September 21, 1965.

[6] Subcommittee on Fiscal Agency Operations of the Committee on Fiscal Agency Operations of the Conference of Presidents (1963, p. 3).

a Reserve Bank operated a book-entry system strictly in its individual capacity, it might – like a private depository – be obliged to continue to hold definitive securities against its book-entry liabilities, a practice that would clearly limit the risk mitigation and cost savings available from a book-entry system.

The need to hold definitive securities could be avoided by providing that a Reserve Bank acted as a fiscal agent of the United States when it created, carried, and extinguished book-entry Treasury securities. However, a Reserve Bank that operated a book-entry system strictly as a fiscal agent might have to continue to safekeep, in definitive form, unpledged securities owned by member banks and others in order to avoid conflicts between its fiscal agency obligations to the Treasury and its custodial responsibilities to the beneficial owners of the safekept securities.[7]

Further complicating the question of whether the Reserve Banks should operate a book-entry system in their individual capacities or as fiscal agents was the recognition that a book-entry system might make a clean distinction between the two roles all but impossible. One early analysis observed that a book-entry system "by its very nature 'meshes' the actions which a Reserve Bank undertakes as custodian on the one hand and as fiscal agent on the other."[8] This suggested that the Banks might have to operate the system in some sort of hybrid capacity.

Placing liens on Treasury securities posed a second problem. Liens were governed by state law and generally required expensive and time-consuming public filings to be effective. However, possession by a pledgee was sufficient if the asset was a definitive security. Since the notion of "possession" of a book-entry security was unclear, there was a distinct possibility that a pledgee who wanted to establish a lien on a book-entry security might have to make a public filing of his or her lien.[9] Any such requirement would sharply reduce the attractiveness of book-entry securities,[10] but the alternative – amending numerous state laws to eliminate the

[7] Debs and Guy (1965, p. 24) stated that "two parallel sets of accounts would have to be maintained."

[8] Letter from the Subcommittee of Counsel on Fiscal Agency Operations, Welford Farmer, Chairman, to Upton Martin, Chairman, Subcommittee on Fiscal Agency Operations, December 3, 1964.

[9] Letter from the Subcommittee of Counsel on Fiscal Agency Operations, Welford Farmer, Chairman, to Upton Marton, Chairman, Subcommittee on Fiscal Agency Operations, December 3, 1964, and Debs and Guy (1965, pp. 16–19).

[10] Rassnick (1971, p. 613) states that if a filing were necessary, "the book-entry procedure would not have been feasible . . ." See also Hoey and Rassnick (1976, p. 181).

need for public filings of liens on book-entry securities – would be time-consuming and costly.

THE FIRST IMPLEMENTATION

In the interest of limiting the range of issues that had to be resolved, Treasury and Federal Reserve officials kept the first version of the book-entry system quite limited. It went into effect on January 1, 1968,[11] and provided just three categories of deposits:[12]

1. member bank securities held for investment and deposited with a Federal Reserve Bank for safekeeping,
2. member bank securities pledged as collateral on a discount window loan from a Federal Reserve Bank, and
3. member bank securities pledged as collateral against federal government deposits.

Left out – at least for the time being – were member bank securities held for trading (rather than investment) purposes, securities safekept by member banks for their customers (including securities owned by nonbank dealers), and securities held by a Federal Reserve Bank as collateral for a purpose other than to secure a Bank loan or federal government deposit.

With respect to securities included in the new system, a member bank could deposit Treasury securities (in bearer or registered form) to its book-entry accounts, withdraw securities (in bearer or registered form) from its accounts,[13] order a transfer of book-entry securities to a book-entry account of another member bank at the same Federal Reserve Bank, or order a CPD transfer of book-entry securities.

The initial implementation of the book-entry system accommodated only two pledgees: a Reserve Bank (pursuant to a discount window loan) and the United States (pursuant to a deposit of public funds). The question

[11] Subpart O of Treasury Department Circular no. 300 (effective January 1, 1968) and Federal Reserve Bank of New York Operating Circular no. 21 (effective January 1, 1968). See also Federal Reserve Bank of New York Circular no. 6075, December 12, 1967.

[12] The idea of limiting the initial system to three categories of deposits originated with Debs and Guy (1965, p. 29).

[13] Bureau of the Public Debt (1984, p. II–6), quoting a memorandum from the Legal Department of the Federal Reserve Bank of New York stating that convertibility of book-entry securities to bearer and registered forms was a "cornerstone to the practical acceptance of the book-entry [system]."

of whether either had to file liens was resolved by relying on the Supremacy Clause of the United States Constitution and the doctrine of federal preemption of state law.[14] The Treasury regulation authorizing the book-entry system simply declared that no filing was necessary and provided that a lien on a Treasury security could be established by making an appropriate entry in the records of the system:

> The making of such entry shall have the effect of a delivery of definitive Treasury securities in bearer form . . . and shall effect a perfected security interest . . . in favor of the pledgee . . . No filing or recording with a public official or officer shall be necessary to perfect the pledge or security interest.[15]

The Treasury did not have to promulgate detailed provisions for security interests on book-entry Treasury securities because its regulation implicitly deferred to state law on all matters other than the method of perfecting a security interest.[16]

Whether the Reserve Banks would operate the book-entry system as principals, as fiscal agents, or in some hybrid capacity was not clearly resolved in the first implementation. Early in the planning process the Conference of Presidents contemplated that, in the interest of simplicity, the system should be operated strictly as a fiscal agency function.[17] That decision allowed the Banks, acting as agents of the United States, to preempt state law on security pledges. Early drafts of the Treasury regulation authorizing the system consequently spoke only of the Reserve Banks operating as fiscal agents of the United States.[18]

During the spring of 1967, Edward Guy, General Counsel of the Federal Reserve Bank of New York, became uneasy that discount window loans

[14] Rassnick (1971, p. 614) and Hoey and Rassnick (1976, p. 181).

[15] Code of Federal Regulations, title 31, part 306, section 118, January 1, 1968, hereafter cited in the form 31 CFR 306.118 (January 1, 1968).

[16] The author is indebted to Lee Rassnick for pointing out the significance of *how* the Treasury pre-empted state law.

[17] The Conference adopted, on September 27, 1965, a recommendation of the Subcommittee of Counsel on Fiscal Agency Operations of the Committee on Fiscal Agency Operations of the Conference of Presidents (1965), based on the analysis of Debs and Guy (1965), that the system should be operated as an agency function. Treasury officials also favored the agency approach.

[18] See the draft dated January 24, 1967, of Subpart O of Treasury Circular no. 300 enclosed in a memo dated January 27, 1967, from Welford Farmer, Chairman, Subcommittee of Counsel on Fiscal Agency Operations, to the members of the subcommittee, and the draft dated June 6, 1967, of Subpart O enclosed with a memo dated June 8, 1967, from Farmer to Edward Wayne, Chairman, Committee on Fiscal Agency Operations.

might not be adequately secured by pledges of book-entry securities recorded in a system operated by the Bank solely as a fiscal agent of the United States.[19] Guy also became uneasy that the Bank might be unable to fulfill its responsibilities to the beneficial owners of unpledged securities that it held in safekeeping.[20]

As a result of Guy's concerns, the final version of the Treasury regulation authorizing the new system provided that:

> The book-entry procedure shall apply to Treasury securities now on deposit or hereafter deposited in accounts with any Reserve Bank
>
> (1) as collateral pledged to a Reserve Bank (*in its individual capacity*) for advances by it,
> (2) as collateral [pledged] to the United States [against deposits of public funds], and
> (3) by a member bank ... for its sole account and in lieu of the safekeeping of definitive Treasury securities by a Reserve Bank *in its individual capacity*.[21]

The references to individual capacity suggest that a Reserve Bank acted, at least in part, in its individual capacity when it held book-entry securities pledged against discount window loans and when it safekept unpledged member bank securities. However, the regulation did not indicate how that assessment could be reconciled with the more specific assertion that, in operating a book-entry system, a Reserve Bank acted as a fiscal agent of the United States.[22]

The first fruits of the new system were modest: only $2.6 billion of bearer securities were converted to book-entry form at the Federal Reserve

[19] Letter from Edward Guy, General Counsel, Federal Reserve Bank of New York, to Welford Farmer, Chairman, Subcommittee of Counsel on Fiscal Agency Operations, April 24, 1967, stating that "it would be doubtful that I would be able to render an opinion to our discount officers that advances by the Federal Reserve Bank of New York secured by book-entry obligations as provided under the terms of the [January 24, 1967] draft could be said to be adequately and legally secured," and memo from Guy to Farmer, June 14, 1967.

[20] Letter from Edward Guy, General Counsel, Federal Reserve Bank of New York, to John Grosvenor, Assistant Chief Counsel, Treasury Department, June 20, 1967, noting the need to "provide assurance that the Reserve Banks would be in a position always to fulfill obligations" to their custodial customers.

[21] 17 CFR 306.117(a) (January 1, 1968). Emphasis added.

[22] 17 CFR 306.115(a) (January 1, 1968), defining a Reserve Bank as "a Federal Reserve Bank ... acting as Fiscal Agent of the United States."

Bank of New York.[23] However, the effort subsequently gained momentum. By the end of 1968, the twelve Reserve Banks had, in aggregate, converted to book-entry form more than 15 percent of the $237 billion of outstanding marketable Treasury securities.[24]

THE SECOND IMPLEMENTATION

Eighteen months after the initial implementation, the Treasury and the Reserve Banks extended the framework of the book-entry system in two directions.[25] First, they expanded the scope of the system beyond the three original accounts and provided that the system could be used for Treasury securities deposited for *any* purpose in additional accounts maintained by the Reserve Banks.[26]

Second, the Treasury extended the scope of its preemption of state law on security interests to include *all* pledgees of book-entry Treasury securities.[27] This action enabled the Federal Reserve Bank of New York to include securities held for the System Open Market Account and pledged against currency issued by the Reserve Banks. In January 1970, $56 billion of bearer securities held for the Open Market Account moved to book-entry form.[28] The expanded pledge provision also allowed the Reserve Banks to include securities pledged to so-called "third parties" – such as state and local governments and federal bankruptcy courts – as performance guarantees and held at Federal Reserve Banks.

The desire of Treasury and Federal Reserve officials to include securities pledged to third parties led to an important change in the operating basis of the book-entry system. Numerous state and local statutes that provided for deposits of securities with a Federal Reserve Bank contemplated that the securities would be deposited with a Bank acting in its individual capacity, rather than as a fiscal agent of the United States. It followed that the securities could not be deposited into a book-entry system operated by

[23] Vollkommer (1970, p. 65).

[24] Federal Reserve Bank of New York Circular no. 7590, March 19, 1975.

[25] Subpart O of Treasury Department Circular no. 300, effective July 15, 1969, and Federal Reserve Bank of New York Operating Circular no. 21, effective August 1, 1969. See also Federal Reserve Bank of New York Circular no. 6379, August 1, 1969.

[26] 31 CFR 306.117(b) (July 15, 1969) and Federal Reserve Bank of New York Operating Circular no. 21, Section 2(b), effective August 1, 1969.

[27] 31 CFR 306.118 (July 15, 1969). [28] Vollkommer (1970, p. 67).

the Reserve Banks strictly as fiscal agents.[29] To facilitate the inclusion of securities pledged to third parties, the regulatory provision for the new accounts stated that:

> The application of the book-entry procedure [to securities deposited in the new accounts] shall not derogate from or adversely affect the relationships what would otherwise exist between a Reserve Bank *in its individual capacity* and its depositors concerning any deposits under this paragraph. Whenever the book-entry procedure is applied to such Treasury securities, the Reserve Bank is authorized to take all action necessary in respect of the book-entry procedure to enable such Reserve Bank *in its individual capacity* to perform its obligations as depository with respect to such Treasury securities.[30]

Federal Reserve officials understood that, pursuant to this provision, the Reserve Banks would accept deposits in a *dual* capacity, both as agents of the United States and in their individual capacities.[31] The second sentence in the quoted provision suggests that a Bank's individual responsibility to depositors might, in fact, trump its fiscal agency responsibilities.[32] Officials described the dual-capacity plan as the "the most significant" aspect of the second implementation of the book-entry

[29] Letter from Welford Farmer, Chairman, Subcommittee of Counsel on Fiscal Agency Operations, to Thomas Winston, Chief Counsel, Bureau of the Public Debt, July 19, 1968, stating that "the term 'Federal Reserve Bank' as used in these statutes ... refers to the Federal Reserve Banks in their individual capacities as distinguished from the Reserve Banks acting as Fiscal Agents," and memo from Subcommittee of Counsel on Fiscal Agency Operations to Committee on Fiscal Agency Operations, "Book-Entry Procedures," December 4, 1968, p. 3, stating that "it appears that the provisions of law applicable to [securities pledged to third parties] might preclude the deposit of the securities with the Reserve Banks if the latter act solely in their capacity as fiscal agents of the United States."

[30] 31 CFR 306.117(b) (July 15, 1969). Emphasis added.

[31] Memo from Subcommittee of Counsel on Fiscal Agency Operations to Committee on Fiscal Agency Operations, "Book-Entry Procedures," December 4, 1968, p. 1, noting that "the proposed revision of Subpart O provides for the Reserve Banks to act in certain circumstances in a 'dual capacity,' i.e., in an individual capacity and as fiscal agents of the United States." A subsequent revision of the book-entry regulations provided that, in operating the book-entry system, a Reserve Bank acted "as Fiscal Agent of the United States and when indicated ... in its individual capacity." 31 CFR 306.115(a) (April 27, 1972).

[32] The Subcommittee of Counsel on Fiscal Agency Operations observed that the quoted provision was "designed principally to minimize ... the risk that the Treasury might take some action in respect of the book-entry Treasury securities or the book-entry procedure that might make it impossible for the Reserve Bank to perform its depository obligations." Memo from Subcommittee of Counsel on Fiscal Agency Operations to Committee on Fiscal Agency Operations, "Book-Entry Procedures," December 4, 1968, p. 4.

system.[33] The introduction of dual capacity settled the matter of the operating basis of the system.

By the end of 1970, the Federal Reserve book-entry system accounted for $121 billion of Treasury securities – almost half of the $248 billion of marketable Treasury debt outstanding.[34] Virtually all of the definitive securities previously held in Reserve Bank vaults had been converted and the System had accomplished the objectives identified in 1963: reducing the risk of misplacing securities and reducing the operating costs of the Reserve Banks.[35]

WHAT REMAINED TO BE DONE

Two important categories of Treasury securities remained entirely outside the book-entry system at the end of 1970: securities owned by member banks for trading purposes and securities safekept by member banks for their customers.[36] The Federal Reserve Bank of New York was anxious to include those securities and to leverage more fully the economic advantages inherent in book-entry securities. As early as 1965, Bank officers had looked forward to the development of a book-entry system because it "appears to be an efficient and effective method of handling Government securities. This Bank has long been of the view that ultimately a book-entry type of procedure for Government securities should be developed to cover all or nearly all holders of such obligations. Over the long run, such a procedure ... would appear to be a more efficient and probably less costly procedure for handing the public debt."[37]

[33] Memo from Subcommittee of Counsel on Fiscal Agency Operations to Committee on Fiscal Agency Operations, "Book-entry Procedures," December 4, 1968, p. 5.

[34] Federal Reserve Bank of New York Circular no. 7590, March 19, 1975.

[35] In announcing the first implementation of the new system, the New York Fed emphasized the economic advantages of the book-entry system: "The ... procedure is designed to help the Treasury Department and the Federal Reserve Banks handle a large volume of Treasury securities through the use of modern high-speed data-processing equipment. Use of the new procedure should lead to increased efficiency in the handling and servicing of Treasury securities by the Federal Reserve Banks." Federal Reserve Bank of New York Circular no. 6022, August 21, 1967. The New York Fed began planning for the introduction of a new computer, the Sigma-5, described in Federal Reserve Bank of New York (March 1972, April 1972, and 1984), to support the new system. The new computer began operation in January 1971.

[36] Vollkommer (1970, p. 70).

[37] Memo from Harold Bilby and Edward Guy to Secretary's Office, Federal Reserve Bank of New York, "Topic II.B.1., Conference of Presidents – September 27, 1965," September 21, 1965.

In the summer of 1968, officials began to seek the cooperation of the large New York clearing banks in developing a more extensive system.[38] The clearing banks expressed interest but believed that change might not come quickly. One official noted that "some expanded form of book entry procedure is inevitable . . . But how to work toward it and at what speed are matters that need further discussion."[39]

[38] Memo from Felix Davis, Vice President, Federal Reserve Bank of New York, to John Lee, Executive Vice President, New York Clearing House, "Program for Expanding Use of Book-Entry Procedure for Treasury Securities," June 10, 1968.

[39] Letter from John Lee, Executive Vice President, New York Clearing House, to Felix Davis, Vice President, Federal Reserve Bank of New York, July 31, 1968.

PART VIII

THE 1970S

Stressful environmental conditions commonly trigger rapid evolutionary change. The seventies had more than their share of stressful conditions, including rising and more volatile interest rates (Chart VIII.1) and sharply higher Treasury financing requirements after 1974 (Chart VIII.2). It is hardly surprising that the decade witnessed significant changes in debt management and the mechanics of open market operations.

With respect to Treasury debt management, the seventies saw the introduction of auction offerings of coupon-bearing securities – a reaction to the growing risk that an unexpected increase in interest rates following announcement of the terms of a fixed-price offering would lead to a failed offering. Coupon auctions also allowed the FOMC to withdraw its commitment to keeping the market on an even keel during an offering, thereby relaxing what would otherwise have become a significant constraint on monetary policy as the frequency of Treasury offerings increased in the second half of the decade.[1] The seventies also saw the extension of regular and predictable offerings, first to short-term notes and later to intermediate-term notes and bonds.

The increasing level and volatility of interest rates limited the attractiveness of providing deep, liquid markets in Treasury debt. At the same time, rising volatility of autonomous reserve factors, including especially float and Treasury deposits at Federal Reserve Banks, made liquidity increasingly important for open market operations. As a result, the Desk continued to expand the scope of its repo operations, introducing repo auctions in 1972 and including bank dealers as eligible counterparties in 1975.

[1] Volcker (2018, p. 88) observes that "as the size and frequency of [Treasury] offerings increased, the Fed's need to maintain [the] so-called even-keel approach became increasingly awkward."

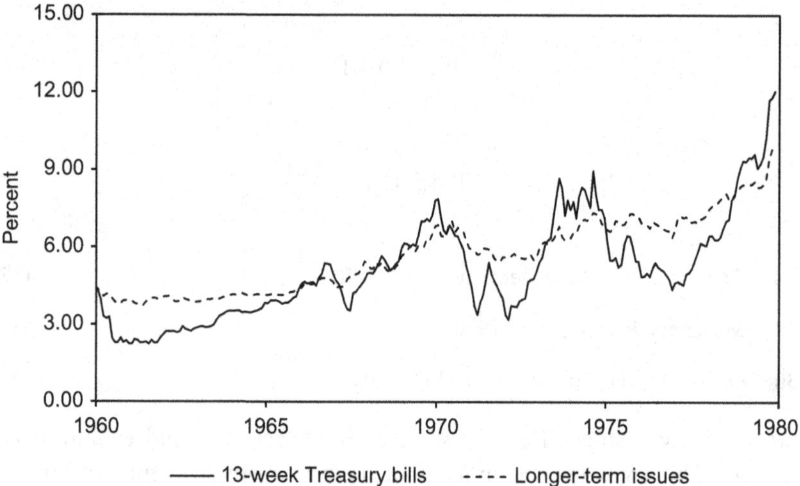

Chart VIII.1 Treasury yields. Monthly averages.
Board of Governors of the Federal Reserve System (1976, tables 12.7A and 12.12A; and 1981, table 22B).

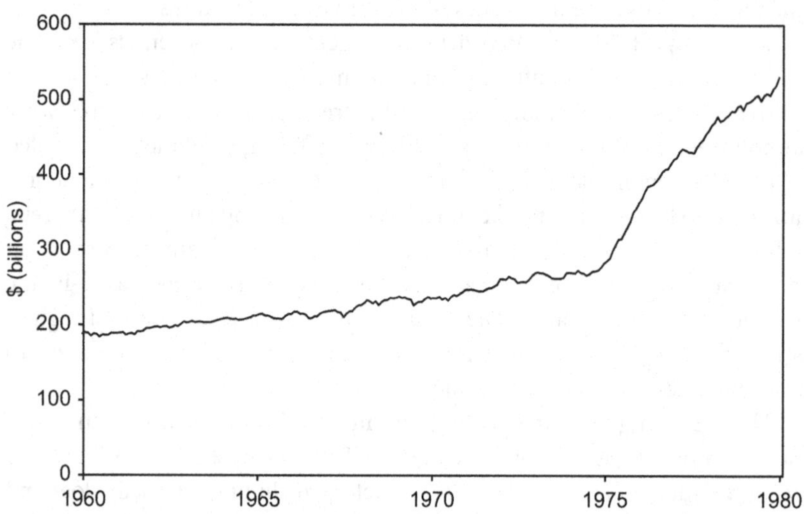

Chart VIII.2 Marketable Treasury debt. End of month.
Board of Governors of the Federal Reserve System (1976, table 13.2; and 1981, table 28).

By the end of the decade, the primary market for Treasury debt looked substantially different than it had at the beginning of the decade – more competitive and less susceptible to idiosyncratic decisions of Treasury officials – and System open market operations were increasingly aligned with the reality of an open, competitive market.

28

Treasury Debt Management in the 1970s

Two shocking events: a mid-quarter refunding that very nearly failed and an historically large peacetime deficit, prompted a rapid evolution in Treasury debt management in the 1970s.

Treasury officials had experienced troubled offerings before, most notably in the summer of 1958, but things reached a tipping point when the May 1970 refunding came within an eyelash of failing.[1] Despite earlier protestations about the importance of effecting a broad distribution of the debt and the belief that unsophisticated investors would decline to participate in auctions that left them exposed to the "winner's curse" of winning an allotment only to find they had paid too high a price, officials decided that they would have to try, for a third time, to introduce auction sales of coupon-bearing debt.[2]

Marketable Treasury debt more than doubled during the 1970s, from $235 billion at the end of 1969 to $531 billion at the end of 1979. The decade divides into two distinct halves: before 1975, when marketable debt increased at an average rate of $9½ billion per year, and after the deep recession of 1974, when it increased at an average rate of almost $50 billion per year (Chart 28.1). The need to raise substantially greater sums of new money in the second half of the decade led officials to extend regular and predictable offerings from bills to notes and bonds.

[1] The 1970 Annual Report of Open Market Operations states (p. A-10) that "a failure of the Treasury's May [1970] cash financing was narrowly averted."

[2] In the post–World War I era, the Treasury tried to auction bonds in 1935 (Garbade, 2012, pp. 286–93) and in 1963 (Chapter 20 above). Both attempts were terminated following the first sign of trouble.

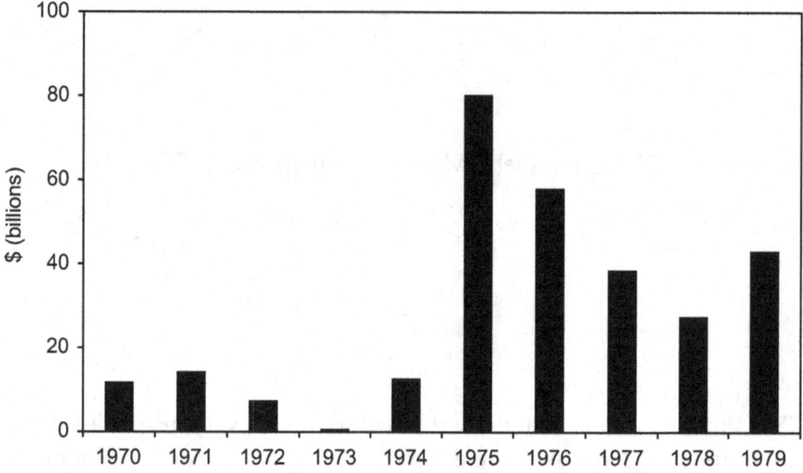

Chart 28.1 Annual change in marketable Treasury debt.
Board of Governors of the Federal Reserve System (1981, table 28).

MARKETABLE TREASURY DEBT IN THE 1970S

Treasury officials issued marketable debt in the form of bills, notes, and bonds in the 1970s. Bills were further divided into regular bills – maturing in thirteen and twenty-six weeks, nine months, and one year – and irregular bills, typically maturing shortly after tax payment dates.

Regular Bills

Regular bills outstanding expanded at a rate of $7.5 billion per year from the end of 1969 to mid-1974, then ratcheted up to $33.7 billion per year through the end of 1975 (Chart 28.2). After 1975, bill issuance was mostly a matter of refinancing maturing bills. Outstanding bills expanded at the much slower rate of $2.5 billion per year from 1976 to 1979.

Thirteen- and Twenty-Six-Week Bills

Chart 28.3 shows that thirteen- and twenty-six-week bill offerings expanded more or less in parallel from 1970 to mid-1974. At the beginning of the decade the Treasury auctioned $1.8 billion of thirteen-week bills and $1.3 billion of twenty-six-week bills every week. By mid-1974 it was

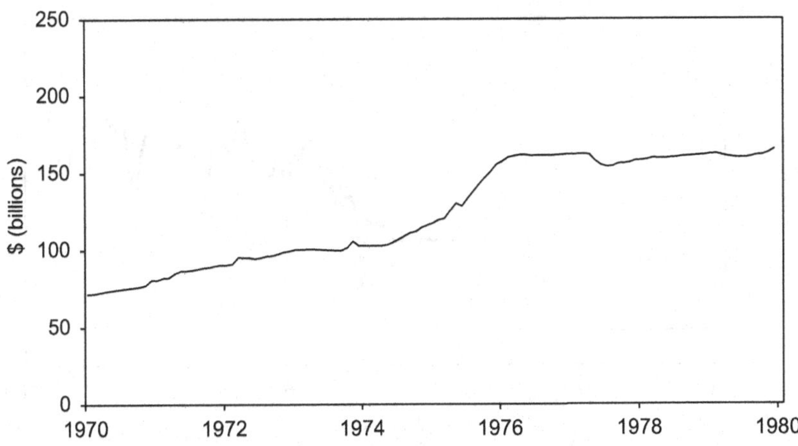

Chart 28.2 Regular Treasury bills. End of Month.
Board of Governors of the Federal Reserve System (1981, Table 28).

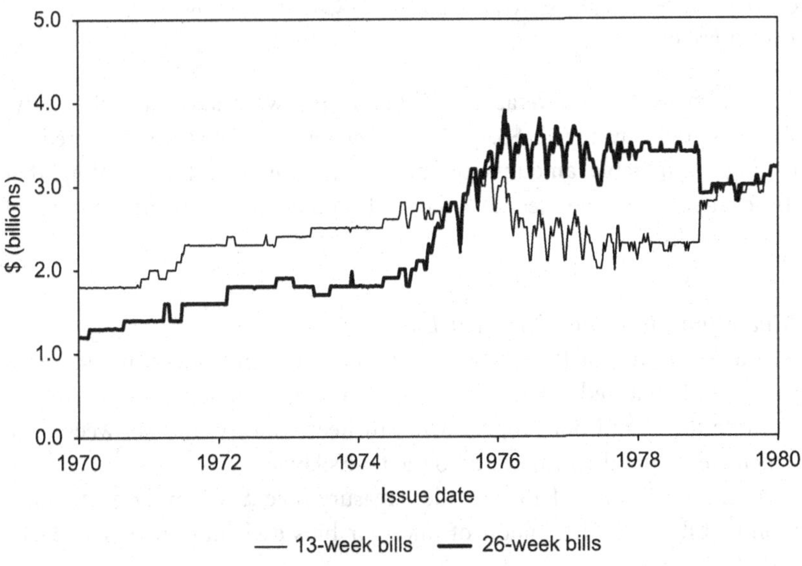

Chart 28.3 Thirteen- and twenty-six-week Treasury bill issuance.
Treasury Bulletin.

conducting weekly auctions of $2.5 billion of thirteen-week bills and $1.7 billion of 26-week bills.

Most of the stepped-up bill issuance after mid-1974 came from increased sales of 26-week bills. Between July 1976 and October 1978, sales

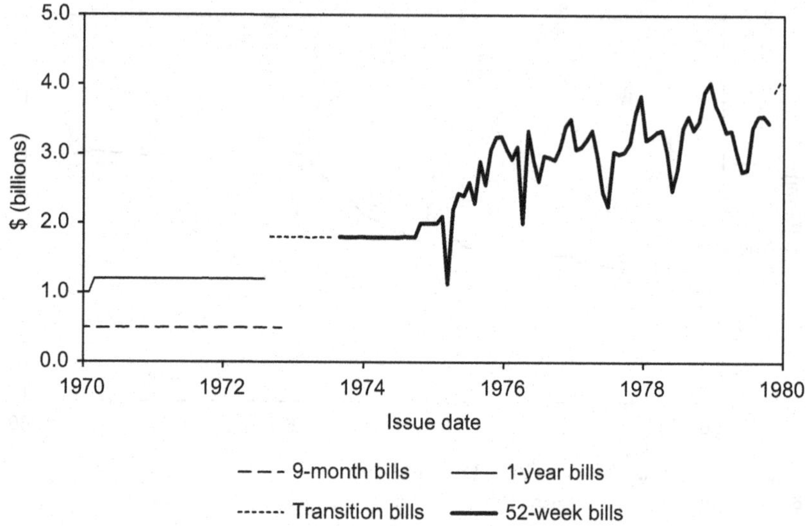

Chart 28.4 Nine-month, one-year, and fifty-two-week Treasury bill issuance.
Treasury Bulletin.

of thirteen-week bills averaged $2.3 billion per week and sales of twenty-six-week bills averaged $3.4 billion per week.[3] Treasury switched to issuing comparable amounts of the two bills in late 1978, stating that the change was "intended to enlarge the potential competitive award of 13-week bills."[4]

Nine-Month Bills and One-Year Bills

At the beginning of the 1970s nine-month bills and one-year bills were issued and matured on the last day of a month. They were, therefore, separate from, and not fungible with, thirteen- and twenty-six-week bills, which were issued and matured on a Thursday.

At the beginning of the decade Treasury sold $500 million of ninie-months bills and $1.2 billion of one-year bills each month (Chart 28.4).

[3] The sawtooth issuance pattern in 1976 and 1977 was the result of a sharp reduction in the bill auctions of June 15 and 22, 1975, triggered by strong tax receipts. "Treasury to Auction $4.5 Billion in Bills," *Wall Street Journal*, June 11, 1975, p. 23. Subsequent auctions at 13-week intervals were similarly reduced because of the smaller refinancing requirements. The oscillations petered out in late 1977.

[4] Treasury statement attached to Federal Reserve Bank of New York Circular no. 8456, November 15, 1978.

Issuance continued at that pace until the summer of 1972, when officials terminated the 9-month series and converted the one-year series to quadweekly offerings of fifty-two-week bills, to be issued on a Tuesday and mature on a Tuesday.[5] The change opened up the month-end dates for regular quarterly offerings of two-year notes, a series that Treasury inaugurated in the fall of 1972.

The last tranche of one-year bills was issued on July 31, 1972, with a maturity date of July 31, 1973.[6] The last tranche of nine-month bills was issued on October 31, 1972, and also matured on July 31, 1973.[7] To refinance subsequently maturing nine-month and one-year bills, Treasury issued a series of twelve transition bills. Transition bills were issued on the last day of a month (beginning in August 1972) with Tuesday maturity dates that were twenty-eight days apart (beginning with Tuesday, August 28, 1973). The first fifty-two-week bill was issued on August 28, 1973, with a maturity date of August 27, 1974.[8]

At the end of the decade the Treasury moved the issue and maturity dates of its fifty-two-week bills from Tuesday to Thursday, so that all regular bills would be issued on a Thursday and mature on a Thursday. The change was made to "reduce the number of separate bill issues outstanding, facilitate market trading, and improve liquidity for the 52-week bills."[9] The change led to another yearlong set of transition bills.[10]

[5] Treasury press release, "Treasury Announces Plans for Restructuring of Monthly Bills," August 18, 1972.

[6] Federal Reserve Bank of New York Circular no. 6974, July 19, 1972.

[7] Federal Reserve Bank of New York Circular no. 7020, October 18, 1972.

[8] Federal Reserve Bank of New York Circular no. 7211, August 16, 1973. The last transition bill was issued on July 31, 1973, with a maturity date of July 2, 1974. Federal Reserve Bank of New York Circular no. 7187, July 18, 1973. Treasury filled in the July 30, 1974, maturity date in October 1973. Federal Reserve Bank of New York, Circular no. 7238, September 27, 1973.

[9] Treasury press release, "52-Week Bill Dating Change," November 1, 1979, attached to Federal Reserve Bank of New York Circular no. 8674, November 2, 1979.

[10] The last fifty-two-week bill maturing on a Tuesday was issued on Tuesday, October 16, 1979, and matured on October 14, 1980. Federal Reserve Bank of New York Circular no. 8652, October 5, 1979. That bill was followed by a series of thirteen 359-day bills, issued on Tuesdays (to refinance maturing fifty-two-week bills) but maturing on Thursdays. The first fifty-two-week bill maturing on a Thursday was issued on Thursday, November 6, 1980 (to refinance the maturing first transition bill) and matured on Thursday, November 5, 1981. Federal Reserve Bank of New York Circular no. 8942, October 24, 1980.

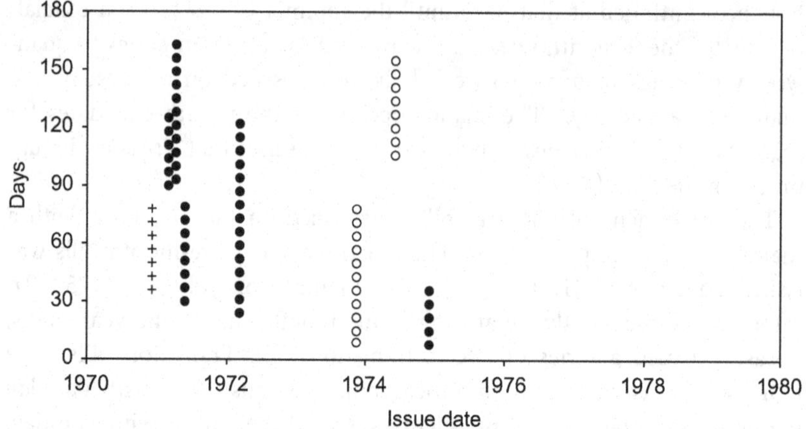

Chart 28.5 Maturities of bills offered in bill strips.
Federal Reserve Bank of New York circulars.

Bill Strips

In the first half of the 1970s Treasury officials supplemented their weekly offerings of thirteen- and twenty-six-week bills with occasional offerings of bill strips. Officials brought eight strip offerings between 1970 and 1974, consisting of from five to fifteen different maturities (Chart 28.5). All of the bills reopened maturities first opened with twenty-six-week offerings. Five strips offered $200 million of each bill, the November 1973 and June 1974 strips offered $100 million of each bill, and the December 1970 strip offered $300 million of each bill. Treasury abandoned the bill strip program when it began expanding its regular weekly offerings of twenty-six-week bills.

Irregular Bills

Treasury officials issued fifty-three irregular bills in the 1970s, eleven more than in the 1960s. Most (but not all) of the bills matured shortly after the major tax payment dates: March 15, April 15, June 15, September 15, and December 15 (Table 28.1). Late April and late June maturities were particularly common.

Table 28.1 *Maturities of irregular bills issued in the 1970s.*

Maturity bracket	Number of irregular bills maturing in bracket
Mar. 15–25	1
Apr. 15–25	22
Jun. 15–25	14
Sep. 15–25	9
Dec. 15–25	2
Other	5
Total	53

Federal Reserve Bank of New York circulars.

The five bills maturing at "other" times included:

- a 299-day $2 billion bill issued on September 14, 1974, maturing on June 30, 1975, that was refinanced at maturity with a 2-year note,
- an 18-day, $1 billion bill issued on August 8, 1975, maturing on Tuesday, August 26, 1975, that was refinanced at maturity with a 52-week bill,
- a 292-day $1.5 billion bill issued on April 14, 1975, maturing on January 31, 1976, that was refinanced at maturity with a 2-year note,
- an 8-day $2.5 billion bill issued on November 7, 1977, maturing on November 15, 1977, that was refinanced at maturity with securities issued in the November 1977 mid-quarter refunding, and
- a 157-day $2.3 billion bill issued on December 10, 1979, maturing on May 15, 1980, that was refinanced at maturity with securities issued in the May 1980 mid-quarter refunding.

The twenty-four irregular bills issued in the first half of the 1970s were similar to irregular bills issued in the 1960s: they were frequently (albeit not always) longer-term bills issued in the second half of a calendar year and scheduled to mature in the first half of the following year. All but two were tax anticipation bills that matured shortly after a tax payment date and were accepted at full face value in payment of taxes, thus giving holders a use-contingent early redemption option. The other two irregular bills were designated "special" bills.[11]

Twenty-five of the twenty-nine irregular bills issued between 1975 and 1979 matured shortly after tax payment dates and were paid down with tax

[11] See Federal Reserve Bank of New York Circular no. 7443, August 21, 1974, and Circular no. 7480, October 16, 1974. The latter bill matured on June 19, 1975, shortly after a tax payment date, but was not accepted at full face value in payment of taxes and was not designated as a tax anticipation bill.

receipts but did not carry the early redemption option of tax anticipation bills. The other four irregular bills matured at other times and, as shown in Table 28.1, were refinanced with conventional offerings.

Short maturities became increasingly common after mid-1975. The first short-dated irregular bill was announced on Wednesday, August 6, 1975, auctioned the next day, issued the day following (Friday, August 8), and matured just eighteen days later, on Tuesday, August 26, when it was refinanced with an offering of fifty-two-week bills. Edwin Yeo, recently sworn in as Under Secretary of the Treasury for Monetary Affairs, stated that the bill represented a new cash management technique: borrowing as needed for short periods of time to buffer transient fluctuations in receipts and expenditures.[12] Irregular bills later came to be known as "cash management bills" regardless of whether they were paid down with tax receipts or refinanced with new issues.[13]

The Fed's Direct Purchase Authority

Cash management bills allowed the Treasury to reduce its reliance on borrowing directly from Federal Reserve Banks when it ran short of cash. As a general matter such direct borrowing was prohibited by a 1935 amendment to Section 14(b) of the Federal Reserve Act,[14] but since 1942 Congress had provided a $5 billion exemption.[15] Treasury officials relied on that authority to bridge temporary cash shortfalls, including three in 1973, one in 1974, and four in 1975.[16]

The Fed's direct purchase authority was widely viewed as a safety net, to be used in the event of an unanticipated emergency, rather than a standing facility suitable for regular use. Resort to the authority complicated the conduct of monetary policy because direct borrowings increased the supply of reserves available to the banking system and forced the Fed to undertake offsetting open market operations.[17]

[12] "18-Day Bill Planned to Help Keep Pace with Spending," *New York Times*, August 7, 1975, p. 55. The Treasury had previously relied on direct borrowings from the Federal Reserve. See also "Treasury Boosts Earlier Estimate of Its Cash Needs," *Wall Street Journal*, August 7, 1975, p. 3; and "New Anti-Inflation Warrior," *New York Times*, August 31, 1975, p. 118.

[13] The first use of the term "cash management bill" in an official Treasury offering notice appears in Treasury press release, "Treasury to Auction Two Cash Management Bills," March 23, 1979.

[14] See the appendix to Chapter 2.

[15] Section 401 of the Second War Powers Act of March 27, 1942.

[16] 1981 Board of Governors of the Federal Reserve System Annual Report, p. 221.

[17] When the first cash management bills were offered in August 1975, the *New York Times* reported Under Secretary Yeo as saying that the bills were "designed to avoid causing

The new short-term cash management bills were so successful that Congress allowed the $5 billion exemption to the prohibition on direct purchases to expire in 1981.[18]

Notes and Bonds

Excluding irregular bills, marketable Treasury debt increased by $244 billion between the end of 1974 and the end of 1979. Notes and bonds accounted for $195 billion of the increase.

There were two differences between a note and a bond in 1970: the maturity of a note could not exceed seven years[19] and the coupon rate on a bond could not exceed 4¼ percent.[20] Secondary market bond yields rose above 4¼ percent in 1965 and the Treasury was thereafter precluded from issuing bonds until 1971, when Congress provided $10 billion of exemptive relief from the 4¼ ceiling.[21] Bonds outstanding declined through the end of 1974, when issuance finally caught up with redemptions, and then began to rise as Congress provided additional exemptive relief (Chart 28.6).[22]

Notes outstanding increased at a rate of $8.9 billion per year from the end of 1969 to the end of 1974 but then accelerated to $34.0 billion per year through the end of 1978. Chart 28.7 shows that bills and notes expanded in parallel before 1976 but that notes carried most of the financing burden

problems for Federal Reserve open market operations." "18-Day Bill Planned to Help Keep Pace with Spending," *New York Times*, August 7, 1975, p. 55. See also "New Anti-Inflation Warrior," *New York Times*, August 31, 1975, p. 118.

18 Garbade (2014).

19 The maximum maturity of a note was originally set at five years by the Victory Liberty Loan Act of March 3, 1919, and extended to seven years by the Act of June 30, 1967.

20 The 4¼ percent ceiling was established by the Third Liberty Bond Act of April 4, 1918.

21 Act of March 17, 1971. The 10-year 7 percent bond of August 15, 1981, issued on August 15, 1971, was the first bond issued after mid-1965. Federal Reserve Bank of New York Circular no. 6767, July 21, 1971; and Circular no. 6768, July 23, 1971. See also "U.S. is Resuming Long-Term Bonds," *New York Times*, July 22, 1971, p.1; and "Treasury Offers 7%, 10-Year Bonds to Individuals," *Wall Street Journal*, July 22, 1971, p. 3.

22 The exemption was increased to $12 billion by the Act of March 15, 1976; to $17 billion by the Act of June 30, 1976; to $27 billion by the Act of October 4, 1977; to $32 billion by the Act of August 3, 1978; to $40 billion by the Act of April 2, 1979; and to $50 billion by the Act of September 29, 1979. The exemption was further increased in the 1980s; see Garbade (2015, p. 25, fn. 19 and p. 55, fn. 1). The 4¼ ceiling was eliminated by Section 6301 of the Technical and Miscellaneous Revenue Act of November 10, 1988.

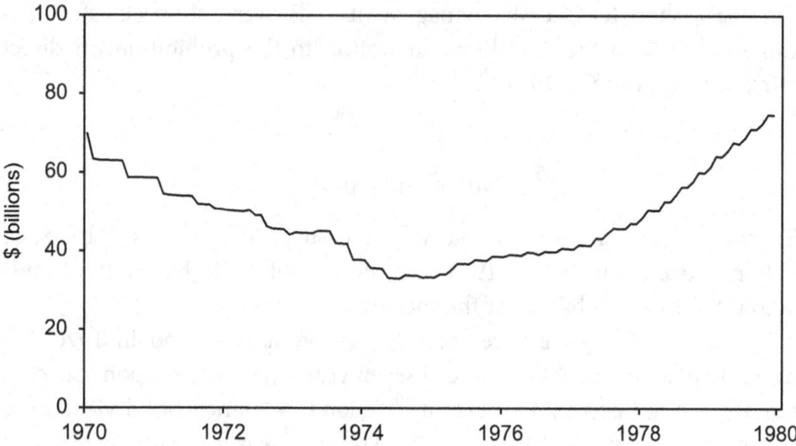

Chart 28.6 Treasury bonds. End of month.
Board of Governors of the Federal Reserve System (1981, table 28).

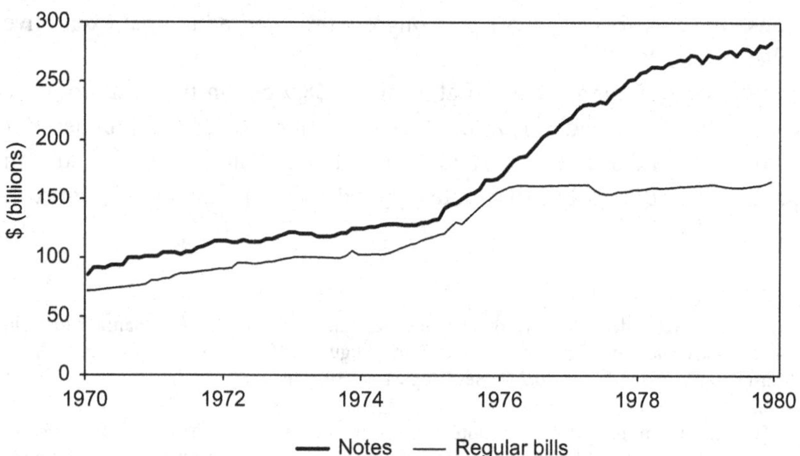

Chart 28.7 Regular Treasury bills and Treasury notes. End of month.
Board of Governors of the Federal Reserve System (1981, table 28).

after 1975. In 1976 Congress extended the maximum maturity of a note to ten years,[23] further facilitating issuance of longer-term debt at yields above 4¼ percent.

[23] Act of March 15, 1976. The 7⅞ percent note of May 15, 1986, issued on May 17, 1976, was the first note with a maturity in excess of seven years. Federal Reserve Bank of New York Circular no. 7864, April 29, 1976, and Circular no. 7865, April 30, 1976. See also

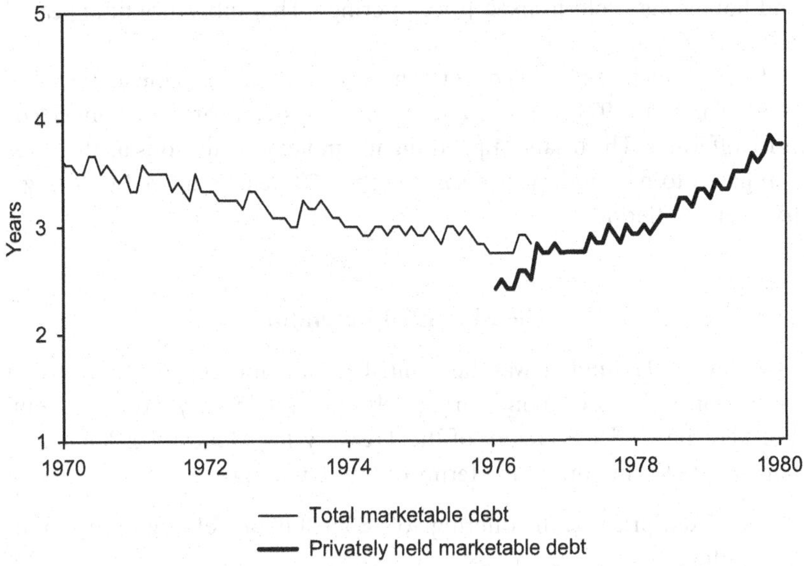

Chart 28.8 Average maturity of marketable Treasury debt.
Treasury Bulletin.

Average Maturity

The average maturity of marketable Treasury debt declined from mid-1965 to the mid-1970s, bottoming out at 2.4 years in early 1976 (Chart 28.8). The trend reversed direction in 1976 as a result of moderating bill issuance and more and longer-term note and bond issuance (facilitated by the increase in the maximum maturity of a note and increases in exemptive relief from the 4¼ ceiling).

THE INTRODUCTION OF TREASURY NOTE AND BOND AUCTIONS[24]

Chapter 20 above observed that bill issuance was dramatically different from note and bond issuance in the 1960s: bills were auctioned while notes

"Treasury Soon Will Begin Sale to Refund $5.6 Billion of Notes Amid Weak Prices," *Wall Street Journal*, April 26, 1976, p. 21, and "Treasury Slates $6.25 Billion Sale of Notes, Bonds," *Wall Street Journal*, April 29, 1976, p. 25.

[24] Some of the narrative in this section first appeared in Garbade (2012, pp. 357–63).

and bonds were sold in fixed-price offerings. That difference disappeared in the 1970s.

The first auction offering of coupon-bearing securities came in the fall of 1970. The year 1971 saw five auction offerings compared to eight fixed-price offerings. The balance tipped slightly in favor of auctions in 1972: six, compared to five, and more decisively in 1973: ten, compared to a single fixed-price offering.

The May 1970 Refunding

The May 1970 refunding was the seminal event that triggered the extension of auction sales to coupon-bearing debt. On Wednesday, April 29, Paul Volcker, the Under Secretary of the Treasury for Monetary Affairs since January 1969, announced the terms of the refunding:

- a fixed-price cash offering of $3.5 billion of eighteen-month notes, and
- a fixed-price exchange offering of 3-year notes and 6¾-year notes for $16.6 billion of maturing securities, $11.7 billion of which was owned by the Federal Reserve.[25]

The subscription books for the cash offering would be open for one day only, on Tuesday, May 5. The books for the exchange offering were set to close on May 6.

In a nationally televised speech on the evening of Thursday, April 30, President Richard Nixon announced that American ground combat forces had crossed over from South Viet Nam into Cambodia in a large-scale operation aimed at eliminating Communist sanctuaries.[26] By Monday, May 4, antiwar protests had erupted at dozens of American colleges, four students had been killed by National Guard troops at Kent State University in Ohio, and (in the words of the *Wall Street Journal*) "the bond markets were battered."[27] Treasury yields rose 25 basis points and the refunding was in danger of failing. The *Journal* reported that "several Government securities specialists thought the Federal Reserve System would consider

[25] Federal Reserve Bank of New York Circular no. 6531, April 29, 1970, and Circular no. 6533, May 1, 1970.

[26] "Nixon Sends Combat Forces to Cambodia to Drive Communists from Staging Zone," *New York Times*, May 1, 1970, p. 1.

[27] "Prices Take Battering from the Shockwaves of Cambodian Invasion," *Wall Street Journal*, May 5, 1970, p. 31.

entering the open market in an attempt to raise prices and lower yields, thereby possibly shoring up the Treasury's operation."[28]

The Fed acted as expected; buying what was described by the *Wall Street Journal* as "large quantities" of Treasury bills.[29] The *New York Times* reported that "the Federal Reserve System was forced to make 'massive' purchases of securities in the open market to prevent the Treasury's $3.5 billion sale of notes . . . from failing . . ."[30] The 1970 Markets annual report states that "Treasury bill purchases totaling $1.5 billion were made in the week ended May 6 and these were supplemented by the execution of $1.2 billion of repurchase agreements."[31] The *Journal* reported that "just prior to [the close of] the Treasury's offering of its 18-month notes, department officials were said to have used some hard-sell tactics in an effort to influence several major commercial banks to participate." A spokesman for one large New York bank acknowledged that "we felt compelled to support the Treasury."[32]

Despite the bill purchases, repos, and strongarm tactics, the Treasury barely covered the offering, receiving subscriptions for only $3.6 billion of the 18-month notes.[33] It filled all subscriptions in full and left subscribers with many more notes than anticipated. The *New York Times* reported that "Wall Street generally expected allotments [on the cash offering] to fall somewhere between 50 per cent and 70 per cent of subscriptions."[34] The *Wall Street Journal* quoted one banker as saying that he guessed "orders [for the cash offering] above $200,000 might receive as much as 60% of their desired amount – but 100% never entered my mind."[35] Following the close of the subscription books for the exchange offerings the Treasury

[28] "Prices Take Battering from the Shockwaves of Cambodian Invasion," *Wall Street Journal*, May 5, 1970, p. 31.

[29] "Treasury and Federal Reserve Join to Place $3.5 Billion Securities," *Wall Street Journal*, May 6, 1970, p. 31.

[30] "Reserve Open Market Purchases Came to Aid of Treasury Notes," *New York Times*, May 8, 1970, p. 50. The *Times* article does not indicate why "massive" is in quotes. The 1970 Annual Report of Open Market Operations, p. A-11, similarly characterized bill purchases in the May 6 statement week as "massive."

[31] 1970 Annual Report of Open Market Operations, pp. A-15 to A-16.

[32] "Refunding Cash Runoff Seemingly High at 31.5% But Treasury Satisfied," *Wall Street Journal*, May 11, 1970, p. 20.

[33] "Bond Note Issue is Barely Sold," *New York Times*, May 8, 1970, p. 50, and "Response to $3.6 Billion U.S. Refunding is Believed Unusually Poor by Dealers," *Wall Street Journal*, May 8, 1970, p. 17.

[34] "Bond Note Issue is Barely Sold," *New York Times*, May 8, 1970, p. 50.

[35] "Response to $3.6 Billion U.S. Refunding is Believed Unusually Poor by Dealers," *Wall Street Journal*, May 8, 1970, p. 17.

announced that 31.5 percent of the $4.9 billion of the publicly held rights had been redeemed for cash.[36]

A month after the refunding the *New York Times* asked Milton Friedman whether Federal Reserve "rescue operations" for Treasury financings might be distorting monetary policy, leaving money market conditions easier than intended. The *Times* reported Friedman as saying that "the fault in these cases lay in the Treasury's funding methods. The Treasury should change to issuing all its financing through open auction instead of attempting to pre-assess market rates."[37]

The First Auction

On Thursday, October 22, Under Secretary Volcker announced the terms of the first leg of the November 1970 refunding: an exchange offering of 3½-year notes and 5¾-year notes for $7.7 billion of maturing securities, $6.0 billion of which was owned by the public.[38] The *New York Times* reported that "many Wall Street bond dealers regarded [the terms of the offering] as not particularly attractive." One dealer described the 7½ percent yield on the 5¾-year note as "chintzy."[39] Attrition on the maturing debt was expected to run as high as 15 to 20 percent. Volcker said he would announce a follow-on cash offering of short-term securities (to cover attrition and to raise new cash) after the exchange offering had been completed.[40]

Between the announcement of the offering and the close of the subscription books on Thursday, October 29, Treasury yields fell about 15 basis points and the offering ended up looking reasonably attractive. Attrition was limited to 10.8 percent of the publicly owned securities.[41]

On Friday, October 30, Volcker announced the second leg of the refunding: a cash offering of $2 billion of eighteen-month 6¾ percent notes. He further announced that, breaking with tradition, the notes would

[36] "Reserve Offers to Buy U.S. Notes," *New York Times*, May 9, 1970, p. 35, and "Refunding Cash Runoff Seemingly High at 31.5% But Treasury Satisfied," *Wall Street Journal*, May 11, 1970, p. 20.

[37] "Friedman Expecting New Money Rein by the Reserve," *New York Times*, June 11, 1970, p. 65.

[38] Federal Reserve Bank of New York Circular no. 6623, October 22, 1970.

[39] "Treasury Notes Register Upturn," *New York Times*, October 30, 1970, p. 59.

[40] "Treasury to Seek Fresh $4.5 Billion Before Year-End," *Wall Street Journal*, October 23, 1970, p. 2.

[41] Federal Reserve Bank of New York Circular no. 6633, November 6, 1970.

be sold on an auction basis. Volcker observed that auctioning securities would give the Treasury "a little more flexibility in a variety of market circumstances," noting that market conditions often change between the time an offering is announced and when the subscription books close.[42]

Treasury officials were cautious in structuring the first public auction offering of coupon-bearing securities in thirty-five years. Rather than auction long-term bonds from the get-go (as they had in 1935[43]), they chose to start with short-term notes and they repeatedly reminded market participants of the similarity between the forthcoming note auction and the well-established bill auctions. The October 30 announcement observed that "the use of the auction method of sale represents an adaptation of the technique used successfully for many years in marketing Treasury bills."[44] Three days later, officials remarked that "bidding and other procedures in the Treasury's new $2 billion cash financing will very closely follow the standard procedure used in regular Treasury bill auctions."[45]

The Treasury received tenders for $5.2 billion of notes – 2.6 times the amount offered. It accepted bids ranging from 100.93 percent of principal (to yield 6.09 percent) down to a stop-out price of 100.69 (to yield 6.26 percent), where there was a 32 percent pro rata allocation. The average accepted price was 100.76 (to yield 6.21 percent).[46] The *Wall Street Journal* characterized the auction as "highly successful."[47]

Subsequent Auction Offerings of Notes and Bonds

Treasury officials brought five auction offerings of notes in 1971, with maturities ranging from fifteen months to five years and two months (Table 28.2). In a speech on March 7, 1972, Volcker characterized the offerings as a "striking innovation": "I cannot claim that [the auction] approach has yet been fully tested in adversity. But I can say it has met or surpassed every expectation so far, to the advantage of the Treasury and the market. I am confident it will pass further testing with larger amounts

[42] "Treasury to Sell in Competitive Auction $2 Billion of 6¾% Notes Due in 1½ Years," *Wall Street Journal*, November 2, 1970, p. 3.

[43] Garbade (2012, pp. 286–93).

[44] Federal Reserve Bank of New York Circular no. 6629, October 30, 1970.

[45] Federal Reserve Bank of New York Circular no. 6631, November 2, 1970.

[46] Federal Reserve Bank of New York Circular no. 6633, November 6, 1970.

[47] "Treasury Note Sale is Highly Successful," *Wall Street Journal*, November 6, 1970, p. 20.

Table 28.2 *Auction offerings of Treasury notes, 1971.*

Auction date	Term	Quantity offered ($ billions)	Quantity bid ($ billions)	Range of accepted yields (percent)	Average accepted yield (percent)
Jun. 22	16 mo.	2.25	4.0	5.71–6.05	6.00
Aug. 5	18 mo.	2.50	4.1	6.44–6.59	6.54
Aug. 31	5 yr., 2 mo.	1.25	3.4	5.92–6.02	5.98
Oct. 15	3 yr., 4 mo.	2.00	4.6	5.46–5.61	5.58
Nov. 9	15 mo.	2.75	4.0	4.79–4.96	4.91

Federal Reserve Bank of New York circulars.

Table 28.3 *Auction offerings of Treasury notes and bonds, 1972.*

Auction date	Term	Quantity offered ($ billions)	Quantity bid ($ billions)	Range of accepted yields (percent)	Average accepted yield (percent)
Mar. 28	3 yr.	1.75	3.8	5.69–5.80	5.78
May 2	1 yr.	1.25	3.3	4.23–4.47	4.44
May 2	9¾ yr.	0.50	1.3	6.23–6.32	6.29
Oct. 11	2 yr.	2.00	4.8	5.77–5.89	5.86
Nov. 1	4 yr.	3.00	7.1	6.16–6.21	6.20
Dec. 20	2 yr.	2.00	5.6	5.72–5.85	5.83

Federal Reserve Bank of New York circulars.

and longer maturities."[48] The Treasury brought six additional auction offerings of coupon-bearing securities in 1972 (Table 28.3), including a 9¾-year bond.

The Treasury began auctioning long-term bonds in January 1973. To meet the objection voiced by Treasury Secretary Anderson in 1959 – that many investors who subscribed to fixed-price Treasury offerings did not have the "professional capacity" to bid in auctions[49] – the Treasury adopted a single-price format in which tenders at or above the stop-out

[48] Volcker (1972). Volcker's speech was reported in "Proposals on Reform of Debt Management Offered by Volcker," *New York Times*, March 8, 1972, p. 57; and "Treasury Seeking to Put More Borrowing on Regular Basis, as with Bill Auctions," *Wall Street Journal*, March 8, 1972, p. 2.

[49] Joint Economic Committee (1959, Part 6A, p. 1148).

Table 28.4 *Auction offerings of long-term Treasury bonds in a single-price format, 1973–74.*

Auction date	Term	Quantity offered ($ billions)	Quantity bid ($ billions)	Yield (percent)
Jan. 4, 1973	20 yr.	0.63	1.67	6.79
May 2, 1973	25 yr.	0.65	1.24	7.11
Aug. 1, 1973	20 yr.	0.50	0.26	8.00
Oct. 1, 1973	19¾ yr.	0.30	1.29	7.35
Feb. 7, 1974	19½ yr.	0.30	1.14	7.46
May 8, 1974	25 yr.	0.30	0.90	8.23

Federal Reserve Bank of New York circulars.

price were awarded securities at the stop.[50] The Treasury observed that "this procedure will provide an incentive to bid at prices sufficiently high to be sure of awards, while also assuring each bidder that, if he bids at a price within the range of accepted bids, he will be awarded bonds at the same price as every other bidder."[51] Over the next sixteen months the Treasury offered long-term bonds in single-price auctions five more times (Table 28.4).

Consequences of Bond Auctions for Advance Refundings

The decision to auction bonds, rather than selling them in fixed-price offerings, led to the termination of advance refundings but did not impede Treasury's continuing efforts at maturity extension.

In the second half of the 1960s, when the 4¼ percent ceiling on bond coupon rates precluded bond offerings in advance refundings as well as in conventional cash and exchange refundings, Treasury officials offered, in "pre-refunding" exchanges, notes for securities due to mature in less than a year (Table 20.2). Following Congressional provision of $10 billion of exemptive relief from the 4¼ ceiling in March 1971[52] officials

[50] Friedman (1960, pp. 64–65) had recommended the single-price format as a way to broaden the primary market.

[51] Federal Reserve Bank of New York Circular no. 7071, December 27, 1972. Volcker (1972) had hinted, in March 1972, at the possibility of auctioning long-term bonds in a single-price format, saying that "we are prepared to explore further variants [of the auction process], including (as the maturity is extended) the possibility of awarding all bids at the stop-out price to encourage wider investor participation."

[52] Act of March 17, 1971.

Table 28.5 *Advance refundings in the 1970s.*

Settlement date	Offer to issue . . .	In exchange for . . .
Feb. 15, 1971	4½-year notes and 7-year notes	\$11.0 billion of securities maturing in 9 months and \$7.0 billion of securities maturing in 1 year
Nov. 15, 1971	7-year notes and 15-year bonds	\$7.3 billion of securities maturing in 6 months and \$6.0 billion of securities maturing in 9 months
Feb. 15, 1972	11-year bonds	\$6.3 billion of securities maturing in 2 years and \$8.1 billion of securities maturing in 2¼ years
Aug. 15, 1972	3½-year notes, 7-year notes, and 12-year bonds	\$2.3 billion of securities maturing in 3 months and \$2.5 billion of securities maturing in 4 months
Aug. 15, 1972	7-year notes and 12-year bonds	\$9.4 billion of securities maturing in 2¼ years and \$7.2 billion of securities maturing in 2½ years

Federal Reserve Bank of New York circulars.

returned to offering bonds (Table 28.5). The advance refunding program ended in 1972 when it proved impractical to structure advance refundings around an auction process. Debt extension nevertheless continued, in the form of cash auction offerings of progressively longer-term debt (Chart 28.9).

Fine-Tuning the Auction Process

By mid-1973, auction sales of notes and bonds had replaced fixed-price offerings. The Treasury had not announced a fixed-price cash offering since August 1970 and the most recent fixed-price exchange offering was in February 1973. However, the auction process did not remain unchanged.

A Failed Auction and the Advent of Yield Auctions

The first setback to Treasury's note and bond auction program came in the August 1973 refunding. To refinance \$4.7 billion of maturing securities held by the public, Treasury officials announced on July 25 that they would auction \$2 billion of four-year 7¾ percent notes, \$500 million of

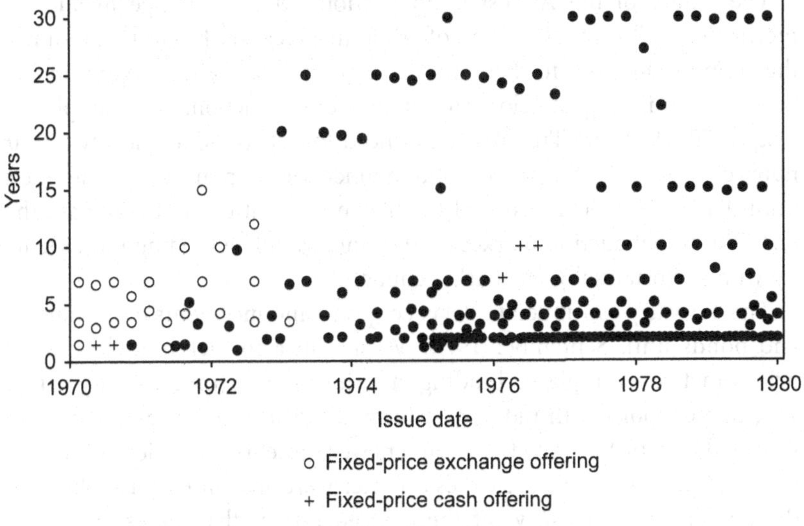

Chart 28.9 Maturities of Treasury note and bond offerings.
Federal Reserve Bank of New York circulars.

twenty-year 7½ percent bonds, and $2 billion of thirty-five-day tax anticipation bills.[53]

Treasury yields rose sharply in late July, victims of an ongoing program of aggressive monetary restraint. Between July 16 and July 30, the yield on five-year notes rose from 7.21 percent to 7.80 percent and the yield on twenty-year bonds rose from 7.21 percent to 7.56 percent.

On July 31, the Treasury received tenders for $2.1 billion of the new 4-year notes, barely more than the quantity on offer. Officials accepted all bids above 99.01 (the lowest price it said it would accept) and 75 percent of the bids at 99.01.[54]

On the following day, the twenty-year bond auction failed. The Treasury received public tenders for only $260 million of bonds. It accepted all of the tenders submitted at or above 95.05, the lowest price it said it would accept. The balance of the offering went to "Government accounts."[55]

[53] Federal Reserve Bank of New York Circular no. 7193, July 25, 1973; and Circular no. 7194, July 26, 1973.

[54] Federal Reserve Bank of New York Circular no. 7201, August 2, 1973; and "Bond Prices Drop in Gloomy Market," *New York Times*, August 1, 1973, p. 51.

[55] Federal Reserve Bank of New York Circular no. 7201, August 2, 1973. The lowest prices the Treasury said it would accept were marginally above the original issue discount

The failure of the August bond auction led to a change in auction mechanics. Following the failed offering, the Treasury began to announce the coupon rate on a forthcoming issue several days after the announcement of the offering and closer to the time of the auction. For example, on August 20, 1973, the Treasury announced that it would auction two-year notes on August 24 but it did not announce the coupon rate on the notes until August 22.[56] This reduced the likelihood (but did not eliminate the possibility) that auction market participants would be bidding for a security with a substantially off-market coupon.

The Treasury continued to delay coupon announcements on new notes and bonds until September 1974, when – in a further modification of prior practice – it replaced bidding in terms of price (on a security with a specified coupon) with bidding in terms of yield (on a security with no specified coupon). Competitive tenders were accepted in order of increasing yield until all of the securities on offer were accounted for. Following the auction, the Treasury set the coupon rate at the highest rate – in increments of one-eighth of a percent – that gave an average price on the accepted tenders not greater than par. Each accepted tender was then invoiced at its own bid yield. The Treasury remarked that "the new bidding method will permit pricing close to par and eliminate the risk of setting a coupon which, because of a change in the market between the coupon announcement date and the auction date, would result, on the one hand, in a price so far above par as to discourage bidders or, on the other hand, result in a price so low that the sale would have to be cancelled."[57]

thresholds of 99 for a four-year note and 95 for a twenty-year bond. US tax law generally provided that the difference between the par value of a note or bond and the issue price, commonly called original issue discount, should be taxed as a capital gain if the security was held to maturity. (Interest payments were taxed as ordinary income as they were received.) However, if a security was issued at a price significantly below par, a purchaser was required to recognize a portion of the original issue discount as ordinary income each year. (This prevented issuers from converting ordinary income into capital gains by issuing notes and bonds at large discounts from par.) The "OID threshold" that separated the two regimes was defined as par minus the number of full years to maturity times ¼ percent. Thus, a twenty-year bond had an OID threshold of 95 percent of par (95 = 100 – 20 years to maturity, times ¼ percent). See also Baker (1976, p. 148).

56 Federal Reserve Bank of New York Circular no. 7213, August 20, 1973; and Circular no. 7215, August 22, 1973.

57 Federal Reserve Bank of New York Circular no. 7456, September 16, 1974. See also Carson (1959, p. 441) and Baker (1976, p. 148, and 1979, pp. 205–6).

The End of Single-Price Auctions

The single-price format used to auction long-term bonds was not popular with dealers. Henry Kaufman, a respected economist at Salomon Brothers, stated bluntly that the format "provides no incentives to . . . dealers to help in the distribution process."[58]

Treasury officials had a different objective in mind when they introduced the single-price format. In response to complaints that the format deprived dealers of an opportunity to buy bonds slightly cheaper than other auction participants, an official pointed out that "the objective is to encourage widespread and confident bidding" and "a broader distribution of our securities." "We're appealing to a type of investor," the official said, "who will be able to bid what he thinks the bond is worth to him without worrying about whether somebody else may get it cheaper."[59]

On May 8, 1974, Deputy Secretary of the Treasury William Simon, formerly a senior partner at Salomon Brothers in charge of the government bond department and the first president of the Association of Primary Dealers in United States Government Securities, was sworn in as Secretary of the Treasury.[60] In the very next refunding, in August 1974, the Treasury switched to a multiple-price auction format for long-term bonds.[61] The Treasury did not state a reason for the change. One money market newsletter reported at the time that "debt managers found no evidence that [the single-price format] was attracting enough additional or different bidders for the bonds to make its use worthwhile."[62] Jack Bennett, the Under Secretary of the Treasury for Monetary Affairs from July 1974 to June 1975, later stated that Simon "made the decision to discontinue the [single-price format] as a result of his judgment, based on his extensive experience in the market for Treasury securities, that the [single-price format] would bring in fewer dollars to the Treasury."[63]

58 Kaufman (1973, p. 170).

59 "Price of Treasury Bonds Decline in Light Trading," *New York Times*, December 29, 1972, p. 39.

60 "Simon Nominated as Treasury Secretary; Nixon to Expand His Own Economic Role," *Wall Street Journal*, April 18, 1974, p. 3. See also "Dent Named Commerce Chief as Expected; Simon of Salomon Bros. No. 2 in Treasury," *Wall Street Journal*, December 7, 1972, p. 3.

61 Federal Reserve Bank of New York Circular no. 7429, July 31, 1974.

62 *The Goldsmith-Nagan Bond and Money Market Letter*, August 3, 1974.

63 Committee on Banking, Housing, and Urban Affairs (1991, p. 409). Baker (1979, pp. 205–6) discusses the decision to adopt a single-price format in 1973 but does not comment on why the Treasury abandoned that format in 1974. Two papers, Tsao and Vignola (1977) and Simon (1994), examine whether the Treasury received more

A Last Harrah for Fixed-Price Offerings

Although by mid-1973 it seemed clear that, going forward, yields on primary market sales of Treasury notes and bonds would be market-determined rather than fixed by Treasury officials, subscription offerings staged a brief comeback in 1976, when officials became particularly anxious to extend the maturity structure of the debt. The 1976 Treasury Annual Report explained that, "to develop a broad market for the coupon financings of the size and frequency necessary to accomplish significant debt lengthening," the Treasury made three fixed-price offerings.[64]

In late January 1976, officials announced the terms of the February refunding: $3 billion of 3-year notes, $3.5 billion of 7-year 8 percent notes, and $400 million of 29¼-year bonds.[65] The shorter note and the bond would be auctioned but, in a surprise to market participants, the seven-year note was offered at a fixed price of par. The 8 percent yield was more than 30 basis points over secondary market yields in the seven-year sector.[66]

Following the close of the subscription books Treasury announced that it had received subscriptions for $29.2 billion of the notes (8.3 times the amount offered) and that, due to the "overwhelming response," it would increase the size of the issue from $3.5 billion to $6 billion.[67] Subscriptions for up to $200 thousand would be filled in full; subscriptions for more than $200 thousand would receive only $200 thousand of the notes.

aggressive bids in the six single-price auctions or the ten multiple-price auctions of long-term bonds held between February 1973 and August 1976. Neither paper comments on why the Treasury abandoned the single-price format. Deputy Assistant Secretary of the Treasury Mark Stalnecker testified in 1982 that the Treasury "analyzed or . . . tried to do some studies on the six [single-price] auctions that we held back in the mid-seventies and the results were inconclusive. It did not appear that there were significant cost savings and frankly our view is that we receive enough bids under our current auction mechanism, and it is well received by both investors and market professionals, so that after selling six securities by the [single-price] auction mechanisms with mixed results we ended that experiment." Committee on Banking, Finance and Urban Affairs (1982, p. 24). Chari and Weber (1992, p. 4) state that the Treasury "abandoned the experiment [with single-price auctions] as largely inconclusive" but do not cite a source.

64 1976 Treasury Annual Report, p. 11.

65 Federal Reserve Bank of New York Circular no. 7807, January 29, 1976.

66 "8% Treasury Notes Draw a Deluge of Orders," *New York Times*, February 6, 1976, p. 39.

67 Federal Reserve Bank of New York Circular no. 7811, February 6, 1976.

Treasury resorted to subscription offerings twice more in 1976, once in the May refunding (when it offered $3.5 billion of ten-year 7⅞ percent notes at par) and again in the August refunding (when it offered $4 billion of ten-year 8 percent notes at par).[68]

The offering yield on the May ten-year notes was not dramatically higher than contemporaneous yields in the secondary market. One dealer remarked that "the new 7⅞s are not the giveaway that the 8s were."[69] Treasury officials received subscriptions for 2.5 times the amount offered and increased the size of the issue to $4.7 billion, filing in full all subscriptions for less than $500 thousand that were accompanied by a 20 percent deposit and allotting 15 percent of the amount subscribed to all other subscribers.[70]

Treasury priced the ten-year notes in the August refunding more attractively and received subscriptions for $24.4 billion of the notes (6.1 times the amount offered). It increased the size of the issue to $7.6 billion, filling in full all subscriptions up to $300 thousand that were accompanied by a 20 percent deposit and allotting $300 thousand to any subscription for an amount in excess of $300 thousand that was accompanied by a 20 percent deposit.[71] The 1976 Treasury Annual Report stated that the ten-year notes were "well distributed with the bulk of [the issue] going to banks and individuals while dealers received very little."[72]

THE ADVENT OF REGULAR AND PREDICTABLE NOTE AND BOND OFFERINGS[73]

During the 1970s, as in the 1960s, the Treasury regularly sold notes and bonds in the second month of each calendar quarter, for settlement on the fifteenth of the month, either for cash or in exchange for maturing debt (Chart 28.10). Sporadically until 1976 it also sold notes and bonds on an as-needed basis in standalone cash auction offerings, that is, offerings for other than mid-quarter settlement, to replenish its cash balances (Chart 28.11).

68 Federal Reserve Bank of New York Circular no. 7864, April 29, 1976; Circular no. 7865, April 30, 1976; and Circular no. 7927, July 29, 1976.
69 "Long-Term Bonds Advance in Price," *New York Times*, April 29, 1976, p. 59.
70 Federal Reserve Bank of New York Circular no. 7870, May 10, 1976.
71 Federal Reserve Bank of New York Circular no. 7932, August 10, 1976.
72 1976 Treasury Annual Report, p. 27.
73 Some of the narrative in this section first appeared in Garbade (2012, pp. 363–67).

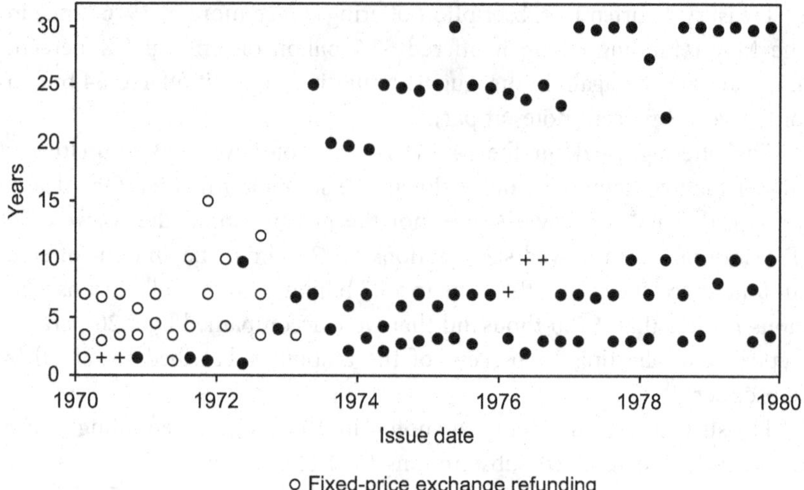

Chart 28.10 Maturities of offerings in mid-quarter refundings.
Federal Reserve Bank of New York circulars.

The Introduction of Two-Year Cycle Notes

A spate of four standalone offerings between June 1971 and March 1972 (Table 28.6) led Treasury officials to begin to think about regularizing coupon offerings outside of the mid-quarter refundings. In March, Under Secretary Volcker revealed that he was considering whether "to routinize or regularize the handling of more of our debt, as we have done for many years in the bill area."[74] In particular, Volcker was considering whether, "in contrast to building up the present concentration of note and bond maturities at quarterly intervals [on the 15th of the second month of each quarter], to be [refinanced] flexibly at the Treasury's discretion," it might not be better to adopt a scheme of "more frequent but also more routine rolling over of relatively short-term notes." Such a scheme might "reduce market uncertainties ... caused by large intermittent financing operations."

Treasury officials took the first step toward putting short-term note offerings on a regular schedule in early October 1972, when they

[74] Volcker (1972).

Table 28.6 *Stand-alone cash offerings in 1971 and 1972.*

Auction date	Issue date	Maturity date	Term (years)	Amount offered ($ billions)
Jun. 22, 1971	Jun. 29, 1971	Nov. 15, 1972	2.3	2.25
Aug. 31, 1971	Sep. 8, 1971	Nov. 15, 1976	5.2	1.25
Oct. 15, 1971	Oct. 22, 1971	Feb. 15, 1975	3.3	2.00
Mar. 28, 1972	Apr. 3, 1972	May 15, 1975	3.1	1.75

Federal Reserve Bank of New York circulars.

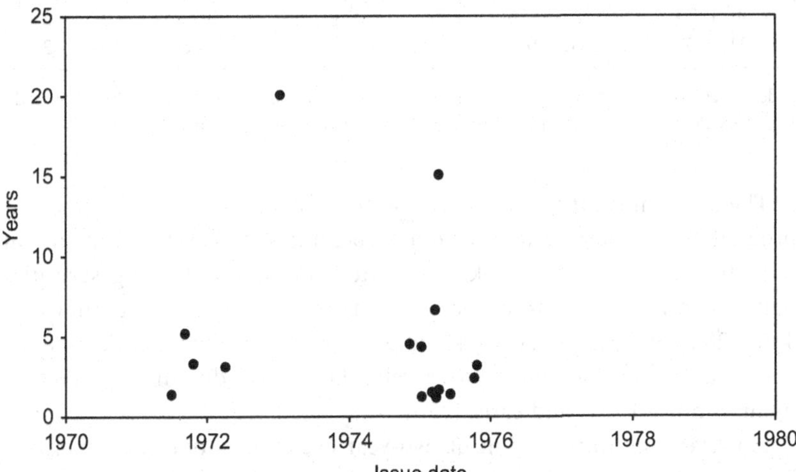

Chart 28.11 Maturities of stand-alone offerings. All of the offerings were cash auction offerings.
Federal Reserve Bank of New York circulars.

announced that they would soon begin to auction two-year notes at regular quarterly intervals. The first tranche – $2 billion of notes maturing on September 30, 1974 – was auctioned on October 11.[75] One market participant praised the new program as "safe, simple, and not at all damaging to the market."[76]

[75] Federal Reserve Bank of New York Circular no. 7013, October 5, 1972; and Circular no. 7014, October 6, 1972.

[76] "Treasury Treads Lightly at Outset of Big Refunding," *New York Times*, October 6, 1972, p. 59.

Table 28.7 *Two-year notes issued prior to 1975 and how they were refinanced at maturity. Two-year notes were not issued in the first half of 1973 because Treasury's cash balances grew unexpectedly large and Treasury did not need the money.*

Two-year notes issued prior to 1975			Refinancing note	
Issue date	Maturity date	Term	Maturity date	Term
Oct. 19, 1972	Sep. 30, 1974	1 yr., 11 mo., 11d	Sep. 30, 1976	2 yr.
Dec. 28, 1972	Dec. 31, 1974	2 yr., 3d	Dec. 31, 1976	2 yr.
Sep. 4, 1973	Sep. 30, 1975	2 yr., 26d	Sep. 30, 1977	2 yr.
Nov. 15, 1973	Dec. 31, 1975	2 yr., 1 mo., 16d	Dec. 31, 1977	2 yr.
Apr. 9, 1974	Mar. 31, 1976	1 yr., 11 mo., 22d	Mar. 31, 1978	2 yr.
May 15, 1974	Jun. 30, 1976	2 yr., 1 mo., 15d	Jun. 30, 1978	2 yr.
Sep. 30, 1974	Sep. 30, 1976	2 yr.	Sep. 30, 1978	2 yr.
Dec. 31, 1974	Dec. 31, 1976	2 yr.	Dec. 31, 1978	2 yr.

Federal Reserve Bank of New York circulars, 1973 Treasury Annual Report, pp. 12 and 22; and "Treasury Postpones $2 Billion Note Offering," *Wall Street Journal*, April 2, 1973, p. 17.

The 2-year note program broke new ground in two ways: it was the first program of regular offerings of coupon-bearing securities with a common term to maturity and it broke the pattern of coupon-bearing securities maturing on the fifteenth of the second month of a quarter. As shown in Table 28.7, officials put two-year notes on a self-sustaining cycle separate and apart from the mid-quarter refundings that dominated Treasury finance in the 1960s and early 1970s.

However, the introduction of two-year cycle notes did not signal that longer-term notes and bonds would soon be sold on a similarly regular and predictable basis. Volcker commented that "regularization and routinization are nice sounding words; straitjacket and rigidity are not. From where I sit, I cannot help but be conscious of the number of times in which particular market or economic objectives may influence the Treasury's thinking as to the form of a particular financing."[77] Officials were not yet ready to abandon tactical discretion.

Extending Regular and Predictable Issuance to Intermediate-Term Notes

The rate of growth of marketable Treasury debt increased sharply in late 1974 and 1975. Outstanding notes and bonds increased by $26 billion

[77] Volcker (1972).

Table 28.8 *Stand-alone cash offerings in 1974 and 1975, exclusive of two-year notes.*

Auction date	Issue date	Maturity date	Term (years)	Amount offered ($ billions)
Oct. 23, 1974	Nov. 6, 1974	May 15, 1979	4.5	1.00
Dec. 30, 1974	Jan. 7, 1975	May 15, 1979	4.4	1.25
Jan. 2, 1975	Jan. 9, 1975	Mar 31, 1976	1.2	0.75
Feb. 19, 1975	Mar. 3, 1975	Aug. 31,1976	1.5	1.65
Mar. 11, 1975	Mar. 19, 1975	Nov. 15, 1981	6.7	1.75
Mar. 13, 1975	Mar. 25, 1975	May 31, 1976	1.2	1.60
Mar. 20, 1975	Apr. 7, 1975	May 15, 1990	15.1	1.25
Apr. 1, 1975	Apr. 8, 1975	Nov. 30, 1976	1.6	1.50
May 22, 1975	Jun. 6, 1975	Oct. 31, 1976	1.4	1.60
Sep. 24, 1975	Oct. 7, 1975	Feb. 28, 1978	2.4	2.10
Oct. 7, 1975	Oct. 22, 1975	Dec. 31, 1978	3.2	2.50

Federal Reserve Bank of New York circulars.

between mid-1974 and mid-1975 and increased by another $19 billion in the second half of 1975. The rapid expansion led Treasury officials to regularize note offerings beyond the two-year sector.

Deficit forecasts deteriorated dramatically during the winter of 1974–75. In November 1974 federal officials estimated that the deficit for the fiscal year ending June 30, 1975, would be about $9 billion[78] and that the deficit for the following year would be $10 to $20 billion.[79] By March 1975, the projections had grown to $45 billion and $80 billion, respectively.[80]

The five-fold growth in the two-year deficit (from $25 billion to $125 billion) meant that the Treasury would have to raise an unprecedented (for a peacetime economy) amount of new money. As early as December 1974 economists were predicting that standalone offerings would be made in nearly every month of the first half of 1975.[81] The Treasury ultimately brought a total of eleven such offerings in late 1974 and 1975 (Table 28.8).

Treasury officials struggled to cope with the expanded funding requirements. In January 1975 they announced an offering of two-year notes

[78] "Estimate of Fiscal '75 Deficit Raised by Ford Aides as Recession Cuts Revenues," *Wall Street Journal*, November 21, 1974, p. 2.

[79] "Fiscal '76 Budget Deficit is Now Likely, in a Range of $10 Billion to $20 Billion," *New York Times*, November 11, 1974, p. 3.

[80] "$37-Billion Rise in Deficit Is Seen," *New York Times*, March 18, 1975, p. 15.

[81] "Treasury Plans Big Borrowings," *New York Times*, December 30, 1974, p. 39.

outside of the quarterly cycle established in 1972.[82] Under Secretary of the Treasury Jack Bennett (who had replaced Volcker in July 1974) stated that "in the coming months, we will be studying the possibility of establishing regular month-end, rather than quarter-end, two-year [cycle] notes . . ."[83] Officials confirmed the new monthly frequency in April.[84]

Treasury officials soon reached the limit of what could be accommodated within the existing debt management framework. On March 20, 1975, the Treasury auctioned $1.25 billion of fifteen-year bonds[85] at the same time that an underwriting syndicate led by Morgan Stanley & Co. brought to market the largest industrial debt offering in history: $300 million of ten-year notes and $300 million of thirty-year debentures from AAA-rated General Motors Corporation.[86] The simultaneous public and private offerings left the bond market in "chaos."[87] One participant described the market as "a disaster," another said it was "a shambles." The *New York Times* reported that the "head-on competition between the most credit-worthy borrowers from the public and private sectors left the bond market in disarray." The chairman of the Joint Economic Committee, Senator Hubert Humphrey, criticized Treasury debt management as "being conducted in an inexplicable and seemingly highly inappropriate fashion."[88]

The deficit had to be financed but closely spaced standalone offerings and head-to-head competition with private-sector borrowers could be minimized with regular offerings. In June 1975 Treasury officials announced $1.75 billion of four-year notes that "might be the first of a 'cycle' of four-year notes maturing at the end of a quarter."[89] "Might" turned to "would" when they announced a second tranche of four-year notes in August.[90]

[82] "Treasury to Sell $10.6 Billion Debt in Three Offers," *Wall Street Journal*, January 23, 1975, p. 23. The offering was made three weeks later. Federal Reserve Bank of New York Circular no. 7569, February 11, 1975, and Circular no. 7570, February 13, 1975.

[83] Committee on Ways and Means (1975, p. 16).

[84] "Official of Treasury Discloses Need for $41-Billion," *New York Times*, April 1, 1975, p. 62.

[85] Federal Reserve Bank of New York Circular no. 7585; March 12, 1975, and Circular no. 7586, March 14, 1975.

[86] "Borrowing Dilemma," *New York Times*, March 20, 1975, p. 57.

[87] "Treasury Bond Auction Creates Chaos; Supply of Money Shows a Record Rise," *New York Times*, March 21, 1975, p. 53.

[88] "Financier for the U.S. Debt," *New York Times*, April 20, 1975, p. 171.

[89] Federal Reserve Bank of New York Circular no. 7657, June 19, 1975, and "2 New Notes, More Bills but No Long-Term Issue," *New York Times*, June 19, 1975, p. 63.

[90] Federal Reserve Bank of New York Circular no. 7684, August 7, 1975, Circular no. 7685, August 8, 1975; and "Treasury Boosts Earlier Estimate of Its Cash Needs," *Wall Street Journal*, August 7, 1975, p. 3, referring to the second tranche of four-year notes as "the second four-year cycle note."

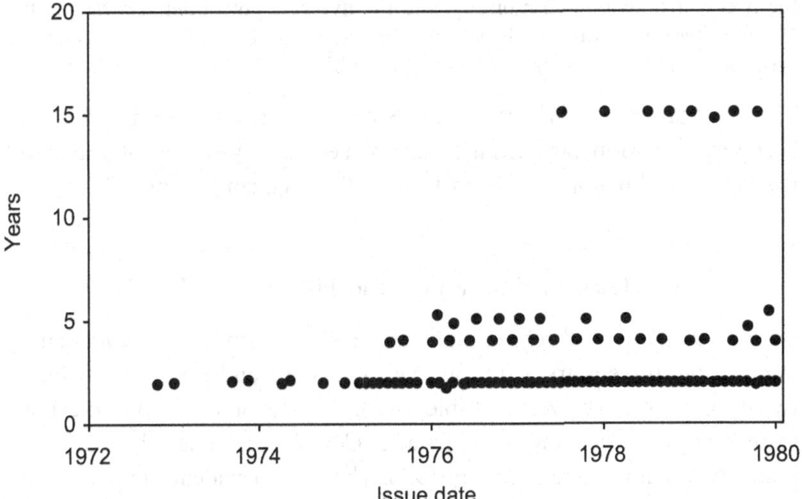

Chart 28.12 Maturities of two-, four-, and five-year note offerings and fifteen-year bond offerings. All of the offerings were cash auction offerings.
Federal Reserve Bank of New York circulars.

In January 1976 Under Secretary Yeo (who had replaced Bennett in August 1975) announced that officials were "seriously considering" adopting a new series of five-year cycle notes.[91] By mid-1976, the Treasury was issuing two-year notes monthly (at the end of each month) and four- and five-year notes quarterly – 5s at the beginning of the first month of a quarter and 4s toward the end of the third month of the quarter (Chart 28.12).

The significance of the regularization of intermediate-term note offerings was widely appreciated. In an interview in late June 1976, Under Secretary Yeo noted the contribution of regular and predictable offerings in limiting the long-run cost of financing the national debt.[92] A primary dealer opined that "regularity makes a lot of sense from a debt management view" and went on to observe that,

> Treasury is making every effort to extend debt maturities and has developed a regular system to accomplish its objective. Two key elements of this program are

[91] "Treasury Plans Heavy Borrowing," *New York Times*, January 28, 1976, p. 58; and "Treasury to Sell $13.8 Billion Bills, Notes and Bonds," *Wall Street Journal*, January 28, 1976, p. 25.

[92] "Treasury Refines Its Management of Federal Debt," *New York Times*, June 28, 1976, p. 50.

the two-year note, offered monthly, and the five-year note, offered each quarter. Making these new issues available on a regular basis gives market participants a better feel for the securities when they are sold.[93]

The *Wall Street Journal* noted that "Secretary William Simon and Under Secretary for Monetary Affairs Edwin Yeo, two veterans of the bond market, played major roles in instituting the financing changes."[94]

Mid-Quarter Refundings and Fifteen-Year Bonds

By late 1974, a typical refunding offered a short-term anchor note maturing in about three years, a six- or seven-year note, and a bond maturing in twenty-five or thirty years (Table 28.9). The tenor of the middle issue varied between seven and ten years after Congress extended the maximum maturity of a note to ten years in 1976. There is no evidence that Treasury officials seriously considered regularizing the maturities of refunding issues in the 1970s.[95]

Anthony Solomon became Under Secretary of the Treasury for Monetary Affairs on March 30, 1977, and promptly initiated a reappraisal of the Treasury's five-year note program. In the course of announcing the terms of the May refunding, Solomon remarked that he was considering replacing the expected July offering of five-year notes with fifteen-year bonds.[96] The Treasury had issued fifteen-year bonds on only two prior occasions in the 1970s,[97] the second of which had not left fond memories. The *New York Times* described the sector as "untested."[98]

[93] "Treasury to Raise $2.5 Billion by Selling 61-Month Notes Despite Bulging Coffers," *Wall Street Journal*, June 28, 1976, p. 15.

[94] "Treasury to Raise $2.5 Billion by Selling 61-Month Notes Despite Bulging Coffers," *Wall Street Journal*, June 28, 1976, p. 15.

[95] The maturities of refunding issues were regularized in the early 1980s to three- and ten-year notes and thirty-year bonds. See Garbade (2007, Charts 2 and 7) and Garbade (2015, Chart 2.2).

[96] "U.S. with Cash Surplus in Quarter, Plans to Pay Off $2 Billion of Debt," *New York Times*, April 28, 1977, p. 85, and "Treasury to Sell $3.75 Billion of Securities," *Wall Street Journal*, April 28, 1977, p. 33.

[97] The Treasury offered a fifteen-year bond in the November 1971 refunding (Federal Reserve Bank of New York Circular no. 6825, October 27, 1971; and Circular no. 6827, October 29, 1971) and as a standalone issue in March 1975 (Federal Reserve Bank of New York Circular no. 7585, March 12, 1975, and Circular no. 7586, March 14, 1975).

[98] "Treasury Plans Sale of $1.5 Billion Bonds," *New York Times*, June 28, 1977, p. 47. Fifteen-year bonds ultimately proved to be unpopular and were replaced with twenty-year bonds in late 1980. Twenty-year bonds were equally unpopular and were terminated in 1986. Garbade (2015, pp. 45–50).

Table 28.9 *Term to maturity of note and bond offerings in mid-quarter refundings.*

	Term to maturity (in years) of . . .		
Refunding	Anchor issue	Middle issue	Long issue
Feb. 1970	1.50	3.50	7.00
May	1.50	3.00	6.75
Aug.	1.50	3.50	7.00
Nov.	1.50	3.50	5.75
Feb. 1971	Not offered	4.50	7.00
May	1.25	3.50	Not offered
Aug.	1.50	4.25	10.00
Nov.	1.25	7.00	15.00
Feb. 1972	Not offered	4.25	10.00
May	1.00	Not offered	9.75
Aug.	3.50	7.00	12.00
Nov.	Not offered	4.00	Not offered
Feb. 1973	Not offered	3.50	6.75
May	Not offered	7.00	25.00
Aug.	Not offered	4.00	20.00
Nov.	2.13	6.00	19.75
Feb. 1974	3.50	7.00	19.45
May	2.13	4.25	25.00
Aug.	2.75	6.00	24.75
Nov.	3.00	7.00	24.50
Feb 1975	3.23	6.00	25.00
May	3.25	7.00	30.00
Aug.	2.75	7.00	25.00
Nov.	Not offered	7.00	24.75
Feb. 1976	3.25	7.25	24.25
May	1.95	10.00	23.75
Aug.	3.00	10.00	25.00
Nov.	3.00	7.00	23.25
Feb. 1977	3.00	7.00	30.00
May	Not offered	6.25	29.75
Aug.	3.00	7.00	30.00
Nov.	3.00	10.00	30.00

(continued)

Table 28.9 (*continued*)

Refunding	Term to maturity (in years) of . . .		
	Anchor issue	Middle issue	Long issue
Feb. 1978	3.25	7.00	27.25
May	Not offered	10.00	22.25
Aug.	3.00	7.00	30.00
Nov.	3.50	10.00	30.00
Feb. 1979	Not offered	8.00	29.75
May	Not offered	10.00	30.00
Aug.	3.00	7.50	29.75
Nov.	3.50	10.00	30.00

Federal Reserve Bank of New York circulars.

Beginning in July 1977[99] and continuing until October 1978, Treasury alternated between issuing five-year notes and fifteen-year bonds at the beginning of each quarter. Fifteen-year bonds were offered for settlement in January and July; five-year notes were offered for settlement in April and October. The move was seen as part of the continuing effort to lengthen the maturity structure of the debt.[100] In October 1978 officials switched to issuing only fifteen-year bonds. In August 1979 they added a new, separate series of five-year notes offered for settlement in the beginning of the third month of a quarter.[101]

The continuing evolution of the maturities of the notes and bonds offered in mid-quarter refundings, and the variation of offerings in the five- and fifteen-year sectors, suggests that while Treasury officials understood the value of regular and predictable issuance they had not yet settled on which maturities should be regularly and predictably issued. That question remained in flux as economic conditions and Treasury financing requirements continued to evolve in the 1980s.[102]

[99] Federal Reserve Bank of New York Circular no. 8131, June 21, 1977.

[100] "$1.5 Billion Bond Issue Planned by Treasury to Replace Notes," *New York Times*, June 21, 1977, p. 56, describing the first 15-year offering as "a move aimed at extending the average maturity of the national debt and thereby making it more manageable."

[101] "Treasury Schedules a $7.25 Billion Sale," *New York Times*, July 26, 1979, p. D7, "Treasury to Raise Additional Cash of $2.42 Billion," *Wall Street Journal*, July 26, 1979, p. 32; Federal Reserve Bank of New York Circular no. 8629, August 22, 1979; and "Treasury to Raise Cash by Selling Notes and Bonds," *Wall Street Journal*, October 25, 1979, p. 36.

[102] See Garbade (2015).

A RECAPITULATION OF TREASURY DEBT MANAGEMENT INNOVATIONS IN THE 1970S

The 1970s witnessed two remarkable innovations in Treasury debt management. The decade began with the successful introduction of auction offerings of short-term Treasury notes. The initial effort was quickly extended out the yield curve. When a failed auction revealed the flaws of auctioning on a price basis, the Treasury switched to yield auctions.

Regular and predictable note issuance began in 1972 with two-year notes and expanded to intermediate-term notes in 1975. Regular issuance reduced the element of surprise in Treasury debt operations and allowed investors to plan future commitments with greater confidence.

Treasury officials have repeatedly asserted the value of regular and predictable issuance. In 1982, Deputy Assistant Secretary Mark Stalnecker expressed the view that "regularity of debt management removes a major source of market uncertainty, and assures that Treasury debt can be sold at the lowest possible interest rate consistent with market conditions at the time of sale."[103] In 1998, Assistant Secretary Gary Gensler observed that "consistency and predictability in [the Treasury's] financing program . . . reduces uncertainty in the market and helps minimize our overall cost of borrowing."[104] And in 2002, Under Secretary Peter Fisher stated that "the Treasury's continuing commitment to a schedule of regular and predictable auction dates is a means, over time, to the end of lowest cost borrowing."[105]

[103] Committee on Banking, Finance, and Urban Affairs (1982, p. 5).

[104] Treasury press release RR-2555, "Assistant Secretary of the Treasury for Financial Markets Gary Gensler, House Committee on Ways and Means," June 24, 1998. Gensler went on to note that "in keeping with this principle, Treasury does not seek to time markets; that is, we do not act opportunistically to issue debt when market conditions appear favorable."

[105] Treasury press release PO-1098, "Remarks of Under Secretary of the Treasury Peter R. Fisher to the Futures Industry Association, Boca Raton, Florida," March 14, 2002.

29

Monetary Policy in the 1970s

Dismayed over the seeming inability of monetary policy to keep inflation under control, in 1970 the Federal Open Market Committee began to shift from managing money market conditions – primarily the Federal funds rate and member bank borrowings at the discount window[1] – on a more or less ad hoc basis to using money market conditions to steer a variety of monetary aggregates toward target growth rates specified by the Committee. The narrowly defined money supply M_1 (currency plus demand deposits) was the most important aggregate but attention focused as well on M_2 (M_1 plus commercial bank time and savings deposits other than large certificates of deposit) and the bank credit proxy (total bank deposits plus liabilities to foreign branches and commercial paper issued by bank holding companies).[2]

1970–1971

The FOMC began actively targeting monetary aggregates in 1970.[3] It set quarterly growth rate targets for the aggregates and instructed the manager

[1] Free reserves were a comparably important index of money market conditions in the 1950s but gradually fell out of favor in the sixties. See Guttentag (1966, text at fn. 3 on p. 28) and Ritter and Silber (1974, pp. 288 and 289).

[2] "Monetary Aggregates and Money Market Conditions in Open Market Policy," *Federal Reserve Bulletin*, February 1971, p. 79 at 91, and Meek and Thunberg (1971, p. 81, fn. 4).

[3] 1970 Annual Report of Open Market Operations, p. 18, stating that, "to a greater degree than in previous years," monetary policy in 1970 was "couched in terms of growth of the money and bank credit aggregates," and p. 21, stating that "the Committee developed a strategy for pursuing desired quarterly growth rates in the money supply and/or bank credit during the course of 1970." See also Ritter and Silber (1974, p. 240), remarking that "at the third [FOMC] meeting in 1970, the monetary aggregates finally were put on a par with interest rates and money market conditions," Meek and Thunberg (1971, p. 80),

of the System Open Market Account to vary money market conditions in response to deviations of the aggregates from their targets, supplying reserves more freely when the aggregates were expanding too slowly and more reluctantly when the aggregates were expanding more rapidly than desired.

The Federal funds rate soon became the most important indicator of money market conditions[4] and monetary policy became a matter of pushing the funds rate up or down in response to deviations of the aggregates from their growth targets. For example, the 1971 Markets annual report states that,

> Through January and most of February the money supply failed to expand as rapidly as was required if the Committee's desire to make up [a fourth quarter 1970] shortfall was to be realized. Having already lowered the Federal funds rate from 6½ percent to 4¾ percent over the fourth quarter the Desk pressed non-borrowed reserves on the banking system until the rate fell to 3½ percent in the second half of February. At this point, the money supply began to grow rapidly. In early April the Committee called for a firming of the money market to curb this expansion.[5]

However, the Committee did not focus exclusively on the aggregates. The 1970 Markets annual report observed that "conditions in the credit markets remained a major, and at times overriding, concern."[6] In addition, the Fed remained committed to maintaining an "even keel" during

noting that "in 1970 the Federal Open Market Committee began to establish longer term objectives for the growth of selected monetary and credit aggregates," "Monetary Aggregates and Money Market Conditions in Open Market Policy," *Federal Reserve Bulletin*, February, 1971, p. 83, stating that "in 1970 monetary aggregates came to play a more prominent role" in the Committee's directive to the Manager of the Open Market Account, and Meulendyke (1998, p. 42), stating that "the inflationary pressures that developed in the late 1960s led to a number of policy initiatives in the early 1970s. . . . In 1970, the Federal Reserve formally adopted monetary targets with the intention of using them to reduce inflation gradually over time."

[4] 1971 Annual Report of Open Market Operations, p. 7, identifying the Federal funds rate as "the most important component of the money market conditions to be achieved by the Desk" and noting that "the Committee's use of the Federal funds rate gives the Manager an objective that he can usually hold within reasonable limits during the statement week."

[5] 1971 Annual Report of Open Market Operations, p. 1.

[6] 1970 Annual Report of Open Market Operations, p. 18. See also "Monetary Aggregates and Money Market Conditions in Open Market Policy," *Federal Reserve Bulletin*, February 1971, p. 83, stating that "the System Account Manager has also been directed, when appropriate, to take account of Treasury financings, liquidity pressures, and the possible impacts of bank regulatory changes in the process of achieving satisfactory conditions in the money market and satisfactory performance of monetary aggregates."

Treasury offerings and remained prepared to undertake rescue operations – as in the May 1970 refunding.

1972–1973

Controlling the aggregates proved more difficult than anticipated, in part because their response to changes in money market conditions was both slow and uncertain. The 1971 Markets annual report observed that "the sluggishness of M_1's response [to Desk operations] in late 1970 and throughout 1971 underscored once again the complexity of the linkages between the Desk's operations, on the one hand and bank behavior, financial flows, and the asset choices of the public, on the other."[7]

In early 1972, the Fed turned to targeting reserves available to support private deposits (RPDs – the reserves needed to support a given distribution of bank deposits other than Treasury and interbank deposits) in an effort to gain better control of the aggregates.[8] Officials expected control of the aggregates to follow inexorably from control of RPDs.

The procedure started with the FOMC setting a tolerance range for the rate of growth of the aggregates.[9] Staff economists would then identify a corresponding tolerance range for RPDs, taking into account the structure of reserve requirements, seasonal shifts between currency and demand deposits, movements of funds between member and nonmember banks, and shifts of deposits between reserve city banks and country banks. The Committee directed the Desk to react to RPD growth above the upper end of the tolerance range by restraining the growth of nonborrowed reserves, thereby forcing member banks to borrow at the discount window and pushing the Federal funds higher – both of which were expected to slow the growth of the aggregates.[10] RPD growth below the lower end of the tolerance range triggered the opposite response.

[7] 1971 Annual Report of Open Market Operations, p. 2.

[8] 1972 Annual Report of Open Market Operations, p. 1, noting the adoption in February 1972 of "a reserve targeting procedure for guiding open market operations." See also Ritter and Silber (1974, p. 240), stating that "early in 1972 the FOMC added . . . reserves available to support private nonbank deposits . . . as an operating target . . ."

[9] 1972 Annual Report of Open Market Operations, pp. 1–3 and 8–10.

[10] 1972 Annual Report of Open Market Operations, pp. 8–9. The notion of a relationship between borrowings and the Federal funds rate was based on how district Reserve Banks administered access to the discount window, a practice that dated to the mid-1960s. (See Chapter 21 above.) The 1982 Annual Report of Open Market Operations succinctly expressed, on p. 17, the basic idea: "Because of administratively controlled access to the Federal Reserve discount window, raising or lowering the pressure to borrow was

Additionally, however, the Committee stipulated that it "wished to avoid both sharp, short-run fluctuations in money market conditions and undesirably large cumulative deviations in money market conditions."[11] Accordingly, the Committee imposed a tolerance range within which the Manager could vary the Federal funds rate between meetings. If the funds rate was at the upper end of the range the Desk refrained from putting additional pressure on the rate, even if RPDs were growing above the upper end of their range.[12]

1974–1979

The FOMC became disenchanted with targeting RPDs by the end of 1973, in part because the relationship between RPDs and the monetary aggregates was not particularly stable over short intervals of time.[13] In 1974, the Committee returned to looking directly to the aggregates. The Committee began by specifying target rates of growth for the aggregates and upper and lower limits for the growth rates. It further specified a target Federal funds rate (which it believed was consistent with the targeted aggregate growth rates) and a tolerance band for the funds rate.[14] The Desk was tasked with keeping the aggregates within their respective tolerance bands, subject to the overriding constraint that the funds rate not move outside of its band. Wider fluctuations in the aggregates were accepted if needed to keep the funds rate within its band.[15]

transmitted to . . . the Federal funds market. As banks, for example, were forced to the window, they turned more aggressively to the funds market and bid up the funds rate. The opposite happened when banks found that nonborrowed reserves were more plentiful."

11 1972 Annual Report of Open Market Operations, p. 9.

12 1972 Annual Report of Open Market Operations, p. 9.

13 1974 Annual Report of Open Market Operations, p. 11, noting that "the Committee found . . . that the actual relationship between RPDs and M_1 often failed to develop as expected, at least in the time period from one meeting to the next." Robert Mayo, president of the Federal Reserve Bank of Chicago, later conjectured that the RPD experiment failed "because we were too timid on the federal funds ranges that we associated with it." Minutes of the Federal Open Market Committee, October 6, 1979, p. 17.

14 1975 Annual Report of Open Market Operations, p. 7, stating that "the FOMC established ranges of tolerance for M_1 and M_2 growth," 1977 Annual Report of Open Market Operations, p. 9, stating that "after each [FOMC] meeting, the Committee supplied the Trading Desk with a set of tolerance ranges for M_1 and M_2," and 1975 Annual Report of Open Market Operations, p. 8, stating that the range of permissible variation in the Federal funds rate "usually centers around the rate believed at the time of the meeting to be consistent with the long-run objectives for the aggregates."

15 Lombra and Torto (1975, p. 9) note that "the Federal Reserve rarely missed the funds rate range but allowed reserves and the money stock to move away from the specified range in about one-half of the two-month control periods." See also 1974 Annual Report of Open

The starting point for determining Desk activity was identifying the operations needed to keep the funds rate at the target level.[16] The calculation began by adding reserves required to be held during a statement week (based on member bank deposit liabilities and vault cash two weeks earlier[17]) to an estimate of the excess reserves that banks were likely to want to hold given the target level of the funds rate. The result was bank *demand* for reserves.

On the supply side the Desk developed projections for each of the autonomous factors that supplied or absorbed reserves (such as float, currency in circulation, and Treasury balances at Federal Reserve Banks), borrowings at the discount window that were consistent with the target funds rate, and securities held in the System Open Market Account (assuming that maturing positions would be rolled over). The sum was the projected *supply* of reserves available to the banking system.

The difference between bank demand for reserves and the projected supply was an estimate of the quantity of reserves that the Desk needed to supply (or absorb) to keep the funds rate on target. If the monetary aggregates were growing within their tolerance limits, the Desk supplied (or absorbed) the indicated reserves.[18] Policy operations (as distinct from defensive operations undertaken to neutralize fluctuations in autonomous factors) would follow if the aggregates were growing above their upper limits or below their lower limits.

However, changes in the funds rate were expected to be "orderly"[19] and the Committee expected the rate to stay within its tolerance band. Raymond Lombra, a staff economist at the Board of Governors, and Raymond Torto, an economist at the University of Massachusetts-

Market Operations, p. 12, stating that "the Manager reacted to new information on the aggregates by altering supplies of nonborrowed reserves in a way that produced an orderly rise or fall in the Federal funds rate. Over the period between meetings, permissible variation in the Federal funds rate was constrained by the FOMC ..."

16 See 1976 Annual Report of Open Market Operations, pp. 14–15.

17 The Board of Governors introduced lagged reserve requirements in 1968. See Federal Reserve Bank of New York Circular no. 6157, April 29, 1968; and Circular no. 6213, September 17, 1968.

18 Lombra and Torto (1975, p. 11) state that "if the money stock is expanding at a rate within its range, then the desired level of the Federal funds rate will probably not be altered to any significant degree."

19 1973 Annual Report of Open Market Operations, p. 9, stating that "the Manager was mindful of the Committee's desire to see an orderly movement in the Federal funds rate," and 1974 Annual Report of Open Market Operations, p. 12, stating that "the Manager reacted to new information on the aggregates by altering supplies of nonborrowed reserves in a way that produced an orderly rise or fall in the Federal funds rate."

Boston, noted that "the significance of the Federal funds range is that it specifically limits the degree of response by the Manager to a deviation of monetary growth from the desired range" and that "the FOMC is willing to tolerate relatively large short-run deviations of monetary growth from desired levels." Lombra and Torto further observed that "if the band on interest rate movements is fairly narrow and inflexible, it is reasonable to question whether or not the money stock is being 'controlled' at all."[20] Ann-Marie Meulendyke, an economist at the New York Reserve Bank, later observed that "during most of the 1970s, the FOMC was reluctant to change the funds rate by large amounts at any one time, even when staff estimates suggested that sizable modification was necessary to achieve ... monetary goals. ... The adjustment in the funds rate often lagged behind market forces, allowing trends in money and prices to get ahead of policy."[21]

COMPLICATIONS

Targeting monetary aggregates successfully was more complicated than the foregoing would suggest. Two quantitatively significant autonomous factors were volatile and difficult to forecast even a few days ahead, making neutralization of fluctuations in those factors problematic. Additionally, bank borrowing at the discount window was not an unambiguous function of the Federal funds rate, so the Desk could not be confident that forcing banks to borrow a particular sum would produce the desired funds rate.

Fluctuations in Autonomous Factors

From a policy perspective, the key issue for the FOMC was whether to tighten to restrain an exuberant economy or ease to encourage economic growth. However, from the perspective of day-to-day operations the important issue was whether the Desk needed to add or drain reserves to compensate for changes in autonomous factors beyond its direct control.[22]

[20] Lombra and Torto (1975, p. 12). [21] Meulendyke (1998, pp. 46–47).

[22] 1977 Annual Report of Open Market Operations, p. 12, observing that "daily open market operations continued to be shaped by large fluctuations in factors that affect bank reserves, principally the Treasury's balances at Reserve Banks, float, and 'as of' adjustments to bank reserve positions."

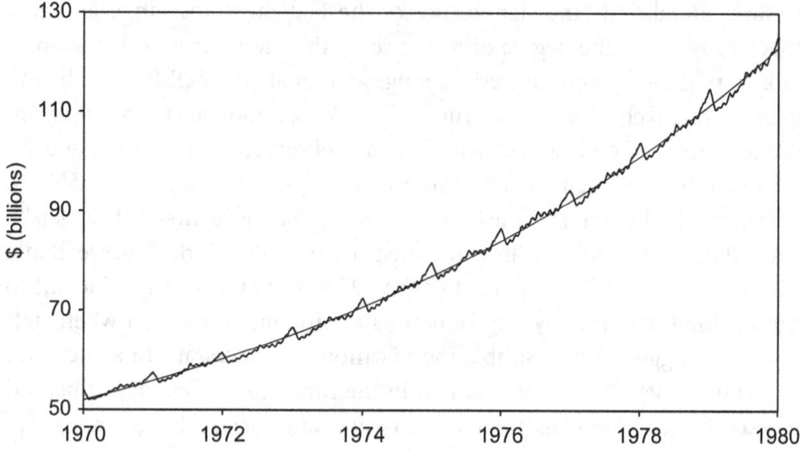

Chart 29.1 Currency in circulation. Weekly averages of daily figures. Least squares regression of weekly values of the natural logarithm of currency between January 1970 and December 1979 on a constant, time (measured in decimal years beginning with a value of zero on December 31, 1969), and time squared gives ln[currency] = 3.949 + (0.0712 + .001504·time)·time. The thin trend line in this figure is a graph of the function exp[3.949 + (0.0712 + .001504·time)·time].
Board of Governors of the Federal Reserve System, *Annual Statistical Digest.*

Currency

Chart 29.1 shows the behavior of currency in the hands of the public during the 1970s. Two facts are immediately clear: currency grew steadily throughout the decade but additionally exhibited regular seasonal variation around the long-run trend.

Fitting a trend line (the thin line in Chart 29.1) to the data facilitates identification of the seasonal fluctuations. As shown in Chart 29.2, currency hit seasonal highs at the end of every year. It increased monotonically from late September or early October, reached a peak in late December, and fell precipitously in January. There was, additionally, a smaller seasonal peak in late June and early July.

Although the variation in currency was large, whether viewed in terms of long-run growth or seasonal departures from trend, the variation was not difficult to neutralize because it was so predictable. Treasury deposits and float were in a different category.

Treasury Deposits at Federal Reserve Banks

Treasury deposits at Federal Reserve Banks, shown in Chart 29.3, were a second and, for a time, exceptionally problematic source of uncertainty.

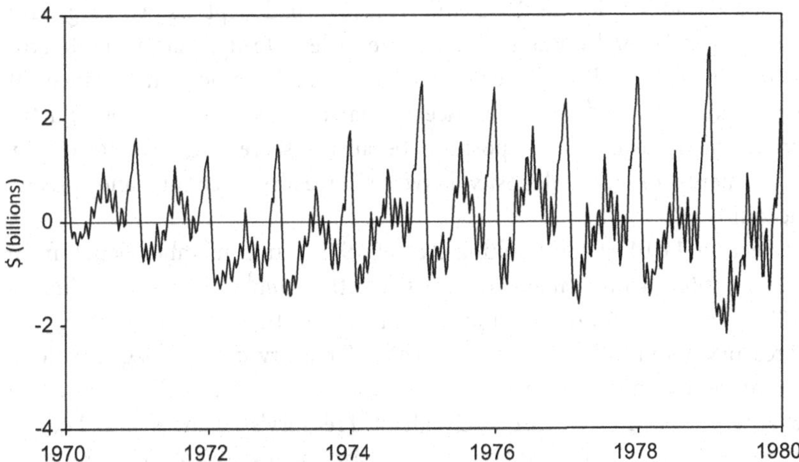

Chart 29.2 Currency in circulation (weekly averages of daily figures) less trend currency.
Currency from Board of Governors of the Federal Reserve System, *Annual Statistical Digest.* Trend currency is the thin trend line in Chart 29.1.

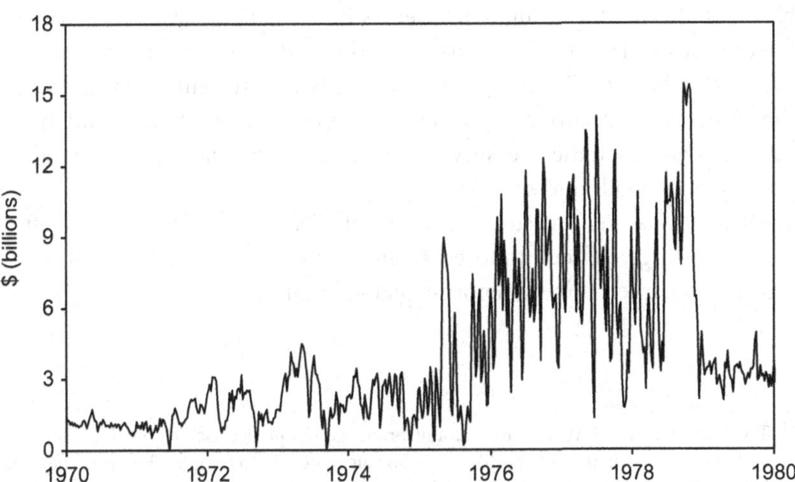

Chart 29.3 Treasury deposits at Federal Reserve Banks. Weekly averages of daily figures.
Board of Governors of the Federal Reserve System, *Annual Statistical Digest.*

For decades prior to 1975 the Treasury had kept its working cash balances at Federal Reserve Banks more or less steady, channeling fluctuations in its overall cash position to Tax and Loan account balances at commercial banks.[23] The practice insulated bank reserves from fluctuations in Treasury's cash position because reserves were unaffected by movements of bank deposits between Treasury accounts and private accounts.

Section 11(b) of the Banking Act of 1933 forbid member banks from paying interest on demand deposits, whether public or private. When a 1974 Treasury study concluded that the restriction was costing the Treasury about $260 million per year,[24] Treasury officials began to look for more remunerative ways to manage their cash balances. They settled on a scheme that moved essentially all of Treasury's balances into Federal Reserve accounts. The Fed had to neutralize the resulting drain of reserves from the banking system by buying Treasury securities, either outright or on repurchase agreements. The Treasury benefitted from the increased interest earnings of the System because the Fed remitted the bulk of its operating income, net of expenses and dividends to member banks, to the Treasury.[25]

The downside of the new policy was that fluctuations in Treasury cash balances affected the volume of reserves in the banking system on a one-for-one basis. Treasury deposits with the Fed rose, and bank reserves declined, when the Treasury received funds in payment of taxes or for the purchase of securities. Conversely, Treasury deposits fell, and bank reserves rose, when the Treasury made social security payments or paid for purchases of goods and services.

Fluctuations in Treasury balances at Federal Reserve Banks after 1974 were large, difficult to forecast, and sometimes difficult to neutralize. The 1977 Markets annual report explained that,

[23] Treasury created the War Loan Account program, the predecessor to the Treasury Tax and Loan program, during World War I. See the appendix to Chapter 3 above. The War Loan Account program was renamed the Treasury Tax and Loan program in 1950. Federal Reserve Bank of New York Circular no. 3518, December 2, 1949.

[24] Department of the Treasury (1974, p. 41, exhibit 11) and Lovett (1978, p. 42).

[25] "Transfer to Treasury of Excess Earnings of Federal Reserve Banks," *Federal Reserve Bulletin*, May 1947, pp. 518–19, Clouse, Henderson, Orphanides, Small, and Tinsley (2003, fn. 90), Board of Governors of the Federal Reserve System, Division of Federal Reserve Bank Operations (1962, pp. 19–20), and Board of Governors of the Federal Reserve System (2018, pp. 61–62).

The Trading Desk was generally successful in offsetting these large variations, though difficulties did arise following major tax receipts in April, September and, to a lesser extent, in December. On these occasions, the Desk was unable to make repurchase agreements in sufficient volume to offset the rise in Treasury balances – primarily because available supplies of securities were low given market expectations of further increases in interest rates.[26]

The 1978 Markets annual report noted similarly that,

In managing reserves, the Desk sometimes encountered difficulty in making a sufficiently large volume of repurchase agreements, particularly at times when the Treasury balance at the Federal Reserve rose sharply. For the most part, large reserve scarcities tended to develop after quarterly tax payment dates. Government securities dealers and other market participants continued to hold small inventories, given the negative carry on them and the expectations of further interest rate increases.[27]

In October 1977, Congress authorized the Secretary of the Treasury to invest in *interest-earning* obligations of banks maintaining Tax and Loan accounts.[28] Following extensive consultation with Tax and Loan depositories, the Treasury adopted a new cash management program in November 1978[29] that, among other things, provided for the payment of interest on Treasury balances at a rate equal to the Federal funds rate less 25 basis points.[30] Officials deemed that rate a reasonable approximation to the open market rate on repurchase agreements which, like Tax and Loan deposits, were collateralized obligations.[31] Treasury moved the bulk of its funds back to commercial banks and, as shown in Chart 29.3, returned to its historic practice of maintaining a steady working balance at Federal Reserve Banks. (The target balance for Treasury accounts at Federal Reserve Banks was initially set at $3 billion.[32])

Float

Float, the Federal Reserve asset that appears when banks are credited for checks sent for collection before the Fed debits the banks on which the checks are drawn, was a second troublesome source of variation in bank

[26] 1978 Annual Report of Open Market Operations, p. 13.

[27] 1978 Annual Report of Open Market Operations, p. 16.

[28] Act of October 28, 1977.

[29] Federal Reserve Bank of New York Circular no. 8452, November 9, 1978.

[30] Lovett (1978, p. 44). Concurrently, the Board of Governors exempted most Tax and Loan account balances from reserve requirements. See Federal Reserve Bank of New York Circular no. 8341, May 9, 1978, Lang (1979, pp. 6–7), and compare 12 CFR 204.1(f)(1)(ii) (January 1, 1978) with 12 CFR 204.1(f)(1)(ii) (January 1, 1979).

[31] Interest rates on repurchase agreements were not widely disseminated in 1979. In contrast, the Federal funds rate was well known to market participants and more acceptable as a benchmark for assessing interest on Tax and Loan account balances.

[32] Madigan and Trepeta (1986, p. 251).

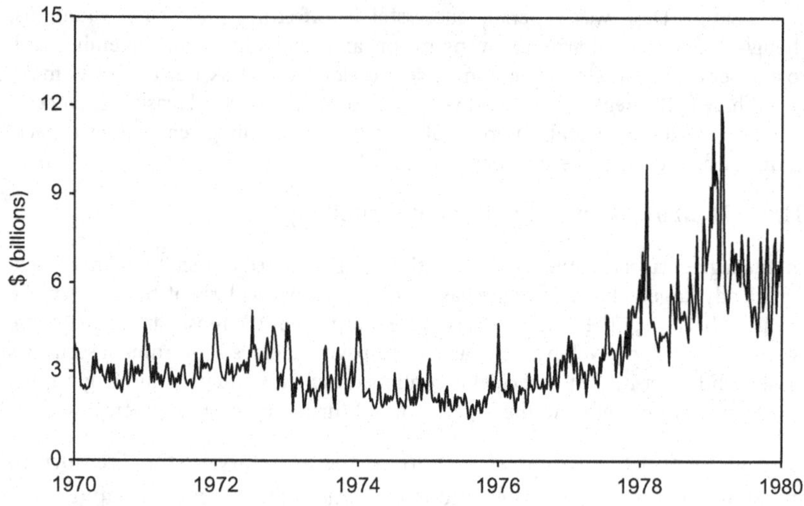

Chart 29.4 Float. Weekly averages of daily figures.
Board of Governors of the Federal Reserve System, *Annual Statistical Digest.*

reserves. As shown in Chart 29.4, float followed something like a mean reverting process, with a seasonal spike at the end of each year and a trend increase after 1975.

Two particularly large transients, in early 1978 and early 1979, resulted from unusually severe winter storms that slowed check collection. The *New York Times* reported in February 1978 that "snowstorms continued to expand reserves in the banking system, raising Federal Reserve 'float' at one point to a record $13.9 billion."[33] A year later the *Wall Street Journal* reported that "the Fed aggressively moved to drain reserves from the banking system to counter technical effects of the severe weather that dumped up to two feet of snow in some parts of the East. The weather problems boosted float . . . and increased bank reserves."[34]

Neutralizing fluctuations in float presented a recurring challenge for the Desk. The 1979 Markets annual report noted that float was "the most volatile and difficult [autonomous factor] to forecast."[35]

[33] "Money Supply Rise Highest in 3 Months," *New York Times*, February 3, 1978, p. D2. See also 1978 Annual Report of Open Market Operations, p. 22, stating that the storms "caused reserve management problems for banks and large reserve projection errors for the Desk as a result of unexpected bulges in float."

[34] "Fed Overcomes Woes of Snow to Produce Its Weekly Figures," *Wall Street Journal*, February 23, 1979, p. 27.

[35] 1979 Annual Report of Open Market Operations, p. 38.

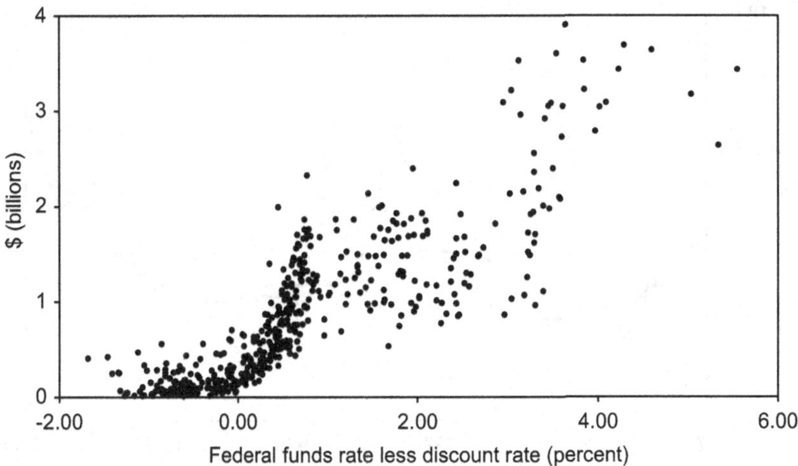

Chart 29.5 Borrowed reserves (daily average over a statement week) as a function of the difference between the Federal funds rate and the Federal Reserve Bank of New York discount rate, January 1970 to December 1979.

Board of Governors of the Federal Reserve System, *Annual Statistical Digest* and Federal Reserve Statistical Release H.15.

Bank Borrowing at the Discount Window

Federal Reserve officials had two reasons for their interest in the relationship between the Federal funds rate and member bank borrowing at the discount window. First, when the monetary aggregates were growing at an acceptable rate, officials needed to identify the volume of borrowing that would maintain the funds rate at its target level. Second, if the aggregates were growing too fast, they needed to identify the volume of additional borrowing that would produce a funds rate at an appropriately higher level, and conversely if the aggregates were growing too slowly.

Chart 29.5 shows the volume of discount window borrowing (daily average over a statement week) as a function of the difference between the Federal funds rate and the discount rate over the period from January 1970 to December 1979. Unsurprisingly, borrowings were an increasing function of the rate spread: banks borrowed more from the Fed when the Fed charged less than the market.

However, the volume of borrowings can hardly be described as a single-valued function of the rate spread. To the contrary, a wide range of borrowings was observed at any given spread, particularly at elevated spreads. Put the other way around, forcing banks to borrow a particular

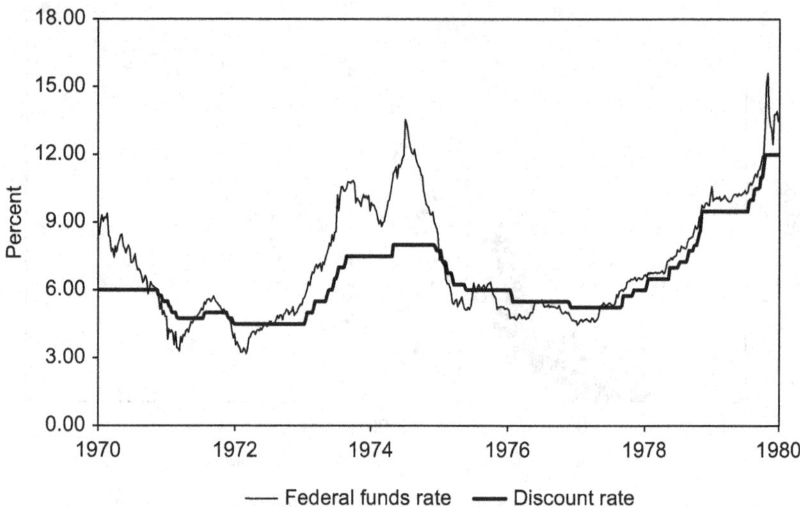

Chart 29.6 Federal funds rate and Federal Reserve Bank of New York discount rate. Daily figures.
Federal Reserve Statistical Release H.15.

amount at the discount window was not reliably associated with a particular rate spread.[36]

Most of the largest differences between the Federal funds rate and the discount rate occurred prior to 1975 (Chart 29.6). Beginning in 1975, officials kept the discount rate much more closely aligned with the funds rate. A comparison of Charts 29.7 and 29.8 shows that the result was a more predictable, but still not unambiguous, relation between the funds rate (relative to the discount rate) and borrowings.

Consequences of Uncertainty

The Fed's imperfect ability to identify in real time the contribution of autonomous factors to reserve availability and its imperfect ability to quantify the volume of discount window borrowings consistent with the target level of the Federal funds rate (given the level of the discount rate) left the funds rate subject to significant random influences that varied from

[36] Similar charts appear in Peristiani (1991, p. 15) and Hamdani and Peristiani (1991, p. 54). Goodfriend (1983) shows how non-price administration of access to the discount window can lead to borrowings that are not a simple function of the contemporaneous spread between the Federal funds rate and the discount rate.

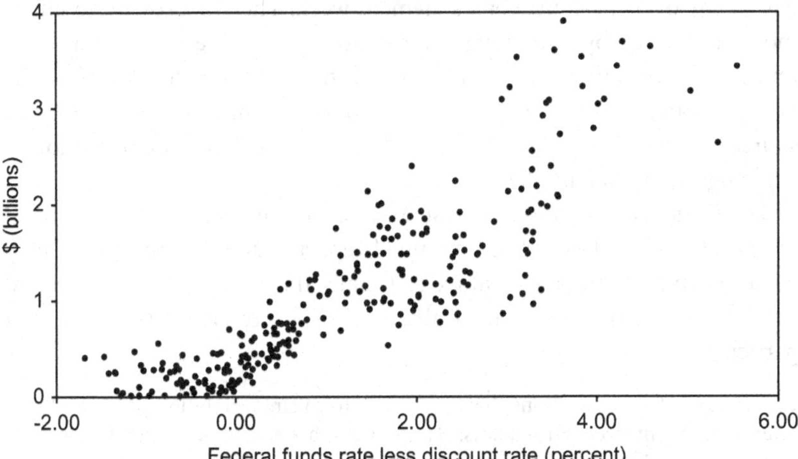

Chart 29.7 Borrowed reserves (daily average over a statement week) as a function of the difference between the Federal funds rate and the Federal Reserve Bank of New York discount rate, January 1970 to December 1974.

Board of Governors of the Federal Reserve System, *Annual Statistical Digest,* and Federal Reserve Statistical Release H.15.

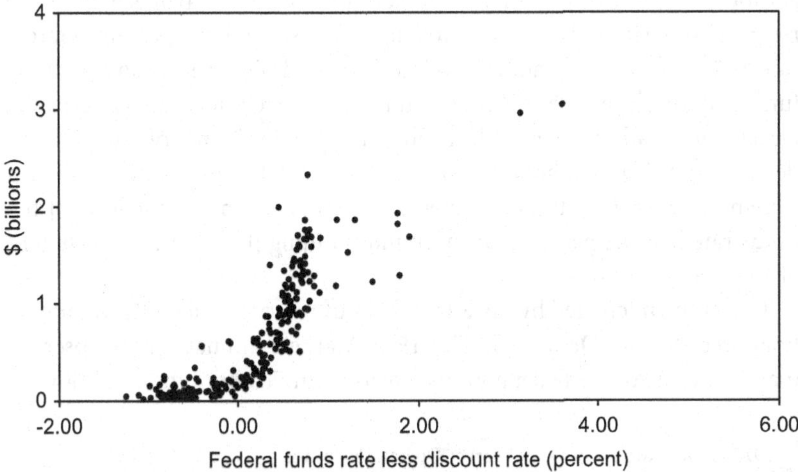

Chart 29.8 Borrowed reserves (daily average over a statement week) as a function of the difference between the Federal funds rate and the Federal Reserve Bank of New York discount rate, January 1975 to December 1979.

Board of Governors of the Federal Reserve System, *Annual Statistical Digest,* and Federal Reserve Statistical Release H.15.

day to day over the course of a statement week. The Desk sought to buffer those influences by extracting information on reserve availability from unexpected movements in the rate. Thus, the 1976 Markets annual report noted that the Desk looked to "the behavior of trading in Federal funds as a source of additional information on the supply and demand forces affecting the money market."[37]

The Desk also conditioned its operations on the behavior of the Federal funds rate.[38] The 1976 Markets annual report stated that the Desk "may defer putting its program into effect until the trading level of Federal funds ... confirms the statistical estimates of reserve availability." In particular,

> Care is taken to avoid actions that might lead to misinterpretation of the System's intentions by market participants. Thus, when a need is anticipated to supply reserves, the Manager may wait for the funds rate to edge up at least to the operational objective before entering the market, or wait for it to edge down at least to or below the objective before entering the market to absorb reserves when an overabundance is projected.[39]

Conditioning open market operations on the level of the funds rate effectively signaled to market participants the rate the Fed was targeting. Banks in need of funds became reluctant to bid much more than the perceived target rate as long as the Fed had time to intervene to supply additional reserves and push the market rate back down; banks with excess reserves were similarly reluctant to lend at rates below the perceived target rate as long as the Fed had time to intervene to drain reserves and push the funds rate back up. Thus, Federal funds were likely to trade close to the target rate, rather than reflect underlying conditions of supply and demand, until a few hours before the close of trading at the end of a statement week. Conditioning open market operations on the level of the funds rate had the perverse effect of undermining the information content of the rate.

The problem created by uncertainty about reserve availability did not go unappreciated by Desk staff. The 1976 Markets annual report observed that "the value of the Federal funds rate as an indicator of the conditions of

[37] 1976 Annual Report of Open Market Operations, p. 16.

[38] "Monetary Aggregates and Money Market Conditions in Open Market Policy," *Federal Reserve Bulletin*, February, 1971, p. 79 at 92, stating that the Federal funds rate "reflects the interaction of the demand for and existing supply of bank reserves and hence provides a basis for making daily decisions as to whether the System should be in the market providing additional or absorbing existing reserves."

[39] 1976 Annual Report of Open Market Operations, p. 16.

reserve availability probably has diminished in recent years" because "large shifts in the Treasury's balances at the Reserve Banks have led to much greater volatility in the level of nonborrowed reserves from day to day. Exposed to such volatility, money position managers at the banks are less likely to react to the immediate ebb and flow of funds since they expect the Federal Reserve to compensate for these massive surges. They appear to be willing to accumulate larger reserve deficits or surpluses before taking offsetting actions in the Federal funds market. Thus, the actual Federal funds rate tends to remain close to the market's perception of the System's objective for the rate until rather late in a statement week."[40]

THE END (SORT OF) OF EVEN KEEL

Although monetary policy in the later 1970s had to deal with a variety of problems, even keel was not one of them. The 1976 Markets annual report observed that,

> "[E]ven keel" considerations have diminished considerably in the past few years. The use of the auction technique for selling coupon issues since 1970 has substantially increased the ability of underwriters [i.e., primary dealers] to adjust their expectations of future rate levels up to the time of the Treasury's sale. The regularization of the Treasury's debt offerings has also reduced uncertainty regarding the size and timing of the Treasury's borrowing.[41]

The report further remarked that the increased frequency of coupon offerings – including monthly two-year notes and quarterly four- and five-year notes – would have placed an intolerable strain on the System's ability to pursue an independent monetary policy in the absence of a retreat from even keeling.[42]

However, the FOMC did not completely abandon the idea of avoiding disruptive policy changes during Treasury offerings. The 1977 Markets annual report observed that when the Desk moved to implement an increase in the Federal funds rate in late October "it was desirable to move

[40] 1976 Annual Report of Open Market Operations, pp. 16–17.

[41] 1976 Annual Report of Open Market Operations, p. 29. Meltzer (2009, p. 832) observes that "auctions reduced the use of even keel procedures but did not, at first, eliminate them," but concludes that "gradually, even keel disappeared as a major constraint on Federal Reserve actions . . ."

[42] 1976 Annual Report of Open Market Operations, p. 29.

[43] 1977 Annual Report of Open Market Operations, p. 32.

promptly since the Treasury was beginning its quarterly financing."[43] Similarly, following the mid-April 1978 FOMC meeting, the Desk "moved quickly to signal the System's firmer posture in advance of the Treasury's two-year note auction ... and the upcoming announcement of its May refunding ..."[44]

[43] 1977 Annual Report of Open Market Operations, p. 32.
[44] 1978 Annual Report of Open Market Operations, p. 26.

30

Open Market Operations in the 1970s

Inflation was the central problem of monetary policy in the 1970s but transient fluctuations in bank reserves was the central focus of open market operations. Neutralizing short-run fluctuations in bank demand for reserves and Treasury balances at Federal Reserve Banks accounted for the bulk of System transactions and continued to prompt evolutionary changes in reserves management. During the 1970s the FOMC introduced competitive repo auctions, admitted bank dealers to participation in its repo operations, and repurposed matched sale-repurchase agreements into a tool for *adding* reserves at times when repo collateral was hard to come by. The 1970s also saw the introduction of outright transactions in federal agency debt.

THE OPERATING ENVIRONMENT

Open market operations in the 1970s were qualitatively similar to those of the preceding decade. As a secular matter, reserves were added from time to time to accommodate growth in the banking system and to replace balances drained off to currency. As a transient matter, reserves sometimes had to be added, and sometimes drained, to neutralize short-term fluctuations in autonomous factors and member bank demand for reserve balances.

As in the 1960s, the Open Market Desk preferred outright transactions for meeting long-term needs and repurchase agreements and matched sale-purchase agreements (MSPs) for satisfying transient requirements. The 1976 Markets annual report observed that,

> The Manager's approach to operations each week is shaped partly with an eye on the extent to which nonborrowed reserves in subsequent weeks are expected to fall

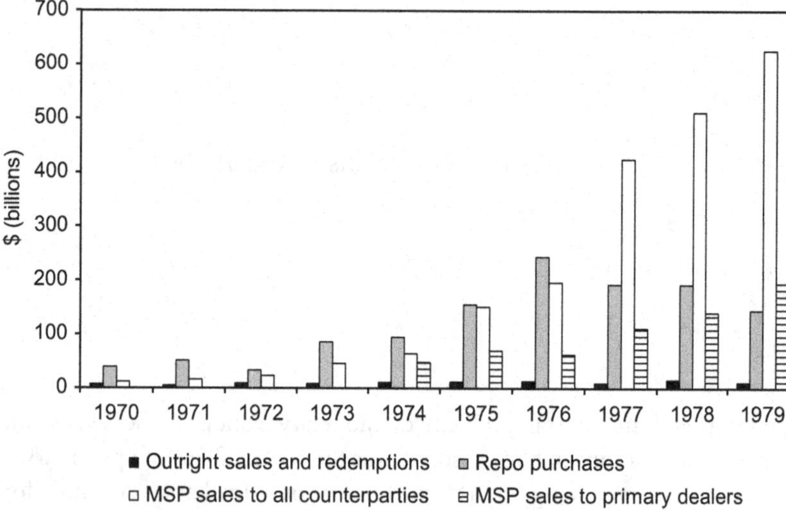

Chart 30.1 Outright sales and redemptions of Treasury securities, repo purchases, and MSP sales in the 1970s.
Annual reports of open market operations.

short of, or exceed, projected reserve requirements. If reserve deficits extend into future weeks, the Desk is more likely to use outright purchases of securities to meet a reserve need. If the need is temporary, greater reliance on repurchase agreements is likely. Conversely, when reserve surpluses are projected over several weeks, outright sales and redemptions of maturing securities may be appropriate. If there is only a temporary need to absorb reserves, matched sale-purchase transactions are employed.[1]

The 1979 Markets annual report noted similarly that "outright transactions were addressed to secular needs or seasonal swings which were expected to persist for several weeks" and that the Desk "continued to use temporary transactions to adjust reserves when the need to add or absorb was not expected to persist or when the magnitude of the required adjustment was too large to be handled entirely through outright transactions."[2]

Chart 30.1 shows that repos and MSPs grew much faster than outright sales and redemptions in the 1970s. (Beginning in 1974, the chart shows MSPs with primary dealers as well as total MSPs. Box 30.1 discusses the reason for showing both series.) Intra- and interweek variation in bank demand for reserves in the early 1970s, and Treasury cash management

[1] 1976 Annual Report of Open Market Operations, p. 15.
[2] 1979 Annual Report of Open Market Operations, pp. A-1 and A-5.

Box 30.1 System MSPs with Foreign Accounts.

Prior to 1974, the Desk generally entered into matched sale-purchase agreements only with primary dealers and only when it wanted to drain reserves from the banking system. In August 1974, the Desk began to enter into MSPs on a regular basis with large foreign accounts, including foreign central banks and sovereign investment authorities.[1] The expansion in the scope of the MSP facility was primarily an accommodation to members of the Organization of Petroleum Exporting Countries (OPEC), the principal beneficiaries of a sharp increase in crude oil prices in the second half of 1973.[2] (The price of West Texas Intermediate, a benchmark American crude, increased from $3.56 per barrel in July 1973 to $10.11 at the end of the year.) From the point of view of an OPEC member, the expanded MSP program was a facility that allowed the country to earn interest on its (suddenly much enlarged) dollar balances while it was deciding how to invest for the longer term.

In some cases an MSP with a foreign account was simply a substitute for an MSP with a primary dealer, an MSP that, in the absence of any interest in lending by a foreign account, the Desk would have undertaken with a primary dealer. In other cases, an MSP with a foreign account was an accommodation to the account that had to be offset with a repo with a primary dealer.[3]

The difference between total MSPs and MSPs with primary dealers in Chart 30.1 was MSPs with foreign accounts. Available data does not disclose what fraction of those MSPs were substitutes for MSPs with primary dealers and what fraction were accommodations to foreign accounts. Available data also does not disclose what fraction of System repos were undertaken to offset accommodative MSPs with foreign accounts.

MSP volume with foreign accounts grew so large that the Desk began to experience difficulty sourcing sufficient dealer interest in offsetting repurchase agreements. In order to avoid an unintended drain in reserves available to the banking system, the Desk increased its outright holdings of Treasury securities in the Open Market Account, i.e., it provided offsetting reserves through outright purchases in lieu of repurchase agreements.[4]

[1] 1975 Annual Report of Open Market Operations, pp. A-4 and C-4.

[2] 1974 Annual Report of Open Market Operations, p. C-1, stating that "the major new element in foreign account activity arose from the investment of the revenues gained by members of the Organization of Petroleum Exporting Countries (OPEC) which resulted from the huge increase in the price of oil."

[3] 1974 Annual Report of Open Market Operations, p. A-4, 1975 Annual Report of Open Market Operations, pp. A-4 to A-5 and C-5.

[4] 1977 Annual Report of Open Market Operations, p. A-2, stating that "the Desk also sought to increase the System's portfolio of outright holdings in order to avoid or limit the need, at times, for very large reserve injections. . . . By the same token, the buildup of a larger outright portfolio increased the need, at times, for large temporary reserve absorptions through matched sale-purchase transactions – but this type of transaction appeared to be more feasible than a comparable volume of repurchase agreements."

practices in the latter half of the decade, were the most important drivers of temporary operations.

Intraweek and Interweek Variation in Bank Demand for Reserves

The Desk regularly supplied and drained reserves on a temporary basis in response to intra- and interweek fluctuations in member bank demand.

The 1970 Markets annual report described the nature of the intraweek fluctuations:

> Banks persistently managed their reserve positions very conservatively. They accumulated excess reserves over the first half of a statement week by bidding strongly for Federal funds and often borrowing heavily from the discount window over the weekend. Then, toward the end of a week, the accumulated excess reserves were sold off, either on Tuesday or Wednesday. Thus, the System would provide reserves aggressively early in a week, only to move to the opposite side of the market sometime after the weekend in order to prevent excessive ease.[3]

A year later, the Markets annual report remarked on the character of interweek fluctuations:

> In 1971 there continued to be a strong tendency for a tight Federal funds market at the end of a statement week to increase the demand for excess reserves by major banks in the following week, especially over the weekend. Conversely, an easy Federal funds market at the end of the week tended to be followed by a more relaxed attitude on the part of money market banks toward the accumulation of reserve deficiencies over the following weekend.[4]

The report provided an example of the interaction between the intraweek variation in demand and the interweek variation:

> [I]n the November 24 statement week . . . the 46 major money market banks were willing to accumulate a reserve deficiency of $3.0 billion over the weekend. The Federal funds rate gave little sign of a $542 million reserve shortfall on Friday or of the large net reserve deficiency building up in the banking system. The Desk's injection of $2 billion of nonborrowed reserves [after the weekend] – the maximum attainable in the circumstances – was not sufficient to prevent the Federal funds rate from rising well above the 4¾ percent desired. Member bank borrowing at the discount window also bulged to almost $2.4 billion on the statement date, which preceded Thanksgiving. Predictably, the 46 money market banks hoarded excess reserves over the following weekend, accumulating $5.4 billion in excess

[3] 1970 Annual Report of Open Market Operations, p. A-8.

[4] 1971 Annual Report of Open Market Operations, p. 10.

reserves by Monday morning. In consequence, the Federal funds rate broke to as low as ¼ percent by the end of the week.[5]

Consistent with the more limited non-price administration of access to the discount window after 1974 (see Chart 29.6), there is little mention of intra- and inter-week management of bank reserves in the second half of the 1970s.

Treasury Cash Management

As discussed in the preceding chapter, Treasury balances at Federal Reserve Banks were exceptionally volatile between 1975 and 1978 (Chart 29.3). The 1976 Markets annual report noted that "the average weekly change in the Treasury's balance at the Reserve Banks amounted to $2 billion in 1976, a 45 percent increase from 1975, and a fourfold increase from 1974. ... As a result, the Trading Desk undertook substantially enlarged operations just to counteract short-run swings in bank reserves."[6] The 1977 report observed that the Desk was unable to add enough reserves following receipt of large tax payments in April and September and that "the Treasury at those times helped alleviate the reserve shortages by temporarily redepositing funds in tax and loan accounts at commercial banks."[7]

THE CONTINUING PROBLEM WITH LIQUIDITY

Desk operations to neutralize fluctuations in Treasury balances at Federal Reserve Banks and to buffer intra- and interweek shifts in bank demand for reserves required counterparties willing and able to buy and sell atypically large quantities of Treasury securities. Suitable counterparties were not always present in the 1970s.

The 1974 Markets annual report observed that, in mid-April, "the Manager found it increasingly difficult to temper the rise in the [Federal] funds rate as banks sought to limit borrowing at the discount window. The Desk found that supplies of securities were often insufficient for open market operations as dealers had sharply reduced their inventories."[8] As a result of the limited liquidity, the FOMC "agreed to permit the funds rate

[5] 1971 Annual Report of Open Market Operations, p. 10.
[6] 1976 Annual Report of Open Market Operations, p. 17.
[7] 1977 Annual Report of Open Market Operations, p. 13.
[8] 1974 Annual Report of Open Market Operations, p. 23.

to move higher than contemplated at its April meeting rather than conduct reserve supplying operations on a scale that would risk market misinterpretation of the System's policy intent." The 1978 annual report noted similarly that,

> In managing reserves, the Desk sometimes encountered difficulty in making a sufficiently large volume of repurchase agreements, particularly at times when the Treasury balance at the Federal Reserve rose sharply. For the most part, large reserve scarcities tended to develop after quarterly tax payment dates. Government securities dealers and other market participants continued to hold small inventories, given the negative carry on them and the expectations of further interest rate increases.[9]

The Desk and the FOMC responded to the need for larger and more frequent operations, and the sometimes-limited interest of non-bank dealers in carrying large positions, by continuing to expand the scope of repurchase agreements. Chapter 22 described how, in the 1960s, the Committee removed the maturity restriction on repo collateral, introduced back-to-back repos that allowed dealers to tender customer collateral, and introduced repos on federal agency securities. The Committee was no less innovative in the 1970s.

Competitive Repo Pricing

The Desk's authority to enter into repurchase agreements derived from the continuing directive of the Federal Open Market Committee. At the beginning of the 1970s, the directive authorized the Desk to buy US government securities and obligations that were direct obligations of, or fully guaranteed as to principal and interest by, any agency of the United States from nonbank dealers on repurchase agreements no longer than fifteen calendar days at rates not less than the lesser of the discount rate of the Federal Reserve Bank of New York and the average issuing rate on the most recent issue of thirteen-week Treasury bills.[10]

The directive did not specify an upper limit on the repo rate and specified a lower limit that could be less than the discount rate whenever the auction rate for thirteen-week bills was lower than the discount rate. Nevertheless, in 1970 the Desk offered repo credit at a rate other than the discount rate on only three days and at rates that differed from the

[9] 1978 Annual Report of Open Market Operations, p. 16.

[10] See, for example, minutes of the Federal Open Market Committee, March 10, 1970, p. 20.

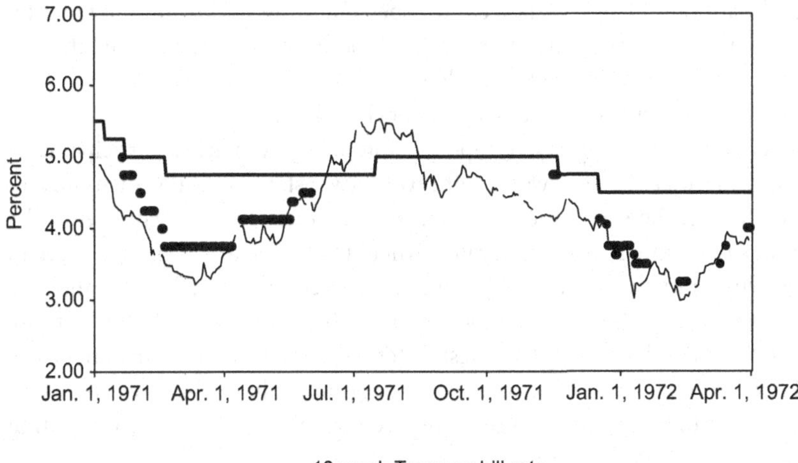

Chart 30.2 Rates on System repurchase agreements that were not equal to the Federal Reserve Bank of New York discount rate. Daily figures.
Federal Reserve Statistical Release H.15 and annual reports of open market operations.

discount rate by only 25 basis points.[11] Setting the repo rate lower than the discount rate engendered complaints from bank dealers that non-bank dealers were being subsidized; setting the repo rate above the discount rate engendered complaints from non-bank dealers that they were being penalized. Alan Holmes, the manager of the System Open Market Account, tried a more flexible form of repo pricing in 1968, setting the repo rate at a spread under the Federal funds rate, but the effort foundered when market participants interpreted a reduction in the repo rate as signaling an imminent easing of monetary restraint.[12]

In 1971 the Desk displayed a greater willingness to price repos at market levels, even if that meant substantial departures from the discount rate (Chart 30.2). When the Desk began pressing reserves on the banking system in January and early February, the weekly average Federal funds rate fell from 4.82 percent (during the statement week ending December 30, 1970) to 3.48 percent (during the week ending February 10, 1971). The thirteen-week bill rate fell from 4.89 percent on December 30 to 3.70 percent on February 10. Over the same period the discount rate fell only

[11] 1970 Annual Report of Open Market Operations, p. E-8. [12] See Chapter 22 above.

50 basis points, from 5½ percent to 5 percent. Instead of continuing to offer repo credit at or near the discount rate (and likely generating little interest), the Desk followed market rates down. By February 18, it was offering repo credit at 3¾ percent, 125 basis points below the discount rate.[13]

The unusually aggressive repo pricing led some market participants to conclude that the Fed was engineering a substantial easing of monetary policy.[14] In the event, the decline in interest rates proved evanescent. The Fed eased up on the accelerator when the monetary aggregates began growing rapidly at the beginning of March, the funds rate and the thirteen-week bill rate rebounded, and the System repo rate followed those market rates back up. The Desk later explained the January and early February repo rate reductions as nothing more than what was necessary "in order to be able to continue using [repurchase agreements] for injecting reserves for short periods."[15]

The difficulties inherent in relying on administratively priced repos resurfaced in late December 1971. On Thursday, December 23, the Desk wanted to provide additional reserves on a temporary basis but had already set the System repo rate about as low as its authority allowed. (On the preceding day it set the repo rate at 4.05 percent, below the 4½ percent discount rate and barely above the most recent thirteen-week bill auction rate of 4.02 percent.[16]) In a move the *Wall Street Journal* described as "shocking," the FOMC suspended the lower limit on System repo rates.[17] The Desk promptly offered nonbank dealers an opportunity to borrow at 3¾ percent, 75 basis points below the discount rate and 27 basis points below the most recent thirteen-week bill auction rate.[18] The Desk

[13] 1971 Annual Report of Open Market Operations, p. E-9.

[14] When the Desk reduced the repo rate to 4¼ percent on February 4 one analyst remarked that "late this year, we may be able to look back upon this action as the starting point for a much easier monetary policy." "Prices of Two Treasury Notes Set Highs; Reserve Believed to Have Injected Funds," *Wall Street Journal*, February 5, 1971, p. 15. When the Desk further reduced the repo rate to 4 percent on February 16, the *Wall Street Journal* reported that "many money-market sources viewed [the move] as an indication that another drop in the discount rate could come at any time." "'Prime' Again Cut; Federal Reserve Assists Dealers," *Wall Street Journal*, February 17, 1971, p. 3.

[15] 1971 Annual Report of Open Market Operations, p. 21. See also p. A-2, stating that the move "became necessary to make the repurchase rate more competitive with prevailing market rates so that the Desk could continue to use this avenue for reserve adjustment."

[16] "Government Securities Dealers Said to Get Federal Reserve Boost," *Wall Street Journal*, December 23, 1971, p. 12.

[17] "Federal Reserve Slashes Key Rate Below Own Floor," *Wall Street Journal*, December 24, 1971, p. 7.

[18] "Move by Reserve Cuts Bill Rates," *New York Times*, December 24, 1971, p. 31.

subsequently offered repos at 3⅝ percent on December 28 and 29, 3¾ percent between December 30 and January 7, 1972, 3⅝ percent on January 10, 3½ percent between January 11 and January 19, and finally at 3¼ percent between February 11 and February 16, all while the discount rate remained unchanged at 4½ percent.[19]

At the regularly scheduled FOMC meeting on January 11, 1972, Holmes suggested that the Committee appoint a staff committee "to investigate whether the [FOMC] should retain its long-standing rule regarding the limit on RP rates; or whether it should consider other options that might provide additional flexibility on a more permanent basis, or that might provide for a competitive determination of repurchase rates which in effect would let the market decide the rate." The Committee agreed and appointed Stephen Axilrod (an associate director of Research and Statistics at the Board of Governors) chairman and designated Karl Scheld (a vice president at the Chicago Reserve Bank and an associate economist on the staff of the Federal Open Market Committee) and Peter Sternlight (a vice president at the New York Bank) members.[20]

Three months later, the Axilrod committee presented its unanimous recommendation: interest rates on System repos should be established through an auction process and bank dealers should be allowed to participate in the auctions.[21] The committee observed that auctions open to all dealers would allow the Desk to inject reserves without appearing to signal anything about prospective changes in monetary policy and without providing a subsidy to, or imposing a penalty on, nonbank dealers. It further observed that more participants would deepen the auctions and help support the steadily expanding size of System repo operations.

Holmes was cautious about the proposed changes but willing to conduct auctions on an experimental basis. Arthur Burns, the chairman of the Board of Governors since February 1970, favored adoption of an auction process, albeit one limited to nonbank dealers. Holmes, the Axilrod committee, and Alfred Hayes, the president of the Federal Reserve Bank of New York, accepted that limitation and the Committee approved a revised directive for the Desk to undertake repurchase agreements "at rates that, unless otherwise expressly authorized by the Committee, shall be

[19] 1971 Annual Report of Open Market Operations, p. E-9; and 1972 Annual Report of Open Market Operations, p. E-9.

[20] Minutes of the Federal Open Market Committee, January 11, 1972, pp. 97–98.

[21] Minutes of the Federal Open Market Committee, April 17, 1972, pp. 6–16.

determined by competitive bidding."[22] The Desk held its first repo auction eight days later, on Tuesday, April 25, 1972.[23]

System Repos with Bank Dealers

In the spring of 1975, the Axilrod committee reviewed the experience with repo auctions and renewed its earlier recommendation that bank dealers be allowed to participate. During a discussion of the committee's report, Sternlight observed that three years of competitive repo auctions had "worked well" and that expanding the auctions to include bank dealers would "put the Desk in touch with a broader range of customers."[24] Holmes agreed, noting that the Desk was likely to get better rates if banks participated.[25] With no objection from Burns or the other Committee members, the FOMC authorized the New York Reserve Bank to include bank dealers in its repo auctions.[26]

Another Way around the Barn

Even with the benefits of competitive repo pricing, and even with the inclusion of bank dealers in repo auctions, the Desk found itself unable, from time to time, to provide sufficient reserves on a temporary basis with repurchase agreements. Increasingly volatile Treasury balances at the Reserve Banks dramatically increased the need for short-term operations, while high and volatile interest rates continued to limit dealer interest in carrying substantial inventories.

In the latter part of the 1970s the Desk developed another way to inject reserves on a temporary basis: by buying securities outright in anticipation of a temporary need and draining funds with MSPs until the need was

[22] Minutes of the Federal Open Market Committee, April 17, 1972, p. 16.

[23] "Federal Reserve's New Repurchase Plan Has a Bumpy Debut," *Wall Street Journal*, April 26, 1972, p. 14. See also "Treasury Bill Rates Over the Short Term Drop Another Notch," *Wall Street Journal*, April 24, 1972, p. 12, and"Federal Reserve Buys Government Securities, Easing Bank Reserves," *Wall Street Journal*, June 1, 1972, p. 15.

[24] Minutes of the Federal Open Market Committee, June 16–17, 1975, pp. 138–39.

[25] Minutes of the Federal Open Market Committee, June 16–17, 1975, pp. 140–41.

[26] Minutes of the Federal Open Market Committee, June 16–17, 1975, pp. 141–42. See also "Rule Changes Set by Reserve Board," *New York Times*, June 18, 1975, p. 81; and "Fed Open Market Unit Will Let Banks Make Repurchase Agreements," *Wall Street Journal*, June 18, 1975, p. 15.

evident and then again after the need had passed.[27] It was, the Desk concluded, easier to find counterparties with money than counterparties with collateral. The new strategy contributed to the decline in the volume of System repos and the increase in the volume of MSPs evident in Chart 30.1.

OUTRIGHT TRANSACTIONS IN FEDERAL AGENCY DEBT

During the winter of 1966–67, the Joint Study took up the matter of outright transactions in federal agency debt. A 1967 staff study provided the factual foundation for virtually all subsequent discussions.[28] The study reported two key findings:

- The $24 billion agency debt market functioned as a single market, even though it included a variety of independent issuers. (The major issuers were the Federal National Mortgage Association, the Federal Home Loan Banks, the Federal Intermediate Credit Banks, and the Banks for Cooperatives.) Yields on the debt of different agencies fell along a single, relatively smooth yield curve, although smaller issues sometimes exhibited significant idiosyncratic deviations.
- About two-thirds of all agency debt was short-term. The liquidity of the short-term agency market was roughly comparable to the liquidity of the market for short-term coupon-bearing Treasury debt.[29]

The study also observed that "agency debt, as obligations of wholly-owned, partially-owned or Government-supervised Agencies, share in the risk-free nature of direct U.S. debt in varying degrees" and that "the fact that the Agencies were created by Congress, are supervised, and in some cases partially owned by the U.S. Government, and in some cases may borrow directly from the Treasury makes their debt in practice almost Government-guaranteed."[30]

[27] The 1978 Annual Report of Open Market Operations states (pp. A-1 to A-2) that "the Desk often found it difficult to negotiate very large volumes of repurchase agreements since collateral was in short supply. In anticipation of such difficulties it often built up the System portfolio in anticipation of when large reserve injections would be needed. Hence, the volume of repurchase agreements arranged during the year was only slightly greater than in 1977, and the bulk of the increase in temporary transactions occurred in matched sale-purchase contracts which were used to drain reserves temporarily."

[28] Peskin (1967). See also Peskin (1971).

[29] Peskin (1967, pp. 6–7).

[30] Peskin (1967, pp. 21–22).

The Joint Study steering committee discussed the merits of outright Federal Reserve transactions in federal agency debt on April 2, 1968. Daniel Brill, the director of the Division of Research and Statistics at the Board of Governors, suggested "a quite marginal volume of transactions" on the grounds that "the prestige and functioning of the Federal agency securities market would be enhanced." He remarked that "the market had developed sufficiently to accommodate the scale of operations that was contemplated."[31]

Holmes challenged Brill's recommendation, arguing that the System did not need to expand its outright operations beyond Treasury debt (even while acknowledging that repos on agency debt had been useful), that small agency issue sizes meant that purchases would have to be spread out over a large number of issues, and that the frequency of agency offerings would create problems with respect to the timing of System operations in the agency market. Finally, he suggested that the "initiation of Federal Reserve operations in agency securities posed the danger of raising false hopes of market support."[32]

In response to a question from Treasury Secretary Henry Fowler, "it was noted that part of the impetus for System operations in agency issues had come from Congressman [Wright] Patman who believed the Federal Reserve might provide an easy means for financing the activities of the Federal agencies." R. Duane Saunders, Special Assistant to the Secretary for Debt Management, observed that "the quite marginal operations in agency issues contemplated by members of the [Joint Study staff] would not relieve the Federal Reserve from political pressures. What Congressman Patman obviously had in mind was sizable System purchases which would significantly influence the market."[33] Under Secretary Deming feared that "pressures to support the agency market would be overwhelming."[34] On the other hand, Stephen Axilrod, then an adviser in the Division of Research and Statistics, noted that those in favor of outright operations "all felt that [agency] securities were essentially the same as direct U.S. Government debt and, given the enabling legislation passed by Congress,

[31] Minutes of the Steering Committee for the Joint Treasury-Federal Reserve Study of the U.S. Government Securities Market, April 2, 1968, pp. 7–8.

[32] Minutes of the Steering Committee for the Joint Treasury-Federal Reserve Study of the U.S. Government Securities Market, April 2, 1968, pp. 8–9.

[33] Minutes of the Steering Committee for the Joint Treasury-Federal Reserve Study of the U.S. Government Securities Market, April 2, 1968, pp. 12–13.

[34] Minutes of the Steering Committee for the Joint Treasury-Federal Reserve Study of the U.S. Government Securities Market, April 2, 1968, p. 9.

there seemed to be no *a priori* argument against outright Federal Reserve transactions in these obligations."[35]

William McChesney Martin, the chairman of the steering committee, concluded that, at least for the time being, "the System should continue to limit its activity in the agency market to repurchase agreements. If the System did undertake outright transactions on a restricted basis, there would be an immediate clamor for larger and more significant operations."[36]

The final report of the Joint Study stated that "outright operations in Federal agency securities would not facilitate, in any material way, the ability of the System to alter the supply of reserves in the market." However, the report also recognized that "market conditions may develop – for example, as a result of further growth in the agency market or the availability of a large floating supply of agency securities – that would make System outright operations more practicable."[37]

Reconsideration

The issue of outright transactions in agency debt resurfaced during the March 9, 1971, FOMC meeting, when Arthur Burns, chairman of the Board of Governors since February 1970, called for comments on near-term monetary policy, including "views regarding the desirability ... of undertaking operations in agency issues."[38]

Speaking first, Hayes remarked that "the proposal for outright operations in agency issues involved important policy questions that had been discussed from time to time in the past but never resolved." He expressed his personal opposition to such transactions, citing the fragmentation of the agency market and the difficulty of avoiding the appearance of supporting new issues.[39] Aubrey Heflin, the president of the Richmond Reserve Bank, and George Clay, the president of the Kansas City Bank, also expressed concern with market fragmentation.[40]

35 Minutes of the Steering Committee for the Joint Treasury-Federal Reserve Study of the U.S. Government Securities Market, April 2, 1968, p. 10.

36 Minutes of the Steering Committee for the Joint Treasury-Federal Reserve Study of the U.S. Government Securities Market, April 2, 1968, pp. 13–14.

37 U.S. Treasury and Federal Reserve System (1969, p. 5).

38 Minutes of the Federal Open Market Committee, March 9, 1971, pp. 58 and 61–62.

39 Minutes of the Federal Open Market Committee, March 9, 1971, pp. 64–65.

40 Minutes of the Federal Open Market Committee, March 9, 1971, pp. 81–82 and 85.

Support for agency operations was stronger among the governors. William Sherrill "believed it was now time to begin outright operations in agency issues, if only to be responsive to the intent of Congress."[41] George Mitchell and J. L. Robertson both thought agency operations could help foster lower long-term interest rates.[42]

Burns concluded the discussion by asserting that a majority of the Committee appeared to favor outright operations in agency debt. He nevertheless deferred an immediate decision pending further study, although he thought it unlikely that the Committee would be any better prepared to act in three or six months.[43]

The FOMC continued discussing the merits of outright agency operations at its April 6 meeting. Burns expressed his support, stating that "there was sentiment in Congress for the System to take steps that would be useful for housing" and that "if the System declined to use the tools Congress had provided, other less desirable legislation might be enacted in the hope of benefiting housing."[44]

The long-running debate over outright operations in agency debt reached a conclusion during the August 24, 1971, FOMC meeting. Burns led off the discussion by once again observing that "a number of members of Congress were of the view that System operations in agency issues would be of substantial benefit [to housing]. They felt that the Committee had demonstrated an uncooperative attitude in the matter, and they had repeatedly raised the question of why the System has not yet utilized the authority to undertake outright operations granted by legislation five years ago."[45] When Heflin protested that "a distinction should be made between the will of Congress and the wishes of particular Congressmen," Burns replied that he thought it fair to say that "Congress as a whole was concerned about the housing problem, and that the feeling was widespread in Congress that the System had not been sufficiently sensitive to that problem."[46]

[41] Minutes of the Federal Open Market Committee, March 9, 1971, p. 73.

[42] Minutes of the Federal Open Market Committee, March 9, 1971, pp. 79 and 95–96.

[43] Minutes of the Federal Open Market Committee, March 9, 1971, p. 96.

[44] Minutes of the Federal Open Market Committee, April 6, 1971, p. 38.

[45] Minutes of the Federal Open Market Committee, August 24, 1971, pp. 108–9. When asked whether the staff thought that System operations in agency debt "would be of significant benefit to the national housing program," Axilrod replied that "in the staff's judgment such operations might be of marginal benefit to housing but probably would not represent a major aid." Minutes of the Federal Open Market Committee, August 24, 1971, p. 108.

[46] Minutes of the Federal Open Market Committee, August 24, 1971, p. 111.

The members of the Committee were dismissive of the prospective benefits of outright agency operations but willing to defer to Burns's judgment. Robertson thought that "operations in agency issues would have only a marginal impact on housing finance" but accepted that "since the Committee had gone into [Treasury] coupon issues it could just as well operate in agency issues." Hayes was concerned that "a Committee decision to undertake such operations would generate expectations about benefits to housing that would not be realized" but was "prepared to defer to the judgment of the Chairman that, on balance, operations with agencies would be desirable." Governor J. Dewey Daane was similarly "prepared to defer to the Chairman's judgment."[47]

At the end of the day the Committee voted unanimously to authorize outright transactions in federal agency debt, but required that the transactions comply with the guidelines shown in Box 30.2.[48] Guidelines 4 and 7 were specifically intended to preclude any expectation that the System would support new agency offerings. Maturing issues would not be rolled over with the issuer and no new issue would be bought until it had been outstanding for at least two weeks. Guideline 5 was intended to limit exposure to small issues with negligible liquidity and susceptible to idiosyncratic price fluctuations.

The Committee announced its decision to initiate outright transactions in agency debt on September 16, 1971, stating that the purpose of the new program was to "widen the base of System open market operations and at the same time to add breadth to the market for agency securities." The Committee further remarked that "because the outstanding volume of many agency issues is small relative to that of U.S. Treasury obligations, Federal Reserve operations in such issues will be on a limited scale. They will not be directed at supporting individual sectors of the agency market or at channeling funds into issues of particular agencies."[49]

Subsequent Events

Desk officials grew more comfortable with the idea of larger positions in individual issues as they gained experience with outright operations in the

[47] Minutes of the Federal Open Market Committee, August 24, 1971, pp. 109–10.

[48] Minutes of the Federal Open Market Committee, August 24, 1971, pp. 112–13.

[49] Federal Reserve Bank of New York Circular no. 6803, September 16, 1971. See also "Reserve Board's Open Market Committee to Buy, Sell All Federal Agencies' Issues," *Wall Street Journal*, September 17, 1971, p. 16; and "Policy Change to Allow Outright Buying and Selling of Issues," *New York Times*, September 17, 1971, p. 61.

Box 30.2 Guidelines for the Conduct of System Operations in Agency Issues, adopted August 24, 1971.

1. System open market operations in Federal agency issues are an integral part of total System open market operations designed to influence bank reserves, money market conditions, and monetary aggregates.
2. System open market operations in Federal agency issues are not designed to support individual sectors of the market or to channel funds into issues of particular agencies.
3. As an initial objective, the System would aim at building up a modest portfolio of agency issues, with the amount and timing dependent on the ability to make net acquisitions without undue market effects.
4. System holdings of maturing agency issues will be allowed to run off at maturity, at least initially.
5. Purchases will be limited to fully taxable issues for which there is an active secondary market. Purchases will also be limited to issues outstanding in amounts of $300 million or over in cases where the obligations have a maturity of five years or less at the time of purchase, and to issues outstanding in amounts of $200 million or over in cases where the securities have a maturity of more than five years at the time of purchase.
6. System holdings of any one issue at any one time will not exceed 10 per cent of the amount of the issue outstanding. There will be no specific limit on aggregate holdings of the issues of any one agency.
7. No new issue will be purchased in the secondary market until at least two weeks after the issue date.
8. All outright purchases, sales and holdings of agency issues will be for the System Open Market Account.

Minutes of the Federal Open Market Committee, August 24, 1971, attachment B.

agency market. In the spring of 1972, Holmes asked that guideline 6 be relaxed to allow the Open Market Account to hold up to 25 percent of an issue. Several committee members pushed back and the Committee compromised, raising the issue limit to 20 percent and imposing a new limit of 10 percent of the total debt of any single issuer.[50] The issue and issuer limits were subsequently raised to 30 percent and 15 percent, respectively, in June 1975.[51]

In July 1974, Holmes suggested that the Committee delete guidelines 4 and 7 to allow the Desk to roll over maturing issues. The recommended

[50] Minutes of the Federal Open Market Committee, April 17, 1972, pp. 18–20.
[51] Minutes of the Federal Open Market Committee, June 16–17, 1975, pp. 132–36.

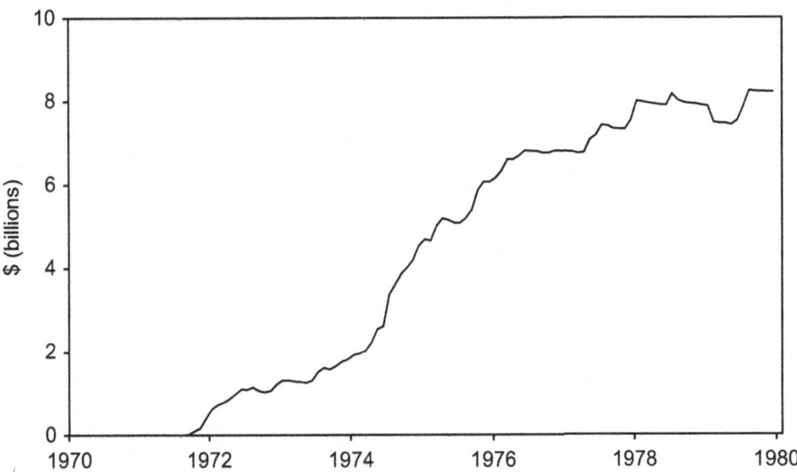

Chart 30.3 Federal agency securities in the System Open Market Account. Monthly average of daily data.
Board of Governors of the Federal Reserve System (1981, table 2A).

action would simplify the management of bank reserves and facilitate the Desk's efforts at accumulating a position in agency debt in line with Committee directives. The Committee acted affirmatively on Holmes' recommendations.[52]

Agency debt in the System Open Market Account increased to about $8 billion at the beginning of 1978 – equal to about 7 percent of total Treasury debt in the Account – and remained at that level through the end of the decade (Chart 30.3).

[52] Minutes of the Federal Open Market Committee, July 16, 1974, pp. 85–86.

PART IX

INFRASTRUCTURE IN THE 1970S

The infrastructure of the government securities market continued to evolve in the 1970s. The introduction of "screen brokers" in the interdealer market and the expansion of the book-entry system to include securities held by member banks for trading purposes and for customers were particularly important. Screen brokerage materially reduced the fragmentation of an over-the-counter market that had previously relied on bilateral verbal communication, fragmentation that otherwise would have worsened as the size of the dealer community almost doubled during the decade. The expanded book-entry system substantially reduced transaction costs by facilitating the replacement of paper securities with electronic storage and transfer.

31

The Secondary Market in the 1970s

Primary dealers – dealers that provided liquidity to the Federal Reserve Bank of New York when that Bank was conducting open market operations – continued to occupy the center of the Treasury market in the 1970s. Their privileged position, relative to other dealers, was reinforced and extended by their access to the interdealer broker market. The gap separating the two classes of dealers widened further when the introduction of electronic quotation systems in the second half of the decade virtually eliminated the fragmentation of trading in the interdealer market and created a central market for Treasury securities.

PRIMARY DEALERS

Membership in the primary dealer community surged from twenty firms at the end of 1969 to thirty-four firms at the end of 1979. Table 31.1 summarizes the additions and departures.[1]

[1] Table 33.1 does not include four relatively short-lived additions.

Paine, Webber, Jackson & Curtis, Inc. was added in September 1972 and departed June 1973 after finding that it was unable to make money as a primary dealer. "Paine Webber Says it Intends to Cease Trading Treasurys," *Wall Street Journal*, June 19, 1973, p. 36, and "Paine, Webber Abandons Active Role in Treasurys," *New York Times*, June 19, 1973, p. 50. As shown in Table 31.1, Paine, Webber returned in August 1977.

Lehman Government Securities, Inc. was added in May 1973 and departed January 1974 following a run of losses, a management succession crisis, and a decision to focus on federal agency securities. "The White Knight at Lehman Brothers," *New York Times*, November 11, 1973, p. 185, "Lehman Brothers Rejects Trading in Treasury Bills," *New York Times*, January 29, 1974, p. 42, and "Treasury-Bond Dealer Finds Job More Hectic as the Market Gyrates," *Wall Street Journal*, August 13, 1975, p.1. As shown in Table 31.1, Lehman also returned in August 1977.

White, Weld & Co., Inc. was added in May 1976 and departed April 1978 following the acquisition of the firm by Merrill Lynch, Pierce, Fenner & Smith, which already had a

Table 31.1 *Additions to and departures from the primary dealer list in the 1970s.*

	Additions	Departures
Jan. 1970		Blyth & Co., Inc.
Jul. 1970	Chase Manhattan Bank, National Association	
Nov. 1971	Bank of America National Trust and Savings Association	
Nov. 1972	A.G. Becker & Co., Inc.	
Feb. 1973	John Nuveen & Co., Inc.	
Jul. 1973		duPont, Glore, Forgan & Co. (originally added under the name Francis I. duPont & Co.)
Nov. 1973	Northern Trust Co.	
Apr. 1974	Donaldson, Lufkin & Jenrette Securities Corp.	
Apr. 1974	First Pennco Securities, Inc.	
Dec. 1974	Blyth Eastman Dillon Capital Markets, Inc.	
Mar. 1975	Goldman, Sachs & Co.	
Nov. 1976	Bache Halsey Stuart, Inc.	
Nov. 1976	Carroll McEntee & McGinley, Inc.	
Aug. 1977	Lehman Government Securities, Inc.	
Aug. 1977	Paine, Webber, Jackson & Curtis, Inc.	
Mar. 1978	E. F. Hutton & Co., Inc.	
Mar. 1978	Dean Witter Reynolds, Inc.	
Jun. 1978	Morgan Stanley & Co., Inc.	
May 1979	Kidder, Peabody & Co., Inc.	
Dec. 1979		Blyth Eastman Dillon Capital Markets, Inc.

Annual reports of open market operations.

primary dealer unit. "Merrill Lynch Buys White, Weld, An Old-Line Firm, for $50 Million," *New York Times*, April 15, 1978, p. 29, and "Merrill Lynch Pays $50 Million for White Weld," *Wall Street Journal*, April 17, 1978, p. 2.

Weeden & Co., Inc. was added in November 1976 and departed May 1978 following losses in its third-market market-making unit that substantially impaired the firm's capital. "Weeden May Quit 'Third Market' and Seek a New Brokerage Role," *New York*

The additions included three banks: Chase Manhattan Bank, Bank of America, and Northern Trust, one bank affiliate: First Pennco Securities (an affiliate of First Pennsylvania Bank), and one independent broker-dealer, Carroll McEntee & McGinley, Inc. The other twelve firms were either full-line broker-dealers or affiliates of full-line broker-dealers.

The three departures reflected idiosyncratic issues at the respective firms. Blyth & Co. left in 1970 following revelations of secret trading and trading on non-public information,[2] duPont, Glore, Forgan & Co. left in 1973 in the wake of operational problems,[3] and the government securities business of Blyth Eastman Dillon Capital Markets was integrated into that of Paine, Webber, Jackson & Curtis following Paine Webber's acquisition of Blyth Eastman Dillon & Co. in 1979.[4]

THE INTERDEALER BROKER MARKET

Government securities dealers relied on interdealer brokers to mask their identity when trading with competitors. A dealer interested in selling to another dealer, whether to test the market or to alter its risk exposure, would give a broker an order to sell a particular amount of a specified security at a designated price. Prior to the mid-1970s the broker would call around to other dealers and "show" the offering. (Until the mid-1970s, virtually all communication among major participants in the government securities market was by telephone.) A dealer who liked the offer could buy the securities at the offer price, paying the broker a modest commission. (To encourage order submission, brokers did not charge commissions to dealers that submitted orders.) Following the execution of the transaction, the broker made a second round of calls, announcing the completion of the trade. Brokers followed a similar procedure in showing bids to buy securities.

Importantly, a broker did not reveal to either party the identity of the counterparty. To settle the transaction, the seller delivered its securities to the broker and the broker redelivered the securities to the buyer. Because the parties remained anonymous, the business of interdealer brokerage was known as "blind brokerage."

Times, January 31, 1978, p. 33, "Weeden Tightens Belt Second Time in Days by Dissolving Unit," *Wall Street Journal*, February 2, 1978, p. 23, and "Weeden Ends 2 Bond Units,' *New York Times*, May 25, 1978, p. D3.

2 See Chapter 23 above. 3 See Morrison and Wilhelm (2007, pp. 235–36).

4 "Paine Webber Set to Buy Blyth," *New York Times*, October 2, 1979, p. D1; and "INA Set to Sell Blyth Eastman to Paine Webber," *Wall Street Journal*, October 2, 1979, p. 4.

Access to the interdealer broker market was important for two reasons. First, interdealer brokers typically offered opportunities to buy modest amounts of Treasury issues – so-called "round lots" – at lower prices, and to sell at higher prices, than those immediately available from customers. Search costs, including time spent uncovering trading opportunities, were so low that only the highest bids and lowest offers attracted attention.[5] Second, the interdealer broker market offered opportunities for a dealer to alter its risk exposure anonymously, without revealing information to competitors. Dealers were more willing to accommodate large customer purchase and sale interests knowing that they could shed at least some of the risk without triggering an adverse move in market prices.

Managing the Risks of Blind Brokerage

Blind brokerage presented an element of risk that was not present in dealer-customer trading because the parties to a transaction had to settle through a broker that typically had little capital.[6] The system worked because brokers and dealers agreed that participation in the interdealer broker market would be limited to adequately capitalized dealers.[7]

The question of who would decide whether a dealer was adequately capitalized was resolved by referring to the list of reporting dealers published from time to time by the Federal Reserve Bank of New York.[8] The Bank had a significant business interest in limiting System operations to

[5] A large block transaction warranted a more extensive search for a compatible trading partner, including inquires directed to institutional investors believed to be interested in taking the other side of a contemplated transaction.

[6] U.S. General Accounting Office (February 1987, p. 62), stating that brokers have "limited capital."

[7] See U.S. General Accounting Office (December 1987, pp. 35–36), quoting a statement of counsel to the Government Securities Brokers Association that blind brokerage services "are provided to counterparties . . . that are known to each other in the sense of belonging to a limited defined group each member of which has agreed to deal 'blindly' with each other member. Therefore, in a blind brokering transaction each counterparty knows that (1) it is buying from or selling to another dealer and (2) that the counterparty dealer belongs to a group that has been approved by each dealer as a party with which it has agreed to transact business."

[8] U.S. General Accounting Office (December 1987, p. 52), noting that, "as a practical matter, requiring all parties gaining trading access to be [reporting] . . . dealers has provided the interdealer brokers a convenient common standard for access . . ."

dealers with adequate capital and it was not unreasonable for interdealer brokers to similarly limit access to their market.

Reliance on the list of reporting dealers for determining access to the interdealer broker market was a mixed blessing for the New York Bank. On the one hand, effectively controlling access to the interdealer market gave the Bank an additional lever to encourage sometimes reluctant dealers to provide the liquidity needed for open market operations. On the other hand, primary dealers repeatedly sought to deepen the Bank's involvement in refereeing access to the market – occasionally at some discomfort to the Bank.

On September 23, 1971, Peter Sternlight, a vice president assigned to the Open Market Desk, attended a meeting of the executive committee of the Association of Primary Dealers called to discuss a controversy that had arisen over access to broker lines, the private-wire telephone lines that directly connected brokers and dealers. The controversy centered around the decision of several brokers to install lines to three dealers that had announced their *intention* to become primary dealers but that had not yet been listed as reporting dealers.

In a memo memorializing the meeting, Sternlight explained that,

> At present, according to my understanding, the dealers with lines to brokers include the twenty dealers on the list of dealers reporting to the Fed, plus Becker, Nuveen, and Bank of America. The criterion seems to be that a dealer should either be on the list of reporters to the Fed, or should be in the position, as are the latter three, of having announced an intention to be a primary dealer.[9]

The primary dealers argued that including a dealer that had merely announced its intention to become a primary dealer was problematic. As Sternlight explained,

> The dealers question . . . how long a firm should be allowed the favored position of having the brokers' lines if they do not succeed in gaining "recognition" from the Fed and being placed on the official "reporting list." Unless there is some time limit, they feel, any firm (including [non-dealer banks with active trading operations]) could declare an intention of being a dealer, get the desired brokers' lines, and then continue merely as a fringe participant in the market without making a real effort to establish a primary dealership.

[9] Memo from Peter Sternlight to Mr. Holmes, Federal Reserve Bank of New York, "Dealer Association Meeting, September 23, 1971," September 30, 1971. The twenty reporting dealers included the twenty dealers identified in Table 23.1 above, less Blyth & Co. (which was de-listed in January 1970), plus Chase Manhattan Bank (which was listed in July 1970).

The dealers suggested that the New York Fed act as a referee, identifying who should get broker lines, but Sternlight was uncomfortable with that role:

> While my mind is not completely made up on the subject, I would feel quite uneasy about the Fed undertaking a major role in deciding who is or is not a "dealer." I grant that there is a problem of deciding who gets brokers' lines, but I think that putting this responsibility on the Fed could lead to much greater problems . . .

Access to broker lines was discussed further during a follow-on meeting two weeks later. The dealers proposed several ways that the Bank might referee access to the brokers' market. Sternlight again expressed his reservations:

> The dealers, it seems to me, have a legitimate concern for seeking to develop and retain a market structure where "dealers" are somehow distinct from "customers" – provided this is done in a way that permits new firms to enter the business. . . .
>
> However, it is something else again to enlist the authority of the central bank in direct support of the dealers' arrangements to restrict access to the brokers' wires. Presumably, the dealers feel that it strengthens their defenses from an anti-trust standpoint if they can lean on [i.e., point to] the Fed in support of their market practices. But this very fact puts a heavy responsibility on the Fed to be sure that its support is, first, perfectly legal and second, that if it is legal it is desirable from a policy standpoint.
>
> Setting aside the legal question as outside my competence . . . it seems to me that on policy grounds . . . the Federal Reserve should stay clear of entanglement with the question of dealer access to the brokers' wires. Our list of trading relationships should be determined wholly on the basis of which relationships can be useful in conducting System open market operations.[10]

Reservations about entanglement notwithstanding, Sternlight suggested a clever solution to the dealers' problem. In keeping with his concern to separate the question of access to broker wires from the question of primary dealer standards, Sternlight remarked that "it would be useful to add a few firms to our list *for reporting purposes only*, without entering into a trading relationship."[11]

Separating Reporting Dealer Status from Primary Dealer Status

When the Federal Reserve initiated the reporting dealer program in 1960, the New York Reserve Bank identified as reporting dealers the same

[10] Memo from Peter Sternlight to Mr. Holmes, Federal Reserve Bank of New York, "Federal Reserve Relationships with Dealers," November 1, 1971.

[11] Memo from Peter Sternlight to Mr. Holmes, Federal Reserve Bank of New York, "Dealer Association Meeting, September 23, 1971," September 30, 1971, p. 4. Emphasis added.

Table 31.2 *Designation as a reporting dealer versus designation as a primary dealer in the 1970s. Delays of more than a month shown in bold.*

	Designated as a reporting dealer	Designated as a primary dealer
Chase Manhattan Bank, National Association	Jul. 1970	Jul. 1970
Bank of America National Trust and Savings Association	Nov. 1971	Nov. 1971
A.G. Becker & Co., Inc.	Nov. 1971	**Nov. 1972**
John Nuveen & Co., Inc.	Nov. 1971	**Feb. 1973**
Northern Trust Co.	Aug. 1973	**Nov. 1973**
Donaldson, Lufkin & Jenrette Securities Corp.	Mar. 1974	Apr. 1974
First Pennco Securities, Inc.	Mar. 1974	Apr. 1974
Blyth Eastman Dillon Capital Markets, Inc.	Dec. 1974	Dec. 1974
Goldman Sachs & Co.	Dec. 1974	**Mar. 1975**
Bache Halsey Stuart, Inc.	Oct. 1975	**Nov. 1976**
Carroll McEntee & McGinley, Inc.	Sep. 1976	**Nov. 1976**
Lehman Government Securities, Inc.	Nov. 1976	**Aug. 1977**
Paine, Webber, Jackson & Curtis, Inc.	Nov. 1976	**Aug. 1977**
E. F. Hutton & Co., Inc.	Nov. 1977	**Mar. 1978**
Dean Witter & Co., Inc.[1]	Nov. 1977	**Mar. 1978**
Morgan Stanley & Co., Inc.	Feb. 1978	**Jun. 1978**
Kidder, Peabody & Co., Inc.	Feb. 1979	**May 1979**

[1] Name changed to Dean Witter Reynolds in January 1978.
Annual reports of open market operations and Federal Reserve Bank of New York reporting dealer notices.

seventeen firms that the Bank had designated as primary dealers. During the 1960s, and initially in the 1970s, the Bank continued to list a firm as a reporting dealer and designate the firm as a primary dealer simultaneously. Chase Manhattan Bank was both listed as a reporting dealer and designated as a primary dealer in mid-July 1970.

Beginning in November 1971, the New York Fed began to add firms to the list of reporting dealers *before* designating them as primary dealers. The list of reporting dealers was necessarily public – dealers who reported their trading activity to the Bank needed to be able to identify whether a trade with another dealer should be classified as a trade with another *reporting* dealer – but the Bank did not have to, and chose not to, reveal whether a reporting dealer was a primary dealer. As shown in Table 31.2, the lag between public identification as a reporting dealer and private designation as a primary dealer sometimes ran a year or more. The new procedure allowed the Bank to put a dealer on the reporting dealer list – thereby giving the dealer access to the interdealer broker market – without requiring that the dealer meet the standards required of a primary dealer.[12]

There is no evidence that the primary dealers were unhappy with the Fed's newly created distinction between reporting dealers and primary dealers, as long as the difference was no more than a transitional matter, where a reporting dealer either moved on to become a primary dealer or was delisted as a reporting dealer. However, they balked when it appeared that the Fed might allow a dealer to remain a reporting dealer without ever becoming a primary dealer.

During a 1976 meeting with Sternlight and other Bank officials, the executive committee of the Association of Primary Dealers expressed its concern that the Bank might add a firm to the list of reporting dealers even though the firm did not make markets in the full spectrum of Treasury securities and was not, therefore, eligible to become a primary dealer. The committee "saw [informal] reporting and then being added to the list [of reporting dealers] as part of the process of achieving a trading relationship with the Federal Reserve" and was concerned that "primary dealers would no longer be distinct as a group" if the Bank allowed dealers that did not intend to make markets across the entire yield curve to report data.[13]

Sternlight did not reject the idea that the Bank might make reporting dealer status more than a transitional matter. He stated that "the reporting list could be viewed as a statistical list of significant participants in the market," that "he could see a case for adding a firm to the list even if it was active only in the coupon sector, provided that it made markets in a broad range of such issues and not just in a few maturities," and that "while the

[12] Separation of reporting dealer status and primary dealer status had the additional advantage of allowing the Bank to terminate a trading relationship with a dealer without the publicity that would follow from removing the firm from the publicly available list of reporting dealers. Bank staff considered public termination of a trading relationship as "terribly difficult ... unless the firm was clearly and publicly withdrawing from active market trading." Memo from Peter D. Sternlight to Mr. Holmes, Federal Reserve Bank of New York, "Federal Reserve Relationships with Dealers," November 1, 1971. When Sternlight suggested that the Bank might list a firm as a reporting dealer without also designating the firm a primary dealer, he additionally suggested that "we might want to consider dropping from the trading list a firm with whom we have had negligible volume in recent months" without also dropping the firm from the list of reporting dealers. Memo from Peter Sternlight to Mr. Holmes, Federal Reserve Bank of New York, "Dealer Association Meeting, September 23, 1971," September 30, 1971.

[13] Memo from Shelia Tschinkel to Securities Department Files, Federal Reserve Bank of New York, "Meeting with Representatives of the Association of Primary Dealers," December 14, 1976.

Federal Reserve would encourage a firm to be active in all sectors, it would not require this."[14] Designation as a reporting dealer nevertheless continued to be a transitional phase on the road to becoming a primary dealer.

THE RISE OF SCREEN BROKERS

As the number of primary dealers increased during the 1970s, interdealer brokers found it increasingly difficult to keep their dealer clients equally well-informed of market developments. Reliance on telephone communication meant that some dealers necessarily found out before other dealers that a new bid or offer had come into the market or that a transaction had taken place.

In mid-decade, interdealer brokers began installing video screens in dealer offices to display the prices and sizes of their active purchase and sale interests. When a dealer called to give an order, the broker keyed the details into a computer and the dealer's bid or offer appeared *simultaneously* on *all* of the dealer screens. A dealer that wanted to trade on the order called the broker to execute the transaction. Announcement of the completed transaction similarly appeared simultaneously on all of the dealer screens.[15] Richard Tilton, the president of Garban, the first firm to use video screens for interdealer brokerage, remarked in 1983 that "screens make the market more efficient by letting everybody see prices at the same time."[16]

Screen brokerage accelerated the pace of interdealer trading and enhanced the liquidity, and reduced the fragmentation, of the interdealer market. E. Craig Coates, the head of the government desk at Salomon Brothers, observed that screen brokerage provided "instantaneous markets to all primary dealers ... at the same time" and was "a substantial improvement over the ... telephone communications for trading that took place prior to the screens."[17]

As a practical matter, screen brokerage went a long way towards making the interdealer market an integrated central market for US government securities. One broker remarked that "brokers are, in effect, an exchange.

[14] Memo from Shelia Tschinkel to Securities Department Files, Federal Reserve Bank of New York, "Meeting with Representatives of the Association of Primary Dealers," December 14, 1976.

[15] Garbade (Summer 1978). See also U.S. General Accounting Office (December 1987, pp. 28–33).

[16] "Big 5 U.S. Securities Dealers," *New York Times*, June 9, 1983, p. D1.

[17] General Accounting Office (February 1987, p. 100).

They provide the Treasury bond market with the same service that the New York Stock Exchange provides to the equity market."[18]

By enhancing the liquidity and reducing the fragmentation of the interdealer broker market, screen brokerage further widened the gulf between primary dealers who enjoyed access to the interdealer market and the other dealers and customers who did not. Dealers that wanted to become primary dealers became increasingly anxious to obtain access to the interdealer broker market and the market attracted the interest of so-called "trading accounts" that wanted to trade actively and at least cost without taking on the burden of being a primary dealer. The conflict between maintaining financial safeguards around trading in a blind brokered market and the demands of those outside the primary dealer community for access to a materially more efficient market would continue in the 1980s.[19]

[18] "Big 5 U.S. Securities Dealers," *New York Times*, June 9, 1983, p. D1. See also Garbade (July 1978).

[19] See, for example, "Lazard Freres Might Seek Privileges of Official Dealers in U.S. Securities," *Wall Street Journal*, January 11, 1985, p. 24, stating that "Lazard [Frères & Co.] says it doesn't want to be a market maker, but it wants access to the wholesale prices on the brokers' screens."

The matter of access to the interdealer broker market became so tangled that Congress mandated, in section 104 of the Government Securities Act of 1986, a study by the General Accounting Office, in cooperation with the Board of Governors, the Department of the Treasury, and the Securities and Exchange Commission, of "the nature of the current trading system in the secondary market for government securities." "Notice of Public Hearing and Request for Comments on the Nature of the Current Trading System in the Secondary Market for U.S. Government Securities," *Federal Register*, January 2, 1987, pp. 220–23, remarking (p. 221) that "in recognition of the complexity of the access issue, the Congress included a provision in the Act for GAO to study the issue . . ."

In addition to conducting numerous interviews, the General Accounting Office organized a public hearing on trading access. See U.S. General Accounting Office (February 1987). The final report was published in U.S. General Accounting Office (December 1987).

32

The Book-Entry System, Part II

At the beginning of the 1970s the Government Securities Clearing Arrangement – hereafter, GSCA – was a fully functioning system for settling transactions in US Treasury securities on a net basis. As discussed in Chapter 25, nine large New York clearing banks settled CPD and intracity transfers with credits and debits to their GSCA clearing accounts during the day. They settled their net account balances with definitive bearer securities at the end of the day.

Also, by the beginning of the 1970s, the Fed had developed the conceptual and legal framework, and put in place the operational foundations, of a book-entry system. The system, separate and distinct from the GSCA, was limited to providing an alternative to definitive securities held in custody at a Federal Reserve Bank.[1] As discussed in Chapter 27, the book-entry system was introduced in early 1968, extended in mid-1969, and accounted for about half of the $248 billion of marketable Treasury debt outstanding at the end of 1970, by which time virtually all of the Treasury securities held at Federal Reserve Banks had been converted to book-entry form.

Two important categories of Treasury securities remained outside the book-entry system: securities owned by member banks for trading purposes and securities safekept in member bank vaults for bank customers.[2] New York Reserve Bank officials had sought the cooperation of the clearing banks in extending the book-entry system to include those

[1] A Federal Reserve book-entry account balance represented actual ownership of securities; a GSCA clearing account balance represented only what was due to or due from the New York Reserve Bank at the end of the day.

[2] Vollkommer (1970, p. 70).

securities.[3] The banks responded with interest but questioned whether change would come quickly.[4]

THE INSURANCE CRISIS

The cost-benefit calculus of expanding the book-entry system changed, swiftly and dramatically, in late 1970. In the wake of several large and well-publicized thefts of bearer Treasury securities – including securities worth $13 million from Morgan Guaranty Trust Company in October 1969[5] – Continental Insurance Company, the leading underwriter of insurance policies covering thefts of securities from commercial banks, announced that it would restrict or terminate coverage in 1971.[6]

Continental's announcement threatened to impose severe limits on trading in Treasury securities, because dealers and clearing banks could not bear the risk of uninsured losses of the magnitudes that had been occurring.[7] Suddenly, the cost of continuing to settle transactions with bearer securities grew immeasurably larger and the idea of expanding the book-entry system became immeasurably more attractive. The threat to market liquidity infused Treasury and Federal Reserve officials, as well as private market participants, with a sense of urgency.[8]

[3] Letter from Felix Davis, Vice President, Federal Reserve Bank of New York, to John Lee, Executive Vice President, New York Clearing House, June 10, 1968, appealing for "your further collaboration" in applying "the book-entry procedure for Treasury securities to those held in custody by members of the Clearing House."

[4] Letter from John Lee, Executive Vice President, New York Clearing House, to Felix Davis, Vice President, Federal Reserve Bank of New York, July 31, 1968.

[5] "Morgan Guaranty Missing $13 Million of U.S. Bills," *Wall Street Journal*, October 24, 1969, p. 14; "Morgan Guaranty Loses $13 Million in Negotiable Notes," *New York Times*, October 24, 1969, p. 1; and "Securities Theft Flurry Prompts Insurers to Mull Halting Coverage on Such Losses," *Wall Street Journal*, November 17, 1969, p. 2. A Treasury official later estimated that about $30 million in bearer Treasury securities were lost or stolen in 1969. "Small-Bond Thefts Up Sharply, Treasury Aides Tell Senate unit," *New York Times*, June 11, 1971, p. 49.

[6] "Loss of Insurance," *New York Times*, December 6, 1970, p. 216. See also "Securities Theft Flurry Prompts Insurers to Mull Halting Coverage on Such Losses," *Wall Street Journal*, November 17, 1969, p. 2; and "Mounting Thefts Cause Some Insurers to Drop Coverage on U.S. Issues," *Wall Street Journal*, June 10, 1970, p. 4.

[7] "Loss of Insurance," *New York Times*, December 6, 1970, p. 216, and Debs (1972, p. 180), noting the risk that "major participants in the market would terminate operations, and the market would cease to function."

[8] "Treasury Announces Move to Thwart Securities Theft," *New York Times*, December 21, 1970, p. 61; "U.S. Help Readied for Bond Market," *New York Times*, December 23, 1970, p. 1; Debs (1972, p. 180), noting that the expansion of the book-entry system was "greatly accelerated" by the insurance crisis; and Ringsmuth and Rice (1984, p. 16), noting that the

Continental agreed to continue coverage, giving the Treasury and the Fed time to act.[9]

EXPANSION OF THE BOOK-ENTRY SYSTEM

The initial effort to expand the book-entry system focused on the clearing banks participating in the Government Securities Clearing Arrangement, because those banks "were the most vulnerable to the problem of insurance coverage."[10]

During the first quarter of 1971 the Federal Reserve Bank of New York worked with the GSCA banks to bring their trading account securities and the securities owned by their customers – including their nonbank dealer customers – into the system. The Bank announced in April that,

> Since December, this Bank has been working with the banks participating in the Clearing Arrangement, as well as the Association of Primary Dealers in U.S. Government Securities, with a view to determining general procedures for establishing the necessary new book-entry accounts and to integrating such accounts into the Clearing Arrangement. Such procedures have been agreed to, and the extended book-entry procedure is available to the twelve New York City banks participating in the Clearing Arrangement.[11]

The expansion of the book-entry system was facilitated by the installation, in mid-January 1971, of a new computer, the Sigma-5, at the Federal Reserve Bank of New York to keep track of securities transfers and account balances.[12] CPD transfers were routed between the Sigma-5 and the eleven other Reserve Banks through an inter-district message switch in Culpepper, Virginia, that opened in August 1970.[13] In a December 1970 review of the current status of the Clearing Arrangement and the

crisis "provided momentum which swept away resistance to the novelty of book-entry procedure[s]."

9 "Bond Insurance Sought in Talks," *New York Times*, December 24, 1970, p. 29, "Continental Insurance Reaches Interim Bond Pact with Banks," *New York Times*, December 25, 1970, p. 47, and "Government Securities Market Structure to Change Radically Under Computer Plan," *Wall Street Journal*, December 28, 1970, p. 4. See also 1970 Annual Report of Open Market Operations, p. 28.

10 Debs (1972, p. 181).

11 Federal Reserve Bank of New York Circular no. 6718, April 26, 1971. See also Government Securities Clearing Arrangement Participant Memo no. 36, March 24, 1971, advising participants of the availability of an expanded menu of "book-entry/clearing accounts."

12 Federal Reserve Bank of New York (March 1972, April 1972, and 1984).

13 Vollkommer (1970, pp. 26–28), Hoey and Vollkommer (1970, pp. 23–24), and Federal Reserve System (1975).

contemplated expansion of the book-entry system, Richard Debs, a senior New York Bank official, observed that "under the new operation – involving the Culpepper computer switch and the national network as well as this Bank's [Sigma-5] computer switch and the local [New York] network – it is expected that the volume and velocity of transfers will be greatly increased and service in general greatly improved." Debs emphasized the importance of the Bank's new computer, observing that "to go beyond a simple book-entry custody account, and to integrate a book-entry account into the [GSCA], we must await the operation of the [Sigma-5]."[14]

In early August 1971, Morgan Guaranty Trust became the first dealer bank to utilize the expanded arrangement when it deposited into the book-entry system Treasury bonds that it held as a primary dealer.[15] Thereafter, any bonds bought by Morgan's trading desk and delivered by CPD or intra-city wire transfer were credited to Morgan's book-entry dealer account (rather than to the bank's GSCA account) and any bonds sold by Morgan's trading desk and delivered via CPD or intra-city transfer were charged to Morgan's book-entry dealer account (rather than to its GSCA account). Most importantly, bonds could be left in the book-entry account at the end of the day and did not need to be transferred, in the form of definitive securities, to Morgan's vaults. The conversion of Morgan's dealer bonds to book-entry form eliminated "the need for physical settlement of the daily clearing balances with respect to the ... issues affected."[16]

In November 1971, Irving Trust, one of the two leading clearing banks for nonbank primary dealers,[17] moved the clearing business of one of its primary dealer customers, Harris Trust and Savings Bank, from a GSCA account to a book-entry account.[18] Four months later Manufacturers Hanover Trust Co., the other leading clearing bank for nonbank primary dealers, converted the Treasury bonds that it held for all of its nonbank primary dealer customers to book-entry form.[19] In July 1972 the New York Fed reported that,

[14] Memo from Richard Debs to Mr. Treiber, Federal Reserve Bank of New York, "Problem of Insurance on Government Securities: Current Status of Book-Entry Procedure and Clearing Arrangement," December 7, 1970, pp. 6 and 12.

[15] Government Securities Clearing Arrangement Participant Memo no. 39, August 4, 1971.

[16] Government Securities Clearing Arrangement Participant Memo no. 39, August 4, 1971.

[17] "U.S. Help Readied for Bond Market," *New York Times*, December 23, 1970, p. 1, "Continental Insurance Reaches Interim Bond Pact with Banks," *New York Times*, December 25, 1970, p. 47, and "Government Securities Market Structure to Change Radically under Computer Plan," *Wall Street Journal*, December 28, 1970, p. 4.

[18] Government Securities Clearing Arrangement Participant Memo no. 41, November 30, 1971.

[19] Government Securities Clearing Arrangement Participant Memo no. 43, March 9, 1972.

> Over the past year, the [book-entry] program has been gradually extended to cover the securities held by [GSCA] banks (a) for account of their customers, including customers which are nonbank dealers in Government securities, and (b) as their 'dealer' inventories in those cases in which the bank is a primary dealer in Government securities.[20]

The expansion of the book-entry system to securities owned by the GSCA banks and by customers of the GSCA banks gave the New York Fed valuable experience operating a settlement system that included securities owned by member banks and by customers of member banks. Bank officials viewed the expansion "as a means of experimenting with … new procedures and developing a basic pattern of book-entry accounts that could accommodate the operations of all member banks."[21]

In March 1973, the Treasury and the Reserve Banks expanded the book-entry system to accommodate Treasury securities held by *any* member bank for *any* customer.[22] The build-out of system infrastructure led to a gradual expansion in the fraction of marketable Treasury debt held in book-entry form, to 65 percent at the end of 1973 and 79 percent at the end of 1975. By the end of the decade almost 94 percent of marketable Treasury debt was held in book-entry form.

CONFRONTING THE LIMITS OF TECHNOLOGY

Settling transactions in Treasury securities on a trade-by-trade basis with definitive bearer securities had the advantage that there could never be more Treasury securities outstanding than the quantity issued by the Treasury. As noted in Chapter 25, that discipline was abandoned (in the interest of facilitating settlements) when the GSCA was introduced in the mid-1960s.

The 1971–73 expansion of the book-entry system allowed the reintroduction of the discipline. A New York Reserve Bank official noted in late 1970 that "the new [book-entry] system has the potential for closer

[20] Federal Reserve Bank of New York Circular no. 6976, July 21, 1972.

[21] Debs (1972, p. 181). See also Federal Reserve Bank of New York Circular no. 6976, July 21, 1972, stating that "in the light of the operating experience … during the past year, operating procedures and book-entry account patterns have been developed to serve as a basis for the extension of the [book-entry] program to all member banks throughout the country."

[22] Subpart O of Treasury Circular no. 300, March 9, 1973; and Federal Reserve Bank of New York Operating Circular no. 21, effective March 30, 1973. See also Federal Reserve Bank of New York Circular no. 7112, March 19, 1973.

coordination of the book-entry accounts maintained at this Bank with the clearing arrangement; instead of providing for a net settlement ... at the end of a day by delivery of physical securities, such deliveries could be virtually eliminated and settlement effected by means of debits or credits to appropriate book-entry accounts."[23]

In February 1974 the Federal Reserve Bank of New York announced "real-time" accounting for book-entry securities.[24] The key element of the new regime was that "securities transfer messages which would cause an overdraft in a book-entry clearing account will be rejected by the Sigma-5 computer." In view of the ongoing replacement of GSCA accounts with book-entry accounts, real-time accounting eventually eliminated any possibility of an over-issue.

Real-time accounting reintroduced the problem that a dealer with a sale and an offsetting purchase due to be settled on the same day, and with no existing position in the security, could not deliver the securities due on the sale until it had received the securities due from the purchase. Avoiding this sequencing problem had prompted the use of fiscal agency stocks of unissued securities when the GSCA was first introduced.

And even if the securities due on the purchase arrived before the close of the book-entry system, there was no guarantee that the securities could be "turned around" before the close. Book-entry transfers reduced the time required to redeliver securities from hours to minutes, but the required turn-around time was still positive. A dealer who received securities shortly before the 2:30 p.m. close might be unable to redeliver the securities and thus be forced to forego receipt of the payment due upon delivery until the next business day, thereby losing interest on the funds.

Within a matter of months after the introduction of real-time accounting, dealers were complaining about "their inability to 'turn-around' transfers received by them just prior to the existing closing hour."[25] They requested that the closing time for out-bound transfers to consenting customers be extended until 2:45 p.m., to give them an extra fifteen minutes to turn around securities received immediately prior to 2:30 p.m. New York Bank officials agreed, subject to the proviso that "the participating banks, rather than [the Reserve Bank], will enforce their

[23] Memo from Richard Debs to Mr. Treiber, Federal Reserve Bank of New York, "Problem of Insurance on Government Securities: Current Status of Book-Entry Procedure and Clearing Arrangement," December 7, 1970, p. 6.

[24] Government Securities Clearing Arrangement Participant Memo no. 54, February 19, 1974.

[25] Government Securities Clearing Arrangement Participant Memo no. 59, May 21, 1974.

agreed-upon closing hours . . . and that the propriety of any transfer . . . is to be determined by the parties to the transaction and not by [the New York Bank]." Provision for what came to be known as "dealer time" continued to be reflected in Bank documents until 1996.[26]

THE END OF THE GSCA AND THE END OF DEFINITIVE SECURITIES

The migration of settlements from GSCA accounts to book-entry accounts gradually eroded the utility of the GSCA accounts. Intra-city and CPD transfers increasingly moved securities into and out of book-entry accounts, reducing the need for end-of-day settlements with definitive securities. The New York Reserve Bank terminated the GSCA in December 1977.[27]

As increasing amounts of Treasury securities were converted to book-entry form, Treasury officials began to contemplate the elimination of definitive securities in new offerings.[28] In August 1976, the Treasury announced that it would stop issuing fifty-two-week bills in bearer form by the end of the year and that it would stop issuing bearer thirteen- and twenty-six-week bills sometime in 1977.[29] The Treasury stopped issuing

[26] See, for example, Government Securities Clearing Arrangement Participant Memo no. 79, November 7, 1977, and Appendix A to Federal Reserve Bank of New York Operating Circular no. 21A, effective January 25, 1984.

In mid-1995 the Federal Reserve System adopted, effective January 2, 1996, a firm closing time of 3:15 p.m. for *all* out-bound wire transfers and deleted references to a separate deadline for dealer-to-customer deliveries, but also stated that it would not object to private agreements for earlier closing times. "Federal Reserve Bank Services," *Federal Register*, August 15, 1995, pp. 42, 411. The Public Securities Association subsequently adopted a 2:45 p.m. cut-off time for customer-to-dealer deliveries and a 3:00 p.m. cut-off time for dealer-to-dealer deliveries. Dealer-to-customer deliveries continued to close at 3:15 p.m. "PSA Amends Good Delivery Deadlines for Extended Fedwire Book-Entry System," *PSA Government Securities Newsletter*, November 27, 1995, p. 2.

Early cut-off times were abandoned in 2009. Treasury Market Practices Group and Securities Industry and Financial Markets Association joint announcement, "Recommended Closing Time Practices for Delivering Fedwire-Eligible Securities," May 28, 2009. See generally Garbade and Keane (2017, pp. 20–23).

[27] Government Securities Clearing Arrangement Participant Memo no. 78, August 11, 1977.

[28] Treasury Department press release, "Formation of a Treasury-Federal Reserve Task Force Established to Expand the Book-Entry Program of Issuing Government Securities," March 1976, reporting that the Treasury and the Federal Reserve would "design and adopt an expanded book-entry system with the ultimate objective of completely eliminating the use of definitive securities in new public debt offerings."

[29] Federal Reserve Bank of New York Circular no. 7939, August 20, 1976.

bearer bonds in September 1982 and did not issue bearer notes after December 1982.[30] The last step came in August 1986, when the Treasury introduced a new book-entry system, TreasuryDirect, designed to accommodate retail investors, and announced that it would no longer issue notes or bonds in registered form.[31]

[30] Federal Reserve Bank of New York Circular no. 9363, September 15, 1982. See also Bureau of the Public Debt (1982).

[31] Federal Reserve Bank of New York Circular no. 10,058, July 17, 1986, and Circular no. 10,064, July 31, 1986. See also Bureau of the Public Debt (1983). Manypenny (1986) summarizes the 1976–86 transition to a book-entry-only Treasury securities market.

33

Coda

This book examined the post-Accord evolution of three US financial institutions:

- Federal Reserve open market operations, including outright purchases and sales, repurchase agreements, and matched sale-purchase agreements;
- Treasury debt management, including what to sell and how to sell it; and
- the secondary market for US government securities, including trading, trade settlement, and financing.

The book focused on how Treasury and Federal Reserve officials went about fashioning the instruments, facilities, and procedures needed to advance their policy objectives in light of the freedoms and responsibilities that followed from the 1951 Accord.

INITIAL ACTIONS

In fixing the terms of the Accord, Federal Reserve officials sought to slip the bonds of their wartime and postwar commitment to a fixed pattern of interest rates and transition to a regime of reserves management with freely fluctuating rates. The Treasury, for its part, wanted to be confident that it would be able to raise new money as circumstances required and to refinance maturing debt. In return for Treasury's acceptance of their objectives, Federal Reserve officials agreed to ensure the success of Treasury offerings priced at market.

Following agreement to the terms of the Accord, Federal Reserve officials took two important actions, one to further their own policy objectives and the other in response to their commitment to the Treasury.

The 1953 Operating Principles

In furtherance of the System's objectives, the Federal Open Market Committee adopted four operating principles in 1953:

1. Intervention in the market was solely to effectuate the objectives of monetary and credit policy.
2. Transactions would be entered into solely for the purpose of providing or absorbing reserves.
3. Operations for the System Open Market Account should be confined to the front end of the yield curve. The Committee expressed a particular preference for conducting operations in the bill market.
4. The System should refrain during a period of Treasury financing from purchasing (a) any maturing issue for which an exchange was being offered, (b) when-issued securities, and (c) any outstanding issue with a maturity comparable to the maturity of a security offered for exchange.

The principles were not iron-clad rules but rather were intended to be guardrails for open market operations, identifying the boundary between (a) routine operations and (b) extraordinary operations to be undertaken only in unusual circumstances and only with the explicit contemporaneous approval of the Committee.

Three considerations prompted the adoption of the operating principles. First, the Committee did not want to slip back into the wartime practice of pegging interest rates. Open market operations would instead focus on managing reserves. Second, the Committee did not want to be obligated to provide direct support for Treasury offerings, although it was prepared to provide liquidity in support of a failing offering. Third, the Committee wanted to encourage the development of a liquid secondary market for government securities. Chairman Martin believed that limiting operations to the bill market and clarity in identifying the boundary between conventional and extraordinary operations would contribute to that goal.

Even Keeling

Undertaken in fulfillment of the Fed's commitment to the success of Treasury offerings priced at market levels, even keeling rose to prominence in 1955 as the economy recovered from a recession and began to expand. Increases in interest rates left dealers unenthusiastic about underwriting new offerings. Martin advanced the idea of keeping the credit markets on an "even keel" during Treasury offerings, suggesting that the Open Market Account "should not do anything in its . . . operations that would appear to interfere with the success of [a Treasury] financing."[1] Episodes of troubled offerings were thereafter relatively rare, with four instances between 1955 and 1960 – in May 1955, November 1955, May 1957, and July 1958 – and one more in May 1970. The five troubled offerings appear to have been matters of bad luck following an announcement of terms rather than purposeful mispricing on the part of Treasury officials.

A METAPHOR FOR CHANGE

In thinking about the evolution of open market operations and Treasury debt management it will be helpful to refer from time to time to a metaphor for institutional change, a way of thinking about why and when change occurs. Thus, think of a bowling ball at the top of a hill, a ball that would roll down the hill but for the fact that it is resting in a local depression. If the depression is shallow a small disturbance might be enough to dislodge the ball and set it rolling; a major shock would be required to dislodge the ball from a deep depression.

Institutional change requires two things. First, an appreciation for the prospective long-run benefits of changing how business is done – how the Desk conducts open market operations and how the Treasury funds the deficit and refinances maturing debt. Change also requires a trigger, a disturbance large enough to fracture the status quo and set the ball rolling. The "why" of change is the perception of market participants, including especially Federal Reserve and Treasury officials but sometimes including also private market participants, of the long-run benefits. The "when" of change is the timing of a trigger large enough to fracture the status quo.

TREASURY DEBT MANAGEMENT

The evolution of Treasury debt management during the quarter century after 1954 was remarkable. By the end of the 1970s, officials had expanded regular and predictable auction offerings from thirteen-week bills to long-term notes and would soon push on to bonds.

[1] Minutes of the Executive Committee of the Federal Open Market Committee, January 25, 1955, pp. 8–10.

Auctions of Coupon-Bearing Debt

Treasury officials recognized, by the mid-1950s, that auctioning coupon-bearing debt would be a distinct improvement over fixed-price offerings. The Treasury had ample experience with auction offerings, having auctioned bills since they were introduced at the end of 1929, so it was not surprising that officials appreciated the benefits of competitive auction pricing. However, the department also had long experience with fixed-price offerings, and it had an established network of banks and broker-dealers that bought and distributed new securities.

During the winter of 1962–63, Under Secretary of the Treasury Robert Roosa tried to auction bonds by emulating a practice used to sell municipal and utility company bonds: offering bonds to competing syndicates of dealers on an all-or-none basis, with the reoffering by the winning syndicate at a fixed price to the public. The first offering went off without a hitch, but the second tranche failed to sell out at the reoffering price.

Seven years elapsed before a shock large enough to trigger another attempt hit the market. The May 1970 mid-quarter refunding very nearly failed following the introduction of ground combat forces into Cambodia. Five months later, Under Secretary Paul Volcker announced the first auction offering of a short-term note. Officials subsequently extended the auction process to progressively longer maturities.

Besides the advantage to the Treasury of selling coupon-bearing securities at competitive prices, the introduction of auction sales allowed the Federal Reserve to wind down its commitment to even keeling.

Regular and Predictable Offerings

By the mid-1950s, two decades of regular weekly offerings of thirteen-week bills had left officials with a clear appreciation of the value of issuing on a regular and predictable basis. The near failure of an offering of one-year certificates in the summer of 1958 spurred the introduction of regular weekly offerings of twenty-six-week bills and quarterly offerings of one-year bills. Surprisingly, however, officials did not go further for more than a decade.

A series of mildly disruptive cash offerings in the second half of 1971 and the first half of 1972 led to the introduction of regular and predictable quarterly offerings of two-year notes in October 1972. Again, however, officials did not go further.

Finally, a sharp increase in the deficit in the spring of 1975, financed with a spate of particularly disruptive cash offerings, led to the introduction of regular quarterly offerings of four and five-year notes. Regular and predictable issuance of longer notes and bonds followed.

OPEN MARKET OPERATIONS

The most striking feature of the evolving scale and scope of open market operations was the steady expansion of System repos. Starting from a limited postwar program, the FOMC,

- suspended the maturity limit on repo collateral during Treasury refundings in March 1965;
- terminated the maturity limit on repo collateral and introduced back-to-back contracts, with nonbank dealers intermediating between their customers and the Desk, in June 1966;
- accepted federal agency securities as repo collateral beginning in December 1966;
- introduced repo auctions in April 1972; and
- accepted bank dealers as counterparties in June 1975.

An airline strike in July 1966 crippled the Fed's check collection system, generated a large and volatile expansion in float, and focused attention on the need for a facility that would allow the Desk to drain large quantities of reserves over short intervals of time in the same way that repos allowed it to supply reserves. Matched sale-purchase agreements were the obvious solution.

FAILED AND SUPPLANTED INITIATIVES

Not every initiative was an enduring success. Some initiatives failed quickly – such as auction offerings of bonds to competing dealer syndicates and "flexible" fixed-rate repo pricing. Others thrived for a while but were ultimately replaced or discarded – as with strip offerings of bills, tax anticipation bills, and advance refundings. But failure and replacement should not be interpreted as signals of a mistaken need for change. Auction pricing of both coupon-bearing debt and repurchase contracts eventually came to pass. And replacement sometimes signaled only that conditions had changed and that new ways could more efficiently achieve old objectives.

INTER-AGENCY ACCOMMODATIONS

In addition to System initiatives aimed at improving the efficacy of open market operations and Treasury initiatives aimed at improving debt management, the two agencies sometimes engineered cooperative modifications to their respective operations. Operation Twist was the most significant, but not the only, example.

Operation Twist

The termination of bills preferably in 1961 was the most dramatic single change in the framework of open market operations during the quarter century after 1954. The FOMC had made a substantial institutional commitment to bills preferably and had defended that operating principle on multiple occasions following its adoption. It took a significant shock to initiate change.

The requisite trigger came in the late 1950s and 1960, when the Treasury and the System struggled to limit foreign central bank demands for gold while encouraging economic recovery. The former required higher, or at least unchanged, short-term interest rates; the latter required ample reserves and lower long-term rates. Committee members sought to resolve the conflict by selling short-term coupon-bearing Treasury debt and buying longer-term issues, in the process abandoning bills preferably as an operating principle.

Treasury Cash Management

Treasury officials generally accommodated System needs by stabilizing Treasury balances at Federal Reserve Banks, thus helping to stabilize reserves available to the banking system even as total Treasury balances rose and fell. The system of War Loan Deposit Accounts (renamed Treasury Tax and Loan Accounts in 1950) dated to World War I but was expanded after World War II to include a broad range of tax payments. The designation of Group C banks in 1955 allowed quicker responses to incipient imbalances.

For a few years in the later 1970s, when the Treasury moved virtually all of its cash balances to Federal Reserve Banks in order to capitalize on rising interest rates, Treasury cash management worked at cross purposes to System needs. By the end of 1978, officials had worked out a system that allowed the Treasury to receive interest on its commercial bank deposits and the Department returned to stabilizing its Reserve Bank deposit balances.

Cash Management Bills

Cash management bills, introduced in August 1975, were useful to both the Treasury and the Federal Reserve. They provided the Treasury with a market-based way to bridge short-term gaps of a few days or weeks between expenditures and receipts and facilitated adherence to the expanding program of regular and predictable issuance. By reducing Treasury's need to borrow directly from the Fed, cash management bills reduced the System's need to undertake reflexive sterilizing operations.

MARKET INFRASTRUCTURE

Following the termination of bills preferably, officials at the Federal Reserve Bank of New York became more directly exposed to operational problems in the markets for intermediate- and longer-term notes and bonds and began to take the lead in crafting solutions to those problems.

Government Securities Clearing Arrangement

The Government Securities Clearing Arrangement was introduced in the second half of the 1960s by the Federal Reserve Bank of New York to reduce the costs of settling transactions in Treasury securities by netting the receive and deliver obligations of a clearing bank. It stands as the only major innovation that cannot be traced to a triggering event. The GSCA is perhaps best viewed as reflecting the increasing concern of the New York Bank with the operational efficiency of the Treasury market, a concern sparked by the Bank's ongoing concern with the liquidity of the market in which it executed monetary policy and with its own operating expenses.

Book-Entry II

The Government Securities Clearing Arrangement and the first, early-stage book-entry system (Book-Entry I, also introduced in the second half of the 1960s) provided concrete evidence of the prospective value of an expanded and automated book-entry and wire-transfer system. However, expanding the system would require the cooperation of hundreds of institutional investors, banks, and broker-dealers.

The requisite shock to the financial system came soon enough, when a large insurance company threatened to withdraw coverage of clearing bank settlement operations following a string of widely publicized thefts and losses of securities in 1969 and 1970. The New York clearing banks agreed that change was urgently needed, and the Federal Reserve Bank of New York developed an expanded, public-facing book-entry system (Book-Entry II).

Securities Lending

Borrowing securities to bridge settlements of asynchronous sales and purchases is hardly different, conceptually, from borrowing money to bridge asynchronously settling purchases and sales. However, while money lending is well understood by the general public, securities lending is an arcane activity commonly associated with short sales aimed at driving down securities prices, not something to be condoned by a government agency. Nevertheless, a surge in settlement fails in 1969, and the prospect of dealers moving to "skip-day" settlement two days after the negotiation of a trade (with a resulting loss of liquidity in the same-day and regular settlement markets), prompted the Federal Open Market Committee to approve short-term loans of securities from the Open Market Account.

The Association of Primary Dealers in US Government Securities

As the New York Reserve Bank became more involved in infrastructure issues it had increasing need for regular contact with market participants to help identify practices and facilities that would reduce transaction costs and enhance liquidity. Dating at least to the time of the Treasury-Federal Reserve Study of the Government Securities Market in 1959, officials believed that institutionalized contact with the primary dealer community would be beneficial. The problem was how to structure such contact without appearing to be an informal regulator. A series of untoward events in 1969 provided the impetus for the formation of the Association of Primary Dealers in United States Government Securities. The Association subsequently played an important role in expanding the book-entry system and in the development of the securities lending facility.

Table 33.1 *Eight important institutional innovations during the quarter century after the Accord.*

Innovation	Triggering event
Abandonment of bills preferably	1960 conflict between the desire for higher short-term rates (to preserve the US gold stock) and lower long-term rates (to promote economic recovery)
Book-entry I	1963 loss of $7½ million of bearer Treasury securities at the Federal Reserve Bank of San Francisco
Government Securities Clearing Arrangement	Introduced in 1965, no specific trigger
Introduction of matched sale-purchase agreements	Unusual level and volatility of float as a result of a 1966 airline strike
Securities lending from the portfolio of the System Open Market Account	Rising settlement fails in late 1968 and 1969
Book-entry II	Threat of loss of insurance coverage due to rising thefts and losses of definitive Treasury securities in the late 1960s
Introduction of coupon auctions	Near failure of the May 1970 refunding
Introduction of interest-earning Treasury Tax and Loan accounts	Problems encountered by the Desk between 1975 and 1978 in neutralizing swings in Treasury cash balances following the decision of the Treasury to keep virtually all of its cash in Federal Reserve Banks

RECAPITULATION

Table 33.1 summarizes eight important institutional innovations during the quarter century from 1954 to 1979. An event or episode of material significance, ranging from problems with Treasury offerings to one-off events like a loss of securities at a Federal Reserve Bank, triggered seven of the eight innovations.

However, not all innovations followed a simple trigger-and-response pattern. The upper half of Table 33.2 shows how regular and predictable offerings of Treasury debt were extended from thirteen-week bills to intermediate-term notes over a span of two decades. The fact that the Treasury had been offering thirteen-week bills on a regular basis since 1938, and the fact that the extension to longer-term notes and bonds continued into the early 1980s, suggests that Treasury officials

Table 33.2 *Two sets of serial innovations during the quarter century after the Accord.*

Innovation	Triggering event
Introduction of regular weekly offerings of 26-week bills in 1958 and regular quarterly offerings of 1-year bills in 1959	Near failure of a subscription offering of 1-year certificates in July 1958
Introduction of regular quarterly offerings of 2-year notes in 1972	Disruptive series of irregular cash offerings in the second half of 1971 and early 1972
Introduction of regular quarterly offerings of 4-year notes in 1975 and regular quarterly offerings of 5-year notes in 1976	Disruptive series of irregular cash offerings in the first half of 1975
1966 elimination of the two-year maturity limit on repo collateral and introduction of back-to-back repos	Prospective need to add substantial reserves to offset currency drains over the July 4 holiday
December 1966 acceptance of agency debt as repo collateral	Desk interest in enlarging alternatives to bills as repo collateral
April 1972 introduction of repo auctions	FOMC interest in greater use of repos when the discount rate was not near the Federal funds rate
June 1975 acceptance of bank dealers as participants in repo auctions	Desk interest in expanding the pool of repo counterparties

were quite reluctant to give up their discretionary control of individual offerings.[2]

The bottom half of Table 33.2 shows a different sort of serial innovation: how the Desk managed the expansion of repurchase agreements from the mid-1960s to the mid-1970s. The incremental expansion of repo terms and procedures reflects the gradual growth in the needs of the Desk, rather than (as with regular and predictable offerings) any strong attachment to past practices.

[2] Paul Volcker (1972) observed, following the introduction of regular and predictable offerings of two-year notes, that, "regularization and routinization are nice sounding words; straightjacket and rigidity are not. From where I sit, I cannot help but be conscious of the number of times in which particular market or economic objectives may influence the Treasury's thinking as to the form of a particular financing."

34

After 1979

Treasury debt management, open market operations, and the infrastructure of the Treasury market continued to evolve after 1979, sometimes in small ways as result of marginally changed circumstances and sometimes in larger ways in response to unanticipated problems.

TREASURY DEBT MANAGEMENT

Federal indebtedness grew at an unprecedented peacetime pace from the mid-1970s to the mid-1990s (Chart 34.1). By 1983, Treasury officials had established a slate of

- regular mid-quarter offerings of three-year and ten-year notes and thirty-year bonds,
- end-of-quarter offerings of four-year and seven-year notes and twenty-year bonds,
- quarterly offerings of five-year notes, and
- monthly offerings of two-year notes, as well as
- weekly thirteen-week and twenty-six-week bills, and
- quad-weekly fifty-two-week bills.[1]

The eleven series proved more than adequate for funding the rapidly growing debt. In fact, the most significant changes in issuance came in the course of pruning less liquid and relatively costly series. Twenty-year bonds were visibly expensive compared to ten-year notes and thirty-year bonds.[2] The twenty-year series was terminated in 1986 and offerings of the latter series expanded. Four-year notes were terminated in 1990 and the

[1] Garbade (2015, ch. 3). [2] See Chart 4.4 in Garbade (2015, p. 49).

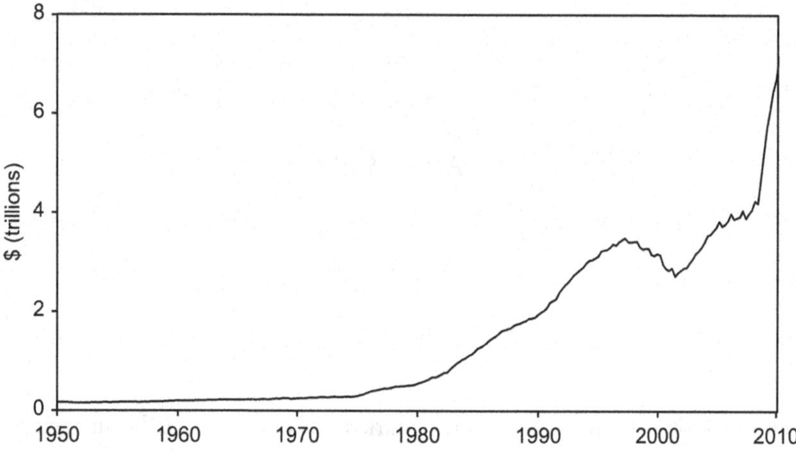

Chart 34.1 Marketable Treasury debt. End of month.
Treasury Bulletin.

more popular five-year series was stepped up to a monthly frequency. Seven-year notes were terminated in 1993 as part of a program aimed at reducing funding costs by shortening the maturity structure of the debt.[3]

The following period of debt paydowns, from 1997 to mid-2001, challenged the continuing commitment of Treasury officials to regular and predictable issuance. Their initial response was to terminate, in 1998, the three-year series and to limit issuance to bills and the more popular two-year, five-year, ten-year, and thirty-year series.[4] When the surplus continued to grow, and indebtedness continued to shrink, officials turned to buying back outstanding debt through reverse auctions – something that had been done on only three prior occasions in the twentieth century.[5] The scale of the buyback program required regular quarterly operations,[6] the success of which illustrated, in a different context, the value of regularity and predictability. (Additionally, the Treasury eliminated most fifty-two-week bill offerings in 2000 and the balance in 2001.[7])

By the middle of 2001, it had become clear that there was no point in continuing to issue long-term bonds that would have to be bought back long before they matured. Officials terminated the thirty-year series in November, leaving only thirteen-week and twenty-six-week bills and two-year, five-year, and ten-year notes.[8]

[3] Garbade (2015, pp. 45–50 and 52–54 and ch. 5). [4] Garbade (2015, pp. 77–80).
[5] Garbade (2012, p. 211). [6] Garbade and Rutherford (2007).
[7] Garbade (2012, p. 94). [8] Garbade (2012, ch. 9).

At the threshold of the new millennium, the concept of regular and predictable issuance had evolved to mean the management of Treasury funding requirements by discretionary management of debt *series* (rather than individual issues), subject to the understanding that a series would be added (and retained for some time) or dropped (and left off for some time) as conditions warranted. Acting under the rubric of regular and predictable issuance, Treasury officials felt free to vary their menu of offerings (but not individual issues) as circumstances dictated. The re-expansion of debt issuance after the attacks of September 11, 2001, and in the wake of the 2008 financial crisis proceeded remarkably smoothly. Three-year notes were reintroduced in 2003 (they were terminated again in 2007 and reintroduced yet again in 2008), thirty-year bonds in 2005, fifty-two-week bills in 2008, and seven-year notes in 2009.[9]

New Securities

Treasury officials introduced several new securities after 1979. The first, adopted during the ramp-up in issuance in 1984, was foreign-targeted Treasury notes: securities intended to attract the interest of non-US investors.[10] Officials offered the notes opportunistically, when market conditions seemed attractive, rather than on a regular and predictable schedule. Dealers never became comfortable with the complicated program and the series died after just four issues.

STRIPS were introduced in 1985.[11] The STRIPS program allowed an investor to exchange ten-year notes and bonds issued after October 1984 for baskets of negotiable single-payment claims representing the individual interest and principal payments due on the notes or bonds. STRIPS were not issued to raise new money: they were intended to reduce financing costs indirectly by enhancing demand for long-term notes and bonds. The program proved successful and was extended to shorter-term notes in 1997.

Officials introduced a third new instrument in 1997: Treasury Inflation-Protected Securities (TIPS).[12] Interest and principal payments on TIPS were not fixed but rather varied with an index of consumer prices. The

[9] Garbade (2015, ch. 11–13). [10] Garbade (2015, pp. 36–43).

[11] Garbade (2015, pp. 31–35).

[12] "Sale and Issue of Marketable Book-entry Treasury Bills, Notes, and Bonds," *Federal Register*, January 6, 1997, pp. 846–874; "Treasury to Auction $7,000 Million of 10-Year Inflation-Indexed Notes," *Treasury News*, January 21, 1997; "Debut of Inflation-Linked Bonds Encourages Treasury Department in Otherwise Quiet Day," *Wall Street Journal*,

securities were intended to appeal to investors interested in hedging against inflation. Not incidentally, the TIPS program was welcomed by economists who had long wanted a market-based measure of inflationary expectations.[13]

Auction Innovations

During the second quarter of 1991, Treasury and Federal Reserve officials learned that Salomon Brothers, a leading dealer in Treasury securities, had systematically violated Treasury auction rules limiting the quantity of securities a single bidder could acquire in a given auction.[14] The ensuing investigation revealed two particularly troubling features of the primary market for Treasury securities: the requirement that bids had to be submitted on paper tenders (to a Federal Reserve Bank or branch) was a burden for many investors, and the multiple-price auction framework put a premium on knowing where others were bidding – to avoid the "winner's curse" of paying more than necessary. As a result, many investors waited to buy in the post-auction secondary market, leaving dealers and other large market participants to underwrite the bulk of the Treasury's offerings.[15]

Revamping the bidding process was straight forward, albeit complex and expensive. The Federal Reserve Bank of New York supervised development of a communication and processing system that allowed bidders to enter auction bids electronically.

How to mitigate the "winner's curse" associated with multiple-price auctions – in particular, whether to reintroduce the single-price auction process abandoned in 1974 – was more problematic. To acquire the data needed to make a decision, Treasury officials undertook a multi-year experiment, auctioning two-year and five-year notes in a single-price framework and three-year and ten-year notes in a multiple-price framework.[16] Officials concluded that the single-price format was marginally

January 30, 1997, p. C21; "New Inflation-Indexed Note Receives a Strong Response," *New York Times*, January 30, 1997, p. D18.

13 "Inflation Notes Will Offer Fed Forecast Tool," *Wall Street Journal*, February 3, 1997, p. C1, and Sack and Elsasser (2004).

14 Committee on Energy and Commerce (1991), Committee on Ways and Means (1991), Securities and Exchange Commission, "In the Matter of John H. Gutfreund, Thomas W. Strauss, and John W. Merriweather," Securities and Exchange Act Release no. 34-31554, December 3, 1992. See also Jordan and Jordan (1996) and Jegadeesh (1993).

15 Department of the Treasury, Securities and Exchange Commission, and Board of Governors of the Federal Reserve System (1992).

16 Malvey, Archibald, and Flynn (1995) and Malvey and Archibald (1998).

superior and announced in 1998 that all future Treasury auctions would be conducted in that format.[17]

MARKET INFRASTRUCTURE

The infrastructure of the Treasury market also continued to evolve after 1979, twice in response to unexpected crises.

Drysdale

In May 1982, Drysdale Government Securities, Inc., a mid-size dealer, failed. Drysdale had previously built a $4 billion short position in long-term bonds. As was customary, the firm invoiced its short sales at the agreed-upon price, plus accrued interest to the settlement date. However, when it borrowed bonds on reverse repurchase agreements to settle the short sales it retained the accrued interest and paid out only the current quoted market price. (It was, at the time, customary for a repo creditor to lend only the quoted price of a bond, leaving the accrued interest as margin in the event the borrower failed. Drysdale, as the creditor on its reverse repurchase agreements, took advantage of that convention.) When the May 15 coupon payment date of some of its bonds arrived, Drysdale was unable to pay the interest due. Total losses amounted to about $200 million.[18]

Federal Reserve officials learned two things from Drysdale's failure. First, contracting conventions for repurchase agreements needed to be revised, to protect those who lent bonds, as well as those who lent money. Second, there was a case for expanded supervision of the Treasury market, beyond the informal oversight of primary dealers that the Federal Reserve Bank of New York had provided since the late 1930s.

Revising the contract conventions for repurchase agreements proceeded with remarkable speed – new conventions were negotiated during the summer of 1982 and implemented in October – largely because the need was readily understandable as well as critically important.[19]

[17] "'Dutch'-Auction Format to be Adopted by the Treasury in More Sales of Issues," *Wall Street Journal*, October 27, 1998, p. A24; and "Remarks by Gary Gensler, Assistant Secretary for Financial Markets, November 1998 Treasury Quarterly Refunding," Department of the Treasury Press Release RR-2782, October 28, 1998.

[18] Committee on Banking, Housing, and Urban Affairs (May 1982), Welles (1982), Committee on Banking, Finance, and Urban Affairs (1983), and Stigum (1983, p. 323).

[19] Garbade (2006).

The issue of expanded oversight, including oversight of dealers other than primary dealers, was an entirely different matter, one where the Fed had to deal with a universe of smaller, mostly unfamiliar, firms sometimes called "secondary dealers." In August 1982, the New York Reserve Bank announced the formation of a new dealer surveillance unit.[20] By the winter of 1983–84, the unit had developed a voluntary monthly reporting program for secondary dealers[21] and crafted a capital adequacy guideline.[22] The relatively simple guideline engendered pushback from larger dealers because it failed to capture some risks and penalized other risks excessively.[23] A revised guideline, released in early 1985,[24] was ultimately adopted by the Department of the Treasury pursuant to rule-making authority provided in the Government Securities Act of 1986.[25]

ESM and Bevill, Bresler

In the early 1980s, ESM Government Securities and Bevill, Bresler & Schulman Asset Management were small government securities dealers that borrowed funds on what were known as "trust-me" repos, where the borrower retained possession of a creditor's repo collateral. Small cities, counties, and school districts were delighted to have an opportunity to earn interest on their relatively modest cash balances without paying a custodian bank to receive, hold, and return collateral. ESM and Bevill, Bresler took advantage of their naiveté and pledged the same collateral to multiple parties, in the process siphoning off the difference between what they borrowed and what they held in their inventories. ESM failed in March 1985, leaving creditors with about $300 million of losses. Bevill, Bresler failed a month later, leaving losses of about $200 million.[26]

20 "Trading Watchdog for New York Fed," *New York Times*, August 23, 1982, p. D2.

21 "Statement Regarding New Reports by Government Securities Dealers," Federal Reserve Bank of New York press release, February 29, 1984.

22 Committee on Banking, Finance, and Urban Affairs (1984, pp. 140–48).

23 Committee on Banking, Finance, and Urban Affairs (1984, pp. 22 and 52).

24 The revised guideline is reproduced in Committee on Government Operations (May 1985, pp. 202–54).

25 "Government Securities Act of 1986; Implementing Regulations; Proposed Rule," *Federal Register*, February 25, 1987, pp. 5660–724; "Implementation of Regulations; Government Securities Act of 1986; Temporary Rule with Request for Comments," *Federal Register*, May 26, 1987, pp. 19642–712; and "Implementing Regulations for the Government Securities Act of 1986; Final Rule," *Federal Register*, July 24, 1987, pp. 27910–59.

26 Committee on Government Operations (April 1985 and May 1985), and Maggin (1989).

The ESM and Bevill, Bresler episodes underscored the problem with "trust-me" repos – collateral might not be where it was said to be, or might not even exist – and proved to be a strong stimulus to the growth of tri-party repo, where collateral was safekept by an agent bank during the term of the repo.[27]

The back-to-back episodes led Federal Reserve officials to rethink whether they wanted to accept responsibility for informally overseeing a large and diverse group of secondary dealers who were not counterparties in open market operations. E. Gerald Corrigan, president of the Federal Reserve Bank of New York, opined, in testimony before the House Committee on Government Operations, that "the current [oversight] arrangements especially as extended to [secondary] dealers, may not be adequate for the future," and stated that "the recent problems in the government securities market have forcefully raised the question whether the market should be subject to some formal regulatory apparatus backed up by explicit statutory authority."[28] Treasury, SEC, and System officials concluded that it was necessary and appropriate to impose a formal regulatory structure on the market[29] and Congress approved the Government Securities Act of October 28, 1986.

The Government Securities Clearing Corporation

The growth in Treasury debt after 1982 (Chart 34.1), the transition of interdealer trading to screen brokers, and continued growth in the number of primary dealers (Chart 34.2) markedly increased the volume of interdealer trades that had to be settled every business day. At first the trades were settled as they had been for decades, on a gross, bilateral basis, with sellers tendering securities to buyers in exchange for payment. Despite the earlier migration to book-entry securities, the result was increasing back office costs.

Members of the primary dealer community and officials of the major clearing banks began to contemplate, in the mid-1980s, the creation of a central counterparty that would net all of the interdealer transactions in a given Treasury security due to be settled on a given day and thus reduce the settlement obligations of each dealer to its net purchases or net sales. Their discussions gave birth to the Government Securities Clearing

[27] Garbade (2006).
[28] Committee on Government Operations (May 1985, pp. 149 and 156).
[29] Securities and Exchange Commission (1985).

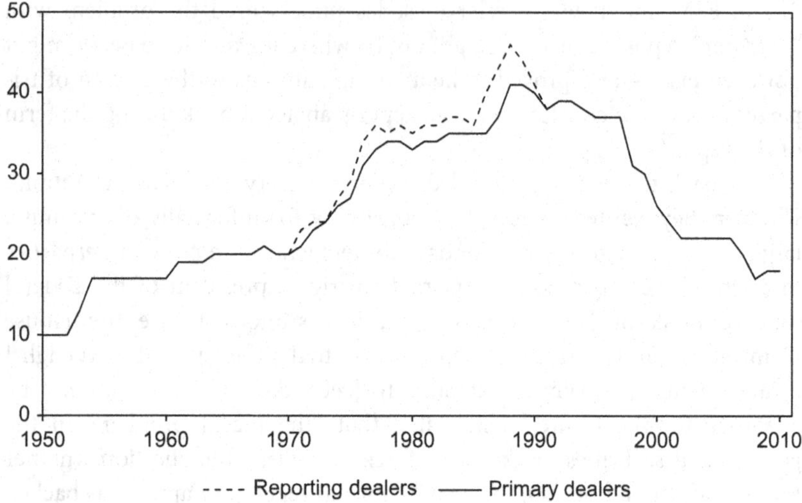

Chart 34.2 Number of reporting dealers and primary dealers.
Constructed from annual reports of open market operations.

Corporation (GSCC, later renamed the Fixed Income Clearing Corporation).[30] Net settlement of bilateral and blind brokered trades began in 1989. Auction takedowns were added in 1994 and repurchase agreements in 1995–96.[31] In 1998 the GSCC introduced a new product, GCF Repo, that substantially enhanced the liquidity of tri-party repos.[32]

Access to the Interdealer Broker Market

For all practical purposes, the advent of screen brokers converted the interdealer market to a continuous central auction. Trading accounts, like hedge funds and other money managers, became interested in acquiring prompt access to information on purchase and sale opportunities in the interdealer market, as well as to information on actual transactions. Some wanted trading access to the market: the ability to hit bids and lift offerings and the ability to submit their own bids and offers.

A 1987 General Accounting Office report, mandated by the Government Securities Act of 1986, concluded that existing proposals for expanded trading access to the interdealer market did not make adequate provision

30 Ingber (2017).
31 Ingber (2017). See also Garbade and Ingber (2005) and Ingber (2006).
32 Ingber (2003) and Fleming and Garbade (2003).

for controlling credit risk but that expanded information access did not raise comparable questions.[33] Nevertheless, the GAO refrained from recommending immediate regulatory action in light of uncertainties about the costs, character, and timing of information access. The GAO suggested that market participants develop a private sector solution.

Three years later there were no visible signs of progress. Impatient with the lack of movement, a GAO update recommended Congressional action to mandate information access to the interdealer market.[34] A joint study by the Treasury, the Securities and Exchange Commission, and the Board of Governors concluded that expanded access to information on interdealer trading would increase market efficiency but despaired of action "absent a federal requirement."[35]

With the Treasury, SEC, Fed, and GAO all in agreement, primary dealers realized that further resistance would not be constructive. In January 1991, the Public Securities Association announced that the dealers and the interdealer brokers had formed a joint venture, GovPX, Inc., to collect real-time interdealer quotations and transaction prices and to make that information available to information vendors like Bloomberg and Reuters.[36] GovPX began operation in June 1991.[37]

At the end of the year, four large interdealer brokers, suffering from reduced earnings and desirous of expanding their market reach, announced that they would grant any GSCC netting member, including members who were not primary dealers, trading access to their markets.[38]

[33] General Accounting Office (1987, pp. 4, 73, and 74).

[34] General Accounting Office (1990, p. 6).

[35] Department of the Treasury, Securities and Exchange Commission, and Board of Governors of the Federal Reserve System (1990, pp. 86–87).

[36] "PSA Joint Venture to expand Access to Government Securities Prices," Public Securities Association press release, January 16, 1991, "Price Data Set on U.S. Issues," *New York Times*, January 17, 1991, p. D18, and "U.S. Securities Price Group Unveils Name, Fee Plan," *Wall Street Journal*, January 17, 1991, p. C18.

[37] "Several Firms Plan to Start Service on Bond Prices," *Wall Street Journal*, June 12, 1991, p. C20.

[38] Department of the Treasury, Securities and Exchange Commission, and Board of Governors of the Federal Reserve System (1992, p. B-91).

References

Adams, Henry. 1887. *Public Debt: An Essay in the Science of Finance*. D. Appleton and Co.: New York, NY.
Anderson, Robert, and William McChesney Martin. 1959. "Summary of Treasury-Federal Reserve Study." *Federal Reserve Bulletin* 45, no. 8 (August): 860–81.
Axilrod, Stephen. 1971. "The FOMC Directive as Structured in the Late 1960s: Theory and Evidence." In *Open Market Policies and Operating Procedures: Staff Studies*. Board of Governors of the Federal Reserve System: Washington, DC.
Baker, Charles. 1976. "Auctioning Coupon-Bearing Securities: A Review of Recent Experience." In *Bidding and Auctioning for Procurement and Allocation*, edited by Y. Amihud. New York University Press: New York, NY.
1979. "The Basis and Practice of Treasury Debt Management." In *The Political Economy of Policy-Making*, edited by Michael Dooley, Herbert Kaufman, and Raymond Lombra. Sage Publications: Beverly Hills, CA.
Balles, John, Norman Bowsher, Harry Brandt, D. R. Crawthorne, Gerald Conkling, J. Dewey Daane, Lewis Dembitz, Douglas Hellweg, Bertram Levin, Spencer Marsh Jr., Seymour Miller, Dorothy Nichols, Parker Willis, Clay Anderson, and Peter Keier. 1959. *The Federal Funds Market: A Study by a Federal Reserve System Committee*. Board of Governors of the Federal Reserve System: Washington, DC.
Banyas, Lawrence. 1973. "New Techniques in Debt Management from the Late 1950s Through 1966." In *Joint Treasury-Federal Reserve Study of the U.S. Government Securities Market, Staff Studies, Part 3*. Board of Governors of the Federal Reserve System: Washington, DC.
Beard, Thomas. 1966. *U.S. Treasury Advance Refunding: June 1960–July 1964*. Board of Governors of the Federal Reserve System: Washington, DC.
Beckhart, Benjamin, James Smith, and William Brown. 1932. *The New York Money Market: External and Internal Relations*, vol. 4. Columbia University Press: New York, NY.
Bierwag, G. O., and M. A. Grove. 1971. "A Model of the Structure of Prices of Marketable U.S. Treasury Securities." *Journal of Money, Credit and Banking* 3, no. 3 (August): 605–29.
Board of Governors of the Federal Reserve System. 1943. *Banking and Monetary Statistics*. Board of Governors of the Federal Reserve System: Washington, DC.

1976. *Banking and Monetary Statistics: 1941-1970*. Board of Governors of the Federal Reserve System: Washington, DC.

1981. *Annual Statistical Digest: 1970-1979*. Board of Governors of the Federal Reserve System: Washington, DC.

2018. *Financial Accounting Manual for Federal Reserve Banks*. Board of Governors of the Federal Reserve System: Washington, DC.

Board of Governors of the Federal Reserve System, Division of Federal Reserve Bank Operations. 1962. *Accounting Manual for Use of Federal Reserve Bank in Preparing Certain Reports to the Board of Governors*. Board of Governors of the Federal Reserve System: Washington, DC.

Bordo, Michael, and Barry Eichengreen. 2013. "Bretton Woods and the Great Inflation." In *The Great Inflation: The Rebirth of Modern Central Banking*, edited by Michael Bordo and Athanasios Orphanides. University of Chicago Press: Chicago, IL.

Bordo, Michael, Owen Humpage, and Anna Schwartz. 2015. *Strained Relations: US Foreign-Exchange Operations and Monetary Policy in the Twentieth Century*. University of Chicago Press: Chicago, IL.

Bremner, Robert. 2004. *Chairman of the Fed: William McChesney Martin Jr. and the Creation of the Modern American Financial System*. Yale University Press: New Haven, CT.

Brunner, Karl, and Allan Meltzer. 1964. *The Federal Reserve's Attachment to the Free Reserve Concept*. Subcommittee Print, Committee on Banking and Currency, Subcommittee on Domestic Finance, U.S. House of Representatives, 88th Congress, 2nd Session, May 7.

Bryan, William. 1972. "Treasury Advance Refunding: An Empirical Investigation." *Journal of Financial and Quantitative Analysis* 7, no. 5 (December): 2139–50.

Bureau of the Public Debt. 1982. *An Analysis of Full Book Entry for Treasury Notes and Bonds, Part I: The Elimination of Bearer Securities*. U.S. Department of the Treasury: Washington, DC.

1983. *An Analysis of Full Book Entry for Treasury Notes and Bonds, Part II: The Replacement of Registered Securities*. U.S Department of the Treasury: Washington, DC.

1984. "Treasury/Federal Reserve Responsibility for the Commercial Book-Entry System." Unpublished paper, U.S. Department of the Treasury.

Burger, Albert. 1969. "A Historical Analysis of the Credit Crunch of 1966." Federal Reserve Bank of St. Louis *Review* 51 (September): 13–30.

Burgess, W. Randolph. 1936. *The Reserve Banks and the Money Market*. Revised edition. Harper & Brothers: New York, NY.

Carr, Hobart. 1952. "Federal Funds." In *Money Market Essays*. Federal Reserve Bank of New York: New York, NY.

1954. "The Treasury and the Money Market." In *The Treasury and the Money Market*. Federal Reserve Bank of New York: New York, NY.

1959. "Why and How to Read the Federal Reserve Statement." *Journal of Finance* 14, no. 4 (December): 504–19.

Carson, Deane. 1955. "Recent Open Market Committee Policy and Technique." *Quarterly Journal of Economics* 69, no. 3 (August): 321–42.

1959. "Treasury Open Market Operations." *Review of Economics and Statistics* 41, no. 4 (November): 438–42.

Cecchetti, Stephen. 1988. "The Case of Negative Nominal Interest Rates: New Estimates of the Term Structure of Interest Rates during the Great Depression." *Journal of Political Economy* 96, no. 6 (December): 1111–41.

Chandler, Lester. 1958. *Benjamin Strong, Central Banker.* The Brookings Institution: Washington, DC.

Chari, V., and Robert Weber. 1992. "How the U.S. Treasury Should Auction its Debt." Federal Reserve Bank of Minneapolis. *Quarterly Review* 16, no 4 (Fall): 3–12.

Childs, C. F. 1947. *Concerning U.S. Government Securities.* C. F. Childs: Chicago, IL.

Clouse, James, Dale Henderson, Athanasios Orphanides, David Small, and Peter Tinsley. 2003. "Monetary Policy When the Nominal Short-Term Interest Rate is Zero." *Topics in Macroeconomics* 3, no. 1: 1088.

Committee of Conference. 1935. "Banking Act of 1935." Report No. 1822, U.S. House of Representatives, 74th Cong., 1st Sess., August 17.

Committee on Banking and Currency. 1935. "Banking Act of 1935." Report No. 742, U.S. House of Representatives, 74th Congress, 1st Session, April 19.

1935. "Banking Act of 1935." *Hearings before a Subcommittee of the Committee on Banking and Currency on S. 1715 and H.R. 7617,* U.S. Senate, 74th Cong., 1st Sess., April 19 to June 3.

1947. "Direct Purchases of Government Securities by Federal Reserve Banks." *Hearing before the Committee on Banking and Currency,* U.S. House of Representatives, 80th Cong., 1st Sess., March 3–5.

1960. "Federal Reserve Direct Purchases - Old Series Currency Adjustment Act." *Hearing before the Committee on Banking and Currency on S. 3702 and S. 3714,* U.S. House of Representatives, 86th Cong., 2nd Sess., June 24.

1963. "Investigation of the Circumstances Surrounding the Disappearance of $7.5 Million of U.S. Government Securities from the Vault of the Federal Reserve Bank of San Francisco, California." *Hearing before a Special Subcommittee of the Committee on Banking and Currency,* U.S. House of Representatives, 88th Cong., 1st Sess., April 22.

1963. "The Mysterious Disappearance of $7.5 Million of U.S. Securities from Vault of the Federal Reserve Bank at San Francisco, California." Report no. 354, U.S. House of Representatives, 88th Cong., 1st Sess., May 29.

1966. "Regulation of Maximum Rates of Interest Paid on Savings." Report no. 1601, U.S. Senate, 89th Cong., 2nd Sess., September 14.

Committee on Banking, Finance, and Urban Affairs. 1982. "Problems Associated with Federal Debt Management." *Hearings before the Subcommittee on Domestic Monetary Policy of the Committee on Banking, Finance, and Urban Affairs.* U.S. House of Representatives, 97th Cong., 2nd Sess., March 23–24.

Committee on Banking, Finance and Urban Affairs. 1983. "Impact on Money and Credit Policy of Federal Debt Management." *Hearing before the Subcommittee on Domestic Monetary Policy of the Committee on Banking, Finance and Urban Affairs.* U.S. House of Representatives, 98th Cong., 1st Sess., April 25.

1984. "An Examination of the Sufficiency of Capital Adequacy Guidelines for Government Security Dealers Proposed by the Federal Reserve Bank of New York." *Hearing before the Subcommittee on Domestic Monetary Policy of the Committee on Banking, Finance and Urban Affairs.* U.S. House of Representatives, 98th Cong., 2nd Sess., May 31.

Committee on Banking, Housing, and Urban Affairs. 1982. "Disturbances in the U.S. Securities Market." *Hearing before the Subcommittee on Securities of the Committee on Banking, Housing, and Urban Affairs.* U.S. Senate, 97th Cong., 2nd Sess., May 25.

1985. "Regulation of Government Securities." *Hearing before the Subcommittee on Securities of the Committee on Banking, Housing, and Urban Affairs.* U.S. Senate, 99th Cong., 1st Sess., May 9.

1991. "The Activities of Salomon Brothers, Inc. in Treasury Auctions." *Hearings before the Subcommittee on Securities of the Committee on Banking, Housing, and Urban Affairs.* U.S. House of Representatives. 102nd Cong., 1st Sess., September 11–12.

Committee on Energy and Commerce. 1991. "Salomon Brothers and Government Securities." *Hearing before the Subcommittee on Telecommunications and Finance of the Committee on Energy and Commerce.* U.S. House of Representatives, 102nd Cong., 1st Sess., September 4.

Committee on Government Operations. 1985. "Ohio Savings and Loan Crisis and Collapse of ESM Government Securities, Inc." *Hearing before a subcommittee of the Committee on Government Operations.* U.S. House of Representatives, 99th Cong., 1st Sess., April 3.

1985. "Failure of Bevill, Bresler & Schulman, A New Jersey Government Securities Dealer." *Hearing before a subcommittee of the Committee on Government Operations.* U.S. House of Representatives, 99th Cong., 1st Sess., May 15.

Committee on the Judiciary. 1942. "Second War Powers Act, 1942." *Hearings before the Committee on the Judiciary.* U.S. House of Representatives, 77th Cong., 2nd Sess., January 30 and February 2.

Committee on Ways and Means. 1975. "Public Debt Ceiling." *Hearings before the Committee on Ways and Means.* U.S. House of Representatives. 94th Cong., 1st Sess., June 2–3.

1991. "Review of Violations in the Marketing of Government Securities." *Hearing before the Subcommittee on Oversight of the Committee on Ways and Means.* U.S. House of Representative, 102nd Cong., 1st Sess., September 26.

Comptroller General of the United States. 1971. *Improvements Needed in the Federal Reserve Reporting System for Recognized Dealers in Government Securities.* B-169905.

Conway, Ed. 2014. *The Summit.* Little, Brown: London, England.

Cooke, Helen. 1954. "Managing the Treasury's Cash Balances." In *The Treasury and the Money Market.* Federal Reserve Bank of New York: New York, NY.

Cooke, Helen, and Kathleen Straus. 1954. "Treasury Tax and Loan Accounts at Commercial Banks." In *The Treasury and the Money Market.* Federal Reserve Bank of New York: New York, NY.

Coombs, Charles. 1976. *The Arena of International Finance.* John Wiley & Sons: New York, NY.

Cooper, Robert. 1967. "Techniques of the Federal Reserve Trading Desk in the 1960's Contrasted with the 'Bills Preferably' Period." Staff study prepared for the Treasury-Federal Reserve Study of the U.S. Government Securities Market. March 28.

Cox, Albert. 1967. "Regulation of Interest on Deposits: An Historical Review." *Journal of Finance* 22, no. 2 (May): 274–96.

Culbertson, John. 1957. "The Term Structure of Interest Rates." *Quarterly Journal of Economics* 71, no. 4 (November): 485–517.

Davis, Andrew. 1910. *The Origin of the National Banking System.* National Monetary Commission. Senate Document 582, U.S. Senate, 61st Cong. 2nd Sess.

Davis, Felix. 1966. "Automating Government Securities Market Operations." Unpublished paper, Federal Reserve Bank of New York. December.

Davis, Felix, and Matthew Hoey. 1973. "Automating Operations in the Government Securities Market." In *Joint Treasury-Federal Reserve Study of the U.S. Government Securities Market, Staff Studies: Part 3*. Board of Governors of the Federal Reserve System: Washington, DC.

Debs, Richard. 1972. "The Program for the Automation of the Government Securities Market." Federal Reserve Bank of New York *Monthly Review* 54, no. 7 (July): 178–82.

Debs, Richard, and Edward Guy. 1965. "The Legal Bases of Proposals for a Book-Entry Procedure in Lieu of the Safekeeping of Government Securities." Unpublished paper, Federal Reserve Bank of New York. May 21.

Department of the Treasury. 1974. *Report on a Study of Tax and Loan Accounts.*

Department of the Treasury, Securities and Exchange Commission, and Board of Governors of the Federal Reserve System. 1990. *Study of the Effectiveness of the Implementation of the Government Securities Act of 1986.*

1992. *Joint Report on the Government Securities Market.*

de Vries, Margaret. 1969a. "The Par Value System: An Overview." In *The International Monetary Fund 1945-1965, Volume II: Analysis*, edited by J. Keith Horsefield. International Monetary Fund: Washington, DC.

1969b. "Setting Par Values." In *The International Monetary Fund 1945-1965, Volume II: Analysis*, edited by J. Keith Horsefield. International Monetary Fund: Washington, DC.

1969c. "Exchange Rate Adjustment." In *The International Monetary Fund 1945-1965, Volume II: Analysis*, edited by J. Keith Horsefield, ed. International Monetary Fund: Washington, DC.

Fand, David, and Ira Scott. 1958. "The Federal Reserve System's 'Bills Only' Policy: A Suggested Interpretation." *Journal of Business* 31, no. 1 (January): 12–18.

Federal Open Market Committee. 1952. *Federal Open Market Committee Report of Ad Hoc Subcommittee on the Government Securities Market.* Reprinted in Joint Committee on the Economic Report. 1954. "United States Monetary Policy: Recent Thinking and Experience." *Hearings before the Subcommittee on Economic Stabilization of the Joint Committee on the Economic Report.* Congress of the United States, 83rd Cong., 2nd Sess., December 6 and 7, 257–307.

Federal Reserve Bank of New York. 1940. *The Place of the Dealer in the Government Security Market.* Unpublished study. May 20.

1952. *Federal Reserve Open Market Operations.* Unpublished study. August 8.

1958. *Speculation in the United States Government Securities Market.* Unpublished study. September 10.

1958. "The Significance and Limitations of Free Reserves." Federal Reserve Bank of New York *Monthly Review* 40, no. 11 (November): 162–67.

1959. *A Proposed Program for the Collection of Statistics on the United States Government Securities Market.* Unpublished study. November 18.

1962. "Possibilities for Lending System Owned Securities to Dealers." Unpublished paper. February 21.
1964. "The Financing of Government Securities Dealers." Federal Reserve Bank of New York *Monthly Review* 46, no. 6 (June): 107–16.
1965. "A Proposal for Reducing the Volume of Securities Deliveries in Connection with Government Bond Dealer Operations." Unpublished paper. February.
1967. "Proposal for System Lending of Government Securities." Unpublished paper. April 19.
1972. "Just Call Me Sigma: My Friends Do." *The Fed* (March).
1972. "Just Call Me Sigma: My Friends Do." *The Fed* (April).
1982. *A Report on Drysdale and Other Recent Problems of Firms Involved in the Government Securities Market.* Unpublished paper. September 15.
1984. "The Sigma Saga." *The Fed* (April).
Federal Reserve Bank of Richmond. 1960. "Federal Reserve Wire Transfer Service." Federal Reserve Bank of Richmond *Monthly Review* (February).
Federal Reserve System. 1975. *The Culpepper Switch.* Federal Reserve Bank of Richmond: Richmond, VA.
Feinman, Joshua. 1993. "Reserve Requirements: History, Current Practice, and Potential Reform." *Federal Reserve Bulletin* 79, no. 6 (June): 569–89.
Fisher, Irving. 1930. *The Theory of Interest.* Macmillan: New York, NY.
Fleming, Michael, and Kenneth Garbade. 2003. "The Repurchase Agreement Refined: GCF Repo." Federal Reserve Bank of New York *Current Issues in Economics and Finance* 9, no. 6 (June).
2007. "Dealer Behavior in the Specials Market for U.S. Treasury Securities." *Journal of Financial Intermediation* 16 (April): 204–28.
Friedman, Milton. 1960. *A Program for Monetary Stability*. Fordham University Press: New York, NY.
Friedman, Milton, and Anna Schwartz. 1963. *A Monetary History of the United States: 1867-1960.* Princeton University Press: Princeton, NJ.
Gaines, Tilford. 1962. *Techniques of Treasury Debt Management.* Graduate School of Business, Columbia University/Free Press of Glencoe: New York, NY.
Garbade, Kenneth. 1978. "The Effect of Interdealer Brokerage on the Transactional Characteristics of Dealer Markets." *Journal of Business* 51, no. 3 (July): 477–98.
1978. "Electronic Quotation Systems and the Market for Government Securities." Federal Reserve Bank of New York *Quarterly Review* 3, no. 2 (Summer): 13–20.
2006. "The Evolution of Repo Contracting Conventions in the 1980s." Federal Reserve Bank of New York *Economic Policy Review* 12, no. 1 (May): 27–42.
2007. "The Emergence of 'Regular and Predictable' as a Treasury Debt Management Strategy." Federal Reserve Bank of New York *Economic Policy Review* 13, no. 1 (March): 53–71.
2012. *Birth of a Market: The U.S. Treasury Securities Market from the Great War to the Great Depression.* MIT Press: Cambridge, MA.
2014. "Direct Purchases of U.S. Treasury Securities by Federal Reserve Banks." Federal Reserve Bank of New York *Staff Report* no. 684. August.
2015. *Treasury Debt Management under the Rubric of Regular and Predictable Issuance: 1983-2012.* Federal Reserve Bank of New York: New York, NY.

2016. "The First Debt Ceiling Crisis." Federal Reserve Bank of New York *Staff Report* no. 783. June.

2017. "Beyond Thirty: Treasury Issuance of Long-Term Bonds from 1953 to 1965." Federal Reserve Bank of New York *Staff Report* no. 806. January.

Garbade, Kenneth, and Jeffrey Ingber. 2005. "The Treasury Auction Process: Objectives, Structure, and Recent Adaptations." Federal Reserve Bank of New York *Current Issues in Economics and Finance* 11, no. 2 (February).

Garbade, Kenneth, and Frank Keane. 2017. "The Treasury Market Practices Group: Creation and Early Initiatives." Federal Reserve Bank of New York *Staff Report* no. 822. August.

Garbade, Kenneth, Frank Keane, Lorie Logan, Amanda Stokes, and Jennifer Wolgemuth. 2010. "The Introduction of the TMPG Fails Charge for U.S. Treasury Securities." Federal Reserve Bank of New York *Economic Policy Review* 16, no. 2 (October): 45–71.

General Accounting Office. 1987. *U.S. Government Securities: An Examination of Views Expressed About Access to Brokers' Services.* GAO/GGD-88-8. December.

1990. *U.S. Government Securities: More Transaction Information and Investor Protection Needed.* GAO/GGD-90-114.

Gilbert, R. Alton. 1986. "Requiem for Regulation Q: What It Did and Why It Passed Away." Federal Reserve Bank of St. Louis *Review* (February): 22–37.

Glass, Carter. 1927. *An Adventure in Constructive Finance.* Doubleday, Page: Garden City, NY.

Goldenweiser, E. A., Henry Edmiston, John Langum, and C. A. Sienkiewicz. 1943. *Dealers in the Government Security Market.* Unpublished report, Federal Open Market Committee. April 6.

Goodfriend, Marvin. 1983. "Discount Window Borrowing, Monetary Policy, and the Post-October 6, 1979, Federal Reserve Operating Procedure." *Journal of Monetary Economics* 12, no. 3 (September): 343–56.

Goodfriend, Marvin, and Monica Hargraves. 1983. "A Historical Assessment of the Rationales and Functions of Reserve Requirements." Federal Reserve Bank of Richmond *Economic Review* 69, no. 2 (March/April): 3–21.

Greenwood, Robin, Samuel Hanson, Joshua Rudolph, and Lawrence Summers. 2014. "Government Debt Management at the Zero Lower Bound." Hutchins Center on Fiscal & Monetary Policy at Brookings, Working Paper #5. September 30.

Guttentag, Jack. 1966. "The Strategy of Open Market Operations." *Quarterly Journal of Economics* 80, no. 1 (February): 1–30.

Haltom, Renee, and Robert Sharp. 2014. "The First Time the Fed Bought GSE Debt." Federal Reserve Bank of Richmond *Economic Brief.* April.

Hamburger, Michael, and William Silber. 1971. "Debt Management and Interest Rates: A Re-Examination of the Evidence." *Manchester School of Economic and Social Studies* 39, no. 4 (December): 261–67.

Hamdani, Kausar, and Stavros Peristiani. 1991. "A Disaggregate Analysis of Discount Window Borrowing." Federal Reserve Bank of New York *Quarterly Review* 16, no. 2 (Summer): 52–62.

Hetzel, Robert, and Ralph Leach. 2001. "The Treasury-Fed Accord: A New Narrative Account." Federal Reserve Bank of Richmond *Economic Quarterly* 87, no. 1 (Winter): 33–55.

Hicks, John. 1939. *Value and Capital.* Oxford University Press: Oxford, England.

Hoey, Matthew, and Leopold Rassnick. 1976. "Automation of Government Securities Operations." *Jurimetrics* 17, no. 2 (Winter): 176–85.

Hoey, Matthew, and Richard Vollkommer. 1971. "Development of a Clearing Arrangement and Book-Entry Custody Procedure for U.S. Government Securities." *Magazine of Bank Administration* 47, no. 2 (June): 21–29.

Holmes, Alan. 1970. "A Day at the Trading Desk." Federal Reserve Bank of New York *Monthly Review* 52, no. 10 (October): 234–38.

Humpage, Owen, and Sanchita Mukherjee. 2013. "Even Keel and the Great Inflation." Federal Reserve Bank of Cleveland Working Paper no. 13–15. October.

Ingber, Jeffrey. 2003. "Gets Complicated Fast: A Review of the GCF Repo Service." *The RMA Journal* (May): 46–51.

2005. "A Decade of Repo Netting." *Legalworks* 26, no. 2 (February): 3–12.

2017. "The Development of the Government Securities Clearing Corporation." Federal Reserve Bank of New York *Economic Policy Review* 23, no. 2 (December): 33–50.

Jarecki, Henry. 1976. "Bullion Dealing, Commodity Exchange Trading, and the London Gold Fixing: Three Forms of Commodity Auctions." *In Bidding and Auctioning for Procurement and Allocation*, edited by Yakov Amihud. New York University Press: New York, NY.

Jegadeesh, Narasimhan. 1993. "Treasury Auction Bids and the Salomon Squeeze." *Journal of Finance* 48, no. 4 (September): 1403–19.

Joint Committee on the Economic Report. 1954. "United States Monetary Policy: Recent Thinking and Experience." *Hearings before the Subcommittee on Economic Stabilization of the Joint Committee on the Economic Report.* U.S. Congress, 83rd Cong., 2nd Sess., December 6–7.

Joint Economic Committee. 1959. "Employment, Growth, and Price Levels." *Hearings before the Joint Economic Committee.* Part 6A: The Government's Management of its Monetary, Fiscal, and Debt Operations. Congress of the United States, 86th Cong., 1st Sess., July 24 and 27–30.

1959. "Employment, Growth, and Price Levels." *Hearings before the Joint Economic Committee.* Part 6B: The Government's Management of its Monetary, Fiscal, and Debt Operations. Congress of the United States, 86th Cong., 1st Sess., August 5–7.

1959. "Employment, Growth, and Price Levels." *Hearings before the Joint Economic Committee.* Part 6C: The Government's Management of its Monetary, Fiscal, and Debt Operations. Answers to Question on Monetary Policy and Debt Management. Congress of the United States, 86th Cong., 1st Sess.

1959. "Employment, Growth, and Price Levels." *Hearings before the Joint Economic Committee.* Part 9A: Constructive Suggestions for Reconciling and Simultaneously Obtaining Three Objectives of Maximum Employment, An Adequate Rate of Growth, and Substantial Stability of the Price Level. Congress of the United States, 86th Cong., 1st Sess.

Jordan, Bradford, and Susan Jordan. 1996. "Salomon Brothers and the May 1991 Treasury Auction: Analysis of a Market Corner." *Journal of Banking and Finance* 20, no. 1 (January): 25–40.

Kaufman, Henry. 1973. "Federal Debt Management: An Economist's View from the Marketplace." In *Issues in Federal Debt Management.* Federal Reserve Bank of Boston: Boston, MA.

Kreps, Clifton. 1952a. "The Commercial Paper Market." In *Money Market Essays*. Federal Reserve Bank of New York: New York, NY.

1952b. "Bankers' Acceptances." In *Money Market Essays*. Federal Reserve Bank of New York: New York, NY.

Lang, Richard. 1979. "TTL Note Accounts and the Money Supply Process." Federal Reserve Bank of St. Louis *Review* (October): 3–14.

Linke, Charles. 1966. "The Evolution of Interest Rate Regulation on Commercial Bank Deposits in the United States." *National Banking Review* 3 (June): 449–69.

Lombra, Raymond, and Raymond Torto. 1975. "The Strategy of Monetary Policy." Federal Reserve Bank of Richmond *Economic Review* 61 (September/October): 3–14.

Lovett, Joan. 1978. "Treasury Tax and Loan Accounts and Federal Reserve Open Market Operations." Federal Reserve Bank of New York *Quarterly Review* 3, no. 2 (Summer): 41–46.

Luckett, Dudley. 1960. "'Bills Only': A Critical Appraisal." *Review of Economics and Statistics* 42, no. 3 (August): 301–6.

Lutz, F. A. 1940. "The Structure of Interest Rates." *Quarterly Journal of Economics* 55, no. 1 (November): 36–63.

Madigan, Brian, and Warren Trepeta. 1986. "Implementation of U.S. Monetary Policy." In *Changes in Money-Market Instruments and Procedures: Objectives and Implications*. Bank for International Settlements, Monetary and Economic Department: Basle, Switzerland.

Maggin, Donald. 1989. *Bankers, Builders, Knaves, and Thieves*. Contemporary Books: Chicago, IL.

Malvey, Paul, and Christine Archibald. 1998. *Uniform-Price Auctions: Update of the Treasury Experience*. U.S. Treasury, Office of Market Finance.

Malvey, Paul, Christine Archibald, and Sean Flynn. 1995. *Uniform-Price Auctions: Evaluations of the Treasury Experience*. U.S. Treasury, Office of Market Finance.

Manypenny, Gerald. 1986. "Book-Entry U.S. Government Securities: Evolution and Effect." Unpublished paper, Stonier Graduate School of Banking.

Markese, John. 1971. *The 'Even-Keel' Policy of the Federal Reserve System*. PhD dissertation, University of Illinois at Urbana-Champaign.

McWhinney, Madeline. 1952. "Member Bank Borrowing from the Federal Reserve Banks." In *Money Market Essays*. Federal Reserve Bank of New York: New York, NY.

Meek, Paul. 1963. *Open Market Operations*. Federal Reserve Bank of New York: New York, NY.

Meek, Paul, and Rudolph Thunberg. 1971. "Monetary Aggregates and Federal Reserve Open Market Operations." Federal Reserve Bank of New York *Monthly Review* 53, no. 4 (April): 80–89.

Meigs, James. 1962. *Free Reserves and the Money Supply*. University of Chicago Press: Chicago, IL.

Meltzer, Allan. 2003. *A History of the Federal Reserve, vol. I: 1913-1951*. University of Chicago Press: Chicago, IL.

2009. *A History of the Federal Reserve, vol. II: 1951-1969*. University of Chicago Press: Chicago, IL.

Meltzer, Allan, and Gert von der Linde. 1960. *A Study of the Dealer Market for Federal Government Securities.* Joint Economic Committee Print, 86th Cong., 2nd Sess.

Meulendyke, Ann-Marie. 1998. *U.S. Monetary Policy & Financial Markets.* Federal Reserve Bank of New York: New York, NY.

Miller, Adolph. 1921. "Federal Reserve Policy." *American Economic Review* 11, no. 2 (June): 177–206.

Modigliani, Franco, and Richard Sutch. 1966. "Innovations in Interest Rate Policy." *American Economic Review* 56, no. 2 (May): 178–97.

1967. "Debt Management and the Term Structure of Interest Rates: An Empirical Analysis of Recent Experience." *Journal of Political Economy* 75, no. 4, part 2 (August): 569–89.

Morrison, Alan, and William Wilhelm, Jr. 2007. *Investment Banking: Institutions, Politics, and Law.* Oxford University Press: Oxford, England.

Morse, Jarvis. 1971. *Paying for a World War.* Unpublished study, U.S. Department of the Treasury.

Murphy, Henry. 1950. *The National Debt in War and Transition.* McGraw-Hill: New York, NY.

Patterson, Robert. 1954. *Federal Debt Management Policies, 1865-1879.* Duke University Press: Durham, NC.

Peristiani, Stavros. 1991. "The Model Structure of Discount Window Borrowing." *Journal of Money, Credit and Banking* 23, no. 1 (February): 13–34.

Peskin, Janice. 1967. *Federal Agency Debt and its Secondary Market.* Unpublished staff study, Joint Treasury-Federal Reserve Study of the U.S. Government Securities Mark. November 14.

1971. "Federal Agency Debt and its Secondary Market." In *Joint Treasury-Federal Reserve Study of the U.S. Government Securities Market, Staff Studies: Part 2.* December.

Porter, Sylvia. 1938. "Gambling in Governments." *Scribner's Magazine* (December): 43–46.

Rassnick, Leopold. 1971. "Certificateless Deposits and Transfers of Securities in the Federal Reserve System." *Business Lawyer* 26, no. 3 (January): 611–15.

Reed, Harold. 1922. *The Development of Federal Reserve Policy.* Houghton Mifflin: Boston, MA.

Riefler, Winfield. 1930. *Money Rates and Money Markets in the United States.* Harper & Brothers: New York, NY.

1958. "Open Market Operations in Long-Term Securities." *Federal Reserve Bulletin* 44, no. 11 (November): 1260–74.

Ringsmuth, Don, and Gary Rice. 1984. "Federal Reserve Bank Involvement with Government Securities." Unpublished paper, Federal Reserve Bank of New York. March 8.

Ritter, Lawrence, and William Silber. 1974. *Principles of Money, Banking, and Financial Markets.* Basic Books: New York, NY.

Roelse, Harold. 1952. "The Money Market." In *Money Market Essays.* Federal Reserve Bank of New York, New York, NY.

Roosa, Robert. 1952. "Integrating Debt Management and Open Market Operations." *American Economic Review* 42, no. 2 (May): 214–35.

1952. "Monetary Policy Again." *Bulletin of the Oxford University Institute of Statistics* 14, no. 8 (August): 253–61.

1956. *Federal Reserve Operations in the Money and Government Securities Markets.* Federal Reserve Bank of New York: New York, NY.

Rouse, Robert. 1952. *Some Current Aspects of the Federal Reserve System and the Government Securities Market.* Lecture at the School of Banking at the University of Wisconsin, April 29.

Ruebling, Charlotte. 1970. "The Administration of Regulation Q." Federal Reserve Bank of St. Louis *Review* (February): 29–40.

Sack, Brian, and Robert Elsasser. 2004. "Treasury Inflation-Indexed Debt: A Review of the U.S. Experience." Federal Reserve Bank of New York *Economic Policy Review* 10, no. 1 (May): 47–63.

Samuel, Lawrence. 1997. *Pledging Allegiance: American Identity and the Bond Drive of World War II.* Smithsonian Institution Press: Washington, DC.

Scott, Robert. 1965. "Liquidity and the Term Structure of Interest Rates." *Quarterly Journal of Economics* 79, No. 1 (February): 135–45.

Securities and Exchange Commission. 1985. *Regulation of the Government Securities Market.* In "Regulation and Supervision of the Government Securities Market." *Hearing before the Subcommittee on Domestic Monetary Policy of the Committee on Banking, Finance and Urban Affairs,* U.S. House of Representatives, 99th Cong., 1st Sess., July 9, 1985, pp. 338–380.

Shulimson, Jack. 1966. *Marines in Lebanon, 1958.* Unpublished paper, Headquarters, U.S. Marine Corps, Historical Branch, G-3 Division: Washington, DC.

Silber, William. 2012. *Volcker: The Triumph of Persistence.* Bloomsbury Press: New York, NY.

Simon, David. 1994. "The Treasury's Experiment with Single-Price Auctions in the mid-1970s: Winner's Curse or Taxpayer's Curse?" *Review of Economics and Statistics* 76, No. 4 (November): 754–60.

Smith, George. 1956. *The Federal Reserve Leased Wire System: Its Origins, Purposes, and Functions.* Unpublished study. Federal Reserve Bank of New York.

Sobel, Robert. 1986. *Salomon Brothers 1910-1985: Advancing to Leadership.* Salomon Brothers: New York, NY.

Solomon, Robert. 1982. *The International Monetary System, 1945-1981.* Harper & Row: New York, NY.

Sproul, Allan. 1964. "The 'Accord' – A Landmark in the First Fifty Years of the Federal Reserve System." Federal Reserve Bank of New York *Monthly Review* 46, no. 11 (November): 227–36.

Steil, Benn. 2013. *The Battle of Bretton Woods.* Princeton University Press, Princeton, NJ.

Stigum, Marcia. 1983. *The Money Market.* Rev. ed. Dow Jones-Irwin: Homewood, IL.

Struble, Frederick, and Stephen Axilrod. 1973. "Even Keel Revisited." In *Issues in Federal Debt Management.* Federal Reserve Bank of Boston: Boston, MA.

Subcommittee of Counsel on Fiscal Agency Operations of the Committee on Fiscal Agency Operations of the Conference of Presidents. 1965. "Book-Entry Procedure for Government Securities." Unpublished paper. August 11.

Subcommittee on Fiscal Agency Operations of the Committee on Fiscal Agency Operations of the Conference of Presidents. 1963. "Book-Entry Procedure for Safekeeping of Government Securities." Unpublished paper. August.

Swanson, Eric. 2011. "Let's Twist Again: A High-Frequency Event-Study Analysis of Operation Twist and Its Implications for QE2." *Brookings Papers on Economic Activity* 42, *no.* 1 (Spring): 151–207.

Taus, Esther. 1943. *Central Banking Functions of the United States Treasury, 1789-1941.* Columbia University Press: New York, NY.

Thomas, Woodlief. 1951. "Lessons of War Finance." *American Economic Review* 41, no. 4 (September): 618–31.

Thomas, Woodlief, and Ralph Young. 1947. "Problems of Post-War Monetary Policy." In *Postwar Economic Studies no. 8: Federal Reserve Policy.* Board of Governors of the Federal Reserve System: Washington, DC.

Timberlake, Richard. 1978. *The Origins of Central Banking in the United States.* Harvard University Press: Cambridge, MA.

Tsao, Che, and Anthony Vignola. 1977. "Price Discrimination and the Demand for Treasury's Long-Term Securities." Unpublished paper, U.S. Department of the Treasury.

Turner, Bernice. 1931. *The Federal Fund Market.* Prentice-Hall: New York, NY.

U.S. Department of Commerce. 1975. *Historical Statistics of the United States, Colonial Times to 1970, Part I.* Government Printing Office: Washington, DC.

U.S. General Accounting Office. 1987. *U.S. Government Securities: Expanding Access to Interdealer Brokers' Services.* February.

1987. *U.S. Government Securities: An Examination of Views Expressed About Access to Brokers' Services.* December.

U.S. Treasury Department. 1960. *Debt Management and Advance Refunding.* U.S. Treasury Department: Washington, DC.

U.S. Treasury and Federal Reserve System. 1959. *Treasury-Federal Reserve Study of the Government Securities Market, Part I.*

1960a. *Treasury-Federal Reserve Study of the Government Securities Market, Part II.*

1960b. *Treasury-Federal Reserve Study of the Government Securities Market, Part III.*

1969. *Report of the Joint Treasury-Federal Reserve Study of the U.S. Government Securities Market.* Board of Governors of the Federal Reserve System: Washington, DC.

1970. *Joint Treasury-Federal Reserve Study of the U.S. Government Securities Market, Staff Studies: Part 1.* Board of Governors of the Federal Reserve System: Washington, DC.

1971. *Joint Treasury-Federal Reserve Study of the U.S. Government Securities Market, Staff Studies: Part 2.* Board of Governors of the Federal Reserve System: Washington, DC.

1973. *Joint Treasury-Federal Reserve Study of the U.S. Government Securities Market, Staff Studies: Part 3.* Board of Governors of the Federal Reserve System: Washington, DC.

Volcker, Paul. 1972. "A New Look at Treasury Debt Management." U.S. Department of the Treasury *News.* March 7.

Volcker, Paul, with Christine Harper. 2018. *Keeping at It: The Quest for Sound Money and Good Government.* Public Affairs, Hachette Book Group: New York, NY.

Vollkommer, Richard. 1970. "*Clearance and Custody of Untied States Government Securities: Solutions to Some Problems.*" Unpublished study, Stonier Graduate School of Banking, Rutgers University.

Walker, Charls. 1954. "Federal Reserve Policy and the Structure of Interest Rates on Government Securities." *Quarterly Journal of Economics* 68, no. 1 (February): 19–42.

Welles, Chris. 1982. "Drysdale: What Really Happened." *Institutional Investor* (September): 73–83.

Warburg, Paul. 1930. *The Federal Reserve System, vol. 1.* Macmillan: New York, NY.

Wicker, Elmus. 1969. "The World War II Policy of Fixing a Pattern of Interest Rates." *Journal of Finance* 24, no. 3 (June): 447–58.

Wood, Elmer. 1955. "Recent Monetary Policies." *Journal of Finance* 10, no. 3 (September): 315–25.

Yeager, Leland. 1966. *International Monetary Relations.* Harper & Row: New York, NY.

Young, Ralph. 1958. "Tools and Processes of Monetary Policy." In *United States Monetary Policy.* The American Assembly, Columbia University: New York, NY.

Young, Ralph, and Charles Yager. 1960. "The Economics of 'Bills Preferably'." *Quarterly Journal of Economics* 74, no. 3 (August): 341–73.

Young, Ralph, Peter Keir, Albert Koch, John Larkin, Robert Mayo, Robert Roosa, and Duane Saunders. 1960. "Implementation of Treasury-Federal Reserve Program of Information About the Government Securities Market, Report of Steering Group." Unpublished paper. January 5.

Index

Printed in the United States
By Bookmasters